The I-Series

Computing Concepts

Complete Edition

The I-Series

Computing Concepts

Complete Edition

Stephen Haag

Daniels College of Business
University of Denver

Maeve Cummings

Kelce College of Business
Pittsburg State University

Alan I Rea, Jr.

Haworth College of Business
Western Michigan University

 **McGraw-Hill Irwin**

Boston   Burr Ridge, IL   Dubuque, IA   Madison, WI   New York   San Francisco   St. Louis
Bangkok   Bogotá   Caracas   Kuala Lumpur   Lisbon   London   Madrid   Mexico City
Milan   Montreal   New Delhi   Santiago   Seoul   Singapore   Sydney   Taipei   Toronto

McGraw-Hill Higher Education ⟨⟩

*A Division of The **McGraw-Hill** Companies*

I-SERIES: COMPUTING CONCEPTS, COMPLETE EDITION

This book is printed on acid-free paper.

domestic   1 2 3 4 5 6 7 8 9 0 QPD/QPD 0 9 8 7 6 5 4 3 2
international 1 2 3 4 5 6 7 8 9 0 QPD/QPD 0 9 8 7 6 5 4 3 2

ISBN 0-07-246401-1

Publisher: *George Werthman*
Sponsoring editor: *Dan Silverburg*
Developmental editor: *Gina M. Huck*
Developmental editor: *Melissa Forte*
Manager, Marketing and Sales: *Paul Murphy*
Lead project manager: *Mary Conzachi*
Lead production supervisor: *Heather D. Burbridge*
Senior designers: *Jennifer McQueen and Mary Christianson*
Cover design: *Asylum Studios*
Interior design: *Asylum Studios*
Photo research coordinator: *Jeremy Cheshareck*
Photo researcher: *Amy Bethea, Denise Simmons*
Lead supplement producer: *Marc Mattson*
Media producer: *Greg Bates*
Compositor: *ElectraGraphics, Inc.*
Typeface: *10/12 New Aster*
Printer: *Quebecor World Dubuque Inc.*

Library of Congress Control Number: 2002100208

INTERNATIONAL EDITION ISBN 0-07-113035-7

www.mhhe.com

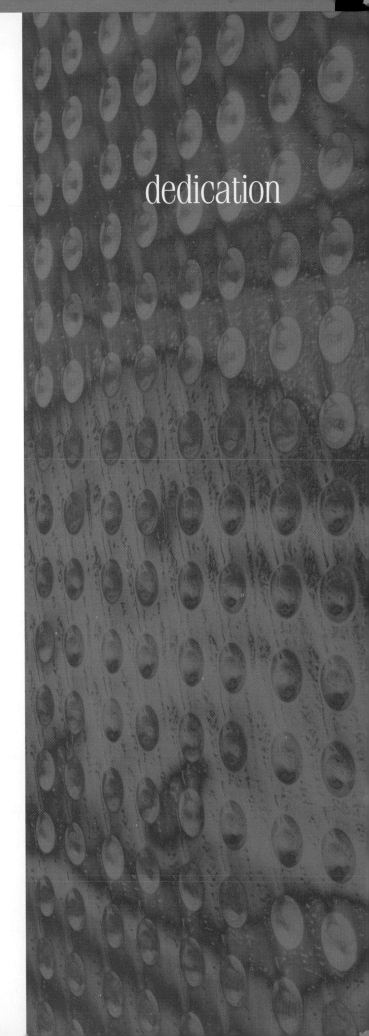

dedication

For Trevor Aaron. My second son—my confirmation that life is more than it's cracked up to be.

STEPHEN HAAG

For Grainne and David, who separately and together, have made my life richer in countless ways.

MAEVE CUMMINGS

To the two most important people in my life: my wife, Lynda, and mother, Susan. Of course, I thank my cats for the occasional rub on the legs as I sat at the computer. I needed that.

ALAN I REA, JR.

InformationTechnology

INFORMATION TECHNOLOGY AT MCGRAW-HILL/IRWIN

At McGraw-Hill Higher Education, we publish instructional materials for the higher education market. In order to expand the tools of higher learning, we publish everything you may need: texts, lab manuals, study guides, testing materials, software, and multimedia products—*the Total Solution.*

We realize that technology has created and will continue to create new mediums for professors and students to use in managing resources and communicating information to one another. McGraw-Hill/Irwin continues to provide the most flexible and complete teaching and learning tools available, as well as offer solutions to the changing world of teaching and learning. Dedicated to providing tools for today's instructors and students, McGraw-Hill/Irwin enables you to successfully navigate the world of Information Technology.

- **Seminar Series and Focus Groups**—McGraw-Hill/Irwin's seminar series and focus groups are offered across the country every year. The seminar series provides you with the latest technology products and encourages collaboration among teaching professionals. We conduct many focus groups year-round where we can hear from you what we need to publish.

- **ITAP-Information Technology Advisory Panel**—This is a "super focus group," where we gather many of the country's top IT educators for three days to tell us how to publish the best IT texts possible. ITAPs are very instrumental in driving our publishing plans.

- **McGraw-Hill/Osborne**—This leading trade division of McGraw-Hill Companies is known for its best-selling Internet titles, Harley Hahn's Internet & Web yellow pages, and the Internet Complete Reference. If we don't have it in CIT/MIS, you can find it at Osborne. For more information, visit Osborne at www.osborne.com.

- **Digital Solutions**—Whether you want to teach a class online or just post your "bricks-n-mortar" class syllabus, McGraw-Hill/Irwin is committed to publishing digital solutions. Taking your course online doesn't have to be a solitary adventure, nor does it have to be a difficult one. We offer several solutions that allow you to enjoy all the benefits of having your course material online.

- **Packaging Options**—For more information about our discount options, contact your McGraw-Hill/Irwin sales representative at 1-800-338-3987, or visit our Web site at www.mhhe.com/it.

WHAT'S THE I-SERIES?

The I-Series is a complete integrated package, including:

- **COMPUTING CONCEPTS**—Introductory (9 chapters) and Complete (13 chapters).

- **APPLICATIONS**—17 different textbooks.

- **SUPPORT MATERIAL**—for instructors and students.

Working together closely as a team, seven authors created *The I-Series* in such a way that the Concepts, Applications, and support material are integrated and act as one presentation.

THE I-SERIES: COMPUTING CONCEPTS

The I-Series: Computing Concepts is designed to provide your students with the most current and relevant information technology content in the most interesting and exciting ways. In creating this approach, we developed six themes, each of which guided our writing efforts.

Consumer/User Focus

We believe that the most effective way to teach technology-related courses is first to show students the immediate benefits of acquiring or using technology. So, *The I-Series: Computing Concepts* focuses first on <u>what</u> your students can do with technology and second on <u>how</u> the technology actually works. Below are just a few of the many examples of a consumer/user focus.

- **WEB AND INTERNET**—We first cover what the Web has to offer, including some really great sites your students will benefit from by visiting, and then we follow with a technical discussion of the Internet infrastructure.

- **NETWORKS**—Networks are an integral part of all technology today, so we introduce your students to various uses of networks in the first five chapters. Chapter 6 addresses the technology-specific aspects of networks including creating a small home network.

- **COMPUTER SOFTWARE**—In the first part of Chapter 3, we cover application software because it helps your students perform tasks that are central to them. We then follow with a discussion of system software.

- **COMPUTER HARDWARE**—Chapter 5 focuses solely on what your students need to know to make an effective and informed purchasing decision. Chapter 6 then introduces your students to the inner technical workings of computers and networks.

- **FILE MANAGEMENT**—We cover the basics of file naming, storing, and organizing in Chapter 3, and we follow in Chapter 8 with a discussion of advanced file management concepts such as defragmentation and zipping/unzipping files.

- **I-BUY**—In this pedagogical element, we address everyday and common—but very important—questions that most of your students have regarding the purchase of a computer. These include desktops vs. notebooks, personal productivity suites, virus protection, and Internet connections, just to name a few.

Integration of Ethics, Security, and Privacy

Reviewers have consistently told us that ethics, security, and privacy are key concerns. So, we've integrated these topics into every facet of *The I-Series* as well as developed a complete chapter on ethics, security, and privacy.

- **COMMON FOCUS BEGINNING WITH CHAPTER 1**—The very first chapter addresses the broad ethical concerns of using technology. Subsequent chapters introduce more detailed discussions.

- **CHAPTER 7**—We've devoted an entire chapter to these vitally important topics. No matter which edition you choose (Introductory or Complete), your students will have this valuable chapter.

- **I-SERIES INSIGHTS**—Where appropriate in the chapters, we've included this boxed feature that discusses ethics, security, and privacy issues. For example, Chapter 1 includes the topic "Are Transactions on the Internet Really Safe?"

- **END-OF-CHAPTER PROJECTS AND EXERCISES**—These topics are so important that we've included an end-of-chapter project category devoted to ethics, security, and privacy.

Changing and Dynamic Nature of Technology

As we created *The I-Series*, we maintained a strong focus on today's emerging technologies and uses of technology. We do cover the "status quo" of today but always strive to inform your students of the emerging technologies we see surfacing.

- **WIRELESS WEB ACCESSING DEVICES—** Wireless Web access with PDAs, cell phones, and pagers is already becoming commonplace. We introduce your students to those possibilities in Chapter 1 and discuss them more in subsequent chapters.

- **HOME NETWORKS—**Microsoft's release of Windows XP ushered in a new home network era. In Chapter 6, your students will learn what it takes to create such a network.

- **CHAPTER 9 EMERGING TECHNOLOGIES—** This chapter focuses completely on emerging technologies. Some are so new and untested that we don't know if they will survive; others, such as automatic speech recognition, certainly will.

- **SOFTWARE RENTING—**Microsoft has already announced its future plans to allow people to rent software over the Internet as opposed to buying it. We think this will be commonplace in a few short years, especially for PDAs.

Innovative and Appealing End-of-Chapter Materials

Reading content is seldom enough for students to actually learn and synthesize key terms and concepts. So, we've created three levels of end-of-chapter projects and exercises that will help your students truly understand and appreciate the chapter content.

- **LEVEL 1 REVIEW OF TERMINOLOGY—**At this level, we include such learning formats as multiple choice and true/false questions, along with an interesting crossword puzzle. The goal is to help your students grasp key terms and definitions.

- **LEVEL 2 REVIEW OF CONCEPTS—**At this level, we help your students develop a more comprehensive understanding of key concepts. Learning formats in this level take on many forms. For example, in many

instances we provide your students with a list of answers and ask them to generate appropriate questions.

- **LEVEL 3 HANDS-ON PROJECTS—**Finally, we ask your students to roll up their sleeves and apply their newly gained knowledge or perhaps even find new information that supports the chapter content. Project categories include:

  1. E-Commerce

  2. On the Web

  3. Ethics, Security & Privacy

  4. Group Activities.

Life-Long Learning

Just because your students complete your course doesn't mean that they stop learning. Indeed, technology is changing every day—some of today's education may be obsolete tomorrow. That's why we've created (and will provide continuous updates to) six *Life-Long Learning Modules* (LLLs) on the Web (www.mhhe.com/i-series). We hope your students will visit these for many years to come.

- **LLL/A ENHANCED WEB DEVELOPMENT—** This module covers basic and advanced Web development techniques including writing scripts, manipulating images, getting a site on a search engine, and many others.

- **LLL/B CARE AND FEEDING OF YOUR COMPUTER—**There are many maintenance and upgrading tasks that your students need to undertake. This module covers many of them such as installing new software, adding more RAM, and even how to clean a keyboard.

- **LLL/C CAREERS IN INFORMATION TECHNOLOGY—**Many of your students may very well consider a career in information technology. This module provides the most current and relevant information concerning IT careers and Web sites devoted to IT careers.

- **LLL/D THE HISTORY OF COMPUTING—** The history of computing is also important because it gives your students some perspective on where we are in light of where we've been. This module will certainly change as we move into a new generation of technology.

- **LLL/E NEW TECHNOLOGIES IMPACTING YOUR LIFE**—This module centers around the latest technologies that are impacting our lives right now—m-commerce and Bluetooth are just a couple of examples.

- **LLL/F COMPUTERS IN YOUR LIFE TOMORROW**—This module focuses on future technologies that are not yet here, as well as how they may impact our lives. This module promises to be a real eye-opener for your students.

Accessible Writing Style

We probably could have discussed the writing style first. All that we have done and will do truly focuses on creating a text that your students will learn from and enjoy. Perhaps that sums up everything about *The I-Series: Computing Concepts*.

THE I-SERIES: APPLICATIONS 2002

The I-Series: Applications 2002 textbooks strongly emphasize that students learn and master applications skills by being actively engaged—by doing. We made the decision that teaching how to accomplish tasks is not enough for complete understanding and mastery. Students must understand the importance of each of the tasks that leads to a finished product at the end of each chapter.

***The I-Series: Applications 2002* includes the following titles:**

- Microsoft Office XP, Volume I
- Microsoft Office XP, Volume II
- Microsoft Word 2002 (Brief, Introductory, Complete editions)—12 Total Chapters
- Microsoft Excel 2002 (Brief, Introductory, Complete editions)—12 Total Chapters
- Microsoft Access 2002 (Brief, Introductory, Complete editions)—12 Total Chapters
- Microsoft PowerPoint 2002 (Brief, Introductory editions)—8 Total Chapters
- Microsoft Windows 2000 (Brief, Introductory, Complete editions)—12 Total Chapters
- Microsoft Windows XP
- Bonus Books to come!

For a close look at *The I-Series: Computing Concepts* and its wide array of pedagogical tools, turn the page . . .

THE I-SERIES: COMPUTING CONCEPTS . . .
THE FUN STARTS HERE!

INVITING . . .

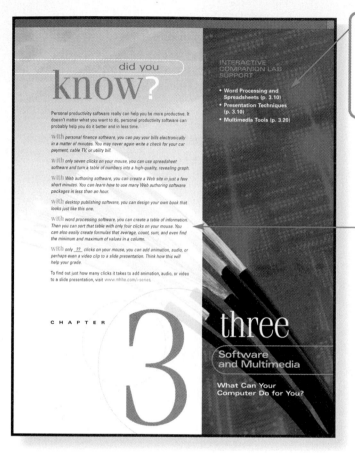

Interactive Companion Lab Support

Featured on the chapter opener, this handy list lets you know which multimedia labs are most appropriate for use with the chapter. Twenty labs are included on the free CD packaged with your text.

Did You Know?

These interesting and fun facts grab your attention right from the start.

Did You Know? Sidebars

Integrated in the margin throughout the text, this feature continues the chapter-opening theme of intriguing facts for your reading enjoyment.

INSIGHTFUL . . .

Four special-interest boxed features sure to engage you are woven throughout the text—bringing concepts to life!

i series insights

Ethics, Security & Privacy

Software That Kills

Software is available today that can actually help you make decisions, especially in the business world. For example, some software can help you determine how much inventory to carry, how to price rooms in a hotel based on seasonal travel, how your customer demographics seem to be changing, and which investment strategies will yield the highest returns. There's even software to help diagnose medical diseases and prescribe treatments.

Software, however, is only as good as the people who develop it. If software has a problem and doesn't produce the correct results, we say that it contains a "bug." Some bugs may not be that bad

(calculating the wrong pay for example), because their errors can be corrected. However, a bug in a medical program can do permanent damage.

Some years ago in the medical industry, software was developed to help determine how to treat cancer patients. It made a mistake and delivered 130 to 250 times the amount of radiation that patients needed. Four of those patients, unfortunately, died.

Software can help people automate tasks. But those tasks must be described in great detail by an expert. Then, the expert must validate that the software works perfectly. We may have some degree of tolerance for variation in personal productivity software but certainly not for software in the medical field that determines radiation levels.

I-Series Insights

Designed to focus on Ethics, Security, and Privacy issues, I-Series Insights provide lively, provocative discussions of these important topics.

i buy

The Ups and Downs of "Always-On" Internet Connections

If your Internet access is via DSL, cable modem, or satellite modem, you probably have an always-on connection, meaning that as long as your computer is on you're connected to the Internet. The up side is that you have instant access to the Internet, and the down side is that you're open to attacks by hackers.

But you can protect yourself. Your first line of defense is passwords. You can protect your files, folders, and disk drives with passwords. The longer the password the harder it is to break. Since it's not always easy to remember long passwords, you can use a phrase that means something to you and cannot be easily associated with you—perhaps something like "TryIt1MoreTime." But be advised that password-cracking software looks for specific phrases and letter combinations, so make the phrase as obscure as you can. If you know words in a language other than English, use a phrase from that language or intersperse the English phrase with non-English words. Throw in some capitalization, digits, and punctuation for good measure. See Chapter 7 for more pointers on passwords.

A good method of protection is a firewall, which is software and/or hardware that protects you from intruders. A software firewall will inform you if someone is trying to gain access to your computer. You can set the program to allow onetime or any-time access to particular people or computers. Some firewall software is available for free.

If you have a home network, you could use a cable/DSL router as a firewall. A router makes your network work more or less invisible to outsiders and can also allow several computers to share one high-speed Internet connection.

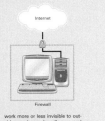

I-Buy

These boxes cover pragmatic topics related to buying and upgrading your own PC. Selected examples include: lease vs. purchase, warranties, and quality of life.

practically speaking

The Best Applications of Virtual Reality

Imagine a world in which the color blue feels like sandpaper, a world in which the only furniture you can sit on must be green, or a world in which a pin dropping on the floor sounds like the cracking of thunder. That's the real world for a person with autism. Autism is a disease that interferes with the development of the part of the brain that processes sensory perceptions. Some autistic people do indeed feel things (sandpaper grinding across the skin) when they see colors.

For autistic people, the world is a mishmash of objects that make no sense to them when they have to deal with them all at once. For example, if you place two differently colored chairs in front of an autistic person and tell him or her that they are both chairs, that person may become confused and disoriented.

A simple world is the best world for individuals suffering from autism. So, many researchers are using virtual reality to teach autistic people to deal with everyday life.

In a virtual reality simulation, researchers can eliminate all forms of background noise, colors, and objects, except those that they want the autistic person to focus on. As the autistic person becomes comfortable with a simple virtual reality simulation, new objects or colors can be introduced without the usual adverse side effects. This allows the autistic person to move from dealing with a simple environment to an environment that includes many objects and colors.

Virtual reality is indeed an emerging and cutting-edge technology, and will dramatically change the way we live our lives and interact with technology. When most people think of virtual reality, they think of games and fun events such as experiencing a roller-coaster ride while sitting in a recliner chair. And there'll be much money made with those types of virtual reality applications.

But the best uses of virtual reality won't necessarily make anyone rich. Instead, they'll help people cope with everyday life. And that's true for all the new technology. It's a multibillion-dollar industry. But perhaps we would all do better to let the money take care of itself, and think more about how technology can aid people in everyday life.

Practically Speaking

These boxes discuss a range of interesting, real-life technology issues. Selected examples include: Internet addiction, speed of speech recognition, and wirelessly wired.

I-Witness

Conveniently located before the end-of-chapter material, I-Witness boxes provide the do's and don'ts of Web site creation and design. Critical thinking is encouraged as you analyze good and bad sites.

i witness

An Up-Close Look at Web Sites

The Blinking Binge

As you've already seen, there are many ways to make your Web site sizzle and its important messages catch the eye. Some of those ways are using different type fonts and styles, using color, and formatting text with bullet points.

Another common method people use to make text eye-catching is

BLINK

to make it blink. Blinking is the simplest form of motion you can put into your Web site. And it's easy to do. You can make single words, sentences, images, or even your whole Web site blink.

Be careful though. Too much blinking can become annoying and it might drive your visitors away. To help you understand how best to use blinking, we've provided three Web sites for you to review. They are

www.mhhe.com/i-series/I-Witness/7-A.html
www.mhhe.com/i-series/I-Witness/7-B.html
www.mhhe.com/i-series/I-Witness/7-C.html

One of those Web sites makes good use of blinking while another uses too much blinking. Which is

the good one and which is the bad one? What would you do to the bad one to better utilize blinking?

Finally, one of the Web sites uses no blinking at all but could benefit from it. How would you incorporate blinking into that Web site to make certain text stand out? You can connect to the site for this text and download these Web sites to your computer. You can then make the changes yourself.

HTML Reference:

The blink tag:

<BLINK>The Blinking Binge</BLINK>—will cause the text "The Blinking Binge" to blink on your Web site.

your guide to the i-series

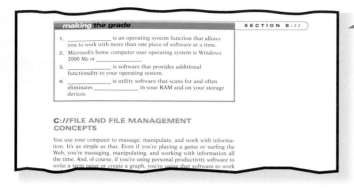

Making the Grade

These checkpoints, made up of short-answer questions, end each major chapter section, making sure you understand the concepts before reading on. Answers appear in an end-of-book Appendix.

INTERACTIVE . . .

End-of-chapter material is organized to follow a 3-level system of instruction. This rich assortment of exercises and projects ensures mastery of the material.

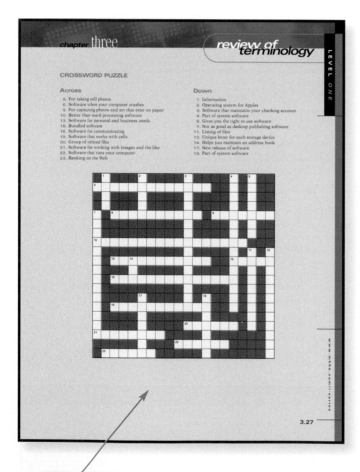

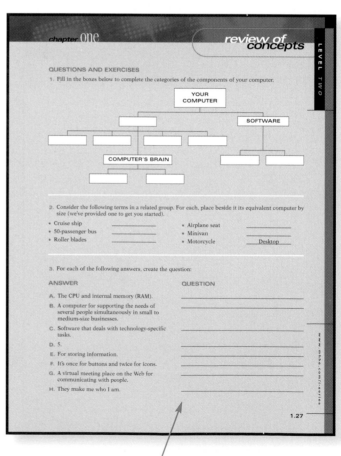

Level One: Review of Terminology

Features a crossword puzzle that makes learning fun!

Level Two: Review of Concepts

Takes you to the next level with various exercise opportunities, including fill-in, answer/question, and more.

xii

chapter three   **hands-on projects**

LEVEL THREE

e-commerce

c. Does the site give you both a map and driving instructions or a combination of the two?

As you travel, would you prefer to have directions from a Web site or use a "fold-up" map? Can the information on a Web site be as reliable as a fold-up map? Or, in reverse, can a fold-up map that was probably printed some time ago be as up-to-date as the information on a Web site?

Below, we've provided four sites that offer online banking. Connect to a couple of them, and let's do some fact-finding concerning online banking.

* www.sfnb.com
* www.netbank.com
* www.delawarefirstbank.com
* www.future-banker.com

First of all, which of these sites are for banks that exist only on the Web? That is, which sites

---

hands-on projects   chapter three

LEVEL THREE

on the web

1. Downloading Free Images, Photos, and Art

In the previous section with e-commerce projects, you visited some Web sites that offer freeware and shareware. And there's a lot more free stuff on the Web. For example, there are thousands of sites that provide free images, photos, and art. All you do is download them and use them as you wish. You can even change the way they look if you wish. Start at your favorite

of choice. Report back to your class the exact set of steps it takes to change a screen saver on your computer.

3. Categorizing Personal Productivity Software

In the computer software ad on page 3.3, we listed some of the more popular personal productivity software packages. What we didn't tell you was in which category of personal productiv-

---

chapter three   **hands-on projects**

LEVEL THREE

ethics, security & privacy

1. Software Piracy

The problem of software piracy grows larger everyday. Software piracy occurs when someone illegally obtains and uses a copy of software. For example, you could create a copy of a game CD-ROM and give it to a friend. That's software piracy. Likewise, someone could post a copy of software on the Web for everyone to copy and use. If that software isn't public domain software

d. If you answered no to the previous question, suggest what the United States should do about the problem. Should the government:

* Clamp down very hard on the nations that pirate software?
* Offer aid in the form of money or software to countries too poor to buy it legally?

---

hands-on projects   chapter three

LEVEL THREE

group activities

1. Game and Entertainment Software

Many people would also include "games and entertainment" as a category in personal productivity software. This particular set of software makes billions of dollars each year in revenue. You can probably find more public domain, shareware, and freeware games and entertainment software on the Web than you can for any other category of personal productivity software. Should "games and entertainment" be a category within personal productivity software? Suppose we asked you to join our author team on the next

4. Adding Sound to a PowerPoint Presentation

As you create a slide presentation, most presentation software such as Microsoft PowerPoint allows you to quickly and easily add sound to a particular slide. As you're creating a slide, all you have to do in PowerPoint to add sound is click on the **Insert** menu option. From there, click on **Movies and Sound** and then **Sound from Gallery.** PowerPoint will then offer you a list of already-prepared sounds you can include in a slide. Start P_____ your presentation

---

Level Three: Hands-on Projects

Helps you put principles into practice with an array of project categories, including e-Commerce, On the Web, Ethics, Security & Privacy, and Group Activities.

Looking Back/Looking Ahead

This unique end-of-chapter feature involves you in summarizing key chapter concepts, while preparing you for what lies ahead.

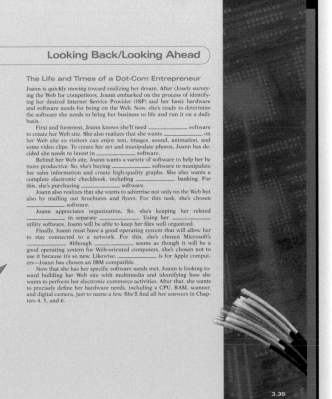

Looking Back/Looking Ahead

The Life and Times of a Dot-Com Entrepreneur

Joann is quickly moving toward realizing her dream. After closely surveying the Web for competitors, Joann embarked on the process of identifying her desired Internet Service Provider (ISP) and her basic hardware and software needs for being on the Web. Now, she's ready to determine the software she needs to bring her business to life and run it on a daily basis.

First and foremost, Joann knows she'll need _____ software to create her Web site. She also realizes that she wants _____ on her Web site so visitors can enjoy text, images, sound, animation, and some video clips. To create her art and manipulate photos, Joann has decided she needs to invest in _____ software.

Behind her Web site, Joann wants a variety of software to help her be more productive. So, she's buying _____ software to manipulate her sales information and create high-quality graphs. She also wants a complete electronic checkbook, including _____ banking. For this, she's purchasing _____ software.

Joann also realizes that she wants to advertise not only on the Web but also by mailing out brochures and flyers. For this task, she's chosen _____ software.

Joann appreciates organization. So, she's keeping her related _____ in separate _____. Using her _____ utility software, Joann will be able to keep her files well organized.

Finally, Joann must have a good operating system that will allow her to stay connected to a network. For this, she's chosen Microsoft's _____. Although _____ seems as though it will be a good operating system for Web-oriented computers, she's chosen not to use it because it's so new. Likewise, _____ is for Apple computers—Joann has chosen an IBM compatible.

Now that she has her specific software needs met, Joann is looking toward building her Web site with multimedia and identifying how she wants to perform her electronic commerce activities. After that, she wants to precisely define her hardware needs, including a CPU, RAM, scanner, and digital camera, just to name a few. She'll find all her answers in Chapters 4, 5, and 6.

3.35

INSPIRING!

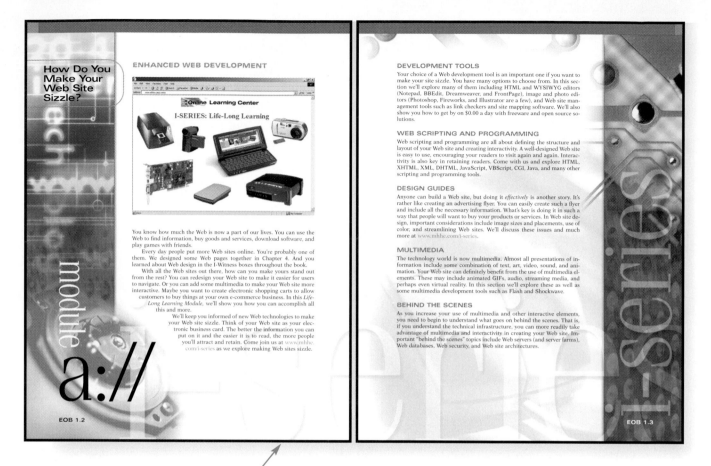

How Do You Make Your Web Site Sizzle?

ENHANCED WEB DEVELOPMENT

You know how much the Web is now a part of our lives. You can use the Web to find information, buy goods and services, download software, and play games with friends.

Every day people put more Web sites online. You're probably one of them. We designed some Web pages together in Chapter 4. And you learned about Web design in the I-Witness boxes throughout the book.

With all the Web sites out there, how can you make yours stand out from the rest? You can redesign your Web site to make it easier for users to navigate. Or you can add some multimedia to make your Web site more interactive. Maybe you want to create electronic shopping carts to allow customers to buy things at your own e-commerce business. In this *Life-Long Learning Module*, we'll show you how you can accomplish all this and more.

We'll keep you informed of new Web technologies to make your Web site sizzle. Think of your Web site as your electronic business card. The better the information you can put on it and the easier it is to read, the more people you'll attract and retain. Come join us at www.mhhe.com/i-series as we explore making Web sites sizzle.

DEVELOPMENT TOOLS

Your choice of a Web development tool is an important one if you want to make your site sizzle. You have many options to choose from. In this section we'll explore many of them including HTML and WYSIWYG editors (Notepad, BBEdit, Dreamweaver, and FrontPage), image and photo editors (Photoshop, Fireworks, and Illustrator are a few), and Web site management tools such as link checkers and site mapping software. We'll also show you how to get by on $0.00 a day with freeware and open source solutions.

WEB SCRIPTING AND PROGRAMMING

Web scripting and programming are all about defining the structure and layout of your Web site and creating interactivity. A well-designed Web site is easy to use, encouraging your readers to visit again and again. Interactivity is also key in retaining readers. Come with us and explore HTML, XHTML, XML, DHTML, JavaScript, VBScript, CGI, Java, and many other scripting and programming tools.

DESIGN GUIDES

Anyone can build a Web site, but doing it *effectively* is another story. It's rather like creating an advertising flyer. You can easily create such a flyer and include all the necessary information. What's key is doing it in such a way that people will want to buy your products or services. In Web site design, important considerations include image sizes and placements, use of color, and streamlining Web sites. We'll discuss these issues and much more at www.mhhe.com/i-series.

MULTIMEDIA

The technology world is now multimedia. Almost all presentations of information include some combination of text, art, video, sound, and animation. Your Web site can definitely benefit from the use of multimedia elements. These may include animated GIFs, audio, streaming media, and perhaps even virtual reality. In this section we'll explore these as well as some multimedia development tools such as Flash and Shockwave.

BEHIND THE SCENES

As you increase your use of multimedia and other interactive elements, you need to begin to understand what goes on behind the scenes. That is, if you understand the technical infrastructure, you can more readily take advantage of multimedia and interactivity in creating your Web site. Important "behind the scenes" topics include Web servers (and server farms), Web databases, Web security, and Web site architectures.

EOB 1.2

EOB 1.3

Life-Long Learning Modules

The learning never ends! That's why the authors created these unique and engaging modules. With a brief introduction in the text, the authors then take you to the text Web site for further exploration of these timely topics. Modules include enhanced web development, careers, new technologies, and more. See for yourself—visit www.mhhe.com/i-series.

We understand that, in today's teaching environment, offering a textbook alone is not sufficient to meet the needs of the many instructors who use our books. To teach effectively, you must have a full complement of supplemental resources to assist you in every facet of teaching, from preparing for class to conducting a lecture to assessing students' comprehension. *The I-Series* offers a complete supplements package and Web site.

INSTRUCTOR RESOURCES

Instructor's Resource Kit

The Instructor's Resource Kit is a CD-ROM containing the Instructor's Manual in both MS Word and .pdf formats, PowerPoint Slides with Presentation Software, Brownstone test generating software, and accompanying test item files in both MS Word and .pdf formats for each chapter. The CD also contains figure files from the text. The features of each of the three main components of the Instructor's Resource Kit are highlighted below.

Instructor's Manual

- Chapter learning objectives per chapter.
- Chapter outline with teaching tips.
- Lecture notes illustrating key concepts and ideas.
- Annotated syllabi (using multiple time formats) depicting a time table and schedule for covering chapter content.
- Suggestions for integrating the teaching of applications.
- Answers to all Making the Grade and end-of-chapter questions.

PowerPoint Presentation

Prepared by Linda Mehlinger,
Morgan State University

The PowerPoint presentation is designed to provide you with comprehensive lecture and teaching resources, including:

- Chapter learning objectives followed by source content that illustrates key terms and key facts per chapter.
- FAQ's (Frequently Asked Questions) to show key concepts throughout the chapter. Also,

lecture notes to illustrate these key concepts and ideas.

- End-of-chapter exercises and activities per chapter as taken from the end-of-chapter materials in the text.
- Speaker's notes are incorporated throughout the slides per chapter.
- Figures/screen shots are incorporated throughout the slides per chapter.

PowerPoint includes presentation software for you to design your own presentation for your courses.

Test Bank

Prepared by Margaret Trenholm-Edmunds,
Mount Allison University

The I-Series Test Bank, using Diploma Network Testing Software by Brownstone, contains over 2,000 questions (both objective and interactive) categorized by topic, page reference to the text, and difficulty level of learning. Each question is assigned a learning category:

- Level 1: Key Terms and Facts
- Level 2: Key Concepts
- Level 3: Application and Problem-Solving

The types of questions consist of 40 percent multiple choice, 40 percent true/false, and 20 percent fill-in/short answer questions.

DIGITAL SOLUTIONS FOR INSTRUCTORS AND STUDENTS

Online Learning Center/Web Site

The Online Learning Center (OLC) that accompanies *The I-Series* is accessible through our Information Technology Supersite at www.mhhe.com/catalogs/irwin/it/. This site provides additional review and learning tools developed using the same three-level approach found in the text and supplements. To locate *The I-Series* OLC/Web site directly, go to www.mhhe.com/i-series. The site is divided into three key areas:

- **Information Center** contains core information about the text, the authors, and a guide to our additional features and benefits of the series, including the supplements.

- **Instructor Center** offers instructional materials, downloads, additional activities and answers to additional projects, relevant links for professors, solutions files, and more.

- **Student Center** contains chapter objectives and outlines, self-quizzes, additional projects, student data files, Web links, and more.

As teachers, we realize that no printed text can be completely up-to-date. The *I-Series: Computing Concepts* Web site augments the printed texts by providing the most up-to-date reviews of technology and much more. Below is just a partial list of exciting topics you'll find on the Web site.

- Personal digital assistants
- Web sites for career searching
- How to use search engines
- Web computers
- Technical Internet resources
- Free image and background sites
- Multimedia authoring software reviews
- Public domain, shareware, and freeware sites
- Web sites that sell software
- M-commerce
- HTML guides
- New CPUs
- Printers and monitors
- Optical storage devices
- Satellite modems
- Bluetooth and WiFi
- Wireless ISPs
- Anti-virus software
- Privacy organizations
- Personal portals
- Automatic speech recognition
- Javascript sites

- Data flow diagramming
- Programming languages
- TQM and BPR
- Leasing a computer
- Groupware suites
- Cultural oddities
- Web hosting services
- Intelligent agents
- Data mining

Online Courses Available—OLCs are your perfect solutions for Internet-based content. Simply put, these Centers are "digital cartridges" that contain a book's pedagogy and supplements. As students read the book, they can go online and take self-grading quizzes or work through interactive exercises.

Online Learning Centers can be delivered through any of these platforms:

- McGraw-Hill Learning Architecture (TopClass)
- Blackboard.com
- Ecollege.com (formerly Real Education)
- WebCT (a product of Universal Learning Technology)

PageOut

As our Course Web Site Development Center, PageOut offers a syllabus page, URL, McGraw-Hill Online Learning Center content, online exercises and quizzes, gradebook, discussion board, and an area for student Web pages. For more information, visit the PageOut Web site at www. pageout.net.

PowerWeb

PowerWeb for Information Technology is an exciting online product available for *The I-Series*. A nominally priced token grants students access through our Web site to a wealth of resources—all corresponding to the text. Features include an interactive glossary; current events with quizzing, assessment, and measurement options; Web survey; links to related text content; and WWW searching capability via Northern Lights, an academic search engine.

STUDENT RESOURCES

Interactive Companion CD

Packaged with the text, this CD-ROM is designed for use in class, in the lab, or at home by students and instructors. The CD combines video, interactive exercises, and animations to cover the most difficult and popular computing concepts. On the first page of each chapter in *The I-Series: Computing Concepts,* you'll find a list of which Interactive Companion Labs are most appropriate for the chapter. You'll also find specific in-text references within each chapter. For example, the Interactive Companion lab titled "E-Mail Essentials" augments the coverage of e-mail in Chapter 2 (The World Wide Web and the Internet).

SimNet XPert

SimNet XPert is a simulated assessment and learning tool. It allows students to study MS Office XP skills and computer concepts, and instructors to test and evaluate students' proficiency within MS Office XP applications and concepts. Students can practice and study their skills at home or in the school lab using SimNet XPert, which does not require the purchase of Office XP software.

For more information on the extensive I-Series supplements package, contact your local McGraw-Hill/Irwin representative or visit our Web site at www.mhhe.com/i-series.

STEPHEN HAAG

Stephen Haag is a professor and Chair of the Department of Information Technology and Electronic Commerce in the University of Denver's Daniels College of Business. Stephen holds a B.B.A. and M.B.A. from West Texas State University and a Ph.D. from the University of Texas at Arlington. Stephen has been teaching in the classroom since 1982 and publishing textbooks since 1984. He has also written numerous articles appearing in such journals as *Communications of the ACM, Socio-Economic Planning Sciences*, and the *Australian Journal of Management*.

Stephen is the author of 34 books including *Management Information Systems for the Information Age, Interactions: Teaching English as a Second Language* (with his mother and father), *Information Technology: Tomorrow's Advantage Today* (with Peter Keen), *Excelling in Finance*, and 17 other books within *The I-Series*. Stephen lives with his wife, Pam, and their three sons—Indiana, Darian, and Trevor—in Highlands Ranch, Colorado.

MAEVE CUMMINGS

Maeve Cummings is a professor of Information Systems at Pittsburg State University. She holds a B.S. in Mathematics and Computer Science; an M.S. in Mathematics; an M.B.A. from Pittsburg State University; and a Ph.D. in Information Systems from the University of Texas at Arlington. She has published in various journals and is on several journal editorial boards. She is the coauthor of *Management Information Systems for the Information Age*, now in its third edition, and *Case Studies in Information Technology*.

Maeve has been teaching for almost 20 years and lives in Pittsburg, Kansas, with her husband, Slim.

ALAN I REA, JR.

Alan I Rea, Jr. is an assistant professor of Computer Information Systems at Western Michigan University's Haworth College of Business. Alan holds a B.A. from The Pennsylvania State University, an M.A. from Youngstown State University, and a Ph.D. from Bowling Green State University. He has published in journals, including the *Mid-American Journal of Business* and *Computers and Composition*. Alan also has coauthored a book chapter in *Web-Based Learning and Teaching Technologies* and serves on various professional committees concerned with teaching and technology.

When not teaching or writing, Alan spends time programming open-source software, playing with his pets, or dating his wife. Alan lives in Kalamazoo, Michigan, with his wife, Lynda, two cats, bearded dragons, and various other forms of wildlife.

FROM STEPHEN HAAG . . .

Throughout my 17 years of publishing, many people have stood by me and supported my efforts. JD Ice really opened the doors of textbook writing for me. Even though he is no longer my editor, I always strive to the level of excellence to which he challenged me. And David Brake, forever my friend in the publishing world, helped me to understand that textbook writing isn't just a job (or an adventure), but a calling that cannot be ignored.

These past 18 months have also reinforced the notion that people can be both friends and business colleagues. Many times, I tested my relationships with Maeve and Alan. Today, we stand together, strong in our friendships and looking forward to future writing efforts.

Finally, there is my family. My parents (Carl and Iona) are second to none. Pam, my wife, never wavered in her support. Bo and Elvis, who are no longer with us, made me smile. And my three sons—Darian, Trevor, and Indy—offered me unconditional love. If I am not remembered for the books I write, I will be content knowing that I am a good father, husband, and son.

FROM MAEVE CUMMINGS . . .

My sincere gratitude goes to the many people who helped directly and indirectly with this project. Thanks to Melanie Buffington who did lots of copy editing; to Cort Buffington who helped with content; to Felix Dreher for his encouragement; to Barbara Clutter, who was invaluable in handling a myriad of details; and to Chris Fogliasso and Mary Wachter, who provided constant moral support.

Thanks to my coauthors, Steve and Alan, who brought great talent and enthusiasm to the project and are the most wonderful people to work with. Thanks to the hundreds of students whom I have met throughout the years who have changed me for the better in a multitude of ways.

Thanks to my wonderfully supportive family: my parents (Dolores and Steve), sisters (Grainne, Fiona and Clodagh), and brother (Colin). To my husband, Slim, constant and unfaltering as the Rock of Gibraltar, I say "thanks—for everything."

FROM ALAN I REA, JR. . . .

Never have I had the opportunity to work on such an intense project with so many dedicated people. I can't name them all, but I want to thank Gina for her continuous stream of supportive e-mail. I also want to thank Maeve, whose biting wit always allowed us to find humor no matter the situation. Finally, I'd like to thank Stephen for putting his trust in a "rookie." He's been my mentor and friend. I'm a better person for it.

I'd also like to thank my colleagues at Western Michigan University. They've created an environment that encourages a student-centered approach to teaching that allows me to embark on adventures such as writing this textbook.

Finally, I'd like to thank my wife, Lynda. She has been my supporter, critic, and front-line editor. Her contributions to this textbook are too numerous to list. Without her, I never would have made it this far.

FROM THE AUTHOR TEAM . . .

This text is certainly not the sole work of just three authors. Rather, it represents the collective efforts of some of the most skilled and innovative people in the publishing industry today. Dan Silverburg, George Werthman, and Rick Williamson each played key roles in providing guidance and motivation. People like Mary Conzachi, Scott Scheidt, Mary Christianson, and Jen McQueen transformed our ideas into the product you see.

And we wish to acknowledge the reviewers of *The I-Series.* They spent countless hours both criticizing and applauding us. The applause was easy to accept; the criticism often difficult. However, we understand their critical analysis of our material was born out of a true love for education and a desire to see their students succeed. Our reviewers were paid only a fraction of their true worth. Even attempting to measure their significance is futile, at best.

Most importantly, Gina Huck and Melissa Forte not only helped us realize our goal but also forged the very path we traveled. Gina and Melissa gave life to *The I-Series,* from the creation of its name to the development of the product vision that guided our writing. *The I-Series* belongs to them as much as it does anyone. Suffice it to say, they should be listed as authors as well. A million thanks is a million too few.

We welcome any and all feedback from you, our valued customer. Please e-mail us at i-series@ mcgraw-hill.com with any suggestions, corrections or noteworthy additions you want to pass along!

brief *brief* contents
Complete Edition

table of contents

3

CHAPTER 3   **3.1**

**SOFTWARE AND
MULTIMEDIA: What Can
Your Computer Do for
You?**

6

CHAPTER 6 6.1

NUTS AND BOLTS OF NETWORKS AND COMPUTERS: How Do Computers and Networks Work?

7

CHAPTER 7 7.1

ETHICS, SECURITY, AND PRIVACY: What's Right, What's Wrong, and How Can You Protect Yourself?

CHAPTER 11   11.1

COMPUTER PROGRAMMING: How Can You Create Your Own Software?

12

13

END-OF-BOOK

Interesting and Current Boxed Features

PRACTICALLY SPEAKING

I-BUY

I-SERIES INSIGHTS: ETHICS, SECURITY & PRIVACY

I-WITNESS: AN UP-CLOSE LOOK AT WEB SITES

People throughout history have always tried to predict the future. Some have been surprisingly successful. Others may have wished they had kept their mouths shut. Let's hear what some people had to say.

"the telephone is inherently of no value to us," according to a Western Union internal memo in 1876.

"everything that can be invented has been invented," according to Charles H. Duell, Office of Patents in 1899.

"who wants to hear actors talk?" asked H. M. Warner of Warner Brothers in 1927.

"stocks have reached what looks like a permanently high plateau," according to Irving Fisher, Professor of Economics at Yale University, in 1929.

"we don't like their sound, and guitar music is on the way out," proclaimed Decca Recording executives in 1962 while reviewing a demo tape of some group called the Beatles.

and last, but certainly not least, "I think there is a world market for maybe __??__ computers," according to Thomas Watson, IBM Chair, in 1943.

To find out just how many computers Thomas Watson of IBM thought there might be a world market for, visit www.mhhe.com/i-series.

CHAPTER

1

one

Computers in Your Life Today

Are You Ready to Become Wired?

We wonder what Mr. Watson of IBM would think now. Just look around your classroom—you can probably see at least five computers right there. And you may very well have two or more computers in your home. By the way, we open each chapter with some really interesting facts, statistics, and quotes. But we always leave one blank and encourage you to visit the Web site for this text (www.mhhe.com/i-series) to fill in the blank. While you're there, check out the other great support we've provided.

The way the Internet has caught on is simply amazing when you think about it. Internet traffic doubles every 100 days. By 2005, there will be over 1 million unfilled jobs that require Internet expertise (check out *Life-Long Learning Module C* on Careers in Information Technology). Online gamblers are expected to lose over $3 billion in 2002. In 1999, only about 100,000 people received their phone service through a local cable TV provider—that number is expected to reach 7 million by 2004.

Times certainly have changed in regard to computers and technology and will change at an even more accelerated rate in the coming years. So we ask you, Do you want to be a part of that change? Can you afford to let it pass you by? Perhaps you don't want to be an Internet expert poised to take your pick of over 1 million unfilled jobs, and that's okay. But you will still need valuable Internet and computer skills to succeed in today's business world, no matter what career you pursue. And for personal and business use you need to know how to make intelligent computer purchasing decisions. Those are two important reasons why we wrote this text: We want you to succeed in the business world no matter what your career, and we want you to become an intelligent computer purchaser and consumer.

A://YOU, YOUR LIFE, AND THE WORLD WIDE WEB

Technology is dramatically changing our lives. Perhaps the most visible and significant new technology is the Internet, or World Wide Web (Web). Right now, let's take a quick tour of the Web and see what it has to offer you.

On the Web, you visit places called Web sites. A **Web site** is a specific location on the Web where you visit, gather information, and perhaps order products. Each Web site has a Web site address. A **Web site address** (or **site address**) is a unique name that identifies a specific Web site on the Web. In Figure 1.1, for example, you can see the Web site for Palm.com. Its Web site address is my.palm.com.

SCHEDULING YOUR LIFE AT PALM.COM
Can the Web Help Me Organize and Manage My Life?

You've probably seen people carrying around small hand-held computers called personal digital assistants, or PDAs. A PDA helps you maintain an address book, schedule appointments, and do some short note taking. Many PDAs can even use wireless technologies to access the Web for you. We'll talk more about Web-accessing PDAs, cell phones, and pagers in Chapter 2.

But you don't have to have a PDA to schedule or organize your life's many events. If you have Web access with a desktop or notebook computer, you can use Palm.com (my.palm.com). For no fee whatsoever, you can register at Palm.com, which will then provide you with a wide array

did you know? in late 1999 there were 250 million people worldwide using the Internet. How many are there today?

F I G U R E   1.1

Many Web sites, such as Palm.com, provide you with free software for organizing your life's many activities.

Maintain your schedule by day, week, month, and even year.

Maintain a contact list.

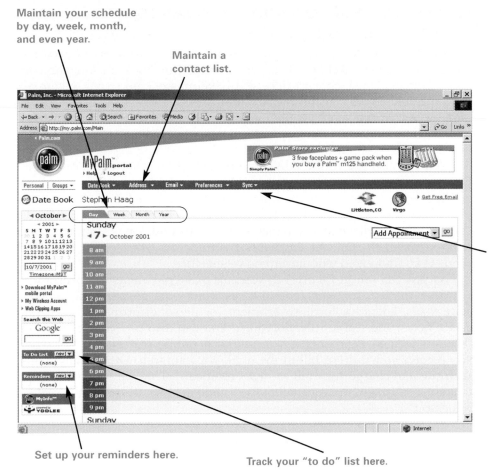

Sync your PDA with your Palm.com information.

Set up your reminders here.

Track your "to do" list here.

of scheduling and organizing software. As you can see in Figure 1.1, Palm.com helps you maintain a calendar and a contact or address book. For your calendar, you can schedule and maintain appointments by day, week, month, or even year. You can even request that Palm.com send you an e-mail note to remind you of important events on your calendar. And when you add a person to your contact list, you can track, sort, and search information by name, address, phone number, fax number, pager number, and e-mail address.

When you register at Palm.com, you are asked several questions, including where you live. Once Palm.com knows this information, you can use it to search for local events in your area. Palm.com will show you only events (movies, sports, plays, concerts, and so on) that are taking place within your area. You can even click on the name of your town to obtain your local weather forecast. This is an example of using a link. A **link** (the technical term is **hyperlink**) is clickable text or an image that allows you to move from one Web site to another or move to different places within the same Web site. So, your town's name is a link to information concerning your local weather forecast.

Palm.com is one of hundreds of Web sites that can help you schedule your life's activities. It's one of hundreds of examples of how the Web is transforming our lives. The Web isn't just a place where you search for useful information or order products or purchase airline tickets. The Web can also really help you be more productive, efficient, and organized.

PAYING BILLS AT OFFICIAL PAYMENTS
Can I Use the Web to Pay Bills?

As you probably already know, you can purchase a vast array of products and services on the Web. For example, you can buy books at Amazon.com (www.amazon.com), concert tickets at ticketmaster.com (www.ticketmaster.com), and jewelry at the Jewelry Mall (www.jewelrymall.com), just to name a few. When most people make purchases on the Web, they do so with their credit cards. Don't worry—using your credit card on the Web is just as safe as using it in a restaurant.

You can also use your credit card on the Web in other ways. At Official Payments (www.officialpayments.com), for example, you can use your credit card to make a variety of payments (see Figure 1.2). It's quite simple. You authorize Official Payments to make a charge against your credit card, and you tell Official Payments to whom and for what purpose to make a payment. Official Payments then charges your credit card and sends that amount to whomever you've specified.

As you can see in Figure 1.2, you can make payments to government entities—the IRS for your federal taxes, your state government for your state taxes, and your local government for personal property taxes, real estate taxes, and traffic rule violations. You can also pay your tuition bill through Official Payments if you attend a public institution. So, when you receive your tuition bill in the mail, you can go to Official Payments' Web site and charge your bill to your credit card. That way you don't have to mail a payment to your school or stand in line to make a payment in person.

F I G U R E   1.2

Web sites like Official Payments can help you make payments to a variety of businesses and the government.

Verify that a payment has been made.

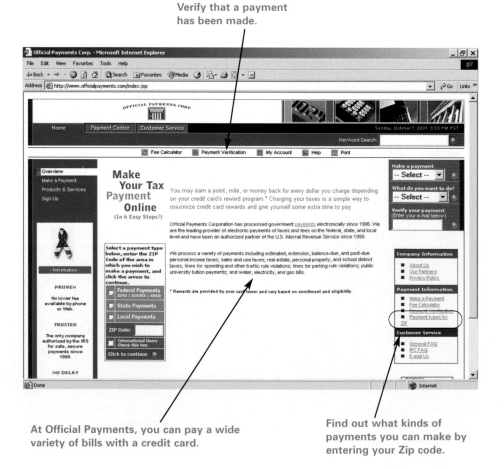

At Official Payments, you can pay a wide variety of bills with a credit card.

Find out what kinds of payments you can make by entering your Zip code.

SHARING YOUR WISDOM AT EPINIONS.COM

Are There Web Sites Where I Can Actually Be Paid for What I Know?

There are hundreds of millions of people using the Web right now. Some are paying bills, some are ordering products and services, some are scheduling their lives, and some are simply enjoying the activity of "surfing" the Web to visit interesting and informative sites. What's more, the Web has become a significant forum for sharing with others your pearls of wisdom, exchanging personal opinions, and discussing recent events in real-time chat rooms.

If this interests you, you should visit Epinions.com (www.epinions.com in Figure 1.3). At Epinions.com, you can read what other people have to say about new products, the latest movie releases, books, and much more. You simply search by a particular topic to find and read whatever interests you. And you can express your own thoughts (or "epinions," which are just electronic opinions). Epinions.com will even pay you in the form of eroyalties every time someone else reads your statements. So, you can actually make money by telling others what you know.

Epinions.com also has numerous chat rooms in which you can discuss topics. A ***chat room*** is a virtual meeting place on the Web in which you can communicate live with other people who happen to be on the Web at the same time. Web sites dedicated to providing just chat rooms are among the most visited sites on the Web. When you enter a chat room, you typically take on an alias of sorts so that no one knows your real identity. This gives you more freedom to express your thoughts and ideas.

Read consumer product reviews before you buy almost anything.

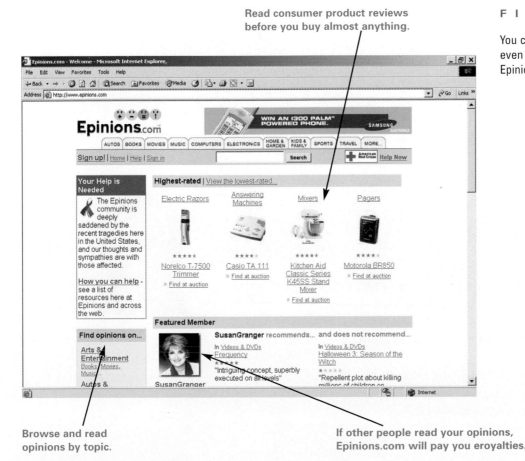

Browse and read opinions by topic.

If other people read your opinions, Epinions.com will pay you eroyalties.

F I G U R E   1.3

You can share your opinions and even get paid for them at Epinions.com.

practically speaking

The Travels of Information throughout History

Today, many people don't read the weather forecast in a local newspaper or even watch for it on television. Instead, they use their personal digital assistants or their car's global positioning system to connect to the Web and obtain up-to-the-minute forecasts.

This now seems almost commonplace to many people. It's how they get their information. If we traverse back through the past, an interesting story unfolds concerning how people have communicated information with each other.

- **3500 B.C. Ancient Rome**—you would write a letter in the form of a pictograph on clay. A messenger service could deliver your clay tablet a distance of 10 miles in about a week.
- **900 B.C. China**—the Chinese developed a postal system, but it could be used only for government purposes.
- **500 B.C. Greece**—the Greeks used trumpets, drums, beacon fires, smoke signals, and mirrors. But these were only for military campaigns.
- **100 B.C. Rome**—the Romans developed their postal system for delivering correspondences on papyrus, animal skins, or bones. You could get a message to a friend in Britain within a couple of months.
- **1400 A.D.**—handwritten books and manuscripts were common among the aristocracy. Chances are that you were not one of the lucky ones who had books or could even read.
- **1661**—American colonies developed a postal system, but you would have had to wait until 1673 to send mail from Boston to New York.
- **1785**—stagecoaches began delivering mail. By 1800, it took only 20 days to deliver mail from Georgia to Maine.
- **1837**—Samuel Morse invented the telegraph.
- **1865**—electromagnetic waves could deliver a short message over a distance of 14 miles without the use of wires.

- **1876**—the telephone was invented.
- **1900**—most people could afford a camera.
- **Early 1900s**—radio became commonplace with 2.5 million radios in the United States alone.
- **1921**—Western Union could send photos via a wire system.
- **1928**—the first televisions were introduced into U.S. homes (three of them, to be exact).
- **1944**—the first digital computer was invented.
- **1975**—you could buy a kit and build your own computer.
- **1982**—IBM introduced its IBM PC.

Since then, we've made quantum leaps in technology and how we deliver information. With a few simple clicks of the mouse, you can be on the Web and virtually anywhere in the world.

We've come a long way. If you're interested in a detailed and informative presentation on the history of technology, visit *Life-Long Learning Module D*.

making the grade

1. A _____ is a specific location on the Web where you visit, gather information, and perhaps order products.

2. A _____ is a unique name that identifies a specific Web site on the Web.

3. A _____ is clickable text or an image that allows you to move from one Web site to another or move to different places within the same Web site.

4. You can go to a _____, a virtual meeting place on the Web, to communicate live with other people who happen to be on the Web at the same time.

B://YOU AND YOUR COMPUTER

The Web is indeed exciting, dynamic, and useful—and all around you. Of course, to access and use the Web you must have a computer of some sort and know how to use it (it's actually possible to access the Web today with a cell phone). To use your computer effectively and efficiently, you need to know something about how and why it works the way it does, what you can do with it beyond just surfing the Web, and the terminology and jargon associated with computers. You also need this knowledge to buy the equipment that will be optimal for you. As we've said, those are the reasons we wrote this book. We want to help you learn about computers so you can be an intelligent user, and—just as crucial, when you think about it—an intelligent purchaser of computer technology.

A *computer* (or *computer system*) is a set of tools that helps you perform information-related tasks. As you've already seen, your computer allows you to surf the Web and find and access a variety of information. Your computer can help you maintain an address book, prepare a report for class, keep a checkbook, and many other tasks. In one way or another, all of these activities deal with *information*. We can say that your computer is a "mind-support" tool. That is, you use your mind to work with information, so your computer is specifically designed to help your mind work with that information. To introduce you at a glance to some common computer terminology, have a look at a computer advertisement shown in Figure 1.4 (shown on the next page).

YOUR COMPUTER HARDWARE AND SOFTWARE

What Are the Major Components of My Computer?

Stated simply, everything in your computer falls into one of two categories—software or hardware. Software is the set of instructions that the hardware devices carry out, while hardware is the physical components of your computer.

Software

Perhaps the most important component of your computer is software. *Software* is the set of instructions that your computer hardware executes to process information for you. As we took a quick tour of the Web, we were using a piece of software—Web browser software. *Web browser software* (or a *Web browser*) is software that allows you to surf the Web.

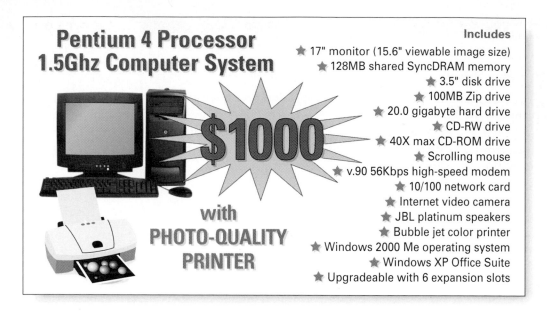

Includes

★ 17" monitor (15.6" viewable image size)
★ 128MB shared SyncDRAM memory
★ 3.5" disk drive
★ 100MB Zip drive
★ 20.0 gigabyte hard drive
★ CD-RW drive
★ 40X max CD-ROM drive
★ Scrolling mouse
★ v.90 56Kbps high-speed modem
★ 10/100 network card
★ Internet video camera
★ JBL platinum speakers
★ Bubble jet color printer
★ Windows 2000 Me operating system
★ Windows XP Office Suite
★ Upgradeable with 6 expansion slots

F I G U R E   1.4

A typical computer ad will tell you everything that comes with the "system."

Another software example would be payroll software for creating new information such as gross pay, overtime pay, deductions, and net pay. Software is fundamental to your computer. Without it, your computer is absolutely worthless.

In our computer ad (Figure 1.4), you can actually see two types of software—system and application. **System software** is the software that details how your computer carries out technology-specific tasks. For example, there are pieces of system software for writing information to a disk, checking for viruses, displaying information on your screen, and converting digitally stored music so it can be piped through your speakers. This software enables your computer itself, so to speak.

Our computer ad lists Windows 2000 Me as system software. Microsoft is the publisher of this system software (known as an operating system), along with Windows 98, Windows 2000 Pro, Windows NT Workstation, and Windows XP (the newest release). Other popular system software includes Mac OS, Linux, and Norton SystemWorks. Both Mac OS and Linux are operating system software, while Norton SystemWorks is utility software. Utility software helps you perform important tasks such as checking for viruses. We'll talk more about these different types of system software in Chapter 3.

F I G U R E   1.5

Microsoft Office XP is a suite of different application software.

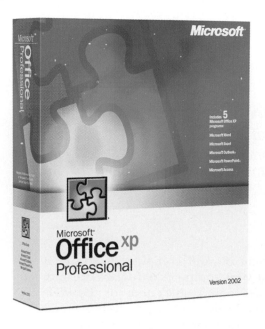

Application software is the software that allows you to perform specific tasks such as writing a term paper, surfing the Web, keeping a home budget, and creating slides for a presentation. In our computer ad, Windows XP Office Suite is application software. It's actually a combination of several different application software packages including Word (for word processing), Excel (for spreadsheets), PowerPoint (for creating slides), and many others.

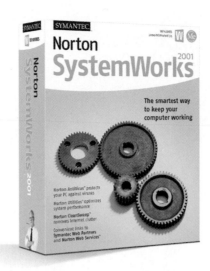

F I G U R E   1.6

Norton SystemWorks is utility software that helps you perform such tasks as checking for a virus.

So, when you buy a computer system, it often comes with the necessary system software and application software you need to get started. We'll explore more about application software in Chapter 3.

Hardware

Hardware includes the physical devices that make up your computer system. You can actually touch these devices (although you shouldn't in some instances). In our computer ad, you can see a variety of hardware including a monitor, 3.5" disk drive, scrolling mouse, Pentium 4 processor, and a high-speed modem. There are many different types of hardware that perform different functions, so let's take a closer look at hardware for a moment.

CATEGORIES OF COMPUTER HARDWARE

What Can My Hardware Help Me Do?

There are five different categories of computer hardware, each devoted to helping you perform one of the following specific tasks (see Figure 1.7 on the next page):

1. Capturing information.
2. Processing information.
3. Presenting information.
4. Storing information.
5. Communicating information to other people.

Capturing Information You Want to Use

For your computer to help you, you must supply it with input information. For example, while we were exploring the Web, we typed in some Web site addresses of places we wanted to go. We did this with a keyboard. So, a keyboard is an input device that helps you capture information. We also used a mouse to point at links on the screen while surfing the Web. You may use your computer and a joystick to play video games. The joystick is an input device that captures information concerning which way you want objects on the screen to move.

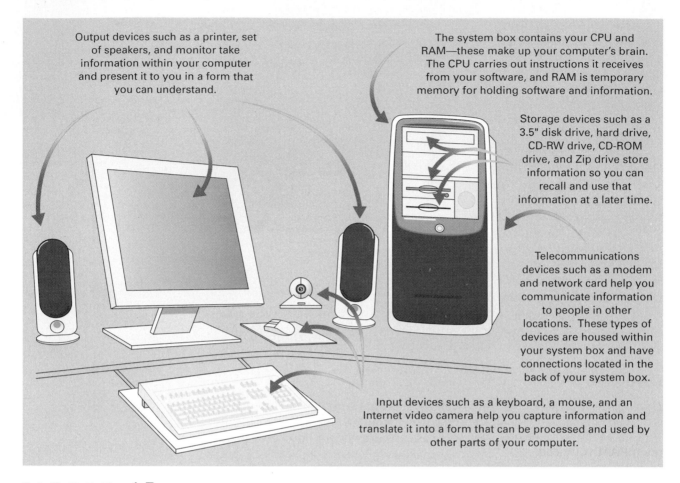

Output devices such as a printer, set of speakers, and monitor take information within your computer and present it to you in a form that you can understand.

The system box contains your CPU and RAM—these make up your computer's brain. The CPU carries out instructions it receives from your software, and RAM is temporary memory for holding software and information.

Storage devices such as a 3.5" disk drive, hard drive, CD-RW drive, CD-ROM drive, and Zip drive store information so you can recall and use that information at a later time.

Telecommunications devices such as a modem and network card help you communicate information to people in other locations. These types of devices are housed within your system box and have connections located in the back of your system box.

Input devices such as a keyboard, a mouse, and an Internet video camera help you capture information and translate it into a form that can be processed and used by other parts of your computer.

FIGURE 1.7

Different components of your computer hardware help you perform different tasks.

FIGURE 1.8

A joystick is an example of an input device.

An ***input device*** captures information and translates it into a form that can be processed and used by other parts of your computer. In our computer ad (Figure 1.4), you can find input devices such as a keyboard, mouse, and Internet video camera. We'll talk more about input devices in Chapter 5.

Processing Information to Create New Information

The original and still most important purpose of your computer is to help you process information. That's the primary responsibility of your computer's brain. Your computer's brain is composed of two distinct parts—the central processing unit and the internal memory. The ***central processing unit*** (***CPU*** or ***processor***) is the chip that carries out instructions it receives from your software (see Figure 1.9). The computer in our ad includes the Pentium 4 processor as its CPU. Other CPUs include the Apple PowerPC, AMD K-6, and Intel Celeron.

The other part of your computer's brain is the internal memory, commonly referred to as RAM. ***RAM*** (***random access memory***) is temporary memory that holds software instructions and in-

F I G U R E   1.9

Your CPU carries out instructions it receives from your software.

F I G U R E   1.10

Along with the CPU, your computer's brain also contains internal memory or RAM.

formation for the CPU (see Figure 1.10). RAM is rather like your short-term memory. When you turn off your computer, all information in RAM is gone.

In our computer ad, RAM is listed as 128MB shared SyncDRAM memory, which is roughly 128 million characters. In Chapter 5, we'll explore the CPU and RAM, including what speed you need (for your CPU) and how much RAM you need.

Presenting Information You Want to See or Hear

For you to effectively use your computer, it must have devices that give information back to you. After all, a computer that processes information is of no use to you if it can't present that information to you in a useful form. As we were surfing the Web, we were watching our surfing on a screen. So, your screen (which we often refer to as a monitor) is an output device that presents information to you. In our computer ad, the output devices include a 17" monitor (15.6" viewable image size), JBL platinum speakers, and bubble jet color printer.

An *output device* takes information within your computer and presents it to you in a form that you can understand. We'll talk more about output devices in Chapter 5.

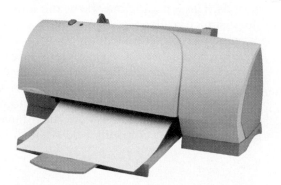

F I G U R E   1.11

A printer is an example of an output device.

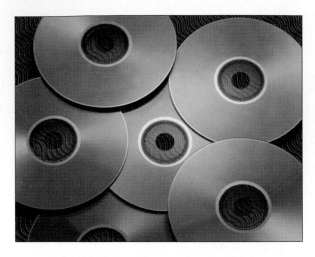

FIGURE 1.12

People store a variety of information and software on storage devices such as 3.5" disks and CD-ROMs.

Storing Information You Want to Use Later

Temporary information storage in RAM is not enough. We need computers to permanently store information so we can recall it at a later time. That's the function of storage devices. When you store information on a storage device, that information is not lost when you turn off your computer. That's why you always hear people telling you to be sure to "save" your information so you won't lose it. That "saving" of information is being done in (or "to") a storage device.

The computer in our ad comes with a variety of storage devices including a 3.5" disk drive, 20.0 gigabyte hard drive, CD-RW drive, and 40X max CD-ROM drive. A *storage device* stores information so you can recall and use that information at a later time. We'll talk more about your storage device needs in Chapter 5.

Communicating Information to Other People

In today's world, communication is vital. Cell phones, e-mail, and digital pagers are an important part of most all our lives. These are all computer-based tools that help you communicate information to people in other locations. Those people may be next door or somewhere around the world—the distance really doesn't matter.

One of the great advantages of the Web is that it helps you communicate information to other people. You can build your own Web site and publish it on the Web for everyone to see (we'll take you through the actual process of building a Web site in Chapter 4). A Web site is one form of communicating information to other people. Of course, to use the Web your computer system must have some special equipment, such as a modem, that connects it to a telephone line.

did you **know?** *every three seconds someone somewhere in the world buys a computer.*

FIGURE 1.13

To use a regular phone line for communication, your computer must include a modem.

A ***telecommunications device*** helps you communicate information to people in other locations. The computer in our ad includes a v.90 56Kbps high-speed modem and a 10/100 network card as telecommunications devices. We'll discuss your needs in this area in Chapters 2, 5, and 6.

To learn more about your computer's hardware and how the various devices work together for you, visit the Interactive Companion Labs and choose "Computer Anatomy."

CATEGORIES OF COMPUTERS BY SIZE

Do Computers Come in Different Sizes and Which Is Best for Me?

Computers do in fact come in different sizes, shapes, and forms. Some are extremely small, so small that you may not even know they exist. Others are almost the size of a telephone booth. Size in some way equates to a computer's power and speed. Smaller computers typically have less power and speed than larger computers.

Personal Digital Assistants (PDAs)

Today, the smallest "portable" computer is not a notebook computer (which we'll discuss in a moment). Rather, we now have personal digital assistants, cell phones, and pagers. You can use all of these devices to manage your personal information, take short notes, and even surf the Web.

Personal digital assistants (PDAs) or "palm-top" computers are small hand-held computers that help you surf the Web and perform simple tasks such as note taking, calendaring and appointment scheduling, and maintaining an address book. PDAs have a small screen that acts as both an input and output device. On the screen, you can display your appointments for the day, and you can also use a special writing stylus to capture information. The PDA screen is touch sensitive, allowing you to write directly on the screen with the screen capturing what you're writing. On the Web site for this text at www.mhhe.com/i-series, you'll find a great review of some of the better PDAs available today.

Notebook Computers for Creating Portable Technology

Moving up the "size" and "power" ladder, next you'll find notebook computers. A ***notebook computer*** (sometimes called a ***laptop computer***) is a small, portable, fully functional computer designed for you to carry around and run on battery power. Notebook computers come completely equipped with all the hardware and software you need. They are, in essence, "portable" computers, some weighing as little as four pounds.

Notebook computers are quickly gaining popularity. Many people need a computer in a variety of settings—at work, at home, at school. Instead of buying a desktop computer for each place, people own one notebook computer that they can take with them wherever they go.

Desktop Computers—Today's Standard

Desktop computers are the most popular choice for personal computing needs, with prices ranging from about $500 to several thousand dollars. Desktop computers come in a variety of physical forms, allowing you to greatly customize not only the system but also your work environment. For example, you can choose a small monitor with a 13-inch viewable screen all the way up to a monitor with a 21-inch viewable screen. You can choose a computer with a horizontal system box (the box is where the CPU, RAM, and storage devices are held) and place a monitor on top of it or choose a computer with a vertical system box (called a tower).

F I G U R E   1.14

Common computers for "personal" use include PDAs, notebook computers, and desktop computers.

Some desktops have horizontal system boxes so you can place the monitor on top.

Other desktop computers have vertical system boxes called "towers." You can place the tower on your desk or on the floor.

Notebooks are fully functional computers which you can easily carry with you wherever you go.

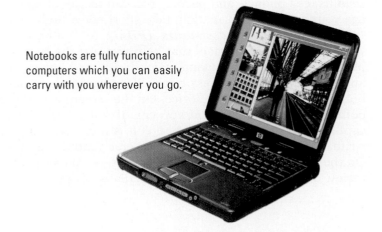

A personal digital assistant (PDA) is a small hand-held computer supporting basic functions such as calendaring, note taking, and maintaining "to-do" lists. You capture information with a PDA by applying a writing stylus or pen directly on the PDA's screen.

i·buy

Notebooks versus Desktops

Throughout this text, we want to help you carry out the process of purchasing a computer. So, you'll find dedicated boxes called I-Buy that address some of the most important questions people have when buying a computer.

As many people approach purchasing a computer today, the question of notebooks versus desktops almost always surfaces. Whether to buy a notebook or a desktop boils down to three issues:

1. Portability.

2. Price.

3. Quality of your interfaces.

First and most important you need to consider portability. Do you really need to be able to take your computer with you? Do you need your computer in some combination of home, work, and school? If you answer yes, then your decision is made. Buy a notebook because you need your computer in at least two different places.

If you answer no or "not really," then you need to consider the other two issues, price and interfaces.

Dollar for dollar, you can buy more computing capability and power with a desktop than with a notebook. (It costs more to build

the same component in a smaller space.) The simple fact is you get more for your money buying a desktop.

Finally, the quality of your interfaces (input and output devices) to your computer is better with a desktop than with a notebook. With a desktop, you can get a larger and more ergonomically correct keyboard than you can with a notebook. You can also get a larger screen with a higher resolution on a desktop. Screen resolution affects the clarity and sharpness of what you see.

Minicomputers, Mainframe Computers, and Supercomputers

Minicomputers, mainframe computers, and supercomputers—the next three categories of computers by size—are very different from the previous three. PDAs, notebooks, and desktops meet the computing needs of a single individual. Minicomputers, mainframes, and supercomputers, on the other hand, meet the computing needs of many people.

A *minicomputer* (sometimes called a *mid-range computer*) is designed to meet the computing needs for several people simultaneously in a small to medium-size business environment. Minicomputers are more powerful and faster than desktop computers but also cost more, ranging from $5,000 to several hundred thousand dollars. Minicomputers are well suited for small to medium-size business environments in which people need to share common information, processing power, and/or certain peripheral devices such as high-quality color printers.

A mainframe computer is a step up in size, power, capability, and cost from a minicomputer. A *mainframe computer* (sometimes just called a *mainframe*) is a computer designed to meet the computing needs of hundreds of people in a large business environment. Mainframes can easily cost in excess of $1 million. With processing speeds greater than 1 trillion instructions per second, mainframes can handle the processing requests of hundreds of people simultaneously.

A minicomputer is well suited for small to medium-size business environments.

FIGURE 1.15

Minicomputers, mainframe computers, and supercomputers can simultaneously process transactions for many people.

Mainframe computers meet the computing needs of hundreds of users in large business environments.

Supercomputers are extremely fast "number crunchers."

Supercomputers are the fastest, most powerful, and most expensive type of computer. Organizations such as NASA that are heavily involved in research and "number crunching" employ supercomputers because of the speed with which they can process information. Other large, customer-oriented businesses such as General Motors and AT&T employ supercomputers just to handle customer information and transaction processing.

SECTION B://

making the grade

1. _____ is the software that details how you would like to perform a specific task.
2. Your ears are to an input device as your _____ are (is) to an output device.
3. A _____ device helps you communicate information to other people in other locations.
4. _____ are the fastest, most powerful, and most expensive type of computers.
5. Every part of your computer is either _____ or _____.

C://YOU, YOUR COMPUTER, AND SOCIETY

Information technology in general (which includes all computers and computer-based products) has had one of the most profound and visible effects of any inventions in modern history. Information technology has become more pervasive (and often invasive) in our lives in a shorter period of time than the automobile, telephone, or cable TV. The technology has even changed our focus in education, to the extent that it has changed *how* we educate people. In 1999, over 2 million students were enrolled in distance learning courses.

Be mindful, however, that every coin has two sides. For every good use, someone has found a way to misuse computers or to exploit them for the wrong purpose. The task ahead of you is to learn to use your computer for the betterment of yourself, your school, your employer, and society at large. Let's take a look at the wrong ways to use a computer and then the right way to use your computer.

THE UNDERUSE OF COMPUTERS

How Can I Use the Full Capabilities of My Computer?

The most common wrong use of a computer is someone's simply not taking full advantage of all the features of the computer. This is not exactly "wrong" in an ethical sense. It's rather like owning a car with a full set of gears and even 4-wheel drive and always driving in only one gear, perhaps even low gear or reverse. You can get where you're going, but it's not always the optimal way to do so.

To avoid the UNDERuse of your computer, you should seek to learn all the capabilities of your software and hardware. For example, Microsoft Word (a word processing package for creating written documents—reports, essays, term papers) includes a function that will automatically build a table of contents for you. Of course, you can build your own table of contents, but it's much faster and easier to use the automated table of contents feature in Word.

Many people underutilize the mouse. Your mouse will probably have two or three buttons and perhaps a scroll ball. But most people just use the left mouse button. The other buttons and the scroll ball can definitely increase your productivity, and it takes only a matter of minutes to learn to use them. The list goes on.

One of our main goals of this text is help you avoid the UNDERuse of your computer.

F I G U R E   1.16

Knowing all the features of a mouse can help you be more productive.

THE ABUSE OF COMPUTERS

Do People Use Computers for the Wrong Reasons?

The real "wrong" way to use a computer is to do so for unethical reasons. These behaviors are a detriment to society and may even be against the law. We refer to this as the ABuse of computers. For example, some people (called hackers) use their computers and the Web to break into other computers and steal information. We'll talk more about hackers in Chapter 7.

And you've probably heard of computer viruses. A **computer virus (virus)** is a piece of software designed intentionally to cause annoyance or damage. Simple viruses can cause your screen to display the wrong information. Deadly viruses can erase all your information

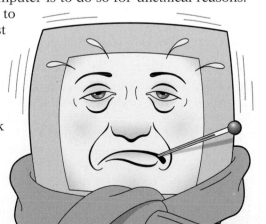

F I G U R E   1.17

Viruses can make a computer sick.

i·series insights

Ethics, Security & Privacy

Are Transactions on the Internet Really Safe?

Many people enjoy surfing the Web, reading interesting material, and e-mailing friends and family. When it comes to ordering products, however, they have a different view. The most common reason people don't order products on the Web is that they believe they're providing their credit card and personal information for everyone to see. Is that true?

The answer is really no. It's just as safe as using your credit card in a restaurant. Think about using your credit card to pay for a meal. You give your card to the waitstaff to take to a back room to process the transaction. What sort of guar-

antee do you have that your credit card information isn't being recorded by the wrong person for the wrong reason? Couldn't the waitstaff record your card information and then use it later for a telephone order or perhaps even an order on the Web?

On the Web, you still have your card in your possession, but it's

true that your credit card information is traveling over a vast network of computers. However, most Web sites that require credit card information do provide some security while your information is traveling. In this instance, the Web site may "scramble" your card information at your computer when you enter it, send it through the Web, and then "unscramble" it when it reaches the Web site.

The process is just as safe as using your credit card in a restaurant. Currently, credit card fraud on the Web is estimated to include less than 1 percent of all transaction fraud in terms of dollars.

on your storage devices. Throughout this text, we'll alert you to these problems and how you can protect yourself against them. On the Web site for this text (www.mhhe.com/i-series), we've also included a list of other Web sites that can alert you to new viruses.

To avoid the ABuse of computers, you should always consider the reason why you're using one. If you honestly must confess that the task you're using your computer for could harm another person or computer (or be against the law), then don't perform that task.

THE ETHICAL USE OF COMPUTERS

How Can I Always Use My Computer for the Right Reasons?

Always use your computer ethically. **Ethics** is the set of principles and standards we use in deciding what to do in situations that affect other people. Ethics may be socially given standards or may be principles that are very personal to you. What might be ethically correct for you might conceivably not be for someone else. Ethics differ from laws. Laws require or prohibit certain actions on your part, with sanctions or punishments to back them up. Ethics, on the other hand, involve how you personally view the rightness or wrongness of your actions, whose outcome is less certain.

As a simple example, consider gossiping. Sharing gossip is not against the law (unless you say something legally defined as harmful or slanderous), but many people consider it unethical. That is, they refuse to pass along demeaning information until they have all the facts, and maybe not even then. Thus, ethics is a matter of personal interpretation. To you, gossip may be unethical, while others may consider it okay.

did you know? **more** *than one-third of all stock trades that occur today happen over the Internet.*

And consider using e-mail to communicate with people. E-mail is a simple, but powerful, tool for communicating electronically. All e-mail software allows you to forward a message. Is that right or wrong ethically? Some people would say that you shouldn't forward an e-mail message (no matter how trivial) unless you obtain the permission of the person who originally wrote the e-mail and sent it to you.

Ethical behavior is essential in our society. Computers have added greatly to ethical dilemmas concerning sharing of all types of information. It's far easier to share information with computers than it ever has been. As you use your computer, you must try to consider the ethics of all people and the ethical standards of society in addition to your own.

To learn more about the critically important topic of ethics, visit the Interactive Companion Labs and choose "Workplace Issues."

---

making *the grade*   SECTION C://

1. We refer to the most common wrong use of a computer as the _____-use of computers.

2. Using a computer for really "wrong," that is, unethical, reasons is called the _____-use of computers.

3. A _____ is a piece of software designed intentionally to cause annoyance or damage.

4. _____ is the set of principles and standards we use in deciding what to do in situations that affect other people.

D://UNDERSTANDING COMPUTER INTERFACES

Being able to work with your computer is all about understanding how to interact with your computer's interfaces. And that includes a lot of things, none of which are difficult to learn. For example, you need to learn how to load paper in your printer and how to load a CD in your CD drive. You also need to know how to clean your keyboard—we discuss many of these "care and feeding" issues in *Life-Long Learning Module B*. Most important, you need to learn how to interact with what you see on your screen. At various times on your screen you'll see forms to fill out, buttons to click on, and icons to choose.

YOUR GRAPHICAL USER INTERFACE
How Do I Tell My Computer What I Want to Do?

When you first turn on your computer, you'll see a screen similar to that in Figure 1.18. This is called your Windows desktop, which is a graphical user interface. A *graphical user interface (GUI)* is a graphic or icon-driven interface on which you use your mouse to start software (such as a Web browser), use that software, and initiate various other functions.

Any GUI typically contains both buttons and icons. A *button* is a graphic representation of something that you click on once with the left mouse button. An *icon* is a graphic representation of something that you click on twice or double-click. In Figure 1.18, you can start Internet Explorer (one of many available Web browsers) with either the button or the

F I G U R E   1.18

Your Windows desktop is a
graphical user interface (GUI)
with buttons and icons.

These are icons. For
example, you can
double-click on the
Internet Explorer icon to
start surfing the Web.

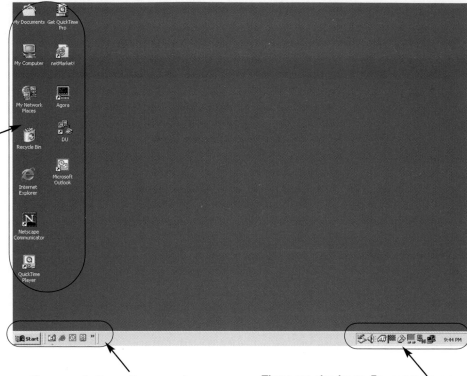

These are buttons. For example, you
can click once on the Internet Explorer
button to start surfing the Web.

These are also icons. For example, you
can double-click on the speaker icon to
adjust the volume.

icon. So, you can click once on the Internet Explorer button located at the
bottom on the screen (that area is called the task bar). Or you can double-
click on the Internet Explorer icon located in the middle left of the screen.
No matter which you choose, Internet Explorer will start and display a
Web site for you. At this point, you're ready to start surfing the Web.

INPUT FIELDS, BUTTONS, AND LINKS
How Do I Use Different Interface Elements?

Figure 1.19 shows Internet Explorer displaying the Yahoo! Web site. Its
Web site address is www.yahoo.com. Within Yahoo!, you can find many
GUI elements. The first is an input field located near the top where you can
enter search terms. To use an input field, just click once in the field and
then type whatever information you want. To submit your request for a
search, you would click once on the **Search** button located to the right of
the input field.

The Yahoo! site also has numerous links. Across the top, you can see
the graphical links for **Calendar, Messenger,** and **Check Email.** To use
any of these, all you have to do is click once on the appropriate link. You
can also see numerous text-based links, such as **Arts & Humanities,
Recreation & Sports,** and **Reference.** Again, to visit any of these portions
of the Yahoo! site all you have to do is click once on the appropriate link.
Text-based links on Web sites are almost always in blue and underlined.

As you begin to explore different types of software, you'll constantly
interface with buttons, icons, links, and input fields. To learn more about
your Windows desktop and various graphical user interfaces, visit the Interactive Companion Labs and choose "User Interfaces."

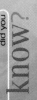

did you know? in *1990, there were about 4,500 Elvis impersonators. Today, there are over 20,000.*

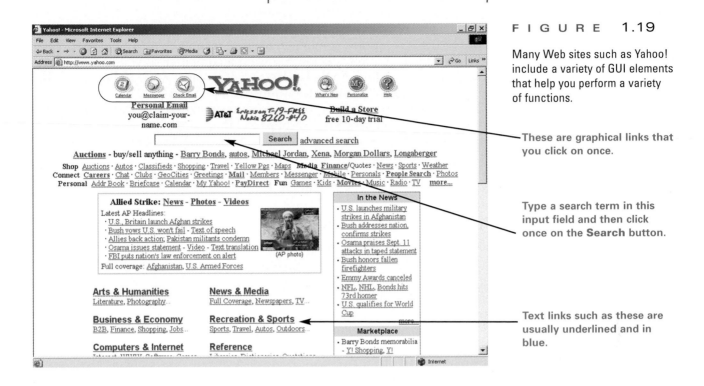

Many Web sites such as Yahoo! include a variety of GUI elements that help you perform a variety of functions.

These are graphical links that you click on once.

Type a search term in this input field and then click once on the **Search** button.

Text links such as these are usually underlined and in blue.

making the grade

1. A _____ is a graphic or icon-driven interface on which you use your mouse to start software, use that software, and initiate various other functions.

2. A _____ is a graphic representation of something that you click on once with the left mouse button.

3. An icon is a graphic representation of something that you click on _____ or double-click.

4. _____ links on Web sites are almost always in blue and underlined.

E://CONSUMER ISSUES

Purchasing a computer isn't necessarily a difficult task, but it's one you shouldn't take lightly. Today, you can buy a fairly robust computer for less than $1,000. But $1,000 may be a lot of money to you, especially if you're working only part time (or maybe not at all).

The bottom line is that purchasing a computer is a very personal decision. We can tell you the advantages and disadvantages of certain computer equipment (and we will in Chapters 2 through 6), but the final decision must rest with you.

IDENTIFYING YOUR NEEDS

Do I Really Need a Computer?

We applaud you for asking this question first. Many people believe they need a computer simply because everyone seems to have one or because computers are one of the hottest topics right now. Those are bad reasons for buying a computer. You should buy a computer for one of two basic reasons. First, you may decide you <u>want</u> a computer so you can do e-mail or spend time surfing the Web. That's a good reason—we all buy a number of products simply because we want them.

Second—and perhaps most important—you may decide to buy a computer because you <u>need</u> one. Perhaps a computer can help you better manage your money. You can certainly benefit in school by having a computer. For example, you can write term papers on a computer, use the Web to research information for that term paper, and create high-quality class presentations using such software as Microsoft PowerPoint.

THE ISSUE OF MONEY

How Much Money Should I Spend?

Once you've determined that you either want or need a computer, it's time to consider money. As we've already stated, computers are not exactly cheap. Further, the price range for a computer can be anywhere from a few hundred dollars to several thousand dollars. As you approach buying a computer, you should first determine how much money you have to spend. When you do, use that figure as an upper limit. Then you'll need to weigh the cost of each component as it relates to your budget. A good way to develop an initial budget is to survey computer ads. See what a typical computer system costs and then determine your budget accordingly.

QUESTIONS AND ANSWERS

1. Won't My Computer Be Obsolete Just as Soon as I Buy It?

The answer here is both yes and no. New, more powerful computers are becoming available every day. What you buy today may be the best today—it won't be tomorrow. But don't let that stop you from buying a computer if you need one. Think of a car—today's best models are quickly replaced by next year's better models. But that doesn't stop people from buying cars.

2. Should I Consider Mail Order or Purchasing Locally?

Depending on the brand, you can get equal quality from either mail order or a local purchase. Many people like to purchase locally because the service center is also local. If you buy through mail order and then have a problem, you often have to pack up your computer and send it off for servicing. But mail order usually provides better flexibility in customizing your computer.

3. Can I Expand My Computer after I Buy It?

The answer here is definitely yes. You can add more memory (RAM), upgrade your CPU to a faster speed, and easily add peripheral devices. Many people specifically plan to expand their computers a few months down the road. This gives you the ability to purchase a basic system now and add more functionality as you have the money.

making the grade

1. Purchasing a computer is a very _____ decision.
2. You should buy a computer if you want one or if you _____ one.
3. Many people like to buy a computer locally because the _____ is local.

F://SUMMARY AND KEY TERMS

You've just been through a very fast but we hope great introduction to computers and what they can do for you. A *computer* (or computer system) is a set of tools that helps you perform information-related tasks. You need to use all the tools in your computer to be effective and efficient. Your computer tools are either hardware or software.

Hardware

- *Input devices* such as a mouse for capturing information.
- *CPU* and *RAM* (your computer's brain) for processing information.
- *Output devices* such as a printer for presenting information.
- *Storage devices* such as a disk for storing information.
- *Telecommunications devices* such as a modem for communicating information to other people.

Software

- *System software* for technology-specific tasks.
- *Application software* for specific tasks such as writing a term paper.

You also learned about the categories of computers by size. These include *personal digital assistants (PDAs), notebook computers, desktop computers, minicomputers, mainframe computers,* and *supercomputers.* As an individual, you'll primarily be using PDAs, notebooks, and desktops for your personal computing needs. Minicomputers, mainframes, and supercomputers address the needs of many computer users simultaneously.

You also explored how to use your computer to gain access to the Web. You learned how to operate within your Windows desktop environment by using a *graphical user interface* that includes *buttons* and *icons.* You also learned the basic functions of *Web browser software,* including how to interact with *links* and the meaning of *Web sites* and *Web site addresses.*

Finally, you opened your eyes to the *ethical* use of computers. You know how to avoid the UNDERuse of your computer and—most important—the ABuse of your computer. Congratulations—you're well on your way to becoming an ethical and expert computer user.

For Chapter 1, we've included a great deal of support on the Web site for this text at www.mhhe.com/i-series for:

- Personal Digital Assistants (PDAs).
- Building Web Sites.
- Careers.
- History of Technology.
- Care of and Feeding Your Computer.

i·witness

An Up-Close Look at Web Sites

Text versus Bullet Points

If you're like most people today, you want to build your own Web site. It may be for informational purposes only (so you can post your resume for example) or because you want to set up shop on the Web and become a dot-com entrepreneur. Whatever the case, we'd like to help. In each chapter, you'll find an I-Witness box in which we take you through many of the do's and don'ts of building Web sites.

Building Web sites is very different from creating traditional print products. For example, Web surfers can leave your site and be at another in the blink of an eye. So, your site must grab and hold the attention of the viewer. Many surfers are sitting at a desk while viewing your site. So your site must be "fast." If it's slow, the viewers will become uncomfortable and either physically get out of their chairs or electronically leave your site in favor of another.

We've provided two Web sites for you to review. You should evaluate each in terms of (1) how long

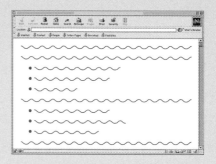

it takes you to read the content and (2) repurposing some of the content so that it appears in the form of bullet points (not just long text). These two sites are:

www.mhhe.com/i-series/i-witness/1-A.html

www.mhhe.com/i-series/i-witness/1-B.html

Which is better in terms of presenting content that you can read quickly? Explain how to shorten the text in the other by using bullet points. You can also connect to the site for this text and download these Web sites to your computer. You can then make the changes yourself.

To download these Web sites, first connect to the Web and then go to the Web site for this text at www.mhhe.com/i-series. Then, click on "Student Center" and then click on the link "I-Witness." Then, click on Chapter 1 and you will see the two file names above: 1-A.html and 1-B.html. To download one of the files, click once on it. You will then see a **Save As** window. Choose the appropriate location and click once on the **Save** button. You will follow this same process for downloading all the Web sites we've provided throughout the text.

KEY TERMS

application software (p. 1.9)

button (p. 1.19)

central processing unit (CPU or processor) (p. 1.10)

chat room (p. 1.5)

computer (computer system) (p. 1.7)

computer virus (virus) (p. 1.17)

desktop computer (p. 1.14)

ethics (p. 1.18)

graphical user interface (GUI) (p. 1.19)

hardware (p. 1.9)

icon (p. 1.19)

input device (p. 1.10)

link (hyperlink) (p. 1.3)

mainframe computer (mainframe) (p. 1.15)

minicomputer (mid-range computer) (p. 1.15)

notebook computer (laptop computer) (p. 1.14)

output device (p. 1.11)

personal digital assistant (PDA) (p. 1.13)

RAM (random access memory) (p. 1.10)

software (p. 1.7)

storage device (p. 1.12)

supercomputer (p. 1.16)

system software (p. 1.8)

telecommunications device (p. 1.13)

Web browser software (Web browser) (p. 1.7)

Web site (p. 1.2)

Web site address (site address) (p. 1.2)

CROSSWORD PUZZLE

Across

3. Also called the processor
6. Set of tools
9. Click on it once
10. Example of an output device
12. Handles technology-specific tasks
15. What defines you
16. Graphical user interface
17. For storing information
19. Portable computer
20. Most popular personal computer
21. Temporary memory
22. Physical devices
24. Helps you surf the Web

Down

1. Handles your specific information-processing tasks
2. Software that can do harm
3. Virtual meeting place
4. Computer for hundreds of users
5. Place on the Web
7. Helps you gather information
8. Example of a telecommunications device
11. Unique identifier for a Web site
13. Instructions
14. Computer for several users in small businesses
18. Personal digital assistant
19. Clickable text or an image
23. Click on it twice

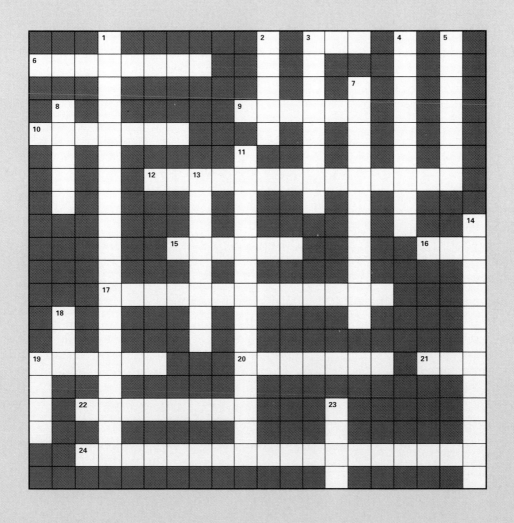

QUESTIONS AND EXERCISES

Multiple Choice

1. A mouse is an example of a(n)
   a. input device.
   b. output device.
   c. storage device.
   d. telecommunications device.
   e. CPU.

2. A disk can help you
   a. capture information.
   b. present information.
   c. process information.
   d. store information.
   e. communicate information.

3. A computer or computer system is
   a. a set of software.
   b. a set of system software.
   c. a set of application software.
   d. a set of tools.
   e. used only for making telephone calls.

4. _____ software is the software that details how your computer carries out technology-specific tasks.
   a. Application
   b. System
   c. Web browser
   d. Payroll
   e. Word processing

5. The following computers meet the computing needs of many people.
   a. Minicomputers.
   b. Desktop computers.
   c. Mainframe computers.
   d. Supercomputers.
   e. a., c., and d.

6. A graphic representation of something that you click on once with the left mouse button is a(n)
   a. button.
   b. task bar.
   c. icon.
   d. keyboard.
   e. input device.

7. The software that allows you to surf the Web is
   a. system software.
   b. Web browser software.
   c. e-mail software.
   d. word processing software.
   e. Internet software.

8. www.yahoo.com is an example of a
   a. client computer.
   b. hardware device.
   c. software program.
   d. Web site address.
   e. notebook computer.

9. The _____ is the chip that carries out the instructions it receives from your software.
   a. RAM
   b. telecommunications device
   c. PDA
   d. CPU
   e. browser

10. _____ is (are) the set of principles and standards we use in deciding what to do in situations that affect other people.
   a. Desktop
   b. Laws
   c. Ethics
   d. Legislative acts
   e. Judicial acts

True/False

11. _____ Links are clickable text or an image that allow you to start another piece of software.

12. _____ Ethics are the same as laws—you must follow them.

13. _____ A computer virus is a piece of hardware designed intentionally to cause harm to another computer.

14. _____ Temporary memory for your computer's brain is RAM.

15. _____ A printer is an example of an output device.

QUESTIONS AND EXERCISES

1. Fill in the boxes below to complete the categories of the components of your computer.

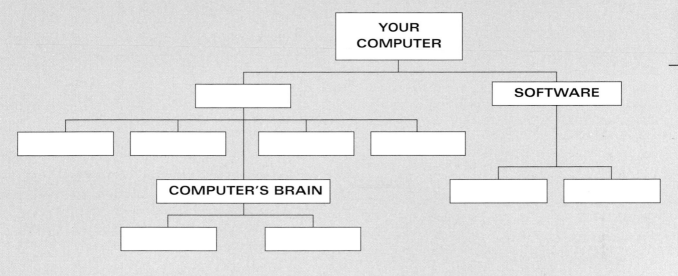

2. Consider the following terms in a related group. For each, place beside it its equivalent computer by size (we've provided one to get you started).

- Cruise ship   _____
- 50-passenger bus   _____
- Roller blades   _____

- Airplane seat   _____
- Minivan   _____
- Motorcycle   _____Desktop_____

3. For each of the following answers, create the question:

ANSWER

QUESTION

A. The CPU and internal memory (RAM). _____

B. A computer for supporting the needs of several people simultaneously in small to medium-size businesses. _____

C. Software that deals with technology-specific tasks. _____

D. 5. _____

E. For storing information. _____

F. It's once for buttons and twice for icons. _____

G. A virtual meeting place on the Web for communicating with people. _____

H. They make me who I am. _____

e-commerce

1. Buying Music

As a consumer, you can buy almost anything on the Web, from concert tickets to sports memorabilia. Here, we want to take a look at buying music. And we focus on buying traditional CDs in this project. To find music of interest to you and (potentially) buy it, connect to two of the following music sites:

- CDNow at www.cdnow.com
- Tower Records at www.towerrecords.com
- MSN eShop at eShop.msn.com
- Amazon at www.amazon.com
- Music Books Plus at www.musicbooksplus.com

While you're at each site, do some music researching and perform the following tasks:

a. Search for a CD by music artist.
b. Search for a CD by title.
c. Search for music by category such as "blues" or "opera."

Now, pick one CD you found that is of interest to you. What is the price? Is there a shipping charge? If so, what is it? How long will it take to have the CD delivered to you? Will the CD arrive by overnight service or parcel service?

Equipped with that information, go to a local music store and find the same CD. Is the price higher or lower on the Web? If there is a difference, speculate as to why the difference exists. Because you can purchase the CD right now in the store, why would people want to shop on the Web for music?

2. Finding a Job

By learning about the Web, you can find employers who are seeking employees. Not only can you search through hundreds of thousands of electronic "want ads," you can also make your resume available in a searchable database. That way, employers can be looking for you while you're looking for them.

To help you learn how to search electronic want ads, we'd like for you to get on the Web and connect to two of the following job database sites:

- Monster.com at www.monster.com
- America's JobBank at www.ajb.dni.us
- CareerNet at www.careernet.com
- headhunter.net at www.headhunter.net

While you're at each site, do some looking around and perform the following tasks:

a. Perform a job search by job title such as "accountant" or "physical therapist."
b. Perform a job search by location such as "Massachusetts" or "international."
c. Perform a job search by company name such as "Microsoft" or "United Airlines."

How many jobs did you find in each instance? Did you ever perform any search and not find any jobs by that search? Which job database site was easiest to use? Why?

3. Buying Groceries

As we've already stated, you can buy almost anything on the Web—and that includes groceries. In many areas of the country, you can have those groceries delivered within 90 minutes. So, your milk will still be cold, and your pizzas will still be frozen. You can do this because many Web-based grocery stores have partnerships with the larger "brick-and-mortar" grocery stores. If one of those grocery stores is in your general vicinity, you may be able to order groceries while on the Web and have them delivered that same day.

For this exercise, we'd like for you to connect to two of the following Web-based grocery sites:

- Groceronline at www.groceronline.com
- Groceries Express at www.grocexp.com
- Peapod at www.peapod.com
- Netgrocer at www.netgrocer.com
- PC Foods at www.pcfoods.com

As you're at each of these sites, do some grocery shopping and answer the following questions:

a. Can you shop for groceries by category such as "fresh fruits and vegetables"?
b. Can you easily add and remove items from your electronic grocery shopping cart?

c. What is the delivery schedule for your groceries? Same day? Two days? Longer?

d. What sort of "extra" delivery charge is there for your Web groceries?

e. Can you create a profile of yourself that you can use when you return to the site for more groceries?

f. What sort of guarantee is offered to you that your groceries will be fresh and undamaged?

Has this experience made you want to order some or all your groceries on the Web? Why or why not?

4. Student Loans

You can also find money all over the Web, for buying a house, for starting your own business (venture capital), and for going to school. That's right—there are a number of sites that offer services to help you find college funding. This funding can be in the form of scholarships, free money you don't have to pay back, and standard student loans.

There are a variety of student loan lenders, ranging from traditional banks and the govern-ment to private parties just wanting to give something back to society. For this exercise, connect to two of the following student funding sites:

- Student Loan Funding at www.studentloanfunding.com
- EStudentLoan at www.estudentloan.com
- Student Loan Marketing Association at www.salliemae.com
- The Student Guide at www.ed.gov/prog_info/SFA/StudentGuide
- CSLF at www.cslf.com

At each, do some looking around and answer the following questions:

a. Can you find loans from the government, banks, private organizations, or some combination of all three?

b. Can you apply for a loan while at the site or must you request paper applications that you need to complete and return?

c. By what sort of categories of funding can you search?

d. Does the site seem sincere in offering funding to you?

on the web

1. Your School's Web Site

Visit your school on the Web. What is the Web site address? Identify the links. Choose one of the links. What is the new Web site address? Now, go back to your school's main site. How did you get there?

2. Using a Search Engine

Connect to the Web and click on the **Search** button on your Web browser. How many search engines can you choose from? Choose two search engines and perform the <u>same</u> search using each. For example, you might want to search on "African safaris" or "the great wall of China." How many sites did each search engine find? Were they all really related to your topic of interest? Why do you think different search engines return different results?

3. Finding Friends and Family

On the Web, you can easily find addresses, phone numbers, and e-mail addresses for family and friends. Connect to the Web and then go to a search engine such as HotBot (www.hotbot.com), AltaVista (www.altavista.com), or WebCrawler (www.webcrawler.com). At those sites, you'll find a feature for searching for people. Try to find several friends, family members, or perhaps even yourself. What information did you have to provide? Was your search successful? How do you personally feel about this type of information being available on the Web?

4. Searching Electronic Newspapers for Jobs

In the e-commerce projects section on page 1.28, we introduced you to finding a job on the Web using a job database site. You can also find jobs by searching the classified ads of electronic newspapers. Get on the Web and connect to the site for your local newspaper. If your local paper doesn't have a site, use another newspaper such as the *New York Times* at www.nytimes.com. At whichever site you choose, perform a few job searches. Report your findings to the class.

5. Finding Medical Advice

On the Web, you can get all sorts of advice, including medical advice. You can even order health-related products and have them delivered right to your door. Connect to WebMD at www.webmd.com. Who supports this site? Is it a "for profit" site or a nonprofit site? Can you get advice there, order products, or both? How comfortable do you feel getting medical advice from the Web? Why?

6. Exploring Yahoo!

Connect to Yahoo! at www.yahoo.com. Then select any one of the many links you see such as "Entertainment" or "Social Science." What did you find? Are there other categories within those categories to choose from? Once you went to the new link, what was the new Web site address? Did you really leave Yahoo! or did you just go to another part of the Yahoo! Web site? Don't links take you to a "new" site? How can it be that you're still in Yahoo!?

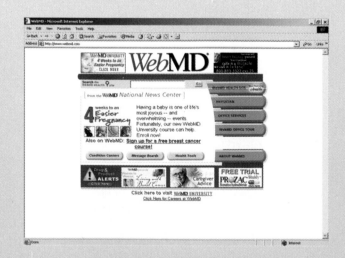

ethics, security & privacy

1. Ethical E-mail

Several years ago (true story), a man working at Chevron distributed what he thought was a funny joke through Chevron's e-mail system. A woman who received the joke was offended by it and sued Chevron to take action against the other employee. After a lot of legal mumbo-jumbo, Chevron paid the woman $2 million to settle out of court. Answer the two sets of questions below:

Question Set #1

a. Who was paying the male employee while he was working?

b. Who owned and maintained the e-mail system he used to distribute the offensive joke?

c. Because he was on company time and using company facilities, was Chevron responsible for his actions?

Question Set #2

a. If you believe Chevron was responsible for his actions, would you mind if your school constantly monitored your e-mail to determine what you're distributing? Why or why not?

b. If you believe Chevron was not responsible for his actions, are you prepared to periodically receive "garbage" e-mail at school and not sue your school if some of it offends you? Why or why not?

2. Your Personal Ethics

Consider the following situation and then answer the questions below and justify your answers. You work at a local flower shop. You also have a great female friend who believes she has met the man of her dreams. At work one day, you see the man ordering flowers for another woman.

a. Do you tell your female friend?

b. Do you tell your female friend if she just got engaged to the man?

c. Do you tell your female friend if you can't confirm that the man wasn't ordering flowers for his mother or sister?

d. Do you tell your female friend if you know she's also seeing another man "on the side"?

3. Ethics and Laws

For each of the following situations, provide what action you would take. Then, determine if your actions are against the law.

a. Leaving school one night, you find a money clip (with no markings) with $10.

b. Leaving school one night, you find a money clip (with no markings) with $1,000.

c. You find a quarter in a pay phone booth. You did not see the person who previously used the phone.

d. You find a quarter in a pay phone booth. The previous person using the phone booth is walking a few paces down the street.

e. You notice two people in class cheating on an exam. You don't know either of them.

f. You notice two people in class cheating on an exam. You know them both and don't like either of them.

g. You notice two people in class cheating on an exam. You know them both and like them very well.

h. Someone asks you for a copy of some software you recently purchased.

group activities

1. Cars and Computers

Consider cars and computers. Both are similar in that they are a collection of tools, and you need to use all the tools. Cars are also similar to computers in that they have the five categories of hardware. For a car, identify at least two instances for each of the five categories of computer hardware.

2. Understanding a Computer Ad

In Figure 1.4 on page 1.8, we provided you with a typical computer ad. Using that ad, identify the following:

Examples of:

- The CPU
- The internal memory
- System software
- Application software
- Input device
- Output device
- Storage device
- Telecommunications device

3. Reviewing Computer Systems

Visit a local computer store and obtain a list of specifications for a computer system being sold there (or perhaps find a computer ad in a newspaper). Now, answer the following questions:

a. What is the CPU speed?

b. How much RAM does it have?

c. How many storage devices are present?

d. How much information can the hard disk hold?

e. Does it come with a printer? If so, what is the printer type?

f. What is the viewable image size of the monitor?

4. Your School's Computers

Go to your school's computer lab and do a little fact finding. What type of computers are there— Macs, IBMs (and compatibles), or both? If both

are present, which is the more dominant? What is the most common system software in your lab? For any given computer, what types of application software are available?

5. Desktops and Notebooks

Find two computer systems for sale that have similar features (for example, CPU speed). One computer system should be a desktop, the other a notebook. What's the difference in price? Review our discussion in the I-Buy box on page 1.15. Is the price difference for notebooks and desktops increasing, decreasing, or staying about the same? Why do you think this is true?

6. Computer Magazines

Computer magazines are a great place to learn more about the field of computers. Visit a local library or bookstore and look through a variety of computer magazines. As you do, answer the following questions for each:

a. What's the name of the magazine?

b. How often is the magazine published?

c. Is the magazine oriented toward personal computing or business computing?

d. What is the subscription rate for the magazine?

e. Is there a Web version of the magazine?

f. Is it a magazine you would be interested in reading periodically?

g. Does the magazine have ads for computer and equipment sales?

7. Starting Your Career Search

Gather a few classmates who are interested in the same field of study as you. Perhaps it's computing, but it could also be accounting, marketing, forestry management, cosmetology, or whatever it may be. Now, find someone in your local business community with a career in that field. Interview that person concerning your field of interest, especially in regard to the necessary computing skills to be successful. Report your findings to the class.

Looking Back/Looking Ahead

The Life and Times of a Dot-Com Entrepreneur

Joann Wu is well on her way to becoming a dot-com entrepreneur and millionaire. Equipped with a really great Web idea, Joann is now turning her attention to putting actions behind her words.

Joann realizes that she has many computing needs. First and foremost, she needs a complete computer system she can take on the road as she travels. For this, she has chosen a _____ computer. A _____ computer simply won't work for Joann because, even though it has everything she would need, it's not portable. Her new system will have a mouse and _____ for gathering information, a monitor for _____ information, a _____ that performs over 700 million instructions per second, 128MB of internal memory or _____, a _____ so she can store information, and a modem for _____ information.

Joann has also decided on a variety of different _____ pieces. She's going to purchase the Microsoft Office XP suite as her primary _____ software. In that suite, Joann knows she'll be using Internet Explorer as her _____ software.

Joann also needs to create a Web presence. She's tentatively decided that her _____ will be www.econfiguration.com. On her Web site, visitors will be able to click on a variety of _____ to obtain more information and visit other sites. As Joann creates her Web site, she'll constantly be considering her own _____ as well as those who might be visiting. She wants to use her computing power in the best interests of society.

As Joann moves forward, she knows she has many more decisions to face. First, she needs to thoroughly understand the Web and the Internet. Then, she needs to decide on exactly what software she needs (both system and application). Then, she'll look to the process of actually creating her Web site. Finally, she must decide on her exact hardware needs. She'll find all her answers in Chapters 2 through 6.

did you

know?

The Web is exploding all around you. Never before has the world seen such a dynamic and exciting technology become a part of our lives so quickly. Many young people growing up today cannot even comprehend life without the Web.

from *the U.S. Postal Service (www.usps.gov) and a variety of other Web sites, you can buy stamps and print them with your printer.*

the *current asking price for the Web site name www.jesus.com (which is used by its owner as a personal ad) is over $10 million.*

uproar.com, *a popular gaming site on the Web, receives over 3 billion visitors each week (many of course are repeats).*

by *the year 2005, U.S. Web surfers will represent only 30 percent of the world's total Web community.*

after *its inception, it took only five years for 20 percent of U.S. households to be surfing the Web. It took over 40 years before 20 percent of U.S. households owned an automobile.*

ebay, *the Web's most popular auction site, currently has over ?? million items up for auction.*

To find out just how many items eBay has up for auction right now, visit www.mhhe.com/i-series.

INTERACTIVE
COMPANION LAB
SUPPORT

- **Internet Overview (p. 2.22)**
- **E-mail Essentials (p. 2.24)**

CHAPTER

two

The World Wide Web and the Internet

How Vast Is Your Virtual Imagination?

The Web (and the Internet) has almost instantly become an important part of all our lives. Many businesses on the Web don't even exist in the physical world. That is, they exist solely in cyberspace, and you can't find them on any street corner. In Chapter 1, we introduced you to the world of computers and technology by briefly surfing a few places on the Web. Let's continue our exploration.

A://THE WORLD WIDE WEB

As we begin, let's define a couple of terms and revisit a few definitions from Chapter 1. First, the World Wide Web and the Internet. The ***Internet*** is a vast network of networked computers (hardware and software) that connects millions of people all over the world. The ***World Wide Web (Web)*** is the Internet in a linked multimedia form. So, in spite of the fact that people use the terms "Internet" and "Web" interchangeably, they are different. The Internet is what really makes the Web possible.

You can access and use the Internet without going through the Web. If you do, you'll see just text information, with no color and with no links. You'll also have to enter character-based commands instead of pointing at and clicking on buttons and menu options. You can think of the Web as a graphical user interface (GUI) that rests on top of the Internet. It allows you to work with and see information in a much richer and more meaningful format.

ADDRESSES, SITES, AND PAGES
What Does a Web Site Address Tell Me?

From Chapter 1, you now know that a Web site is a specific location on the Web where you visit, gather information, and perhaps order products and that a Web site address is a unique name that identifies a specific site on the Web. For example, the *USA Today* is a Web site, and its Web site address is www.usatoday.com (see Figure 2.1). Let's go there and do some exploring.

FIGURE   2.1

Most Web sites include many Web pages. At the *USA Today* Web site, for example, you can click on **Sports** to go to a Web page devoted entirely to that topic.

Click here to go to the
Sports Web page.

FIGURE 2.2

The structure of a Web site and its Web pages is most often in a hierarchical form.

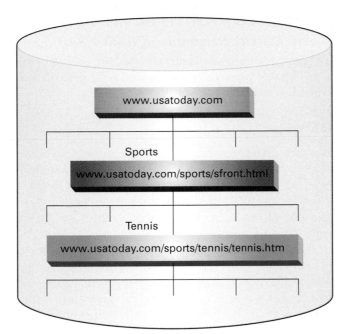

Most Web sites include several and perhaps even hundreds of Web pages. A *Web page* is a specific portion of a Web site that deals with a certain topic. Some Web sites may actually contain only a single Web page, but that's not the case most of the time. At the *USA Today,* for example, you can click on **Sports,** which is a Web page within the *USA Today* Web site. From there, you can click on **Tennis,** which is another Web page within a Web page (**Sports**) within the *USA Today* Web site. Like the *USA Today,* most Web sites contain Web pages in a hierarchical form (see Figure 2.2). People tend to use the terms Web site and Web page interchangeably—in this text we'll most often use the term Web site. Incidentally, **Sports** and **Tennis** are both examples of links.

Addresses for Web sites and pages can actually become quite long, like the ones in Figure 2.2. But you don't need to remember addresses. All you have to do is add them to your Favorites list in your Web browser software. Once you find a site or page you like, simply click on **Favorites** in the menu bar and then **Add to Favorites . . . .** Your Web browser software will add the logical name (for example, USA Today Latest News) to your Favorites list for you. Whenever you surf the Web again, all you have to do is display your Favorites list and click on the logical name. Your Web browser recalls the address and instantly takes you there.

FIGURE 2.3

Using your **Favorites** list, you can organize the sites you visit frequently.

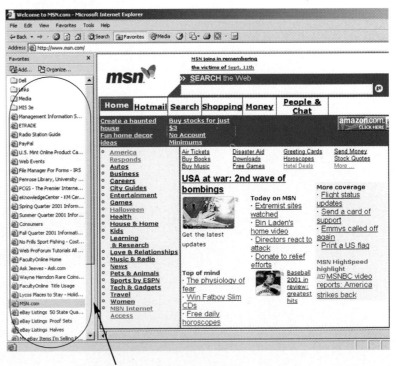

You can organize your favorite Web sites within folders or list them individually.

WEB SITES WORTH SURFING

Where Do You Recommend I Start Surfing on the Web?

There are literally millions of sites on the Web, and the ones you like are simply your personal preferences. Let's get you started by looking at some we think will interest you.

Careers

In many ways, computers (and technology in general) can help you land a really great job. First and foremost, you need computer skills in jobs today. So, just learning about computers is a step in the right direction. You can also use the Web to search for jobs and post your resume in a database. Employers, in turn, search these databases to find potential employees (and it could be you).

To search for a job and post your resume for employers to review, we recommend that you start with such sites as Monster.com (www.monster.com shown below), hotjobs.com (www.hotjobs.com), and headhunter.net (www.headhunter.net). There are numerous other great sites that can help you find a job. For a comprehensive list, please visit the site for this text at www.mhhe.com/i-series. At any of these sites, you simply type in a job you want (and possibly a desired location), and you'll instantly see a list of available jobs.

FIGURE   2.4

To begin your career search, consider visiting sites such as Monster.com.

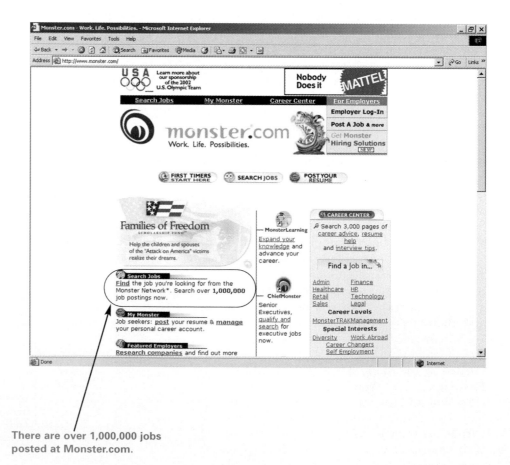

There are over 1,000,000 jobs posted at Monster.com.

Information and Reference

The Web is a wealth of information at your fingertips. You can find everything from recipes to the latest sports scores on the Web. Some information and reference sites you visit are purely for your personal enjoyment and pleasure. Others, however, can benefit you greatly. For example, you can find research material at Electric Library (www.elibrary.com). That site allows you to search newspapers, books, magazines, radio transcripts, and even maps.

You can find information and reference sites that deal with a particular topic that might interest you, as well. At Consumer World (www.consumerworld.org), for example, you can research products you're considering purchasing. You can read about the latest safety reviews of automobiles, find the best rates for investments, and learn more about the newest prescription drugs.

FastWeb (www.fastweb.com in Figure 2.5) is certainly a site worth visiting. FastWeb can help you find funding for your education. It has everything from government loans to free money you don't even have to pay back. Millions of dollars in scholarships each year go unclaimed because no one completes an application. FastWeb can help you find those scholarships and much more.

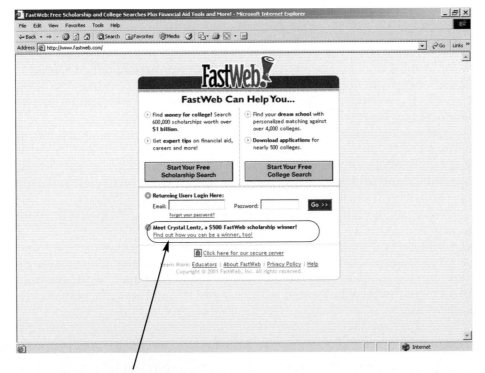

FIGURE 2.5

FastWeb and many other sites offer information and reference material that can greatly benefit you.

Once you begin using FastWeb, you're automatically entered into a daily drawing for education funding.

FIGURE 2.6

You can do more than just order computers on the Web. Sites such as PCSupport.com provide answers to your technology questions.

Computing

While you're using your computer to find sites on the Web, you might want to think about computer-related sites. Computer-related sites cover a broad range of topics and electronic commerce activities. At Dell (www.dell.com), for example, you can customize your own computer system and pay for it with a credit card.

Other sites cover specific aspects of computers such as software. At software.net (www.software.net) you can buy almost any kind of software you want. While browsing for software, you can do so by category (desktop publishing or graphics), by software name (Word or Excel), and even by publisher (Microsoft or Lotus).

What might really interest you are the sites that can help you be more productive in using your computer or help you fix something on your computer. For example, PCSupport.com (corporate.pcsupport.com) and service911.com (www.service911.com) are both sites devoted to answering your computer-related questions. You can read FAQ pages, send an e-mail to an expert (who will respond within 24 hours), and even participate in a chat room.

Travel

In virtual space (the Web, that is), traveling is fun and easy. Just start typing in Web site addresses and clicking on links and you'll soon be in places all over the world. The Web can also help you visit real places and go on vacations. It doesn't matter if you have your eye on a cruise or simply need to fly home for the holidays; there are many travel and travel-related Web sites that can help.

did you

know?

The word "stressed" spelled backwards is "desserts."

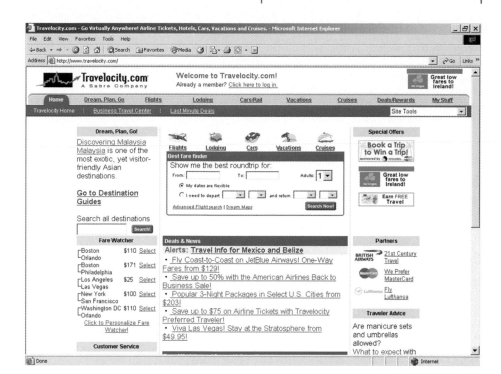

F I G U R E   2.7

The Web is now a great place to schedule all your travel arrangements.

At Travelocity.com (www.travelocity.com shown in Figure 2.7), you can book airline travel, rent cars, and make reservations at hotels around the world. You can even find "fire sale" deals, which are nothing more than extremely cheap airline tickets. They may not be for exactly where you want to go, but, if you don't care and just want to get away, they may be perfect.

Other popular travel sites include Expedia (www.expedia.com), TravelSecrets (www.travelsecrets.com), and HotWire (www.hotwire.com). None of these sites require a fee for their use, and all you need is a credit card to pay for your travels.

USING A SEARCH ENGINE

What if I Don't Know Which Site I Should Be Visiting?

Finding information on the Web can often be easy; other times it can be extremely difficult. What if you need information, but don't know exactly where to find it? Fortunately, you can find your information (and probably more than you want) by using a search engine. A **search engine** is a facility on the Web that allows you to find Web sites by key word or words.

There are two main types of search engines—directories and true search engines. A **directory search engine** organizes listings of Web sites into hierarchical lists. A **true search engine,** on the other hand, uses software agent technologies (we'll discuss these in more detail in a later chapter) to search the Web for key words and place them into indexes.

Suppose, for example, that you wanted to find out who won the Academy Awards in the year 2001. To do so, you could use a directory search engine such as Yahoo! (see Figure 2.8). You would first go to the Yahoo! site by typing www.yahoo.com into the address field. Then, you would click on **Arts & Humanities, Awards, Movies and Films@, Academy Awards,** and **Coverage of the 73rd Annual Academy Awards.** You can then select whatever Web site seems to offer the information you want.

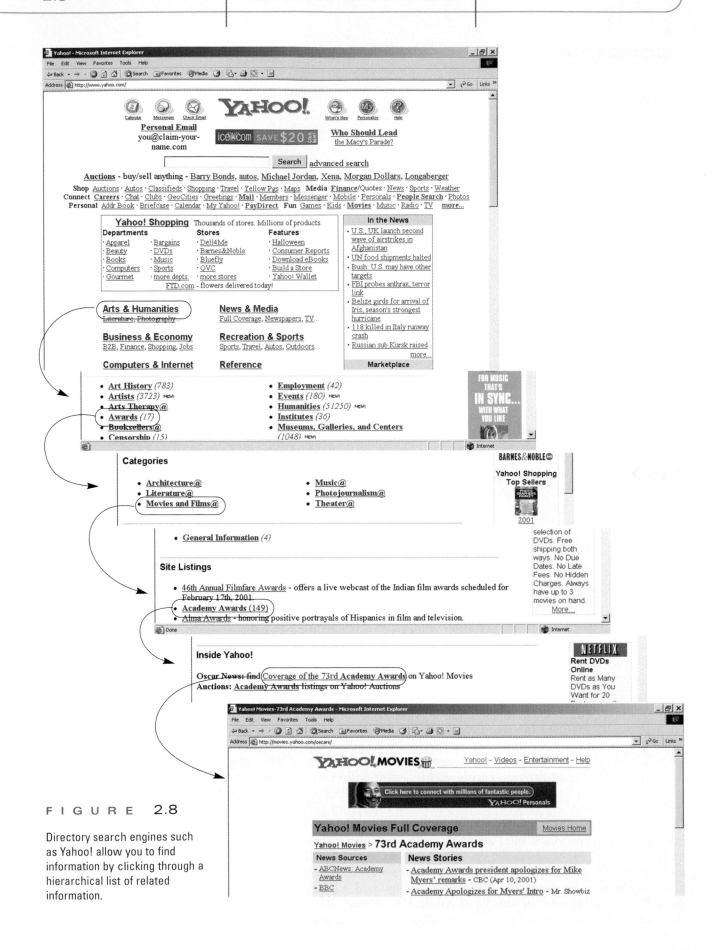

Directory search engines such
as Yahoo! allow you to find
information by clicking through a
hierarchical list of related
information.

On the other hand, you could use a true search engine, such as Ask Jeeves, to find the same information. Ask Jeeves is a search engine that allows you to enter a question concerning what information you'd like to find. To do so, you would first go to Ask Jeeves by typing www.askjeeves. com into the address field. Then, you would enter the question, "Who won the Academy awards in 2001" (without the quote marks), and click on Ask (see Figure 2.9). As you can see in the second screen, Ask Jeeves then provides a list of Web sites with the information you want.

We definitely recommend that you become acquainted with both types of search engines. Other popular search engines include Mamma.com (www.mamma.com), AltaVista (www.altavista.com), Excite (www.excite. com), HotBot (www.hotbot.com), Lycos (www.lycos.com), and Web-Crawler (www.webcrawler.com).

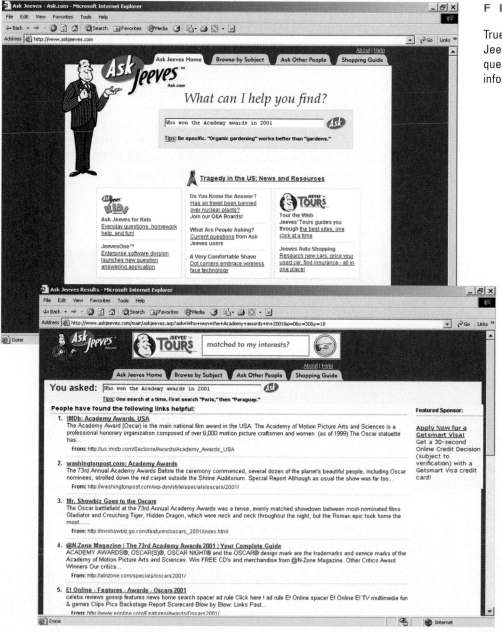

F I G U R E 2.9

True search engines such as Ask Jeeves allow you to enter a question related to the information you want to find.

i·series insights

Ethics, Security & Privacy

Getting Conned by Dot-Coms

The "brick-and-mortar" business world is full of shady deals and scams. So is the "click-and-mortar" business world of the Web. And it's even harder to pursue and prosecute criminals in the virtual world of the Web. Hiding behind Web site addresses is often an effective mechanism. Here's just a sampling of a few shady deals that have gone down on the Web.

- One-time auction houses advertised for several weeks about an upcoming auction. When the auction was over and money was collected, no goods were shipped.

- Typical credit card fraud in which card numbers were used to illegally order other products.

- "All expenses paid" vacations that ended up including a hotel that wasn't free.

- A variety of health care products that turned out to be snake oil. This is a big scam on the Web.

One Web site even offered free access to adult-oriented material. But it turned out not to be free. Once you went there, the site disconnected your phone call through your modem, kept your line active, and used it to call a long-distance number to another service provider outside the United States.

Be careful when you're ordering products and services on the Web. Deals that seem to be too good to be true probably are. If you feel you've been scammed on the Web, immediately contact the Federal Trade Commission at www.ftc.gov.

SECTION A://   *making* **the grade**

1. The _____ is a vast network of networked computers (hardware and software) that connects millions of people all over the world.

2. A _____ is a specific portion of a Web site that deals with a certain topic.

3. If you find a site you'd like to visit frequently, you should add it to your _____ list.

4. A _____ is a facility on the Web that allows you to find Web sites by key word or words.

5. A _____ organizes listings of Web sites into hierarchical lists.

B://HARDWARE AND SOFTWARE FOR SURFING THE WEB

By now, we hope, you're excited about the prospects of surfing the Web. It's actually quite easy to do, and the Web offers something for everyone. Let's take a step back and discuss what hardware and software you need for surfing the Web.

HARDWARE FOR WEB SURFING
What Hardware Do I Need for Surfing the Web?

You can use a variety of hardware configurations to surf the Web—anything from a very expensive notebook or desktop to a relatively inexpensive cell phone. Many people are choosing to access the Web in a variety of ways. They just can't seem to get enough of the Web. You may fall into that category.

Today's Typical Computer Systems

Today's typical computer system that you can buy offers all the hardware you need to surf the Web, including hardware devices such as keyboard, mouse, monitor, and modem. A **modem** is a device that connects your computer through a phone line to a network of other computers. To use your modem, all you have to do is connect it to a phone line and then dial up another computer that's already connected to the Web. We'll talk more about this connection process when we discuss connectivity software in a moment.

Web Computers

There are many people today who want a computer just to surf the Web. They're not really interested in investing a lot of money to have a great deal of CPU speed or a lot of RAM (internal memory). For these people, a Web computer is a nice solution. A **Web computer** is a scaled-down version of today's typical computer system that provides Web access and costs about half the price.

Again, these are great computer systems if you're primarily interested in surfing the Web. They also allow you to use a variety of personal productivity software such as word processing and personal information management. However, if you also want to do a lot of video editing and other intensive tasks, these types of machines are not for you. For a list of Web computers and their capabilities, visit the site for this text at www.mhhe.com/i-series.

Television-Based Web Surfing Machines

As technology becomes more prevalent and widespread, you can expect to see a convergence of devices that offer you access to information. One such convergence that's already occurring is Web access through your television. Many cable TV providers today offer access to the Web through your cable line. If so, your television actually becomes your monitor.

Other products, such as WebTV, offer something similar. If you buy a WebTV system, you get a box that connects to a phone line and your television. The system also comes with a wireless mouse and keyboard. So, you can sit back in your favorite chair and surf the Web on your television from across the room (see Figure 2.10 on the next page).

However, a WebTV system doesn't include such devices as a disk, CD, or DVD drive. So, you can't do anything with your WebTV system except surf the Web. WebTV systems cost about $100, and then you pay a monthly fee of about $25 to surf the Web.

Web Phones

For people on the go, there are a variety of wireless Web surfing machines, namely, personal digital assistants and Web phones. A **Web phone** is a

F I G U R E   2.10

Television-based Web surfing machines such as WebTV bring the Web to your television screen.

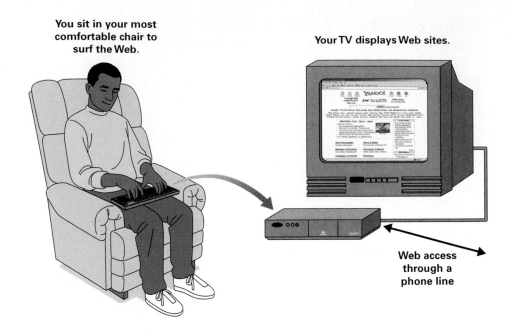

You sit in your most comfortable chair to surf the Web.

Your TV displays Web sites.

Web access through a phone line

special type of cell phone that allows you to access the Web. Most important, Web phones include a microbrowser. A ***microbrowser*** is Web browser software for Web phones that can display text information in a small amount of space.

Web phones today also offer you other nice features, mainly in the form of personal information management software. So, in addition to making phone calls and accessing the Web, you can use your Web phone to keep appointments, maintain an address book, and take short notes.

Don't buy a Web phone if you want to enjoy hours of Web surfing with cool graphics, animation, and sound. Web phones are ideal for fast access to bits and pieces of information—flight schedules, weather reports, sports scores, and news. This information will come to you primarily in text form (we expect that to change soon).

Pagers

Pager services these days do more than just deliver phone numbers and short text messages—they also give you Web access. The most popular Web-accessing pager today is the Blackberry. While providing basic e-mail services, the Blackberry also delivers content from Bloomberg News, StockSmart Stock Quote, Hollywood.com, and a variety of other Web sites.

Personal Digital Assistants (PDAs)

Many of today's personal digital assistants also provide you with access to the Web. Using a small antenna that neatly folds away, you can dial the Web and access specific Web sites (just as with a Web phone) and receive "Web clippings" from other sites that include *The Wall Street Journal*, ABC News, and Etrade (just as with a Blackberry pager).

We believe that accessing the Web wirelessly with various devices, especially PDAs, is the wave of the future. This will definitely lead to an explosion of m-commerce, or mobile commerce, which we'll discuss in Chapter 4.

Special cell phones called Web phones give you access to the Web. But don't expect great graphics or color.

Some high-end pagers such as a Blackberry offer you paging capabilities, e-mail capabilities, and Web access.

Many PDAs today come equipped with a wireless modem and antenna that allow you to access the Web.

FIGURE 2.11

Web phones, pagers, and PDAs now bring the Web to you wherever you are.

SOFTWARE FOR WEB SURFING

What Software Do I Need for Surfing the Web?

Almost any computer you buy today comes with the software that you need to surf the Web—connectivity software and a Web browser. You're already familiar with Internet Explorer, Microsoft's popular Web browser software. Another popular Web browser is Netscape Communicator. Web browser software is probably the easiest software to learn and use, even on your own with no book or instructions.

Connectivity Software

Connectivity software enables you to use your computer to "dial up" or connect to another computer. When you want to access the Web from home, you must connect your computer to another computer that's already connected to the Web. These computers that are already connected to the Web are owned and maintained by companies such as AOL or Netzero and perhaps even your school.

Let's consider using your school to connect to the Web. When you start your connectivity software (which comes standard on today's computer systems and is usually an icon on your Windows desktop screen), you'll see a box similar to that in Figure 2.12. All you have to do is enter your user name and password, enter a phone number or verify that the existing phone number is correct (contact your school's IT support department for the correct phone number), and click once on the **Dial** button. Your connectivity software will then take over, make a phone call to your school's computer through your modem, and establish a connection between your computer and your school's computer. Then, you simply start your Web browser and you're on the Web.

No matter which Internet service provider you choose, you'll follow a similar process to access the Web. In the next section, we'll explore some of the more popular Internet service provider options.

F I G U R E   2.12

Connectivity software allows you to "dial up" another computer so you can access the Web.

We should also point out that accessing the Web through a telephone line and modem is not the only way to do so. As we've already discussed, you can access the Web wirelessly with a PDA, pager, or cell phone. You also have several other "wired" and "wireless" options that we'll discuss in Chapter 6.

Making Your Decision

For software, your choices are pretty straightforward and simple. The connectivity software you need is already on your computer, so there's no decision to make. For Web browser software, it depends. If you're using AOL to connect to the Web, it provides its own Web browser for you to use, as do most other Internet service providers. If you're using your school to connect to the Web or an Internet service provider that doesn't offer a Web browser, then your choice is either Microsoft's Internet Explorer or Netscape Communicator. The choice is really up to you.

SECTION B : //   making the grade

1. A _____ is a device that connects your computer through a phone line to a network of other computers.
2. A _____ is a scaled-down version of today's typical computer system that provides Web access at about half the price.
3. A popular television-based Web surfing system is _____.
4. A _____ is Web browser software for Web phones that can display text information in a small amount of space.
5. A _____ is a popular Web-accessing pager.

C://INTERNET SERVICE PROVIDERS

To access the Web, you need an Internet service provider. An *Internet service provider (ISP)* is a company that provides individuals, organizations, and businesses access to the Internet. ISPs can include your school (you probably have access to the Internet from your school's computer lab), your place of work, and typical for-profit companies such as AOL and Juno. Which you choose is an important decision.

COMMERCIAL INTERNET SERVICE PROVIDERS

Do Some ISPs Offer More than Just Internet Access?

Commercial ISPs charge you a monthly fee, just as your telephone company charges you a monthly fee for phone service. This ISP fee can range from just a few dollars to about $20 per month. Some commercial ISPs may also place a limit on the amount of time you can spend connected to the Internet. If you exceed that time limit, you may have to pay extra by the minute or hour.

Popular worldwide commercial ISPs include Microsoft (MSN), AOL, CompuServe, and AT&T WorldNet, just to name a few (see Figure 2.13). You can also find regional commercial ISPs that serve just your local area. If want to find these, just look in the business listings of your phone book.

In addition to providing access to the Internet, commercial ISPs offer a number of other features and services. For example, most commercial ISPs provide you with Web space. *Web space* is a storage area where you keep your Web site. You can't actually keep your Web site on your home computer and have people access it. So, you need Web space to publish your Web site for everyone to see.

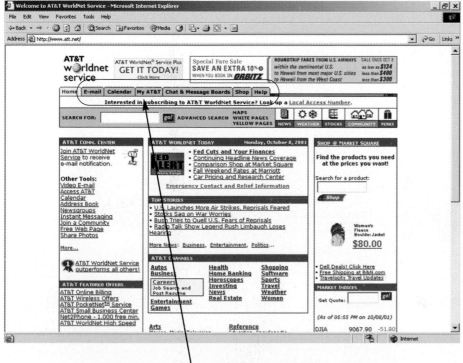

F I G U R E   2.13

AT&T WorldNet is a commercial ISP that provides you with a number of features and customization capabilities.

As with most commercial ISPs, AT&T WorldNet provides you with e-mail, chat rooms, customized pages, and many other features.

Commercial ISPs also offer free e-mail, chat rooms, and instant messaging. With instant messaging, someone can send you a message and it will immediately appear on your screen as opposed to going to your e-mail box. Most commercial ISPs also offer very good 24-hour technical support in case you have any problems. If you want to shop around and find the right ISP (commercial, or free, which we discuss in a moment), we recommend that you visit internet.com (thelist.internet.com), FindAnISP (www.findanisp.com), or ISP Finder (www.ispfinder.com).

FREE INTERNET SERVICE PROVIDERS

Can I Find an ISP That's Basically Free?

Although commercial ISPs don't cost too much, many people opt for free ISPs. Free ISPs are absolutely free, as their names suggest—you don't pay a setup fee, you don't pay a monthly fee, and you may have unlimited access to the Web. But there are some catches. When you use a free ISP, a banner ad will almost always appear on your screen (see Figure 2.14). You can move it around and from side to side, but you can't get rid of it.

Technical support is often limited with a free ISP. Some offer only e-mail support, while others do offer phone support but no toll-free number. Finally, free ISPs offer you limited Web space, if any at all. And you need Web space if you want to put up a Web site.

Popular free ISPs include FreeLane (www.freelane.excite.com), FreeInternet.com (www.freei.com), Ifreedom.com (www.ifreedom.com), Juno (www.juno.com), and NetZero (www.netzero.com).

F I G U R E   2.14

Juno is a popular free ISP.

Even if you sign up for Juno's platinum service, you will still see banner ads.

YOUR SCHOOL OR WORK

Can I Access the Internet through School or Work?

One of the nice side benefits of going to school or being employed is that you often get free Web access through school or your work. While in school, you can have access to the Web in a lab and often from home. All you have to do is connect to your school's computer with connectivity software and you're ready to surf.

Most work environments with offices offer Web access to their employees. And most places allow you to have Web access while at work and while at home. Again, all you have to do is dial in to your place of work's computer with connectivity software and you're ready to surf.

Something important to consider while using your school or work as an ISP is that many schools and places of work monitor your movements on the Web, and they have the right to do so. Some even restrict where you can go on the Web. That's definitely a downside. The upside is that the service is probably free.

MAKING YOUR DECISION

What Are the Guidelines for Choosing an ISP?

So, which type of ISP is right for you? We can't answer that question but we can offer you some guidelines.

- **Do you need Web space?** If you want to publish your own Web site, free ISPs may not be for you. Your employer may not let you publish your own site.
- **Is great technical support important?** If you want a no-hassle Web experience with solid support, definitely choose a commercial ISP.
- **Is money a serious consideration?** If saving money is the way to go for you, choose a free ISP, your school, or your work.
- **Is privacy important to you?** All ISPs track who's doing what and going where. However, your school and place of work may be the nosiest.

You might also want to consider looking for a package deal with a new computer you buy. Many new systems come with several hundred dollars in rebates as long as you're willing to subscribe to the services of a commercial ISP for a year or more. So, you can buy a computer at the regular price and get commercial ISP service essentially for free, for a period of time.

making the grade   SECTION C://

1. An _____ is a company that provides individuals, organizations, and businesses access to the Internet.
2. _____ ISPs charge you a monthly fee to access the Internet.
3. _____ is a storage area where you keep your Web site.
4. Juno is a _____ ISP.
5. If you want free access, you can choose from among a free ISP, your school, or your _____.

D://THE INTERNET BEHIND THE WEB

So far, we have been exploring the Web and some of the many great sites to visit. Underneath or behind the Web are the Internet and all its technologies. Let's pop the hood and see what it looks like.

THE STRUCTURE OF THE INTERNET

What Exactly Is the Internet?

The Internet is what makes the Web possible. While surfing the Web, using technologies such as a Web browser, a keyboard, a mouse, a monitor, perhaps a modem for connecting over a phone line to an ISP, and so on, you're relying on and taking advantage of the Internet—the vast network of computers that connects millions of people all over the world.

Internet Technologies

The Internet is a collection of hardware and software in the form of a worldwide network. A **network** is simply a collection of computers that support the sharing of information and hardware devices. The **Internet backbone** is the major set of connections for computers on the Internet (see Figure 2.15). A **network access point (NAP)** is a point on the Internet where several connections converge. At each NAP is at least one computer that simply routes Internet traffic from one place to the next. These NAPs are owned and maintained by a network service provider. A **network service provider (NSP),** such as MCI or AT&T, owns and maintains routing computers at NAPs and even the lines that connect the NAPs to each other. (In Figure 2.15, you can see that Dallas is a NAP, with lines converging from Atlanta, Los Angeles, Kansas City, Houston, and Austin.)

At any given NAP, an ISP such as AOL may connect its computers to the Internet. In turn, you connect your computer to an AOL computer (by dialing it up with connectivity software). So, your ISP provides you access to the Web by allowing you to connect your computer to the Internet through its computer.

F I G U R E   2.15

The Internet backbone is the major set of connections for computers that make up the Internet.

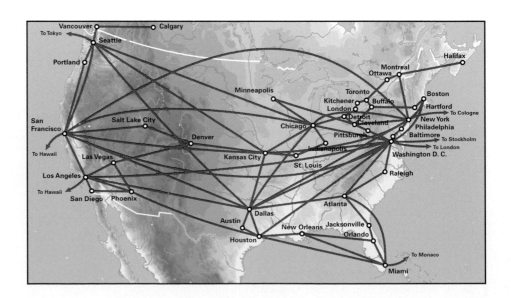

FIGURE   2.16

The anatomy of a URL is very similar to the path name for a file located on your computer.

Internet Addresses and Domain Names

When you access a certain site, you do so with its address, such as www.usatoday.com (for the *USA Today*). Technically, this address is a domain name. A **domain name** identifies a specific computer on the Internet and the main page for an entire site. If you visit a particular Web page within the *USA Today* such as Sports, its address is www.usatoday.com/sports/sfront.htm. The technical name for this address is a URL (see Figure 2.16). A **URL (uniform resource locator)** is an address for a specific Web page or document within a Web site. Again, domain name and URL are the technical terms. Almost everyone today uses the terms *Web site, Web page,* and *address* instead of "domain name" and "URL."

Domain names tell you a lot about the site you're visiting, as www.etrade.com tells you the site name (Etrade) and that it's a commercial organization by the last three letters—"com." This last three-letter extension can take on other forms—edu, gov, mil, and many others—and is referred to as the **top-level domain** (see Figure 2.17). Thus, www.ucla.edu is the site address for UCLA, an educational institution.

Domains	Description
Com	Commercial or for-profit business
Edu	Educational institution
Gov	U.S. government agency
Mil	U.S. military organization
Net	Internet administrative organization
Org	Professional or non-profit organization
Int	International treaties organization

FIGURE   2.17

Top-level domains are three-character extensions that tell you what type of organization you're accessing.

practically speaking

How Old Is the Internet?

You may send e-mail and surf the Web almost every day and take them for granted. Have you ever stopped to realize that not long ago neither of them existed? What was merely an idea 50 years ago today is a vast collection of computers and applications such as the World Wide Web criss-crossing the planet.

It all began in 1957 when the U.S. government formed a military research agency to keep up with its cold war enemy the Soviet Union, which had launched the first satellite, called Sputnik 1. The United States wanted to remain technologically ahead of the Soviets so it formed DARPA (Defense Advanced Research Projects Agency) whose scientists investigated new technologies.

With new knowledge came new vulnerabilities. Worried about having to keep what they were investigating and learning all in one location, DARPA sought to protect the nation's information by linking together computers so as to guard against losing all the information should a key computer fail. These connected computers formed the ARPANet (Advanced Research Projects Agency Network), which scientists also used to talk to one another and share files. This was the grandparent of the Internet as we know it today. The ARPANet started with only four computers in 1969. Today over 95 million across the world form our Internet. That's a pretty phenomenal spurt of growth for just over 30 years, don't you think? Of course the Internet is still growing.

The World Wide Web is even younger than the Internet. It is *very* recent. In 1991, a computer scientist named Tim Berners-Lee created a program that worked on his employer's computer system enabling people to link their documents and files together. Future Web surfers, however, still lacked one thing: software. It wasn't until a couple of years later that Marc Andreessen released *Mosaic for X,* a graphical Web browser. He went on to cofound Netscape and a Web browser called Netscape Navigator. Soon companies such as Microsoft were making Web browsers as well. The Web caught on. In 1993 there were only 130 Web sites. Think of it—less than 10 years ago few people had ever heard of the Web. Today you can visit more than 25 million Web sites.

To learn more about the history and growth of the Internet, visit our Web site at www.mhhe.com/i-series.

1969
ARPANet

Today's
Internet

FIGURE 2.18

FTP servers such as Zdnet.com/downloads maintain many files that you can download to your computer.

COMPUTERS ON THE INTERNET

Are There Different Types of Computers on the Internet Performing Different Functions?

There are two basic types of computers on the Internet—servers and clients. A **server computer** (also called a **host computer**) is a computer on the Internet that provides information and services to other computers and Internet users such as you. Server computers can be high-end workstations, minicomputers, and even mainframe computers. A **client computer** is essentially the computer you use to move around the Internet and access the information and services on a server computer. So, a client computer can be your desktop or notebook, your cell phone, or even your TV-based computer system.

There are many types of server computers on the Internet. The one we've focused on is a Web server. A **Web server** provides information and services to Web surfers. So, when you access www.census.gov to obtain government census data, you're accessing a Web server with your client computer. Most often, you'll be accessing and using the services of a Web server.

Other servers on the Internet include mail servers, FTP servers, and IRC servers. A **mail server** provides e-mail services and accounts. An **FTP server** maintains a collection of files that you can download (see Figure 2.18). These files can include software, music files, and games. An **IRC (Internet relay chat) server** supports your use of discussion groups and chat rooms. IRC servers are popular hosting computers for sites such as www.epinions.com (which you visited in Chapter 1).

INFORMATION ON THE INTERNET

How Does Information Move from Computer to Computer on the Internet?

As information moves around the Internet, bouncing among network access points until it finally reaches you, it does so according to various communications protocols. A **communications protocol (protocol)** is a set of rules that every computer follows to transfer information.

Protocols are very necessary in a network environment because different types of computers handle information internally in different forms, and there are many types of computers on the Internet—server computers that can be minicomputers, perhaps hand-held computers such as your cell phone, everybody's desktops. If we want them all to communicate effectively, computers must have common protocols for moving information among themselves on the Internet.

TCP/IP

TCP/IP (Transport Control Protocol/Internet Protocol) is the basic communications protocol that makes the Internet work. It defines the rules that allow various computers to communicate across the Internet. It doesn't matter if you're viewing a multimedia presentation from a Web server, transferring a file from an FTP server, or chatting across an IRC server, TCP/IP is the foundation for the movement of the information.

Hypertext Transfer Protocol (http)

Hypertext transfer protocol (http) is the communications protocol that supports the movement of information over the Web, essentially from a Web server to you. That's why Web site addresses start with "http://." That beginning portion of the address informs all the Internet technologies that you want to access something on the Web. For example, it tells your browser software that you want to access a Web site. Most browser software today assumes that you want to access a Web site on the Internet. So, you don't even have to type in the "http://" if you don't want to. Essentially, http://www.whitehouse.gov is the same thing as www.whitehouse.gov.

If you recall, the Web is the Internet in multimedia form. So, when you access a Web site, your computer is using both TCP/IP (to transfer any type of information over the Internet) and http (because the information you want is Web-based).

File Transfer Protocol (FTP)

File transfer protocol (FTP) is the communications protocol that allows you to transfer files of information from one computer to another. FTP servers are popular stops for Web surfers who want to download a variety of different types of files—software such as games and music are the most common. When you download a file from an FTP site, you're using both TCP/IP (the basic Internet protocol) and FTP (the protocol that allows you to download the file).

If you'd like to read more about the technical Internet, we've provided a list of books and resources on the Web site for this text at www.mhhe.com/i-series. You can also visit the Interactive Companion Labs and choose "Internet Overview."

did you know?

An *Audi TT two-door coupe sells for $35,650 on the Web. A local dealership quoted $35,800 for the car.*

1. A _____ computer (also called a host computer) is a computer on the Internet that provides information and services to other computers and Internet users such as you.

2. A _____ is a point on the Internet where several connections converge.

3. A _____ is the technical term of an address on the Internet.

4. A _____ is a set of rules that every computer follows to transfer information.

5. _____ is the communications protocol that supports the movement of information over the Web, essentially from a Web server to you.

E://CONSUMER ISSUES

E-MAIL

How Can I Use E-Mail to Communicate with Other People?

E-mail (short for **electronic mail**) is software you use to electronically communicate with other people. You send an e-mail message instead of writing a letter and sending it through the postal system. Using e-mail is almost as simple as using a Web browser. To receive e-mail messages, you need an e-mail address. An **e-mail address** is a unique address for a person using an e-mail system. Consider Stephen Green, a student at UCLA. His e-mail address could appear as stephen_green@ucla.edu. Not all e-mail systems use a person's full first and last name; some will simply use the first initial with the last name such as sgreen@ucla.edu.

To give you a short demonstration of e-mail, we'll use Microsoft Outlook, a Microsoft product (most e-mail software looks and acts very similar to Outlook). In Figure 2.19, you can see a sample of an electronic mailbox. An open envelope beside a message indicates mail you've already

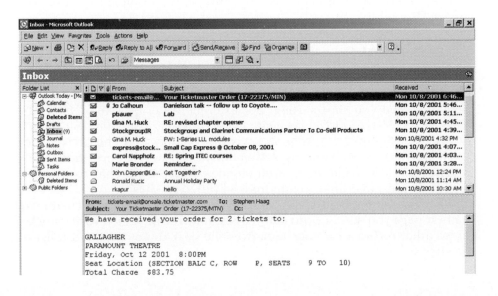

FIGURE 2.19

A Microsoft Outlook mailbox shows you your received messages.

FIGURE   2.20

When you reply to a message, a "reply to" form like this one makes it easy for you to respond to an e-mail.

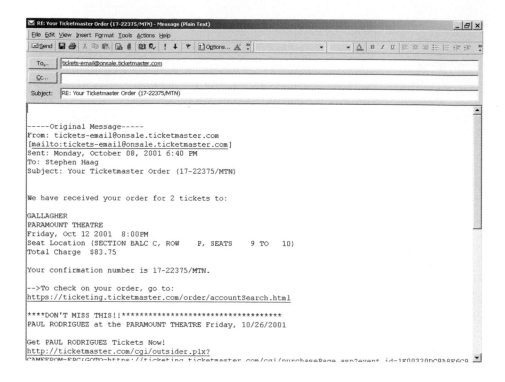

read; an unopened envelope indicates new mail you haven't read. You can easily read any message by double-clicking on it.

You can respond to a message by simply clicking on the **Reply** button. Outlook will display a "reply to" form and automatically fill in the **From, To,** and **Subject** fields (see Figure 2.20). Outlook also includes the message you originally received. All you have to do is type in your response and click on **Send.** It's that easy.

You can also send someone an e-mail message without first receiving one from them. In this case, you click on the **New** button. Outlook will display a form similar to the "reply to" form. In this instance, you have to enter information in the **To** and **Subject** fields, compose your message, and click on **Send.**

As we said, e-mail is easy to use, and you can learn it in a short time. To learn more about e-mail, visit the Interactive Companion Labs and choose "E-mail Essentials."

WEB PORTALS

Where Do I Start on the Web?

Most Web browser software is already configured to take you to a certain Web site when you start surfing. For example, Internet Explorer usually starts at the Microsoft Network site (MSN at www.msn.com). Sites such as MSN (see Figure 2.21), Yahoo! (www.yahoo.com), and The Go Network (www.go.com) are Web portals. A *Web portal* is a site that provides a wide range of services, including search engines, free e-mail, chat rooms, discussion boards, and links to hundreds of different sites.

The nice thing about Web portals is that they often let you customize the first page you see. So, you can request a ticker of your favorite stocks, the weather forecast for your area over the next three days, and a list of the sites you most commonly visit.

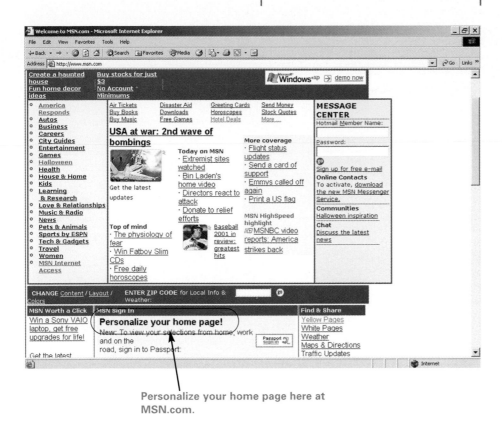

F I G U R E   2.21

Web portals such as MSN.com offer many services and most often allow you to customize your home page.

Personalize your home page here at MSN.com.

QUESTIONS AND ANSWERS

1. How Fast Can I Surf the Web?

Speed, as far as surfing the Web is concerned, means how fast you can access and load Web sites into your Web browser. In your school's computer lab, it may seem very fast. At home, however, it may be another story. What determines this speed is bandwidth. **Bandwidth** is the amount of information that can travel from one place to another in a given amount of time. We most often measure bandwidth in terms of bytes per second. So, if you have a 56k modem, your computer can receive information at a rate of 56 kilobytes per second. So in general, the faster your modem the faster you can surf the Web.

2. Can I Spend Too Much Time Surfing the Web?

Yes, you can. This is a real problem for many people, and this problem is a mental health issue. Some people become so addicted to the Web that they stay up all night to surf the Web, miss classes or work, and even eat their meals right in front of their computer. Too much of anything is not good. If you need to check your e-mail every 30 minutes or can't seem to stay out of chat rooms, you need some time away from the Web.

3. Will the Web Ever Go Away?

Definitely not. The Web is not the "technology fad of the month." Businesses and individuals alike are becoming increasingly dependent on the Web. Millions of people couldn't do without it. And that's okay. We would have a difficult time surviving without electricity. It, too, is just a technology, and it was also once "new."

i·witness

An Up-Close Look at Web Sites

Images

One of the fastest and easiest ways to make your Web site sizzle is to incorporate images. Images are simply artwork or photos that enhance the visual appeal of your Web site. Of course, you need to be careful not to add too many images to your Web site. Images can be fairly large, requiring a longer time for them to load. If the viewer can't load your Web site quickly, he or she may move on.

We've provided three Web sites for you to review. One Web site includes good use of images and loads fairly quickly. The second Web site includes too many images and takes too long to load. Finally, the third Web site has no images. These three sites are:

www.mhhe.com/i-series/I-Witness/2-A.html

www.mhhe.com/i-series/I-Witness/2-B.html

www.mhhe.com/i-series/I-Witness/2-C.html

Which makes the best use of images and loads quickly? Which

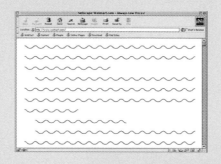

has too many images and takes too long to load? Which has no images at all?

For the Web site with no images, make some recommendations concerning what images might be appropriate and where they would appear. You can connect to the site for this text and download these Web sites to your computer. You can then make the changes yourself. If you'd like a list of Web sites that offer free images, connect to www.mhhe.com/i-series.

As a final note, Web sites can usually only display images in formats that include JPG, JPEG, or GIF.

HTML Reference:

- Insert an image
  <IMG SRC="filename.ext">

- Center an image
  <CENTER><IMG SRC="filename.ext"></CENTER>

- Right justify an image
  <IMG SRC="filename.ext" ALIGN=RIGHT>

SECTION E:// making the grade

1. _____ is software you use to electronically communicate with other people.

2. An _____ is a unique address for a person using an e-mail system.

3. A _____ is a site that provides a wide range of services, including search engines, free e-mail, chat rooms, discussion boards, and links to hundreds of different sites.

4. _____ is the amount of information that can travel from one place to another in a given amount of time.

F://SUMMARY AND KEY TERMS

The **World Wide Web (Web)** is the Internet in multimedia form. On the Web, you can enjoy sound, animation, images, photos, and even video. A **Web site** is a specific location on the Web where you visit, gather information, and perhaps order products. Most Web sites are composed of **Web pages,** a specific portion of a Web site that deals with certain topics. Most Web sites include numerous—if not hundreds of—Web pages.

If you need to find information on the Web but don't know where to go, you can use a **search engine.** There are two types of search engines—a **directory search engine** and a **true search engine.** Both use a key word or words to classify Web sites.

Hardware and software for surfing the Web include:

Hardware

- Today's typical computer systems which have everything you need.
- **Web computers** that are scaled down versions of typical computers systems at about half the price.
- Television-based Web surfing machines such as WebTV.
- **Web phones,** a special type of cell phone that allows you to surf the Web.
- Pagers such as a Blackberry that deliver content from specific sites.
- Personal digital assistants (PDAs) that deliver "Web clippings" from certain sites.

Software

- **Connectivity software** that enables you to use your computer to "dial up" or connect to another computer.
- Web browser software that allows you to surf the Web. Web browsers for cell phones are **microbrowsers.**

To connect to the Web, you need an **Internet service provider (ISP),** a company that provides individuals, organizations, and businesses access to the Internet. ISPs can be commercial such as AOL, free such as Juno, and perhaps even your school or place of work.

Behind the Web is the **Internet,** a vast network of computers that connects millions of people all over the world. Much of the **Internet backbone** is owned and operated by **network service providers (NSPs).** These NSPs maintain **network access points (NAPs),** places on the Internet where several connections converge and ISPs can connect their computers.

A **domain name** is the technical term for a server computer and Web site and identifies the main page for an entire site. **URL** is the technical term for a Web page or document within a Web site. You access these server computers and Web sites with your **client computer.** Popular servers include **Web servers, mail servers, FTP servers,** and **IRC servers.**

Communications protocols are sets of rules that every computer follows to transfer information on the Internet. **TCP/IP** is the communications protocol that all information transfers on the Internet follow. If you're visiting a Web site, you're also using the ***hypertext transfer protocol (http).*** If you're downloading information from an FTP server, you're also using the ***file transfer protocol (FTP).***

Finally, we've provided a great deal of support for this chapter on the Web site for this text at www.mhhe.com/i-series. That supports includes:

- Career sites.
- Search engines.
- Web computers.
- Technical Internet resources.

KEY TERMS

bandwidth (p. 2.25)

client computer (p. 2.21)

communications protocol (protocol) (p. 2.22)

connectivity software (p. 2.13)

directory search engine (p. 2.7)

domain name (p. 2.19)

e-mail (electronic mail) (p. 2.23)

e-mail address (p. 2.23)

file transfer protocol (FTP) (p. 2.22)

FTP server (p. 2.21)

hypertext transfer protocol (http) (p. 2.22)

Internet (p. 2.2)

Internet backbone (p. 2.18)

Internet service provider (ISP) (p. 2.15)

IRC (Internet relay chat) server (p. 2.21)

mail server (p. 2.21)

microbrowser (p. 2.12)

modem (p. 2.11)

network (p. 2.18)

network access point (NAP) (p. 2.18)

network service provider (NSP) (p. 2.18)

search engine (p. 2.7)

server computer (host computer) (p. 2.21)

TCP/IP (Transport Control Protocol/Internet Protocol) (p. 2.22)

top-level domain (p. 2.19)

true search engine (p. 2.7)

URL (uniform resource locator) (p. 2.19)

Web computer (p. 2.11)

Web page (p. 2.3)

Web phone (p. 2.11)

Web portal (p. 2.24)

Web server (p. 2.21)

Web space (p. 2.15)

World Wide Web (Web) (p. 2.2)

review of
terminology

CROSSWORD PUZZLE

Across

1. Web browser for cell phones
9. Connects businesses and people to the Internet
11. No more snail mail
12. Unique for you in e-mail
14. Device for connecting your computer to an ISP
15. Not a directory search engine
16. Hypertext transfer protocol
18. Same as URL
19. Server that supports chat rooms
24. Cell phone for accessing the Web
26. Standards by which computers communicate
27. For transferring files among computers
29. Provides services to you

Down

2. Software to connecting your computer to another computer
3. The Internet to you
4. Server that supports e-mail
5. Connection point on the Internet
6. Same as domain name
7. For finding Web sites by key words
8. Search engine that creates hierarchical lists
10. What determines speed on the Internet
13. Where you keep your Web site
17. Personalized Web starting point
20. The basic communications protocol of the Internet
21. Biggest network there is
22. Supporting structure of the Internet
23. Your computer on the Internet
24. Portion of a Web site
25. Two or more computers connected together
28. Business that supports the Internet

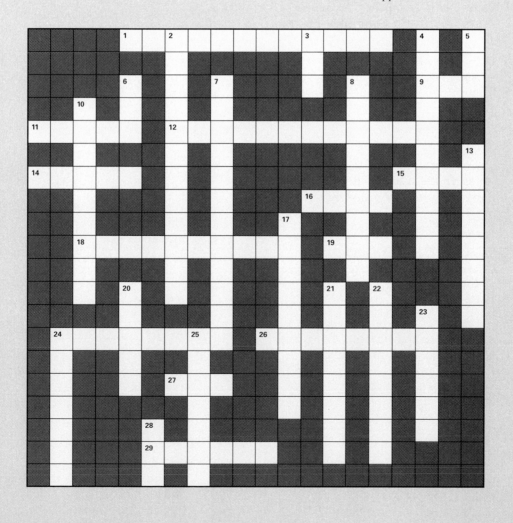

QUESTIONS AND EXERCISES

Multiple Choice

1. A specific portion of a Web site that deals with a certain topic is a
   a. Web server.
   b. Web page.
   c. Web site address.
   d. Web page address.
   e. URL.

2. The Internet is an example of a
   a. network service provider.
   b. network access point.
   c. network.
   d. Web.
   e. communications protocol.

3. You use your client computer to access a _____ computer on the Internet.
   a. modem
   b. Web browser
   c. search engine
   d. server
   e. cookie

4. A _____ is a site that provides a wide range of services, including search engines, free e-mail, chat rooms, discussion boards, and links to hundreds of different sites.
   a. Web computer
   b. Web portal
   c. Blackberry
   d. communications protocol
   e. Web phone

5. _____ is the amount of information that can travel from one place to another in a given amount of time.
   a. Bandwidth
   b. Communications protocol
   c. ISP
   d. NAP
   e. NSP

6. An example of a television-based Web surfing machine is
   a. a Web portal.
   b. a server computer.
   c. a client computer.
   d. a search engine.
   e. WebTV.

7. Web browser software for Web phones is a
   a. microbrowser.
   b. search engine.
   c. Web portal.
   d. cookie.
   e. modem.

8. _____ software enables you to use your computer to "dial up" or connect to another computer.
   a. http
   b. Connectivity
   c. Communications
   d. Web browser
   e. Microbrowser

9. A(n) _____ is a company that provides individuals, organizations, and businesses access to the Internet.
   a. NAP
   b. NSP
   c. cookie
   d. ISP
   e. Internet backbone

10. Most commercial ISPs provide you with
    a. a cookie.
    b. Web space.
    c. a Web phone.
    d. a microbrowser.
    e. a Blackberry.

True/False

11. _____ The Internet is a vast network of computers that connects millions of people in the United States.

12. _____ A network access point is a point on the Internet where several connections converge.

13. _____ A network service provider provides you with free e-mail and Web space.

14. _____ Technically, a Web site address is a domain name.

15. _____ Technically, a Web page address is an NRL.

QUESTIONS AND EXERCISES

1. In the real world, you can find many equivalents to the Internet and all its technologies. For each real world concept below, provide the Internet equivalent.

1234 Main Street _____

1234 Main Street Apt #12A _____

Stop light _____

Interstate _____

Yellow pages _____

Motorcycle _____

Telephone company _____

1-800 number _____

Post office box _____

State, such as Maine _____

Handshake _____

Application form _____

Water hose _____

2. For each of the following answers, create the question:

ANSWER

QUESTION

A. Most of the time, http://. _____

B. A collection of Web pages. _____

C. 4 million. _____

D. Your frequently visited Web sites. _____

E. Connects your computer through a phone line to a network of other computers. _____

F. About half the price of today's typical computer systems. _____

G. Web browser software for a cell phone. _____

H. Partner to connectivity software. _____

I. NSP. _____

J. Where you keep your Web site. _____

K. Juno. _____

L. What your school can be. _____

M. Major set of connections for computers on the Internet. _____

N. For hosting discussion groups or chat rooms. _____

O. The basic communications protocol for all Internet traffic. _____

e-commerce

1. Games

Some of the most popular sites on the Web are those where you can buy, sell, and trade games and even play games online. Of course, many sites even offer free games (called freeware and shareware, which we cover in the next chapter).

Below, we've provided four sites where you can buy, sell, and trade games. Connect to a couple of these and let's see what's there.

- GamEscapes—www.gamelover.com
- GameSpot—gamespot.com
- GameStop.com—www.funcoland.com
- Blockbuster—www.blockbuster.com

For the two sites you visit, answer the following questions:

a. How can you search for games—by title, publisher, category, etc.?

b. Can you buy both new and used games?

c. Are chat rooms present so you can talk to other gamers?

d. Are product reviews provided?

e. Are tips provided concerning how to play certain games and achieve really high scores?

f. Can you demo video games or perhaps watch short clips of them on your screen?

g. What's the return policy for a game you buy but would rather not keep?

2. Books

Buying books on the Web is a simple process. Just connect to any one of hundreds of sites selling books, find the ones you want, pay for them (usually by credit card), and wait for them to arrive in the mail. Let's see how this process works. Below, we've provided four sites that sell books. Connect to two of them.

- Amazon—www.amazon.com
- Barnes & Noble—www.barnesandnoble.com
- Borders—www.borders.com
- Fat Brain—www.fatbrain.com

Now, think of a book that you'd like to buy (it can be one you already own or perhaps even a textbook like this one). For that book, perform the following tasks and answer the following questions:

a. How can you search for that book—by author, title, category, or perhaps some other way?

b. Can you buy the book in either soft-cover or hard-cover format?

c. Does the site recommend other books you might be interested in based on the one you're looking for?

d. Is there a shipping fee? If so, what is it?

e. How can you pay for the book? Do you have to use a credit card?

Now, armed with that information, visit a local bookstore and find the same book. Is it cheaper in the local bookstore or on the Web?

Finally, what steps are brick-and-mortar bookstores taking to keep people from shopping on the Web? Do they offer extra services? Can any of those services be duplicated by click-and-mortar bookstores?

3. Auctions

One of the truly great things about the Web is that it has brought together people from all over the world with common interests. You can discuss issues in chat rooms, join fan clubs, and buy and sell items in auction houses. If you have a particular hobby or enjoy collecting memorabilia, auction houses will probably be a place you'll want to visit. Below, we've listed several popular auction houses on the Web.

- eBay—www.ebay.com
- Haggle Online—www.boxlot.com
- AuctionAddict.com—www.auctionaddict.com
- AuctionUS—www.auctionus.com

All of these auction houses offer similar features. So, let's just visit one and do some fact finding. Pick one that interests you and answer the following questions:

a. What process do you go through to register as a buyer or seller?

b. Can you search for items without registering first?

c. Does the auction house guarantee the quality and authenticity of items being sold?

d. What sort of mechanism is used to rank the quality of buyers and sellers?

e. What search capabilities can you use to find items that might interest you?

f. How does the auction house make money by simply letting other people buy and sell products?

Auction houses are one of the most popular stops on the Web, with eBay leading the way. Why do you think this is true? Are people getting good deals on items they buy or sell? If people are selling items for a high price (getting a good deal), then aren't buyers paying too high a price?

4. Finding an Internet Service Provider (ISP)

Finding an ISP is certainly not a difficult task. There are many to choose from and most have similar fees and features. The two major categories of ISPs are free and commercial, with commercial ISPs charging fees but offering more features and services.

Below, we've provided four Web sites that will help you find the right ISP. Visit a couple of these and find at least two ISPs that might interest you.

- Internet.com—thelist.internet.com
- FindAnISP—www.findanisp.com
- ISP Finder—www.ispfinder.com
- Netscape ISP Locator—home.netscape.com/ computing/isp_locator/index.html

For the two ISPs you're interested in, answer the following questions:

a. What is the monthly subscription rate?

b. For how long must you sign an agreement?

c. Is an e-mail service provided?

d. Is Web space provided?

e. How fast can you surf the Web? That is, what's the bandwidth speed?

f. Do you have to download and install any software?

g. What sort of technical support is provided?

h. Based on your answers to the questions above, which ISP would you choose? Why?

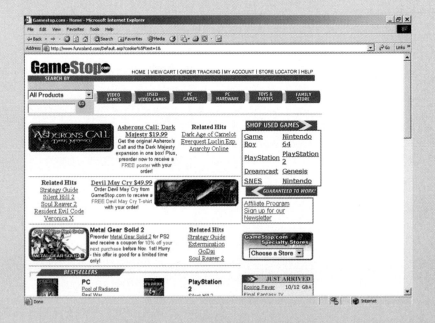

on the web

1. Your School's Web Site Structure

At the beginning of this chapter, we took a brief look at the *USA Today* Web site and how it creates a well-organized hierarchy of Web pages. This is key to developing a good Web site. Visit your school's Web site (its address is probably www.schoolname.edu where schoolname is your school's actual name or abbreviation). As you click on various links, draw the hierarchy of your school's Web site, just as we did in Figure 2.2 on page 2.3. Is your school's Web site well organized and easy to follow? How easily can you find a list of classes for the upcoming term? A list of faculty members by department? A list of majors and minors? How would you reorganize your school's Web site from a student point of view?

2. Free E-Mail

If all you want is e-mail, you certainly don't need to pay for it. Many Web portal sites such as Microsoft Network (MSN at www.msn.com) and The Go Network (www.go.com) offer free e-mail to anyone who wants it (you don't even have to use these sites as your ISP). Connect to one of those sites and subscribe to a free e-mail service. What information do you have to provide? How do you get to pick your e-mail address? Did you find perhaps that someone had already chosen the e-mail address you wanted? After a few days, connect to your new free e-mail again. Do you have any e-mail messages? Whom are they from?

3. Library Resources

The Web can certainly help you write your term papers. You no longer need to spend endless hours in the library trying to find past issues of magazines. You can simply connect to any one of several library resource sites and find almost everything you need. Connect to a couple of sites we've listed below.

- IFLA—www.ifla.org
- Library of Congress—www.loc.gov
- Internet Public Library—www.ipl.org
- Cline Library (Northern Arizona University)—www.nau.edu/~cline/

While you're there, try to look up some information for a term paper you have to write. Can you find information in books, magazines, or other periodicals? Can you print information you want or request that it be sent to you? Do you have to pay any fees to obtain information? Can the Web really help you gather information for a term paper?

4. Humor on the Web

As we've stated many times, you can find almost anything on the Web. Often, it's fun and entertaining just to see what's out there. Explore the Web for humor. That's right—humor. You can connect to any search engine site and type in such words as "humor," "jokes," and even "cartoons." In fact, you might want to start at:

- CartoonBank—www.cartoonbank.com
- Comics.com—www.comics.com
- The Onion—www.theonion.com

Some of these sites will even let you e-mail a cartoon to a friend. You can also register and have cartoons sent to your e-mail on a daily basis. How are these sites making money? Did you find any site that requires you to pay a monthly fee?

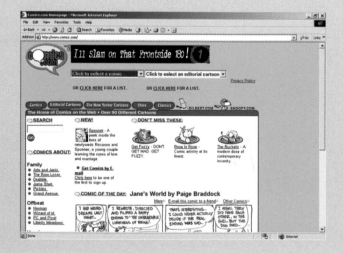

ethics, security & privacy

1. Finding Personal Information on the Web

Information about you is all over the Web. You may not have even given your permission, but it's there for everyone to see. Most commonly, you can find information about people by using people searches. We've listed a few below—access these and try to find yourself, a friend, or a family member and then answer the questions below.

- WhoWhere?—www.whowhere.lycos.com
- Netscape PeopleFinder—www.home.netscape. com/netcenter/whitepages.html
- Yahoo! PeopleSearch— www.people.yahoo.com

a. How easy was it to find someone?

b. What information were you able to find?

c. Do you like the fact that you can look up people on the Web?

d. Do you like the fact that people can look you up on the Web?

e. Young children today are growing up with the Web. In 10 years, will these people have any problems with their information being so easily available?

2. Government-Posted Information on the Web

Many government agencies also post information on the Web about you. At www.douglas.co.us/as-sessor (Douglas county in Colorado), for example, all you have to do is type in a street address and you can obtain owner name, sales history of the property, building characteristics, actual and assessed values, and much more.

a. Should this type of information be available on the Web for everyone to see?

b. How can someone use this information in a bad way?

c. How can someone use this information in a good way?

d. Should government agencies be required to receive your permission before letting everyone know what you paid for your house?

3. Finding E-Mail Addresses on the Web

At many schools (and yours may be one), you can easily look up people to find their e-mail addresses. All you have to do is type in a first name or last name. You don't even need to know the correct spelling. The school will tell you if that person is a registered student (or faculty member) and how to contact them by e-mail.

a. Is this good or bad? Why?

b. Did you know that your school might offer this type of service?

c. Should your school get your permission before making this type of information available to anyone who has access to the Web?

d. Does your school actually provide this type of service?

4. The Government's Role in Privacy in the Web

Let's talk about this whole issue of privacy and access to the information on the Web. Develop some answers for the questions below.

a. At what level of government should legislation be enacted to ensure your privacy of information on the Web?

b. For that matter, is your right to privacy an important consideration? Is it inevitable that all your information will someday be on the Web for everyone to see?

c. What is too much information? Maybe you think your name and address is okay, but what about your hair color, your shoe size, and perhaps even your grades?

hands-on projects

group activities

1. Finding a Regional ISP

In the e-commerce projects earlier, you explored finding an Internet service provider (ISP) through several Web sites. Now, let's focus on finding a regional ISP by using a phone book and phone. Flip back to the yellow pages of your phone book and find ISPs. Make a phone call to a couple of listed ISPs and determine their monthly fees and features. Did any seem to be better or cheaper than the ISPs you found while completing the e-commerce projects? Are the regional ISPs really located in your town or perhaps a town close by? Would you rather use a well-known commercial ISP such as AOL or a regional ISP you've never heard of?

2. Connecting to the Web through Your School

Contact your school's technical support group that can tell you how to use your school to connect to the Web. Answer the following questions:

a. What connectivity software must you have?

b. Is that connectivity software already on your own computer or do you have to download it?

c. What is the phone number you call to make a connection between your computer and your school's computer?

d. Is there a time limitation for staying connected to the Web through your school?

e. Does your school provide FTP software so you can download files from the Web?

f. Does your school provide Web space so you can publish your own Web site?

3. What Your School's Computer Lab Has to Offer

Visit one or more of your school's computer labs. While you're there, answer the following questions:

a. What Web browser software is on the computers?

b. What are the versions of the Web browser software?

c. Can you use FTP software to download files from the Web? If you can, can you download to the computer's hard disk or just a floppy disk you provide?

d. What sort of anti-virus software is present to keep you (and the computers) from getting a virus while surfing the Web?

e. Does your school restrict you from accessing certain types of Web sites?

4. Finding a Web-Accessing Cell Phone

Cell phones are certainly emerging as a way for you to connect to the Web while you're on the go. As a group, do some exploring of the latest and best cell phones that come equipped with micro-browsers and Web access. Prepare a report for your class that provides the following information.

a. At least two cell phones that provide Web access (their cost, manufacturer, and capabilities).

b. What process you go through to activate the cell phones for Web access (including the monthly fee).

c. What Web sites you can access with each cell phone.

d. What it takes to subscribe to an e-mail service with the cell phones.

e. The length of contract you must sign to have a cell phone with Web-accessing capabilities.

Looking Back/Looking Ahead

The Life and Times of a Dot-Com Entrepreneur

After having a good review of technology and briefly surfing the Web, Joann is now ready to specifically look at what she'll need to set up a Web shop. Joann knows her first priority is to decide on a _____, which will uniquely identify her Web site. She knows that the technical name for this is a _____. Within her Web site, Joann wants to create many well-organized and easy-to-navigate _____ that each deal with specific topics which will interest her visitors. The technical name for the address of each of these is a _____.

As she envisions her visitors, Joann understands that they'll be using a variety of hardware to access her site. Most will use today's typical computer systems, but some will also use _____, which cost about half the price of a typical computer system. Some will even want to use _____ software on a cell phone because they always seem to be on the go.

To create her site on the Web, Joann needs _____, a storage area where she can keep her Web site. Because she needs that, Joann has chosen AOL as her _____. She simply can't use many of the _____ because they don't provide her with 24-hour technical support.

When visitors arrive, Joann wants them to be able to access Web pages, download various types of information, and participate in chat rooms. Each of these capabilities requires that visitors use different types of communications protocols. No matter what they do, her visitors will always use _____, the basic communications protocol that makes the Internet work. Other protocols include _____ for downloading files, _____ for accessing her Web site, and _____ for participating in a chat room.

Armed with that knowledge, Joann is now ready to look toward her software needs, including the software she needs to run her business and make her more productive. She'll learn about that software in Chapter 3. Then, she must begin the process of actually building her Web site and Web pages. For this, she'll be writing html code, which she can learn about in Chapter 4.

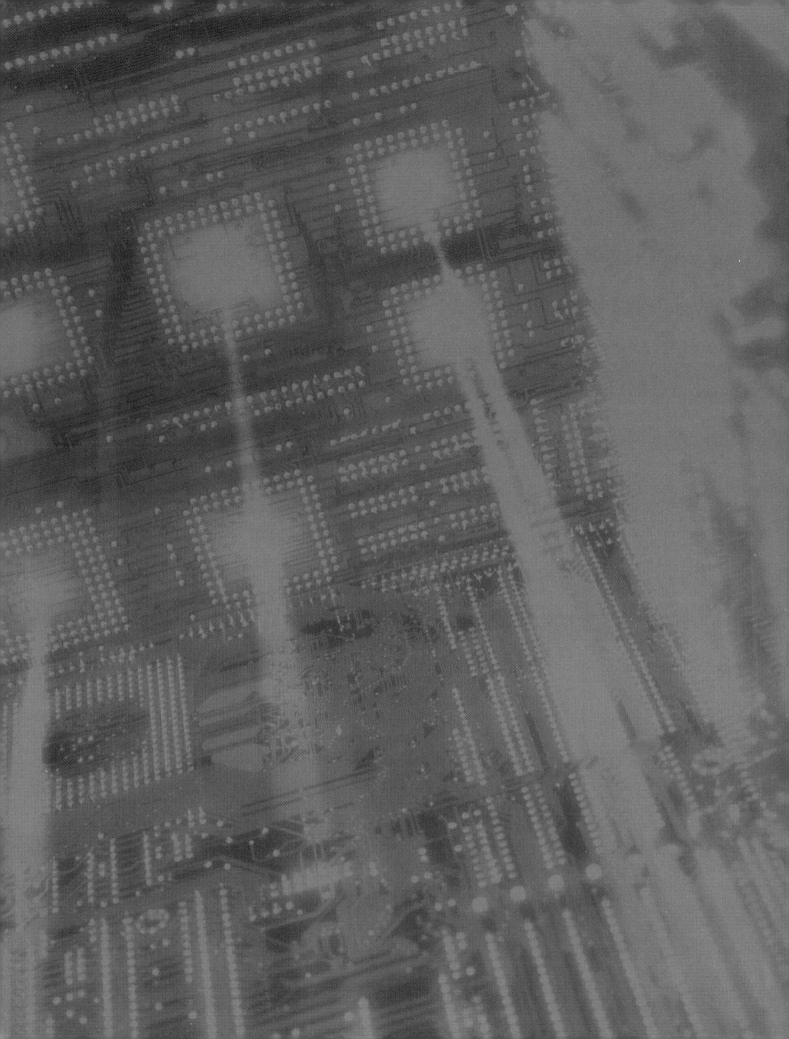

did you
know?

Personal productivity software really can help you be more productive. It doesn't matter what you want to do, personal productivity software can probably help you do it better and in less time.

with *personal finance software, you can pay your bills electronically in a matter of minutes. You may never again write a check for your car payment, cable TV, or utility bill.*

with *only seven clicks on your mouse, you can use spreadsheet software and turn a table of numbers into a high-quality, revealing graph.*

with *Web authoring software, you can create a Web site in just a few short minutes. You can learn how to use many Web authoring software packages in less than an hour.*

with *desktop publishing software, you can design your own book that looks just like this one.*

with *word processing software, you can create a table of information. Then you can sort that table with only four clicks on your mouse. You can also easily create formulas that average, count, sum, and even find the minimum and maximum of values in a column.*

with *only ?? clicks on your mouse, you can add animation, audio, or perhaps even a video clip to a slide presentation. Think how this will help your grade.*

To find out just how many clicks it takes to add animation, audio, or video to a slide presentation, visit www.mhhe.com/i-series.

CHAPTER

3

three

Software and Multimedia

What Can Your Computer Do for You?

As you read in Chapter 2, you need both hardware (mouse, keyboard, and modem are examples) and software (Web browser software, for example) to surf the Web. The same is true for maintaining your electronic checkbook—you need both hardware and software. In this instance, the software is personal finance software such as Intuit Quicken or Microsoft Money. Simply put, to do anything with your computer you need both hardware and software. In this chapter we want to help you decide what software you need (in Chapter 5 we'll help you determine what hardware to buy).

There are two major categories of software—system and application (see Figure 3.1). *System software* is the software that details how your computer carries out technology-specific tasks. These tasks include getting your computer going when you turn it on, writing information to a disk, checking for viruses, and a host of other activities. Because system software deals with technology-specific tasks, we say that it's the layer of software closest to your computer.

FIGURE 3.1

Application software is the layer of software closest to you, while system software is the layer closest to your computer.

APPLICATION SOFTWARE

Surfing the Web

Keeping a home budget

Processing payroll

Communicating with others

SYSTEM SOFTWARE

Writing information to a disk

Checking for viruses

Converting digitally stored sound for your speakers

Application software is the software that allows you to perform specific tasks such as writing a term paper, surfing the Web, keeping a home budget, and creating slides for a presentation. Because application software deals with specific information-related tasks you want to perform, we say that it's the layer of software closest to *you*.

First, we discuss application software and then system software. Why in that order? Because application software is key when deciding which computer system you'll buy. If you make a list of what you want to do with your computer, most if not all the tasks would be directly related to application software. So, let's cover it first.

A://THE APPLICATION SOFTWARE YOU NEED

As a personal computer user (and buyer), you'll most often be interested in a subset of application software called personal productivity software. *Personal productivity software* helps you with personal tasks that you can probably perform even if you don't own a computer. Writing a letter, creating slides for a presentation, maintaining your checking account bal-

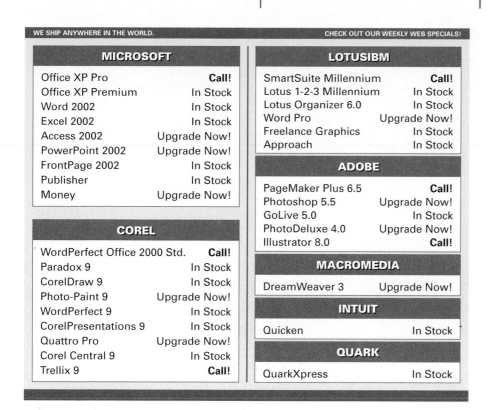

F I G U R E   3.2

Ads for computer software are often organized by publisher and include such information as the version number.

ance, and creating a graph are all examples of these tasks. In Figure 3.2, we've provided an ad for software that you might see in your local newspaper or in a computer magazine. Now, the question becomes, Which of that software—if any—do you need?

SOFTWARE PUBLISHERS, NAMES, AND VERSIONS
What's in a Software Title?

Let's take a look at Corel's Paradox 9. Without even knowing what that software can help you do, you can identify three of its characteristics. First, Corel is the software publisher for Paradox. Second, its name is Paradox. And finally, its version number is 9. Most people identify software by its publisher. Just as in the ad in Figure 3.2, most ads group software this way. However, if you buy software on the Web (try www. cdw.com if you wish), you can also look up software by category—word processing, Web authoring, and so on.

A **software version (version)** tells you which iteration of the software you're using. For Paradox, it's version 9. Version 9 is newer than all other versions of Paradox with lower numbers. As a general rule, you should always buy the newest version of software available. Some software publishers use years instead of version numbers. So, Microsoft Excel 2000 came out in 2000 and is newer than Excel 98 or 95. Most recently, Microsoft came out with a new version of its office products called XP. These are newer than the Office 2000 products. Some publishers use terms such as "Standard," "Pro," and "Premium." These terms identify what group or suite of software is included.

	Microsoft Office XP Pro	Microsoft Office XP Premium	Corel WordPerfect Office 2000 Standard	LotusIBM SmartSuite Millennium
Word processing	Word	Word	WordPerfect	Word Pro
Spreadsheet	Excel	Excel	Quattro Pro	Lotus 1-2-3
Presentation	PowerPoint	PowerPoint	Presentations	Freelance Graphics
Desktop publishing	Publisher	Publisher	Trellix	
Personal finance	Money	Money		
Personal information management			Central	Organizer
Web authoring	FrontPage	FrontPage	Trellix	FastSite
Graphics		PhotoDraw		

APPLICATION SOFTWARE SUITES

Can I Buy Software in Bundles or Just Specific Packages?

Most computer users have common fundamental personal productivity software needs—some combination of word processing, spreadsheet, presentation, desktop publishing, personal finance, personal information management, Web authoring, and graphics. You can buy all these individually if you want to, or you can buy them in a suite. **Software suites** are "bundles" of related software packages that are sold together.

There are four software suites listed in the ad in Figure 3.2—Microsoft Office XP Pro, Microsoft Office XP Premium, Corel WordPerfect Office 2000 Standard, and LotusIBM SmartSuite Millennium. In Figure 3.3, you can see what each software suite includes. Notice that they all seem to include a different combination of personal productivity software. Purchasing all the software individually in any suite will usually cost you two to three times as much as the suite. So, even if you don't need everything in a suite, it's still cheaper to purchase the suite than the exact software you need.

LET YOUR NEEDS DRIVE YOUR PURCHASE

If I Know What I Want to Do, Can I Decide What Software to Buy?

Now back to our original question. Which software in the computer ad should you buy? We can tell you this: Buy the software that will meet your needs. But what are your needs? In the area of personal productivity software, your needs will generally fall into some mix of seven categories (see

What you want to do	What software you need
Create mainly text (letters, term papers, flyers, etc.)	• Word processing software or • Desktop publishing software
Build Web sites	• Web authoring software
Create photos and art	• Graphics software
Build a slide presentation	• Presentation software
Work with numbers, calculations, and graphs	• Spreadsheet software
Manage personal information	• Personal information management software and/or • Personal finance software
Communicate with other people	• E-mail software and/or • Web browser software

FIGURE 3.4

Always choose which software to buy according to what you want to do.

Figure 3.4). It's a relatively simple process of picking which of the seven needs you have to determine which software to buy. Of course, if you need word processing software (most people do), you must then decide if you want Microsoft Word, Corel WordPerfect, or Lotus Word Pro.

In our short time together in this text, we can't really explore each of the seven categories in great detail. Besides, the class you're taking may include learning many of these different types of software. So, let's just hit the highlights of each.

WORD PROCESSING AND DESKTOP PUBLISHING SOFTWARE

What Software Do I Need for Creating Term Papers, Letters, Advertising Flyers, and the Like?

If you need to create documents that consist primarily of text, you need word processing or desktop publishing software. **Word processing software** helps you create papers, letters, memos, and other basic documents. **Desktop publishing software** extends word processing by including design and formatting techniques to enhance the layout and appearance of a document.

This book is a good example. As authors, we created this textbook using Microsoft Word (word processing software). We then gave it to a book production expert who imported our Word documents into QuarkXPress. The book production expert created the various formatting you see, the color, the "Did You Know?" features in the sidebar, the art and photos and special headings, and all the backgrounds. We simply couldn't perform some of those tasks with word processing software.

WEB AUTHORING SOFTWARE

What if I Want to Build My Own Web Site?

If you want to build your own Web site, you should probably consider acquiring Web authoring software. **Web authoring software** helps you design and develop Web sites and pages that you publish on the Web. Most Web authoring software includes an easy-to-use graphical user interface (GUI) and drag-and-drop capabilities.

Web authoring software helps you design and create Web sites and pages that you publish on the Web.

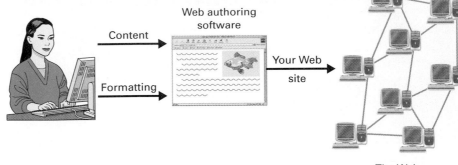

So, all you do is design the layout of your site, put in all the content you want, and the Web authoring software will generate the HTML code for you. Later, if you want to make changes, you don't change the HTML code—you simply make your changes in the design and content, and your Web authoring software will do the rest (see Figure 3.5). We'll explore various Web authoring software and ways in which you can build your Web site in Chapter 4.

GRAPHICS SOFTWARE

What if I Need to Work with Photos and Art?

As you create any type of document, you may want to employ photos and art. **Graphics software** helps you create and edit photos and art. Using graphics software, you can crop (adjust) photos to an appropriate size, add captions, change colors, and even combine photos to create a photo collage. You can also use your computer to create free-hand art, choosing colors, shapes, and perhaps even 3-dimensional images.

If your computer's operating system is Microsoft Windows, you already own a couple of basic graphics software packages—Kodak Imaging for Windows (for photo editing) and Microsoft Paint (for art).

Graphics software helps you create and edit photos and art, including 3-dimensional images.

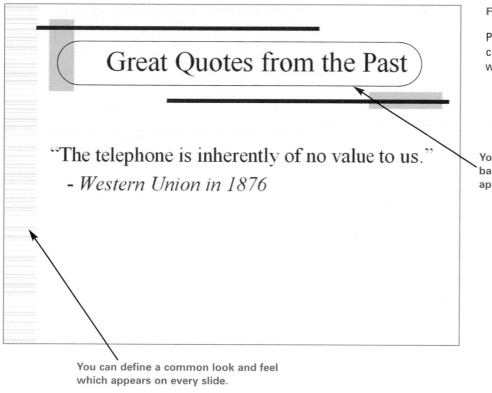

Presentation software helps you create and edit information that will appear in electronic slides.

You can define a banner which will appear on every slide.

You can define a common look and feel which appears on every slide.

PRESENTATION SOFTWARE

What if I Need to Create Slides for a Presentation?

To increase the effectiveness of your class presentations and public speaking, presentation software can definitely help you. **Presentation software** helps you create and edit information that will appear in electronic slides. And the information you include can be text, photos, art, tables, graphs, sound, animation, and even video.

As you create your slides, presentation software helps you define a consistent look and feel, change background colors, and add banners. You can also add links to your slides so you can demonstrate a Web site. If you do include a link in your presentation and click on it, your presentation software will instantly start your Web browser software and go directly to the Web site for which you created a link.

SPREADSHEET SOFTWARE

What if I Need to Work with Numbers, Calculations, and Graphs?

Spreadsheet software helps you work primarily with numbers, including performing calculations and creating graphs. With spreadsheet software, you enter numbers in cells (a cell is the intersection of a row and column), and then use the cells' identifiers or addresses in formulas and functions to create new information. If you change the information in a cell, your spreadsheet software will automatically recalculate all the formulas and functions.

FIGURE 3.8

With spreadsheet software, you can easily create revealing and high-quality graphs with a few clicks of your mouse.

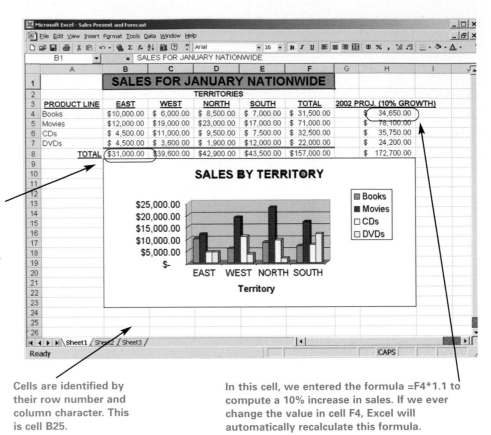

In this cell, we entered the function =SUM(B4:B7) to sum the sales for the East territory. If we change any of the values in B4 through B7, Excel will automatically recalculate this function.

Cells are identified by their row number and column character. This is cell B25.

In this cell, we entered the formula =F4*1.1 to compute a 10% increase in sales. If we ever change the value in cell F4, Excel will automatically recalculate this formula.

Spreadsheet software can also help you transform your numeric information into graphs. With a few simple clicks, you can turn a table of information into a revealing and high-quality graph. Figure 3.8 shows a 3-D column graph for sales by territory. It took only seven clicks on the mouse to create that graph.

PERSONAL INFORMATION MANAGEMENT AND PERSONAL FINANCE SOFTWARE

What if I Need to Manage My Personal Information and Finances?

Personal information management (PIM) software helps you create and maintain (1) to-do lists, (2) appointments and calendars, and (3) points of contact. PIM software is the primary software for personal digital assistants, which we discussed in Chapters 1 and 2. If you don't have a PDA, you can still purchase PIM software for your notebook or desktop computer (or use Web-based PIM software as we demonstrated in Chapter 1).

Using PIM software, you can easily track your appointments and scheduled activities by the day, week, or month. You can enter your class schedule, for example, and have the PIM software show those class times for the rest of the semester or quarter. You can ask your PIM software to remind you of important dates or events. So, your PIM software can inform you of an important upcoming exam.

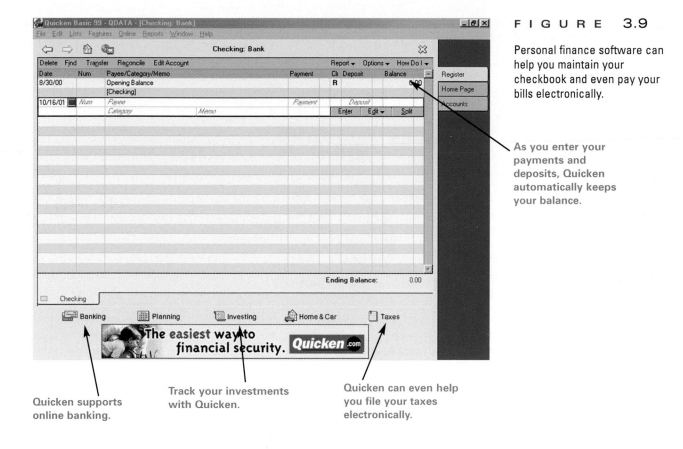

FIGURE 3.9

Personal finance software can help you maintain your checkbook and even pay your bills electronically.

As you enter your payments and deposits, Quicken automatically keeps your balance.

Quicken supports online banking.

Track your investments with Quicken.

Quicken can even help you file your taxes electronically.

Also in the area of managing your personal information, ***personal finance software*** offers you capabilities for maintaining your checkbook, preparing a budget, tracking investments, monitoring your credit card balances, and even paying bills electronically (see Figure 3.9). If you can pay bills with your personal finance software, then it supports what we call online banking. ***Online banking*** is the use of your computer system to interact with your bank electronically, including writing checks, transferring funds, and obtaining a list of your account transactions.

COMMUNICATIONS SOFTWARE
What if I Need to Communicate with Other People?

In both Chapters 1 and 2, you learned about communications software, specifically e-mail, Web browser software, and connectivity software. ***Communications software*** is software that helps you communicate with other people through the use of your computer. Communications software is now a standard feature on almost all new computer systems. That's why you don't see any communications software listed in the ad on page 3.3.

i·buy

Can My Software Really Help Me Be More Productive?

Yes, personal productivity software can really help you be more productive, but—we want to emphasize this—only if your basic skills are already good. What if you decide you need personal finance software? You always seem to lose your ATM receipts and you seldom log your checks. Will personal finance software help you? Absolutely not. Software can't help you not lose your receipts, nor can it make you log your checks.

The same is true for word processing software. Can it help you become a better writer? Well, it can help you spell check and grammar check your documents. It avoids the drudgery of a typewriter by allowing you to move text about. But it can't really make you a better writer—that's your job. Of course, you can buy learning software that will help you increase the effectiveness of your writing skills.

It all boils down to this. If you're doing something wrong, a computer will only help you do it wrong millions of times faster! If you're doing something *right,* then a computer (and software) does help you become more productive. So, if you are doing things right, we recommend that you start with a basic personal productivity software suite as your software choice. Start using it, and see if it meets all your needs. If not, consider purchasing other software that will help you be more productive.

To learn more about personal productivity software, visit the Interactive Companion Labs and choose "Word Processing and Spreadsheets" or "Presentation Techniques."

SECTION A://   *making the grade*

1. _____ software extends word processing software by including design and formatting techniques to enhance the layout and appearance of a document.
2. _____ software helps you create and edit photos and art.
3. Spreadsheet software allows you to enter numbers in _____, the intersections of rows and columns.
4. _____ is the use of your computer system to interact with your bank electronically.

B://YOUR CHOICE OF SYSTEM SOFTWARE

Simply put, system software is the task manager for your entire computer system. It gets your computer going when you first turn it on, allows you to specify which software you want to run, notifies the printer when you want a paper copy of a document, manages your system resources such as internal memory (RAM), and checks for viruses. It even gives you the option of which screen saver you want to display.

There are two categories of system software—the operating system and utility software. As we look at both, we'll keep an eye out toward helping you decide what you need.

OPERATING SYSTEM FUNCTIONS

What Does My Operating System Do?

Your **operating system software** is system software that controls your application software and manages how your hardware devices work together. Operating system software supports a variety of helpful and useful functions:

- *Multitasking*—allows you to work with more than one piece of software at a time (see Figure 3.10).

- System resource management—for example, managing your RAM and its contents, managing your devices such as your disk drive, and even notifying you when to add paper to your printer.

- Security—including password protection to ensure the safety of your computer.

Now that you know something of the basic capabilities that your operating system provides, let's look at the more popular personal operating systems today.

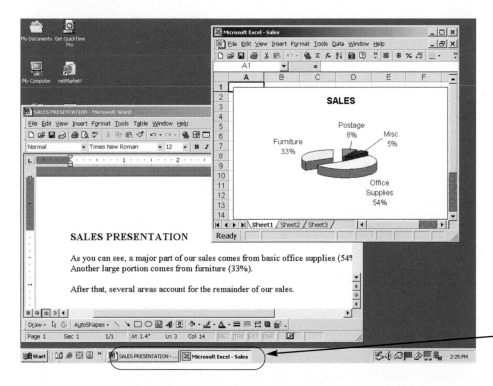

F I G U R E   3.10

Your operating system supports a number of useful functions such as multitasking, which allows you to work with more than one piece of software at a time.

The task bar area tells you what software you're currently working with.

THE MICROSOFT FAMILY OF OPERATING SYSTEMS

What Are the Most Popular Operating Systems?

Microsoft is the leading provider of personal operating systems, with a variety to choose from. Although Windows XP Home and Windows XP Professional are the newest (published in 2001), many people still use Windows 2000 Millennium and Windows 2000 Professional.

Microsoft Windows 2000 Millennium (Windows 2000 Me) is an operating system for a home computer user with utilities for setting up a home network and performing video, photo, and music editing and cataloging. With Windows 2000 Me, you can easily set up a small network in your home, sharing printers, scanners, and perhaps access to the Web.

FIGURE　3.11

Microsoft's Windows XP Home
helps you easily create different
users for the same computer and
create a home network of
computers that you can control
from any machine in your home.

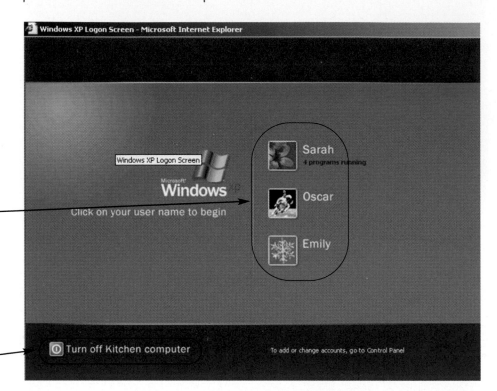

Create unique users for
the same computer.

Control other computers
in your home from any
computer.

Microsoft Windows XP Home (Windows XP Home) is Microsoft's newest home computer user operating system. Windows XP Home is an upgrade to Windows 2000 Me and includes many new and advanced features. Most notably, Windows XP Home provides great support for allowing multiple people to use the same computer (although not at the same time), each with unique names and passwords. As you can see in Figure 3.11, you can create different users. You can network all your home computers together and control any of them from any machine.

If you visit most computer stores on the Web such as Dell at www.dell.com to buy a computer, they will probably recommend either Windows 2000 Me or Windows XP Home. So, if you want to buy a computer that you'll use primarily at home and Microsoft Windows is your preference, Windows 2000 Me or Windows XP Home is the way to go.

If you have a computer that you'll be connecting to a network of other computers in a workplace environment or perhaps at school, Microsoft offers Windows 2000 Professional and Windows XP Professional. *Microsoft Windows 2000 Professional (Windows 2000 Pro)* is an operating system for people who have a personal computer connected to a network of other computers at work or at school. Windows 2000 Pro offers increased security over Windows 2000 Me and Windows XP Home, making it more suitable for computers that run on a network.

Microsoft Windows XP Professional (Windows XP Pro) is Microsoft's newest operating system for people who have a personal computer connected to a network of other computers at work or at school. So, if you're buying a notebook that you'll be connecting extensively to a network at school or work, Windows XP Pro is one alternative for you, with the other being Windows 2000 Pro.

If you are purchasing a computer that you'll be using for school, we recommend that you contact your school's technology support department. That department will help you determine which operating system is best.

LINUX AND MAC OS

What Non-Microsoft Operating Systems Are Available?

Linux is an open-source operating system that provides a rich operating environment for high-end workstations and network servers. For that reason, you probably won't find it on very many personal computers in a home or workplace environment. If your computer is for personal use such as surfing the Web, typing documents, sending e-mail, and the like, Linux is probably not the operating system for you.

Mac OS is the operating system for today's Apple computers. It supports a graphical user interface similar to Windows operating systems, although the look and feel is a little different (see Figure 3.12). With the newest release of Mac OS, you enter your password by speaking it. So, you must not only know what the password is, you must also be able to speak it in a way that matches how you originally recorded it. If you buy an Apple computer, Mac OS is your choice of operating system software.

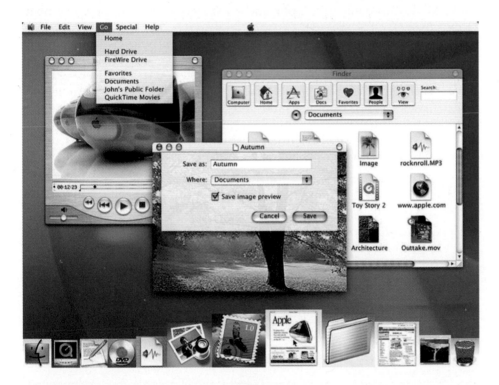

FIGURE 3.12

Mac OS is the operating system for Apple computers and supports a graphical user interface similar to most Windows operating systems.

THE RIGHT PERSONAL OPERATING SYSTEM FOR YOU

So, What Operating System Should I Buy?

First, you need to decide if you want an Apple computer or an IBM/compatible computer. If Apple is your choice, then your operating system is Mac OS. If you go the other route, you need to consider how and where you'll use your computer. If you'll keep your computer at home most of the time, get Windows 2000 Me or Windows XP Home. If your computer will be connected to a network at school or work most of the time, go with Windows 2000 Pro or Windows XP Pro.

At the time we wrote this text, Microsoft was just releasing Windows XP Home and XP Pro. Therefore, it's difficult at this moment to recommend which operating system you should choose if you'll use your computer primarily at home (Windows 2000 Me or Windows XP Home). When making your choice (and all such choices), you should definitely seek advice from other people, especially your instructor and your school's technology support department.

Again, we do not recommend Linux for the majority of today's personal computer users.

UTILITY SOFTWARE
What Other System Software Is on My Computer?

The second category of system software is utility software. ***Utility software*** is software that provides additional functionality to your operating system. However, don't get the idea that utility software is simply "optional" and not required. You definitely need several pieces of utility software. Some will come with your operating system, and some you'll need to purchase.

The most important utility software today is anti-virus software. ***Anti-virus software*** is utility software that scans for and often eliminates viruses in your RAM and on your storage devices. Viruses are everywhere today, with 200 to 300 new ones surfacing each month. Viruses can be very destructive to your computer, and you should definitely have anti-virus software to combat them.

Anti-virus software is essential. Beyond that, there's some other utility software you should consider having:

- ***Crash-proof software***—utility software that helps you save information if your system crashes and you're forced to turn it off and then back on again.

- ***Uninstaller software***—utility software that you can use to remove software from your hard disk you no longer want.

- ***Disk optimization software***—utility software that organizes your information on your hard disk in the most efficient way (we'll talk more about this in Chapter 8).

FIGURE 3.13

Anti-virus software scans for and helps eliminate viruses from your RAM and storage devices.

Specify if you want to scan your whole computer or just certain storage areas.

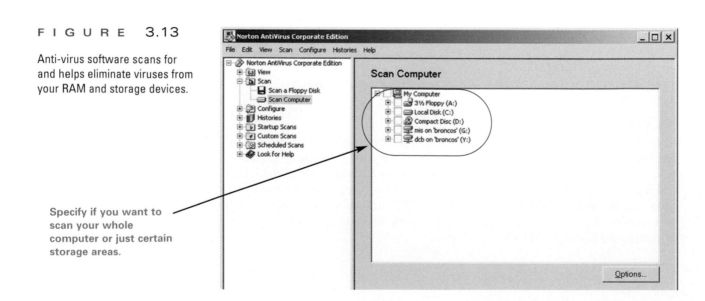

making the grade

1. _____ is an operating system function that allows you to work with more than one piece of software at a time.

2. Microsoft's home computer user operating system is Windows 2000 Me or _____.

3. _____ is software that provides additional functionality to your operating system.

4. _____ is utility software that scans for and often eliminates _____ in your RAM and on your storage devices.

C://FILE AND FILE MANAGEMENT CONCEPTS

You use your computer to massage, manipulate, and work with information. It's as simple as that. Even if you're playing a game or surfing the Web, you're massaging, manipulating, and working with information all the time. And, of course, if you're using personal productivity software to write a term paper or create a graph, you're using that software to work with information.

Within your computer, most of the information you work with is stored in files (and on storage devices such as your hard disk or CD). A *file* is a collection of information you need to use your computer effectively. For example, while writing a term paper with word processing software, you would create a file that contains the contents of your term paper. As you call up that file and refine and enhance your term paper, you make changes to the file and continually save those changes to your storage device.

You'll store many different types of files on your computer. For example, the software (word processing) you use to create and refine your term papers is stored in a file. And the ID and password you use to log on to your computer is stored in a file. Videos are each stored in a different file, as are audio clips and Web pages you create.

There's actually much for you to learn about files and file management concepts, including file types, optimizing the location of files, creating backups, and so on. We'll cover those topics in Chapter 8. Right now, let's focus on what you need to know about files just to perform basic functions with your application and operating system software.

FILE NAMING CONVENTIONS

How Do I Specify a File Name?

When you create a file, you must give it a filename. A *filename* is a unique name that you give to a file of information. A filename is usually followed by a filename extension. A *filename extension* (most often just called an *extension*) further identifies the contents of your file usually by specifying the file type. For example, you could create a file with the filename **Finance Term Paper 3-12-02.doc**. The portion appearing before the period or dot is the unique filename you provide (**Finance Term Paper 3-12-02**). The portion appearing after the period or dot is the extension. In this case, the extension is **doc,** which Microsoft Word automatically provides when you create a document using that software.

As you use most application software to create files, the application software will provide its recommended extension. For example, Excel provides **xls,** Access provides **mdb,** and PowerPoint provides **ppt** (all Microsoft products and extensions).

When you provide a filename, it must adhere to the rules of your chosen operating system (called file naming conventions; see Figure 3.14). For the most part, you have a great deal of flexibility in choosing filenames. We certainly recommend that you use filenames that are as descriptive as possible to help you recall them. For example, **Finance Term Paper 3-12-02** is more descriptive than just **Finance Term Paper**, because you have a date associated with the first but not the second.

F I G U R E   3.14

File naming conventions are rules that you must follow in creating filenames and differ according to your operating system.

	Linux	Mac OS	Windows 2000 & XP
Maximum filename length	256	31	255
Are spaces allowed?	No	Yes	Yes
Are numbers allowed?	Yes	Yes	Yes
Special characters not allowed	! @ # $ % ^ & * ( ) { } [ ] " \ ' ; < > ?	None	\ ? : " < >	* /
Is it case sensitive?	Yes	Yes	No

ORGANIZING FILES

With So Many Files, How Can I Organize Them Effectively?

To help you manage your files, your operating system includes utility software called file manager utility software. *File manager utility software* is utility software that helps you manage, organize, find, copy, move, rename, and delete files on your computer. To use your file manager utility software effectively, you need to know something about device letters, directories, folders, pathnames, and filenames (which we just discussed).

Identifying Your Storage Devices with Device Letters

As you probably already know, you can store and access files of information on different storage devices such as a floppy disk, hard disk, and CD (or DVD). Each of these devices has a device letter. A **device letter** is a unique identifier for each different storage device on your computer (see Figure 3.15). On almost all personal computer systems, the device letter for the floppy disk is A. So, we refer to it as Drive A. The hard disk is almost always Drive C. The drive letters for your other storage devices depend on the computer you have as well as your operating system.

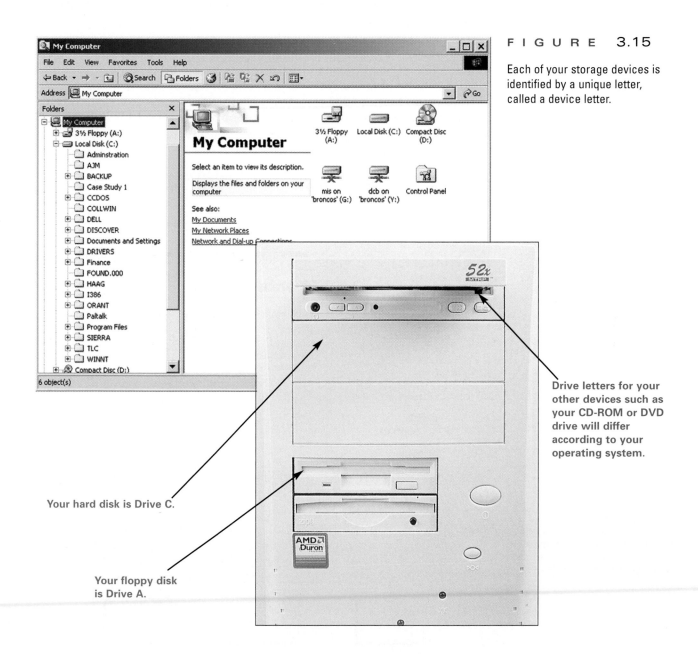

F I G U R E   3.15

Each of your storage devices is identified by a unique letter, called a device letter.

Drive letters for your other devices such as your CD-ROM or DVD drive will differ according to your operating system.

Your hard disk is Drive C.

Your floppy disk is Drive A.

Using Directories and Folders for Organizing Files

Each of your storage devices contains a directory. A ***directory*** is a list of the files (and folders, which we'll discuss next) on a particular storage device.

This main directory is often called the *root directory*. If you have many files, the root directory must contain them all, unless you create subdirectories or folders. A ***folder*** (which your operating system will display as a manila folder icon) is a special portion of your root directory into which you can place files that have similar information. For example, you can create a folder called **Finance** and in it store all the files you create for your Finance class (see Figure 3.16).

You can create folders within folders (these are called subfolders). So your **Finance** folder could contain the subfolders **Finance 3212** and **Finance 4032.** Your purpose in creating these would be to store all your files related to your Finance 3212 class in one subfolder and all your files related to your Finance 4032 class in another subfolder. In doing so, your file management system would begin to look like a pyramid (or hierarchical tree structure; see Figure 3.16), with the root directory at the top.

F I G U R E   3.16

Your file management system contains files within folders.

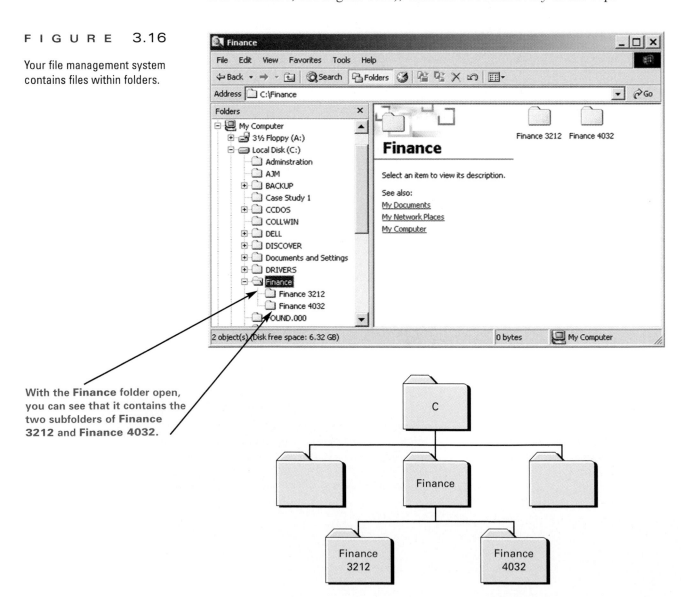

With the **Finance** folder open, you can see that it contains the two subfolders of **Finance 3212** and **Finance 4032.**

Using Pathnames to Identify File Locations

As you begin to organize your files by storage device and folders, you need to learn how to create and read a pathname. A *pathname* is the device letter, folder, subfolder (if present), filename, and extension that describe a particular file and its location. In our previous example, there could be a file called **Finance Final Analysis.xls** stored in the **Finance 4032** subfolder within the **Finance** folder on Drive C. The pathname for that file is

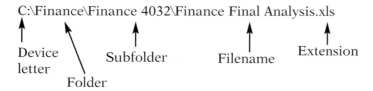

Why is this important? You may, from time to time, share a disk of information with friends or classmates. If you want to direct them to a particular file, you'll need to do so with the pathname. Of course, if you're passing around a disk, it's probably understood that the device letter is A.

Again, exactly how file manager utility software works and displays information and how it designates device letters is unique to your particular operating system. But the <u>concepts</u> of organizing files, folders, filenames, and extensions are the same regardless of your computing environment. If you take a class using a textbook that teaches you how to use different types of application software, we encourage you to read the section in the textbook on file manager utility software.

---

making the grade   SECTION C://

1. A _____ is a collection of information you need to use your computer effectively.

2. A filename _____ further identifies the contents of your file usually by specifying the file type.

3. A _____ is a list of the files on a particular storage device.

4. A _____ is a special portion of your root directory into which you can place files that have similar information.

D://MULTIMEDIA

Multimedia truly enhances the richness of the presentation of information on computers today. *Multimedia* is a presentation of information that can include sound, text, graphics, video, and animation and over which you have some sort of control. That's why we say that the Web is the Internet in multimedia form. On the Web, you experience sound, text, graphics, video, and animation. You have the ability to control where you want to go and what information you want to see or hear and in what order you want to see and hear information.

FIGURE 3.17

Encyclopedia Britannica at
www.britannica.com is one of
many multimedia sites on the
Web.

Multimedia includes text, art,
photos, and other presentations
of information.

With multimedia, you have some
control. By clicking on links, you
can choose what to see.

If you visit Encyclopedia Britannica at www.britannica.com, you can
view topical information in a multimedia format (see Figure 3.17). That is,
you decide what information you want to view (click on America's Stonehenge to read more about it), and you can see or hear information in a variety of formats (text, photos of Stonehenge, and so on).

Multimedia doesn't have to be purely Web-based. Earlier, in reference
to improving your writing skills, we discussed learning software, which
can help you practice a skill set or learn new knowledge. Almost all learning software you buy at a local computer store comes on a CD or DVD. So,
you don't even have to be connected to the Web to enjoy multimedia. If
you want to see some examples of multimedia on a CD, we would encourage you to view the presentations on the Interactive Companion CD
that comes with this textbook. All the Interactive Companion CD presentations are in fact multimedia. You can also choose the "Multimedia
Tools" lab to learn more about multimedia and its tools.

COMPUTER EQUIPMENT FOR USING MULTIMEDIA
What Do I Need on My Computer to View Multimedia?

Because multimedia presents information to you in a variety of formats,
you need a variety of computer equipment to experience it. Fortunately,
today's standard computer system (even notebooks) comes fully equipped
with everything you need to enjoy multimedia (see Figure 3.18 on the next
page).

- **A Fast CPU**—while viewing multimedia, your CPU (the real brains
  of your computer) must work especially hard to simultaneously
  pipe sound into your speakers and display text, images, video, and
  animation on your screen.

- **Speakers**—standard devices.

Each *month, about 8 percent of computers encounter a virus. That's one computer in every 12.*

did you know?

Your monitor is connected to your CPU with a graphics card.

Your speakers are connected to your CPU through a sound card.

Many multimedia applications come on CD or DVD.

A really fast CPU creates real-life multimedia presentations.

FIGURE 3.18

Hardware for viewing multimedia includes speakers, a monitor, and a CD or DVD player.

- **Monitor**—another standard device.
- **CD or DVD player**—multimedia you buy from a local computer store will come on either CD or DVD.

Many of these devices vary greatly in quality and price. In Chapter 5, we'll directly address these issues when we take you through the process of buying a computer.

COMPUTER EQUIPMENT FOR BUILDING MULTIMEDIA

What Special Equipment Do I Need to Create My Own Multimedia?

To build a multimedia application, you'll need some special hardware and software. Some of this hardware and software may be standard on your computer, and you'll have to purchase the rest.

Special Hardware Needs

Special hardware for building multimedia includes a microphone, scanner, digital camera, and digital video camera. A *microphone* is an input device that captures live sounds such as your voice or perhaps a dog barking. All operating systems today come with the necessary software that allows you to record sounds.

A *scanner* is an input device that helps you copy or capture images, photos, and artwork that exist on paper. With a scanner, for example, you might easily and quickly capture (or scan in) a photo of yourself or an associate. In our earlier example of Stonehenge at Encyclopedia Britannica,

FIGURE 3.19

To create multimedia, you'll need such hardware as a scanner, digital camera, and/or digital video camera.

A scanner can help you capture images, art, and photos that exist on paper.

A digital camera can help you capture live photos and transfer them directly to your computer.

A digital video camera can help you capture live video and transfer them directly to your computer.

there were several photos that were captured with a scanner. There are many types of scanners, and they vary greatly in quality and price. We'll talk more about scanners in Chapter 5.

A *digital camera* is an input device that helps you capture live photos or pictures and transfer them directly to your computer. With a regular camera, you would need to develop the film and then scan the photo. A digital camera, however, connects directly to your computer so that you can quickly transfer your photos. Some digital cameras even store photos on a disk that you would then use in your computer's disk drive. We'll talk more about digital cameras in Chapter 5.

Finally, if you want video in your multimedia application, you'll need a digital video camera. *A digital video camera* is an input device that helps you capture live video and transfer them directly to your computer. As with digital cameras, some digital video cameras connect directly to your computer while others store the video on a disk.

Special Software Needs

Of course, capturing the information you want in your multimedia application is only half the battle. You still need to integrate all your information into an exciting and meaningful presentation with multimedia authoring software.

Multimedia authoring software is software that you use to build your multimedia application. Popular multimedia authoring software is Adobe After Effects, CorelDRAW, Director 7 Shockwave, MediaForge, and Dazzler-Max. With multimedia authoring software, you define the look and feel of your multimedia application, adding buttons and links. You create the timing for your presentation by identifying which information should appear when. For example, you can specify that text should roll on to the screen from the right or the left as a narrator makes comments. To do this, you have to specify the timing of the text in conjunction with the narrator's voice.

For a review of some of the better multimedia authoring software packages, please visit the Web site for this text at www.mhhe.com/i-series.

SECTION D://   *making* **the grade**

1. Multimedia is a presentation of information, which can include sound, text, graphics, video, and animation and over which you have some _____.

2. A _____ is an input device that captures live sounds such as your voice or perhaps a dog barking.

3. A _____ is an input device that helps you capture live photos or pictures and transfer them directly to your computer.

4. _____ is software that you use to build your multimedia application.

E://CONSUMER ISSUES

YOUR RIGHTS TO YOUR SOFTWARE

When I Buy Software, Do I Really Own It?

When you buy software, you don't actually own it; rather you've purchased the right to use that software. Software you purchase includes a *software license,* which defines the way in which you can use the software. It may even include the stipulation that the warranty is void if you change the way the software works.

There are many types of software licenses. The most common for personal productivity software, personal operating systems, and utility software is a shrink-wrap license. A **shrink-wrap license** is a document that is shrink-wrapped to the outside of the software box. It states that by opening the shrink-wrap you agree to the terms of the license. For this reason, you may not be able to return software for a refund if you've already opened the box.

FREEWARE, SHAREWARE, AND PUBLIC DOMAIN SOFTWARE

Is Free or Almost-Free Software Available?

There is a variety of software available at little or no cost. This software can be public domain software, shareware, or freeware. **Public domain software** is software that you can copy, distribute, and even modify without obtaining permission, because someone has developed the software and then decided to place it within the public domain for anyone to use however they wish.

Shareware is software that you can "test drive" or "try before you buy." With shareware, you usually receive a license that gives you the right to use the software for a trial period. The license states that after the trial period you must pay a fee for continued use.

Finally, **freeware** is software that is also public domain software, meaning you can use it as you wish free of charge. People often use the term freeware in confusing conjunction with shareware, so, you should closely check your licensing agreement about this.

For a list of Web sites that offer public domain software, shareware, and freeware connect to the site for this text at www.mhhe.com/i-series.

QUESTIONS AND ANSWERS

1. Is Installing Software a Difficult Task?

No, installing most software is not difficult. When you purchase software, it usually comes with a short set of instructions that tells you how to perform the installation process. Most often, an ".exe" file accompanies the software, and all you have to do is execute that file (by double clicking on it) and answer a few questions. Be careful with public domain software, shareware, and freeware—you may not get installation instructions with these types of software.

2. Can I Buy Utility Software as a Suite Just like Personal Productivity Software?

Today, three suites dominate the utility market. These include McAfee Office Pro, Norton SystemWorks Professional Edition, and Ontrack System-Suite. Each includes all the software we discussed (anti-virus, crash-proof, uninstaller, and disk optimization), plus some other utilities. You may also find that a complete computer system you buy today will include one of these suites. If it doesn't, we recommend that you spend the money to get one. These suites usually sell in the $50 to $100 range.

3. Is My Software Compatible with Other Publishers' Software?

Maybe so, maybe not. Most popular software packages such as Word and WordPerfect do include utilities that can easily read files created using different software packages. In fact, most popular software packages even give you ability to save a file specifically for a different software package. So, you can use Word to create a document and then save that document in a WordPerfect format.

i·series insights

Ethics, Security & Privacy

Software That Kills

Software is available today that can actually help you make decisions, especially in the business world. For example, some software can help you determine how much inventory to carry, how to price rooms in a hotel based on seasonal travel, how your customer demographics seem to be changing, and which investment strategies will yield the highest returns. There's even software to help diagnose medical diseases and prescribe treatments.

Software, however, is only as good as the people who develop it. If software has a problem and doesn't produce the correct results, we say that it contains a "bug." Some bugs may not be that bad

(calculating the wrong pay for example), because their errors can be corrected. However, a bug in a medical program can do permanent damage.

Some years ago in the medical industry, software was developed to help determine how to treat cancer patients. It made a mistake and delivered 130 to 250 times the amount of radiation that patients needed. Four of those patients, unfortunately, died.

Software can help people automate tasks. But those tasks must be described in great detail by an expert. Then, the expert must validate that the software works perfectly. We may have some degree of tolerance for variation in personal productivity software but certainly not for software in the medical field that determines radiation levels.

SECTION E:// making the grade

1. A _____ defines the way in which you can use your software.

2. _____ is software that you can "test drive" or "try before you buy."

3. _____ software is software that you copy, distribute, and even modify without obtaining permission.

4. A _____ license is a document that is shrink-wrapped to the outside of the software box.

F://SUMMARY AND KEY TERMS

Software is the most important part of your computer system. ***Application software*** is the software that allows you to perform specific tasks such as writing a term paper and creating slides for a presentation. ***System software,*** on the other hand, is the software that details how your computer carries out technology-specific tasks (such as writing information to a disk or checking for viruses).

Within the realm of application software, you'll focus mostly on using personal productivity software:

- ***Word processing*** and ***desktop publishing software*** for creating mainly text documents.
- ***Web authoring software*** for building and maintaining a Web site.

i·witness

An Up-Close Look at Web Sites

Text Color

To make certain text on your Web site stands out, you can adjust its color. When building your Web site, you can adjust the color of text in two ways. First, you can change the default text color of black to any other color. If you do this, all text in your Web site will take on the new color. Second, you can adjust the color of just certain text. So, text within your Web site can be all one color (default black or any other color you choose) or many different colors.

Of course, you should use color wisely. Changing text color just for the sake of having different colors is not a wise move. Change your text color only if it makes sense and makes your Web site more appealing. Wild variations can detract.

We've provided three Web sites for you to review. One uses only the default black text color. The remaining two alter the text color in some way. These sites are:

www.mhhe.com/i-series/I-Witness/3-A.html

www.mhhe.com/i-series/I-Witness/3-B.html

www.mhhe.com/i-series/I-Witness/3-C.html

Evaluate the two Web sites that change the text color for their effec-tiveness. Would you change either of them? Do they perhaps use too much color or not enough?

For the Web site that uses no color, make recommendations as to how to incorporate different text colors. You can also connect to the Web site for this text and download these Web sites to your computer. Then you can make the changes yourself.

HTML Reference:

- To change the default color for the whole Web site
  <BODY TEXT="color name"> -
  <BODY TEXT="blue">
  would change all the text to blue

- To change the color for just certain text
  <FONT COLOR="color name"> -
  <FONT COLOR="blue">new color</FONT>
  would display new color, while not changing the color of any other text

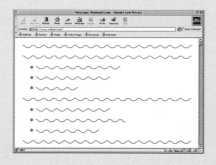

- **Graphics software** for creating photos and art.
- **Presentation software** for building a slide presentation.
- **Spreadsheet software** for working with numbers, calculations, and graphs.
- **Personal information management** and **personal finance software** for managing personal information.
- **Communications software** for communicating with other people.

System software is your operating system and utilities. **Operating system software** is system software that controls application software execution and manages how your hardware devices work together. Popular operating systems include **Microsoft Windows 2000 Me, Microsoft Windows 2000 Pro, Microsoft Windows XP Pro, Microsoft Windows XP Home, Mac OS,** and **Linux.**

Utility software provides additional functionality to your operating system. This includes anti-virus software, crash-proof software, uninstaller software, and disk optimization software.

When you store information on your computer, you do so in the form of a *file*—a collection of information you need to use your computer effectively. A file has a unique *filename* that describes it, as well an *extension* that further specifies the file type. To be organized, you should keep related files in *folders,* which are special portions of your *directory* (lists of files) into which you can place files that have similar information.

Most important, you understand that what software you choose to use should be driven by your needs, not the other way around. Choose software that meets your needs, and you'll instantly be productive. (However, never expect software to improve your basic personal habits and skills—you have to do that yourself!)

On the Web site for this text at www.mhhe.com/i-series, we've provided a great deal of support as you learn about software. That support includes:

- Multimedia authoring software.
- Public domain software.
- Shareware.
- Freeware.
- Web sites that sell software.

KEY TERMS

anti-virus software (p. 3.14)

application software (p. 3.2)

communications software (p. 3.9)

crash-proof software (p. 3.14)

desktop publishing software (p. 3.5)

device letter (p. 3.17)

digital camera (p. 3.22)

digital video camera (p. 3.22)

directory (p. 3.18)

disk optimization software (p. 3.14)

file (p. 3.15)

file manager utility software (p. 3.16)

filename (p. 3.16)

filename extension (extension) (p. 3.16)

folder (p. 3.18)

freeware (p. 3.23)

graphics software (p. 3.6)

Linux (p. 3.13)

Mac OS (p. 3.13)

microphone (p. 3.21)

Microsoft Windows 2000 Millennium (Windows 2000 Me) (p. 3.11)

Microsoft Windows 2000 Professional (Windows 2000 Pro) (p. 3.12)

Microsoft Windows XP Home (Windows XP Home) (p. 3.12)

Microsoft Windows XP Professional (Windows XP Pro) (p. 3.12)

multimedia (p. 3.19)

multimedia authoring software (p. 3.22)

multitasking (p. 3.11)

online banking (p. 3.9)

operating system software (p. 3.11)

pathname (p. 3.19)

personal finance software (p. 3.9)

personal information management (PIM) software (p. 3.8)

personal productivity software (p. 3.2)

presentation software (p. 3.7)

public domain software (p. 3.23)

scanner (p. 3.21)

shareware (p. 3.23)

shrink-wrap license (p. 3.23)

software license (p. 3.22)

software suite (p. 3.4)

software version (version) (p. 3.3)

spreadsheet software (p. 3.7)

system software (p. 3.2)

uninstaller software (p. 3.14)

utility software (p. 3.14)

Web authoring software (p. 3.5)

word processing software (p. 3.5)

CROSSWORD PUZZLE

Across

6. For taking still photos
8. Software when your computer crashes
9. For capturing photos and art that exist on paper
10. Better than word processing software
13. Software for personal and business needs
15. Bundled software
16. Software for communicating
19. Software that works with cells
20. Group of related files
21. Software for working with images and the like
22. Software that runs your computer
23. Banking on the Web

Down

1. Information
2. Operating system for Apples
3. Software that maintains your checking account
4. Part of system software
5. Gives you the right to use software
7. Not as good as desktop publishing software
11. Listing of files
12. Unique letter for each storage device
14. Helps you maintain an address book
17. New release of software
18. Part of system software

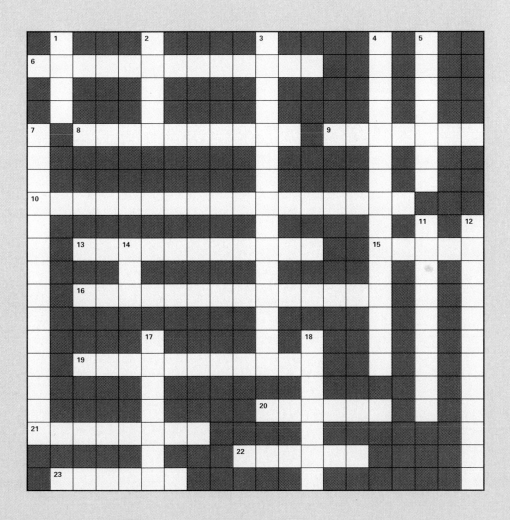

QUESTIONS AND EXERCISES

Multiple Choice

1. File manager utility software is utility software that helps you _____ files on your computer.
   a. organize
   b. copy
   c. move
   d. rename
   e. do all of the above to

2. Software that helps you work with numbers, calculations, and graphs is
   a. presentation software.
   b. word processing software.
   c. calculation software.
   d. spreadsheet software.
   e. database management software.

3. Software that helps you with tasks that you can probably perform even if you don't have a computer is
   a. word processing software.
   b. desktop publishing software.
   c. presentation software.
   d. communications software.
   e. all of the above.

4. Enhanced word processing software is
   a. communications software.
   b. multimedia authoring software.
   c. desktop publishing software.
   d. Web authoring software.
   e. none of the above.

5. System software that adds to the functionality of your computer system is
   a. operating system software.
   b. utility software.
   c. communications software.
   d. desktop publishing software.
   e. presentation software.

6. _____ is an operating system function that allows you to work with more than one piece of software at a time.
   a. OLE
   b. Multitasking
   c. System resource management
   d. Linux
   e. Crash-proof

7. _____ software can help you maintain an address book, your calendar, and your to-do list.
   a. Personal finance
   b. Word processing
   c. Utility
   d. Graphics
   e. Personal information management

8. Multimedia authoring software helps you build
   a. term papers.
   b. class notes.
   c. multimedia.
   d. number calculations.
   e. Web sites.

9. A pathname consists of a
   a. device letter.
   b. folder (and subfolder if present).
   c. filename.
   d. extension.
   e. all of the above.

10. Application software can help you
    a. write a term paper.
    b. surf the Web.
    c. keep a home budget.
    d. create slides.
    e. do all of the above.

True/False

11. ___ When you buy licensed software, you can do whatever you want with it, including selling it to someone else.

12. ___ Operating system software includes screen savers and anti-virus software.

13. ___ Windows XP Pro is a Microsoft operating system for the typical home computer user.

14. ___ Connectivity software falls in the category of application software.

15. ___ A digital camera can help you capture live photos.

QUESTIONS AND EXERCISES

1. In the left-hand column below, write down every class you're currently taking. In the right-hand column, write down all the applicable personal productivity software that could help you in each class.

CLASSES

PERSONAL PRODUCTIVITY SOFTWARE

2. For each of the following operating systems, write down the number one reason for choosing it.

OPERATING SYSTEM

NUMBER ONE REASON FOR CHOOSING IT

Mac OS

Windows XP Home

Windows XP Pro

Linux

3. Multimedia is a presentation of information, which can include sound, text, graphics, video, and animation and over which you have some control. Keeping that in mind, address the following:

a. How is a movie you rent a multimedia presentation? How is a movie you rent <u>not</u> a multimedia presentation?

b. How is your radio a multimedia presentation? How is your radio <u>not</u> a multimedia presentation?

c. How is the Interactive Companion CD that accompanies this text a multimedia presentation? You may need to take a look at it if you haven't already.

d. How is an ATM a multimedia presentation? How is an ATM <u>not</u> a multimedia presentation?

e-commerce

1. Freeware and Shareware

The computer field today is full of software, with literally thousands of packages for you to choose from. Some you have to pay for, but there are many more for free (or almost free). It's what we call freeware and shareware.

Connect to a couple of the following sites and do a little fact-finding concerning freeware and shareware.

- www.freeware-downloads.com
- www.freewareworld.com
- www.shareware.cnet.com
- www.jumbo.com

As you visit these sites, look around for some software that might interest you. As you visit each site, answer the following questions.

a. Who owns and maintains the site?

b. How does the site owner make money "giving away" software?

c. Can you search by category such as games or entertainment?

d. Is there any "free" software for which you must actually pay a fee?

Finally, consider the issue of your computer's security. Are you worried about downloading software from the Web and getting a virus? Do any of the sites guarantee that you won't get a virus from their software?

2. Buying and Renting Videos

Videos are another hot electronic commerce aspect of the Web. Not only can you buy and rent videos on the Web, you can also watch them on the Web. Right now, let's just focus on buying and renting videos.

When you buy or rent videos on the Web, you'll be able to choose from beta, VHS, or DVD. You'll be able to search by name, category, and even actor or actress. Connect to a couple of the sites listed below and let's see what we can find.

- www.blockbuster.com
- www.columbiahouse.com
- www.video.com
- www.videoflicks.com

As you visit each site, perform the following tasks and answer the following questions.

a. Search for a video by name. Do you have to know the exact name?

b. Search for videos by category. What categories are available?

c. Search for videos by actor or actress. Do you have to know the name of the actor or actress or can you choose from a list?

What about renting a video? Which sites will let you rent a video instead of buying it? If you can't find such a site in our list, go to a search engine site and track one down (there are many). How does renting a video on the Web work?

3. Maps and Directions

You need never be lost again in a city or traveling across the country. Why? Because the Web is full of sites that can offer you driving directions. At many of these sites, you simply type in where you are and where you want to go. The site will then give you a detailed map along with specific driving directions, often telling you exactly how far to travel on each leg of your journey.

Let's visit a few of these sites and see what they have to offer. Below is a list of four Web sites that offer maps and directions. Connect to a couple of them.

- www.maps.expedia.com
- www.mapquest.com
- www.maps.com
- www.maps.yahoo.com

At each site you choose, pick a starting point and a destination for your journey. Now, try to enter that information to receive driving instructions. As you do, answer the following questions.

a. How easy is it to specify your starting point and destination?

b. Do you have to know exact addresses or can you pick a location by something such as a business or hotel name?

c. Does the site give you both a map and driving instructions or a combination of the two?

As you travel, would you prefer to have directions from a Web site or use a "fold-up" map? Can the information on a Web site be as reliable as a fold-up map? Or, in reverse, can a fold-up map that was probably printed some time ago be as up-to-date as the information on a Web site?

4. Online Banking

Believe it or not, many people are predicting that brick-and-mortar banks will soon go out of business in favor of click-and-mortar banks on the Web. That's already becoming true to a certain extent. Recall that personal finance software supports online banking so you can pay your bills, transfer money, and even check your account balances all from the comfort of your home.

And many banks and savings and loans now charge for you to go inside and perform a transaction with a teller. That's right. You can use an ATM for free, but you have to pay to see a teller at several banks.

Below, we've provided four sites that offer on-line banking. Connect to a couple of them, and let's do some fact-finding concerning online banking.

- www.sfnb.com
- www.netbank.com
- www.delawarefirstbank.com
- www.future-banker.com

First of all, which of these sites are for banks that exist only on the Web? That is, which sites support a bank that has no brick-and-mortar presence on some street corner?

Now, pick one specific site and answer the following questions.

a. What's the process for opening an account? Can you apply online and instantly open an account or do you have to complete some forms by mail?

b. If you were to open an account, how do you get money into your account?

c. Is there a minimum balance requirement for opening an account? For maintaining an account?

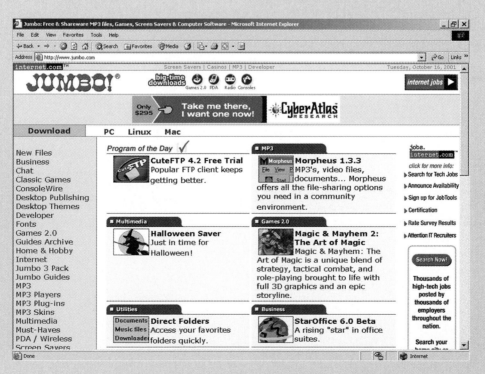

on the web

1. Downloading Free Images, Photos, and Art

In the previous section of e-commerce projects, you visited some Web sites that offer freeware and shareware. And there's a lot more free stuff on the Web. For example, there are thousands of sites that provide free images, photos, and art. All you do is download them and use them as you wish. You can even change the way they look if you wish. Start at your favorite search engine and find sites that offer free images, photos, and art. Report to your class some of the better sites you found as well as what it takes to download images, photos, and art from the Web.

2. Finding Free Screen Savers

Another category of free stuff on the Web is screen savers. Screen savers are interesting to look at, but they also serve a very important purpose. If your screen displays something too long, that "something" can actually burn a "ghost" image of itself onto your screen. And it will be there forever. Perform another search on the Web and this time find free screen savers you can download. Download one of the screen savers and determine how to make it your screen saver

of choice. Report back to your class the exact set of steps it takes to change a screen saver on your computer.

3. Categorizing Personal Productivity Software

In the computer software ad on page 3.3, we listed some of the more popular personal productivity software packages. What we didn't tell you was in which category of personal productivity software each package belonged. For example, is Corel Trellix Web authoring software, desktop publishing software, or some other type? As a group, visit a Web site that specializes in the sale of personal productivity software and determine the category of each of the software packages listed in that ad. It might surprise you to find that a couple of the packages actually fall into more than one category.

4. Updating Your Anti-Virus Software

When you buy software (or get it for free), you'll usually be able to use it for a couple of years before considering an upgrade. But that's not true with anti-virus software. New viruses spring to life each day. That being the case, you need to constantly update your anti-virus software so it will find the new viruses. When you update your anti-virus software, you're actually just updating a file of information that describes each type of virus. Visit the Web site for the anti-virus software you have on your computer and download the new file. What are the steps involved in doing this? After you download the new file, what do you have to do on your computer to use it? Why don't anti-virus software publishers charge for the updated file?

ethics, security & privacy

1. Software Piracy

The problem of software piracy grows larger everyday. Software piracy occurs when someone illegally obtains and uses a copy of software. For example, you could create a copy of a game CD-ROM and give it to a friend. That's software piracy. Likewise, someone could post a copy of software on the Web for everyone to copy and use. If that software isn't public domain software, then it's software piracy.

Software piracy is a particular problem on a global scale. In some parts of the world, you can buy a copy of Microsoft Windows operating system software for just a few dollars. Two of the countries in which the practice of software piracy is the most rampant are Russia and China. The Software Publishers Association estimates that in those countries more software is pirated than obtained legally.

You should understand that the per capita gross domestic product of the people in Russia is about $5,000 per year; in China it's even less, at about $2,500. In the U.S. on the other hand, the per capita gross domestic product is $27,000.

Consider the following questions in relation to software piracy.

a. Given that the path to economic prosperity in today's world involves having and knowing how to use information technology, what will happen to the relative economic position of poor countries if they can't get modern software?

b. Will increased poverty in a large part of the world adversely affect U.S. trade, and in turn the U.S. economy?

c. Is it OK for poor countries to acquire software illegally if they can't afford it since without it they're heading for economic suicide?

d. If you answered no to the previous question, suggest what the United States should do about the problem. Should the government:

   • Clamp down very hard on the nations that pirate software?

   • Offer aid in the form of money or software to countries too poor to buy it legally?

   • Ignore the problem and take the heat from software publishers?

e. If you think it's OK for poorer countries to pirate software (you answered yes), answer the following questions:

   • Do people who create software or music or who write books have a right to profit from their intellectual property?

   • Is there an upper dollar limit to that right?

   • If it's OK to pirate software, is it OK to steal other things, like computers or cars?

   • How poor do you have to be to have a right to steal?

All these issues and questions relate to what we call "the great digital divide." The great digital divide basically states that the division between the "haves" and "have nots" is now defined by technology, not money or even education. If you're interested, there's a lot of great reading concerning the digital divide in books and on the Web.

group activities

1. Game and Entertainment Software

Many people would also include "games and entertainment" as a category in personal productivity software. This particular set of software makes billions of dollars each year in revenue. You can probably find more public domain, shareware, and freeware games and entertainment software on the Web than you can for any other category of personal productivity software. Should "games and entertainment" be a category within personal productivity software? Suppose we asked you to join our author team on the next edition of this text and asked you to write a section on games and entertainment software. What would it look like? What specific software packages would you mention?

2. Using Microsoft Paint

Microsoft Paint is graphics software that comes with the Microsoft Windows operating system. To find it, click on the **Start** button, then **Programs,** then **Accessories,** and finally **Paint.** Paint is quite easy to use—on the left you'll find your drawing tools (pencil, spray can, brush, and so on), and at the bottom you'll find your color selections. Choose a few drawing tools as well as some colors and create a free-hand drawing. What did you draw? How easy was it to learn the basic functions of Paint? Did you use the shapes such as rectangle and oval?

3. Your School's Operating System Software

Go on a fact-finding mission and visit your school's computer lab. If there are several, visit at least two of them. While you're there, determine which operating systems are on the various computers. Do some of the computers have different operating systems? If your school's computer lab is a network, inquire which operating system is used to run the network. Is it the same as the operating system on the individual computers? Also, inquire about the licensing agreement your school has to run a particular operating system on multiple computers.

4. Adding Sound to a PowerPoint Presentation

As you create a slide presentation, most presentation software such as Microsoft PowerPoint allows you to quickly and easily add sound to a particular slide. As you're creating a slide, all you have to do in PowerPoint to add sound is click on the **Insert** menu option. From there, click on **Movies and Sound** and then **Sound from Gallery.** PowerPoint will then offer you a list of already-prepared sounds you can include in a slide. Start PowerPoint (or your presentation software), create a blank slide, follow the process of adding sound, and then select one of the sound options. When you view that slide, how do you know the sound is there? During a presentation for which you were in the audience, would sound be annoying or enhancing? Why?

5. Exploring Application Software on a Computer System

Visit a local computer store and find a computer for sale that would interest you. What application software comes with the computer system? Is it a suite of software, individual software packages, or perhaps a combination of the two? Which additional application software would you need to buy? What is the operating system software that comes with the computer system? What utility software comes with the computer system?

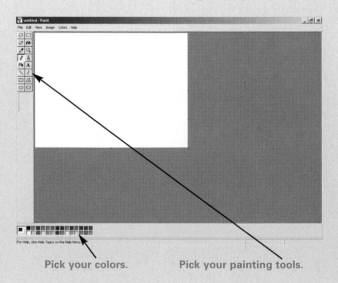

Pick your colors.   Pick your painting tools.

Looking Back/Looking Ahead

The Life and Times of a Dot-Com Entrepreneur

Joann is quickly moving toward realizing her dream. After closely surveying the Web for competitors, Joann embarked on the process of identifying her desired Internet Service Provider (ISP) and her basic hardware and software needs for being on the Web. Now, she's ready to determine the software she needs to bring her business to life and run it on a daily basis.

First and foremost, Joann knows she'll need _____ software to create her Web site. She also realizes that she wants _____ on her Web site so visitors can enjoy text, images, sound, animation, and some video clips. To create her art and manipulate photos, Joann has decided she needs to invest in _____ software.

Behind her Web site, Joann wants a variety of software to help her be more productive. So, she's buying _____ software to manipulate her sales information and create high-quality graphs. She also wants a complete electronic checkbook, including _____ banking. For this, she's purchasing _____ software.

Joann also realizes that she wants to advertise not only on the Web but also by mailing out brochures and flyers. For this task, she's chosen _____ software.

Joann appreciates organization. So, she's keeping her related _____ in separate _____. Using her _____ utility software, Joann will be able to keep her files well organized.

Finally, Joann must have a good operating system that will allow her to stay connected to a network. For this, she's chosen Microsoft's _____. Although _____ seems as though it will be a good operating system for Web-oriented computers, she's chosen not to use it because it's so new. Likewise, _____ is for Apple computers—Joann has chosen an IBM compatible.

Now that she has her specific software needs met, Joann is looking toward building her Web site with multimedia and identifying how she wants to perform her electronic commerce activities. After that, she wants to precisely define her hardware needs, including a CPU, RAM, scanner, and digital camera, just to name a few. She'll find all her answers in Chapters 4, 5, and 6.

INTERACTIVE
COMPANION LAB
SUPPORT

- **Multimedia Tools (p. 4.17)**
- **Photo Editing (p. 4.22)**
- **Internet Overview (p. 4.23)**

did you know?

Since its "official" arrival in 1994 the World Wide Web has experienced phenomenal growth.

your dictionary has been emptied onto the Web. Type in any English word as a domain name and you'll probably hit a site.

every month 750,000 people access the Web for the first time.

thousands of job sites are on the Web. Many job seekers turn to the Web before their local newspaper.

over half a million people have placed their resume on the Web. Many companies now encourage applicants to post a resume at their Web site.

in October 1994, Jeff Bezos wanted to name his new Web venture "Cadabra": like "abracadabra." But his attorney convinced him that this magical name sounded a bit too much like "cadaver." Reluctantly, Bezos went with his second choice: Amazon.com.

in 1998, 7.9 percent of Americans over the age of 14 made online purchases. By 2002, __??__ over the age of 14 will.

To find out just how many people will make purchases, visit www.mhhe.com/i-series.

CHAPTER

4

four

E-Commerce, Web Multimedia, and Web Authoring

How Do You Harness the Power of the Web?

You've probably noticed the e-commerce projects at the end of each chapter. But until now, we haven't formally defined electronic commerce. *Electronic commerce (e-commerce)* is really just commerce, but it's commerce that technology facilitates and enhances. The technology aspect of e-commerce allows you to reach more customers, distribute information quickly, establish strong and lasting relationships, and be innovative in how you perform all types of commerce functions.

In this chapter we focus on e-commerce on the Web. First we explore types of e-commerce, e-commerce purchasing, building your own e-commerce site, and mobile commerce. Then you'll learn how businesses are using Web multimedia and interactivity to attract your attention. Web multimedia and interactivity include such things as plug-ins, players, and streaming media.

Finally, we want to help you start a Web site that will include your resume. Using the Web to reach potential employers should be significant to you.

A://ELECTRONIC COMMERCE

Electronic commerce is a broad topic and field. More important, e-commerce (and technology in general) is a hot topic in business. E-commerce is not simply the "fad of the month" in business or your personal life. It's here to stay.

E-COMMERCE BUSINESS

What Types of Businesses Are Out There?

You can categorize a business in different ways—whether it's product or service oriented, whether it sells primarily to individual customers or to other businesses, or by its industry (food, manufacturing, health care, etc.). You can also categorize a business according to how you can interact with it through e-commerce.

Brick-and-Mortar Businesses

If you can interact with a business only by visiting a physical location such as a store, then it's a brick-and-mortar business. A *brick-and-mortar business* exists only in the physical world and performs no e-commerce functions. Before the Web, almost all businesses fit into this category. (An exception would be mail-order businesses.) Some locally owned businesses are still in this category, but even that's rapidly changing.

Click-and-Mortar Businesses

Today most businesses that exist in the physical world are also on the Web. These are click-and-mortar businesses. A *click-and-mortar business* has both a presence in the physical world (such as a store) and a Web site that supports some type of e-commerce. For some click-and-mortar businesses, e-commerce may be a Web page with a phone number and directions. Other businesses such as JCPenney place their catalogs on the Web so you can buy items with your credit card and have them delivered to your home (see Figure 4.1).

F I G U R E   4.1

JCPenney is a click-and-mortar business. You can make purchases both on the Web and in its stores.

Click-and-Order Businesses

Some businesses don't even have a place where you can go to shop. They exist only on the Web. Although they store their products in warehouses and run their operations from offices, they interact with you as a customer only through the Web. A ***click-and-order business*** exists solely on the Web with no physical presence that you can visit to buy products and services. Amazon.com and CDNow are click-and-order businesses (see Figure 4.2).

F I G U R E   4.2

CDNow sells you music on the Web but not in stores. It's a click-and-order business.

TYPES OF E-COMMERCE ACTIVITIES

How Are Businesses and Consumers Interacting through E-Commerce?

Different e-commerce activities have different purposes. Is the business targeting consumers like you or does it cater to another business? Maybe the e-commerce isn't even a company, but someone trying to sell something to someone else on the Web.

Business to Consumer E-Commerce (B2C)

Business to consumer electronic commerce (B2C e-commerce) occurs when a business sells products and services through e-commerce to customers who are primarily individuals. Hundreds of thousands of B2C e-commerce businesses exist on the Web. They include Dell (a click-and-order business) and Barnes and Noble (a click-and-mortar business).

B2C e-commerce businesses have been the most visible. However, only about 3 percent of all e-commerce revenues are B2C. The other 97 percent are mostly B2B e-commerce revenues.

Business to Business E-Commerce (B2B)

Business to business electronic commerce (B2B e-commerce) occurs when a business sells products and services through e-commerce to customers who are primarily other businesses. For example, Gates Rubber Company makes rubber- and synthetic-based products such as belts and hoses for cars. But Gates doesn't sell directly to you. Instead, parts stores and automakers buy its products.

A type of B2B e-commerce called electronic data interchange existed before the Web. ***Electronic data interchange (EDI)*** is a set of guidelines for electronically handling the ordering, billing, and paying for goods and services. EDI eliminates paper in the transaction. EDI is very nearly a requirement in B2B e-commerce today. For example, General Motors won't buy products from a supplier who cannot perform EDI. Many suppliers such as Gates offer EDI capabilities over the Web, as shown in Figure 4.3.

FIGURE 4.3

If you were an automaker, you could buy hoses and belts from the Gates Rubber Company over the Web without using any paper. This is business to business e-commerce.

The two industries Gates Rubber Company does business with.

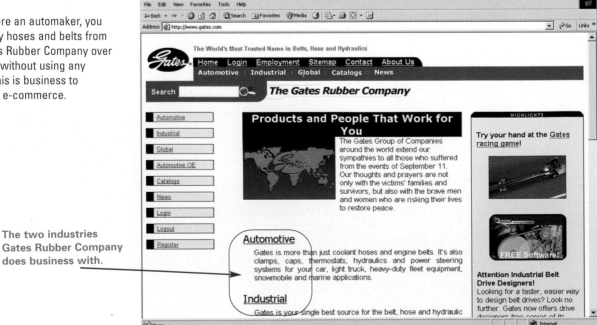

Consumer to Consumer E-Commerce (C2C)

Finally there's consumer to consumer electronic commerce. ***Consumer to consumer electronic commerce (C2C e-commerce)*** occurs when a person (such as you) sells products and services to another person through e-commerce. The most well-known Web site that supports C2C e-commerce is eBay (www.ebay.com). EBay is a form of a click-and-order business, but it does no more than provide an electronic marketplace where you can buy and sell products with other people. We'll look at eBay later.

E-COMMERCE PURCHASING

How Can a Business Make Me Want to Purchase Something through E-Commerce?

Every day people buy a product or service on the Web for the first time. But some don't do it again. Perhaps they couldn't find the Web site a second time, weren't comfortable using their credit card online, couldn't contact the company to ask questions, or didn't like the product once they got it. Let's see what e-commerce businesses are doing to ensure you're a repeat customer. To illustrate, we'll visit Amazon.com.

Personalization

Have you ever been to a store that tracks what you buy and then recommends items that you might like? This is called personalization and it's certainly possible on the Web. ***Personalization*** on the Web is the process of customizing a Web page or series of Web pages according to a customer's preferences. For example, you can create your own account at Amazon.com. Through it, Amazon.com will track your purchasing preferences, shipping information, and more. It keeps some of this information about you in a cookie. A ***cookie*** is a small text file containing information about you that's stored on your computer's hard drive. This cookie stores your Amazon.com log-in ID as well as computer-generated codes that locate information about you in Amazon.com's database.

In Figure 4.4, an Amazon.com screen shows a personalized Web page.

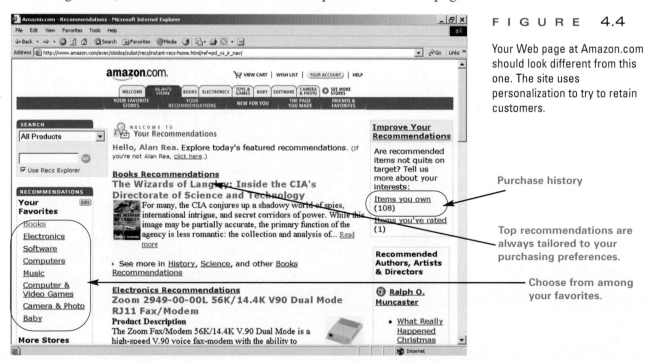

FIGURE 4.4

Your Web page at Amazon.com should look different from this one. The site uses personalization to try to retain customers.

Purchase history

Top recommendations are always tailored to your purchasing preferences.

Choose from among your favorites.

If you create an account at Amazon.com, it won't look exactly like the one in Figure 4.4. Instead, it will display <u>your</u> preferences and information. You should try it.

Usability

Often a Web page's personalization isn't enough to bring you back. The Web page also must be easy to use. ***Usability*** refers to how easy or difficult it is to use a Web page or site. Usability is key to generating sales. Figure 4.4 shows how Amazon.com has mastered usability. You can choose to buy one of its recommendations, like the book *The Wizards of Langley* or a new fax/modem for your computer. There are ways to manage your account, check how much you've purchased, and even change your recommendations and preferences. So Amazon.com has made it easy for you to personalize your shopping experience. This is one reason why Amazon.com is such a successful click-and-order business.

Customer Service

If something you buy at a store doesn't work, it's easy to return to the store for help. On the Web, customer service is more complicated. ***Customer service*** means making sure that a customer knows about the product and has no questions about buying it or what happens afterward. To improve customer service, many click-and-order businesses include a return package and postage with your purchase. Some allow you to print a postage-paid label off their Web site.

Product Information

When you go to a bookstore, you can browse the shelves, read a few pages of a book, ask a friend or another customer his or her opinion, and maybe even sip a cup of coffee. But these advantages—except perhaps for the coffee—are not lost online. If you want to learn about *The Wizards of Langley* book at Amazon.com, you click on the book icon, which takes you to the Web page shown in Figure 4.5. Here you have many options. You can look at the book's table of contents, read editorial reviews, or see if other readers endorse it.

FIGURE 4.5

You can learn a lot about a book before deciding whether to buy it at Amazon.com.

Read sample pages from the book.

Purchase the book.

Amazon even predicts how well you will like the book.

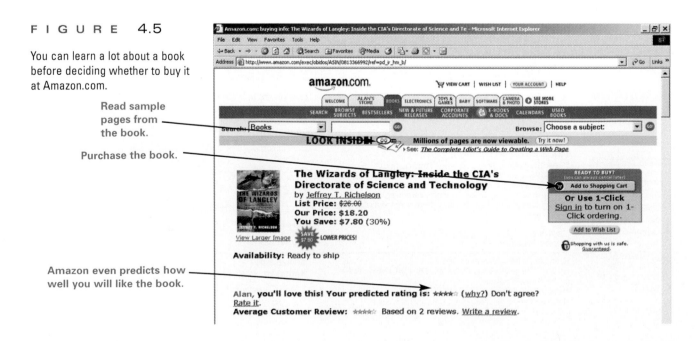

Ordering

If the feedback convinces you to buy the book, ordering is easy. In the middle right of Figure 4.5 is an "Add to Shopping Cart" button. A ***shopping cart*** is software that stores information about your e-commerce purchases. Clicking on the "Add to Shopping Cart" button allows you to provide your shipping and billing address, enter your credit card information, and print a copy of your invoice.

Security

Before sharing sensitive information such as a credit card number on an e-commerce Web site, make sure you're involved in a secure transaction. A ***secure transaction*** uses specific protocols to transfer sensitive information. ***Encryption*** is the technology used to hide the information and make it secure. You can tell if you're using a secure transaction by looking for the lock icon on your browser (see Figure 4.6). Don't order from an e-commerce site that doesn't provide a secure transaction. We've provided more information on protecting your information at www.mhhe.com/i-series.

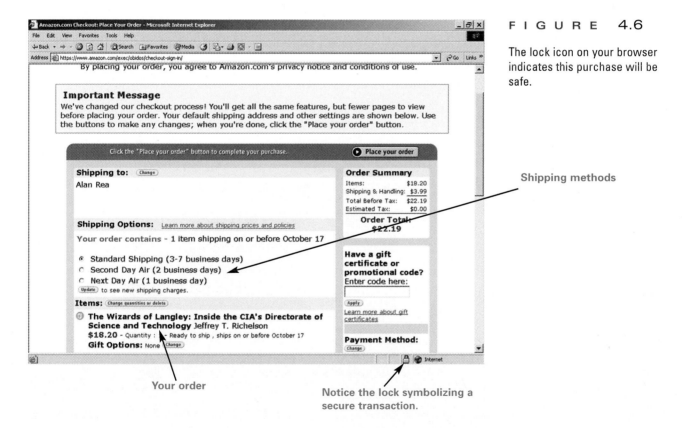

Your order

Notice the lock symbolizing a secure transaction.

Shipping methods

F I G U R E   4.6

The lock icon on your browser indicates this purchase will be safe.

Shipment

Next you'll need your product shipped to you. Most e-commerce Web sites offer shipping options based on how fast you want the product. As Figure 4.6 shows, Amazon.com allows you to choose a shipping option.

Personalization, usability, customer service, product information, ordering, security, and shipment options are all important facets of successful e-commerce Web sites. If you ever decide to open your own click-and-order business, keep these in mind as you develop your business and your site.

BUILDING YOUR E-COMMERCE WEB SITE

How Can I Sell Products on the Web?

Now that you're familiar with e-commerce, you may have decided that you want to sell some products—your old computer system, some CDs, or a video game—on the Web. Fortunately, for whatever you want to sell, there's probably someone who wants to buy it. To sell your products, you can do so through C2C or B2C e-commerce.

Consumer to Consumer E-Commerce Selling

If you want to sell products but not as a formal business, you should use a C2C site. The most popular is eBay. Here you list your products in a virtual auction. You specify everything from a minimum price and description to how long the auction will run. Other individuals will bid on your products, with the highest bidder winning the auction. So, eBay is a virtual marketplace that supports C2C e-commerce.

Figure 4.7 shows eBay's many options for sellers. These include services that will help you process secure transactions with credit cards and digital money. ***Digital money*** allows you to purchase items using a bank account balance instead of a credit card. As a seller, if you'd rather not receive payment in electronic form, you can specify that you'll accept only other payment forms such as cash, money orders, or cashier's checks.

FIGURE 4.7

EBay helps you safely sell products to other consumers on the Web.

The many tools available at eBay

Categories

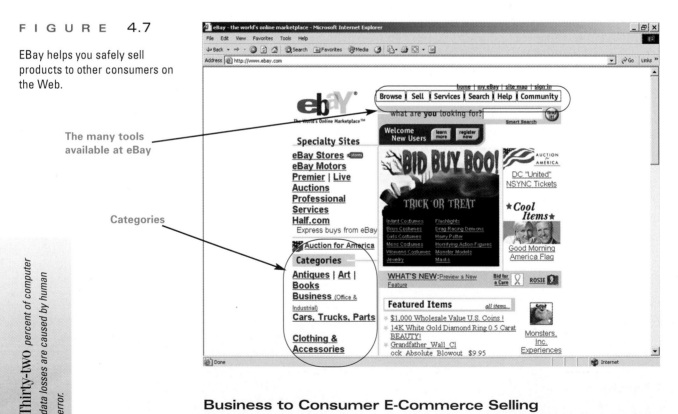

Business to Consumer E-Commerce Selling

The easiest way to open a click-and-order business and sell products regularly is to use an e-commerce enabled Web site host. An ***e-commerce enabled Web site host*** allows you to build a virtual storefront, create a catalog, process secure payments, provide customer service, and manage your e-commerce Web site.

i·series insights

Ethics, Security & Privacy

Security, Privacy, and Trust in E-Commerce

If you read *The Wall Street Journal* or follow the stock market, you'll hear that e-commerce will continue to grow. But e-commerce does face some challenges. Most important, many people still don't trust doing e-commerce on the Web. And that hesitancy is warranted. Before you join the e-commerce bandwagon, keep the following in mind.

Security

From the very beginning, you'll want to check regularly that each of your e-commerce transactions is secure. Check your credit card statements carefully. If you use dig-

ital money, monitor your account balances.

Privacy

As Web sites collect more information about you, you're relinquishing privacy in return for convenience. Monitor how they can use your personal information and decide whether to submit this information in return for information and services.

Check the privacy policies at the e-commerce Web sites you

shop. Do they sell your buying habits to other companies? What happens to this information if the company merges with another?

Trust

Whether the e-commerce Web site adheres to industry's privacy codes determines if you can trust it. Look for a TRUSTe logo, which means that the Web site follows certain standards. TRUSTe is a nonprofit organization that sets privacy standards and monitors its member Web sites for violations of privacy standards. You can learn more about TRUSTe at www.truste.org.

Experts call many of these virtual or Internet malls. Like a regular mall, an **Internet mall** provides the Web space and utilities (in this case, software) and you supply the information and products. Two of the most popular e-commerce enabled Web site hosts are Yahoo! Stores and Amazon zShops. We show you how to establish a click-and-order business through an e-commerce enabled Web site host at www.mhhe.com/i-series.

M-COMMERCE

Do I Have to Sit in Front of My Computer to Perform E-Commerce?

E-commerce businesses don't want to force you to sit at a computer to shop. A new form of e-commerce, called m-commerce, is becoming more prevalent. **M-commerce,** or **mobile e-commerce,** allows you to use wireless devices such as cell phones or PDAs to buy and sell products and services. As Web-enabled cell phones and PDAs become common, expect to see m-commerce explode.

It's not that we think you'll soon use your cell phone or PDA to buy a television or stereo on the Web. But what if you could buy a soda or pay for your gas without cash or a credit card? What if you could check the movie schedule as you drove by the theater? All this will be possible with m-commerce. In fact, people in Japan do it now with DoCoMo's imode.

You can find out more about m-commerce at www.mhhe.com/i-series. Check back and we'll keep you up to date on this trend.

E-COMMERCE MARKETING AND ADVERTISING
How Do Businesses Attract People to Their Web Sites?

Once you've visited an e-commerce site and made a purchase, that business knows what kind of items you'll buy. Now it can market similar items to you. But how can e-commerce businesses attract new customers? They can use a variety of marketing and advertising techniques, as we'll discuss next.

Banner Ads and Click-Throughs

Have you ever visited a Web site and noticed a small advertising banner at the top of the page? This is a banner ad. A ***banner ad*** is a graphical advertisement that will take you to an e-commerce site if you click on it. Some sites place banner ads in small Web pages that "pop up" when you enter the Web site. A ***pop-up ad*** is a small Web page containing an advertisement that appears on your computer screen outside of the current Web site loaded in your Web browser. Pop-ads are designed to draw attention to their content by appearing where you don't expect them.

Most ads target a specific audience. In Figure 4.8, for example, the banner ad is for Oracle software. This ad appears on CNET (www.cnet.com), a site people interested in technology frequently visit.

F I G U R E   4.8

Oracle hopes that if you visit CNET.com, you'll want to check its Web site, too. Notice its banner ad.

The Oracle banner ad ————

To monitor the effectiveness of banner ads (and perhaps pay for them), e-commerce sites track click-throughs. A ***click-through*** is information that is captured when you click on a banner ad to go from one Web site to another. For payment purposes, the business that placed the banner ad must pay the hosting site for every click-through. So, if you have a site and sell banner ad space, the more click-throughs you record (called a click-through count), the more money you can make.

Companies such as Double Click (www.doubleclick.net) and Engage (www.engage.com) specialize in helping you create your own banner ads to place on other Web sites.

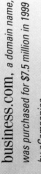

business.com, a domain name, was purchased for $7.5 million in 1999 by eCompanies.

did you know?

Affiliate Programs

To make money by hosting banner ads, you must first attract people to your Web site. One way to do this is by joining an affiliate program. An *affiliate program* (or an *associate program*) allows you to sell goods and services via another e-commerce site.

Let's say you create a Web site about online gaming. On your site you recommend books, software, and gaming items (controllers, joysticks, etc.) through an affiliate program such as Affiliate.net (see Figure 4.9) from Barnes & Noble (www.bn.com). For every person who "clicks through" from your site to Barnes & Noble, you get a commission. So, you can make money just by creating a Web site people want to visit.

FIGURE 4.9

Services such as Barnes & Noble's Affiliate.net help you bring e-commerce to your own Web site.

Businesses make it easy to join their affiliate network.

Opting In and Opting Out

Click-throughs usually record basic information about you, such as what site you came from and the date and time. But when you want to purchase a product, a Web site will want even more information—your name, e-mail address, phone number, age, and gender along with your likes and dislikes. And if it's an e-commerce site, it'll probably want payment information as well.

But did you know that most businesses allow you some control over the information they collect about you? They give you the choice of "opting in" or "opting out." *Opting in* is when you give permission for alternative uses of your personal information. *Opting out* is when you say no to alternative uses of your personal information.

Would you rather have businesses ask you first before using your information (opt out) or simply assume you are willing to allow them to use it (opt in)?

Viral Marketing

Some e-commerce businesses let you play games and have the chance of winning money or prizes in exchange for your personal information. An example is www.grab.com (see Figure 4.10).

These sites then use your name and e-mail address for their promotional purposes and sell it to other businesses as well. This is the concept of viral marketing. **Viral marketing** is a technique that e-commerce businesses use to gather personal information about you, use that information in their own promotional campaigns, and sell that information to other e-commerce businesses. If you participate in viral marketing as a consumer, your e-mail will soon be full of advertisements and offers from hundreds—if not thousands—of e-commerce businesses. Some you may be interested in, some you may not.

SECTION A:// *making* **the grade**

1. E-commerce is really just commerce, but it's commerce facilitated and enhanced by _____.

2. A _____ business exists solely on the Web with no physical location that you can visit.

3. _____ is a well-known site that supports C2C e-commerce.

4. A _____ is software that stores information about your e-commerce purchases.

5. _____ is when you say no to alternative uses of your personal information.

B://WEB MULTIMEDIA AND INTERACTIVITY

Interactive gaming—such as what you'll find at Grab.com—requires Web multimedia. **Web multimedia** is the use of audio, video, animation, and other elements to allow interactivity on a Web site or page. Web multimedia helps Web businesses attract and retain customers because it improves personalization, usability, and product presentation. So let's explore Web multimedia and see how your Web pages can incorporate it.

USING WEB MULTIMEDIA

What Software Do I Need to Enjoy Web Multimedia?

Your favorite song pulses through your computer speakers as you play a game with a friend in Russia and watch a preview of an upcoming movie. All of this is possible using Web multimedia, but you might need to install some software to make it happen.

Plug-Ins

Have you ever gone to a Web page only to have a message tell you that you need a plug-in? A *plug-in* is software that works within your Web browser to play multimedia. For example, you may need a Shockwave plug-in to play an Internet game with your friend in Russia. Getting and installing a plug-in isn't difficult. Figure 4.11 shows Netscape's resource site for all available plug-ins.

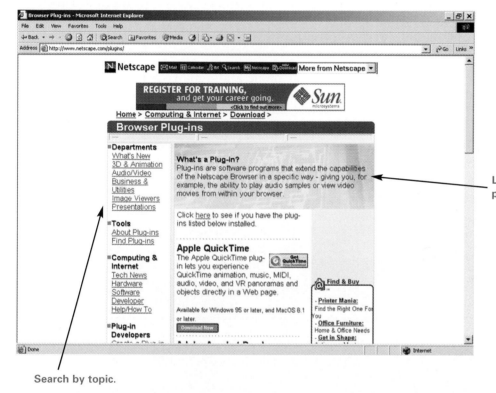

Search by topic.

F I G U R E   4.11

You can download free software called plug-ins to help you use Web multimedia. Netscape offers plug-ins at its Web site.

Learn more about plug-ins.

Players

A plug-in isn't the only way to view multimedia on the Web—you also can use a player. A *player* (or a *viewer*) is software that works outside your Web browser to play multimedia. Players combine a plug-in with software you install on your computer to view multimedia files. The most popular are Windows Media Player (which comes installed on computers with Windows as the operating system) and RealNetworks RealPlayer. Macromedia also has a Shockwave player for interactive games and animation. Combine these with a few plug-ins and you'll be able to access most of the multimedia on the Web.

MULTIMEDIA FORMATS

So, What Multimedia Can I Access?

Now that you know what you need to access multimedia, let's look at what you can access.

Audio

Your computer makes beeps or other sounds as you open, use, and close software. Most of these sounds are wave (.wav) or audio (.au) files. These also can become Web audio in Web pages. **Web audio** is all of the sounds and music on the Web.

Video

Similarly, **Web video** is all of the movies on the Web. You can download and play video on your Web page using plug-ins. You also can download video files and view them on a player such as the QuickTime Player or Windows Media Player. Video files come in many file formats. QuickTime formats and Windows AVI are the most common. You may need more than one player to view all of the video formats. The Windows Media Player in Figure 4.12 is one of the many free players available.

F I G U R E   4.12

The Windows Media Player lets you enjoy music and video
without having to wait until your browser downloads all of the file.

The tabs along the edge help you find content.

The controls are similar to a VCR or CD player.

Current movies, television, and music are featured.

Current type of media being played

Streaming Media

Because of their size, some audio and video files take a long time to download if you have a slow connection. What if you could use audio and video without the long download times? Streaming media allows you to do this. *Streaming media* continually sends small parts of a large file to your Web browser as you watch or listen to what you've already downloaded. Thus, you don't have to wait until an entire file downloads to start watching a video. You need to use either the Windows Media Player, RealNetworks RealPlayer, or the QuickTime Player to access streaming media.

OTHER INTERACTIVE ITEMS
How Do I Get to the Cutting Edge?

Watching movies and listening to music are only the beginning of what you can enjoy through Web multimedia. More and better multimedia and interactive technology are surfacing each day. We'll keep you up-to-date on our Web site at www.mhhe.com/i-series. Now let's discuss the more popular technologies on the Web.

Flash and Shockwave

Many Web pages use Flash technology. Designed by Macromedia, *Flash* is software that helps you create animated and interactive Web pages. Instead of nonmoving (static) images, you can use Flash to incorporate animation, moving images, and sounds on your Web page. All of these use relatively small files so Web pages are quick to load and access. You can access pages that use Flash with a free plug-in from Macromedia (see Figure 4.13).

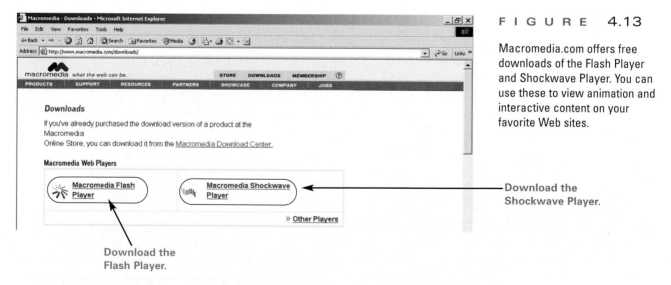

FIGURE 4.13

Macromedia.com offers free downloads of the Flash Player and Shockwave Player. You can use these to view animation and interactive content on your favorite Web sites.

For Web pages with even more multimedia such as gaming interactivity, look for "shocked" Web pages. Shocked Web pages use Macromedia's Shockwave technology. *Shockwave* is software that helps you create Web pages with significant interactivity through Web multimedia. A "shocked" Web page lets you play games on the Web and view animations. You can also download games and play them with the Shockwave player (see Figure 4.13).

If you want to develop Web multimedia in either Flash or Shockwave, you'll need to learn how to use Macromedia's software.

Are You Addicted to the Internet?

Do you glance at the clock and realize that you've spent more time than you wanted to surfing the Web? Or do you find yourself checking e-mail throughout the day and being disappointed when you don't have any? Do you find yourself looking forward to more time on the Internet? If you answered yes to any one of these questions, you may be addicted to the Internet. You just can't seem to get enough of it, and, when you try to quit, you can't.

Dr. Kimberly Young is one of the first "cyber-psychologists." She is a professor at the University of Pennsylvania and author of articles and books on cyber-addictions. On her Web site (www.netaddiction.com), Dr. Young notes that cyber-addiction takes many forms—cyber-relationships, online gambling, and excessive chat room use. Over 60 percent of the respondents to a survey of Dr. Young's who were deemed addicted to the Internet spent their time in interactive activities such as chat rooms and other virtual environments.

New forms of Internet addiction appear each day. They include day trading on the stock market, Internet gaming use, and excessive Web surfing for information. Dr. Young suggests answering certain questions to determine if you're addicted:

- How often do your grades or schoolwork suffer because of the amount of time you spend online?
- How often do you check your e-mail before something else that you need to do?
- How often do you find yourself anticipating when you will go online again?
- How often do you lose sleep because of late-night log-ins?

Internet addiction is serious. Although it's very different from being addicted to a substance (a chemical or physical dependence), psychological addiction can be even more powerful and more difficult to break. With the increase in the number of ways the Internet can be accessed such as through cell phones and PDAs, anyone can get an "Internet fix" anytime and anywhere.

If you're wondering if you have an Internet addiction, go to the NetAddiction Web site and take its survey.

VRML

Through Web multimedia, you can view information on the Web in many forms, such as animation. But what if you could interact with that animation so that you felt as though you were physically inside it? It's possible through VRML. *VRML,* or ***Virtual Reality Modeling Language,*** creates a virtual world in which users have the illusion that they are physically participating in the presentation of the Web multimedia. So, VRML allows you to create representations of objects (such as views of an art gallery in Figure 4.14) and allows users to interact with them.

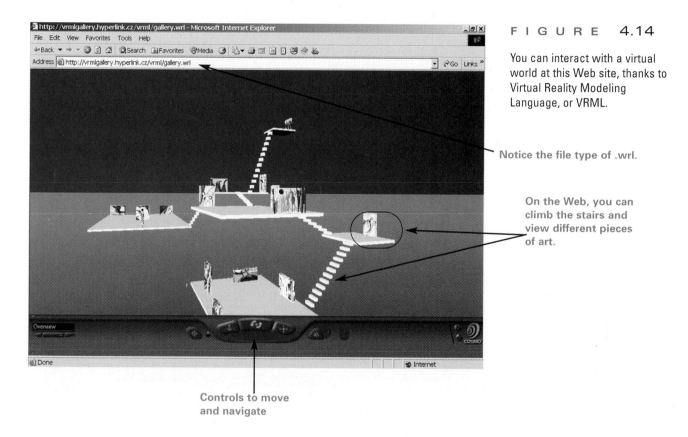

FIGURE 4.14

You can interact with a virtual world at this Web site, thanks to Virtual Reality Modeling Language, or VRML.

Notice the file type of .wrl.

On the Web, you can climb the stairs and view different pieces of art.

Controls to move and navigate

VRML shows great promise. Imagine if, when shopping on the Web, you could try on clothes using a representation of yourself (called an *avatar*) to make sure everything fit. What if you could experience the beaches of Hawaii before deciding to vacation there? On the Web site for this text at www.mhhe.com/i-series, we've included links to Web sites that use VRML. VRML is a Web-based version of virtual reality (we'll discuss virtual reality in Chapter 9). To learn more about the many types of multimedia (including virtual reality), visit the Interactive Companion Labs and choose "Multimedia Tools."

SECTION B://   *making the grade*

1. Audio, video, animation, and other interactive elements on a Web page are all _____.

2. To use multimedia within your Web browser you'll need a _____.

3. A _____ lets you use multimedia outside your Web browser.

4. _____ continually sends small parts of a large file to your Web browser and enables you to view a multimedia file while you download it.

5. _____ creates a virtual world on the Web in which users have the illusion that they are physically participating.

C://WEB AUTHORING AND WEB SITE MANAGEMENT

Before you can build your own Web site, you must be familiar with Hypertext Markup Language. **HTML** *(Hypertext Markup Language)* is the basic language used to create Web pages. Let's look at how you might build and publish your own e-resume as we study HTML.

FIGURE 4.15

You can make an e-resume like this one by starting with an HTML document.

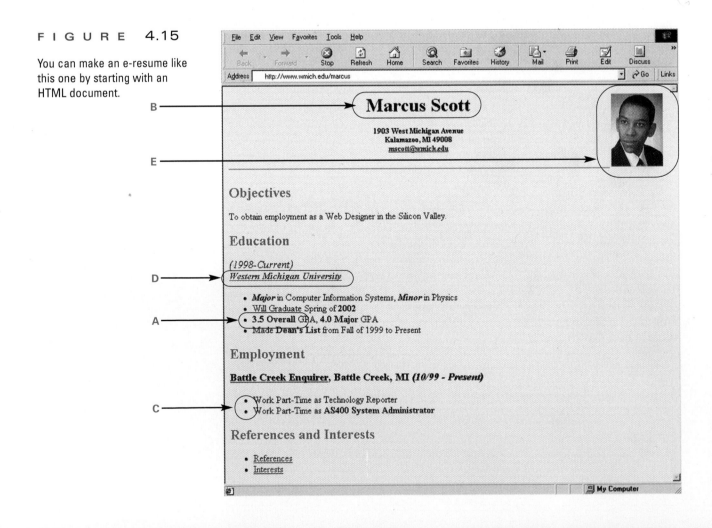

Gloria – 908 – 405 – 1662

HTML

How Do I Create a Web Page?

HTML lets you decide what information will appear on your Web page and how it will look. To format your page, you place commands in angle brackets **< >** to tell the Web browser what, where, and how you want the information to appear. We call these commands HTML tags. ***HTML tags*** specify the formatting and presentation of information on a Web page.

But first you must create an HTML document in your Web space. An ***HTML document*** is a file that contains HTML tags and the information you want to appear on your Web page. Thus, a Web page is simply an HTML document visually displayed in a Web browser. Figure 4.15 shows a Web page with an e-resume and Figure 4.16 shows the HTML document that created it.

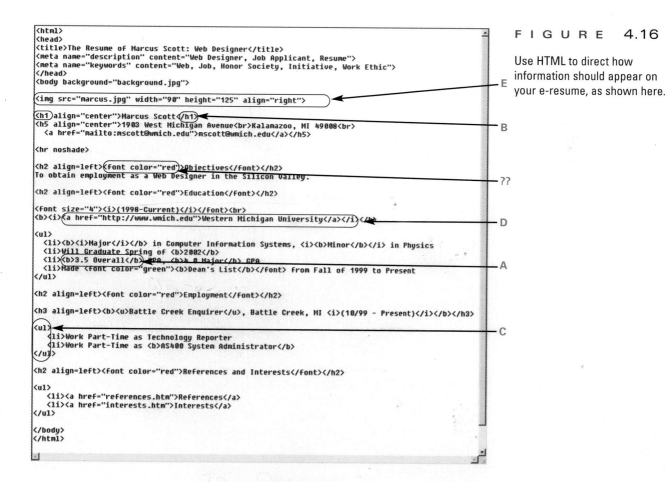

F I G U R E   4.16

Use HTML to direct how information should appear on your e-resume, as shown here.

As we explore how Marcus created his e-resume in Figure 4.16, we'll refer to Figure 4.17 (on page 4.21), which lists basic HTML tags and describes their purposes. You're also able to compare the HTML tags in Figure 4.16 with the resulting e-resume in Figure 4.15. For more information and examples, visit the Web site for this text at www.mhhe.com/i-series (*Life-Long Learning Module A* "Enhanced Web Development").

General Tags

While creating your HTML document, you'll make use of several general tags including basic formatting tags, heading tags, and font tags. **_Basic formatting tags_** are HTML tags that tell a Web browser how to display text in formats such as bold (**** and ****), italics (**<i>** and **</i>**), and underline (**<u>** and **</u>**). Marcus used these basic formatting tags on information such as his GPA and the fact that he made the Dean's List (see the HTML code marked A in Figure 4.16 and the corresponding Web page information in Figure 4.15).

    Heading tags are HTML tags that make certain information, such as titles, stand out on your Web page. Heading tags range from **<h1>** and **</h1>** to **<h6>** and **</h6>,** with **<h1>** being the largest. As you can see from the code marked B in Figure 4.16, Marcus used the **<h1>** tag to make his name large and bold. Another way to change the size of text is to use font tags. **_Font tags_** are HTML tags that allow you to change the size of your text, specify a font type, and/or specify a color. Can you find examples of where Marcus used font tags to change the size of text and specify a color?

List Tags

When you create any Web page, you usually want to present text in the most concise manner. Your visitors simply won't read a series of long paragraphs. **_List tags_** are HTML tags that allow you to present information in the form of a list, either numbered (using **<ol>** and **</ol>**) or unnumbered (using **<ul>** and **</ul>**). Notice that Marcus used such a list to present his primary work responsibilities at the _Battle Creek Enquirer_ (see the HTML code marked C in Figure 4.16).

Link Tags

Notice that Marcus also included in his e-resume links to his other Web pages as well as related Web sites (the HTML code marked D in Figure 4.16). He did this using link tags. **_Link tags_** are HTML tags you use to create links on your Web page to other sites, pages, downloadable files such as audio and video, and e-mail.

    To create a link to Western Michigan University, Marcus wrote in HTML: **<a href="http://www.wmich.edu">**Western Michigan University**</a>**. This link tag may look complicated, but it's not. Between the quote marks after the equal sign (**=**), you place a Web site or page address. Then, after the greater than sign (**>**) and before the **</a>** closing tag, place the text you want to appear on the screen. That's all.

Image Tags

To personalize his e-resume, Marcus used an image tag (the HTML code marked E in Figure 4.16) to insert a photo of himself. **_Image tags_** are HTML tags you use to insert photos and other images onto your Web page. So, Marcus's HTML document includes: **<img src="marcus.jpg" width="90" height="125" align="right">**. This tag identifies the name of the file in which Marcus captured his photo (marcus.jpg) and several property settings. The property settings determine the size of the photo (in pixels identifying width and height) and justification (right).

FIGURE 4.17

Here are some of the basic HTML tags you'll need to design a Web page. These are just a few of the hundreds of tags you can use to create your Web page. Learning to use these tags is easy. Designing the right look and feel for your Web page and defining the content is the challenging part.

HTML Tag	Description/Use
<html></html>	Frames your HTML document. Always start your HTML document with <html> and end it with </html>.
<head></head>	Creates a header area for your HTML document. Within it, you place your Web page title and key words by which search engines will find your Web page.
<title></title>	Creates a title for your Web page which will appear on the title bar.
<body></body>	Surrounds the content of your Web page. <body> comes immediately after </head>, and </body> comes immediately before </html>.
 	Creates a line break. For example, Hello world! would display Hello World
<p></p>	Creates paragraph standard formatting with a blank line after the paragraph.
<b></b>	Bolds whatever text is in between.
<i></i>	Italicizes whatever text is in between.
<u></u>	Underlines whatever text is in between.
<h1></h1>	Creates large, bold heading text. Numbers can vary from 1 to 6, with 1 being the largest and 6 being the smallest.
<font></font>	Changes the size, font type, and/or color of text. For example, <font color="blue">Color</font> would display Color, while <font size ="2">Size</font> would display Size.
<hr>	Creates a horizontal line.
<ul></ul>	Creates a bulleted list. All items between these tags that start with <li> will appear as separate bulleted items. Marcus's e-resume includes an example of this.
<ol></ol>	Creates a numbered or ordered list. All items between these tags that start with <li> will appear as separate numbered items.
<a href></a>	Creates a link. For example, <a href="http://www.mhhe.com/i-series">I-Series Books</a> would create the link I-Series Books. If you click on this link, you will go to the Web site for this text.
<a href></a>	Can also create a link for e-mailing someone. For example, <a href="mailto:shaag@du.edu">Book Author</a> would create the link Book Author. If you click on this link, you will be able to send an e-mail message to one of the authors.
<img src>	Places an image within your Web page. For example, <img src="sample.gif"> would place the image contained within the file sample.gif in your Web page. You must have the image file in your Web space.
<body bgcolor>	Creates a background color for your Web page. For example, <body bgcolor="red"> would create a red background.

When you place an image on a Web page, you're providing a reference to an image file. This image file needs to be in a specific image format. *Image formats* contain instructions to create and store information about an image. The two most-used image formats on the Web are GIFs (Graphics Interchange Format) and JPEGs (Joint Photographics Expert Group). Another format making its way onto the Web is the progressive network graphic (PNG). To learn more about working with images, visit the Interactive Companion Labs and choose "Photo Editing."

To create his e-resume Marcus used several other HTML tags. See Figure 4.17 for a description of these. Also, visit the Web site for this text (*Life-Long Learning Module A* "Enhanced Web Development") at www.mhhe.com/i-series to learn more about HTML tags.

WEB AUTHORING SOFTWARE
What Should I Use to Write HTML?

Many professional Web developers use Notepad or another simple text editor to work on their HTML. They also use specially designed tools. If you develop Web pages regularly, you may want to use Web authoring software, which we discussed in Chapter 2. Web authoring software is also known as HTML editing software.

Web authoring software packages vary in capability and price. The most common programs are Netscape Composer, shown in Figure 4.18,

Notice the many commands
available for HTML editing.

F I G U R E   4.18

Netscape Composer is one of
the more common Web
authoring software packages.

In this area, you can
change the font type,
color, and size.

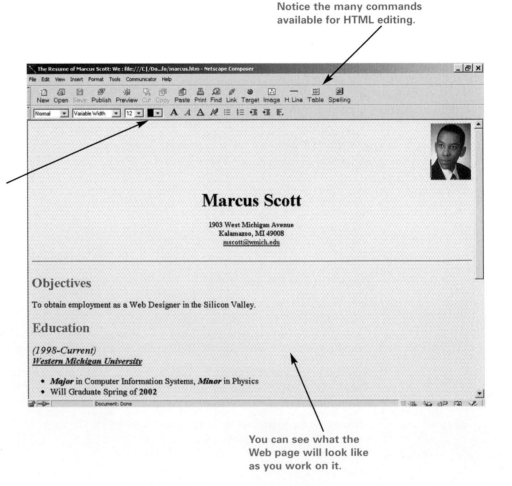

You can see what the
Web page will look like
as you work on it.

and Microsoft's FrontPage Express. Both are free to use. Both also are WYSIWYG HTML editors. **WYSIWYG HTML editors,** or "What You See Is What You Get" HTML editors, display how your Web page will look. These editors allow you to change the displayed version, which results automatically in changes to the actual HTML document. You can still manipulate the HTML document if you wish.

Other Web authoring software packages help you not only to develop Web pages but also to maintain your Web pages and Web site. These have become Web site management software. **Web site management software** allows you to create, update, and manage all of your Web pages quickly and efficiently. For example, you can create a template. Then, when you add pages to your Web site, they will look similar to existing ones—an important aspect of effective Web site design. Macromedia Dreamweaver and Microsoft FrontPage are popular Web site management software packages.

PUBLISHING AND MAINTAINING YOUR WEB SITE
How Do I Get My Site on the Web?

Once you've built your Web site, you'll want to share it with others. You'll have some decisions to make about publishing your Web site. Let's look at these.

Web Space

If you have an account that you use to check e-mail and connect to the Internet, you may already have Web space. You learned in Chapter 2 that Web space is a storage area where you keep your Web site. To store Web pages and images in your Web space (which is on a Web server) you'll need a File Transfer Protocol (FTP) program. An **FTP program** moves files from your computer to your Web server so people can view them on the Web. You'll need to get information about your account from your Internet service provider (ISP). Remember that you must decide whether to use your school ISP, a commercial ISP (like AT&T), or a free ISP. All have benefits and drawbacks. Look at Chapter 2 for a refresher on these. You also might want to look again at the Interactive Companion Labs and choose "Internet Overview."

Maintaining a Web Site

The Web changes fast. Keep your site "up to speed" with fresh content. People quickly notice an outdated Web site. Don't keep dead links, either. Links to other sites fail as the Web changes. If your friend removes her Web site, your link to it dies. Check your links regularly to make sure they work.

BEYOND HTML
What Else Can I Do with My Web Site?

If you're like most creators of a new Web site, you're asking, "What's next?" The short answer: "A whole lot." Let's briefly look at opportunities ahead of you.

Cascading Style Sheets

Cascading style sheets (CSS) are a method of creating one file that contains your entire theme (color, fonts, etc.) for your Web site. On each of your Web pages you reference the style sheet. When you want to change your theme, you change one file. The theme is then changed on all of your Web pages.

JavaScript

Have you ever been to a Web page with images or text that changed when you placed your cursor over it? This site is probably using JavaScript. *JavaScript* is a scripting language that allows you to add interactivity and other features to a Web page. Shopping carts at e-commerce sites are often in JavaScript.

Java Applets

Sometimes when you visit a Web page a "loading Java" message appears at the bottom of your browser. What's happening? Your Web browser is starting a program to run a Java applet. *Java applets* are small pieces of software that enable applications to run on a Web page. These can be moving images, games, or even programs that access databases and files on the Web. Many Java applets are available for your use (see Figure 4.19). Only your programming skills limit the use of Java applets.

F I G U R E　4.19

In this Java applet you can manipulate the 3-D image. For example, the blades on this helicopter spin as you rotate it.

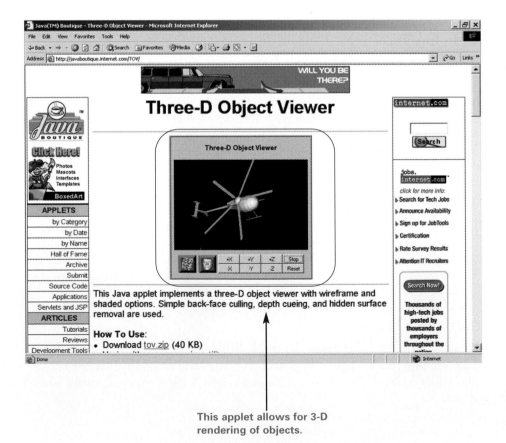

This applet allows for 3-D rendering of objects.

XML

Have you used a search engine that returned so many Web pages you didn't know where to start? Extensible Markup Language, or XML, is remedying this. **XML (eXtensible Markup Language)** allows you to use key words to identify similar items and organize information on the Web. If a Web site uses XML correctly, your search will return Web pages containing the information you need.

---

making the grade   SECTION C://

1. _____ is the basic language used to create Web pages.
2. _____ allows you to use key words to identify similar items and organize information on the Web.
3. _____ tags are HTML tags you use to insert photos and other images onto your Web page.
4. An _____ moves files from your computer to the Internet.
5. Java _____ are small pieces of software that enable applications to run on a Web page.

D://CONSUMER ISSUES

Whether you're visiting an e-commerce Web site or developing one of your own, you need to consider many issues. Below, we address a few.

EFFECTIVE WEB DESIGN GUIDELINES
How Do I Make My Site Sizzle?

No matter why you build a Web site, you'll want to make it attractive and easy to use, so as to encourage people to visit your site and return many times. For a list of effective Web design guidelines, see Figure 4.20. You can also learn more about how to make your Web site sizzle in *Life-Long Learning Module A* "Enhanced Web Development" introduced at the end of the text and continued on the text Web site at www.mhhe.com/i-series.

- Create a consistent theme and stay with it throughout your Web pages.
- Create a theme that targets your specific audience.
- Always place navigation links in the same place on each Web page.
- Each Web page should include a "Home" link that returns the user to the main page.
- Use visuals only if they have a purpose. "Dressing up" your Web site typically isn't a good purpose.
- Don't create lengthy paragraphs of text. If you need a lot of text, break it into lists.
- Always proofread your content for errors.
- Include the date when you last updated your site.
- Avoid the "blinking binge." This can be very annoying.
- Test your Web site for compatibility with all popular browsers.

FIGURE 4.20

Follow these effective Web design guidelines and you'll be on your way to a good Web site.

Themes

A *theme* is the coordinated presentation of colors, text, and other elements that appear on your Web site. You'll want to develop the theme with your intended audience in mind. For example, if you're creating a Web site for children, use primary colors such as red, blue, and yellow. If the site is for college students, however, you'll want it to be more "edgy" with dramatic color contrasts and perhaps a black background.

Image Use

As you develop your theme, consider the purpose of your images. Images can enhance the quality of your site, or they can be distracting—and they do take time to load. Thus, include an image only if you can justify its necessity. To learn more about working with images, visit the Interactive Companion Labs and choose "Photo Editing."

Developing for Different Web Browsers

You should always consider how your Web page will appear in both Internet Explorer and Netscape Navigator. These Web browsers interpret some HTML tags in different ways. So, as you develop your site, check it in both Web browsers.

You've also learned about microbrowsers for cell phones and the use of PDAs to access the Web. When developing Web sites for these devices (some of which have only four lines), you'll need to consider different methods of Web development. We have some examples at the Web site for this text at www.mhhe.com/i-series.

GETTING SEARCH ENGINES TO FIND YOUR SITE
How Do Search Engines Categorize My Site?

Most people find a Web site by using a search engine such as Yahoo! or Ask Jeeves, as we discussed in Chapter 2. You can register your site with these search engines and specify key words by which your Web site would appear on a search list.

You also can embed some of these key words into your HTML document. Figure 4.21 shows how Marcus's HTML document does this. Notice the line that starts as **<meta name="keywords"** . . . and lists terms such as Job and Initiative. These are key words by which search engines will find and categorize Marcus's site.

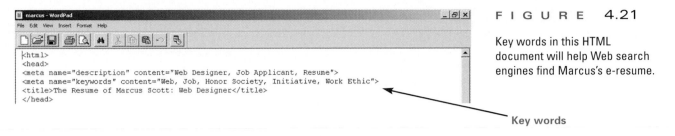

F I G U R E   4.21

Key words in this HTML document will help Web search engines find Marcus's e-resume.

Key words

QUESTIONS AND ANSWERS

1. What Web Authoring or Site Management Software Should I Buy?

Before buying software to help maintain Web pages, try the free Web authoring tools. Netscape Communicator has built-in Web authoring software and Microsoft offers FrontPage Express as a free download. Or a text editor such as Notepad may be enough for your needs. Services such as AOL also offer Web authoring software.

If you do decide to buy software, consider whether you'll need it to create Web pages or to manage multiple Web sites. Your choices range from Claris Home Page to more powerful site management software such as Microsoft FrontPage or Macromedia Dreamweaver. You can learn more at www.mhhe.com/i-series.

2. Where Can I Find the Best E-Commerce Web Sites?

Some Web sites rank e-commerce businesses according to their security, customer service, and other business practices. BizRate (www.bizrate.com) ranks C2C e-commerce sites according to customer feedback. The Better Business Bureau (www.bbb.org) runs the Better Business Bureau Online (www.bbb.online.org) that monitors Web businesses. Also, ask your friends which e-commerce Web sites work best for them.

3. Should I Create My Own Site or Hire Someone to Do It?

If you plan to build a site that will hold your e-resume and perhaps provide information about a student organization, consider developing the Web site yourself. On the other hand, if you want to open a full-scale click-and-order business, you may need to hire a Web developer. A **Web developer** is a professional who creates Web sites.

Web developers are expensive. In a typical company, Web developers make between $30,000 and $150,000 annually. If you hire a Web developer as a consultant, expect to pay between $50 and $300 per hour.

---

making the grade

S E C T I O N   D : / /

1. A _____ is the coordinated presentation of colors, text, and other elements that appear on your Web site.

2. When creating a Web site, you should always make sure it works in _____ Web browsers.

3. Search engines find and categorize Web sites according to _____.

4. A _____ is a professional who creates Web sites.

i·witness

An Up-Close Look at Web Sites

Navigation

As you know, most Web sites arrange Web pages in a hierarchy. There's a reason for this. As surfers navigate a site, they need to know where they are in the overall site, how to proceed down, how to return to the top, and perhaps even how to move sideways. **Navigation** refers to how easily surfers can find what they need on a Web page or Web site.

If surfers get lost on your site, they won't take the time to get their bearings straight. They'll simply go somewhere else. And they'll remember that your site is difficult to navigate and won't return.

Creating a navigable Web site requires linking pages logically. When building your Web site follow these guidelines:

- On each page include a link that returns to your main page, or "Home."

- Always place your navigation links in the same place on each page. At the top or to the left is standard.

- If your site is large, consider including a site map. A **site map** is a sketch or diagram of how all of your Web pages work together. Visit eBay's site map (www.ebay.com) for a great example.

Here are two Web sites for you to review that illustrate both good and bad uses of our navigation guidelines. The two sites are:

www.mhhe.com/i-series/I-Witness/4-A.html

www.mhhe.com/i-series/I-Witness/4-B.html

First, determine which site follows our guidelines. Once you do, identify characteristics that make it easy to navigate.

For the site that's difficult to navigate, recommend how you'd reorganize the site using our navigation guidelines.

You can also connect to the Web site for this text and download these Web sites to your computer. Then you can make the changes yourself.

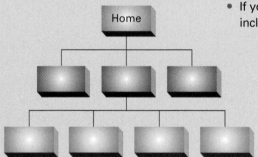

E://SUMMARY AND KEY TERMS

Electronic commerce is exploding on the Web. **Electronic commerce (e-commerce)** is really just commerce, but it's commerce that technology facilitates and enhances. Different types of businesses are **brick-and-mortar, click-and-mortar,** and **click-and-order.** Of these three, the last two are types of e-commerce businesses. E-commerce businesses are classified according to who their customers are:

- **B2C e-commerce**—a business that sells products and services through e-commerce to customers who are primarily individuals.

- **B2B e-commerce**—a business that sells products and services through e-commerce to customers who are primarily other businesses.

- **C2C e-commerce**—an individual who sells products and services to another individual through e-commerce.

To attract you as a new customer and retain you as a repeat customer, e-commerce businesses employ a variety of techniques including ***personalization*** of their Web site, making sure they have good ***customer service,*** and providing you with a ***secure transaction*** so you'll trust sending personal information over the Internet.

Of course both e-commerce businesses and other Web sites also want your attention. In addition to ***banner ads,*** many Web sites use Web multimedia to attract and keep you coming back. ***Web multimedia*** is the use of audio, video, animation, and other elements to facilitate interactivity on a Web site or page. To enjoy Web multimedia, you'll need certain software, which might include a plug-in and/or a player. With these, you also can enjoy ***streaming media***—viewing small parts of a video you've already downloaded while your Web browser continues to download the rest. Other interactive items include ***Flash, Shockwave,*** and ***VRML.***

When you create a Web page, you use ***HTML,*** the basic language used to create Web pages. HTML allows you to specify what information you want on your Web page and how that information will look. You achieve the "how" part with ***HTML tags.*** You can write the HTML yourself or use ***WYSIWYG*** Web authoring software or ***Web site management software.***

You can extend the interactivity of your Web site by using ***cascading style sheets, JavaScript, Java applets,*** and ***XML.***

On the Web site for this text at www.mhhe.com/i-series, we've provided more information on the above topics as well as information on using an e-commerce enabled Web site host, m-commerce, HTML, and VRML Web sites, to name a few.

KEY TERMS

affiliate program (associate program) (p. 4.11)

banner ad (p. 4.10)

basic formatting tag (p. 4.20)

brick-and-mortar business (p. 4.2)

business to business electronic commerce (B2B e-commerce) (p. 4.4)

business to consumer electronic commerce (B2C e-commerce) (p. 4.4)

cascading style sheet (CSS) (p. 4.24)

click-and-mortar business (p. 4.2)

click-and-order business (p. 4.3)

click-through (p. 4.10)

consumer to consumer electronic commerce (C2C e-commerce) (p. 4.5)

cookie (p. 4.5)

customer service (p. 4.6)

digital money (p. 4.8)

e-commerce enabled Web site host (p. 4.8)

electronic commerce (e-commerce) (p. 4.2)

electronic data interchange (EDI) (p. 4.4)

encryption (p. 4.7)

Flash (p. 4.15)

font tag (p. 4.20)

FTP program (p. 4.23)

heading tag (p. 4.20)

HTML (Hypertext Markup Language) (p. 4.18)

HTML document (p. 4.19)

HTML tag (p. 4.19)

image format (p. 4.22)

image tag (p. 4.20)

Internet mall (p. 4.9)

Java applet (p. 4.24)

JavaScript (p. 4.24)

link tag (p. 4.20)

list tag (p. 4.20)

m-commerce (mobile
e-commerce) (p. 4.9)

navigation (p. 4.28)

opting in (p. 4.11)

opting out (p. 4.11)

personalization (p. 4.5)

player (viewer) (p. 4.13)

plug-in (p. 4.13)

pop-up ad (p. 4.10)

secure transaction (p. 4.7)

Shockwave (p. 4.15)

shopping cart (p. 4.7)

site map (p. 4.28)

streaming media (p. 4.15)

theme (p. 4.26)

usability (p. 4.6)

viral marketing (p. 4.12)

VRML (Virtual Reality Modeling
Language) (p. 4.17)

Web audio (p. 4.14)

Web developer (p. 4.27)

Web multimedia (p. 4.12)

Web site management software
(p. 4.23)

Web video (p. 4.14)

WYSIWYG HTML editor
(p. 4.23)

XML (eXtensible Markup
Language) (p. 4.25)

CROSSWORD PUZZLE

Across

1. eXtensible Markup Language
5. Hiding information
7. When you sell goods and services over the Internet to another person
8. A scripting language used on the Web
10. This one doesn't go with milk
11. File transfer protocol
12. Customize your Web page
13. Right after d-commerce
17. Continuous media
18. Another word for viewer
19. This map helps you find your way around the Web

Down

2. Going mobile
3. Hypertext Markup Language
4. An ad on a small Web page containing an advertisement
6. Clicking from one Web site to another
9. Some Java that helps applications run on the Web
14. Guidelines for electronically handling the ordering, billing, and paying for goods and services
15. How easy or hard a Web site is to use
16. This helps you create your own world online

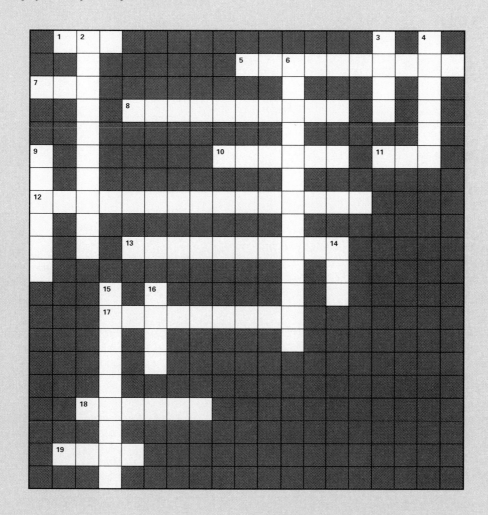

QUESTIONS AND EXERCISES

Multiple Choice

1. _____ is the basic language used to create Web pages.
   a. JavaScript
   b. HTML
   c. ASP
   d. Hypertext
   e. Java

2. The HTML _____ tag allows you to change the size of text.
   a. structure
   b. font
   c. color
   d. image
   e. link

3. The _____ HTML tag places an image on a Web page.
   a. `<img here>`
   b. `<insert>`
   c. `<img src>`
   d. `<a href>`
   e. `<font>`

4. _____ is the use of audio, video, animation, and other elements to facilitate interactivity on a Web site or page.
   a. Flash technology
   b. Shockwave
   c. Streaming media
   d. JavaScript
   e. Web multimedia

5. E-commerce is really just _____, but it's commerce that technology facilitates and enhances.
   a. the fad of the month
   b. the fad of the year
   c. commerce
   d. C2C selling
   e. B2C selling

6. A _____ business has both a presence in the physical world and a Web site.
   a. brick-and-mortar
   b. click-and-mortar
   c. click-and-order
   d. B2B
   e. B2C

7. A small text file stored on your hard disk that contains information about you is a _____.
   a. database
   b. record
   c. Web space
   d. cookie
   e. cake

8. A _____ is software that stores information about your e-commerce purchases.
   a. cookie
   b. cake
   c. shopping cart
   d. secure transaction
   e. JavaScript

9. A(n) _____ allows you to offer goods and services to users via another e-commerce site.
   a. affiliate program
   b. viral marketing campaign
   c. opting in policy
   d. opting out policy
   e. secure transaction

10. A _____ is the coordinated presentation of colors, text, and other elements that appears on your Web site.
    a. cookie
    b. JavaScript
    c. Java applet
    d. theme
    e. Web developer

True/False

11. _T_ You can develop Web pages without Web space.

12. _F_ An HTML document isn't the same thing as a Web page.

13. _F_ You can use any type of image format on the Web.

14. _F_ You can purchase products and services on the Web without a credit card.

15. _T_ M-commerce involves purchasing items with a cell phone.

QUESTIONS AND EXERCISES

1. Search your school's Web site for your instructors this semester or quarter. Find the ones who have Web pages. In the left-hand column below, list the instructors who have Web pages. In the right-hand column, note what types of HTML tags and Web multimedia each uses.

INSTRUCTORS

HTML TAGS AND WEB MULTIMEDIA

_____

_____

_____

_____

_____

_____

_____

_____

_____

_____

_____

_____

_____

_____

2. For each of the following types of e-businesses, describe what each does and provide an example.

E-BUSINESS

DEFINITION AND EXAMPLE

B2B

_____

_____

_____

B2C

_____

_____

_____

C2C

_____

_____

_____

_____

3. Much like a printed resume, an e-resume contains academics, work history, and other experience needed to get a job. But there are differences. Keeping this in mind, answer the following:

a. When might you use a resume instead of an e-resume?

b. Looking at your resume, what parts do you think might work well in an e-resume?

c. What can you do with an e-resume that you can't do with a regular resume?

e-commerce

1. Finding an Internship

Sometime in your college career you'll probably take an internship to learn more about the field you'll work in. Besides the resources on your campus, there are Web sites to help you find an internship.

Connect to the following Web sites and search for internships in a career field that interests you.

- Internships.com—www.internships.com
- InternshipPrograms.com— www.internshipprograms.com
- InternJobs.com—www.internjobs.com
- InternWeb.com—www.internweb.com

Now, answer the following questions:

a. Which internships did you find interesting?

b. Which features helped you find the types of internships you wanted?

After you've created a list of internships, visit your college's career center (or other office with internship information) to see how it organizes and offers internships.

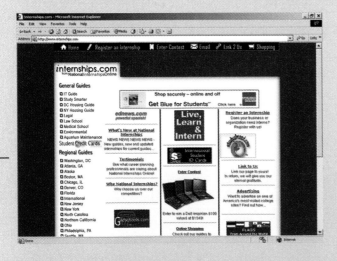

2. Classified Ads

The classified ads in your local paper don't need to be the only place you look for a used bike, apartment, or job. On the Web you can check specialized classified ads or look at newspapers from cities around the world. Visit a couple of the sites below to look for an item, a job, or an apartment.

- Honolulu Advertiser.com— www.hawaiiclassifieds.com
- BayArea.com Classifieds— classifieds.bayarea.com
- New York Times Classifieds— www.nytimes.com/classified
- Mlive.com Marketplace— www.mlive.com/marketplace

As you visit these sites, consider how they organize and present the material versus your local paper or other Web sites.

a. Were you able to find what you were looking for in the Web sites?

b. Which classifieds were easier to use?

c. Can you see a difference in price, descriptions, etc., in items in these few classified Web sites?

Now get copies of your local paper from different days. Compare items in the Web classifieds with your local paper. Better yet, see if your local paper (or one nearby) has Web classified ads. Compare the print and the Web classified ads.

d. What's the difference between print and Web classified ads?

e. Why do you think there are differences? If there aren't any, why do you think it's that way?

f. Which would you rather use? Why?

g. Could you think of some situations when you would want to use print over Web? What about Web over print? Make sure to explain why.

3. Using Intelligent Agents

Intelligent agents are Web-based software tools that efficiently find information for you. They can perform repetitive tasks and even do large Web searches while you sleep. The potential of intelligent agents is enormous. Many researchers are developing new types of intelligent agent software to help you work more efficiently on the Web. The following Web sites contain relevant information:

- BotSpot Home Page—www.botspot.com
- UMBC Agent Web—agents.umbc.edu

Intelligent agents also can help you find a good bargain on the Web. Intelligent e-commerce agents can search through e-commerce sites to find the best deal for you.

Why don't you try it? Conduct a search for a computer system, or printer, or PDA. Or maybe you want a new digital camera. In any case find the best technology deal at the following sites:

- Computer Shopper—www.zdnet.com/computershopper/
- CNET.com—www.cnet.com
- MySimon—www.mysimon.com

As you use these sites, note which one makes it easiest to find your item. Answer the following questions:

a. Were you able to find what you wanted? How easy was it to find? If you didn't find what you wanted, why do you think that's the case?

b. Which Web site gave you the best deal? Which provided the most information on the item? Was it the same site?

4. Buying Software

You learned about freeware and shareware software in Chapter 3. And you may have downloaded and tried some by now. But did you know that you can also shop and buy software packages such as Microsoft Office on the Web?

There are two methods for buying software packages on the Web. The first is a conventional e-commerce transaction: You pay for it on the Web; then the company ships it to you.

The other purchase involves an electronic download. After you buy the software, you get an access code or small program that allows you to download the software package. Sometimes this download is available only for a limited time after the purchase date or for a limited number of downloads. Either way, you never receive a CD-ROM or printed manuals. Digital manuals are part of the download.

Check out some of these sites and search for a specific software package. Find at least one electronic download.

- Buy.com—www.buy.com
- Amazon.com—www.amazon.com
- Micro Warehouse Inc.—www.warehouse.com

Answer the following questions:

a. Were you able to find your software package at all the sites?

b. Did you find an electronic download version? Was there a substantial price difference between it and the physical software package? (Remember, you don't have to pay shipping on an electronic download.)

c. Armed with a few price quotes on software packages (electronic download and physical delivery), go to a store that sells the software package. Which option saves you more money?

ESD Superstore
electronic software delivery
ESD refers to the electronic delivery of software and other digital goods, such as music, over the Internet to your desktop. Downloading software from buy.com is as simple as Buy, Download, and Launch.

on the web

1. Finding Web Development Resources

In this chapter you saw how to build a Web page using HTML. There's much more information on the Web about how to effectively develop a Web site. Using a search engine, look for "Web development" resources. As you search for Web development resources, find sites for the following topics: basic HTML, JavaScript, Java applets, design guidelines, and free images and backgrounds. Report to your class the Web sites you found interesting and useful. Explain how they could help someone develop Web sites.

2. Experiencing Web Multimedia

We discussed Web multimedia in this chapter. Now it's time to experience some of it. Conduct a search for "streaming media" sites, find a few sites containing streaming media that interest you, and try to view the content. Did you have to download and install any players to view the content you found? Explain the process of accessing streaming media to your class. Discuss why you think streaming media will or won't take the place of other forms of multimedia.

3. Effective Sites for Web Shopping

In this chapter we discussed what makes an effective e-commerce experience. We discussed making an Amazon.com purchase and how the Web site assisted us. Now it's your turn to look at an effective (or not so effective) e-commerce Web site. Find a site that interests you and discuss why you will or won't shop there. Your reasons should relate to the following topics: personalization, usability, customer service, product information, ordering, security, and shipping.

4. Secure Transactions

Encryption and secure transactions are part of e-commerce. Without them, we wouldn't be able to safely purchase products and services. Search for "secure transactions" on a search engine. Discuss the Web sites you found that help e-commerce conduct secure transactions over the Web. Finally, consider the real "security" that's provided on the Web. If people can write software to encrypt information, can't other people write other software to decrypt the information and then steal it?

5. E-Commerce Enabled Web Site Hosts

One of the easiest ways to get your click-and-order business going on the Web is to use the services of an e-commerce enabled Web site host. Find three such sites on the Web. Answer the following questions for each:

a. Does the site offer various "levels" of service?

b. Does the site limit the amount of Web space you'll have?

c. Does the site charge you for the amount of traffic that comes to your site?

d. What types of usage reports does the service provide?

e. What is the fee (if any) associated with the service handling credit card transactions for you?

ethics, security & privacy

1. What's Your View of Cookies?

The *New Yorker* cartoon below illustrates how most people view surfing the Web. Most think they can move from site to site without leaving information about themselves.

This is not true. Many sites write "cookies" or small text files to the "cookie folder" on your computer. Cookies for a specific Web site might include when you visited a site, what Web pages you looked at, and any information you gave the Web site, such as your name and e-mail address. Each time you return to that Web site, it can access the cookie it wrote to your hard drive. Some companies set the cookies to "expire" after some time, but others leave them on your computer for as long as possible. Most companies use cookies responsibly in order to personalize your Web experience at their site. As you consider the use of cookies on the Web, answer the following questions:

a. Did you know companies were storing information about you and your activity at their site? What do you think about this?

b. Most Web sites use cookies to personalize a visit for you. The result may be you don't have to log in, or your local weather and favorite sports team automatically appear. Which do you prefer: having a personalized visit or having privacy?

c. If you answered that you prefer privacy in the preceding question, would you consider turning off cookies? Some Web sites won't work at all. Is this sacrifice worthwhile?

d. You can also set your Web browser to tell you each time a Web site wants to give you a cookie. Is doing this enough? Do you want to have a message pop up on your Web browser every time a Web site wants to give you a cookie? How will this affect your Web surfing experience? Should you be forced to do this?

e. Do Web sites have a right to use cookies? Why or why not?

f. Some companies have found ways to track Web surfing from site to site instead of just at their own. Now you leave a "cookie trail" at all the sites you visit. If you listen to a certain kind of music at one site, there is a possibility that when you visit a Web CD store, that type of music CD will appear on your Web page. Is this something you want to happen? What are the possible effects of this?

"On the Internet, nobody knows you're a dog."

hands-on projects

group activities

1. Using Web Authoring Software

When designing Web pages, you can use various Web authoring software. We mentioned some in the chapter and have more references to them at www.mhhe.com/i-series. As a group, choose a Web authoring tool. You can either use what you or your school already has or download and install a trial copy. Demonstrate to your class how this software works and what it can do for a Web developer. Is the software you chose free? A WYSIWYG tool? Really Web site management software?

2. Demonstrating a Web Multimedia Player

Using a Web multimedia player, such as RealNetworks' RealPlayer or Microsoft Windows Media Player, prepare a demonstration of the types of media you can access and use with this particular software application. If your class has access to a computer connected to the Internet, consider a live demonstration. Discuss with the class the strengths and weaknesses of the Web multimedia that you found.

3. Surveying E-Commerce Habits

Conduct a survey of computer users and their e-commerce habits. As a group prepare a list of questions to use, such as:

a. How often do you buy things on the Web? If you don't, why not?

b. Which e-commerce Web sites do you use?

c. What is your favorite e-commerce Web site and why?

You can go to your school's computer labs, visit the dorms, or ask people questions as you walk around campus. Prepare your findings using presentation software for the class. Were your findings a surprise? Are more or fewer people using e-commerce than you thought? If you have the chance, ask a friend at another school to do the same survey. Do your results differ?

4. Building a Basic E-Commerce Web Site

As a group, create a basic e-commerce Web site. Develop some Web pages and discuss why each is needed for an effective e-commerce Web site. Don't worry about developing a secure transaction for your project or even providing ordering capabilities—your site can simply advertise products you have to sell. If your class has access to the Internet, take them to e-commerce Web sites and discuss the good and bad of each site.

5. B2B E-Commerce Web Sites

In this chapter we focused on B2C e-commerce because it has a very real and direct impact on your life. When you enter the business world, your attention will turn to B2B e-commerce. Search the Web and find some sites devoted to B2B e-commerce. Have you heard of many of these e-commerce businesses? Are they click-and-order or click-and-mortar? If 97 percent of all e-commerce revenues occur in the B2B space, why has the B2C space received so much more attention?

Looking Back/Looking Ahead

The Life and Times of a Dot-Com Entrepreneur

Joann has the necessary software she needs to run her business. Using an existing computer system, she decides to install her Web authoring software and develop her own Web site to tell others about her business. She is also considering starting her own e-commerce Web site, complete with ordering capabilities.

Joann knows that even though she's using a _____ Web authoring software that allows her to see what her Web pages will look like on the Web, she still needs some basic knowledge of _____ tags and how she can use them to create her Web site. She knows that _____ tags provide the framework for a Web page and _____ tags tell the Web browser how to display text. She also wants to make sure that she uses the correct image _____ to display her graphics on the Web.

She wants to make sure that all of her colors, images, and text form a coherent _____ so people will enjoy her site. Joann considers using _____, or audio, video, and animation on her Web site, but instead decides to use _____, a scripting language that adds interactivity to her Web site.

Joann also considers hiring a _____ to help her develop an e-commerce Web site. Joann wants to sell to consumers. As a business, she would create a _____ e-commerce Web site. Realizing that she will need a _____ host, she calls her ISP to make sure it can provide her with a _____ to encrypt and exchange information for a _____ transaction. Luckily it can.

Joann decides to allow her customers to pay with either a credit card or _____ for those who don't want to use a credit card. She also will allow customers to use _____ so they can quickly send all their information securely. Joann does decide that her site will use _____ to customize each customer's session by storing their information in a small text file on their computer. Joann wants to make sure that each customer's experience is _____ according to his or her preferences and that her Web site has sufficient _____ to answer any customer questions about a purchase.

Joann has a good idea of where her business is going, but now she needs to make sure she has the hardware to run all of her software effectively. She'll find the answers in Chapters 5 and 6.

did you

know?

In 1982, IBM brought microcomputers to the business world with its release of the IBM PC. Back then, for $2,500, you could purchase an IBM PC that would fit on top of a desk with a central processing unit (the 8088 chip) capable of performing 330,000 operations per second. Today, you can spend less than a third of that amount and get a system capable of performing an amazing more than 2 billion operations per second.

If other industries had progressed at a similar pace, we would be able to purchase a

set *of automobile tires for $1 that would last over 50 million miles.*

car *(if you buy the tires, you might as well have the car) that would get roughly 80,000 miles to the gallon.*

ticket *for an around-the-world airline flight that would last less than a minute (no in-flight movie on this trip!).*

CD *with 3,000 cuts for 1 cent.*

home *for $ __??__ that would occupy __??__ million square feet.*

To find out the cost of a home and how many millions of square feet it would occupy, if the home construction industry had reduced costs at the rate computers have, visit our Web site at www.mhhe.com/i-series.

CHAPTER

5

five

A Consumer's Guide to Computer Systems

What Do You Need to Know When Buying a Computer?

Buying a computer system is in many ways like buying a new car—it's an investment that will make your life better and more fun, and sometimes the range of options can make you dizzy. A *computer system* is a set of tools that helps you perform information-related tasks. Car buyers and computer system buyers fall into one of two categories. The first knows what the various components are, what they do, and how they can be used. The second, more sophisticated group, understands how a car or computer works.

In this chapter, we'll discuss buying the hardware components that go with the software that you learned about in Chapter 3. So, this chapter is really a consumer's guide to buying the hardware for a computer system. In the next chapter, Chapter 6, we'll discuss how the parts of your computer work together. For more information, visit the Interactive Companion Labs, and choose "Computer Anatomy" and "Purchasing Computers."

A://INSIDE THE BOX

The box that people often refer to as the "computer" is called the system unit. The *system unit* is the case or box in which the motherboard and storage units are housed. For desktop computers, you have a choice of various sizes and shapes, such as the traditional desktop box, tower, mini-tower, micro tower, and even an all-in-one model in which the screen and system unit are combined. No matter what kind of system unit you have, inside you'll find a motherboard that connects all the components of your computer to the CPU. The *motherboard,* also called the *main board,* or *system board,* is the large circuit board inside your system unit that holds the CPU, memory, and other essential electronic components (see Figure 5.1). Usually, storage devices such as floppy and hard disk drives, and CD and DVD drives are also inside the system unit.

FIGURE 5.1

The motherboard holds your CPU, memory, and other essential electronic components.

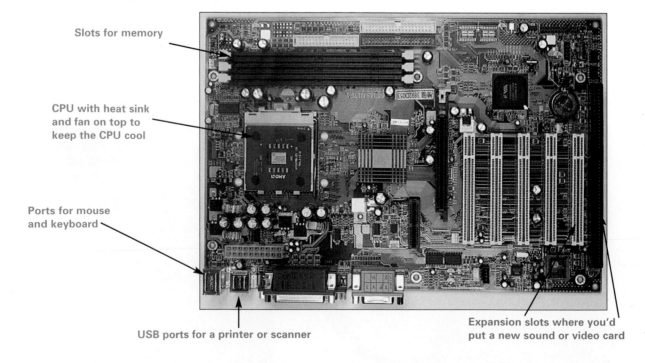

Slots for memory

CPU with heat sink and fan on top to keep the CPU cool

Ports for mouse and keyboard

USB ports for a printer or scanner

Expansion slots where you'd put a new sound or video card

FIGURE 5.2

Computer systems on the inside differ, and those differences affect price and how well your computer system will perform for you.

Computer systems at a glance

In general, with a more powerful system you
1. See better graphics and video.
2. Get faster downloads of large files from the Web.
3. Have a more realistic gaming experience with smoother animation and sound.
4. Realize better performance when running several applications at the same time.
5. Pay a higher price.

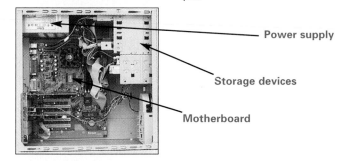

Power supply

Storage devices

Motherboard

THE BASIC SYSTEM

How Do Desktop Computer Systems Differ?

When you buy a new car, you can usually expect to get certain essentials such as wheels and an engine—and the more powerful the engine the more the car costs. Similarly, when you buy a computer, you must choose a CPU (or processor), which is your computer's "engine." You'll also have to decide how much memory you want. Memory holds the software instructions, such as Microsoft Word software, that the CPU carries out. Together, the CPU and memory largely determine the power level or speed of your computer—and hence, usually the price.

If you want to use your computer only to generate simple Word documents, you won't need a very powerful computer system. If, on the other hand, you want to run multimedia software, that is, software with graphics, sound, and other features, you'll need more power. The more complex your software, the more instructions it takes to make it work, so the more space in memory it needs, and the faster the CPU needs to run. In the next sections, we'll examine these two components, CPU and memory, in more detail.

THE CENTRAL PROCESSING UNIT (CPU)

What Do I Need to Know about Buying a CPU?

The CPU or processor is your computer's brain, housekeeper, conductor, and commander. The ***central processing unit (CPU*** or ***processor)*** is the chip that carries out instructions it receives from your software. You'll also hear the CPU referred to as a microprocessor or a CPU chip. The type and speed of the CPU is generally one of the first things that computer ads tell you about.

FIGURE 5.3

CPUs come in various types and speeds—even from the same manufacturer.

Manufacturer name and processor name

System 1	System 2	System 3
Intel Celeron processor at 800 MHz	AMD Athlon XP Thunderbird CPU at 1.6 GHz	Intel Pentium 4 up to 2.0 GHz

This CPU processes software instructions at a rate of 800,000,000 cycles per second.

This CPU processes software instructions at a rate of 2,000,000,000 cycles per second.

CPU at a glance

1. If you're using your computer for simple tasks such as Word text documents, you don't need the latest and greatest CPU. However, the more you're into graphics and animation, the more you'll need as much speed as you can get.
2. While CPU speed is a big factor in overall performance, it's not the only one, and a faster CPU alone may not improve performance appreciably.

The CPU carries out both system software and application software instructions. Operating system software (such as Windows 2000, Windows XP, and Linux) is a type of system software and keeps your computer functioning. Application software allows you to use your computer as a tool. For example, Web browser software lets you use your computer to surf the Web. Figure 5.3 shows three different CPUs.

The most helpful information for comparing CPUs is their relative speeds. CPU speed is usually quoted in megahertz or gigahertz. **Megahertz (MHz)** is the number of *millions* of CPU cycles per second. **Gigahertz (GHz)** is the number of *billions* of CPU cycles per second. The number of CPU cycles per second determines how fast the CPU carries out the software instructions—more cycles per second means faster processing.

Since the CPU carries out instructions from the software, it makes sense that the faster it does so the better. However, you'll notice speed, or the lack of it, more in some applications than in others. For example, while you're using your computer to create Word documents, you might not see great improvement with extra speed. However, if you're a gaming enthusiast, or work with video or complex graphics, which require many more calculations and hence many more instructions than a Word document does, you'll probably find that more CPU cycles per second makes a big difference.

Keep in mind that while your CPU speed is a big factor in determining how fast your computer runs, it's not the only one. The amount of memory you have is also a major factor. Another factor is how fast information moves between memory and the CPU. Yet another is the size of cache memory, which is a kind of waiting-room memory for the CPU,

did you know?

A modern supercomputer can process 12 trillion (that's 12,000,000,000,000) operations in one second.

where instructions stay briefly before being used by the CPU (more on this in Chapter 6). So a faster CPU alone will not necessarily provide enough improvement in performance to justify its cost. For more information on CPUs, visit our text Web site at www.mhhe.com/i-series.

MEMORY

What Does RAM Do and How Is the Amount Important?

Along with the speed of your CPU, how much memory, or RAM, you have in your computer makes a big difference in how fast your computer runs. ***RAM (random access memory)*** is temporary memory that holds software instructions and information for the CPU.

RAM holds

- Operating system instructions that must be available to the CPU all the time the computer is on, since they are necessary to keep the computer functioning.
- The application software instructions you're using (such as Word or a Web browser).
- The document, picture, spreadsheet, copy of Web site, etc.
- Keyboard strokes and mouse movements.

Figure 5.4 shows three examples of how advertisements describe memory.

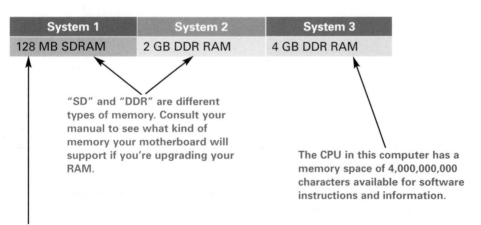

System 1	System 2	System 3
128 MB SDRAM	2 GB DDR RAM	4 GB DDR RAM

"SD" and "DDR" are different types of memory. Consult your manual to see what kind of memory your motherboard will support if you're upgrading your RAM.

The CPU in this computer has a memory space of 4,000,000,000 characters available for software instructions and information.

This computer has a memory space of 128,000,000 characters available for software instructions and information.

F I G U R E   5.4

The memory in a computer system is usually described with a size and type.

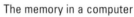

RAM at a glance

1. The amount of RAM is more important than the type for most consumers.
2. A shortage of memory will slow down processing time.
3. The more sophisticated the software you're using, the more memory you'll need.

CAPACITY AND TYPE OF RAM
How Much Memory Is 4 GB?

The "MB" in System 1 in Figure 5.4 stands for megabytes, which is *millions* of characters of space available for instructions and information for the CPU to use. The "GB" in Systems 2 and 3 stands for *billions* of characters.

We measure the amount of space available for storage in RAM (or on storage devices such as a hard disk, which we'll discuss in the next section) in terms of the number of bytes it can hold (see Figure 5.5). A byte is equivalent to a character.

F I G U R E   5.5

A gigabyte stores a lot of information.

Unit	Exact size in bytes	How much is that?
Kilobyte (KB or K)	1,024	A double-spaced typed page of text requires approximately 1K of storage since it has about 1,000 characters including spaces. It could take up a little more or less storage depending on the font size and type, the margins, and so on.
Megabyte (MB or M or Meg)	1,048,576	1 MB would store about 1,000 pages of typewritten text. A ream of paper that you'd buy for your printer comes in 500-sheet packages. So 1 MB would store all that you could type on 2 reams of paper.
Gigabyte (GB or Gig)	1,073,741,824	To type 1 billion characters, you'd need 1 million sheets of paper, which would be about 2,000 reams—a stack that would stand about 325 feet high.
Terabyte (TB)	1,099,511,627,776	Corresponds to about 1 billion pages, or 2,000,000 reams, or a stack about 325,000 feet high (about 62 miles). The Library of Congress houses a total of about 20 terabytes of information.
Petabyte (PB)	1,125,899,906,843,624	How many pages of double-spaced text would you need for a petabyte?
Exabyte (EB)	1,152,921,504,607,870,976	If a ream of paper weighs 5 lbs., what would a stack of paper weigh that had 1 exabyte written on it?
Zettabyte (ZB)	1,180,591,620,718,458,879,424	If a floppy diskette holds 1.4 Meg, how many would it take to accommodate 1 zettabyte?
Yottabyte (YB)	1,208,925,819,615,701,892,530,176	If you put all the sheets of paper that had a yottabyte written on them end to end (a sheet of paper is 11 inches long), how far would the line stretch?

- A *kilobyte* (*KB* or *K*) is about 1,000 bytes (a kilobyte is exactly 1,024 bytes, but we round down to 1,000 for the sake of simplicity).
- A *megabyte* (*MB* or *M* or *Meg)* is roughly 1 million bytes.
- A *gigabyte* (*GB* or *Gig)* is about 1 billion bytes.
- A *terabyte* (*TB)* is approximately 1 trillion bytes.

RAM AND VIRTUAL MEMORY

How Much RAM Is Enough and What Effect Does a Shortage Have?

Software packages have different memory requirements. Usually the publisher's packaging or Web site will tell you a *minimum* RAM requirement for the product. "Minimum" means that the software won't run at all with less. For optimum performance, you'll probably need much more memory than is stated on the package. Microsoft recommends that if you want to run Office XP you should have a Pentium with a speed of at least 133 MHz (make that 400 MHz, if you want speech recognition capabilities) and at least 128 MB of RAM. Adobe recommends more than 256 MB of RAM for its *After Effects* software, which lets you put motion and graphics effects into your Web authoring project. Don't forget that you'll probably want to run several applications at once (multitasking), which will increase your memory requirements.

So how does a shortage of RAM, which stores instructions, slow down your processing? Let's say you're writing a report on the cost of computer systems. So, you'll need to have Word open. You'll need to consult the Web to get current prices, and you might want to use Excel to do the calculations. Also, while you're doing all this, you'd like your e-mail software to check for incoming mail every 10 minutes. Your CPU must process the instructions for all four applications as well as those of the operating system. All the instructions must be in RAM before the CPU can access them.

When the instructions don't all fit into memory at the same time, some are stored on the hard disk and then moved into RAM when needed (see Figure 5.6). *Virtual memory* is the space on your hard disk space that holds software instructions for a program currently in use. If your RAM isn't large enough to hold all the instructions for all four applications along with everything else that has to be there, the most used instructions will be in RAM and the less used will be in virtual memory. Then, your CPU will swap out instructions between RAM and virtual memory as it needs them. This swapping back and forth slows down processing. It takes much longer to move instructions from the hard disk to RAM and then to the CPU, than it does to move them directly from RAM, which is where they have to be before the CPU can access them to carry them out. For more information on memory, visit our Web site at www.mhhe.com/i-series.

When you turn off the power to your computer, the contents of RAM disappear. So, we need a way of storing software and information long term. This is why we use peripheral storage devices such as hard disks, floppy disks, CDs, and DVDs, the contents of which stay put until you change or delete them. In upcoming sections we examine storage.

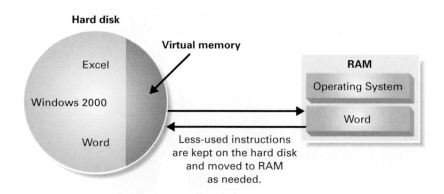

FIGURE 5.6

When there's not enough space in RAM for all the necessary instructions, some instructions are stored in virtual memory on the hard disk.

i·series insights

Ethics, Security & Privacy

A Spy Inside Your Computer?

When it first came out, the Pentium III CPU had one very controversial feature. This was an internal processor serial number (PSN) which was put onto the chip during the manufacturing process and couldn't be removed or changed. However, utility software in the operating system can enable or disable the PSN. This means the software can make the ID number available or not to software running either on your computer or on another computer that you're connected to. Interesting.

Intel, which makes the Pentium CPU, thought that the PSN would provide security for computer users. For example, if you bought something from a Web site, software at that site could check your PSN to verify your identity. It makes good sense for authenticating transactions. Companies would also be better able to keep track of the computers on their networks and would be able to detect an unauthorized connection.

Consumer privacy advocates, on the other hand, saw the PSN as an invasion of privacy in that anyone on the Internet could track you online more easily. IBM, in response to the controversy, started disabling the PSN on its computers. Then, under the threat of a boycott, Intel announced in April 2000 that it would not put the PSN into future generations of Pentium chips. What do you think? Is the cost of reducing fraud worth the price of less privacy?

BAYS FOR STORAGE UNITS

Where Do Storage Units Go in the System Unit?

Storage drives can be fixed or removable. Hard disks are usually the only fixed media on consumer computers. Other media, such as floppy disks, CDs, and DVDs, are removable. The drives for both fixed and removable storage media fit into bays in your system unit. A **bay** is a place in the system unit reserved for a storage unit (see Figure 5.7). The number of storage bays you get in your system unit depends largely on the size of the system unit. It's nice to have extra bays in case you want to add another storage device later.

FIGURE 5.7

System units have 3.5-inch and 5.25-inch external bays for removable storage units.

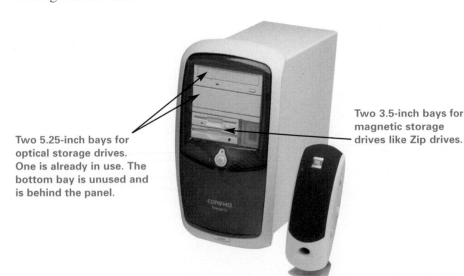

Two 5.25-inch bays for optical storage drives. One is already in use. The bottom bay is unused and is behind the panel.

Two 3.5-inch bays for magnetic storage drives like Zip drives.

System units have two types of bays: internal and external. The internal bays are for hard disks, and you always get at least one of these. The external bays are where your drives for removable storage media such as floppy disks, CD-ROMs, and DVDs are located. External bays come in two sizes: 3.5-inch bays for magnetic storage, such as Zip disk drives, and 5.25-inch for optical storage devices such as CD and DVD drives. The more bays your system unit has, the more storage devices you can add to your system.

See Figure 5.8 for an overview of the storage devices that you'll see in subsequent sections.

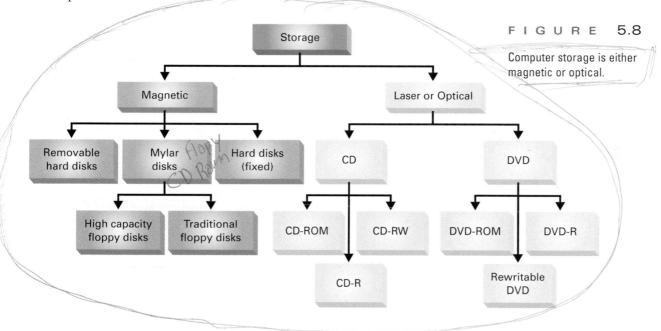

FIGURE   5.8

Computer storage is either magnetic or optical.

HARD DISK DRIVES

What Do I Need to Know about Choosing a Hard Disk?

Most computer systems come with a hard disk drive as standard equipment, but sizes vary. A ***hard disk*** is a magnetic storage medium, usually fixed inside the system unit, consisting of one or more thin platters or disks that store information. Magnetic storage devices all work on the same basic principal—a thin layer of magnetic iron oxide compound coats either metal or plastic and is magnetized to represent information. Read/write heads access the information on the disk surfaces (both top and bottom) and transfer copies to and from RAM. The heads "read" information while copying it from the storage medium to RAM and "write" it when copying it from RAM to the storage medium.

FIGURE 5.9

Hard disks come in many different capacities.

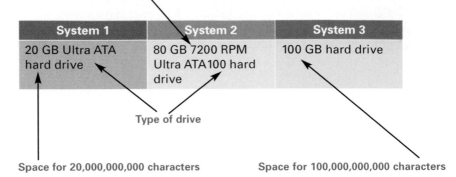

The 7,200 RPM is telling you the rotation speed of the hard disk platters. The faster they spin the more quickly the read/write heads can access information.

System 1	System 2	System 3
20 GB Ultra ATA hard drive	80 GB 7200 RPM Ultra ATA100 hard drive	100 GB hard drive

Type of drive

Space for 20,000,000,000 characters   Space for 100,000,000,000 characters

Hard drives at a glance

Buying as much hard disk space as you can afford is usually a good idea because

1. It gives you space for new software.
2. It gives you space for new versions of software, which tend to be larger than older ones.
3. It gives you space for large video or music files. Even MP3 files, which are compressed music files, take up a lot of space if you download lots of them.
4. Some software lets you put part onto the hard disk and the rest onto a CD or DVD. But access to the hard disk is faster so the more you can put there, the faster the software will run.

Your hard disk is where you store your operating system and application software long term (see Figure 5.9). When you start up your system, the operating system instructions are copied from your hard disk into RAM. When you launch an application, a copy of the software goes into RAM so that the CPU can execute the instructions. The CPU can't carry out software instructions directly from any storage device; they must go into RAM first.

Since the hard disk is where you keep most of your software until you want to use it, and you'll probably add new software from time to time, it's generally advisable to get a hard disk as big as you can afford. Hard disk capacity is usually measured in gigabytes, that is, billions of characters.

When choosing hard disk capacity, remember that new versions of software are usually larger than previous versions. Music, graphics, animation, and video files gobble up storage. An uncompressed video file uses about 1 GB of space per minute of video.

If you buy software on a CD, you often copy only part of the software onto a hard disk and then use the CD too when you want to run software. For example, say you bought *Street Atlas*, which is software that has street maps and information on points of interest for all 50 states. You can use the software to generate maps and look up addresses, and find landmarks or facilities such as museums, hotels, and restaurants. You can run *Street Atlas* with the CD in the CD drive, or you can copy all 700 MB of information from the CD onto your hard disk and not use the CD anymore. You might want to do the latter because the software instructions can be transferred to RAM much faster from the hard disk than from a CD. You'll notice an appreciable difference since the software draws maps—graphics—on the screen, and that means a lot of instructions need to be transferred, so you want all the speed you can get. A full CD takes up almost three-quarters of a gigabyte, so if you copy many such CDs onto your hard disk, you'll use up a lot of hard disk space very quickly.

REMOVABLE MAGNETIC STORAGE MEDIA
What Kind of Removable Magnetic Storage Disks Can I Get?

Removable storage media, such as floppy disks and CD-ROMs, can be removed from the drive, unlike hard disks which are fixed inside the hard disk drive unit. Removable storage media come in two varieties: magnetic and optical. In this section, we'll discuss the magnetic variety and in the next section the optical variety.

Removable magnetic storage media come in two basic types. The first stores information on a floppy Mylar disk housed inside a plastic casing. Mylar disks are thin, flexible plastic disks, and in turn come in two types: traditional 3.5-inch floppy disks and high-capacity floppy disks.

1. *Traditional 3.5-inch floppy disks* are removable magnetic storage media that hold about 1.44 megabytes of information. **Floppy disks** are also called simply **floppies** or **diskettes.** Most computer systems come with a floppy disk drive although this is not likely to continue much longer because of the proliferation of higher-capacity storage alternatives.

2. *High-capacity floppy disks* come in different types and sizes depending on the manufacturer. Two examples are the Superdisk and Zip disk.

   - *Superdisk™*, also known as *LS 120*, is a removable magnetic storage medium that holds 120 MB, much more capacity than traditional floppies. The Superdisk drive will also read from and write to traditional 3.5-inch floppies.

   - *Zip® disk* is a removable storage medium that comes in two sizes: 100MB or 250MB; the 250MB drive can also read and write 100MB Zip disks. You can't use the Zip drive to read from or write to floppies.

The second type of removable magnetic storage disk stores information on one or more metal platters instead of on Mylar disks. These are sometimes called removable hard disks. The metal platters provide a higher storage capacity. The Jaz® disk is an example of this type of removable hard disk and has a capacity of up to 2 GB.

OPTICAL STORAGE

Should I Buy CD and/or DVD Drives?

CDs and DVDs are both examples of optical or laser discs and are great for storing large amounts of information on one removable disc. (Note that when we're discussing magnetic disks, the word "disk" ends in "k" and when we're talking about optical discs, the word "disc" ends in "c.") Most software that you buy comes on CDs or DVDs. You'll need an appropriate drive to be able to use the CD or DVD. CD-ROMs, DVD-ROMs, CD-Rs, CD-RWs, and recordable DVDs are all examples of optical storage media. See Figure 5.10 for examples of how optical storage is advertised.

F I G U R E   5.10

DVDs and CDs are optical storage and have three formats: read only, write once, and rewrite.

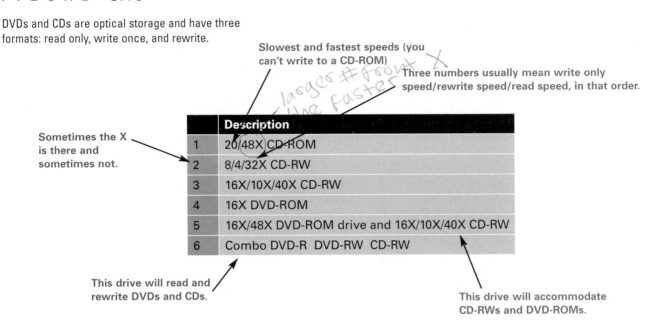

Slowest and fastest speeds (you can't write to a CD-ROM)

Three numbers usually mean write only speed/rewrite speed/read speed, in that order.

larger # = time Faster

Sometimes the X is there and sometimes not.

	Description
1	20/48X CD-ROM
2	8/4/32X CD-RW
3	16X/10X/40X CD-RW
4	16X DVD-ROM
5	16X/48X DVD-ROM drive and 16X/10X/40X CD-RW
6	Combo DVD-R DVD-RW CD-RW

This drive will read and rewrite DVDs and CDs.

This drive will accommodate CD-RWs and DVD-ROMs.

Optical storage at a glance

1. Optical discs are said to last between 50 and 300 years.
2. –ROM: It came from the factory, and you can't change it.
3. –R: You can write to it one time only, i.e., you can't change the contents, but you can delete.
4. CDs can store up to a maximum of about 800 MB, whereas DVDs have different capacities.
5. DVDs that you can write to and change have many different names and formats, and a disc created in one type won't necessarily work in a different type of drive.
6. Optical storage discs are good for "heavy" files such as music, video, graphics, and photos, and as backup media.

Read-Only Optical Storage Media

CD-ROMs and DVD-ROMs that you buy with software, graphics, music, or movies are optical discs that come from the factory with information already written on them, and you can't change or delete anything on the disc. This is the type of CD you buy to play in your stereo.

A **CD-ROM (compact disc read-only memory)** is an optical or laser disc whose information cannot be changed once it has been created. The manufacturer "closes" the CD, so that no more information can be written to it. You can store up to about 800 MB on a CD-ROM—about the same amount of information as 550 floppies would hold. That much information is equivalent to an entire set of encyclopedias. One CD-ROM will hold up to 8,000 photos (depending on resolution), over 20 hours of speech, or about 80 minutes of compressed video, or some combination. Many computer systems come with a CD-ROM drive as standard equipment.

The speed at which CD-ROM drives transfer information is usually shown as a number with an "X." For example, 48X means that the drive transfers information at 48 times the rate of the first CD-ROM drives that transferred information at 150 KB per second. The larger the number before the X the faster the information transfer.

A **DVD-ROM** is an optical storage medium whose information can't be changed, but which has a larger capacity than a CD-ROM. Note that some people say that DVD stands for *digital video disc* or *digital versatile disk*, and others say it stands for nothing in particular. DVD-ROMs come in four varieties with four different storage capacities (see Figure 5.11). You can purchase a combination DVD/CD-ROM drive that will read both CD-ROMs and DVD-ROMs.

DVD Disc Type	1 side 1 layer	1 side 2 layers	2 sides 1 layer	2 sides 2 layers
Capacity	4.7 GB	8.5 GB	9.4 GB	17 GB
Hours of Video	2 hours	4 hours	4.5 hours	8 hours

FIGURE 5.11

The capacity of a DVD-ROM depends on the number of layers of information stored and the number of sides used.

One-Time Writable Optical Storage Media

A **CD-R (compact disc—recordable)** is an optical disc to which you can write one time only. You might use a CD-R for information you want to keep indefinitely, such as your photos. You can write information to a CD-R using a CD-RW drive. If you record your buddies' rock band on a CD-R and you close it, you can probably play it in your stereo CD player. If you have information on there other than music, you can read it with a CD-ROM or CD-RW drive (see below). For more capacity, you could use a DVD-R. A **DVD-R (DVD—recordable)** is an optical disc to which you can write one time only and which has a higher capacity than a CD.

Fully Read-and-Write Optical Storage Media

CD-RWs and DVD-RWs are like hard disks or Zip disks in that you can add, delete, and change information on them.

Are Deleted Files Gone?

How "gone" a file is depends on where it was stored in the first place—and how much trouble you're prepared to go to to get it back. Let's look at three separate cases: a file stored (1) on removable storage media; (2) on a hard disk; (3) on a server.

Files on Removable Media

When you choose to delete a file, you'll get a message asking you whether you're sure you want to delete this file. If you answer yes, the name of the file will disappear from the directory or list of your folder or disk contents. That means that the name of the file has been marked in the directory as no longer needed, and the space is now available for saving new files. However, the file is not physically gone. It's still on the disk, and you can get it back with special utility software—it's a lot of trouble, but you can do it. Note that even though you can't change the information on a CD-R, you can still delete a file. The delete process doesn't remove the file, it just makes it unavailable for normal reading.

Files on the Hard Disk

When you delete a file that's on the hard drive you get a slightly different message before the deed is done. The little box asks you whether you want the file to go to the recycle bin. If you answer no, the file stays where it is. If you answer yes, the file simply moves to another folder called the recycle bin. From there, you can undelete it by dragging it back to whatever folder you want it in. In other words, you have a backup copy until you empty the trash can.

Files on a Server

If you get e-mail, you can set your e-mail software to take your messages off the server or not. If you choose to take them off the server, be warned there may well still be copies at your Internet service provider (ISP). Responsible ISPs make regular backups of all their files. Some reuse the same backup medium every day, but others may keep copies for a long time. Also, e-mail messages are stored in several places as they make their way from sender to recipient, so it's almost impossible to get rid of an e-mail message completely.

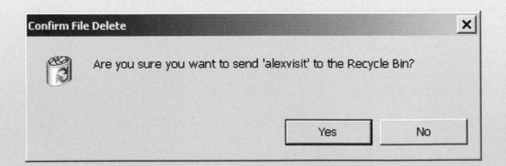

A *CD-RW (compact disc—rewritable)* is a compact disc storage medium that allows you to save, change, and delete files. CD-RWs work in some CD-ROM drives. CD-RWs on which you record music will also play in certain stereo systems. When describing rewritable optical media, manufacturers generally give three numbers (16X/10X/40X): The first usually represents the rate at which new information can be written to CD-Rs (write rate). The second number is the rate at which information can be rewritten to CD-RWs (rewrite rate). And the third is the rate at which the information on the disc can be read (read rate).

A *DVD-RW* (also called *DVD-RAM,* or *DVD+RW* by different manufacturers) is an optical storage medium that allows you to save, change, and delete files but has a larger capacity than a CD-RW. It's similar to a CD-RW in its rewritable feature and to a DVD-ROM in capacity. There are various types of recordable DVDs from various manufacturers, each of which must have its own special drive. This is a relatively new technology and no clear standard has yet emerged.

making the grade   SECTION A://

1. The brain of your computer is the _____.
2. _____ is temporary storage that holds software instructions and information for the CPU.
3. A terabyte is one _____ bytes.
4. Zip disk drives are an example of removable _____ storage.
5. You can write information to a CD-R _____ time(s).

B://OUTSIDE THE BOX

Essential components that you need outside the system unit are basic output devices (such as a monitor) and input devices (such as a keyboard and mouse). Apart from these essentials, you usually get speakers and a modem as standard equipment, and you may also get a printer as part of the package. You can then purchase other components such as a microphone for Internet phone calls, a digital camera to take photos you can store on your computer and send to family and friends, a scanner to copy printed material into your computer, and many other extras.

KEYBOARD AND MOUSE

Are There Choices When It Comes to Keyboards and Mice?

Keyboards and mice come in different styles. Some keyboards are wireless, so that you're not tied to the desk while you're surfing. Some keyboards have a set of special keys for multimedia that give you one-touch access to Web sites and e-mail, as well as controls to play CDs, MP3 files, and DVDs.

i·buy

Saving Your Neck—and All the Rest of You

Whether it's typing documents, memos, and letters or simply surfing the Web, people may sit for long periods using their keyboards and mice, which can lead to physical problems. To avoid physical problems and this misery, consider buying ergonomic computer devices.

Ergonomics deals with how you arrange and use your technology to reduce discomfort and avoid health problems. For example, there are many styles of keyboards and mice that are built to minimize strain on your neck, back, and arms. You should try several and find ones that suit you. Even the most expensive keyboards and mice aren't really that expensive (probably in the neighborhood of $100). That's a small price to pay for avoiding or alleviating pain.

At the same time you do need to sit correctly at your computer.

Here are some sitting guidelines to follow:

- Position your screen about the length of your arm away and so that you look slightly down at it.
- Your feet should be flat on the floor.
- Your elbows, knees, and hips should form right angles.
- Your back should be at a right angle to the floor.
- Rest your eyes by looking away from the screen frequently.
- Stretch your shoulders, back, arms, and wrists at least every 30 minutes.
- Stretch your hands downward and backward frequently.

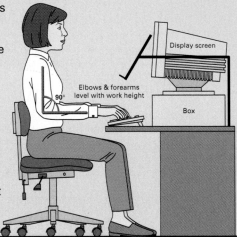

Display screen

Elbows & forearms level with work height

90°

Box

Feet flat on the floor or use a footstool or footrest

Most important, always listen to your body when it tells you that you're uncomfortable and *do something about it.*

FIGURE 5.12

This optical mouse uses light to sense movement and transmits the information along a wire. A wireless version would transmit the movement information with radio waves or infrared light (like your remote control for the TV).

The point-and-click user interface of today's software requires a pointing device, such as a mouse or a touchpad. A touchpad is a little dark gray rectangle that you often see on the base of notebook computers, but you'll find a touchpad on some standard keyboards too. You move your finger around the ***touchpad*** and the cursor moves accordingly.

If a mouse is your preference, you can choose from various types.

- A standard ***mouse*** has a ball on the bottom that causes the cursor on the screen to move as the ball rolls. Most mice are available with a scroll wheel that scrolls up and down without your having to use the scroll arrows on the side of the screen.
- A ***trackball*** is a mouse with the ball on the top, and you move it with your fingers or thumb.
- An ***optical mouse*** senses movement with red light and moves the cursor accordingly. An optical mouse doesn't have to be on a flat surface, so you can sit back from the computer and move the mouse along your arm or some other surface (see Figure 5.12).
- A ***wireless mouse*** sends signals to the computer by means of waves. You can get a wireless mouse either with a ball or as an optical mouse. You'd plug the cable on the sensor into the mouse connector and position the sensor so that the signal from the mouse has an unobstructed path.

MONITORS

What Kind of Monitor Should I Get?

Monitors come in two varieties: CRT or flat panel display (see Figure 5.13). **CRTs** are the monitors that look like TV sets. They're the most common type of monitor. **Flat-panel displays** are thin, lightweight monitors and take up much less space than CRTs.

Flat-panel displays are usually either gas plasma or LCD screens. **Gas plasma displays** shine light through gas to make an image. **LCD (liquid crystal display)** screens shine light through a layer of crystalline liquid to make an image. LCDs are the most usual type of flat-panel screens for computers and come in two types: passive matrix and active matrix. **TFT (thin film transistor)** displays are flat-panel displays with active matrix screens. **Active matrix screens** have a separate transistor for every pixel, or dot, on the screen and update faster providing a higher-quality, crisper image.

The features you should watch for when evaluating monitors are the screen size, the resolution, and the dot pitch.

FIGURE   5.13

Monitors are either CRT or flat-panel and their resolution tells you how sharp the image is.

Side view of flat-panel display

Front view of flat-panel display

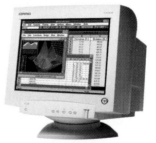

CRT

	Resolution	
Type	Horizontal	Vertical
VGA	640	480
SVGA	800	600
XGA	1,024	768
SXGA	1,280	1,024
UXGA	1,600	1,200
HDTV	1,920	1,080
QXGA	2,048	1,536

Monitors at a glance

A flat-panel display
- Usually costs much more than a CRT with a comparable screen size.
- Takes up less space than a CRT.
- Is lighter and less awkward than a CRT.
- Gives off less heat than a CRT.
- Is usually better than a CRT for static images.
- Is usually not as good as a CRT (with more blurring) if you move the cursor quickly or play video or animation.
- Has less glare than a CRT, especially if you tilt it down slightly.

Screen Size

The viewable area of your monitor is measured from corner to opposite corner. CRTs are usually quoted with two numbers—the size of the screen and the size of the image. In a CRT, the picture doesn't fill the screen; there's a black border around it (that's true for your CRT TV set too). So, the important information is how big the image is. The image on a flat-panel display fills the screen so the size of the screen is the size of the image.

Resolution

The **resolution of a screen** is the number of pixels it has. **Pixels (picture elements)** are the dots that make up the image on your screen. The number of dots varies with the type of monitor you have, but larger numbers are better than smaller ones.

Dot Pitch

Dot pitch is the distance between the centers of a pair of like-colored pixels. Color monitors make images with three pixel colors—red, green, and blue. Instead of telling you the exact size of the pixel, ads for monitors usually tell you the distance between the centers of the pixels (i.e., dot pitch). A monitor with .24 mm dot pitch is better than one with .28 dot pitch because the dots are smaller and closer together giving you a better-quality image. For more information on monitors, go to our text Web site at www.mhhe.com/i-series.

PRINTERS

Will I Get a Printer with My Computer System?

Sometimes a printer is included with a computer system and sometimes you have to buy it separately. People buying printers for home or school usually buy either an inkjet or a laser printer (see Figure 5.14). Both types make images with dots. A printer's sharpness and clarity depend on its resolution. The **resolution of a printer** is the number of dots per inch (dpi) it produces, which is the same principle as the resolution in monitors. The more dots, the better the image, and usually, the more costly the printer. A laser printer may advertise a resolution of 1,200 × 1,200 dpi. Multiplying these numbers together gives you 1,440,000 dots per square inch. That resolution would yield a better image than a printer that boasts 1,440 × 720 dpi (1,036,800 dots per inch). Also note that the 1,440 × 720 tells you that there are more dots per inch horizontally than vertically. An even distribution of dots (like 1,200 × 1,200) gives you a better-quality image.

Inkjet Printers

Inkjet printers are the most popular type of printer. They're great for color as well as black and white printouts. **Inkjet printers** make images by forcing ink droplets through nozzles. The top speed of an inkjet is about 15 ppm (pages per minute).

Laser printer

Inkjet printer

F I G U R E   5.14

Laser and inkjet printers both make pictures with dots, but they use entirely different methods.

Printers at a glance

1. Both laser and inkjet printers make pictures with dots and the more dots per inch there are, the better the picture.
2. A printer that prints the same number of dots horizontally as vertically tends to make a better-quality image.
3. Inkjet printers are available in 4 or 6 colors—the 6-color versions provide better color shading.
4. The cost of toner for color laser printers is four times that of a black-only laser because of the three extra cartridges.

Most inkjets have black, cyan (blue), magenta (purplish pink), and yellow ink, which come in little receptacles called tanks. You can buy inkjet printers for which the tanks for the four colors are in four separate cartridges or alternatively in two cartridges, one for black and one for the other three colors. Many inkjet printers combine the print nozzles with the ink tanks so that you get new nozzles when you replace the tanks. This helps to avoid the clogging that used to be a problem with inkjet printers.

Some inkjet printers are specially designed to produce high-quality images and are often advertised as photo printers. These have six colors (a second shade each of magenta and cyan) and so provide a better range of colors and shades.

Laser Printers

Laser printers usually generate better-quality output than inkjets, but they're also more expensive—especially the color ones. A *laser printer* forms images using an electrostatic process, the same way a photocopier works. Laser printers print between 3 and 30 pages per minute depending on type. The color laser has two different speeds—the faster one for black only. It takes either three or four passes, depending on the type of printer, to print the color image, so color is slower.

Black-only laser printers have one toner cartridge. Color laser printers require four, which increases the cost of cartridge replacement considerably.

Multifunction Printers

A printer that will scan, copy, fax, as well as print is a *multifunction printer.* A multifunction printer can be either an inkjet or laser unit. You would typically pay less for a multifunction printer than you would if you bought the devices separately. The multifunction unit will also take up less space on your desk. For more information on printers, visit our Web site at www.mhhe.com/i-series.

CONNECTING PRINTERS (AND OTHER DEVICES) TO THE SYSTEM UNIT

How Do I Know What to Connect Where?

Different devices have different types of connectors for linking components to the motherboard and CPU. Many devices have two or more connectors. Different printers, for instance, have a variety of different types of connectors, and many have at least two. Common types are USB, Firewire, serial, and parallel. Connectors plug into ports, which are usually located on the back of the system unit. USB or Firewire ports are the exception to this rule. They can be on the front of the system unit, or even on your keyboard or flat-panel display monitor. Look at Figure 5.15 to see what common connectors and ports look like.

FIGURE 5.15

Computers have many different types of ports for different types of connectors on peripheral devices.

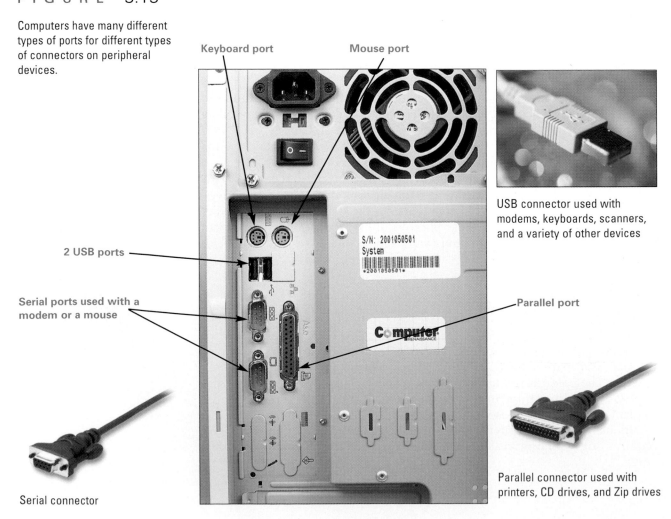

Keyboard port

Mouse port

2 USB ports

Serial ports used with a modem or a mouse

Parallel port

S/N: 2001050501
System
2001050501

USB connector used with modems, keyboards, scanners, and a variety of other devices

Serial connector

Parallel connector used with printers, CD drives, and Zip drives

USB (universal serial bus) connectors and ports are becoming the most popular means of connecting devices to computers. There are usually at least two USB ports on desktop computers and one on notebooks. The day will probably come when most devices have USB connectors. A USB connector allows hot-swap Plug and Play. With **Plug and Play** you can add devices to your computer and the operating system will find and install the drivers automatically without your having to go through a manual installation. If you don't already have the right device driver on your system, the operating system will prompt you to insert the appropriate disk or CD-ROM.

Firewire connectors are similar to USB connectors, except they're faster. Firewire lets information move more than 30 times faster than USB.

A **serial connector,** which plugs into a serial port, usually has 9 holes but may have 25, which fit the corresponding number of pins in the port. The computer knows serial connections internally as COM1, COM2, and so on.

A **parallel connector,** which plugs into a parallel port, has 25 pins, which fit into the holes that are in the port. You often use a parallel connector for your printer. Internally, parallel connections are named LPT1, LPT2, and so on. So if you're installing a new printer that's plugged into a parallel port, Windows may ask you where it's connected, and give you a list to choose from that includes LPT1 and LPT2.

IrDA (infrared data association) ports are for wireless devices, and work in essentially the same way as the remote control to your TV does. To use a wireless device, you must have one port on the device and another one on your computer. You'd use an IrDA port for sending information from your notebook to a wireless printer.

making the grade
SECTION B://

1. A(n) _____ mouse senses movement with red light and moves the cursor accordingly.

2. The _____ of your screen is the number of pixels it has.

3. _____ printers make images by forcing ink droplets through nozzles.

4. The kind of connector you might find on a keyboard or flat-panel display would be a _____ connector.

5. An IrDA port is for _____ devices.

C://NOTEBOOK COMPUTERS

The chief advantages of notebook computers are their small size, light weight, and portability. Recall that in Chapter 1 in the I-Buy section we discussed the three issues that separate notebooks from desktop computers: portability, price, and quality of interfaces. The notebook wins only on the portability factor because it's small and can run on a battery, but for many people portability is more important than the other two factors. (In some parts of the world, in places where power is unpredictable, people may buy notebooks because they run on batteries, to avoid power surges.)

Keyboard with touchpad

The length of time the battery power lasts in a notebook varies a great deal. The advertised length of time is usually a maximum. Under normal working conditions your battery will probably not last that long. It might be well worth the investment to buy a second battery so that you have a spare when the first one starts fading. If you're using your notebook somewhere you can plug it in, do so and save the battery.

The monitor or screen on a notebook computer is usually an LCD screen. Some have side lighting and some screens are back lit, making the lighting more even and the screen more readable.

As a pointing device, some notebook computers come with a touchpad on the keyboard. Others have a trackball built into the keyboard.

ADDING PERIPHERAL DEVICES TO A NOTEBOOK
Will I Need to Add Devices to My Notebook?

For adding devices to your notebook, there are usually two openings, one on top of the other, on the side or front of a notebook called PC Card slots. That's where you connect external devices with a PC Card (see Figure 5.16). A *PC Card* (which is an updated version of the traditional *PCMCIA card*) is the expansion card you use to add devices to your notebook computer. PC Cards often look like fat credit cards and slide into the side of a notebook computer without your ever having to open the case. For example, if you wanted to add a CD-ROM drive, you'd slide a PC Card into the slot and then connect the CD-ROM drive to the connector on the PC Card. One of the great things about PC Cards is that you can hot-swap devices. *Hot-swap* means that you can change, or swap out, cards without shutting your computer down.

If you're buying a notebook, think carefully about what extras you might want, such as a modem or DVD drive, and try to choose a system which has devices built in since your expansion possibilities are limited unless you use a docking station. A *docking station* is a small platform into which you can plug your whole notebook computer. Then you can plug any peripherals you want into the docking station.

FIGURE 5.16

To add devices to a notebook computer you need a PC Card.

SECTION C:// **making** *the grade*

1. A notebook computer can run when plugged into a wall outlet or off a _____.
2. The main advantage of a notebook is its _____.
3. The pointing device on a notebook is usually a trackball or _____.
4. An expansion card for a notebook is called a _____ Card.
5. The term _____ means you can change or swap out devices without turning off the computer.

D://CONSUMER ISSUES

Computers are by nature very versatile machines. You can turn your computer into a gaming paradise or an electronic dark room.

FOR GAMING ENTHUSIASTS

What's the Best I Can Get for Gaming?

You have two options for computer gaming—playing locally or on the Web. Here are some suggestions to improve your gaming fun.

- *Joystick for input:* If you're serious about gaming you'll need a good joystick, gamepad, or some other input device that gives you good control. Try out different types in the store and get one that feels good to you (see Figure 5.17).

- *Speakers for output:* Game surround sound can make a real difference in your gaming experience. So, you might consider investing in good speakers. The four-speaker, surround-sound type with 3-D audio produces great sound effects.

- *Speed for processing:* Your biggest advantage in gaming is speed. To increase your speed, without getting a new computer or even a new CPU, you'll need lots of RAM and lots of hard drive space. You can increase your speed by copying CD-ROM or DVD-ROM information to your hard disk for additional speed. If you're gaming online, you'll need a fast Internet connection.

F I G U R E   5.17

A joystick or a gamepad makes for a better gaming experience.

FOR PHOTOGRAPHY ENTHUSIASTS

How Can I Use My Computer for Photography?

You can process photos faster and easier than was ever possible in dark rooms, and you can adjust photos in ways previously only possible in photo-finishing enterprises. Even if you want to work with photos produced by traditional cameras, you can do wonders.

- *Digital cameras for input:* A digital camera, as you saw in Chapter 3, is an input device that lets you capture photos and transfer them directly to your computer. Camera resolution is often quoted in **megapixels,** which is the maximum number of dots, in millions, that make up the image. One-megapixel cameras are fine if all you want to do is send photos via e-mail or to your Web site. If you

FIGURE 5.18

Digital cameras and scanners can serve as input devices.

This digital camera uses memory sticks to store photos on. Other cameras use compact flash memory, mini-CDs, or even a tiny hard disk.

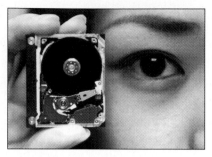

IBM Japan's one-gigabyte Microdrive is being marketed for cameras and other portable electronic devices.

This scanner converts slides into electronic form.

want to print out your photos, look for at least two megapixels, particularly if you want to print copies 8" × 10" or bigger.

Some digital cameras have compact flash memory cards, which look like mini–removable floppy disks. Others have memory sticks that are like small, thin, elongated credit cards. Still others use miniature CD-Rs that are about 3 inches in diameter.

You can even produce photos from negatives and slides with a special scanner. A scanner simply converts an image into electronic form.

- *Printers for output:* You can print nice photos with a color laser printer. Or you can get inkjet printers designed especially for photos. Some photo printers let you plug the camera's compact flash memory card right into the printer, bypassing the computer altogether.
- *Speed for processing:* You need lots of RAM and hard disk space since pictures take up lots of space. You'll also need good editing software.

QUESTIONS AND ANSWERS

1. Do I Need a Docking Station for My Notebook Computer?

A docking station is a small platform into which you can plug your whole notebook computer. Then you can plug a regular monitor and keyboard, and any other peripherals you want simply by inserting the notebook into the docking station. With a docking station, you still have access to the hard disk drive on your notebook with all the software and information you have stored there, without the inconvenience of the small screen and keyboard. Or you can use a docking station just for its power supply (so you don't run the notebook off its battery) and to connect to your network.

2. Do I Need to Buy a Video Card?

No matter what kind of monitor you have, it must be connected to the CPU by means of a video card. A video card converts the information from RAM into an image on your screen. Nowadays, computers usually come

did you know?

About 80 percent of the world's motherboards are manufactured in Taiwan.

with a video card already installed or even integrated into the motherboard. You might, however, want to install a specialized video card, particularly if you want very sophisticated graphics or animation. Video cards usually have their own CPU and memory dedicated to image processing, freeing up the main CPU for other tasks (see Figure 5.19).

FIGURE 5.19

Video cards have their own CPU and memory to take some of the load off the main CPU.

3. Do I Automatically Get a Sound System with My Computer?

Sound systems are standard on most computers on the market today. You usually get a sound card (on the motherboard or integrated into the motherboard) and a set of speakers. The sound card lets you record sound with a microphone (the input device) and play it back with speakers (the output device).

If you're a music lover you might want to upgrade your sound system. If so, you'd probably get a new sound card and speakers. The *Sound Blaster* sound card was one of the first sound cards for the PC and has become the standard over time. You'll often see sound cards advertised as being "Sound Blaster-compatible" or "Blaster emulation." This means that hardware components that work with a Sound Blaster will work with that sound card.

---

making the grade

SECTION D://

1. A joystick is a(n) _____ device.
2. Both video and _____ cards are usually installed on the motherboard or integrated into it when you buy your computer system.
3. The resolution of digital camera images is measured in _____.
4. Video cards often have their own CPU and _____.
5. A small platform into which you can plug your whole notebook computer is called a _____ station.

i·witness

An Up-Close Look at Web Sites

Using Different Type Fonts, Sizes, and Styles

Your personal Web site should be taking on a nice form by now. As you proceeded through the first four chapters, you learned how to use bullets (as opposed to text), incorporate images, add color, and navigate. Now let's take a look at variations for how your text itself can be set.

It's very important to create a Web site that's visually appealing. You can do this with images and color—and also by varying your type fonts. A type character's *font* is its shape or design. Each font family has a different name such as Arial, Courier, CG Times, etc. Such varying fonts have a very different quality and feel. *Font sizes* are given in "points" and refer to the actual size of the characters. A 10 or 12 point font is standard, but you

can also have very small characters (6 point) or very large (72 point) ones. Then, the text type characters of whatever font can be further stylized—underlined, bolded, or italicized—for emphasis.

We've provided two Web sites for you to review. One makes good use of various font families, sizes, and styles. The other is just "plain" text. Review the first and note how we've incorporated font variations. For the second Web site, make suggestions concerning how to make it look better with font adjustments. Of course, remember that as with your use of images, it is possible to "have too much of a good thing." The two Web sites are:

www.mhhe.com/i-series/I-Witness/5-A.html

www.mhhe.com/i-series/I-Witness/5-B.html

You can also connect to the site for this text and download these Web sites to your computer. You can then make the changes yourself to the second one.

HTML Reference:

Font Styles

- <B>—bold. <B>outrageous</B> displays **outrageous**

- <I>—italics. <I>outrageous</I> displays *outrageous*

- <U>—underline. <U>outrageous</U> displays <u>outrageous</u>

- <B><U>—bold and underline. <B><U>outrageous</B></U> displays **<u>outrageous</u>**

Font Sizes

- <FONT SIZE=??>—change font size. <FONT SIZE=20>outrageous</FONT> displays outrageous

Font Families

- <FONT NAME=?name?>— change font family. <FONT NAME=Courier>outrageous</FONT> displays word outrageous in Courier.

E://SUMMARY AND KEY TERMS

Just as you need to know about brakes, antilock brakes, tire types, horsepower, mileage per gallon, type of transmission, and many other things when you're buying a car, you need to know about the hardware components of a computer system, too, when you buy one. The *system unit* is the case or box in which the motherboard and storage units are housed. The *motherboard* is where all the components eventually connect to the CPU. It's also where the CPU and memory are housed. The *central processing unit (CPU or processor)* is the chip that carries out instructions it receives from your software. The speed with which the CPU carries out instructions is measured in *megahertz (MHz)* and *gigahertz (GHz).* Memory or *RAM (random access memory)* is temporary memory that holds software instructions and information for the CPU. Its capacity is measured in megabytes or gigabytes. A *megabyte* is roughly one million bytes. A *gigabyte* is about one billion bytes.

Long-term storage devices can be magnetic or optical. Magnetic storage devices include hard disks, traditional floppy disks, high-capacity floppy disks, and removable hard disks. Optical discs include CD-ROMs and DVD-ROMs. The major difference between CDs and DVDs is that DVDs have much greater capacity.

- *CD-ROMs* and *DVD-ROMs* are both optical or laser discs whose information cannot be changed.
- *CD-Rs* and *DVD-Rs* are optical discs to which you can write one time only.
- *CD-RWs* and *DVD-RWs* (or *DVD-RAM* or *DVD+RW*) are optical storage discs that you can write to many times and change.

Of the computer components outside the system unit, the most essential are the monitor, keyboard, pointing device, and printer. Monitors come in two types: CRT and flat-panel display. A *CRT* is the monitor that looks like a TV set. *Flat-panel displays* are thin, lightweight monitors. Flat-panel displays are either gas plasma or LCD screens. The image quality of a screen is determined by screen size, *resolution,* and *dot pitch.*

Most printers that people buy for home or school are either laser or inkjet. The resolution again determines the quality of the image that is produced.

Devices connect to the system by means of connectors plugged into ports. The four main types are

- *USB,* which is becoming the most popular.
- *Serial,* which usually has 9 holes but may have 25.
- *Parallel,* which has 25 pins that fit into holes in the port.
- *IrDA* for wireless devices.

For Chapter 5, we've included a great deal of support on the Web site for this text at www.mhhe.com/i-series for

- CPUs
- Memory
- Optical storage
- Printers
- Monitors

KEY TERMS

active matrix screen (p. 5.17)

bay (p. 5.8)

CD-R (compact disc—recordable) (p. 5.13)

CD-ROM (compact disc read-only memory) (p. 5.13)

CD-RW (compact disc—rewritable) (p. 5.15)

central processing unit (CPU, processor) (p. 5.3)

computer system (p. 5.2)

CRT (p. 5.17)

docking station (p. 5.22)

dot pitch (p. 5.18)

DVD-R (DVD—recordable) (p. 5.13)

DVD-ROM (p. 5.13)

DVD-RW (DVD-RAM, DVD+RW) (p. 5.15)

ergonomics (p. 5.16)

Firewire (p. 5.21)

flat-panel display (p. 5.17)

floppy disk (floppy, diskette) (p. 5.11)

gas plasma display (p. 5.17)

gigabyte (GB, Gig) (p. 5.6)

gigahertz (GHz) (p. 5.4)

hard disk (p. 5.9)

hot-swap (p. 5.22)

inkjet printer (p. 5.18)

IrDA (infrared data association) (p. 5.21)

kilobyte (KB, K) (p. 5.6)

laser printer (p. 5.19)

LCD (liquid crystal display) (p. 5.17)

megabyte (MB, M, Meg) (p. 5.6)

megahertz (MHz) (p. 5.4)

megapixel (p. 5.23)

motherboard (main board, system board) (p. 5.2)

mouse (p. 5.16)

multifunction printer (p. 5.20)

optical mouse (p. 5.16)

parallel connector (p. 5.21)

PC Card (PCMCIA card) (p. 5.22)

pixel (picture element) (p. 5.18)

Plug and Play (p. 5.21)

RAM (random access memory) (p. 5.5)

resolution of a printer (p. 5.18)

resolution of a screen (p. 5.18)

serial connector (p. 5.21)

system unit (p. 5.2)

terabyte (TB) (p. 5.6)

TFT (thin film transistor) (p. 5.17)

touchpad (p. 5.16)

trackball (p. 5.16)

USB (universal serial bus) (p. 5.21)

virtual memory (p. 5.7)

wireless mouse (p. 5.16)

CROSSWORD PUZZLE

Across

2. Like USB, but faster
3. A dot on a monitor
4. This type of memory is actually on the hard disk
6. Active matrix flat-panel display
8. Memory
9. A wireless port
11. The computer component that provides the base for connections to the CPU
12. This printer works like a photocopier
15. A billion bytes
18. This type of card lets you add devices to your notebook computer
20. A thousand bytes
21. Many connectors are of this type
23. This type of port has 9 or 25 holes
25. Looks like a CD, but stores much more information

Down

1. A billion cycles per second
3. This type of connector is often found on a printer
5. How you measure the resolution of a digital camera
7. A trillion bytes
10. A monitor that looks like a TV
13. Hot _____—you don't have to shut down the computer to change devices
14. In this printer, ink squirts out through nozzles
16. _____ pitch—the distance between the dots
17. The _____ unit is the box that houses many computer components
19. The "brain" of your computer
22. Where you install a hard disk drive
24. A type of flat-panel display

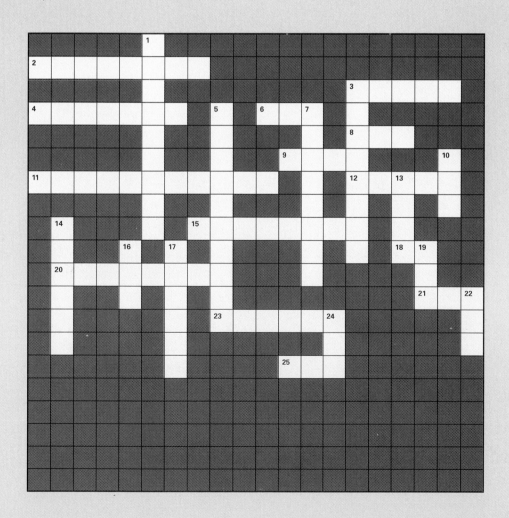

review of terminology

QUESTIONS AND EXERCISES

Multiple Choice

1. The central processing unit (CPU)
   a. stores information long term.
   b. carries out the instructions it receives from the software.
   c. carries information around the motherboard.
   d. is usually found outside the motherboard.
   e. is a peripheral device.

2. The motherboard
   a. is housed in the system unit.
   b. is peripheral storage.
   c. can have a maximum of three components on it at any one time.
   d. is the only circuit board in a computer.
   e. is none of the above.

3. The most important feature of a CPU is
   a. its size.
   b. its speed.
   c. its color.
   d. its manufacturer.
   e. none of the above.

4. The speed of the CPU can be quoted in
   a. dpi.
   b. RAM.
   c. megahertz.
   d. gigabytes.
   e. TFT.

5. RAM is
   a. a term that describes how a computer is built.
   b. the computer's brain.
   c. a type of monitor.
   d. temporary storage that holds instructions and information for the CPU.
   e. a term that measures storage space.

6. A terabyte is
   a. 1,000 bytes.
   b. 1,000 bits.
   c. 1,000,000 bytes.
   d. 1,000,000,000 bytes.
   e. 1,000,000,000,000 bytes.

7. A flat-panel display
   a. looks like a TV set.
   b. can't be used with a computer.
   c. can be active matrix.
   d. has an image that doesn't fill the screen.
   e. is none of the above.

8. A hard disk
   a. is a Mylar disk in a casing.
   b. is an optical storage medium.
   c. is part of the CPU.
   d. is fixed inside your system.
   e. is none of the above.

9. The RAM on your computer stores
   a. the operating system.
   b. the instructions for the application you're using.
   c. keystrokes and mouse movements.
   d. the document or file you're working on.
   e. all of the above.

10. A DVD-ROM
    a. is an optical storage medium.
    b. stores more than a CD.
    c. stands for double virtual density.
    d. is a. and b. only.
    e. is b. and c. only.

True/False

11. ____ You can write or change information on a CD-R many times.

12. ____ RAM holds only application software instructions.

13. ____ A floppy disk is a magnetic storage medium.

14. ____ A microphone is a device that you use to input sound into your computer.

15. ____ Plug and Play means that you can add a device to your computer and the operating system will automatically install the device driver.

QUESTIONS AND EXERCISES

1. Match the motherboard components to the picture above.

COMPONENT	NUMBER IN PICTURE
CPU	_____
RAM slots	_____
Expansion slots	_____
Ports	_____

2. For each of the following answers, create the question:

ANSWER	QUESTION

A. It's the feature that allows me to add devices without having to manually install the drivers.

B. It's the housing for the motherboard and storage devices.

C. It's better for gaming than a mouse.

D. It's a type of flat-panel display.

E. It's the feature that allows you to swap peripheral devices without shutting down your computer.

F. It means millions of pixels.

G. The place where instructions and information are stored temporarily while waiting to be processed by the CPU.

e-commerce

1. Buying a Computer

When buying a computer you have many choices of where to go, including click-and-order businesses on the Web. Visit the following sites and see for yourself what's available at click-and-order businesses. Choose a computer system and compare the prices at the various sites for similar systems. Choose a CPU, an AMD Athlon or Intel Pentium 4. Compare the RAM available on the system you choose in the packages offered at the different sites.

- PC Nation—www.pcnation.com
- Comp-U-Plus—www.compuplus.com
- Buy.com—www.buy.com
- Internet Shopping Outlet—www.shoplet.com

Answer the following questions:

a. What are the return policies of the sites?
b. Do these sites sell software too?
c. Do the sites have any provision for technical support? How about customer support?

When you've got your comparative prices from the click-and-order stores, check them out against the brick-and-mortar stores. Find comparable systems at one or more of these stores and see if prices differ. If these stores have Web sites, see if there is a difference in the prices there compared to the prices offered to the walk-in customers.

2. Writing a Resume

If you're applying for a job, your resume may be scanned by a computer and entered into a database before a human being ever sees it. The rules for writing scannable resumes are different from those that apply to traditional paper resumes. The advice job-seekers used to get was to use heavy paper with a high rag content to send a message of quality to the interviewer and to use decorative fonts and columns in the layout. These features don't work well for scanned resumes—computers can't feel paper. They might even hurt your chances of making the cut since the fonts and columns could obscure vital information

about you. To find out how to tailor a resume to fit you, the job you're seeking, and the type of resume you're expected to submit, connect to the following sites:

- The Resume Shop—www.cyber-north.com
- The University of Minnesota—www1.umn.edu/ohr/ecep/resume
- Proven Resumes—www.provenresumes.com
- The Monster Career Center—content.monster.com/resume
- How to Write a Good Resume—www.nhlink.net/employme/how.htm

While you're at each site, do the following:

a. Check to see if the site gives free help in writing your resume or if you have to pay for the service.
b. Check to see if the site will post your resume for prospective employers.
c. Check to see if the site will critique your resume.

3. Radio Stations

There are radio stations online for every listener's taste. You can listen to stations that feature music from a particular decade or play only rock, jazz, country, or classical. Or you can listen to talk radio. You can even listen to radio broadcasts in another country, which might be helpful if you're studying a foreign language—you can practice your comprehension skills. Or perhaps you're homesick and want to hear some hometown radio. Whatever your needs or taste, you'll probably find a radio station on MIT's list of radio stations that appeals to you. The address is www.radio-locator.com/cgi-bin/home.

For this exercise, go to the following sites and answer the questions.

- Radio Casablanca—www.maroc.net/rc
- Irish radio—www.rte.ie
- Amarillo Junior College's station—www.kacvfm.org/listen.html
- National Public Radio—www.npr.org

a. Can you listen to the station at that site?

b. If the answer to the previous question is yes, what software did the station require you to have for you to be able to listen to the music?

c. What kind of station or stations did you find at each site?

d. Was the station for a particular community?

4. Restaurant Food Delivery

More and more people are "outsourcing" their meals by eating out, having food delivered, or getting take-out. The Web has many, many sites that can accommodate your every taste and culinary need. You can get prepared meals that have been prefrozen. You can get gourmet meals or meals that cater to a special diet. There are sites that specialize in particular types of food, such as seafood, and many more that can provide you with ethnic and regional dishes. Try out the sites below and then answer the questions.

- Food.com—www.food.com
- Waiters on Wheels—www.waitersonwheels.com
- Meals To Go.com—www.mealstogo.com
- Grocer Online—www.groceronline.com
- The Impromptu Gourmet—www.impromptugourmet.com

a. Do you need to leave personal information, such as your name and address, before you're allowed to see what food is being offered at the site?

b. What types of food are available at the site?

c. Is the food cooked before you get it?

d. Does the site act as a clearing house for other sites or for restaurants?

e. Are there restrictions on the cities the site will deliver to?

on the web

1. Evaluating Price and CPU Speed

Connect to two computer vendors on the Web. For example, you could use Dell (www.dell.com) and Gateway (www.gateway.com). Find the cheapest and the most expensive computer system that each site is offering. (*Hint:* usually the faster the CPU, the more expensive the computer system). What type of CPU is each vendor including in its most and least expensive packages? How fast is each CPU?

2. Evaluating RAM

At those same sites in #1, for the same computer systems, check out how much RAM each system has. What type of RAM does each system use?

3. Evaluating Multimedia Capabilities

Look again at the two computer manufacturer sites. Can you get a computer in different colors? What colors? Do the computer specifications say anything about multimedia capabilities? If so, what type of multimedia capability are they advertising?

For Exercises 4, 5, and 6 you might want to use a "shopbot" (shopping robot). A shopbot is a site you go to and type in what you're looking for, after which the bot will visit lots of sites looking for your item and return with a list of prices, descriptions, and sellers. Here are some shopbots you could use:

- Bottom Dollar—www.bottomdollar.com
- b silly—www.bsilly.com
- Price Watch—www.pricewatch.com
- dealspin—www.dealspin.com
- Deal Time—www.dealtime.com

4. Evaluating Peripheral Devices and Connectors

Look on the Web and find information about peripheral devices. See what kind of connectors the peripheral devices below come with. For each one specify whether there is a choice of connectors and if so, what are those choices.

- Laser printer with black ink only.
- Color laser printer.
- Scanner.
- CD-ROM drive.
- DVD-ROM drive.

5. Evaluating Tower Units

Go to Dell's Web site and look at its tower system units. Then look at Compaq's site at www.compaq.com. Compare the design of the Compaq's tower computer with Dell's. Which do you like better? Do you see any connectors on the front of either computer? What connectors would you put on the front of a computer instead of the back?

6. Comparing Notebooks and Desktops

Find two comparable computer systems: a tower or desktop computer and a notebook. They will be comparable if they have the same CPU with the same speed and the same amount of RAM. Which is cheaper? What is the difference in price?

7. Replacing a Lost Manual

Let's say that you've lost the user's manual to your computer and you want to add memory, but don't know what kind to get. Look at four computer equipment sites and see if you can find out what kind of RAM goes with a particular computer.

ethics, security & privacy

1. Using a Global Positioning System

Many years ago, the Department of Defense installed more than 20 satellites in space over the equator for the purpose of helping the military identify positions on earth. This global positioning technology is now available to anyone who has a GPS. A GPS (global positioning system) is a small device that can tell you where you are to within a few feet. You can buy a hand-held GPS or it can be part of another system.

The first commercial GPSs showed only longitude and latitude, but by adding processors, memory, and map information to GPS capabilities, you can link the longitude and latitude to specific street names, and even houses on those streets. You can also tell what direction you're moving and at what speed. GPSs already have many applications, and have many more possibilities.

Let's examine some of the implications of this technology.

- **Automobiles:** Some cars have GPSs linked to maps that show on a screen positioned where the driver can see it. Some cars go even further. Cadillac and other GM products, for example, have the OnStar system. When you turn it on, it sends a continuous stream of information to the OnStar center about your position. The OnStar employees then monitor the cars on their computers.

a. Would it be good to have the OnStar system come on with the engine and stay on, so that if your car were stolen, the police could locate it faster for you?

b. What if you had a company car and had to have the OnStar system on all the time so that your boss could tell where you were at all times?

c. Wouldn't parents want to be able to keep track of their teenagers when they borrow the car?

- **Babies:** Parents could use their computers and the Internet to monitor the whereabouts of their babies when they're not with them.

a. Do you think that parents would want to put a chip into a baby's body at birth so that babies in the hospital could no longer be swapped by mistake?

b. Do you think that parents would like to know whether the baby-sitter took their baby out of the house and where they went?

c. Would a chip be good for locating a baby who was kidnapped?

- **Older Children:**

a. If you think that identifying chips implanted in babies is a good idea, then at what age should we remove the chip? 10? 14? 18? 21? Never?

b. If you think that implanted chips are too much, how about something less intrusive? For example, you could put the tracking system in the book bags of school-age children. Then parents and the school administrators could still keep track of the children. Do you think that a school should be able to mandate this for every pupil?

group activities

1. Understanding Software

As you now know, the CPU takes the instructions it gets from software and carries out those instructions. The CPU will do exactly what the instructions say to do, no more and no less. The CPU will assume absolutely nothing that the instructions don't tell it. To get some idea of how precise those instructions have to be, get different people in the group to play the various roles in the processing of software instructions. Play computer and make a peanut butter and jelly sandwich.

This is ideal for two-person teams. Let one person be the CPU and carry out the instructions that the other person gives—exactly. See how many ways there are to interpret any given instruction. For example, if the "instruction" person says, "put peanut butter on the knife," but hasn't yet instructed the "CPU" person to open the jar, the CPU person should say "ERROR."

2. CPUs at Your School

Do a little fact finding at your school and find out what types of CPUs the computers in your computer lab have. Are they all the same or are some newer than others? How much RAM do the computers have?

3. Ports at Your School

In your computer lab look at the ports on the back (or front) of two computers and answer these questions.

a. Do they have USB ports? If so, what if anything, is plugged in there?

b. Do they have parallel ports? Use Figure 5.15 on page 5.20 for comparison.

c. How many serial ports does each machine have?

4. Understanding the Magnitude of Memory

In this exercise make some comparisons of area with amounts of memory. Let's say for argument's sake that 1 kilobyte of memory takes up 1 square inch of space. (You know that it's actually much, much smaller, or we couldn't fit so much RAM into such little chips.) How much memory would fit into the following areas?

Area	Amount of storage
A 500-square-foot apartment. (*Hint:* 1 square foot is equal to 144 square inches.)	_____
A 3,000-square-foot house.	_____
A football field which is 120 yards × 53.33 yards. (*Hint:* 9 square feet make up 1 square yard.)	_____
A field that covers 1 acre. (*Hint:* An acre is 43,560 square feet.)	_____

5. Finding CPUs All around You

List all the everyday items you can think of that have CPUs in them. For example, if you're wearing a watch, it probably has a CPU and unless your car is very old, it has many CPUs in it.

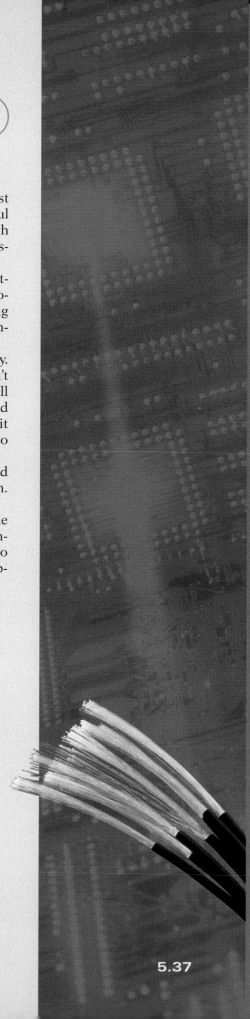

Looking Back/Looking Ahead

The Life and Times of a Dot-Com Entrepreneur

Joann is thinking about getting a new computer. She would like the fastest _____ she can get, but she knows that the most powerful ones are also the most expensive. She would also like to have enough _____ so that when she has lots of applications open, the system won't slow down any more than necessary.

She'd like a color printer. She knows that the _____ printers are more expensive to run than _____ printers, but produce a crisper image. Since the _____ connector is becoming the industry standard, she might try to get a printer with that type of connector.

Now Joann is considering which other devices she might want to buy. She thinks she'd like a(n) _____ mouse since she wouldn't need a flat surface to roll it on. She'd like to make her own CDs so she'll need a _____ to give her the greatest flexibility. She's decided get a DVD drive so that she can watch movies on her computer. Since it has much more capacity than a CD, she's wondering if it would be good to buy a _____ now for backup storage.

When Joanne has the kind of computer equipment she wants, she'd like to make a Web page to become part of the great e-commerce boom. She'll need to set up her Web page and also make sure it's secure.

She thinks it would be nice to have a little network at home since she and her husband both have computers at home and would like to share information electronically. In that case she'll need to find out about how to set up a network and how to protect it from cyberspace intruders. Chapters 6 and 7 will help her do just that.

did you know?

The trend in computing is toward smaller, cheaper, and more powerful technology. And this has been so since computers began to be taken seriously in the 1960s.

the *first electronic computer measured 1,280 cubic feet. It could perform 26,000 operations per second. In contrast, a modern hand-held PDA occupies about 4 cubic inches and can perform 60,000,000 operations per second.*

the *average American depends on more than 264 computers each day, from the smallest microprocessor to the biggest mainframe.*

when *he got married in 1957, Dijkstra (one of the first computer gurus) listed his profession as "programmer." The authorities made him change it saying that there was no such profession.*

nine *out of 10 computers sold in the year 2000 were sold to people outside the United States.*

a *72-gigabyte hard disk has enough room to hold 12 characters (or a word like "organization") for every man, woman, and child on our planet (over 6 billion people).*

intel's® Pentium 4 has __??__ million transistors built into the chip.

To find out just how many transistors are on the Pentium 4 chip, visit the Web site for this text at www.mhhe.com/i-series.

CHAPTER

6

six

Nuts and Bolts of Networks and Computers

How Do Computers and Networks Work?

In the last chapter you learned about the various components of a computer. You saw that buying a computer is similar to buying a car in that you have to make lots of choices about features. In this chapter we're going to take a closer look at how computers work, by themselves and with each other in networks. As with your car, it's good to know something about how computers work.

If you have a car, for example, you need to know that if you use the lights, radio, or fan while the engine is off, they're all running off the battery and if the battery runs down, the car won't start. It wasn't so long ago that you had to know a lot more than that about how a car works. For instance, you had to be careful not to flood the engine when trying to get it started. That's not a problem anymore now that we have fuel-injection engines. In general, cars are more user-friendly than they once were; we use them with little thought beyond changing the oil periodically. The computer industry has not by any means reached such a state of maturity; computers demand far more of our attention if we want them to work well for us. So it's very helpful to know more about computers than simply what the various peripheral devices are.

Another thing—we connect computers together in networks for added flexibility and power. (This is something we can't do with cars, except in the extreme circumstances of jump-starting one or towing a broken-down one.) In later sections of this chapter we'll see how to create a small network in your home or dorm room, how businesses use networks, and how to connect computers to the Internet.

A://WHAT'S GOING ON INSIDE YOUR COMPUTER

The first thing to know is how information is represented inside a computer. In written English, our communication symbols include 56 alphabetic characters (A . . . Z and a . . . z); 10 numeric symbols (0 . . . 9); and miscellaneous characters such as the dash, the dollar sign, quotation marks, and so on. Other Western languages have similar symbol sets. Many Asian languages employ thousands of symbols.

At the most basic level, the tiniest computer components function based on whether electricity is present or not. Thus they have two states—on and off. That's all there is to work with. We use 1 and 0 to correspond to the computer's on state and off state, respectively, and thus have to convert all our human communication symbols into 1s and 0s. Each 1 or 0 is called a *bit*. "Bit" is a contraction of the term ***binary digit***. All software, keyboard strokes, mouse movements and clicks—all information of any kind that moves around or is stored in your computer—are in the form of 1s and 0s, or bits. Everything becomes numbers since that's the only form of information a CPU can process.

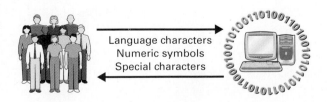

Language characters
Numeric symbols
Special characters

REPRESENTING INFORMATION INSIDE A COMPUTER

How Is Information Converted into 1s and 0s?

The challenge, then, is to convert our natural complex language into the 1s and 0s, or binary code, that the computer can manipulate. The obvious way to do that is to group the bits so that each unique pattern of 1s and 0s represents one natural language character. But how many bits should be in the pattern for one character?

If we used 2 bits, then an A might be represented by 00, a B by 01, a C by 10, and a D by 11. But then we'd be out of possible patterns and still have lots more characters to represent. If we had 4 positions for bits, we'd have enough different patterns for 16 characters, that is, 2^4. Think of a 0 or 1 filling each of the 4 different positions—that's 16 possibilities. Still not enough.

By combining bits into groups of 8, we can make 256 (2^8) different patterns, and that's enough to represent the basic set of symbols we use in English and similar alphabets.

Since this 8-bit group can form enough unique patterns for what we need, it has become the standard over time. A group of 8 bits that represents one natural language character is called a ***byte.*** Each byte has a unique pattern of 1s and 0s. That is, each of the 8 bits in a byte can be a 1 or a 0. For example, if you were to type the word "COOL" on the keyboard, it would change into four bytes—one for each character—that would look like the following so it could be stored in RAM:

01000011	01001111	01001111	01001100
C	O	O	L

For more information on binary numbers, visit the Interactive Companion Labs and choose "Binary Numbers."

ASCII, EBCDIC, and Unicode

For software and information to be transferable from computer to computer, we need a standard method of converting human communication symbols into binary code. The particular set of patterns, or coding system, that you saw used above for the characters in the word "COOL" is called ASCII.

ASCII (American Standard Code for Information Interchange), pronounced ASK-ee, is the coding system that most personal computers and minicomputers use (see Figure 6.1 on the next page). IBM mainframes use another set of patterns called ***EBCDIC.***

The 256 patterns that we get from the ASCII and EBCDIC encoding systems work well in languages that use alphabets similar to the English alphabet, but are inadequate for encoding languages that have many more symbols than English does. The solution to this problem is Unicode. ***Unicode*** is a coding system that uses 16 bits instead of 8, allowing for approximately 65,000 (2^{16}) different patterns. This is enough patterns to incorporate the characters required by the government standards of many Asian countries including Japan, Korea, China, and Taiwan. Additionally, Unicode also accommodates symbols used in the West that don't fit into the 256 patterns of ASCII such as various mathematical symbols, recycling symbols, and currency symbols such as the peso.

FIGURE 6.1

ASCII and EBCDIC are different ways of representing natural language characters in binary code.

Your Characters	ASCII	EBCDIC
(space)	00100000	01000000
!	00100001	01011010
#	00100011	01111011
$	00100100	01011011
&	00100110	01010000
0	00110000	11110000
1	00110001	11110001
2	00110010	11110010
3	00110011	11110011
4	00110100	11110100
5	00110101	11110101
6	00110110	11110110
7	00110111	11110111
8	00111000	11111000
9	00111001	11111001
A	01000001	11000001
B	01000010	11000010
C	01000011	11000011
D	01000100	11000100
E	01000101	11000101
a	01100001	10000001
b	01100010	10000010
c	01100011	10000011
d	01100100	10000100
e	01100101	10000101

Because the first 256 patterns are the same as ASCII, Unicode is usable on ASCII computers too. The Windows NT operating system, for example, uses Unicode.

did you know? **Sixty-two** *percent of American households have personal computers.*

Representing Numbers

Your computer stores numbers in one of two ways based on the type of number. The first type is numbers that are generally not needed to solve a math problem, such as a social security number or a phone number; these numbers are stored as characters like any other. The second type is those used in calculations, that is, numbers that represent an amount. These are stored a bit differently; they're represented in binary as quantities, rather than as separate digits (see Figure 6.2 to see how this works).

THE CPU

What Does the CPU Do?

Now that you know that information used by the computer is in the form of 1s and 0s, let's examine what the CPU does with the information. In Chapter 5 we defined the ***central processing unit (CPU),*** also called the ***microprocessor*** or ***processor,*** as the chip that carries out the instructions it receives from your software. The CPU's role in your computer system is

Base 10	Binary (Base 2)
0	0
1	1
2	10
3	11
4	100
5	101
6	110
7	111
8	1000
9	1001
10	1010
11	1011
12	1100
13	1101
14	1110
15	1111
16	10000

In binary code there are only two symbols, 0 and 1. When we want to express numbers larger than 1 we simply go to the next position as we do in base 10, with what we call the 10 digits (0–9) that we use all the time.

With the 10 digits, when we get to 9 we've used up all our digits so the next quantity is expressed in two positions—10. Then we keep increasing the lowest-level position to 1 and 2 and 3 and so on until we run out and start on the second position, and continue in this fashion.

With binary digits we run out of symbols faster. So binary 0 is base-10 0 and binary 1 is base-10 1, but to represent 2 we have to go to the next position, i.e., 10, and so on.

F I G U R E   6.2

Numbers that are used in calculations are represented as quantities.

When adding # w/ 1 + 0 can be answer only if not go to closer # w/ this #'s

analogous to the role of your brain. Your brain is your body's processor. It performs two types of tasks. The first is to keep your body functioning; your brain controls your breathing, heartbeat, digestion, and so on. Your computer's equivalent is system software. Beyond these "housekeeping" tasks, your brain also has control over those jobs that your body performs because you want it to. Your brain tells your legs and arms how to move when you want to run. Your computer's equivalent is application software.

For your brain to process either system instructions (to keep your body going) or application instructions (to carry out particular tasks you direct your body to perform), obviously it has to be connected to your body parts through your nervous system. Similarly, all computer components must be connected to your computer's brain, the CPU. The motherboard provides the base for these connections (see Figure 6.3). The processor is seated into the motherboard and tiny wires radiate from it out to all computer components, which are either positioned on the motherboard (like RAM) or connected to the motherboard through special plugs or connectors (as is your monitor).

F I G U R E   6.3

The motherboard provides the base for connecting all computer components to the CPU.

Physically, a CPU is a collection of millions of tiny transistors connected to each other on a small rectangular slice of silicon. The silicon slice is embedded into a small plastic or ceramic block with metal connectors that enable it to connect into the motherboard. Computer engineers are constantly striving to shrink transistors even further. The tinier the transistors are, the shorter the distance the electrical charges have to travel, and the faster the processing.

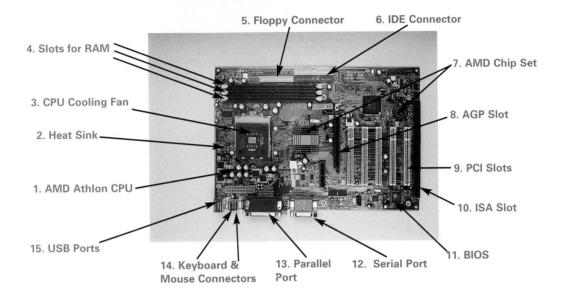

1. **CPU:** Central processing unit is the chip that carries out the instructions it receives from the software. This one is an Athlon from AMD Corp.
2. **Heat sink:** Absorbs heat from the CPU, which gets very hot during processing.
3. **CPU fan:** Blows the heat away from the heat sink.
4. **DIMM sockets:** This is where the RAM chips are located. They come on small circuit boards called sticks. This motherboard is designed for the DIMM type of memory stick.
5. **Floppy connector:** This is where the cable from your floppy drive plugs in.
6. **IDE connectors:** You plug storage devices, such as a hard disk or CD-ROM drive, into these two IDE connectors. This is not the only way to connect storage devices. You can also connect them with an SCSI card, or even with a USB port.
7. **Chip set:** One or more chips working together as a unit that directs information around the motherboard. The chip set controls the flow of information to and from the expansion slots, connectors, etc.
8. **AGP slot:** This is where you would plug in an AGP video card.

9. **PCI slots:** Slots for expansion cards that connect your peripheral devices to the motherboard. For example, a sound card could go into one of these slots and then you could connect your speakers and microphone to the panel of the sound card that is visible at the back of your computer.
10. **ISA slot:** This is an older type of slot for expansion cards. It's not used very much any more, and some motherboards don't have one at all.
11. **BIOS:** This is the chip where low-level start-up instructions are kept. It's these instructions that the CPU uses to start your computer and to load the operating system into RAM.
12. **Serial port:** This is the place to plug in devices such as a printer or mouse, although there is a special connector for a mouse on the motherboard too.
13. **Parallel port:** You'd plug a printer in here. You can tell where to plug a device in by the shape of the connector on the end of the attached cable.
14. **Keyboard and mouse connectors:** This is where you usually plug in the mouse and keyboard.
15. **USB ports:** Here you'd plug in devices such as a scanner or digital camera. You usually get at least two of these.

How the CPU Carries Out Instructions

Here's an analogy for how the CPU carries out software instructions. Say you want to make a memorable dinner for a special person in your life. Perhaps this person likes spinach lasagna. Your grandmother knows how to make every kind of lasagna. So you call her and ask her to give you directions. She stays on the phone (she's a very patient person) and gives you the instructions, one by one, from beginning to end, as you make the lasagna. Each time you carry out one instruction, you go back for the next. In this analogy your grandmother is RAM—where the instructions are stored. You're the CPU asking for each instruction as you need it. As you get each instruction, you carry it out. When a CPU and RAM act like you and your grandmother fixing lasagna, it's called a machine cycle or a CPU cycle. A *machine cycle* or a *CPU cycle* consists of retrieving, decoding, and executing the instruction, and returning the result to RAM.

For the CPU to do its job, the instructions (software) must be in RAM. When you load (or open) a program, you're telling your computer to send a copy of the program from the storage device (hard disk or CD) into RAM. In carrying out the instructions in the software the CPU repeatedly performs machine cycles as follows:

1. *Retrieve an instruction:* The CPU sends to RAM for the next instruction and the information it needs. For example, if the instruction says to add 4 and 6, the two numbers travel as information with the add instruction.

2. *Decode the instruction:* The CPU examines the instruction to see what needs to be done, in this case, add 4 and 6 (see Figure 6.4 on the next page).

3. *Execute the instruction:* The CPU then does what the instruction says to do. In our example, it sends the two numbers to the arithmetic logic unit to be added. The *arithmetic logic unit (ALU)* is a component of the CPU that performs arithmetic operations.

4. *Store the result in RAM:* The CPU then sends the result of the addition, 10, to RAM.

For more information on how a computer works, visit the Interactive Companion Labs and choose "Computer Anatomy."

CPU Speed

You'll sometimes hear the CPU speed referred to as the "clock speed." This refers to the CPU clock. Every CPU has its own *CPU clock,* which is simply a sliver of quartz that beats at regular intervals in response to an electrical charge. The beat of the CPU clock is like the drummer in a marching band. Just as the drummer keeps everyone marching in time, the CPU clock keeps all your computer's operations synchronized. Each beat or tick of the CPU clock is called a *clock cycle* and is equivalent to a CPU cycle, also called a machine cycle. The CPU uses the CPU clock to keep instructions and information marching through your CPU at a fixed rate. The CPU completes a machine cycle for every tick of the CPU clock. Nothing outside your CPU moves that fast.

FIGURE 6.4

Cache memory holds instructions and information for the CPU.

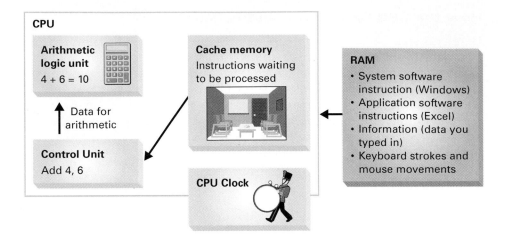

Some instructions are complex and take more than one machine cycle and others are simpler and take less, so the number of instructions processed per second is not the same as the number of clock cycles. Some tasks require a lot more instructions than others. For example, putting graphics on the screen requires a lot more CPU time than text because it takes lots of calculations to color each dot (pixel) on the screen the right intensity to form the image. Lots of calculations means that lots of instructions are needed and, hence, lots of machine cycles. So if your application is taking a long time, maybe several seconds, to complete a task, it's probably because it's carrying out complex operations that take a lot of instructions.

CPU speed, however, is not the only determinant of processing time. Other components strongly impact how fast your computer works. Cache memory, which is a sort of waiting-room memory, is one such factor. *Cache* memory is where instructions and information wait for processing after they arrive in the CPU from RAM (see Figure 6.4). The size of your cache affects processing speed. Another speed factor is the system bus, which, in our Grandma and the lasagna story, would be the phone line.

BUSES

How Does Information Move around the Motherboard?

Buses, or data buses, carry information in the form of bits around the motherboard in your computer. The pathway that carries information between RAM and the CPU is part of the system bus. The *system bus* consists of electrical pathways which move information between basic components of the motherboard, including between RAM and the CPU. The number of bits that can travel side by side at one time helps to determine the speed of a bus. Obviously, the more the bus can accommodate, the faster the transfer of information, in the same way that multiple lanes on our traffic highways allow more vehicles to reach their destinations more quickly.

Much of the elaborate circuitry that you can see on the top and bottom of the motherboard is part of the expansion bus, which is another system of pathways along which information moves. The *expansion bus* forms the highway system on the motherboard that moves information coming from and going to devices outside the motherboard such as your microphone or printer.

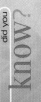

Various types of buses make up the expansion bus. Here are three examples of common expansion buses.

- The **ISA (industry standard architecture) bus** is the oldest and slowest type of expansion bus. Newer motherboards have either one or none of these.

- The **PCI (peripheral component interconnect) bus** is the most common in modern computers. The PCI bus moves information about four times faster than the ISA bus.

- The **AGP (accelerated graphics port) bus** is dedicated to carrying complex graphics between the CPU and the AGP video card in the AGP slot on the motherboard. Unlike the ISA and PCI buses, AGP is usable only for carrying information to the monitor.

EXPANSION CARDS, PORTS, AND CONNECTORS

How Does Information Get from a Device to the Expansion Bus?

The expansion bus, in its various forms, carries information to and from devices outside the motherboard. So how does the information get from the devices to the expansion bus?

Like roads coming into a city, one end of the expansion bus highway system goes to the CPU. The other end spreads out on the motherboard and terminates in interface hardware. **Interface hardware** is the hardware that connects external devices to the motherboard and can be one of two types.

The first type of interface hardware is an expansion board in an expansion slot. An **expansion slot** is a long skinny socket on the motherboard into which you insert an expansion board. An **expansion board** (or **card**) is a circuit board that you insert into the expansion slot on the motherboard and to which you connect a peripheral device. There are three types of expansion slots: ISA, PCI, and AGP (see Figure 6.5). The **ISA slot** (on a modern motherboard you'll see one or none of these) is usually black, and terminates the ISA bus. The **PCI slots** (usually white) terminate the PCI bus. And the **AGP slot** (usually brown) is the end of the line for the AGP bus. Into these slots you plug expansion cards such as video cards, sound cards, or modem cards. These cards or boards have ports on the edge that are visible on the back panel of your computer and that's where you plug in the connector on the end of the cable attached to the device (recall what you learned about slots and connectors in Chapter 5).

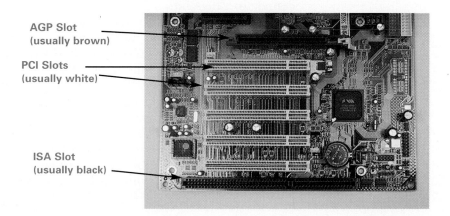

AGP Slot
(usually brown)

PCI Slots
(usually white)

ISA Slot
(usually black)

FIGURE 6.5

Most motherboards will have PCI and AGP slots and may also have an ISA slot.

i·series insights

Ethics, Security & Privacy

Big Brother in England: A Network of Cameras

In England, almost every town, from the teeming city of London to the smallest hamlet, has surveillance cameras on the corners of buildings and incorporated into street lamps. Victoria Station, one of the most famous spots in London, has about a dozen cameras in its vicinity. The cameras are trained on the streets to record activity.

The surveillance has three uses: (1) It continuously monitors street activity, (2) stores images of events for possible future use, and (3) identifies wanted persons.

The cameras in the surveillance network deliver images to a monitoring center where officials keep an eye on what's happening on the streets. The monitoring centers are also connected to a huge

database of photos of people wanted by the police. The images captured by the cameras are fed to software that compares each one

with the pictures in the database and signals when a match is found. The images are then stored in case they're needed in the future.

Opinions in England differ as to whether such surveillance is a good or bad thing. Opponents feel that the system is an invasion of privacy and violates the rights of law-abiding citizens. Those in favor point to a huge reduction in crime (95 percent in car theft alone) as proof that street cameras make England a safer place to be since they enable the police to stop crimes in progress. Also, a videotape of the actual commission of a crime provides ironclad evidence for prosecutors, increasing their conviction rate and getting criminals off the street.

FIGURE 6.6

The CPU sends information along the expansion bus to the interface hardware then through the parallel connector and cable to the printer.

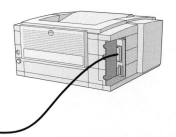

Parallel connector

The second type of interface hardware is integrated directly into the motherboard. In this case you don't need to plug in any expansion card so you won't see any expansion slots. What you do see are the ports on the motherboard. They're positioned so that they're accessible on the back panel of your system unit. This is where you connect various peripheral devices.

Check out your printer, for example. Your printer, unless it's wireless, has a cable with a connector on the end, let's say a parallel connector. This connector plugs into a port, in this case, a parallel port, in the back of the system unit. Most likely, the port is directly on the motherboard, although it could be on an expansion card. If so, the expansion card would be inserted into a PCI slot (the terminal of the PCI bus).

When the CPU sends information to the printer, it travels along the expansion bus into the interface hardware (either the PCI slot with expansion card inserted or the integrated version). Then it travels through the port to the connector, along the cable, to the printer. And then the text or image prints on the paper in the printer (see Figure 6.6).

Wireless Devices

For a printer or mouse or any other wireless device, you'll need a wireless port on your notebook or desktop (see Chapter 5). One type is the IrDA that you learned about in Chapter 5. IrDA wireless connections use infrared waves as your TV remote control does. So when the CPU sends information to a wireless printer, it travels on the expansion bus to the port on the computer as usual. But instead of being carried to the printer by cable, it becomes waves that move through the air and are captured by the IrDA port on the printer itself (see Figure 6.7). Infrared signals are suitable for short-range communication only and are generally used for devices such as printers and mice.

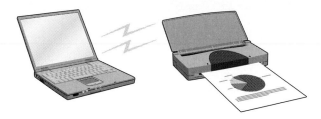

F I G U R E   6.7

Wireless devices send and receive information as waves through the air.

To get more information on what's happening and what can cause problems within your computer, visit the Interactive Companion Labs and choose "Computer Troubleshooting."

making the grade

1. A _____ is a 1 or a 0.
2. A group of 8 bits is called a _____.
3. The coding system that most personal computers and minicomputers use is _____.
4. The _____ bus forms the highway system on the motherboard that moves information coming from and going to devices such as printers.

B://SMALL NETWORKS

Nowadays you don't use just one computer. Anytime you use e-mail or visit a Web site, your computer becomes part of a network and interacts with other computers. A *computer network* (which we refer to simply as a network) is a collection of computers that support the sharing of information and hardware devices.

Networks come in all sizes from two computers connected to share a printer, to the Internet, which is the largest network on the planet, joining millions of computers of all kinds all over the world. In between are business networks, which vary in size from a dozen or fewer computers to many thousands. For more information on networks, visit the Interactive Companion Labs and choose "Network Connections."

Some basic principles apply to all networks, large or small.

- Each computer on a network must have a network card (either as an expansion card or integrated into the motherboard) that provides the connection between the CPU in that computer and the other computers.

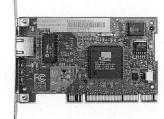

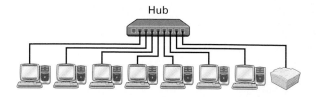

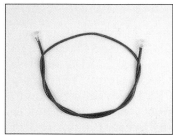

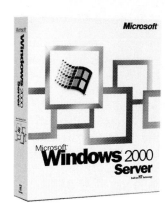

- There's usually at least one connecting device (such as a hub or a router) that acts as a sort of switchboard for transporting messages from one computer to another.
- There must be a communications medium, such as cables or radio waves, which moves information between and the connecting device.
- Each computer must have a network operating system that allows the movement of information in and out.

HOME AND DORM NETWORKS

Can I Create a Network in My Home or Dorm?

You can set up a simple peer-to-peer network at home or in your dorm with just a few computers. A ***peer-to-peer network*** is a network in which a small number of computers share hardware (perhaps a printer) and information.

Suppose you have a computer with a printer attached and link it to another computer so that both computers can use the printer. What you have now is a peer-to-peer network. Each computer independently stores its own software and information, but can access the information on the other computer, and both computers on the network can use the same printer.

A fairly typical home network has Ethernet cards and a dedicated network cable. For this type of network you need

- An Ethernet network interface card for each computer.
- A hub or home router as a connecting device.
- Cable to link the computers.
- A network operating system.

You must first install a network interface card into each computer. A ***network interface card (NIC)*** is an expansion card or PC Card (for a notebook) that connects your computer to a network and allows information to flow between your computer and the rest of the network (see Figure 6.8 on the next page). An ***Ethernet card*** is the most common type of network interface card. Ethernet cards are available to fit either an ISA or a PCI expansion slot.

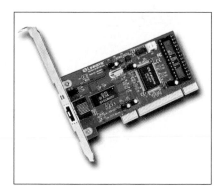 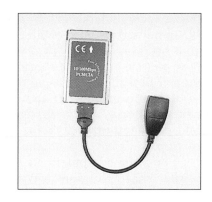

F I G U R E   6.8

Ethernet cards provide a network connection for desktop computers, and PC Cards do the same for notebook computers.

As a connecting device, you'd get a hub or a home router. A **network hub** is a device that connects multiple computers into a network. Each computer that you plug into the hub becomes part of the network, and a message sent from one computer travels into the hub and out to the recipient computer. A **router** is a device that acts as a smart hub connecting computers into a network, and goes a step further by separating your network from any other network it's connected to (see Figure 6.9). So if you're accessing the Internet from your home network, the router offers you a measure of protection from intruders. Hubs for small networks and home routers, such as LinkSys Cable/DSL routers, are not expensive.

You would connect the computers to the hub with Cat 5 cable. **Cat 5** or **Category 5 cable,** also called **Ethernet cable,** is twisted pair cable (like phone cable), except that there are more pairs of wires, and the pairs are twisted around each other. On each end of the cable is an **RJ-45 connector** (also called an **Ethernet connector**), which looks like a telephone connector except that it's larger. One end of each strip of cable plugs into the Ethernet card on a computer and the other end plugs into the network hub (see Figure 6.10).

As always, when you have hardware, you need software to make it work, in this case a network operating system. A **network operating system (NOS)** is the operating system that runs a network, steering information

F I G U R E   6.9

A router is a smart hub, which connects computers into a network, but also separates your network from any other network it's connected to.

F I G U R E   6.10

A network interface card, a cable, and a hub connect a computer to a network.

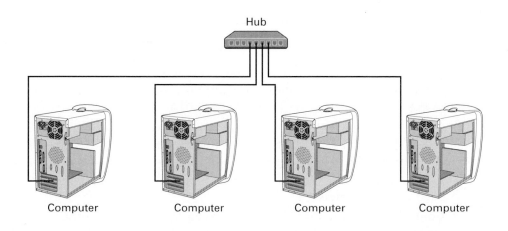

between computers and managing security and users. If you have Windows (95 or newer) installed on all computers, then you already have the NOS for your peer-to-peer network. To make files available to another computer, you have to turn on the file-sharing option in Windows. The files on one computer will then appear as additional folders on the others.

If you want to limit access to certain directories, you can select specific directories and/or drives to share. You can also go one step further and password-protect them. Then the person trying to get to that information will have to enter the correct password before access is granted.

For your computers to share a printer, you'll have to turn on the printer sharing option in Windows and you'll have to install the printer driver on all computers in the network. It doesn't matter which computer the printer is physically connected to; it will appear in the list of printer choices on all computers on the network.

SECTION B://   *making* **the grade**

1. A(n) _____ is an expansion card that connects your computer to a network and allows information to flow between your computer and the rest of the network.

2. A(n) _____ is a smart hub.

3. The operating system that runs a network is called a(n) _____.

4. The most common type of NIC is a(n) _____ card.

C://LARGE NETWORKS

You've probably heard the term "LAN." A *local area network (LAN)* is a network of computers that are contained within a limited geographic area, a building or a campus. A LAN is often a client/server network. A *client/server network* is a network in which one or more computers are servers and provide services to the other computers, which are called clients. In the small peer-to-peer networks you learned about above, all computers were equal. Each one had its own files and devices, sharable with the other computers.

As the number of computers increases, a peer-to-peer network becomes inefficient and less secure. So large organizations, businesses or educational institutions, where many people need access to the same software and information, tend to use client/server networks. It's usually cheaper and more efficient to have software on a server where everyone can access it:

- A network license allowing everyone on the network to use a software package is usually cheaper than buying separate copies of the software for each computer.
- It's easier to update one server copy of software than to update each copy separately.
- Control of software and information is easier if they're on the server.
- Viruses and other security problems are easier to control from a server because protective software can be installed there and sent out to all client computers.

did you **know?** A CPU fabrication plant is tens of thousands of times cleaner than a hospital operating room.

BUSINESS NETWORKS

How Is a Business Network Different from a Home Network?

Surprisingly, a large business network is not conceptually very different from our small home network but is much more complex in its implementation. See Figure 6.11 for two obvious differences. First, there are multiple hubs and routers, which are larger and more complex than the home models. Second, there are servers, which are usually the most powerful computers on the network. Servers have hardware, software, and/or information that the client computers can access. Servers are often dedicated to certain tasks such as e-mail or handling database access.

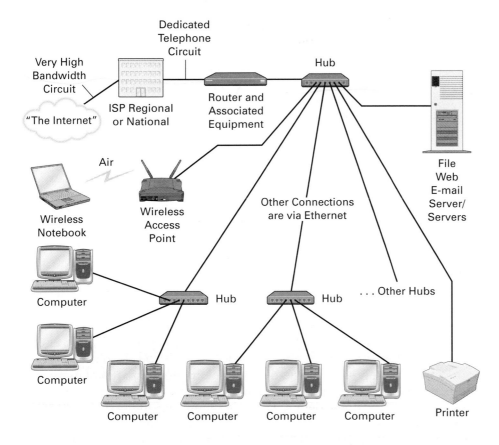

F I G U R E   6.11

A large network has more hubs and routers than a small home network and is much more complex to implement.

Saying that large networks are theoretically similar to small ones is by no means saying that they're almost as easy to build and maintain. The more computers you have, especially if they're different types, and the more scattered the computers are, the more complicated the system becomes. Volumes have been written about how networks work. Good network specialists are in great demand and command high salaries because the task is so complex. There might be literally thousands of computers in a network that must all talk to each other.

In large networks there are many, many considerations. For example, you may have to install special network processors such as multiplexors, which collect transmissions from several communications media and send them over a single line that operates at a higher capacity. You also have to consider the type of topology (how the computers are connected to each other and to the server), and what sort of protocol to use. A protocol is a "language" or a set of rules that every computer follows in communicating with the other computers. Recall that in Chapter 2 you learned about

TCP/IP (Transport Control Protocol/Internet Protocol), which is the protocol that computers connected to the Internet use to communicate.

Then there's the issue of a communications medium. You could use metal cables or fiber optic cable, very thin glass or plastic fiber through which information flows as pulses of light. Or you could go wireless and use microwave or satellite transmission. Depending on the situation you might use a combination. These are only a few of the many complications involved in running large networks.

USING A LARGE NETWORK

How Is Using a Network Different from Using My Own Computer?

Usually the first thing you notice that's different is that you have to log onto a network computer. The **network administrator,** who is the person in charge of the network, will give you your log-in name. You'll usually be allowed to choose your own password. In the I-Buy box later in this chapter you'll see some guidelines for choosing passwords.

Using software on your network computer is usually not very different from using your own home computer. Suppose your college network has a statistics software package called Minitab that you're required to use. When you double click on the Minitab icon, the program loads into your RAM. But the difference is that if Minitab is on the server, it isn't copied from your hard disk, but rather from the server computer (see Figure 6.12). You really don't notice any difference since the program is in the RAM on your computer and your information is usually being processed by the CPU in your computer. The person sitting next to you can also get a copy of the same software from the server and use it on his or her computer.

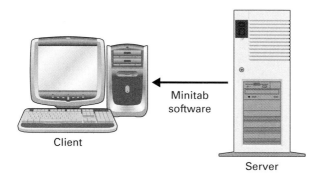

FIGURE 6.12

The Minitab software comes from the server rather than from the hard disk on the computer you're using.

Minitab software

Client

Server

Depending on how the network is configured, servers may process information for client computers. The server may be a very powerful computer, perhaps even as big and powerful as the supercomputers you learned about in Chapter 1, that client computers use for processing jobs requiring more speed or RAM than the client computer has. Then the client computer becomes just a terminal, that is, a screen and keyboard using the server's CPU, RAM, and disk space.

In a large organization, information that is needed by many people is kept on the server. Then, when someone needs it, they can access it from the server. To restrict access to certain files, the network administrator can password-protect them so that only those who are authorized can have access.

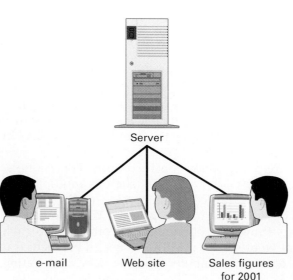

Server

e-mail

Web site

Sales figures for 2001

LARGE NETWORK OPERATING SYSTEMS

Do Network Computers Need Special Hardware and Software?

In a client/server network you'll need a special network operating system, which consists of separate software for the server and the clients. The server software handles ID tracking, requests for software and information, and devices such as printers. The client software, which must be installed on every client computer, is responsible for such tasks as sending information to the network printer and the network disk drives.

A client/server network often includes a local intranet. An intranet is a network available only to members of a business or organization (you'll learn more about intranets in Chapter 12). However, to the people using the intranet, it looks like the Internet with Internet features such as Web pages, e-mail, and so on.

WIRELESS NETWORK CONNECTIONS

How Do I Get Wireless Network Access from My Notebook Computer?

Each computer (or other device) that is to be part of the wireless network must have a wireless adapter. A *wireless adapter* for your desktop computer or a *wireless PC Card* lets you wirelessly access a network. Also, the network would have to have a wireless network access point.

A *wireless network access point* is a device that allows computers to access a wired network using radio waves (see Figure 6.13). The wireless network access point device on the network (1) transforms information into waves and sends it to the notebook and (2) receives information in the form of waves and transforms it into electrical pulses for the wired network. Each wireless network access point device has a receiver, a transmitter, and antennas to provide for bidirectional information flow. The notebook's wireless network PC Card also has a receiver and transmitter so that it can send and receive radio wave transmissions. Instead of using an infrared wireless connection of the type used for a wireless printer,

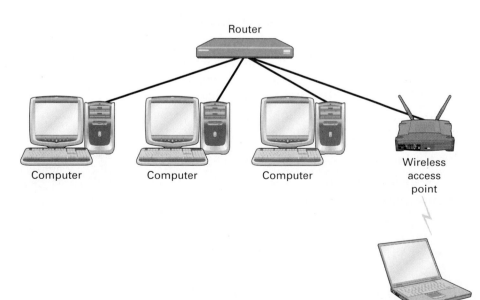

Router

Computer Computer Computer Wireless access point

Wireless notebook computer

FIGURE 6.13

A wireless access point on a network allows you to access the network without wires or cables.

notebook computers usually transmit information using radio waves. Radio and infrared waves have different frequencies.

The type of radio wave transmission often used is WiFi. **WiFi** (formerly known as IEEE 802.11b) is a way of transmitting information in radio wave form that is reasonably fast and is often used for notebooks. A relatively new and competing wireless technology for short-range wireless connections, also using radio waves, is called Bluetooth. Named for a Viking king, **Bluetooth** technology provides entirely wireless connections for all kinds of communication devices. For example, Bluetooth could replace the cable connecting a notebook computer to a cellular telephone. Virtually all digital devices, such as keyboards, joysticks, printers, and so forth, can be part of a Bluetooth system. Bluetooth is also adaptable to home appliances such as refrigerators, microwaves, and so on. To read about the latest developments in Bluetooth and WiFi technology, visit the Web for this text at www.mhhe.com/i-series (and select "Wireless Standards").

Many universities and businesses have networks with wireless network access points so that as soon as you're within range, perhaps as you enter the building, you're on the network. And you also have access to the Web if your network supports it.

SECTION C://   *making* **the grade**

1. The person in charge of a network is the _____.
2. _____ technology provides entirely wireless connections for all kinds of communication devices.
3. A network of computers contained within a small area such as a room or a building or campus is called a _____.
4. A _____ is the operating system that runs a network.

D://A SUPER-SIZED NETWORK

The largest network in the world is the Internet and it's the most familiar network for most people. The Internet is a WAN. A **wide area network (WAN)** is a network of networks that extends over a large geographic area. You can connect to the Internet with

1. A telephone modem.
2. Digital Subscriber Line (DSL).
3. A cable modem.
4. A satellite modem.
5. A wireless connection.

TELEPHONE MODEM

How Does a Telephone Modem Work?

Simply put, a telephone modem is a telephone for your computer. You use a traditional telephone to talk to other people. A computer uses a modem to communicate with other computers. For accessing the Internet, a ***telephone modem (modem)*** is a device that connects your computer through a phone line to a network of other computers. The modem lets you access your Internet service provider (ISP) via the phone line and your ISP then connects you to the Internet. Most people refer to a telephone modem simply as a "modem." A modem changes computer signals, which are digital, into phone line signals, which are analog, so that they can travel along phone lines. That is, a modem first **mo**dulates the signal. At the receiving end, another modem converts the analog signals back to digital signals. That is, it **dem**odulates them (see Figure 6.14).

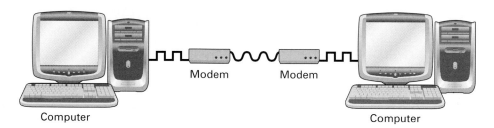

Modem   Modem

Computer   Computer

F I G U R E   6.14

A telephone modem changes outgoing computer signals, which are digital, to telephone signals, which are analog, and then reverses the process on the receiving end.

So, to access the Internet with a telephone modem, you need: (1) a telephone modem; (2) a phone line; (3) an Internet service provider; and (4) connectivity software.

Most modems today are internal modems, meaning that the modem is either built into the motherboard or is an expansion card that plugs into the motherboard. A modem expansion card plugs into either an ISA or PCI expansion slot, depending on the type of modem. New computer systems often come with a modem installed. A modem generally has two telephone jacks, called RJ-11s, which are accessible on the back panel of your computer. And you connect your modem in the same fashion as you would an answering machine. Usually you get connectivity software packaged with your modem.

A telephone modem is the slowest type of Internet connection you can get. The fastest a telephone modem can go is 56 Kbps (or 56 thousand bits per second). To get a faster connection to the Internet, you can use DSL, cable modem, a satellite modem connection, or a wireless connection.

DIGITAL SUBSCRIBER LINE (DSL)

How Does DSL Compare to Regular Phone Line Internet Access?

A **DSL (Digital Subscriber Line)** is a high-speed Internet connection using the phone line, which allows you to use your phone for voice communication at the same time. There are many kinds of DSL systems—ADSL (asymmetric DSL), SDSL (symmetric DSL), HDSL (high-bit-rate DSL), to name a few. One popular type of DSL system, ADSL, divides your phone line into three channels, one for sending information, one for receiving information, and the last one for your regular voice phone line. That means that you can talk on the phone while you're surfing the Web (see Figure 6.15).

FIGURE 6.15

A DSL modem brings you Internet access on your phone line, but you can still make calls even when you're on the Web.

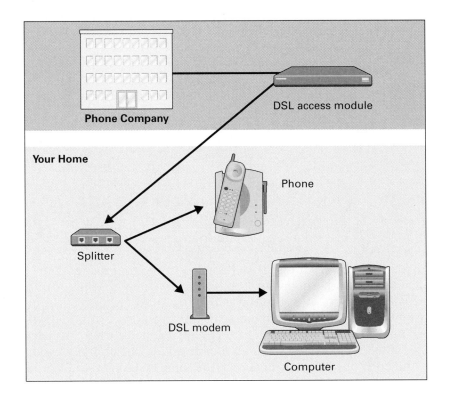

A DSL modem has four big advantages over a regular telephone modem: (1) DSL is much faster—up to 100 times faster than a phone modem; (2) DSL is usually an "always-on" connection giving you instant Internet access without having to dial in; (3) you can still use the same phone line for voice connections; and (4) if you have a home network with a router, you can use the same DSL connection for all the computers on your network.

The big drawback with DSL is that you have to live within a certain distance of your telephone company to be able to use it. That distance will determine the speed of DSL service that your phone company can offer.

CABLE MODEM

How Does a Cable Modem Work?

You know that your cable TV comes to you on a coaxial cable that connects to your TV set. This same cable can connect you to the Internet as well. Both the cable TV signal and your Internet connection travel from the cable company on one wire.

A splitter at your home routes the TV signal to your TV and the Internet connection to your cable modem. A **cable modem** is a device that uses your TV cable to produce an Internet connection (see Figure 6.16). The cable from the cable modem attaches to either an Ethernet card or a USB port (see Chapter 5) in your computer. The speed of transmission with a cable modem is between 20 and 100 times faster than a telephone modem.

A cable modem has most of the same advantages as DSL: It's faster than phone modem access, it's an always-on connection, you can still use your phone line to make calls, and you can use one Internet connection for several computers on a network. However, unlike a DSL connection, cable modem Internet access may slow down with an increase of users on the cable system.

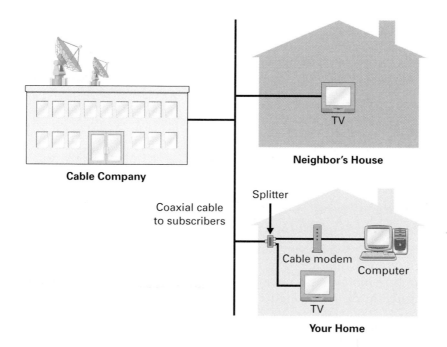

FIGURE 6.16

A cable modem gives you Internet access using the same wiring that brings you cable TV.

i·buy

The Ups and Downs of "Always-On" Internet Connections

If your Internet access is via DSL, cable modem, or satellite modem, you probably have an always-on connection, meaning that as long as your computer is on you're connected to the Internet. The up side is that you have instant access to the Internet, and the down side is that you're open to attacks by hackers.

But you can protect yourself. Your first line of defense is passwords. You can protect your files, folders, and disk drives with passwords. The longer the password the harder it is to break. Since it's not always easy to remember long passwords, you can use a phrase that means something to you and cannot be easily associated with you—perhaps something like "TryIt1MoreTime." But be advised that password-cracking software looks for specific phrases and letter

combinations, so make the phrase as obscure as you can. If you know words in a language other than English, use a phrase from that language or intersperse the English phrase with non-English words. Throw in some capitalization, digits, and punctuation for good measure. See Chapter 7 for more pointers on passwords.

A good method of protection is a firewall, which is software and/or hardware that protects you from intruders. A software firewall will inform you if someone is trying to gain access to your computer. You can set the program to allow one-time or any-time access to particular people or computers. Some firewall software is available for free.

If you have a home network, you could use a cable/DSL router as a firewall. A router makes your net-

Firewall

work more or less invisible to outsiders and can also allow several computers to share one high-speed Internet connection.

SATELLITE MODEM

Can I Get Satellite Internet Access?

Until quite recently, you could only download via satellite. But you can now get two-way Internet access from a satellite dish using a satellite modem. A **satellite modem** is a modem that allows you to get Internet access using a satellite dish (see Figure 6.17). For this, you'll need the right type of

F I G U R E   6.17

A satellite modem gives you access to the Internet via satellite.

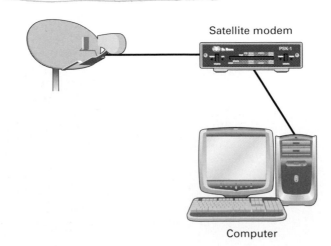

antenna (i.e., the satellite dish). You can get an antenna for Internet access alone or one that gives you both Internet access and TV reception. Then, you'll need a satellite modem, which usually plugs into a USB port. And, of course, you'll need the software to make it work. That comes with the satellite modem. To learn more about the latest developments in satellite modems, visit the Web site for this text at www.mhhe.com/i-series (and select "Internet Connections").

WIRELESS INTERNET CONNECTIONS

How Can I Get to the Internet with a Wireless Connection?

You already saw that if your notebook has a wireless PC Card and the network you're accessing has a wireless access point, you can wirelessly join that network. And if the network has Web access, you can get to it too. But what if you don't have access to such a network?

In that case, you'll still need the wireless PC Card and you'll also need a wireless Internet service provider. A **wireless Internet service provider (wireless ISP)** does the same job as a standard Internet service provider except that you don't need a wired connection for access. In fact, some ISPs provide both wired and wireless connections. If you travel a lot, you'll need a wireless ISP with a wide geographic reach, just as you do with a cellular phone.

If you want to reach the Web with something smaller than a notebook computer, you can use a hand-held wireless device such as a PDA, Web phone, or pager, which you learned about in Chapters 1 and 2. These small devices allow you to access the mobile Web or any other network that is appropriately configured for wireless communication.

PDAs will probably be the dominant hand-held wireless device of the future for Internet access. Distinctions between hand-held devices, however, are already blurring. Some manufacturers are already combining cellular phones and PDAs. Some are mostly phones with PDA capabilities, and others are PDAs with phone capabilities.

Recall from Chapter 1 that a **personal digital assistant (PDA)** is a small hand-held computer that helps you surf the Web and perform simple tasks such as note taking, calendaring and appointment scheduling, and maintaining an address book. There are two types of PDAs: (1) **Palms** and **Handspring** and (2) **PocketPCs.** The difference between Palms/Handspring and PocketPCs is similar to the difference between PCs and Macs in that they use different operating systems. The Palms/Handspring–type PDAs run on the **Palm Operating System (Palm OS),** while PocketPCs run on **Windows CE** (also called **Pocket PC OS**). Palm OS–based PDAs are more popular with about 80 percent of the market, but CE has been gaining ground.

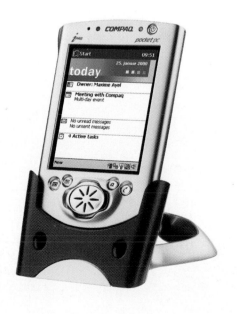

Wireless ISPs support one or the other or both, so if you plan on buying a wireless PDA for Internet access, check it out. For example, SkyWriter and YadaYada support only Palms, while OmniSky and Go.Web support both. Be sure to check on what services are available to you. And if you're going to do much traveling, you should check into what wireless ISPs cover the places you'd be visiting. On the Web site that supports this text at www.mhhe.com/i-series, we've provided a review of many wireless devices (select "Networks").

Disadvantages of Wireless Web Access

In general, don't expect to surf the Web with a hand-held wireless device the way you would with a notebook or desktop computer. The various wireless service providers use one of several standards that were designed for cell phones and, while they're fine for talking, they're too slow for good Web access. Your notebook would most likely use a faster type of wireless Internet access. The drawbacks of using hand-held devices for Web access are

- Access is very slow—this is the biggest problem.
- Access is not all that reliable.
- You won't get good readability on the small screen.
- Not all Web features are available on wireless devices (your wireless ISP determines the type and level of services you can expect to get).

Most wireless network users currently take advantage of wireless Internet service providers that offer specific services such as e-mail, games, stock quotes, travel, and so on. In fact, most (about 70 percent) of the wireless Web subscribers currently use their wireless devices for e-mail only.

Faster wireless technology is in the pipeline and improvement is expected in 2003 with the introduction of new standards. But really fast (2 megabits per second) transmission is projected to arrive three or four years later. As access becomes faster and more reliable, experts expect that about 23 million people will be using wireless devices to access the Web by the middle of the decade, compared to only 2 million in 2001.

SECTION D://   *making the grade*

1. A _____ modem is a device that connects your computer to your phone line.
2. A _____ modem is a device that uses your TV cable to deliver an Internet connection.
3. A _____ does the same job as the standard ISPs except you don't need a wired connection for access.
4. PocketPCs use the operating system _____.

E://SUMMARY AND KEY TERMS

Information inside a computer is represented with 0s and 1s called *bits.* We collect bits into groups of eight, called *bytes,* because that gives us enough patterns to represent our basic set of English-language symbols. All information stored in or used by a computer is in this binary code of 1s and 0s.

The *CPU* processes both system instructions to keep the machine running and application instructions to do the work you want done. To carry out software instructions, the CPU loads a copy of the software into *RAM.* Then it retrieves the software instructions one-by-one. The instructions travel on the *system bus* to the CPU, which carries out each one in turn. The *expansion bus* is the highway system that carries information between the CPU and devices connected to your computer.

did you know? The largest McDonald's in the world is in Moscow, Russia.

i·witness

An Up-Close Look at Web Sites

Backgrounds

You may have noticed that many Web sites you visit have different backgrounds, ranging from simple colors to textures to photos and images. Altering the background of your Web site can definitely increase its appeal. But on the other hand, it may instead be distracting. Dark backgrounds tend to make your text harder to read, and backgrounds with too many graphics can be almost blinding.

Altering the background of your Web site is a simple process—it takes only one HTML tag. To change the color of your background from the default white to blue requires the following statement at the beginning of the <BODY> section:

<BODY BGCOLOR="blue">

That's all. Simply insert the color you want between the quote marks and you're done.

Changing your background to a texture or image doesn't require much more. You simply need a .jpg file that contains the texture or image you want. The HTML statement for that is:

<BODY BACKGROUND="filename.jpg">

That's all. Simply insert the file name between the quotes that contains your texture or image.

We've provided three Web sites for you to review that use varying forms of backgrounds. These sites are

www.mhhe.com/i-series/I-Witness/6-A.html

www.mhhe.com/i-series/I-Witness/6-B.html

www.mhhe.com/i-series/I-Witness/6-C.html

Which makes the best use of a background? Which makes the worst use and why?

On the Web site for this text at www.mhhe.com/i-series, we've provided you with a list of Web sites that offer free background textures and images. Take a moment, download one you like, and insert it into your Web site.

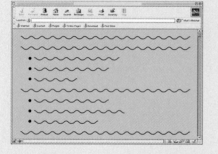

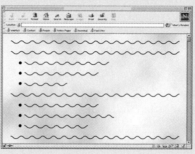

When you connect computers together you create a **computer network.** Generally, each computer on a network has a **network interface card (NIC),** a connecting device such as a hub or router, a connecting medium such as cable, and an operating system that supports networking. A **peer-to-peer network** is a network in which a small number of computers share information and hardware.

A **client/server network,** on the other hand, has one or more computers called servers that provide services to the other computers, called clients. Large business networks are usually client/server networks with multiple hubs and/or routers. Business networks are very complex and require highly skilled individuals to build and maintain them.

Wireless connections are usually infrared for devices such as printers and mice. For short-range communication, notebook computers usually use **WiFi.** A competing wireless standard is **Bluetooth.**

To join the largest network in the world—the Internet—you can use a **telephone modem,** a **DSL modem,** a **cable modem,** a **satellite modem,** or a wireless connection. DSL, cable modems, and satellite modems are faster than telephone modems. Wireless Internet access for hand-held devices is still slow since it uses technology developed for voice communications.

On the Web site that supports this text at www.mhhe.com/i-series, you can find more information about topics in this chapter, including:

- Satellite modems.
- Bluetooth and WiFi.
- Internet service providers.
- CPUs and RAM.
- Hand-held devices.
- Sites with free images and backgrounds.

KEY TERMS

AGP (accelerated graphics port) bus (p. 6.9)

AGP slot (p. 6.9)

arithmetic logic unit (ALU) (p. 6.7)

ASCII (American Standard Code for Information Interchange) (p. 6.3)

bit (binary digit) (p. 6.2)

Bluetooth (p. 6.18)

byte (p. 6.3)

cable modem (p. 6.21)

cache (p. 6.8)

Cat 5 (Category 5 cable, Ethernet cable) (p. 6.13)

central processing unit (CPU, microprocessor, processor) (p. 6.4)

client/server network (p. 6.14)

clock cycle (p. 6.7)

computer network (p. 6.11)

CPU clock (p. 6.7)

DSL (Digital Subscriber Line) (p. 6.20)

EBCDIC (p. 6.3)

Ethernet card (p. 6.12)

expansion board (or card) (p. 6.9)

expansion bus (p. 6.8)

expansion slot (p. 6.9)

Handspring (p. 6.23)

interface hardware (p. 6.9)

ISA (industry standard architecture) bus (p. 6.9)

ISA slot (p. 6.9)

local area network (LAN) (p. 6.14)

machine cycle (CPU cycle) (p. 6.7)

network administrator (p. 6.16)

network hub (p. 6.13)

network interface card (NIC) (p. 6.12)

network operating system (NOS) (p. 6.13)

Palm (p. 6.23)

Palm Operating System (Palm OS) (p. 6.23)

PCI (peripheral component interconnect) bus (p. 6.9)

PCI slot (p. 6.9)

peer-to-peer network (p. 6.12)

personal digital assistant (PDA) (p. 6.23)

PocketPC (p. 6.23)

RJ-45 connector (Ethernet connector) (p. 6.13)

router (p. 6.13)

satellite modem (p. 6.22)

system bus (p. 6.8)

telephone modem (modem) (p. 6.19)

Unicode (p. 6.3)

wide area network (WAN) (p. 6.18)

WiFi (p. 6.18)

Windows CE (Pocket PC OS) (p. 6.23)

wireless adapter (wireless PC Card) (p. 6.17)

wireless network access point (p. 6.17)

wireless Internet service provider (wireless ISP) (p. 6.23)

CROSSWORD PUZZLE

Across

2. Contraction of binary digit
7. This bus moves information to and from peripheral devices
9. A server on a network provides services to this type of computer
10. This type of card lets you connect to a network
12. CPU _____—the component that synchronizes CPU cycles
13. Short-term, waiting-room memory
14. Has over 65,000 different patterns for 1's and 0's
17. Is a type of operating system for a PDA
18. American Standard Code for Information Interchange
19. A small hand-held computer
21. The device that connects computers into a network

Down

1. This bus moves information between the CPU and RAM
2. A standard for radio wave transmission over short distances
3. A standard for wireless transmission of information
4. A network that you might find in a building
5. A wireless network _____ point lets you connect wirelessly to a network
6. You can get Internet access this way
8. Eight bits
11. The card that each computer on a network must have
15. The type of modem that lets you access the Internet using your TV cable
16. You can talk on the phone and still use the phone line for Internet access with this
17. These expansion slots are usually white
18. This slot is for an AGP video card
20. A part of the CPU that does arithmetic

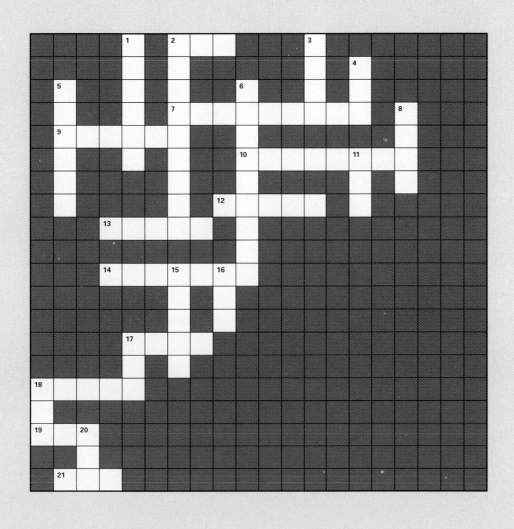

QUESTIONS AND EXERCISES

Multiple Choice

1. A computer's CPU performs two types of tasks. They are
   a. accessing the hard disk and running the printer.
   b. keeping the computer running and performing the tasks you specify.
   c. turning the computer on and off.
   d. none of the above.
   e. all of the above.

2. A bit is
   a. a 1 or a 0.
   b. a contraction of binary digit.
   c. the form that information is in within your computer.
   d. all of the above.
   e. none of the above.

3. A client/server network is
   a. a network in which all the computers are equal.
   b. a network which has one or more computers that provide services to the other computers, called clients.
   c. the traffic cop in that it directs information around the motherboard.
   d. a device that carries information between the CPU and RAM.
   e. none of the above.

4. The expansion bus is
   a. composed of lots of different types of buses.
   b. the same as the system bus.
   c. in the CPU.
   d. a device that carries information between the CPU and RAM.
   e. none of the above.

5. Unicode is
   a. used in IBM mainframe computers.
   b. an 8-bit set of patterns.
   c. a 16-bit set of patterns.
   d. a type of RAM chip.
   e. none of the above.

6. The PCI bus is
   a. the most common type of bus.
   b. one that usually incorporates several slots.
   c. often where you plug in a sound card.
   d. often where you plug in a modem card.
   e. all of the above.

7. A technology that provides wireless connections is called
   a. Bluetooth.
   b. routing.
   c. a wide area network.
   d. Cat 5.
   e. none of the above.

8. Communication that travels without cables is called
   a. wireless.
   b. Cat 5 cable.
   c. fiber optic cable.
   d. NIC cable.
   e. network cable.

9. You can get wireless Web access from
   a. a notebook.
   b. a PDA.
   c. a Web phone.
   d. a pager.
   e. all of the above.

10. Wireless Internet access is
    a. slow.
    b. very cheap.
    c. limited compared to desktops.
    d. not possible yet.
    e. none of the above.

True/False

11. __T__ The CPU is also called a processor.

12. __T__ A byte is 8 bits.

13. __F__ An intranet is a network that a business sets up for its customers.

14. __T__ A DSL modem allows you to have Internet access over your phone line and talk on the phone at the same time.

15. __F__ A PDA is larger than a breadbox.

QUESTIONS AND EXERCISES

1. Match the computer terms on the left to the non-computer terms on the right.

COMPUTER TERMS	NON-COMPUTER TERMS
A. 1 or 0	Doctor's waiting room
B. ALU	The New York subway
C. CPU	Light switch
D. Cache	Brain
E. Expansion bus	Calculator
F. Computer network	Metronome
G. CPU clock	Professional organization

2. For each of the following answers, create the question:

ANSWER

QUESTION

A. It has enough 1s and 0s to represent one English character.

B. The coding system used for languages that need more than 256 patterns.

C. The coding system that most personal computers and minicomputers use.

D. It's a network that has one or more computers that provide services to the others.

E. You can talk to your brother on the phone and simultaneously buy him a birthday present from a Web site using this type of connection.

F. It carries information to and from the expansion cards in the PCI slots.

G. A network of a few computers that allows computers to share hardware and information.

H. 48

I. The most common type of network interface card.

J. This one computer has special duties.

K. Performance degrades as more people access the Web by this method.

e-commerce

1. Buying Gifts

Most online stores will send gifts to other people for you. Many will gift-wrap your purchases for you before sending them out. Often they will also keep the names and addresses of people you send presents to in case you need them in the future. Visit these sites, then answer the questions that follow:

- Wish List—www.wishlist.com
- The WeddingChannel.com— www.weddingchannel.com
- The Wedding Registry for the Environmentally Conscious—www.wedding-registry.net
- Gifts of History—www.giftsofhistory.com

a. Are the gifts on the site for a special occasion?

b. Are the gifts on the site for a particular type of product? If so, what product or class of products?

c. Are the gifts for a particular market segment, such as families with babies or pet owners?

2. Buying Clothes/Return Policies

Buying clothes on the Internet is similar to buying them by mail order in that you can't try them on first. To overcome this problem, most e-tailers, like mail-order merchants, let you send garments or shoes back if, for any reason, you don't want to keep them.

Look at four clothing and/or shoe e-tailers and answer the questions below. You can use your own preferred Web sites or the ones that follow:

- Eddie Bauer—www.eddiebauer.com
- Old Navy—www.oldnavy.com
- Nordstrom—www.nordstrom.com
- Nike—www.nike.com
- Customatix.com—www.customatix.com

a. Does the site have a measurement guide explaining the measurements that correspond to sizes?

b. Does the site tell you whether you can get your money back or store credit only?

c. Can you design your own shoes at the shoe sites? (*Hint:* Try the Customatix.com Web site.) Can you return the shoes if you find you don't like them?

d. Do the shoe sites have detailed foot-measuring methods?

3. Cruises

How would you like to take a cruise to Bora Bora or sail around the Cape of Good Hope? If days or weeks on a large ship with wonderful food, lots of leisure activities, blue sky above you, and green sea all around you add up to your idea of fun, you can use the Internet to set it all up.

However, a word of caution here. One of the top-10 online scams, according to the Federal Trade Commission, is the sale of vacations that turn out to be less than promised or even nonexistent, so be wary of any deal that looks too good to be true—it probably is.

e-commerce

You can book cruises at most of the usual online travel agencies such as Expedia.com, Travelocity.com, and so on. You can also book directly from cruise specialists.

Try these Web sites, then answer the following questions:

- Carnival Cruises—www.carnival.com
- Travelocity—www.travelocity.com
- Expedia—www.expedia.com

a. What was the longest cruise you could find?

b. How much did it cost?

c. What was the cheapest cruise you could find?

d. Did the cost include airfare to the port of departure?

e. Did the site offer a money-back guarantee?

4. Reading Books Online

If you like reading, you'll be pleased to know that you can find a wealth of reading material on the Web. You can download books onto your computer and read them on-screen or print out the pages. On some sites you can read the book right there on the Web site. If you'd like to have a more portable online book, you can buy an e-book, which is a little hand-held screen into which you can download books. You can then take the e-book with you on a plane flight, to bed, up into the hills, or wherever you like to read. You can also download a book to your PDA.

For e-book reading devices check out www.eBook-Gemstar.com. With an e-book reading device you can read in the traditional manner, but you get more than just words on a screen. You can do key word searches, make annotations, and consult a built-in dictionary. eBook-Gemstar even has a built-in modem so that you can download books using the phone line. There's enough memory for about 20 books and you can upgrade to many times more than that. A big advantage of online books is that you can adjust the text size to suit your needs.

Look at these sites, then answer the following questions for each site:

- Glassbook—www.glassbook.com
- CyberRead—www.cyberread.com
- eBooks 'n Bytes—www.ebooksnbytes.com

a. Do these sites let you download to your computer or do you need an e-book device?

b. Can you read the book online at these sites?

c. Do you have to pay for the online book?

d. If you have to pay for the book, can you read a sample and can you get book reviews?

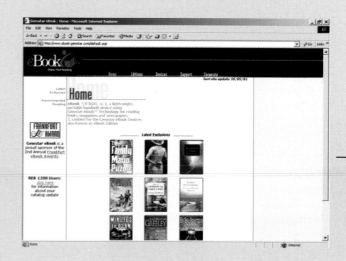

on the web

1. Researching Cache Memory

Cache memory is special memory where instructions that are likely to be needed by the CPU stay during processing. The purpose of cache is to speed up processing by keeping instructions closer to the CPU so that a minimum of time is lost by the CPU waiting for instructions to come all the way from RAM. Computers are sold with different amounts of cache. Look at Web sites that sell computers and see what they say about cache memory.

2. Finding the Right PDA

Look for wireless devices on the Web. Go to a site that sells electronic devices and compare four PDAs according to

a. Price.

b. Amount of memory included.

c. Price of additional memory.

3. Finding Parallel-Processing Computers

Some motherboards allow for multiple CPUs. This is called parallel processing. Parallel processing has been the norm in supercomputers for quite some time now, but this technology has only recently become available to the average computer user's PC. To take advantage of parallel processing, you need a motherboard with multiple processor sockets (with processors in them, of course) and an operating system (some versions of Windows for example) which can handle more than one processor. Then you'll need to use application software that knows how to utilize parallel processing. Look at some Web sites that sell computers and see if you can find any that advertise parallel processors or that are parallel-processor ready.

4. Researching Video Cards

On the Web, find four different video cards. How much does each one cost? How much memory does each one have? What special features do these video cards offer that might interest you?

5. Notebook Docking Stations

If you have a notebook computer, you might want a docking station. Find three different docking stations on the Web and compare them under the following headings:

a. Price.

b. Connectors (how many and what kind).

c. Extra features.

6. Firewall Software

Find three different firewall software packages on the Web. A good place to start looking would be the sites that sell anti-virus software. Compare the firewall software on price and features.

7. Satellite Internet Access

Find out about satellite Internet access. For example, try Direct PC at www.directpc.com and find out where its service is available and how much it costs. Find out if you have to buy a special satellite dish.

ethics, security & privacy

1. Using Software to "Categorize" People

Although companies have always offered preferential treatment to their more profitable customers, the speed and capacity of computers today are making the segmenting of customers possible to a degree unheard of just a few years ago. Businesses now have the ability to gauge whether individual customers are worth the trouble of making them happy. For example, if you called the bank that issued you your credit card and said that you didn't want to pay the annual fee any more, the bank could look at your activity and decide whether your business is worth giving in on the annual fee issue.

Visa uses this type of software as a way to help the company spot fraud and to determine which of their customers might default or go bankrupt. The First Union Bank has software that categorizes people into red, green, and yellow depending on the customer's history and value to the bank. Customers who are "green" might get better credit card rates than customers who are "red" and are judged to add less to the bank's bottom line.

Financial institutions are not the only ones doing this. Catalina Supermarkets, for example, keeps track of which customers buy which products, how frequently, and what price they pay. The supermarket chain has increased its percentage of high-value customers by offering them services such as free home delivery.

The movie business is also getting in on the act. Twentieth Century Fox slices and dices the information in its databases to determine the most popular movies, actors, and plots in certain theaters, cities, and areas of the country. The result, however, may be that people in certain areas will not get the chance to see certain movies.

There was a time when certain neighborhoods or geographic regions were "redlined" by lending institutions and others. That meant that banks and other businesses wouldn't deal with anyone who lived in the redlined areas. Some people think that electronic market segmentation or customer categorization is a new form of redlining. Following are some questions for you to answer regarding this practice.

a. Do you think that the segmentation practices described above are fair?

b. Do you think you should get better treatment if you're a better customer?

c. How do you feel about being pigeonholed by computer software?

d. Would it help if you knew what the criteria were and how the determination was made?

e. Is it reasonable to predict future behavior of customers based on their previous actions?

f. Is this the same as redlining, or is it okay because it categorizes individuals by actual behavior rather than by assuming characteristics because of membership in a particular group?

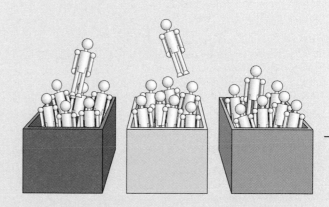

group activities

1. Your School's Network Workings

Find out what kind of network your school has. Ask the technical people how many computers are on the network, and how many hubs and routers they use. Determine what role the server computer or computers play in supporting the needs of people on the network.

2. Your Access to the Internet

Write a report on what sort of Internet connections are available close to you. How many ISPs offer telephone modem access? Is DSL available to you? Is it available to anyone in your area? Does your cable company offer a cable modem? Compare each available service on price and on extras such as a help line, or people who will come out to your home and help you if you're having difficulties. What type of Internet connection do you currently use? Do you plan to upgrade in the future? If so, to what type of connection? If not, why not?

3. Researching Bluetooth

Research Bluetooth technology. What companies are committed to this new wireless protocol? Can you find any home appliances that are already, or are shortly scheduled to be, outfitted with Bluetooth? What household appliances would you most like to run with a remote control (other than the TV)?

4. Researching Server Computers

Compare a high-end desktop computer designed to be a network server and a typical computer designed for a single individual. What's the difference in the CPU chips? What's the difference in price? How many CPUs are there in the server? Is there a difference in the memory (the amount and type) in the two machines? How about the hard disk drives? Is there any sort of automatic backup on the server? Would you like such an automatic backup system on your computer? Why or why not?

5. Wireless Web Access

Find out whether any ISPs in your area offer wireless Web access. Find out what type of transmission standards the ISP supports (TDMA, GSM, or CDMA). If no company in your area offers wireless Web access, then check three cellular phone companies and find out which of the above standards they use.

6. Build Your Own Network

Investigate how much it would cost you to build your own home network. Assume you have the computers already and just need to link them together. Find prices for hubs and routers on the Web. Also research Ethernet cards and cables. If you were to get a high-speed Internet connection, such as a cable modem or DSL modem, how much would it cost? Can you buy your own or would you have to rent the modems from the phone or cable company?

Looking Back/Looking Ahead

The Life and Times of a Dot-Com Entrepreneur

Joann now knows a bit more about how computers and networks work. The CPU gets instructions one by one from _____ and processes them. Information moves around the motherboard on _____. There are two types of buses. The first is a _____ bus, which moves information between the CPU and RAM, and the second is the _____ bus, which moves information to and from connectors and the expansion slots.

If Joann wants an Internet connection (and who doesn't?) she has several choices. One is to get a _____, which uses the phone line. With this connection, she won't be able to talk on the phone while she's on the Internet. However, she could also get a _____, which would bring an Internet connection through a satellite dish or a _____ modem connection where her Internet access would come with her cable TV.

Joann doesn't think that her business is big enough to need a _____ network. She doesn't have enough computers or departments to need a server to provide services to the other computers. But she might get a _____ network so that all her computers can use the same color laser printer.

Joann realizes that she and her business are a part of a very interconnected world. So, she wants to run her business in the most ethical way and protect it from people who do not consider ethics to be important. She'll learn about ethics, security, and privacy in Chapter 7.

What Joann would also like to know about is how files and databases work and how application systems are developed. She would also like to know more about how businesses leverage information technology for competitive advantage. All these topics are coming up shortly.

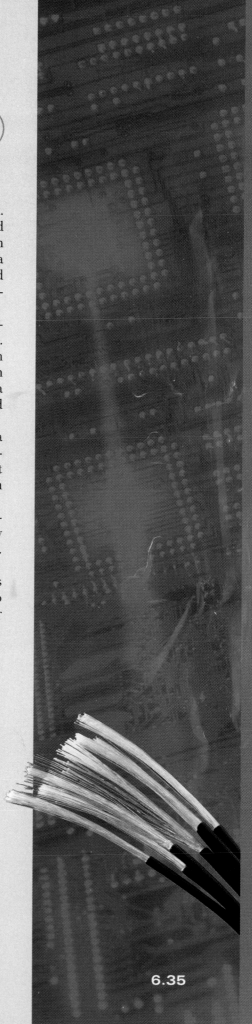

did you
know?

The widespread use of computers brings us enormous power and freedom from drudgery but also a new kind of vulnerability to observation by others.

in *March 2000 the* Business Week/*Harris Poll reported that 57 percent of the population wants the government to pass laws on how personal information is collected.*

the *U.S. Federal Trade Commission (FTC) says that 92 percent of Americans are concerned about misuse of their personal information.*

a Time *magazine poll found that 95 percent of Americans believe that employers should not be allowed to listen in on their employees' phone conversations.*

the *lie detector was outlawed in 1988 as a preemployment screening device because of its notorious inaccuracy.*

the *American Management Association found that 78 percent of large U.S. businesses monitor their employees' communications.*

most *hackers are young men aged ??   to ?? *

To find out how old a typical hacker is, visit www.mhhe.com/i-series.

CHAPTER

7

seven

Ethics, Security, and Privacy

What's Right, What's Wrong, and How Can You Protect Yourself?

The "gift of fire" is how Sara Baase describes computers in her book on computers and ethics. Like fire, computers are a tremendous force for good. Computers free you from all sorts of paperwork drudgery. They enable you to do so many things faster and better. They give you convenience and accessibility. Computers even save lives: Without computers, many of the diagnostic and corrective medical procedures in use today wouldn't be possible. However, as with fire, there's a downside. Computers can be used as weapons to cause harm, to steal, to hurt people.

In this chapter we'll examine the ethical use of computers, good manners in cyberspace, privacy, how computers are used to commit crimes, and how you can protect yourself.

A://ETHICS AND MANNERS

Computers are tools that you use to communicate and interact with other people. What you do when you interact with other people affects them in ways big and small. Our societal rules regarding how we interact with one another fall into two categories:

- *Ethics* covers those actions that have serious consequences in the lives of others. These are the sorts of actions that you label "right" or "wrong."
- *Manners* color our day-to-day behavior toward others in situations whose effects are not likely to be far-reaching. These are behaviors you might label either "polite" or "rude."

Ethics and manners are the rules and guidelines that evolve over time in a society with the objective of enhancing our human coexistence. Ethics provide you with a measure of protection from the darker side of human nature while manners make day-to-day living more pleasant.

ETHICS IN THE USE OF COMPUTERS
How Do I Use My Computer Ethically?

Your behavior in using computers is an extension of your sense of ethics in other parts of your life. As an ethical person, you try to live by certain principles, but from time to time you'll face ethical dilemmas, which are situations in which determining what the "right thing" is becomes a difficult matter. Ethical dilemmas usually arise in situations in which you have to reconcile conflicting demands, responsibilities, and goals.

Consider this dilemma: A young woman is engaged to a young man who has developed a medical condition that causes him constant pain. Medicine is available to treat this illness and relieve the pain, but it's very expensive and the young man doesn't have insurance to cover it. The young woman hasn't much money either. If the man had the medicine he could lead an almost normal life, but without it he's seriously disabled. The young woman has the skills necessary to break into the local pharmacy's computer and get the medicine. She knows how to alter the records to show that the medicine is paid for and get it sent to her fiancé.

But she knows that hacking (breaking into someone else's computer) and theft are unethical—not to mention illegal. On the other hand, someone she cares deeply for is suffering and she has the ability to fix it quickly and easily. What does she do? That will depend on her ethics.

did you **know?** **About** *2 billion people in the world have no steady supply of electric power.*

Ethics is the set of principles and standards we use in deciding what to do in situations that affect other people. Sometimes these principles are so strongly and widely held that they have become laws. Murder is an example. In cyberspace, the same ethical rules that apply in the brick-and-mortar world also apply.

In general we can say that it's unethical to

- Use your computer to harm others. It may or may not be illegal, but it's certainly unethical.
- Use your computer to steal.
- Abuse your power. As is true in the brick-and-mortar world, in cyberspace certain people know and can do more than others. However, the ability to do something doesn't give you the right to do it.
- Use or access someone else's computer resources without permission.
- Copy copyrighted software either for your own use or to give to others. It's also illegal. This is the law that's probably broken the most often in the world of computing.

Copyright

A *copyright* is a type of legal protection accorded to intellectual property (see Figure 7.1). A copyright protects an expression of an idea. Many people who write music copyright their compositions. A copyright means that although other people may of course use the same musical notes or even phrases in their creations, no one else can sell music that is too similar to the copyrighted tune or song. Again, if you invent a cool video game and you copyright it, you can't prevent others from developing their own video games, but they can't sell a game that looks too much like yours.

Furthermore, you can't just borrow or tape copyrighted material for your own use. It's illegal to copy a copyrighted video game or other software, a picture, text, video, or anything else, without permission, whether it's on the Internet or not. This would be making someone else's expression of an idea your own without asking permission or paying to do so.

Fair Use Doctrine

Having a copyright doesn't mean that you have absolute rights to your intellectual product under every circumstance. There are certain exceptions. For example, a TV program could show your video game without your permission. This would be an example of the use of copyrighted material for the creation of new material—the TV program—and, under the Fair Use Doctrine, it's perfectly legal.

The *Fair Use Doctrine* defines the situations in which copyrighted material may be used. These include when copyrighted work is used in the creation of new work and, within certain limits, when it is used for teaching purposes. Generally, the determining factor in copyright disputes is whether the copyright holder has been or is likely to be denied income based on the infringement. Courts will also consider other factors such as how much of

F I G U R E   7.1

You may not copy copyrighted material without permission.

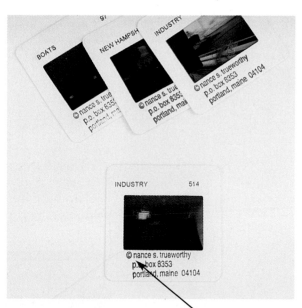

If you see this symbol, it's protected by a copyright.

the work was used and for what purpose. For instance, a teacher may copy only a specified amount, or number of words, of a story or book to hand out to students without getting permission from the author.

When you buy copyrighted software, what you're paying for is the right for you, the buyer, to use it. Generally, by breaking the shrink-wrap on the package you're agreeing to the copyright statement. Actual copyright terms vary among software publishers. Some software companies state emphatically that you may not install the software on more than one computer—even if the additional computers are yours and no one else ever uses them. Other companies allow you to put a copy of the same software on multiple machines—as long as only one person is using the given software package at any one time.

To copy software and give it to a friend in violation of the copyright statement would be copyright infringement and the copy is pirated software. ***Pirated software*** is copyrighted software that is copied and distributed without permission of the owner. Furthermore, copyright law demands that you protect copyrighted material, so knowingly letting someone make a copy of your computer game would violate copyright law as much as if you had done the copying yourself. Not all software is copyrighted, however. Software can also be shareware, freeware, or public domain (see Figure 7.2). Refer back to Chapter 3 for details. For more on downloadable freeware and shareware, visit www.mhhe.com/i-series.

FIGURE   7.2

The creator of the software determines what others may do with it.

Type	Your Rights
Copyright	Buy a license to use it
Shareware	Try before you buy
Freeware	Use, copy, share
Public domain	Use, copy, share, sell

There's one universal exception to all software copyright statements. You may always make one copy of copyrighted software to keep for backup purposes. After that, the number of legal copies you may make depends on the copyright agreement that comes with the software package.

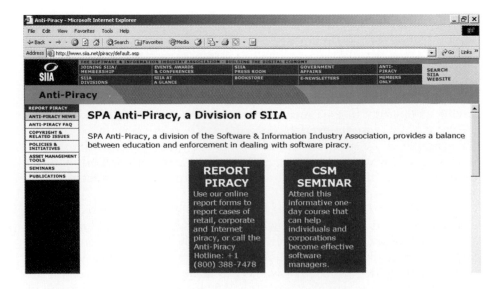

CYBER-MANNERS

Are There Any Guidelines Concerning How I Should Behave in Cyberspace?

Ethics address the serious issues of what's right and wrong in how we treat each other. But we also have another set of rules for human behavior applicable in common situations that are less consequential. These we refer to as good manners. Good manners are the guidelines for everyday

General Cyberspace Netiquette

DO

- DO remember that in cyberspace people deserve the same courtesy and respect that you would give them in the brick-and-mortar world.
- DO use unambiguous date formats. For example, January 2, 2001, should not be written as 1-2-2001, since a large part of the world would write the same date as 2.1.2001.
- DO remember that people can't see you and get cues from your body language. Make sure it's clear if you mean a comment as irony or sarcasm. You can do this by including emoticons, like a smile :-), to indicate that what you wrote is meant to be funny and not critical.

DON'T

- DON'T expect people to answer you immediately or to feel as strongly about issues as you do. Your projects, opinions, requests, and e-mail are not everyone else's top priority.
- DON'T overuse acronyms such as FYI (for your information), IMHO (in my humble/honest opinion), and BTW (by the way). They can be very annoying. And annoying people is bad manners.
- DON'T use offensive language. And DON'T call people names.
- DON'T ever give your user ID or password to another person.

E-Mail Netiquette

DO

- DO be careful what you say about others. Remember how easy it is to forward e-mail.
- DO be careful about addressing e-mail. Sometimes it looks as if e-mail is going to one person when you're actually sending it to many.
- DO put a subject heading in your e-mail that gives the receiver a good idea of what the e-mail is about. It's a good idea to send only one message per e-mail.
- DO edit out irrelevant parts of messages that you're quoting to others.
- DO take e-mail messages off the server and, if you want to save them, keep them on your own hard disk or some other storage medium.

DON'T

- DON'T ever assume that your e-mail is private. If you wouldn't write your message on a post card, don't put it in e-mail. E-mail gets stored at various points on its journey to you, so it's not at all a private communication.
- DON'T send copies of everything to everyone you know. You're wasting their time if you do, and that's bad manners.
- DON'T send huge attachments to your e-mail friends. Many e-mail systems don't allow attachments larger than about 1 MB and even if they do, the recipient may have to take a lot of time to complete the download. It's useful to include the size of the file in the e-mail message so that the receiver will know what to expect.
- DON'T forward personal e-mail to mailing lists or Usenet without the author's permission.
- DON'T capitalize words in e-mails except for helpful emphasis. Capital letters can be the equivalent of shouting, and seem very rude.
- DON'T send off-color jokes or pictures to anyone with whom you don't have a close personal relationship.

To find more netiquette guidelines, visit www.mhhe.com/i-series.

i·series insights

Ethics, Security & Privacy

The E-Mail You Send Can Get You Fired

When you use e-mail, remember that it's not private. There are no laws protecting e-mail like those that protect snail mail. If you are using the company computer system at your job to send e-mail, be aware that your employer has the right to monitor your messages. Courts have consistently ruled in favor of employers in cases involving employer monitoring of employee e-mail.

Many people have lost their jobs because they thought their e-mail at work was private. Here are some recent examples.

- The *New York Times* fired more than 20 people for sending or forwarding e-mail that the paper considered offensive.

- The First Union Bank fired 7 employees for the same reason.

- The Dow Chemical Company investigated complaints about inappropriate e-mail and as a result of the inquiry, hundreds of employees stood accused of sending and receiving such e-mail. When it was all over, 50 employees had been fired, some of whom had worked for Dow for more than 10 years.

- The Nissan Motor Corporation fired two people who received and saved sexually suggestive messages.

Apart from getting you fired, what you write in an e-mail can also be used against you in a court of law. For example, in 1991, a police officer involved in the Rodney King beating sent an e-mail message to a friend stating that he hadn't beaten anyone that badly in a long time. He mistakenly thought his e-mail was private. Of course, he was mistaken about a lot of things.

When deciding what to put into an e-mail message, a good policy to follow is "if in doubt, leave it out." If you don't, it could cost you your job.

---

behavior that enable people to live together in relative harmony. Good manners, sometimes called etiquette, grace the spirit of human interaction. We know what good table manners are—at the least you don't throw your food at the cook just because you don't like the taste of it. We have manners for shopping—it's not polite to shove someone out of the way because that person is not paying fast enough at the checkout counter. We also have rules for behavior in cyberspace—sometimes referred to as "netiquette." **Netiquette** is good manners or courtesy in cyberspace.

The guiding principles in netiquette, as in good manners in general, are consideration and respect. It's easy to forget that interaction in cyberspace is between human beings because you can't see the other people. But it's important to remember that the person you're communicating with has real feelings and sensitivities. The old adage that "sticks and stones may break my bones, but names can never hurt me" is simply not true. The hurt from words can be very strong and can last a long, long time, especially if the words are in written form. The Golden Rule can help here: Treat others as you would have them treat you. For more specific guidelines, refer back to Figure 7.3 on page 7.5.

making the grade

1. The set of principles and standards we use in determining what to do in situations that affect other people is called _____.

2. The _____ says that copyrighted material may be used in certain specified situations.

3. When you buy copyrighted software, you're buying only the _____ to use it.

4. _____ is copyrighted software that is copied and distributed without the permission of the owner.

B://THREATS IN CYBERSPACE

Computers are weapons and targets of computer crime. They're weapons in that computers are used to steal money, customer lists, personal identities, credit card numbers, and so on. They're used to spread rumors, harass people, and snoop into private files. None of these are new crimes of course; they've just taken on a new, electronic form.

Computers are also the targets of computer crime. Some people, popularly called hackers, make determined efforts to get access to other people's computers. Their reasons vary. Some hackers merely want to prove they can break in, others want to cause annoyance or damage, and still others want to steal information.

First we'll take a look at the ways in which people use computers to commit crimes, and then we'll examine some of the exploits of hackers.

Downloading Credit Card Numbers and PINs Now...

COMPUTERS AS WEAPONS

How Can People Steal Online?

Theft by computer takes many forms. It could be credit card fraud, identity theft, or some sort of scam.

Credit Card Theft

Stealing your credit card number, rather than the card itself, is much safer for thieves. If you notice your credit card is missing, you'd inform the credit card company and have the card canceled. But if someone steals just the number, you have no way of knowing that your card has been compromised—until you get the bill. Thieves can get your credit card number in one of several ways.

- First, thieves can use skimmers, which are small devices that scan the number off credit cards. The drawback is that the thieves have to get your name and address elsewhere.

- Second, they can buy magnetic strip readers, which read the name, number, expiration date, and a unique code off the card as well as the number.
- Third, they can sometimes break into databases of credit card bureaus, banks, or other institutions that keep credit card records.

When you shop on the Internet, be sure you're on a secure site before you volunteer your credit card number. It's possible for thieves to get credit card numbers that are traveling from one computer to another unless the information is encrypted (converted into a secret code). To decrypt, or read the code, the receiving Web site must have the decryption key. You'll usually see a warning box that pops up before you enter a secure site (see Figure 7.4). You'll know the site is secure if you see an "s" on the end of the http (https://) (see Figure 7.5). Your Web browser will also usually show a little padlock in the bottom right-hand corner.

A person armed with your social security number, driver's license, and a fake credit card can get credit or debit cards in your name. Experts estimate that this happens to 1,000 people in the United States every day. Theft costs all of us a lot of money, since to cover the cost of purchases made on stolen or faked credit cards, credit card companies raise interest rates and charges.

Identity Theft

Imagine that you've been working and earning money for 20 years. You've always paid your bills on time and have a very good credit rating. Now imagine a thief trolling for a good mark. This person is looking for someone like you—a person with good credit.

So, having found you, the thief steals your financial identity and becomes you—on paper. This is when your problems start and you probably

FIGURE 7.4

Sites that encrypt information will let you know that their sites are secure.

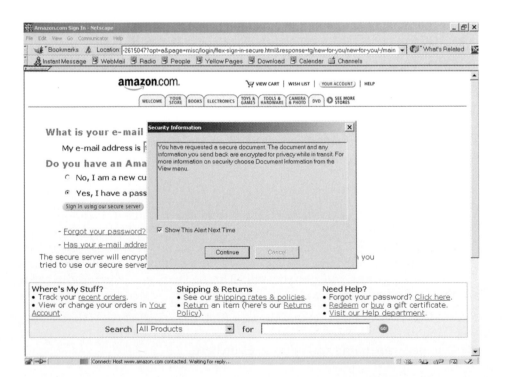

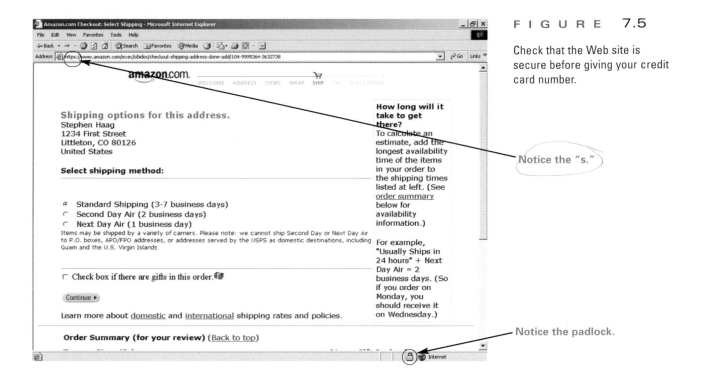

F I G U R E   7.5

Check that the Web site is
secure before giving your credit
card number.

won't even know it. The thief runs up a huge credit card debt, takes out
loans, writes bad checks, travels to exotic destinations, all the while pre-
tending to be you, financially speaking.

Then one day you find your financial reputation is ruined. You can't
cash a check, your credit cards are refused, and you can't get a bank loan.
This is when you discover that you've become the vic-
tim of identity theft. **Identity theft** is the impersonation by a thief of someone with good credit. The thief
essentially uses the victim's credit to steal products
and services. If you're the victim, you won't usually
have to pay the debts, but your financial good name
no longer exists. Often times, your only choice is to
shut yourself down financially. That means you have
to start building a good financial reputation again.
And it's not that simple. It's hard to get a second social
security number and driver's license since these numbers are designed to stay with you for life.

Since social security numbers are the key to finding almost all other information about you, experts
suggest that you be very careful with your social security number and not use it as your driver's license
number or have it printed on your checks.

Dot-Cons

Many criminals who used to operate in the brick-and-mortar world have moved their operations to cyberspace, and new crooks have joined them. There, they can work in a more protected, more comfortable environment. The scams they perpetrate include get-rich-quick schemes, travel and vacation fraud, phone fraud, health care fraud, and many others. Here are some specific examples:

- Buy and sell votes: During the 2000 presidential election, a Chicago-based Web site was offering a "presidential vote auction." In other words, you could sell your vote, which, incidentally, is illegal. Payment was offered ($12.38 for an Illinois vote and $19.61 for a California vote) in exchange for a promise to vote a certain way.

- The CD-Universe blackmail case: Criminals broke into CD-Universe's customer database and stole thousands of credit card numbers. They then threatened the company that they would publish the credit card list on the Internet unless CD-Universe paid them ransom money. The company refused and the criminals duly published the credit card numbers.

- McDonald's payroll system: This case involved a 15-year-old who broke into McDonald's payroll records and gave raises to his friends.

- Stock price manipulation: A junior college student put false rumors on the Internet about Emulex Corporation, a California-based technology company. The stock price plummeted and he bought up lots of stock. When the panic subsided and the price went back up, he sold the stock and made a tidy profit.

Dot-Con Scams

The U.S. Federal Trade Commission (FTC) is on the trail of Internet criminals and has published a list of the Top 10 Online Frauds (www.ftc.com). Here are some examples.

- **Travel/vacation fraud**: You're offered a luxury trip with all sorts of "extras" at very low prices. Then you find that what you get is much lower quality than was promised. Or, you're hit with hidden charges after you've paid.

  FTC says: Make sure you have all promises in writing, including the cancellation policy, before you sign up.

- **Bogus business opportunities**: You see an offer to stay at home, be your own boss, and earn big bucks. But then you find that the scheme is a bust and you're probably worse off than before.

  FTC says: Check with others who have started businesses with the company. Get all promises in writing and get an attorney or accountant to check the contract.

- **Online auction fraud**: In this case you get something less valuable than what you paid for, or you might even get nothing at all.

  FTC says: Always use a credit card or an escrow service.

- **Internet service provider scams**: You get a check for a small amount ($3 or $4) in the mail and cash it. Then you find you're trapped into long-term contracts with ISPs which exact huge penalties if you cancel.

  FTC says: Read ALL the information about the check before you cash it and watch for unexpected charges.

- **Credit card fraud**: You get an offer which says you can view adult-oriented Web sites for free if you provide a credit card number—just to prove you're over 18. Then your credit card bill has charges for goods and services you never purchased.

  FTC says: Always examine your credit card statement carefully for unauthorized charges. You'll only have to pay up to $50 of the charges if your card was misused.

COMPUTERS AS TARGETS

How Do People Attack Computers?

There's lots of malware floating around in cyberspace. **Malware** is malicious software that is designed by people to attack some part of a computer system. Two of the most notorious types of malware are viruses and denial-of-service attacks.

Viruses

The term "computer virus" is a generic term for lots of different types of destructive software that spreads from file to file. A **computer virus (virus)** is software designed intentionally to cause annoyance or damage. There are two types of viruses, benign and malignant. The first type of virus displays a message or slows down your computer but doesn't destroy any information.

Malignant viruses, however, do damage to your computer system. Some will scramble or delete your files. Others shut your computer down, make your Word software act strangely, or damage the compact flash memory in your digital camera so that it won't store pictures any more.

One of the most prevalent types of computer viruses is the macro virus. **Macro viruses** are viruses that spread by binding themselves to software such as Word or Excel. If your computer is infected, and you send an infected file to someone else as an e-mail attachment, the recipient's computer will get the virus as soon as the attachment is opened. The virus will then make copies of itself and spread from file to file, destroying or changing the files in the process. You can also get infected if you download an infected file from the Internet or open a file on an infected disk.

A **worm** is a computer virus that spreads itself, not only from file to file, but from computer to computer via e-mail and other Internet traffic. A worm finds your e-mail address book and sends itself to the e-mail addresses in your list. One of the more famous worm viruses is called the "Love Bug." It arrives in your e-mail as an attachment to an e-mail. The subject of the e-mail is "I LOVE YOU"—a message that's hard to resist. Take a look at Figure 7.6 on the next page to see what it does.

A virus can't do anything unless the virus instructions are executed. That usually means that you have to open the attachment to become infected because that's where the harmful code is. So be very careful about opening up an attachment if you're not sure what it is and where it came from. Also, be aware that some e-mail programs have the ability to execute macros (small blocks of code) and these may be executed when you open the e-mail itself, releasing the virus. Consult your e-mail program vendor for more information.

There are even virus hoaxes. A **virus hoax** is e-mail distributed with the intention of frightening people about a nonexistent virus. People who get such an alert will usually tell others, who pass the information on. The effect of the hoax is to cause people anxiety and lost productivity. The cost to companies can be very severe since business must be suspended while computer professionals spend time and effort looking for a non-existent virus in hundreds, perhaps thousands, of computers on one or more networks.

Viruses are scary, but a virus can't hurt your hardware, your monitor or processor, except in rare, isolated cases. Viruses can't hurt any files they weren't designed to attack either. For example, a virus designed for Microsoft's Outlook generally doesn't infect Qualcomm's Eudora or any other e-mail application. Viruses can't infect files on write-protected disks or infect compressed files.

FIGURE 7.6

The Love Bug worm gets busy once
it's released in your computer.

1 The virus arrives in
an e-mail marked
"I LOVE YOU."

2 When you open the
attachment, you turn
the virus loose in
your computer.

3 It goes to your address
book to mail itself to
all your friends.

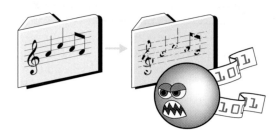

4 The virus starts
destroying files.

5 The virus looks for
passwords that it can
send back to
its creator.

Denial-of-Service Attacks

Many e-businesses have been hit with denial-of-service attacks. ***Denial-of-service (DoS) attacks*** cause thousands of access attempts to a Web site over a very short period of time, overloading the target site and shutting it down. The attacks may come from one or many thousands of computers. In either case the objective is to flood the targeted computer, usually belonging to an e-business, with so many access attempts as to prevent legitimate customers from getting into the site to do business. One such DoS is the "Ping of Death" (see Figure 7.7 for details on it works). E*Trade, Amazon.com, and Yahoo!, among others, have been victims of the "Ping of Death."

For some companies, such as an online stockbroker, denial-of-service attacks can be disastrous. The timing of stock trading is often crucial, and it matters very much whether the sell or buy order goes in this hour or the next. And since stockbrokers need a high level of trust from customers to do business, the effect of having been seen to be so vulnerable is very bad for business.

Combination Worm/DoS

A form of worm first discovered in July 2001 combines the worm's ability to propagate and denial-of-service attack's ability to bring down a Web site. The first worm of this kind was called "Code Red." It attacked only servers (the computer on a network that provides services to the other

FIGURE 7.7

The objective of a denial-of-service attack is to shut down the target computer.

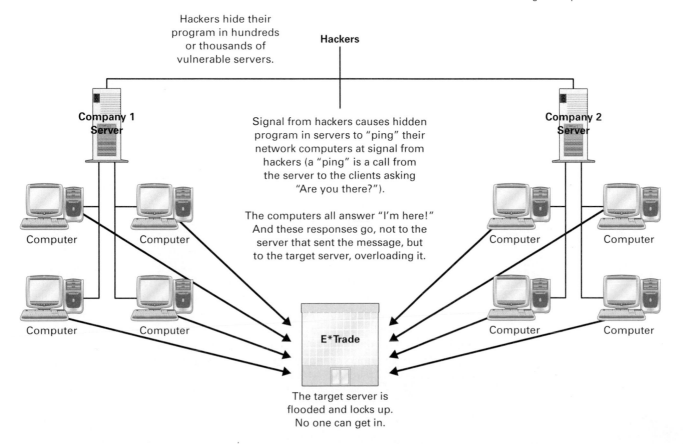

Hackers hide their program in hundreds or thousands of vulnerable servers.

Hackers

Signal from hackers causes hidden program in servers to "ping" their network computers at signal from hackers (a "ping" is a call from the server to the clients asking "Are you there?").

The computers all answer "I'm here!" And these responses go, not to the server that sent the message, but to the target server, overloading it.

Company 1 Server

Company 2 Server

Computer

Computer

Computer

Computer

Computer

Computer

Computer

Computer

E*Trade

The target server is flooded and locks up. No one can get in.

network computers) running specific system software. Code Red again used e-mail address books to send itself to lots of computers, but it was very efficient, with the ability to infect as many as 500,000 other servers per day. When it infected a server it had two tasks to perform. First, it defaced the server for 10 hours before going dormant. Second, it initiated 99 separate threads (or tasks), which all scanned (sought out) other servers to infect for 19 days. On day 20 all infected computers launched denial-of-service attacks against a White House Web server.

This type of worm has the potential to do an extraordinary amount of damage. Code Red affected the performance of network equipment and caused slowdowns for cable Internet providers. Code Red cost an estimated $2.4 billion in prevention, detection, and cleanup, even though it didn't destroy files or otherwise do much damage. What has computer security experts worried is that the potential for this particular type of malware is very great and future versions may carry a much nastier payload.

THE PERPETRATORS

Who Are the People Who Spread Viruses and Denial-of-Service Attacks?

People who break into computer systems are often called hackers. **Hackers** are very knowledgeable computer users who use their knowledge to invade other people's computers. They're usually under 25 years of age and are generally very talented individuals. There are many types of hackers.

White-Hat Hackers

White-hat hackers follow a "hackers' code" and, while they break into computers they have no right to access, they often report the security leaks to the victims. Their thrill is in being able to break in and their reward is usually the admiration of their fellow hackers.

Black-Hat Hackers

Black-hat hackers are hackers with malicious intent—they're cyber vandals. They exploit or destroy the information they find, steal passwords, or otherwise cause harm. They may deliberately cause trouble for people just for the fun of it by creating viruses and bringing down computer systems.

Crackers

Crackers are hackers who hack for profit. They might break into a system to blackmail, bribe, or get revenge with the information they find. Crackers are the people who engage in corporate espionage.

Hacktivists

Hacktivists, or **cyber terrorists,** are politically motivated hackers. Hacktivists use the Internet to send a political message of some kind. The message can be a call to end world hunger, an alteration of a political party's Web site exhorting you to vote for the opposition, or a slogan for or against a particular religious or national group. Some terrorist organizations hide maps and sabotage plans inside graphic images on Web sites for easy access by group members.

did you **know?** The FBI says that 90 percent of businesses have detected security breaches in the last year.

Script Bunnies

Script bunnies or *script kiddies* are people who would like to be hackers but don't have much technical expertise. They download click-and-point software that automatically does the hacking for them. An example is the young man who started the Kournikova virus in Holland. That virus was very similar to the Love Bug worm in that it sent itself to all the people in your Outlook address book. Tens of millions of people received e-mail with the infected attachment, and a large portion of those opened the attachment hoping to see a picture of Anna Kournikova, the very attractive Russian tennis player.

Ethical Hackers

Given the proliferation of viruses, denial-of-service attacks, and other types of intrusions, it's no surprise that the number of computer security firms is increasing. These companies find the vulnerable spots in a business network and strengthen them against attack. They offer advice on how to prevent problems and install protective software and hardware. Usually such firms have "ethical hackers" on staff who use the same methods that malicious hackers use to probe for weaknesses on the network. However, these hackers have the company's permission to break into the computer system. For more on hackers, visit www.mhhe.com/i-series (and select "Malware").

---

making the grade   SECTION B://

1. _Identity_ theft is the impersonation by a thief of someone with good credit.
2. A _Hacker_ is a very knowledgeable computer user who uses his or her knowledge to invade other people's computers.
3. A computer _Virus_ is software designed intentionally to cause annoyance or damage.
4. When thousands of computers overload a target site by trying to access it at the same time, the target site may be a victim of a _DOS_ attack.

C://PRIVACY MATTERS

There's lots of personal information about you, and everyone else, on the Internet—so much, in fact, that you would hardly believe it—and so much that many people are becoming increasingly concerned about what they see as an assault on their privacy. *Privacy* is the right to be left alone when you want to be, to have control over your own personal information, and not to be observed without your consent. It's the right to be free of unwanted intrusion into your private life.

Most of us value our privacy, but we know that there are intrusions that are just a part of life. For example, the electric company can send a bill to your home whether you want one that day or not, so they don't have to leave you alone completely.

If the neighbors see you going to school at certain times each day and notice how you're dressed, you'd probably just consider that to be part of living in a community. You probably wouldn't win a lawsuit to prevent people from looking out their own windows at you. But if they were looking in *your* windows, you might have a case.

Sometimes you exchange some of your privacy for something you want. You have to give your name, address, and social security number to get a driver's license. So you're giving up some personal information, hence some privacy, in exchange for the privilege of being able to drive. In order for businesses to offer products and services that you want, they need to have information about you. If government agencies are to fulfill their missions, they need information about the people they're there to serve. The primary debate centers around how much and what kind of information organizations should be allowed to collect, and to whom they allow access to that information.

Should you be able to look at the information that companies have about you? Should you be able to change things that are wrong? Should you be able to delete information you don't want them to have? Europeans think so. The European Union has implemented the Directive on Protection of Personal Data. The rights accorded citizens of member countries include the right to know the marketer's source of information, the right to check personal information, the right to correct it, and the right to specify that information can't be used for direct marketing.

Before computer use was so widespread, massive amounts of paper records were collected and kept. But the paper system naturally limited the amount of information collected and its accessibility. Cross-tabulation isn't easy with paper files. The people who collected information about your health stored it in one place; those who recorded your grocery shopping habits kept the information somewhere else. With computers, multiple types of information can be cross-referenced quickly and easily, creating a picture of you that is quite detailed and, in the opinion of many, too intrusive.

FIGURE 7.8

There are three ways businesses can get information about you.

Companies know about you and your preferences through
- Information you volunteer such as when you register for sweepstakes at a store or at a Web site.
- Information that organizations collect based on your contact with them. Credit card companies have information on what you buy, and Web sites can see what pages you look at and for how long.
- Information that organizations can buy from one another.

INFORMATION ON YOUR BUYING HABITS AND PREFERENCES

How Do Companies Get Information about Me?

Companies get information about your preferences and identity three ways: (1) from information you explicitly provide, (2) from information organizations collect through contact with you, and (3) from information about you that organizations get from other organizations (see Figure 7.8).

Information You Volunteer

Some ways in which you provide personal information to organizations are

- *Contests and promotions:* If you've ever signed up for a contest at your local supermarket, you've offered personal information to the store in exchange for a chance to win.

- *Warranty cards and rebate offers:* When you send in a warranty card or respond to a rebate offer, you give the manufacturer information about your buying habits along with your name and address.
- *Registration at Web sites:* If you've ever registered at a Web site to receive products or services or to enter a contest, you've given the Web site personal information.

There's personal information on most adults in hundreds of databases. Using the Internet to access databases that sell personal information, you can find out virtually anything about anyone. You can find out what people earn, where they live, how much they paid for their home, where they lived before, and so on.

Information Collected by Contact

When you use credit cards or checks, you're giving the store information about yourself, which can be linked to your receipt showing your buying habits and preferences. Not surprisingly, the companies with the largest databases of personal information are those that have direct contact with consumers—retailers, financial services companies, and telecommunications companies. The Federal Trade Commission says that 92.8 percent of Web sites gather at least one type of identifying information, at least your name or e-mail address. More than half collect at least one type of demographic information, perhaps your gender or age. Those with the largest databases include the Chase and First Union banks and retailers such as Wal-Mart, Kmart, the Limited, and Sears. In fact, Wal-Mart has the largest data warehouse outside the government with about 101 terabytes of information. It uses the information to keep hundreds of stores stocked with products in the colors, sizes, and prices attractive to consumers living in the vicinity of each store.

Retailers and banks collect and keep information to make decisions about how to run their businesses. Web sites do the same thing, except they collect information on you by observing you at their sites. They see which Web pages you go to, how long you stay there, what you buy, and so forth, and make judgments about your needs and interests from that information. They sometimes even store information about you on your own hard disk drive in the form of "cookies."

A *cookie* is a small text file containing specific information about you that is stored on your computer's hard drive. This information is always helpful to the site that placed it there. Sometimes it's helpful to you too. For example, if you want to repeatedly visit a site that requires an ID and password, a cookie can keep that information and provide it to the Web site so that you don't have to type it in every time. When you visit that Web site, your Web browser looks for the cookie information for that Web site. If it finds it, your Web browser sends the information on to the Web site. If you put products into a wish list or an electronic shopping cart, that information stays in a cookie so that the next time you visit the site, that site can access the information. When you buy a product or take it out of the shopping cart, the cookie on your hard disk is altered accordingly.

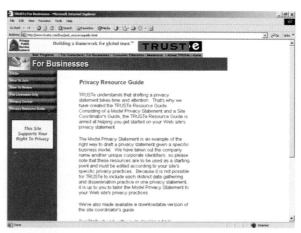

You can turn cookies on and off, and best of all, you can get your Web browser to tell you when a site wants to send you a cookie (see Figure 7.9).

FIGURE   7.9

You can set your Web browser to accept cookies, to not accept cookies, or to warn you that a Web site wants to set a cookie.

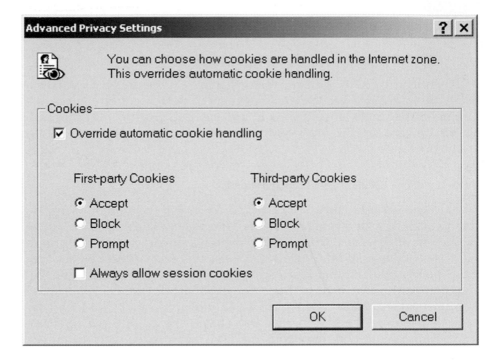

Information Sold from One Company to Another

Many companies with huge databases of information sell that information to others. Credit card companies sell information on consumers although many claim that they don't sell personal information with names attached. There are companies that specialize in the collection and sale of information. Retail companies like big spenders. Market researchers know that there are certain online consumers who spend $8,000 or more every year, for instance, and commercial online companies will pay to find out who these people are.

Among the Web companies that collect information, the most famous are DoubleClick and Engage. They follow you around the Web and then sell the information on your activities to other Web sites that want to sell you products and services. Some companies also collect information from chat rooms and discussion groups. So, a prospective employer wanting to know more about you can, for a fee, get access to what you have said. For more information on the workplace, visit the Interactive Companion Labs and choose "Workplace Issues."

With a cookie, Web sites can tell who you are by looking at the cookie information. But that's not the only way they keep track of you. They can also use sniffers. A **sniffer** is software that sits on the Internet analyzing traffic. The software tries to find out who you are. It tries several approaches until it finds one that works.

Armed with information on who you are, the software can engage in *Web tracking*. It can track what pages you visit, how long you stay there, what files you download, and what documents you open. This information is then stored in a database, where it can be analyzed along with information from other Web visitors.

did you

know?

The *cost of a computer virus infection to a business can range from $2,000 to $200,000.*

Companies use this information in many ways. They make business decisions with it, they define target markets, they send you advertising, and so on. Companies can send you either customized or mass advertising. If companies know who you are and think you're likely to shop with them, they display ads on a site that you're likely to visit. If they increase their click-through count (the number of people who click on the ad) by only one-half of one percent, they're happy and consider their advertising dollars well spent.

Mass advertising is the posting of ads where lots of people are likely to see them, such as TV advertising. On the Web, mass advertising reaches you when you visit a Web site or by junk e-mail, which is called "spam."

Spam is electronic junk mail or unsolicited mail, usually from commercial businesses attempting to sell you products and services. The Dot-cons, or scams, are heavy users of spam, which is often sent out to 10,000 or more people at the same time. It's cheap and easy since lists of e-mail addresses are readily available and so is bulk e-mail software.

Would you be interested in increasing Energy Levels by 84%?
Would you like to increase your Muscle Strength by 88%?
While at the same time reducing Body Fat by 72%?

Of course you would! We offer Wonder Drink, the Most Potent Formula available to help you achieve all of this and more!

In thousands of clinical studies, our Wonder Drink has been shown to accomplish the following:
- Reduce body fat and build lean muscle without exercise!
- Remove wrinkles and cellulite!
- Lower blood pressure and improve cholesterol profile!
- Improve sleep, vision, and memory!
- Restore hair color and growth!
- Strengthen the immune system!
- Increase energy and cardiac output!
- All this in only 6 months of usage!!!

Testimonial:
"As a straight-ahead bicycle racer, I used to have to wait a minute and a half after sprinting for my heart rate to come down to where I could sprint again. After a month on Wonder Drink, I can now sprint again after only 45 seconds! Wonder Drink cut my waiting time in half!"—Ed Caz, CA

Spammers often "spoof" their addresses to make it hard for you to find them. **Spoofing** is forging the return address on an e-mail so that the e-mail message appears to come from someone other than the sender. Spammers can also relay their spam through several different servers, making it difficult to trace.

GOVERNMENT RECORDS

What Information Does the Government Keep on Individuals?

The various branches of government need information to administer entitlement programs, social security, welfare, student loans, law enforcement, and so on. Government agencies have about 2,000 databases containing personal information on individuals. It's fairly safe to assume that any time you have contact with any branch of government, someone will subsequently store information about you. For example, if you get a government-backed student loan, you must provide personal information

i·buy

Get Yourself Virus Protection

There are more than 50,000 viruses in circulation, and the rate of infection keeps increasing. Therefore it makes sense for you to use anti-virus protection on your computer, particularly if you use e-mail and access the Internet, as most of us do nowadays.

Many ISPs have anti-virus software that checks incoming e-mail for viruses. Some ISPs will simply delete the infected message. Others send it on with a message telling you your e-mail is infected, and still others clean off the virus and send the message on its way to you.

Even if your ISP has anti-virus software, you'd be well advised to have your own. You can choose from many anti-virus software packages. We recommend that you set up your anti-virus software to scan all disks that you insert into your system and all files that you download from the Internet, including those from bulletin boards and

e-mail attachments. To do this your anti-virus software must run all the time your computer is on.

Remember to update your anti-virus software frequently since new viruses come along every day. Some anti-virus vendors, Symantec, for instance, the company that sells Norton AntiVirus software, have an automatic update option. That means that you can set up your anti-virus software to go out to the Web and download updates automatically to your computer.

Following are some sites at which you can find anti-virus software.

- McAfee at www.mcafee.com
- PC-cillin at www.pc-cillin.com

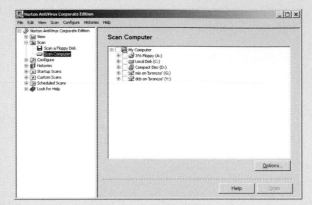

- Dr. Solomon Anti-Virus Toolkit at www.drsolomon.com
- Norton AntiVirus at www.symantec.com
- Inoculate IT at www.antivirus.cai.com

For more on anti-virus software, visit www.mhhe.com/i-series.

such as your name, address, income, parents' income, and so on. That information is then stored with other pertinent facts, such as the school you're attending, the bank dispersing the loan, and later your repayment records. Following are some other examples of government agencies that collect a lot of information.

The **NCIC (National Crime Information Center)** is a huge database with information on the criminal records of more than 20 million people. You've often heard about someone being arrested for a grievous crime after a routine traffic stop for some minor infraction like a broken taillight. The Oklahoma City bombing perpetrators were caught

U.S. Laws on Information

The United States doesn't have a consistent set of laws protecting citizens from misuse of information. Laws are spotty and apply to only certain groups or industry segments.

- The **Privacy Act** restricts what information the federal government can collect; allows people to access and correct information on themselves; requires procedures to protect the security of personal information; and forbids the disclosure of name-linked information without permission.

- The **Freedom of Information Act** says that citizens have the right to access the information that federal agencies have collected on them.

- The **Computer Matching and Privacy Protection Act** says that government agencies can't compare certain records trying to find a match. However, most records are not covered by this act.

- The **Bork Bill** (officially known as the **Video Privacy Protection Act**) prohibits the use of video rental information on customers for any purpose other than that of marketing goods and services directly to the customer.

- The **Communications Assistance for Law Enforcement Act** requires that telecommunications equipment be designed so that authorized government agents are able to intercept all wired and wireless communications being sent or received by any subscriber. The Act also requires that subscriber call-identifying information be transmitted to a government agency when and if required.

- The **Health Insurance Portability and Accountability Act** gave the health care industry until April 2002 to formulate and install policies and procedures to keep patient information confidential.

- The **Financial Service Modernization Act** requires that financial institutions protect personal customer information and that they have customer permission before sharing such information with other businesses.

this way. Usually the arrest comes about after the officer stops the car and runs a check on the license plate and driver's license through the NCIC, finding an outstanding warrant.

The IRS (Internal Revenue Service) has income information on all taxpayers. The IRS also has access to other databases. For example, the IRS keeps track of vehicle registration information so that they can check up on people buying expensive cars and boats to make sure they're reporting a corresponding income level.

The Census Bureau collects information every 10 years on all the U.S. inhabitants the agency can find. Everyone is requested to fill out a census form, and some people get a very long and detailed form requiring them to disclose a lot of personal information. The information that the Census Bureau collects is available to other government agencies and even to commercial enterprises.

making the grade

1. _____ is the right to be left alone when you want to be.

2. A _____ is software that analyzes Web traffic.

3. _____ is electronic junk mail.

4. _____ is forging the return address on e-mail.

D://HOW TO PROTECT YOURSELF

Cyberspace is a great place to visit. You can work, shop, and play there. But you have to be just as careful as you are in the brick-and-mortar world.

SECURITY BEFORE YOU ENTER CYBERSPACE

How Do I Protect My Computer and Files?

Here are two rules you should remember: (1) If it can be stolen, lock it up. (2) If it can be damaged, back it up.

Now that many people use notebooks, the number of computers that are stolen is skyrocketing. You can buy security cable with padlocks for your notebook to make it harder to steal when it's not by your side. The cable and padlocks are like those you see in department stores for expensive products that the store wants you to be able to look at but not take without paying.

The best protection for files is backups. Losing hardware, a Zip disk, or hard drive, is seldom your biggest problem. The real value is most likely in the files. Replacing those may well be much more expensive in time and effort than replacing the hardware.

SECURITY IN CYBERSPACE TRANSACTIONS

How Do I Protect Myself in Cyberspace?

If you buy goods and services on the Web, you need to do what you do in the brick-and-mortar world—use common sense.

Credit Card and Identity Theft

- Give your credit card number only to reputable companies that you trust.
- Use only secure sites, i.e., those with http**s**://.
- Never give out your social security number unless the law demands it. Your social security number is the key to most information about you.
- Use passwords of at least 10 characters and numbers.
- Use different passwords for different systems/sites.

Dot-Cons

- Be very skeptical about claims of extraordinary performance or earnings potential.
- Always read the fine print.
- Always look at the site's privacy policy.
- Be wary of a company that doesn't clearly state its name, address, and phone number.
- Immediately report any fraudulent, deceptive, or unfair practices to the Federal Trade Commission.

Protecting Personal Information

Don't give out personal information without thinking about it first. Think about whether you want the recipient to have this information, keeping in mind that you lose control of the information once you hand it over. Look for the privacy policy of the site you're dealing with. But be aware that the bankruptcy courts have held that customer records are assets that may be sold to pay off debts.

Anti-Tracking Software

You can buy software (SurfSecret is an example) that prevents your being tracked while you're surfing. It runs continuously in the background (like your anti-virus software) and erases the information that accumulates during your Web activity. For example, it will clear your history and cookie files if you want it to.

Avoiding Spam

Spam can be very irritating. The more times you give your e-mail address to e-commerce businesses and post it to online message boards, the more spam you can expect to get. A general rule is not to believe anything that spammers say—including how to get off their list. By replying, even to the "unsubscribe" option, you're really just confirming that your e-mail address is active.

Protecting a Computer or Network from Intruders

A *firewall* is hardware and/or software that protects computers from intruders. The firewall examines each message as it seeks entrance to a network, like border guards checking passports. Unless the message has the "right" markings, the firewall prevents it from entering the network.

If you have just one computer, firewall software is probably enough to protect your system and information from intrusion when you're connected to the Internet. The firewall software permits nothing to enter or leave that shouldn't. For example, McAfee has firewall software called Personal Firewall (available at www.mcafee.com). Another product is Zone Labs' ZoneAlarm (available at www.zonelabs.com) and you can download the basic edition free.

If you have more than one computer with a cable modem or a DSL connection, you would be well advised to invest in a hardware firewall. With a router, such as Linksys (www.linksys.com), you can link all your computers to the router and to each other (see Figure 7.10). Then the router will check all incoming traffic and deny access to any that looks suspicious.

FIGURE 7.10

A firewall kicks out any incoming traffic that looks suspicious.

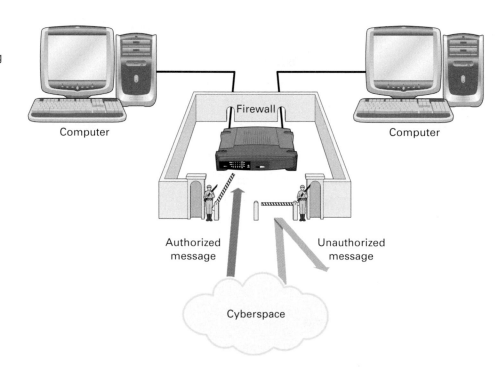

SECTION D://   *making the grade*

1. A _____ is hardware and/or software that protects computers from intruders.
2. _____ software prevents your being tracked while you're surfing.
3. The _____ tracks consumer fraud of all kinds.
4. Your _____ is the key to most information about you.

i·witness

An Up-Close Look at Web Sites

The Blinking Binge

As you've already seen, there are many ways to make your Web site sizzle and its important messages catch the eye. Some of those ways are using different type fonts and styles, using color, and formatting text with bullet points.

Another common method people use to make text eye-catching is

to make it blink. Blinking is the simplest form of motion you can put into your Web site. And it's easy to do. You can make single words, sentences, images, or even your whole Web site blink.

Be careful though. Too much blinking can become annoying and it might drive your visitors away. To help you understand how best to use blinking, we've provided three Web sites for you to review. They are

www.mhhe.com/i-series/I-Witness/7-A.html

www.mhhe.com/i-series/I-Witness/7-B.html

www.mhhe.com/i-series/I-Witness/7-C.html

One of those Web sites makes good use of blinking while another uses too much blinking. Which is

the good one and which is the bad one? What would you do to the bad one to better utilize blinking?

Finally, one of the Web sites uses no blinking at all but could benefit from it. How would you incorporate blinking into that Web site to make certain text stand out? You can connect to the site for this text and download these Web sites to your computer. You can then make the changes yourself.

HTML Reference:

The blink tag:

<BLINK>The Blinking Binge</ BLINK>—will cause the text "The Blinking Binge" to blink on your Web site.

E://SUMMARY AND KEY TERMS

Ethics is the set of principles and standards we use in deciding what to do in situations that affect other people. Our ethics in how we use computers is an extension of our ethics in other parts of our lives.

A *copyright* protects the expression of an idea. The *Fair Use Doctrine*, however, says that you may use copyrighted material in certain situations. *Pirated software* is copyrighted software that is copied and distributed without permission of the owner. *Netiquette* is good manners or courtesy in cyberspace.

Identity theft is the impersonation by a thief of someone with good credit. *Hackers* are very knowledgeable computer users who use their knowledge to invade other people's computers. *Crackers* are hackers who hack for profit. *Computer viruses* are software that was written with malicious intent to cause annoyance or damage. *Macro viruses* spread by binding themselves to software such as Word or Excel. A *worm* is a computer virus that spreads itself, not only from file to file, but from computer to computer via e-mail and other Internet traffic. *Denial-of-service attacks* cause thousands of computers to try to access a Web site at the same time, overloading the target site and shutting it down.

Privacy is the right to be left alone when you want to be, to have control over your own personal information, and to not be observed without your consent. A *sniffer* is software that sits on the Internet analyzing traffic.

A *cookie* is information placed on your hard disk by a Web site that you visit. *Spam* is electronic junk mail, i.e., unsolicited mail, usually from commercial businesses attempting to sell you goods and services. *Spoofing* is forging the return address on an e-mail.

A *firewall* is hardware and/or software that protects computers from intruders. As added support, we've provided more information on the Web site that supports this text at www.mhhe.com/i-series concerning the following topics:

- Downloadable freeware and shareware
- Hackers
- Anti-virus software

KEY TERMS

black-hat hacker (p. 7.14)

computer virus (virus) (p. 7.11)

cookie (p. 7.17)

copyright (p. 7.3)

cracker (p. 7.14)

denial-of-service (DoS) attack (p. 7.13)

ethics (p. 7.3)

Fair Use Doctrine (p. 7.3)

firewall (p. 7.23)

hacker (p. 7.14)

hacktivist (cyber terrorist) (p. 7.14)

identity theft (p. 7.9)

macro virus (p. 7.11)

malware (p. 7.11)

NCIC (National Crime Information Center) (p. 7.20)

netiquette (p. 7.6)

pirated software (p. 7.4)

privacy (p. 7.15)

script bunny (script kiddie) (p. 7.15)

sniffer (p. 7.18)

spam (p. 7.19)

spoofing (p. 7.19)

virus hoax (p. 7.11)

white-hat hacker (p. 7.14)

worm (p. 7.11)

CROSSWORD PUZZLE

Across

1. This type of theft steals your financial identity
4. The legal protection of an expression of an idea
6. _____ Use Doctrine-exceptions to the copyright law
8. This type of virus attaches itself to Word or Excel
9. Software that attacks some part of a computer system
10. The principles and standards we use in dealing with others
11. Someone who breaks into computers for ideological reasons
14. This type of software is procured illegally
15. Software or hardware that protects your computer or network from attack
17. Forging the return address on an e-mail
19. This "bunny" or "kiddie" gets hacking tools off the Internet
20. A Web site puts this on your hard drive
21. It sends itself to people in your e-mail address book

Down

2. Good manners online
3. You have a right to this
5. Code created by someone to do damage
7. A profitable hacker
12. Electronic junk mail
13. Someone who breaks into other people's computers
16. A hacker with this color hat invades computers to look around
18. Has over 20 million records on criminals, stolen goods, missing persons
19. This software watches Web traffic

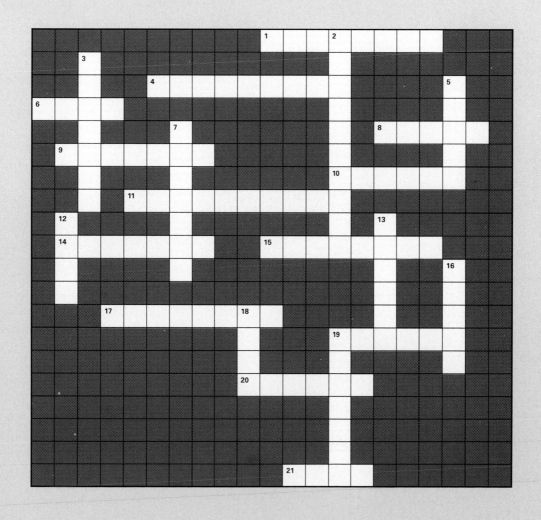

QUESTIONS AND EXERCISES

Multiple Choice

1. The set of principles and standards we use in deciding what to do in situations that affect other people is called
   a. ethics.
   b. privacy.
   c. good manners.
   d. the law.
   e. none of the above.

2. Something that's legal is ethical.
   a. sometimes
   b. always
   c. never
   d. at the beginning of the month only
   e. none of the above

3. The Fair Use Doctrine says that
   a. you can copy anything you like.
   b. you can copy copyrighted material under certain circumstances.
   c. you can use anyone's computer as long as you don't use it to commit a crime.
   d. you can use any software as long as you are not using it to commit a crime.
   e. none of the above.

4. What can you NOT do with freeware software?
   a. copy the software
   b. change the software
   c. sell the software
   d. give away the software
   e. You can do all of the above.

5. What can you NOT do with public domain software?
   a. copy the software
   b. change the software
   c. sell the software
   d. give the software to a business
   e. You can do all of the above.

6. The information that a Web site places on your hard disk is called a
   a. spam.
   b. sniffer.
   c. cracker.
   d. cookie.
   e. firewall.

7. Spoofing is
   a. spreading jokes on the Internet.
   b. sending unsolicited e-mail.
   c. forging the return address on e-mail.
   d. collecting personal information.
   e. none of the above.

8. A firewall
   a. could be hardware.
   b. could be software.
   c. protects your computer from intruders.
   d. is all of the above.
   e. is none of the above.

9. A company can get information
   a. directly from you.
   b. from contact with you as a customer.
   c. from a third party who collected the information.
   d. from all of the above.
   e. from none of the above.

10. Privacy is
    a. the right to be left alone if you want to be.
    b. the right to have control over your own personal information.
    c. the right to be free of observation from others.
    d. all of the above.
    e. none of the above.

True/False

11. ___I___ Netiquette is good manners or courtesy in cyberspace.

12. ___I___ Spamming is sending unsolicited e-mail.

13. ___I___ Federal law says that no one can use your personal information without your permission.

14. ___F___ Anti-virus software prevents people from developing viruses.

15. ___I___ A copyright protects the expression of someone's idea.

QUESTIONS AND EXERCISES

1. Describe the cyberspace equivalent for the following brick-and-mortar situations.

   A. Getting junk mail in your mailbox.

   B. Having someone follow you around a mall writing down which stores you go into and how long you stay there.

   C. Checking all the doors on someone else's car, and finding a back door open, letting yourself in to look around and examine what's in the glove box.

   D. Breaking into someone's car to steal the stereo and sell it to someone else.

   E. Making a "flu bug" in your basement and getting onto an airplane to let it loose.

   F. Having someone read the mail in your mailbox without your permission.

   G. Standing at an intersection writing down the tags of passing cars.

   H. Making photocopies of a book and handing them out to your friends.

2. For each of the following answers, create the question:

ANSWER	QUESTION
A. A teacher who copies a page out of a copyrighted article to make a point.	_____
B. Forging the return address on an e-mail.	_____
C. How a thief uses a computer.	_____
D. It shows that you're at a secure site.	_____
E. It's the "key" to personal information about you.	_____
F. An e-mail that offers you a diploma without tests, classes, books, or interviews.	_____
G. Kind of attack by which hackers shut down e-businesses.	_____
H. Many employees have been fired for this type of computer misuse.	_____
I. You should report Internet fraud to these people.	_____
J. 15 and 25.	_____
K. Someone who creates and spreads a virus.	_____
L. Has records on citizens.	_____
M. How we treat each other.	_____

e-commerce

1. Renting a Hotel Room

If you're going to a town where you have no relatives or friends (or perhaps because you do), you might need a hotel room. You can find lots of hotel information on general travel sites such as www.expedia.com or www.travelocity.com. Here are some hotel-chain Web sites. Visit a few of them and answer the questions that follow.

- Marriott International—www.marriott.com
- Motel 6—www.motel6.com
- Super 8—www.super8.com
- Hilton Group—www.hilton.com
- Holiday Inn—www.holidayinn.com

a. Which chains have hotels in other countries? On what continents do they offer hotel rooms?

b. Which hotel chains have properties in your hometown or in the town where you're going to college?

c. Can you get airline miles for staying at any of these chains?

d. Which Web sites give you a picture of the rooms?

e. Which sites offer a privacy policy?

f. Which sites have a consumer protection seal such as TRUSTe?

2. Making Airline Reservations

Almost all airlines sell tickets on their Web sites. But you can also go to general travel sites and compare flight times and prices there.

For discounted first-class and business-class tickets try 1stair.net. For some of the best deals, you should check out the sites that compare prices for you, such as www.farechase.com or www.airlineguides.com.

Look at the following airline Web sites and answer the questions that follow.

- American Airlines—www.aa.com
- Delta Airlines—www.delta.com
- Southwest Airlines—www.southwest.com
- United Airlines—www.ual.com

a. How much luggage can you have on each airline? How many pieces of carry-on can you take and what's the size limit?

b. Pick a destination at least 1,000 miles from where you are now and compare

Prices—which is cheapest? Which is the most expensive? Does the time of day or day of the week matter?

Number of stops—can you fly nonstop?

How long it takes you to get to the destination airport—does the number of stops have something to do with the time it takes?

c. Which site was the easiest to navigate? Why?

d. Did any of the sites give you a list of cities they serve? How were you able to choose from the list of cities?

e. Which sites offer a privacy policy?

f. Which sites have a consumer protection seal such as TRUSTe? If you found a seal other than TRUSTe, which was it?

3. Renting a Car

You might want to rent a car at your destination. You'll need a valid driver's license and a credit card. You can rent pretty much any kind of vehicle you want from recreational vehicles to buses. Visit a few of the following sites and compare them answering the questions that follow.

- Avis—www.avis.com
- Rent-A-Wreck—www.rentawreck.com
- Dollar Rent-A-Car—www.dollar.com
- National Car Rental—www.nationalcar.com
- Alamo—www.alamo.com
- Enterprise Rent-A-Car—www.enterprise.com

a. Can you rent a car in every state in the United States? Are some states more expensive than others?

b. Can you rent a car overseas? Do you have to obtain a special driver's license for certain countries?

c. Do they give you maps and/or weather information?

d. Do they have frequent user programs? Is it easy to enroll in one?

e. Do they share information with any other companies? (You can tell this by looking to see if you can swap frequent programs with other companies.)

4. Buying Event Tickets

You may want to go to a concert, a football game, a rodeo, an opera, a dog show, wrestling, show jumping, or some other event. If so, you can probably find tickets for these events on the Web, and buying tickets on the Web is often easier than over the phone. You pick your event, enter the number of seats you want, and specify your desired price level. The site will tell you if seats are available and offer you a map of the stadium or arena and allow you to select your seats. Here are some sites to look at (pick one and answer the questions that follow).

- Tickets.com—www.tickets.com
- Ticket Master—www.ticketmaster.com
- Sport-Hospitality.com—www.sports-hospitality.com
- Culturefinder.com—www.culturefinder.com
- Pacific Northwest Ticket Service—www.nwtickets.com

a. Does the site provide tickets for more than 10 different types of events?

b. Does the site offer tickets primarily for one category of events, sports, concerts, etc.?

c. Does the site offer events in a particular city?

d. Does the site have a privacy statement?

LEVEL THREE

www.mhhe.com/i-series

on the web

1. Parental Control Software Packages

To protect your family, you can get software that prevents children from connecting to undesirable sites. The software launches when a person starts the Web browser. This software looks at every Web address that someone tries to connect to in two ways. First, it compares the address to its database list of thousands of objectionable sites. If the address is on that list the software blocks the retrieval of the site. Second, if it doesn't find the address in the list, it checks the content of the site, looking for specific words that might indicate an objectionable site.

Search the Web and find at least two different parental control software packages. What features do they include? Are they free to download?

2. Codes of Ethics

Various professional organizations have codes of ethics. The accounting profession, for example, has a thick book with small print called Generally Accepted Accounting Principles. This book includes rules for how accountants should deal with difficult situations that might arise during performance of their professional duties. The Association for Computing Machinery (ACM), which is an organization for computing professionals, has a similar, although much simpler, set of codes. Go to the ACM site at www.acm.org and summarize the guidelines cited there for members of ACM and computing professionals.

3. Exploring Anti-Virus Software

In this chapter you learned how important it is to have anti-virus software. Viruses spread very fast and you need to have the current version of your anti-virus software to have some hope of detecting and removing the latest viruses. In the text we gave you some sites to look at.

- McAfee—www.mcafee.com
- PC-cillin—www.pc-cillin.com
- Dr. Solomon Anti-Virus Toolkit— www.drsolomon.com
- Norton AntiVirus—www.symantec.com
- Inoculate IT—www.antivirus.cai.com

Go to each of these sites and check out the cost of each anti-virus package. Also examine each site's list of current viruses and find five that are common to all sites.

4. Privacy Standards for Health Care Agencies

The Health Insurance Portability and Accountability Act (HIPAA) was signed into law by President Clinton in August of 1996. The final rule was published in August 2000. The HIPAA is due to become law on October 16, 2002. This law stipulates security and privacy standards for health care agencies. Visit the Web and find out what the privacy standards are according to this law.

5. Cybercrimes According to the FBI

Go to the Federal Bureau of Investigation (FBI) site at www.fbi.gov and click on **Congressional Statements** (under **Press Room**) and look at the latest report on Cybercrime. What are the categories of crimes listed there?

ethics, security & privacy

1. Napster

Napster was started by 19-year-old Northeast University student Shawn Fanning, who set up a music site with software that allowed people to link their computers together and share their music in MP3 format. The site kept a list of the people who shared their music through Napster, and also provided search capabilities so that you could easily find someone who had the music you wanted.

The Recording Industry Association of America (RIAA) representing 18 recording companies including the "Big Five"—Sony, Warner, Universal, BMG, and EMI—filed suit to stop Shawn and Napster. The basis for the legal action was that Napster provided a service that enabled and facilitated piracy of music on an enormous scale. You have to show injury in such a case, and RIAA claimed that Napster's piracy facilitation was cutting into its $14-billion-a-year sales.

Napster, in its defense, claimed that the site actually stimulated CD sales. They also referred to the Audio Home Recording Act of 1992, which allows people to copy music for personal use. Napster said it wasn't guilty of copyright infringement since no music was stored on its site, so it didn't give any music to anyone.

A digital rights management firm called Reciprocal Inc. commissioned a study to try to measure the effect of Napster on music sales. Pre-sumably assuming that college students used Napster most heavily, the study surveyed retail stores that sold CDs within a 5-mile radius of college campuses. The results showed sales in these stores declined 4 percent. This was in contrast to sales overall, which increased over the same period. A separate study suggested that 73 percent of college students used Napster at least once a month. Thus, the conclusion was that Napster was hurting CD sales.

What do you think about these studies? Can you think of other reasons that sales were down in CD stores around colleges other than students using Napster? Below are some possible explanations for sales declining. Referring to your own experience, rate each possible explanation on how much effect you think it might have had. Give 5 to those reasons that you think had the most influence and 0 to those that had none.

REASON	EFFECT (0–5)
A. Napster (and other similar sites)	_____
B. The increasing cost of CDs	_____
C. Online CD sales (CDNow etc.)	_____
D. College store CDs are sometimes more expensive than other outlets	_____
E. The availability of CD-Rs and CD-RWs so that you can copy someone's CD yourself	_____
F. Ability to listen to cuts online to see if you like a CD	_____
G. The lack of music written and performed for college-aged people	_____

group activities

1. Government Databases

Make a list of government databases where there might now, or might someday, be information about you. Here are some examples: (1) tax records, (2) bankruptcy records, (3) voter registration lists.

2. Helping a Friend

Suppose you fully intend to spend the evening working on an Excel assignment that's due the next day when a friend calls who is stranded miles from home and desperately needs your help. It takes most of the evening to pick up your friend, bring him home, and return to your studying. However, you're so tired when you get home, you just fall into bed and sleep.

The next day your friend, who completed his assignment earlier, suggests you just make a copy of his, put your own name on it, and hand it in as your own work. Should you do it? Isn't it only fair that since you helped your friend, your friend should do something about making sure you don't lose points because of your generosity? What if your friend promises not to hand in his own work so that you can't be accused of copying? Your friend wrote the assignment he has given you so there's no question of copyright infringement. What will you do?

3. Providing Personal Information

Each member of your group should think of three times he or she provided personal information in exchange for something. Make a table of what information each person gave and what they received for providing the information.

4. Ethics and Laws

Make a table of what's legal but might still be unethical. Think of five laws, past or present, at home or abroad, that you would consider unethical to obey and state why. Also think of five behaviors that are legal, past or present, at home or abroad, that you would nevertheless consider unethical. State why you would consider the behaviors unethical.

5. Debating Privacy

The European Parliament has decreed that citizens of all member countries have the following rights:

- The right to know where a marketer obtained personal information.
- The right to look at any personal information that any company has.
- The right to correct any inaccurate information.
- The right to prevent personal information from being used for direct marketing.
- The right to never have sensitive information such as race, religion, and sexual orientation divulged without express permission.

Half of your group should take the privacy advocate's side and give reasons why these rights should be written into U.S. law. The other half should take the opposing viewpoint and give reasons why this might not be a good thing for this country.

Looking Back/Looking Ahead

The Life and Times of a Dot-Com Entrepreneur

Now that Joann has her own Web site and is involved in e-commerce, she needs to understand the dangers as well as the opportunities in cyberspace. Joann knows the basics. For example, she knows that you can't copy someone else's software and put it on your computer—that would be _____ infringement. She also knows that in certain cases you can use parts of copyrighted material because of the _____ Doctrine. She is also mindful of _____, which means acting politely toward others in cyberspace.

Joann has also learned that she needs to be very careful about giving out her personal information because someone might steal her financial good name and make her a victim of _____. She also knows that there's a lot of truth to the old adage, "if it sounds too good to be true, it probably is," so she'll be watching out for _____, fraudulent schemes on the Internet.

She will be careful to protect her computer with _____ software to lessen her chances of getting a computer virus. She'll also need to decide on a way to protect her computers from being invaded by _____, who might break into her computer and steal her customer list. Joann knows that there are lots of different kinds of _____ in cyberspace who break into computers for a variety of reasons. She'll need a _____ to stop people from getting into her computer. Since she's doing business with her computer, she might also become a victim of a _____ attack.

Now that she's strongly invested in computing and is depending on computers for her continued business success, she'd like to know more about databases so that she can organize and access her information with ease. She'd also like to know about developing applications so that if she hires someone to write custom software, she'll understand the process. Joann would also like to know how other businesses use information technology to advance their goals and objectives. In the coming chapters she'll find information about all these topics.

did you
know?

Today people must process more information than ever before. Databases help organize this information and apply it in various situations.

databases *help promote democracy. Uganda created a registered voter database so each citizen uses only one voter ID card.*

databases *are helping U.S. politicians. A database containing information for about 130 million registered voters has grown to 100 gigabytes.*

you *don't have to be an expert to create an online database. Services provide databases you manage with Excel.*

a *survey of more than 500 database developers found that one-third are designing wireless or mobile device applications.*

individuals *and not businesses create the most information. People create 500 times as much information with e-mail than all the Web pages in existence.*

the *DNA project has more than ?? bits of data—at least twice the contents of the U.S. Library of Congress.*

To find out just how much DNA data geneticists have stored, visit www.mhhe.com/i-series.

CHAPTER

8

eight

Files and Databases

How Do You Organize Information?

How does living in the "information age" affect your daily life? Probably more than you realize, especially when you consider how new ways of organizing information have made our latest conveniences possible. For example, did you e-mail friends today using an online address book? Did you press a speed dial button on your cell phone to leave a voice mail at home? And which would you prefer to do—wait while the campus registrar searches file cabinets or check your class schedule posted on the Web?

In just a few minutes in today's information age, you can access, assimilate, and apply more information than your grandparents had available to them in a single day (or more likely, week) when they were your age. All that information would easily overwhelm you if you were unable to organize it in a meaningful way. That's where databases come in, and in this chapter we'll see how and why they work.

First, we'll discuss how you can manage information using the basic elements of a database. Then, we'll discuss the various databases you can use and show you the more popular kinds of databases. From there we'll dive into the ways a database can help you manage information, as well as explore how databases contribute to e-commerce. We'll discuss how databases are revolutionizing how you surf the Web and shop online, and what you need to be aware of concerning your personal information and privacy as database use increases. Finally, we'll end by looking at how you can begin to manage and maintain your own information device—your computer.

A://MANAGING INFORMATION

You arrive at the airport excited about taking a vacation. You need to remind yourself of your gate and when your plane is leaving. After checking in at the ticket counter you look at your boarding pass and head to your gate.

DATA VERSUS INFORMATION
Is Data Different from Information?

Your boarding pass has provided you with essential information, such as the gate number and departure time (and without it you probably wouldn't be able to get on the plane, either).

This information comes from data the airline keeps about flights, departures, gate assignments, and so on. Take a look at Figure 8.1. There you can see the difference between data and information. **Data** are distinct items that don't have much meaning to you in a given context. For example, in Figure 8.1, you can see the items **NW843, 1140,** and **23,** but you

FIGURE 8.1

The difference between data and information is extraordinary. Which would you rather look at to find your flight?

Data

NW843, MSP, ANC, 1140, 1444, 6.4, 757, 23

Information

Flight Information							
Flight	Origin	Destination	Departure	Arrival	Flight Time	Airplane	Gate
NW 843	Minneapolis (MSP)	Anchorage (ANC)	1140 AM	0244 PM	6 hr. 4 min.	Boeing 757	23

don't know what they mean. Once someone organizes these data, in the appropriate context, it becomes clear that your flight (NW 843) leaves at 11:40 A.M. from Gate 23. The data have been transformed into information. **Information** is *organized* data whose meaning is clear and useful to you in a given context. Both presentations in Figure 8.1 contain the same items, but one is more useful than the other, because one is meaningfully organized for you. Which would you rather use when trying to find your flight?

DATABASE STRUCTURES AND ORGANIZATION

How Can I Organize Data in a Meaningful Way?

Whether it's sorting through an electronic address book, registering for classes on the Web, or organizing flight information for a major airline, you need a database. In the broadest sense, a **database** stores and organizes data. In many ways, a database is like an electronic filing cabinet.

As you saw in Figure 8.1, creating usable information from data is vitally important. Storing the data in an organized manner is essential to creating the information. You need a way to organize data, and for this you use data files. **Data files** contain organized data destined for use in a database. Data files use specific data *structures* to help organize the data so a database can use them.

Structures

Data files, like filing cabinets, structure data to make sure it's accurate and as easy to understand as information. **Data structures** organize data in a uniform manner. The structure of a filing cabinet is straightforward—it holds drawers that contain information on cards arranged alphabetically.

Our electronic data file also uses certain structures that maintain accurate and accessible data. In Figure 8.1, each column in the data file is a field. A **field** is the smallest piece of *meaningful* data. In Figure 8.1, the flight, departure, gate, and the others are field names. **Field names** describe what's in the fields. Fields have specific properties. A **property** is the *type* of data in a field (for example, numeric, date, and currency).

Figure 8.2 displays a data file containing organized data from a car dealer's database. Let's call this car dealership Retread Auto. Here the **Name** field contains only text, while the **Mileage** field contains only numbers. So one field's property is text while the other's is numeric.

FIGURE 8.2

This data file (cars.dat) shows some of Retread Auto's sales. Notice the many fields Retread Auto uses to organize the data, which creates information.

License	Name	Address	Phone	DOB	Purchased	Car	Year	Color	Mileage	Price
M23405-2382	Tavis Marten	122 Anyplace Drive, Kalamazoo, MI	616-555-4587	January 4, 1980	December 18, 2000	Jeep Cherokee	1995	Blue	101,034	$8,032
M25868-8583	Susie Jones	8675 State Street, Portage, MI	616-555-7425	June 23, 1975	March 3, 1994	Geo Metro	1994	Red	67,009	$6,348
M57346-0488	Manny Smith	3453 Ada Ave., Galesburg, MI	616-555-2255	May 6, 1984	May 7, 2000	Chevy Camaro	1997	Black	88,000	$12,023

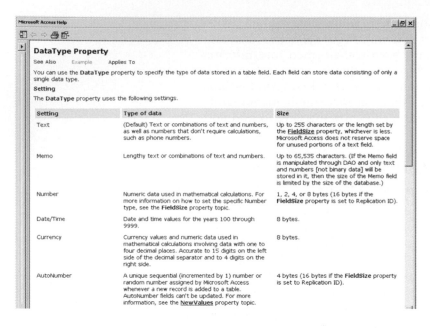

F I G U R E   8.3

When you're in Microsoft Access you can press the F1 key and search for the field data types chart.

The **Year, DOB,** and **Purchased** fields have the date/time property. Some fields can be tricky. For example, the **Phone** field is text and not a number. Can you guess why? Have you ever had to add or subtract phone numbers? Probably not. The number field allows you to perform calculations. More field types or properties are shown in Figure 8.3.

Fields run vertically in columns in our data file. The horizontal rows are records. A *record* is a complete data entry. A record contains data from the fields in our data file and forms an entity. An *entity* is a distinct item in a database. In Figure 8.1 (on page 8.2) an entity is a particular flight and in Figure 8.2 (on page 8.3) an entity is a car dealer customer.

A list of records makes up a data file. Link a data file or collections of data files together and you form a database.

Organization

Let's return to our metaphor of an electronic filing cabinet to see how a database and a cabinet are similar—and different. Your local used car dealer, Retread Auto, keeps a filing cabinet of all the used cars he sold. The filing cabinet has three drawers in it, the first drawer for people with last names from A–L, the second for M–S, and the third for T–Z. In each drawer he arranges cards alphabetically for each person. Figure 8.4 shows this manual system.

F I G U R E   8.4

Here's Retread Auto's filing card system with three drawers. It's easy to find customers by name, but what happens when you want to search by automobile type or purchase date?

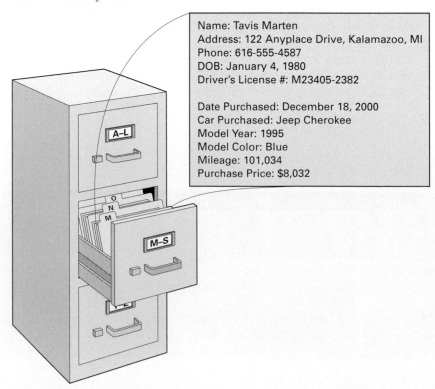

Name: Tavis Marten
Address: 122 Anyplace Drive, Kalamazoo, MI
Phone: 616-555-4587
DOB: January 4, 1980
Driver's License #: M23405-2382

Date Purchased: December 18, 2000
Car Purchased: Jeep Cherokee
Model Year: 1995
Model Color: Blue
Mileage: 101,034
Purchase Price: $8,032

When the dealer wants to find information on Mr. Marten, for instance, he looks up Mr. Marten's card under the letter "M." But what happens when the dealer wants to know who bought cars in the current year so that he can thank them for their recent business? Or what if he wants to know who owns a car older than 1995 to see if they are ready to replace it? This dealer can't efficiently find this information unless he remembers customers by name.

What if the dealer was able to have the filing cabinet automatically reorganize the data to produce the information that he wanted? You're probably thinking that a database can do this. Retread Auto thought so too and acquired one. And our Figure 8.2 is a good starting point to understanding the database.

When you look back at the data file in Figure 8.2 (on page 8.3), it becomes easier to see how a database is the answer to our questions. If the dealer wants to send cards to recent customers, he can quickly scan the **Purchased** column to see who recently bought a car. If he wants to know whose cars are older than 1995 models, he looks at the **Year** column and contacts those customers to ask if they want to look at newer models. To learn more about database structures and organization, visit the Interactive Companion Labs and choose "Introduction to Databases."

---

making **the grade**   SECTION A://

1. To store and organize data you use a _____.
2. A _____ is the smallest piece of meaningful data.
3. The type of data in a field is its _____.
4. A _____ is a complete data entry.
5. A distinct item in a database is an _____.

B://DATABASES

Now that you know the basic structure and organization of data files, let's look at the types of databases available to organize your data files.

HIERARCHICAL AND NETWORK DATABASES

What Were the First Types of Databases?

In the past most databases were either hierarchical or network oriented. A *hierarchical database* uses the inverted directory tree structure you learned about in Chapter 3. Just like file management systems, this database organizes data under different directories. Certain records belong to certain directories. Parent directories are the main directories. A *parent* is a directory similar to a folder in file systems. Each parent directory has its children. The *children* are subdirectories or subfolders. In other words, records belonging to a directory are children and the directory is the parent.

This parent-child analogy often describes the data organization. In a hierarchical database children can have only one parent. The *network database* uses a tree structure similar to the hierarchical database but its children can have more than one parent. The ability for a child subdirectory to have more than one parent directory is the main difference between a network database and a hierarchical database.

RELATIONAL DATABASES

What's the Most Popular Type of Database Today?

Relational databases are the most common database today. Microsoft Access, Oracle, Sybase, DB2, FileMaker, and other database programs support relational databases. Links to database programs are available at www.mhhe.com/i-series (select "Databases and DBMS Software"). **Relational databases** store data in tables that have rows and columns. **Tables** are organized collections of records. The tables have fields (columns) and records (rows) to organize the data. Figure 8.5 is the Customer table from our Retread Auto example.

F I G U R E   8.5

Here's the Customer table from the Retread Auto Microsoft Access database. Notice the fields and the records in this relational database.

Records

Fields

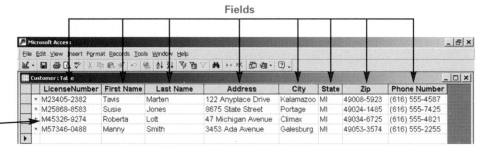

The Customer table (Figure 8.5) contains field names such as **License Number, First Name,** and **Address.** And, of course, these fields have properties. In Figure 8.5, all the properties are text. Look at each row and see that each contains a complete record. Of course, each record represents an entity. In this table, each entity is a Retread Auto customer. We'll discuss relational databases in greater detail in a moment.

OBJECT-ORIENTED DATABASES

Which Database Type Might Become the Most Popular Next?

Most computer experts agree the next type of database that will become popular will be object-oriented. **Object-oriented databases** use objects to represent entities rather than fields in tables. An **object** is one item that contains distinct information. In an object-oriented database, each object has its own properties or attributes. An **attribute** is a quality that an object possesses. For example, a car object would have a color attribute as well as a model, year, and price attribute. Similar objects all belong to the same class. For now, think of a **class** as a collection of similar objects. We'll learn more about object-oriented concepts in Chapter 11. Figure 8.6 shows how you'd organize the Car class in a Retread Auto object-oriented database.

F I G U R E   8.6

This is how we might view objects if we used an object-oriented database for our Retread Auto example.

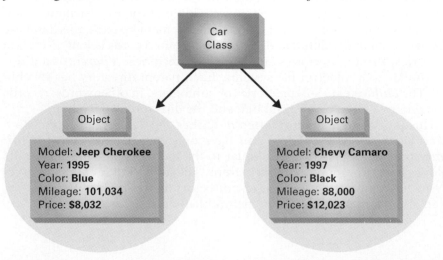

WORKING WITH A RELATIONAL DATABASE

How Can I Make a Database Work for Me?

You've now had a glimpse at many options available when you must organize data. You could store cards in a filing cabinet, organize your data in a single data file, or select a hierarchical, network, relational, or object-oriented database.

Chances are that you'll work with a relational database using such software tools as Oracle, Sybase, Microsoft Access, FileMaker, MySql, or DB2.

Relationships

From the day you were born, you've been creating information with the data you collect from the world around you. Most of this information is from associations or relationships. You may have touched a hot stove and learned to stay away from it. (Of course, later in life you learned to use the stove correctly.) A **relationship** is an association between database entities. For example, if we were to create a Retread Auto relationship, we could say that each owner has a car. The relationship would look something like Figure 8.7.

FIGURE 8.7

This entity relationship represents the statement "Each owner has a car."

The relational database relies on associations, or relationships, between the various tables in the database. When you create relationships between tables you can choose among three types: one-to-one, one-to-many, and many-to-many. Figure 8.8 illustrates how you'd represent these relationships. Let's discuss how we'd use them for Retread Auto.

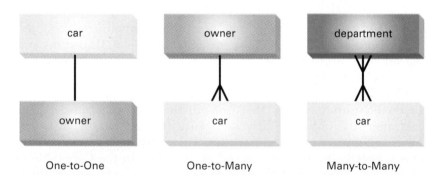

One-to-One   One-to-Many   Many-to-Many

FIGURE 8.8

Relationships in a database can vary, as shown here for Retread Auto.

A **one-to-one relationship** means that *one* record of a record type can be related to only *one* other record in a record type. For example, one car can have only one owner. A **one-to-many relationship** means that *one* record of a record type can be related to *many* records of another record type. One owner can own many cars. Finally, a **many-to-many relationship** means that *many* records of a record type can be related to *many* records in another record type. For example, many departments (such as sales, service, and body shop) keep track of many cars. Many of these same cars are tracked by many of the same departments. We'll work more with relationships later in this section.

Organizing and Structuring Data

Tables store all data in a relational database. We need three tables to store the data in our Retread Auto example. Figure 8.9 displays the Cars, Customer, and Service tables.

The *U.S. Patent and Trademark Office database includes all patents dating from 1790, a total amounting to 6.5 million.*

did you know?

FIGURE 8.9

Here are the three tables Retread Auto used to build its database.

Roberta Lott owns the Honda Civic.

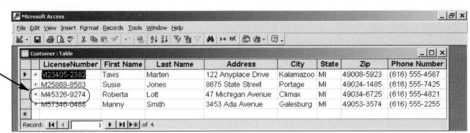

Cars Table

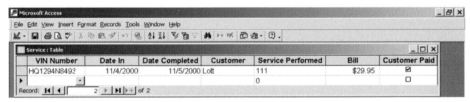

Customer Table

Service Table

Each table has fields in columns and records in rows exactly like the car dealer data file (see again Figure 8.2 on page 8.3). But instead of having all the information in one data file, we've created tables and established relationships between them. Figure 8.10 shows these relationships.

You'll notice that all of the relationships are one-to-many. The **LicenseNumber** field is the "one" in the Customer table because each customer has only one driver's license number. In the Customer table **LicenseNumber** is the primary key. The *primary key* in a table is the field that is specific to only one record in the table. In the Cars table there can be "many" driver's licenses because a customer can buy more than one car.

Notice in Figure 8.10 that the primary keys are in bold type. **License Number** (Customer table) and **VIN** (Cars table) are easy enough to recognize. But the Service table has both the **VIN** and **DateIN** as the primary key. A *compound primary key* occurs when two or more fields identify a distinct record. **VIN** won't work alone because a car can be serviced more than once. So, the database uses **DateIN** as well.

Now that we've set up our tables and relationships, we are ready to sort and arrange our data to produce information. From the tables in Figure 8.9, you can see that the Honda Civic (Cars table) belongs to Roberta

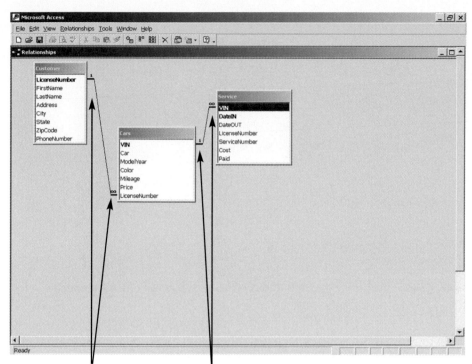

F I G U R E   8.10

Notice the Retread Auto table relationships and primary keys. Without them this database wouldn't work correctly.

Notice the one-to-many relationships represented with the 1 to infinity sign (∞).

Lott (Customer table) and it has been recently serviced (Service table). But there's an easier way to get this information from these tables than by looking at them as we've been doing. We'll need a database management system.

making the grade

1. A _____ uses a tree structure similar to the hierarchical database.

2. _____ store data in tables that have rows and columns and are the most-used databases.

3. To link tables you must establish a _____ between them.

4. A field specific to each record in a table is called the _____.

C://DATABASE MANAGEMENT

To manage the many tables we've created for our Retread Auto database (Figure 8.9 on page 8.8), we'll need a database management system. A **database management system (DBMS)** is application software that allows you to arrange, modify, and extract data from a database to create

F I G U R E   8.11

This table lists some of the available DBMS software packages.

Name	Web Site
Access	www.microsoft.com/office/access/
Adabas	www.softwareag.com/adabas/
DB2	www.ibm.com/software/data/db2/
FileMaker	www.filemaker.com
Informix	www.informix.com
MySQL	www.mysql.com
Oracle	www.oracle.com
POET (Object-Oriented)	www.poet.com
PostgreSQL (Object Relational)	www.postgresql.org
Sybase	www.sybase.com
Versant (Object-Oriented)	www.versant.com
Visual FoxPro	msdn.microsoft.com/vfoxpro/

Note: Unless otherwise noted, all DBMSs are based on the relational data model.

information. DBMSs work on everything from a PDA to a large mainframe computer. Figure 8.11 lists some common DBMSs.

DATABASE MANAGEMENT FEATURES
What Can a DBMS Do for Me?

With a DBMS you can work more easily with data you store in the database. You also can make sure that all data in your database conforms to your standards. For example, you can make sure that no one adds a new customer to the Customer table in Figure 8.9 (on page 8.8) without a current driver's license number. But DBMSs can do more than this. Let's look at a few general features before moving into some specific examples using Microsoft Access.

Storage

You know that a database allows you to keep more data in one place. A filing cabinet would soon fill up with cards and require another filing cabinet. Adding a filing cabinet also would require reorganizing your cards. But you can add data as necessary to a database with a DBMS.

If the database gets too large, you can archive the data. An ***archive*** is a copy of older data that becomes historical records. In our Retread Auto database, we might archive all cars purchased in the 1980s and use only data dating from 1990. This maximizes storage and allows you to efficiently maintain your database.

Retrieval

A DBMS makes it easier for you to find and retrieve data. A filing cabinet lets you find data by only one parameter, such as a last name, but a DBMS allows you to retrieve varying pieces of data. You'll find out how in just a moment.

i·buy

Where Can I Buy Data Online?

You locate information on the Web with a search engine, which lists Web sites that can help you find information. You can even search for a friend's e-mail address using specialized Web databases. You can find a cousin's phone number at www.bigfoot.com or locate your high school sweetheart at www.classmates.com.

But what if you need large amounts of data on city residents, such as how many people live in apartments? Would you want to search an entire online phone book for information? Or, what if you wanted to find out a job applicant's driving record or possible criminal history? This information is not readily available with a simple search on the Web.

Instead there are massive collections of data that you can access only through services called data brokers. **Data brokers** are companies that search many databases and return information to you. Companies such as ChoicePoint (www.choicepointinc.com) will search databases from the U.S. Census Bureau, the FBI files, gov-

ernment documents, real estate transactions, marketing data, and many other databases. You can search many of these databases yourself, but it would take time to compile all the information you might need. Data brokers use specialized software that helps them meet your request quickly. Most data brokers will generate easy-to-read reports and put a copy of the data on a CD-ROM.

Companies that need large amounts of data to make business decisions employ their own data brokers, but there are also data brokers who will search for information for anyone who requests it. Think of them as Internet private eyes.

Organization

A DBMS lets you reorganize your data for specific purposes. What if you want to know only the people who bought cars before 1995? A DBMS can instantly reorganize and present that information to you. A filing cabinet can't.

A DBMS can accomplish this organization because it uses a data dictionary. A **data dictionary** defines the basic organization of a database. It contains a list of all the data files, records, and names and types of fields in a database.

Distribution

Most DBMSs also have report generator functions. A **report generator** creates a written or Web report of information you request. For example, you could make a list of all customers who bought a car this year. Then you could generate "Thank You" cards with personalized greetings.

Assimilation

With a DBMS, you can also import data files to create new data files. Bringing external files into a database is an important function because the more data a database can effectively assimilate, the more information a DBMS can produce.

Integrity

A DBMS can also check for data integrity. ***Data integrity*** makes sure the right type of data is in each field. For example, data integrity won't allow you to enter a name in the date field. DBMSs can enforce ***alphabetic validation*** to make sure only letters appear in a field or ***numeric validation*** to make sure only numbers appear in a field.

Types of validation checks vary depending on the DBMS. In our Retread Auto database, we can make sure our DBMS doesn't accept a new customer unless he or she has a valid driver's license.

Security

For security reasons, you can use a DBMS to decide who can access the database. ***Data security*** restricts database access for viewing, organizing, and updating data files. Levels of access can differ according to users' IDs and passwords. For example, a database might allow all salespeople to view records, but allow only the manager to update records.

Queries

By scanning the data in our Retread Auto data file (see again Figure 8.2 on page 8.3) and tables (Figure 8.9 on page 8.8) we've been able to answer questions such as "Who purchased a 1995 blue Jeep Cherokee?" (Tavis Marten did.) But what if we have more entries or more complicated questions? It would be difficult to scan 2,000 entries to answer, "How many Jeep Cherokees have been sold in the last five years?" We might as well be at a filing cabinet.

A DBMS helps us answer these questions quickly and without effort. With a DBMS you can ask for specific data by using a query. A ***query*** asks a question to a database in a language it understands—query language. A ***query language*** uses English statements to extract data from a database and create information. ***Structured Query Language (SQL)*** is the default query language for most databases. We can use SQL to identify people who bought cars from 1995 and earlier from our cars data file in Figure 8.2 (on page 8.3):

SELECT Name, Address, Phone FROM "cars.dat" WHERE Purchased <= 1995

To try an SQL query for yourself, visit the Interactive Companion Labs and choose "SQL Queries."

DATABASE MANAGEMENT APPLICATIONS
How Do I Use a DBMS to Meet My Needs?

Now that you know the basic DBMS functions, let's look at how to use a DBMS. For this section we'll use Microsoft Access, because it's the most common DBMS software in personal productivity environments.

Querying

You know that you can get data from a database with a query. Remember, queries can help you answer questions such as "Who bought what car?" In Access you use a query-by-example to ask your questions with the DBMS. A *query-by-example (QBE)* allows you to graphically represent what information you'd like to see from the database. Using this example, the DBMS then displays the information you want by creating an SQL statement so you can query the database. Figure 8.12 shows a simple QBE.

In this example, the QBE pulls data from the Customer and the Car tables of our Retread Auto database. Using a one-to-many relationship between the tables, the DBMS is able to link all sold cars by a customer's license number. Each time you run, or execute, the query, the DBMS assimilates any new data and produces new information in whatever format you choose.

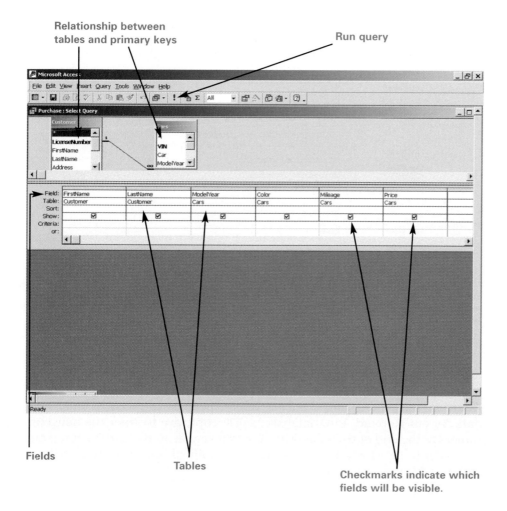

Relationship between
tables and primary keys

Run query

Fields

Tables

Checkmarks indicate which
fields will be visible.

FIGURE 8.12

This Access query-by-example (QBE) will help us generate the necessary information we need.

Reports

Once you complete your query, you can display your results in an easy-to-read format. **Reports** are graphical displays of your data. You can create printed reports as in Figure 8.13. You also can create Web pages. With Microsoft Access you can even integrate your reports into other Microsoft Office applications such as Word or PowerPoint. You can run reports regularly (weekly, for example) or you can generate a report whenever someone needs one.

F I G U R E   8.13

Here's an Access Report generated from a QBE. We can use this information to print out a report or even create a Web page.

Database fields displayed in a report format

Customers			
First Name	Tavis		
Last Name	Marten		
License #	M23405-2382		

Price	VIN Number	Car	Mileage
$8,032.00	MJ4563H9	Jeep Cherokee	101,034.00

First Name	Susie
Last Name	Jones
License #	M25868-8583

Price	VIN Number	Car	Mileage
$6,348.00	JD5768D6	Geo Metro	67,009.00

First Name	Roberta
Last Name	Lott
License #	M45326-9274

Price	VIN Number	Car	Mileage
$14,025.00	HQ1294N8	Honda Civic	45,021.00

First Name	Manny
Last Name	Smith
License #	M57346-0488

Price	VIN Number	Car	Mileage
$12,023.00	ZZ9384N3	Chevy Camaro	88,000.00

Forms

After you've created your database tables, people will need to enter new data. In our Retread Auto database, salespeople are to enter the new customers at the end of each day. They could give you all the data to enter, but it's easier to develop a form. **Forms** are graphical interfaces that make it easy to add or delete data.

i·series insights

Ethics, Security & Privacy

Databases and Privacy

We've discussed how databases can store, modify, and access data to create information. Databases can also make a business more efficient and can customize your e-commerce experience. But these same abilities may chip away at your privacy. If you want to be alone, you can close your door. It's harder, however, to keep your personal information from businesses with databases.

You disclose this information when you fill out a marketing survey, apply for a credit card, fill out a warranty, apply for a driver's license, or enter a Web sweepstakes.

Each time, businesses collect data on you and store it in databases. And as database use increases, more companies are selling such information to each other. We discussed this in Chapters 4 and 7.

Sometimes you may want people to know about you. Maybe you'd like e-mail about CD bargains on your favorite artist. But first check the business's privacy policy.

Ultimately, it's up to you to protect your personal data. If you don't want someone to know what you bought, use cash instead of a credit card. If you don't want someone to know your address, get a post office box. To stop unwanted e-mail, use a separate e-mail account for the surveys you fill out online.

Learn more about your privacy rights and how to protect them. We've created a list of helpful organizations at www.mhhe.com/i-series.

Figure 8.14 shows the Retread Auto form displaying the first record from the Customer table. The salesperson can also add new customers as long as you've set the database security to allow this. To learn more about using Microsoft Access as your DBMS, visit the Interactive Companion Labs and choose "Introduction to Databases."

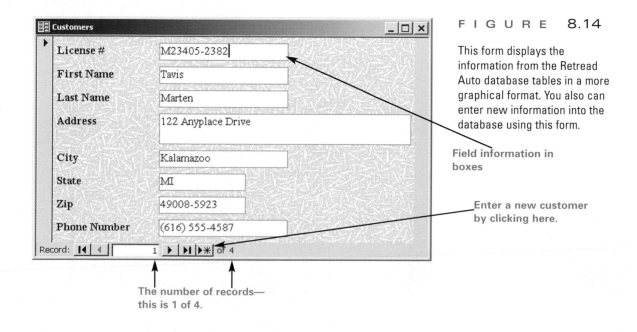

FIGURE 8.14

This form displays the information from the Retread Auto database tables in a more graphical format. You also can enter new information into the database using this form.

Field information in boxes

Enter a new customer by clicking here.

The number of records— this is 1 of 4.

1. A _____ is application software that allows you to arrange, modify, and extract data to create information.
2. A _____ defines the basic organization of a database.
3. Database _____ can be printed or made into Web pages.
4. Restricting database access for reading and updating data files is a part of _____.
5. You use a specialized language called a _____ for extracting data from a database.

D://DATABASES IN ELECTRONIC COMMERCE

In Chapter 4 we discussed electronic commerce, or e-commerce, as the buying and selling of goods and services on the Web. But e-commerce can be more than that. E-commerce can also mean using the Web to conduct business. Databases play a key role in helping businesses conduct e-commerce by making their business tasks more effective and efficient.

Many businesses are using the Web to provide their employees with access to information. Figure 8.15 shows an interface a business can use to access its supply database through the Web.

The Web has encouraged businesses to think about how they can best provide information to you, the consumer, too. You use databases when you look at a Web catalog or search the Web using a search engine. You use them even when you visit a Web site that personalizes weather forecasts and other information.

FIGURE   8.15

The Web interface to a supply chain system allows employees to access their business's database from anywhere in the world.

Employees log in here.

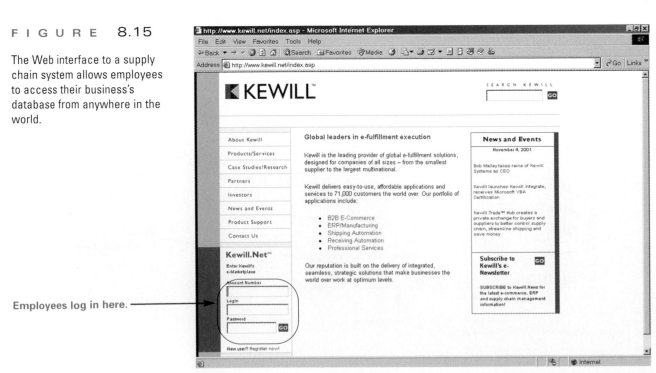

With the growth of databases on the Web, security is an issue for businesses and individuals. Only authorized people should be able to access secure areas of a database, such as those containing credit card numbers. You should know how secure your own data is and who's using it.

USE IN BUSINESS

How Might I Use a Database at Work?

Most databases now use a client/server network. You learned about these networks in Chapter 2 and Chapter 6. The network may be at one location (intranet), many business locations (extranet), or anywhere in the world (Internet). It even can be a combination of all three.

Typically you'll be able to access portions of databases through the access privileges the DBMS grants you. Once you've logged onto the network, the DBMS will recognize you. But how does the DBMS know whom to let in and what access to grant them? People who administer databases play a key role.

To develop and keep databases running, businesses depend on database administrators. **Database administrators (DBAs)** design, implement, and maintain solutions to business challenges using databases. They also work with Web developers to integrate databases with the Web. To see listings of database jobs, visit the Interactive Companion Labs and choose "Introduction to Databases."

WEB-ENABLED DATABASES

How Can I Access Information Online?

Many people use Web browsers to surf the Web. Businesses use Web browsers to access databases, which allows them to share documents with one another, monitor business transactions, and sell goods and services to you. They use Web technologies such as eXtensible Markup Language (XML) to make the information from databases appear on Web pages as in Figure 8.16. You learned in Chapter 4 that XML helps organize and present information in a Web browser. In most cases, XML gets its information from a Web-enabled database.

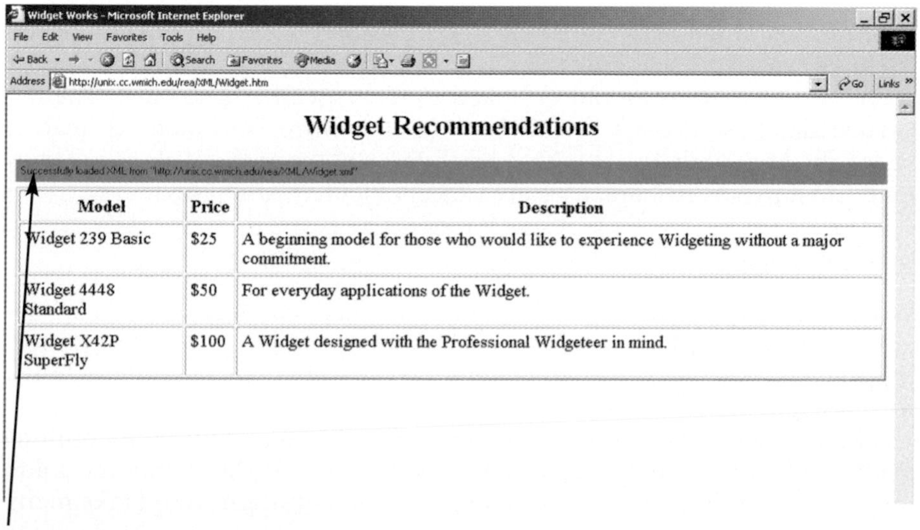

The Web browser informs you that XML has been successful.

FIGURE 8.16

A business can use XML to present database information using a standard Web browser.

Web-enabled databases access, modify, and present information through a Web browser. A Web-enabled database offers all the functions of a DBMS. In most cases, a Web-enabled database uses the same DBMS (such as Access or Oracle) with a program, or middleware, to make the database available on the Web. *Middleware* is a software application that works between two different software applications and allows them to talk to each other. In this case, middleware allows the DBMS and the Web browser to exchange information.

Web Search Engines

When you use a Web search engine such as Yahoo!, Altavista, or Google, you're accessing data from a database. Web search engines are Web-enabled databases that search, sort, and categorize Web addresses. Web search engines store Web addresses and short descriptions of the Web page's content in a searchable database. When you send your query to the database, it returns Web pages likely to contain the information you requested. Daily updates keep these databases current with Web content. Figure 8.17 displays results from Google, a popular Web search engine.

F I G U R E   8.17

Google, a popular Web search engine, uses a hypertext database to present a list of Web sites most relevant to your search criteria.

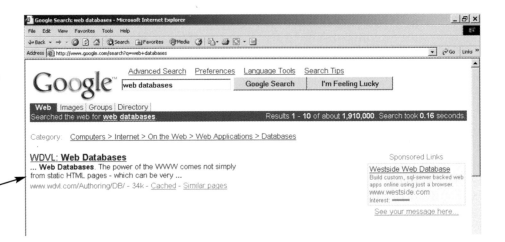

**Notice the hyperlink,
the URL, and the short
Web site description.**

Web search engines use a hypertext database to generate a list of hyperlinks with Web page descriptions for you. *Hypertext databases* list each Web address as an object linked to its respective Web page. The hypertext database doesn't keep a copy of the entire Web page. Instead it keeps the hyperlink object with a brief description of the Web page's content. Most hypertext databases are object-oriented databases.

Web Catalogs

When you shop on the Web by browsing through catalogs, you're also accessing databases. *Web catalogs* use a database to provide images, information, and pricing on available items. The database displays these items formatted on a Web page.

Businesses such as Dell Computer sell computers with many options available to you. You can choose hard drive size, RAM, computer color, and more. Listing every possible computer configuration would take many

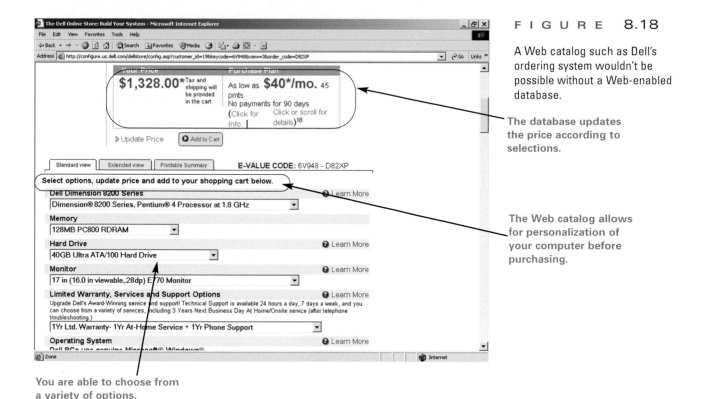

FIGURE   8.18

A Web catalog such as Dell's ordering system wouldn't be possible without a Web-enabled database.

The database updates the price according to selections.

The Web catalog allows for personalization of your computer before purchasing.

You are able to choose from a variety of options.

Web pages. Instead, Dell uses a database to allow you to select your configuration. It then displays your customized computer with its price, as in Figure 8.18. You can see your configuration choices and your purchasing options. None of this would be possible without a database-driven Web catalog.

Web Personalization

When you want to make a purchase at a Web catalog, you need to enter information such as your name, shipping and billing addresses, and credit card number. If you shop the Web catalog regularly, you might prefer that the business keep a record so you don't have to enter this information each time.

Just as our car dealer can keep customer information, so can an e-commerce Web site. By placing your name and information in a database, the e-commerce Web site allows you to use a log-in ID and password to access this information. We discussed this process in Chapter 4, but we didn't note that it's a Web-enabled database that allows for this Web personalization.

You're using a Web-enabled database when you visit a Web catalog that knows what you'd like to purchase or a Web site that knows your local weather. Businesses use the data they collect from you to personalize your experience at their sites.

F I G U R E   8.19

You can customize a Web site with the information most relevant to you with a personal portal such as Octopus.

Your search engine of choice is ready to use.

Recommended reading is listed according to your interests.

Your favorite Web page is here.

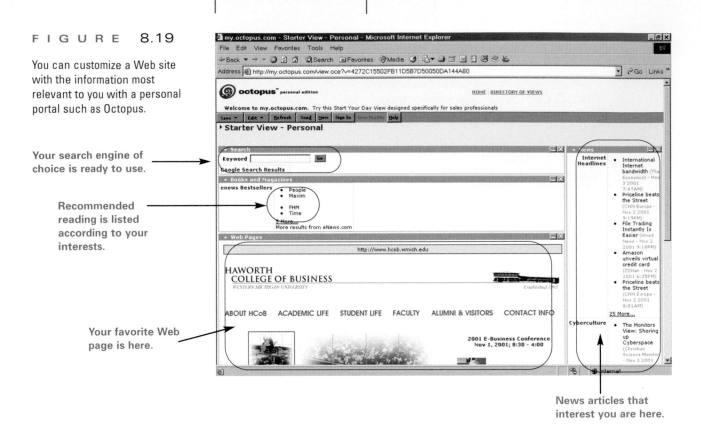

News articles that interest you are here.

Figure 8.19 is a personalized Web site. Here you can create an account and tailor the site to display what you want. If content or a favorite Web page isn't available, the personalized Web site allows you to import your favorite Web page. The personalized Web site is called a personal portal. A ***personal portal*** integrates all of your information into one Web site.

SECURITY AND PRIVACY
When Is My Data Not Mine?

Web personalization is just one method businesses use to collect information about you. Today it's easier than ever before for businesses to compile information about you in their databases. It happens every time you fill out a customer survey or a warranty or enter a contest.

Security

Most businesses work hard to protect data about you. Access privileges limit who can modify your data. But one operator mistake can create headaches for you when businesses share data. Consider a credit agency database. What if a mistake by a person entering data causes you to have a bad credit rating? Credit companies that access this database may refuse to give you loans or credit cards.

Security lapses increase as more databases become available over the Web. Hackers can break into databases containing credit card numbers from e-commerce sites, Internet banking sites, and online medical records. Links to sites that track these occurrences are at the text Web site at www.mhhe.com/i-series.

Privacy

More businesses are compiling data about you in their databases as it becomes easier to do so. This also makes you a target of one-to-one marketing. **One-to-one marketing** allows businesses to provide you with goods and services they tailor to your buying habits. We discussed these techniques in Chapter 4 when we covered e-commerce.

As businesses merge, so do their databases. Other businesses make money by selling information about you. It's always good to know a business's privacy policy before volunteering information. Many organizations, such as the Electronic Frontier Federation (www.eff.org), help you with privacy concerns and questions.

---

making the grade

SECTION D://

1. _____ design, implement, and maintain database solutions to business challenges.

2. _____ access, modify, and present their information through a Web browser.

3. _____ is a software program that works between the database and the Web browser.

4. _____ uses database information to make your visit to a Web site unique.

5. _____ tailors service and product offers to your buying habits.

F I G U R E   8.20

This table lists a few files either you or your computer use on a regular basis.

E://FILES

In Chapter 3 you learned about the importance of files. Your computer needs files to function. You need files to run a program (executable file), to store a report (text file), or to keep your favorite song (MP3 file). We've listed some of these file types in Figure 8.20.

Before you can use these files, you must be able to access, or open, them. Sometimes this means you click on an icon. But before your computer can respond, it needs to know where the files are. In Chapter 3 you learned how your computer organizes files in directory structures, pathnames, and hierarchies. Now we'll show you how your computer keeps track of and stores your files. It does this using file management and allocation tables.

Batch File	Same as command file. This file contains operating system instructions.
Binary File	Contains data or instructions in binary format (0s and 1s).
Command File	Contains operating system instructions.
Data File	Contains data used in databases or file storage.
Directory File	Contains information about files that are below it in the hierarchy.
Document File	Contains a file for programs such as Microsoft Word.
Executable File	Contains a program or commands in an executable format.
Image File	Contains a graphic. Window uses bmp files, but gif and jpg are also common.
Object File	Contains code that has been compiled.
Spreadsheet File	Contains a spreadsheet file for programs such as Microsoft Excel.
Text File	Contains textual data (that is, data that can be read by humans), including files you create with a text editor and any file in ASCII format.

We'll also discuss how you can help your computer run more efficiently. Sometimes this requires freeing up space on your hard disk or making sure you arrange files efficiently.

FILE MANAGEMENT

How Do I Know Where My Files Are?

What happens when you double-click on a Microsoft Word file (for example, **essay.doc**)? Your computer must start the **word.exe** executable file that starts the Microsoft Word program. Then Microsoft Word opens the file. The computer's file management system is important in this process. A *file management system* coordinates how the computer organizes and keeps track of files.

Think of file management systems as a basic DBMS. Part of a DBMS's task is to make sure a database stores data efficiently. A file management system does the same with files on your computer. In most cases, it makes sure that the computer stores all files in a hierarchical fashion (as discussed in Chapter 3). Windows Explorer is a built-in file management system that comes with Microsoft Windows. In Figure 8.21, Windows Explorer helps you look through folders to see where files are sitting on your computer. You can find out the type, size, and date of each file. You can also delete and rename files, but don't do it unless you know what you're doing.

Within a file management system, you can create backups of your files. *File backup systems* copy files and store them in a safe place. To learn more about managing files, visit the Interactive Companion Labs and choose "File Organization."

FIGURE 8.21

Windows Explorer can help you organize your computer files.

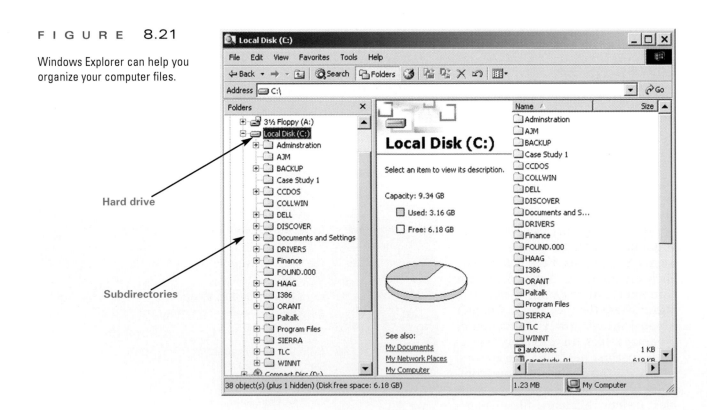

FILE ALLOCATION TABLES (FAT)

How Does My Computer Find My Files?

You use a file's pathname or click on an icon to tell your computer to open a file. But do you know that this file doesn't exist all in one place on your computer's hard drive? A computer places parts of files in different locations, or sectors, to maximize the hard drive space. A *sector* is a single area that can hold a certain number of bytes of data. (Usually this number is 512 bytes.) The computer groups sectors into a cluster. A *cluster* is an organized collection of sectors. A cluster can hold from 512 bytes to 256 kilobytes, depending on the hard drive and the operating system.

So if you have a 5 KB file and your computer uses 4,086 byte clusters, your computer places part of the file in an area where 4,086 bytes are free and the rest where 914 bytes are free. When you add to the file, the computer will find yet another place to add the data.

So how does your computer keep track of where it places your file? Your computer uses its file allocation table to record where it places all the pieces of the file. The *file allocation table (FAT)* is a file that stores information about the physical location of every file on the computer's hard disk. The FAT also tracks used areas on the disk so files don't overwrite each other.

Fragmentation

As you create, edit, and delete files, your clusters change and the FAT changes to keep track of where files are. As your computer moves and rewrites files, your hard disk fragments. *Fragmentation* occurs when your computer places parts of files over many hard disk areas. Too much fragmentation reduces your hard drive's efficiency.

As you allow your computer's hard drive to fragment, you increase the chance that your computer won't work as well. *Access speed*—the time between when you ask for a file and when the computer delivers it to you—slows as your hard disk fragments. Increased fragmentation also leads to file and hard disk failures that can destroy data.

To manage fragmentation, you'll run a defragmentation program regularly. *Defragmentation programs* reallocate file clusters and decrease fragmentation. To learn more about how disk fragmentation happens (and how to fix it), visit the Interactive Companion Labs and choose "Disk Fragmentation."

FILE COMPRESSION

How Can My Computer Hold More Files?

When you compress something, you make it smaller. Using *file compression,* you can shrink a file or files into a smaller file. This smaller file is a *compressed file.* In order to use this compressed file, you need to *decompress* or "unshrink" it back to its original size.

You can control the file size by setting a compression ratio. A *compression ratio* determines how small you want the compressed file to be. If you set a compression ratio of 30:1, the compressed file will be 30 times smaller than its original.

Compression Software

If you want to compress a file or files, you'll need compression software (see Figure 8.22). ***Compression software*** is utility software that allows you to compress a file or files. PKZip, ZipIt, and WinZip are popular compression software programs. They've become so popular that most people refer to compressing a file as ***zipping*** and decompressing a file as ***unzipping.*** Zipped files have a **.zip** extension.

You can also compress files before sending them over e-mail or putting them on a floppy disk. A smaller file will travel more quickly and take up less space in an e-mail account. On a floppy disk, you'll be able to store more files.

F I G U R E   8.22

WinZip is compression and decompression utility software available to you.

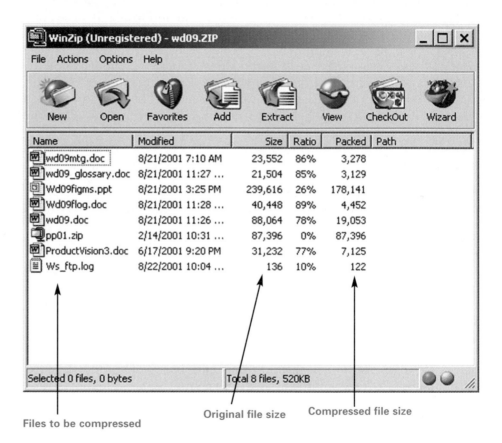

Files to be compressed

Original file size

Compressed file size

Disk Compression

Similar to file compression, disk compression will shrink files on a hard disk and create an area for these files. You need to use a compression utility to manage disk compression. A ***disk compression utility*** operates between the compressed files and the operating system. When you save a file to the compressed disk, the utility automatically compresses the file. When you open the compressed file, the utility automatically decompresses it. Using a disk compression utility slows down file access time, but it also allows you to save almost twice the data on your hard disk. Some versions of Windows have a built-in disk compression utility called DriveSpace.

i·witness

An Up-Close Look at Web Sites

How Do You Use Tables Effectively?

Basic HTML provides you with formatting of text. You can use different fonts and styles, change colors, create paragraphs, and place items in lists. But you also may want to place information in multiple columns that span the screen. Unfortunately, this isn't as simple as using the tab key. To do it, you must create a table.

Building a simple table requires that you:

1. Use the tags to create the table itself (**<table>** and **</table>**)

2. Use the tags to create a row in the table (**<tr>** and **</tr>**)

3. Within a row, use the tags to specify the information, which is essentially a column (**<td>** and **</td>**)

4. Repeat steps #2 and #3 until done.

You can also use tag and tag parameters to alter column widths, hide the bordering of a table, merge cells across a row, merge cells down a column, create a table caption, and much more.

Two Web pages will help you learn more about building and using tables. They are:

www.mhhe.com/i-series/I-Witness/8-A.html

www.mhhe.com/i-series/I-Witness/8-B.html

The first provides you with more information about building

and using tables in a Web site. Read it closely and print it out if you wish. The second is a Web site that contains a lengthy list of items with three subcategories. Your task is to convert that list into a three-column table. You can connect to the site for this text and download the second Web site to your computer. You then can make the changes yourself.

---

making the grade

1. A _____ coordinates how the computer organizes and keeps track of files.

2. _____ slows as your hard disk fragments.

3. The _____ stores information about the physical location of every file on the computer's hard disk.

4. As your computer moves and rewrites files, your hard disk _____.

5. In order to use a compressed file, you need to _____ it back to its original size.

F://SUMMARY AND KEY TERMS

The amount of **data** we need to manage to create **information** is increasing. **Databases** can organize and store data efficiently and effectively.

Understanding the different types of databases, such as **hierarchical, relational,** or **object-oriented,** helps you understand how they function. No matter which you choose, a **DBMS** can make sure that your data maintains **integrity** by validating data and providing **security.**

A **relational database** such as Microsoft Access will help you create **forms** and **reports,** run **queries** with **SQL,** and modify **records.** Make sure you establish the correct **relationships** though. You can choose from **one-to-one, one-to-many,** or **many-to-many.**

After you've created your database, you might want to use XML to create a **Web-enabled database** or a **Web catalog.** With these you can either start an e-commerce Web site or use **Web personalization** to attract people to your Web site. Make sure to consider issues of security and privacy of information.

You should also maintain your primary information system—your computer. **File management systems** can help. **Compressing** files, using **file backup systems** and **disk compression utilities** can help maintain the efficiency of your computer's hard disk. To maintain an effective **access speed,** check the level of hard disk **fragmentation.** You may need to run a **defragmentation program** to reallocate file **clusters.**

Remember, you can use file and database managers to control your own data. Or perhaps you'd like to consider becoming a **DBA** to help others build databases.

For Chapter 8, we've included a great deal of support on the text Web site at www.mhhe.com/i-series. We've provided additional resources on topics including:

- Databases and DBMS software
- Privacy organizations
- Security tracking
- Personal portals

KEY TERMS

access speed (p. 8.23)

alphabetic validation (p. 8.12)

archive (p. 8.10)

attribute (p. 8.6)

children (p. 8.5)

class (p. 8.6)

cluster (p. 8.23)

compound primary key (p. 8.8)

compressed file (p. 8.23)

compression ratio (p. 8.23)

compression software (p. 8.24)

data (p. 8.2)

data broker (p. 8.11)

data dictionary (p. 8.11)

data file (p. 8.3)

data integrity (p. 8.12)

data security (p. 8.12)

data structure (p. 8.3)

database (p. 8.3)

database administrator (DBA) (p. 8.17)

database management system (DBMS) (p. 8.9)

decompress (p. 8.23)

defragmentation program (p. 8.23)

disk compression utility (p. 8.24)

entity (p. 8.4)

field (p. 8.3)

field name (p. 8.3)

file allocation table (FAT) (p. 8.23)

file backup system (p. 8.22)

file compression (p. 8.23)

file management system (p. 8.22)

form (p. 8.14)

fragmentation (p. 8.23)

hierarchical database (p. 8.5)

hypertext database (p. 8.18)

information (p. 8.3)

many-to-many relationship (p. 8.7)

middleware (p. 8.18)

network database (p. 8.5)

numeric validation (p. 8.12)

object (p. 8.6)

object-oriented database (p. 8.6)

one-to-many relationship (p. 8.7)

one-to-one marketing (p. 8.21)

one-to-one relationship (p. 8.7)

parent (p. 8.5)

personal portal (p. 8.20)

primary key (p. 8.8)

property (p. 8.3)

query (p. 8.12)

query-by-example (QBE) (p. 8.13)

query language (p. 8.12)

record (p. 8.4)

relational database (p. 8.6)

relationship (p. 8.7)

report (p. 8.14)

report generator (p. 8.11)

sector (p. 8.23)

Structured Query Language (SQL) (p. 8.12)

table (p. 8.6)

unzipping (p. 8.24)

Web catalog (p. 8.18)

Web-enabled database (p. 8.18)

zipping (p. 8.24)

CROSSWORD PUZZLE

Across

1. A complete data entry
3. A smaller file than the original
7. Database administrator
9. File allocation table
10. An object's quality
12. A graphical interface used to add and delete data
13. A portal designed just for you
14. Query by example
16. Decompress a file
18. An association between database entries

Down

1. A graphical display of your data
2. An item that contains distinct information
4. Works between two other software applications
5. Decreases fragmentation
6. A copy of older data
8. Organized data
11. An organized collection of records
15. Ask a question to a database
17. A collection of objects
19. Structured Query Language

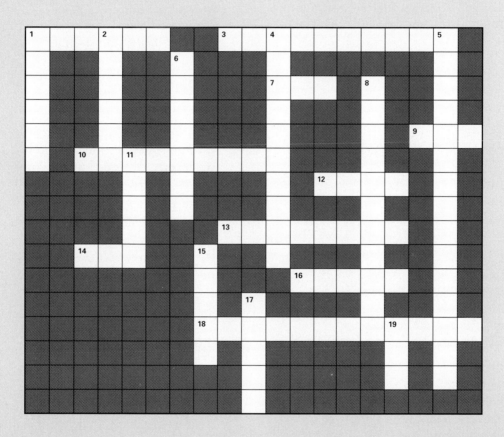

QUESTIONS AND EXERCISES

Multiple Choice

1. _____ is organized _____ from a database.
   a. Data, information
   b. Information, data
   c. A record, files
   d. Record, properties
   e. none of the above

2. _____ organize data in a uniform manner.
   a. Fields
   b. Records
   c. Disks
   d. Data structures
   e. Entities

3. Databases use _____ validation to make sure only letters appear in fields.
   a. numeric
   b. alphanumeric
   c. alphabetic
   d. character
   e. security

4. _____ store data in tables.
   a. Relational databases
   b. Hierarchical databases
   c. Network databases
   d. Object-oriented databases
   e. None of the above

5. SQL stands for
   a. Structured Query Language.
   b. Simple Query Language.
   c. Structured Questioning Language.
   d. Simplified Questioning Language.
   e. none of the above.

6. A _____ relationship means that one record of a record type can be related to only one other record in a record type.
   a. many-to-many
   b. one-to-many
   c. one-to-one
   d. many-to-one
   e. none-to-one

7. _____ copy files and store them in a safe place.
   a. Databases
   b. Computers
   c. File backup systems
   d. File systems
   e. Hard drive

8. How fast a computer delivers a file when it's requested is the
   a. megahertz.
   b. access speed.
   c. fragmentation level.
   d. file per hour time.
   e. none of the above.

9. A _____ of 30:1 means that the original file is 30 times larger than the _____ file.
   a. compression ratio, decompressed
   b. fragmentation, compressed
   c. compression ratio, compressed
   d. decompression ratio, decompressed
   e. compression ratio, secondary

10. A(n) _____ operates between the compressed files and the operating system.
    a. disk compression utility
    b. application
    c. compression ratio
    d. file system
    e. DBMS

True/False

11. _____ A cluster is smaller than a sector.

12. _____ A DBMS is a database management system.

13. _____ A hierarchical database doesn't use a tree structure.

14. _____ Webware is a software application that works between the database and the Web browser.

15. _____ A personal portal integrates all your information in one place.

QUESTIONS AND EXERCISES

1. In the left-hand column list activities you've done this week that you think may have used a database. In the right-hand column explain why you think a database was involved.

ACTIVITY

_____

_____

_____

DATABASE INVOLVED

_____

_____

_____

_____

_____

2. In class or at home, find the file management system on your computer. In the left-hand column we've listed what to find on your computer. List an example of what you find in the right-hand column. For example, you might use your word-processed research paper for your Microsoft Word file.

ITEM

    Microsoft Word file

    Microsoft Access file

    A directory

    A subdirectory

    Pathname to a file

    A compressed file

ON YOUR COMPUTER

_____

_____

_____

_____

_____

_____

3. Most databases are managed with a database management system. Keeping in mind what a database does and how it's managed, answer the following:

a. When you check out a library book with your school ID, how might the data be managed? How does your school know which books you checked out and when they are due?

b. When you rent movies with your movie card or membership, how might a database be used? Besides knowing you've checked out a movie, why might the video store want to know what you rent?

4. Databases play a large role on the Web. Think about Web sites you've visited. Do you think any of them used a Web-enabled database? Why? How? List your answers below.

WEB SITE

_____

_____

_____

HOW IT USED A WEB DATABASE

_____

_____

_____

_____

e-commerce

LEVEL THREE

www.mhhe.com/i-series

1. Entering "Free" Contests

"Win a free computer." "Win a free shopping spree." You've seen these advertisements on Web pages or banner ads as you surf the Web. For the most part these contests are legitimate. These Web sites help you find free giveaways, contests, and prizes:

- Free Stuff Center—www.freestuffcenter.com
- TotallyFree Stuff—www.totallyfreestuff.com
- The FreeSite.com—www.thefreesite.com

Before entering any contests or giveaways, read how these sites use your information. You'll need to look at the "small print." Now, answer the following questions:

a. What kind of information does the site want? Are you willing to provide this information?

b. Is the site clear about why it wants this information? Does it say what it will do with it?

c. Are you willing to share this information in exchange for a free item or a chance in a giveaway?

Before giving away your personal information, learn about your personal privacy rights. We list helpful Web sites at www.mhhe.com/i-series.

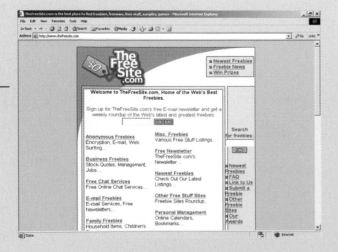

2. Using Personal Portals

Many Web sites allow you to personalize their sites by creating an account and selecting the items you want to appear on your Web page. You can select weather, news, sports, or other information. Some of the more popular Web sites are:

- MSNBC—www.msnbc.com
- ESPN.com—www.espn.com
- The Weather Channel—www.weather.com

Look at the above Web sites and then answer the following questions:

a. What personalization do these sites permit?

b. Are there limits to what you can do? For example, can you arrange the page content to suit yourself?

For greater personalization, you'll want to create a personal portal. A personal portal integrates all of your information in one place. As you look at the Web sites below, consider how they differ from those that offer only limited personalization:

- OnePage—www.onepage.com
- BackFlip—www.backflip.com
- Octopus, Inc.—www.octopus.com
- Yodlee—www.yodlee.com

Now, answer the following questions:

c. Would you use a personal portal? If so, what would you use it for?

d. Are there major differences among what these personal portals offer? Why might you use one over another?

e. What services do personal portals offer that some personalized Web sites lack?

f. Why might you use a personal portal? When would you need one instead of a personalized Web site?

Whether you use a personal portal or not, it's good to understand what these Web sites can offer. As the size of the Web increases, so will the availability of portals to manage the information. We'll keep you up to date at www.mhhe.com/i-series.

e-commerce

3. Renting an Apartment

You'll probably need to look for an apartment if you haven't already. You could check classified ads or bulletin boards to find an apartment. But what if you need an apartment in another city? Let's check some Web sites that can help you find an apartment. As you use these sites, enter the same criteria to search for your apartment. For example, you might need a one-bedroom that allows cats for under $600 a month. Choose your own criteria and search the following Web sites:

* HomeStore.com—www.homestore.com
* ApartmentLinks—www.apartmentlinks.net
* Apartment Living/Rental—
  apartments.about.com

Now, answer the following questions:

a. Were you able to find an apartment using these sites? Was one site easier to use than another? Why or why not?

b. What if you wanted a roommate? Is it possible using these services? Would you use them to do this? Why or why not?

Now look through the apartment listings in your local newspaper. Search for the same criteria as you did at the Web sites above. Note any differences.

4. Applying for a Credit Card

Most people buy goods and services on the Web with a credit card. In the United States e-commerce purchases using credit cards have almost doubled each year since 1998. Thus businesses have made it easier to apply for credit cards. Most of the major companies have applications on the Web:

* American Express—
  www.americanexpress.com
* Discover Card—www.discovercard.com
* MasterCard—www.mastercard.com
* Visa International—www.visa.com

Look at these Web sites and answer the following questions:

a. How easy is it to apply for a credit card on each site? Is the application clearly marked?

b. Would you consider applying for a credit card over the Web? Why or why not?

c. What advantages do you see using the Web instead of a paper application or a phone call? Are there any?

Before applying for a credit card, know the issues and responsibilities of owning one. The National Association of Colleges and Employers estimates that more than one-fourth of college students exceed $7,500 in credit card debt.

hands-on projects

on the web

1. Finding File Management Systems

Windows has its own file management system—Windows Explorer—built into its operating system. Many other file management systems are available on the Web. Search the Web for three different file management systems. Write down their names, Web addresses, and what they offer to users like you. Download one of them and try it out. Discuss the differences between your chosen system and Windows Explorer. Report your findings to the class.

2. Ranking Database Management Systems

Businesses rely on databases to manage data. Find three database management systems using a search engine. Make sure you record the title, the Web address, and the main features of the DBMS. Rank the three programs you find and discuss your rankings. Were there major differences among the programs? Why might a business choose one over the other? Report your findings to the class.

3. Customizing a Computer

Computer manufacturers now allow you to customize and order computers on the Web. Visit at least two Web catalogs and customize a computer. Use previous chapters to determine what hardware and software you'll need. Compare and contrast the shopping experience on each site. Which site was easier to use? Which would you buy a computer from? Which Web catalog did you like the most? Why? Share your findings with the class.

4. Personalizing Your Own Web Site

Web personalization is available on many Web sites. Search the Web for what you think are the three best Web sites that allow you to personalize their content and information. Sign up for one of the sites and personalize it for yourself. Report to the class the Web sites you found and how you personalized your own Web site. If a computer is available, show the class your personalized Web site.

5. Database Security

Protecting data is an ongoing challenge for many DBAs. Most businesses use specific software and techniques to protect valuable information from competitors, hackers, and others who could benefit from the stolen information. Search the Web for three sites that discuss the importance of database security. Share the Web sites with the class. Also, list five steps you can take to check for database security on the Web.

6. Finding a Free Database

Many people use Microsoft Access because it's included in their Microsoft Office software. But what if you don't have Access? Are there other databases you can use? Are they free (or available at a low cost)? Search the Web and find at least three free databases. Explain to the class what types of databases you found. Would you use any of them? Why or why not?

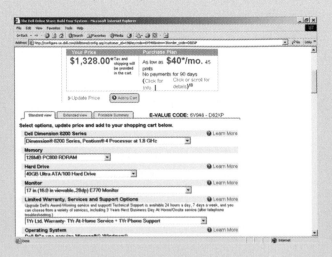

ethics, security & privacy

1. How Secure Is Your Personal Information?

Databases are an important part of e-commerce. Without them, businesses wouldn't be able to have interactive Web catalogs, process your credit card payment, or let you track your order. Businesses couldn't keep their inventories stocked or tell you about items that might interest you. Databases can store all of this data and produce information almost instantaneously.

Yet all this convenience comes with a price. It's the risk of people breaking into e-commerce Web sites. Crackers attack regularly. Most attempts fail, but some don't. And businesses don't often report the attacks because they don't want to damage their reputations. Consider these questions that relate to database security:

a. Would you work with or provide information to a business that a cracker had broken into? What if the business demonstrated it had improved its security after the break-in?

b. Who should be responsible for protecting data? Many businesses assume the software they use can withstand an attack. They blame the software developers when a cracker finds a vulnerability.

c. Software developers blame businesses that don't monitor their daily "bug reports" on software systems. Bug reports discuss vulnerabilities and offer solutions. Should businesses be responsible for keeping their software current? Or should software developers notify businesses? Who should keep the system updated?

Many Web sites and organizations also inform people about software vulnerabilities and the latest cracks into e-commerce systems. Should you be responsible for monitoring the latest problems with database security? You can look at these Web sites to find out if a particular business was ever cracked. We have links to these sites at www.mhhe.com/i-series.

Ultimately, who should be responsible for protecting valuable data that you provide to businesses?

2. How Much Information Is Available on the Web?

Have you ever wanted to look for relatives in another state, trace your genealogy, or find a lost love? Because of the power of Web-enabled databases, you can now search millions of phone numbers and addresses on the Web.

Before these Web-enabled databases, you had to scan phone books. Now with the Web and the power of databases, you can find almost anyone. And anyone can find you.

Check out these Web sites and look for someone:

- 555-1212.com—www.555-1212.com
- Bigfoot.com—www.bigfoot.com
- Yahoo! People Search—people.yahoo.com

Now, consider the following questions:

a. Were you surprised at whom you were able to find?

b. Should this information be accessible? Why or why not?

c. What if someone doesn't want this information on the Web? What choices are available to them? Should they have a choice? Why or why not?

group activities

1. Digging for Databases

Compile a list of databases that people use on your campus. Ask your friends if they use any databases. Go to computer labs and see what databases are on computers. Ask professors if they use any databases in their research. Search the library's Web site for reference databases or ask a reference librarian what databases are available. For each database note its name, purpose, and location. What did you find about the number of databases on campus? Present your findings to the class.

2. Whom Do You Trust?

The nonprofit organization TRUSTe has established privacy guidelines to protect your personal information. Web sites that apply and meet these guidelines get the "trustmark" logo.

Go to www.truste.org and read its criteria for becoming a trusted site. Then, look at five e-commerce sites—two certified and three that aren't. Describe how the two Web sites meet the TRUSTe guidelines.

Prepare a class presentation in which your group discusses TRUSTe and its guidelines. Then show the two Web sites that meet those guidelines and discuss why they do. Finally, show the three that don't. Point out why they can't be certified.

3. Create Your Own Database

In this chapter, we showed how a car dealer could take records from a filing cabinet and create a relational database using Microsoft Access.

Your group's task is to find some organization or entity that could use a database to organize its data. For example, you could organize someone's CD collection or create a club membership directory.

For this exercise your group won't create the entire database. Instead, create the appropriate tables with fields, records, and a primary key. Make sure you follow the guidelines in this chapter. You can use Microsoft Access to create the tables or create them just using Microsoft Word. Ask your instructor which program to use. When the tables are complete, present them to the class.

4. Making Some Tables

At the Web site for this text (www.mhhe.com/i-series and click on "chapter8"), you'll find a Word document for this exercise. It contains a list of database fields.

Your group needs to decide the best way to create tables using these fields and input them into Microsoft Access. Make sure to select field characteristics and set a primary key. At the Web site for this text, we provide tips on how to work through this exercise.

5. Top 5 DBMSs

Most businesses use only one or two database management systems. Conduct research on the Web to determine which ones your group considers the top five business DBMSs. Rank and discuss each DBMS's strengths and weaknesses. What is the primary purpose of each DBMS? Present your list in class and see how your results compare with other groups.

Looking Back/Looking Ahead

The Life and Times of a Dot-Com Entrepreneur

Joann's business and Web site are doing well. She's aware of the many ethics, security, and privacy issues associated with a Web site and technology in business, so she knows she'll need to be careful as she grows her business.

Joann has been doing so well that she needs to reorganize how she stores important data about her business. She stores contacts, sales, billing, and other items in a filing cabinet. Joann decides to move them into an electronic filing cabinet or _____. In this way she can take all her individual pieces of _____ and create _____ to help her make better decisions. She knows a _____, an application program that allows her to arrange, modify, and extract data to create information, will be sufficient. She chooses Microsoft Access.

Since Joann is using Access, she will be creating a _____ database. As she builds her tables she is careful to choose her _____, the smallest units of data, and give them appropriate _____ to identify the type of data. She uses a _____ in each table to identify unique records.

Joann establishes _____ between the tables so she can quickly create printed _____ and use _____ to enter data. Even though she's not a professional database administrator, or _____, she is careful to create validation rules to maintain _____. She also restricts access to the database for increased _____.

Joann knows that someday she will create a _____ database so that she and her customers can access data over the Web, but her concerns with database _____ and online _____ cause her to wait.

For now, Joann is happy with her new database. With a simple question, or _____, she can use _____, or SQL, to find the information she needs. Before leaving for the day, she checks the file organization on her computer with a _____ and checks the _____ level to see if she needs to run a _____ program to reallocate file clusters on her hard disk.

Joann's business is running well, but she'd like to know what new technologies are out there to help her improve her business. She'll find out more in Chapter 9.

did you know?

"The future is only a day away." That means a lot with respect to computers. Technology will change so rapidly that some people may get left behind. Let's see what some experts are predicting for the very near future.

$100,000,000$ plus—*the number of cell phones expected to be sold in 2002.*

$273,000,000$—*the estimated number of Internet appliances worldwide in 2004.*

$1,500—*projected cost of an Internet-enabled toilet, currently being developed by Matsushita.*

2002—*the year in which gadgets such as cell phones, game systems, and personal digital assistants will begin to outsell computers.*

$1,000,000$—*the number of titles an e-book will be able to hold by 2003.*

__??__ —*the number of Americans who will have wireless access to the Web in 2003.*

To find out just how many millions of Americans will have wireless access to the Web in 2003, visit the Web site for this text at www.mhhe.com/i-series.

CHAPTER

9

nine

Emerging Technologies

How about a Preview of Coming Attractions?

Technology is certainly not static—it changes every day. New versions of software become available, prices drop for hardware, and that same hardware becomes smaller, faster, and better. But changes in technologies we already use are just the tip of the iceberg. In this chapter we survey some new and emerging technologies and look at how those technologies will change your life. Let's look into tomorrow to see what's coming next.

On the horizon, there are emerging technologies (and innovative uses of technology) that will dramatically change how you interact with your computer and forever change how you live your life. For the most part, these new technologies and the changes they will bring are inescapable.

Ten years ago, there were only a handful of people on what is now known as the World Wide Web (Web) and most people had never heard of it. In the business world today, it's almost impossible to ignore the Web. That's how fast things have changed—and will change.

Today, people have telephones in their homes and separate cell phones to carry around. In the near future, we'll completely replace home telephones and simply have one cell phone for all our calls. Today, people primarily use a mouse and keyboard to enter information. Those devices are destined to be replaced by speech recognition and biometrics.

In this chapter, we'll explore with you emerging technologies that are already here and becoming widespread and others that will take a while longer before we fully embrace them. We'll conclude the chapter by taking a look at some extreme emerging technologies. Your life as you now know it is about to change.

For even more information on new technologies that are emerging every day, visit *Life-Long Learning Module E* (New Technologies Impacting Your Life) and *Life-Long Learning Module F* (Computers in Your Life Tomorrow).

FIGURE 9.1

Emerging technologies such as biometrics and holographic devices will dramatically change your life.

TOUCHING YOUR SENSES
- Automatic speech recognition
- 3-D
- Biometrics
- Virtual reality

E-COMMERCE
- E-cash
- Renting software
- Push technologies
- Just commerce

The Future

YOUR INTELLIGENT HOME
- Information supplier convergence
- Talking to your home
- Staying in touch with your home
- Intelligent home appliances

PUSHING THE ENVELOPE
- Technology in the walls
- Implant chips
- Holographic devices
- Computer-controlled cars
- Computers in your shoe

A://TOUCHING YOUR SENSES

Perhaps the most visible emerging technologies are those that incorporate all your senses. Traditionally, you view information on a screen or hear it through a set of speakers. You also use input devices such as a keyboard and mouse to capture information. But technology will soon move beyond those traditional forms of interaction. You'll soon be able to talk to your computer, view real 3-D images, provide identification through biometrics, and participate in virtual reality.

AUTOMATIC SPEECH RECOGNITION

When Will I Talk to My Computer?

In the movies at least, for many years now, people have been carrying on conversations with their computers. Think of "Hal" in *2001*. To a certain extent, you can expect that to become an everyday reality in your lifetime. (But no, your computer won't try to take over.) Automatic speech recognition is the emerging technology that will help you talk to your computer.

An ***automatic speech recognition (ASR)*** system captures your speech and can distinguish your words and word groupings to form sentences. ASR systems include many IT components such as a microphone (an input device), a sound card (another piece of hardware), software to distinguish your words, and databases that contain words and language rules. An ASR system uses these components to process your speech in three steps (see Figure 9.2).

FIGURE 9.2

Automatic speech recognition (ASR) is a three-step process.

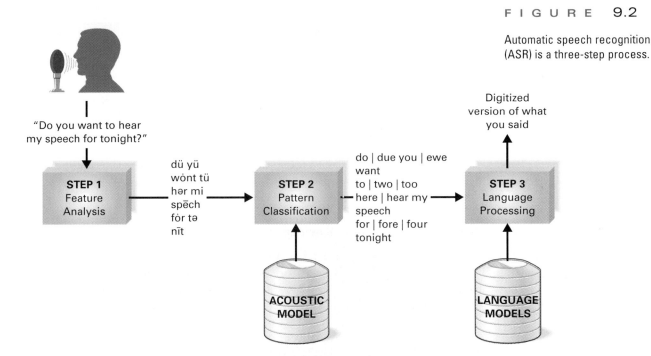

- **Step 1 Feature Analysis—*Feature analysis*** captures your words as you speak, converting the digital signals of your speech into phonemes. A *phoneme* is the smallest unit of speech, essentially a syllable. In Figure 9.2, you can see that the ASR system captured the word "Do" and converted it into the phoneme "dü." The phonemes are then passed to step 2.
- **Step 2 Pattern Classification—*Pattern classification*** attempts to recognize your spoken phonemes by locating a matching phoneme (or phoneme sequence) among words stored in an acoustic model database. An acoustic model database is your ASR system's vocabulary. For the phoneme "dü," pattern classification may find multiple words such as "do" and "due." Whatever the case, it sends all possible matching phonemes to step 3.

- **Step 3 Language Processing—***Language processing* attempts to make sense of what you're saying by comparing the possible word phonemes to rules in a language model database. Your language model database includes grammar rules, task-specific words, and sentences you might frequently use. As an example, in Figure 9.2 you're asking a question. So, your language model database would determine that your first spoken word is "do" and not "due."

Language processing is the key step. When you listen to someone, you can easily determine which words they're using within the context of your conversation. That's difficult for a computer. Consider the sentence, "Fruit flies like a banana." What does that mean? Well, in the gardening Olympics (if there is such a thing), that statement implies that if you were to toss a piece of fruit in the air, it would "fly" in the same way a banana would. More realistically, though, it means that a winged insect called a fruit fly is particularly fond of the taste of a banana.

Type	Description
Discrete	Requires you to pause between each spoken word.
Continuous	Can process continuous streams of words—that is, normal speech patterns.
Speaker-independent	Can be used by anyone; contains a limited vocabulary.
Speaker-dependent	Lets you "train" it to recognize only your voice; contains an expandable vocabulary.

The best ASR system is a combination of continuous, speaker-independent, and speaker-dependent.

Automatic Speech Recognition Today and Tomorrow

ASR is already all around you. Most telephone service providers use ASR when you call information to obtain a phone number. Most cell phones today include some sort of ASR so you can speak a person's name instead of dialing his or her phone number. Many of today's new home appliances (which we'll discuss further in a moment) include ASR. So, all you have to say is "cold water, delicate rinse, no fabric softener," and your washing machine sets itself appropriately.

In the future, ASR will become more and more widespread. We expect that most standard computer systems will come equipped with ASR within the next couple of years. But don't expect to be carrying on normal conversations with your computer for several years. We say this for a variety of reasons. First, ASR systems must become flexible enough to recognize the voices of many different people, not just yours. And they must be able to recognize your voice even when you have a head cold.

Second, ASR systems are somewhat limited in recognizing continuous speech patterns. In a normal conversation, you drop many ending consonants and run words together. Other people can understand what you're saying, but it becomes extremely difficult for a computer to do. So, step 1 (feature analysis) must become more sophisticated in converting your speech into phonemes.

Finally, step 3 (language processing) currently doesn't attempt to understand your speech within the context of a conversation or perhaps a term paper you're speaking. For true conversations to occur between you and your computer, your ASR system must be able to <u>understand</u> your words and sentences in the greater context of your conversation.

Nonetheless, ASR is here and here to stay. Even in its current form, ASR can be a great productivity tool for you. You can probably talk much faster than you can type. Even if your ASR system incorrectly interprets your words five times per page, fixing those errors is much faster for most people than typing the entire page. On the Web site for this text at www.mhhe.com/i-series, we've provided a list of the better ASR systems today. And in *Life-Long Learning Module F* on the future of technology, we've included more information. You should definitely read that module—you'll like what you see.

REAL 3-D

Will My Computer Show Me Things in "Real Life"?

Traditionally, you view information on your screen (even your TV screen) in two dimensions or pseudo three dimensions. In Figure 9.4, for example, you can see two graphs. The first shows information in only two dimensions. The second shows the same information in pseudo three dimensions. It achieves this by adding depth and shadowing. But it still isn't real three-dimensional.

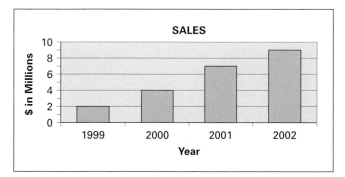

Two-dimensional presentations of information show only height and width.

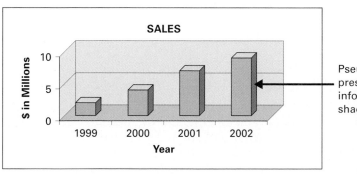

Pseudo three-dimensional presentations of information incorporate shadowing to show depth.

FIGURE 9.4

Most software today produces two-dimensional and pseudo three-dimensional representations.

FIGURE 9.5

Many sites on the Web provide high-quality 3-D images.

Real ***three-dimensional (3-D)*** technology presents information to you in such a way that you have the illusion that the object you're viewing is actually in the room with you. You can see the depth of the image, turn it to reflect different angles and perspectives, and in some way understand the density of the object. You can already find 3-D presentations of information on many Web sites and included in many different types of learning software. For a list of great Web sites with 3-D presentations of information, visit the Web site for this text at www.mhhe.com/i-series.

FIGURE 9.6

Some keyboards come equipped with biometric scanning devices for fingerprint identification. Other fingerprint ID devices can be plugged into the back of your computer.

The Future of 3-D Technologies

Like ASR, 3-D is here and here to stay. It's really only a matter of time before 3-D becomes commonplace. In the past, other technologies such as hard disk capacity and the speed of your CPU have limited the use of 3-D. However, with today's better, faster, and cheaper machines, 3-D is just around the corner.

BIOMETRICS
Will We Ever Get Rid of Passwords?

Today, the standard security mechanism is a password. You have to remember it, and you need to change it frequently. But that will soon change with the emerging technology of biometrics. ***Biometrics*** is the use of physical characteristics, such as your fingerprint, the blood vessels in the retina of your eye, or perhaps the sound of your voice, to provide identification. Already, biometrics is widely used in high-security environments such as military installations.

The concept is quite simple. You can copy someone's password, but you can't copy a fingerprint or retina scan. Many banks are currently converting

ATMs to use biometrics, specifically a retina scan. When you open an account and request ATM use, the bank doesn't issue you an ATM card. Instead, the bank scans your retina and captures a copy of it. To use an ATM, you allow the machine to scan your retina and it matches you to your account. You can then perform whatever transaction you wish.

Home computers may someday be devices that commonly include biometrics. You can already find keyboards that have a special scanning device for your fingerprint. You can't turn on and use your machine until you provide a fingerprint scan. It makes sense when you think about it.

VIRTUAL REALITY

How Can I Truly Experience Places and Events?

Imagine snow skiing on the slopes of Colorado while standing in your home. Imagine walking the white sandy beaches of the Hawaiian Islands and experiencing a luau while sitting in your office. It's coming and the technology that will support you is called virtual reality. *Virtual reality* is a three-dimensional computer simulation in which you actively and physically participate. To achieve this, virtual reality uses some special input and output devices, including gloves, headsets, and walkers.

A *glove* is an input device that captures the shape and movements of your hand and fingers. A *headset* is a combined input and output device that (1) captures the movement of your head from side to side and up and down and (2) includes a special screen that covers your entire field of vision. Finally, a *walker* captures the movement of your feet and body as you walk or turn in different directions.

Consider a simple virtual reality application in which you're trying to shoot monsters in a swamp. When you put on your headset, you see the swamp in front of you in 3-D. As you begin to walk on the walker, the headset adjusts its display to give you the illusion you're walking into the swamp. Your walker may also tighten its tension, making it more difficult for you to walk as you move through water. Finally, in your glove you have a gun. When you move your gun into your field of vision, the headset shows you your hand and gun. Now, when a monster enters your vision, all you have to do is aim and fire (hopefully, you'll vaporize the monster).

Virtual reality applications are very popular in games such as the one we described. You can fly an airplane, ski snowy slopes, and even play golf in virtual reality. The business world also uses virtual reality for a variety of purposes. Volvo, for example, lets you virtually experience a car wreck to learn how air bags work. And many airlines use virtual reality to train pilots how to react to mechanical failures and adverse weather conditions.

Cybersickness—The Downside of Virtual Reality

The reality of virtual reality is that there are downsides. That is to say, virtual reality has both advantages and disadvantages. People who participate in virtual reality sometimes experience cybersickness, including

FIGURE 9.7

Virtual reality makes use of special input and output devices such as gloves, headsets, and walkers.

The Best Applications of Virtual Reality

Imagine a world in which the color blue feels like sandpaper, a world in which the only furniture you can sit on must be green, or a world in which a pin dropping on the floor sounds like the cracking of thunder. That's the real world for a person with autism. Autism is a disease that interferes with the development of the part of the brain that processes sensory perceptions. Some autistic people do indeed feel things (sandpaper grinding across the skin) when they see colors.

For autistic people, the world is a mishmash of objects that make no sense to them when they have to deal with them all at once. For example, if you place two differently colored chairs in front of an autistic person and tell him or her that they are both chairs, that person may become confused and disoriented.

A simple world is the best world for individuals suffering from autism. So, many researchers are using virtual reality to teach autistic people to deal with everyday life.

In a virtual reality simulation, researchers can eliminate all forms of background noise, colors, and objects, except those that they want the autistic person to focus on. As the autistic person becomes comfortable with a simple virtual reality simulation, new objects or colors can be introduced without the usual adverse side effects. This allows the autistic person to move from dealing with a simple environment to an environment that includes many objects and colors.

Virtual reality is indeed an emerging and cutting-edge technology, and will dramatically change the way we live our lives and interact with technology. When most people think of virtual reality, they think of games and fun events such as experiencing a roller-coaster ride while sitting in a recliner chair. And there'll be much money made with those types of virtual reality applications.

But the best uses of virtual reality won't necessarily make anyone rich. Instead, they'll help people cope with everyday life. And that's true for all the new technology. It's a multibillion-dollar industry. But perhaps we would all do better to let the money take care of itself, and think more about how technology can aid people in everyday life.

eyestrain, simulator sickness, and flashbacks. You may experience eyestrain if you remain too long in a virtual reality application that uses a low-resolution headset. And most virtual reality headsets do have a lower resolution than what you see on most standard computer systems today.

Other people experience simulator sickness when the physiological inputs and outputs are out of sync in a virtual reality application. For example, if you move your head and the headset takes an extra second to adjust to what you're seeing, then you may become dizzy and nauseated. Finally, some people experience flashbacks or a form of déjà vu several hours after participating in virtual reality. This can cause a temporary disassociation with "real" reality.

The Future of Virtual Reality

In spite of its current limitations and drawbacks, virtual reality is an emerging technology that's destined to take its place in your future. Prices are quickly dropping for in-home virtual reality kits that include gloves, headsets, and walkers. And when speed is no longer an issue on the Web, you can expect to visit hundreds (if not thousands) of sites that will offer you free virtual reality experiences.

making **the grade**   SECTION A://

1. An _____ system captures your speech and can distinguish your words and word groupings to form sentences.

2. Real _____ technology presents information to you in such a way that you have the illusion that the object you're viewing is actually in the room with you.

3. _____ is the use of physical characteristics to provide identification.

4. _____ is a three-dimensional computer simulation in which you actively and physically participate.

5. A _____ captures the movement of your feet and body as you walk or turn in different directions.

B://ELECTRONIC COMMERCE TOMORROW

Electronic commerce is one of the hottest topics today not only in the business world but also in your personal world. As e-commerce evolves and becomes more important, the changes will be unbelievable. We discuss some of them in this section. On the Web, you'll start to use e-cash and rent software instead of buying it. You'll also begin to notice that e-commerce will begin to take on the form of a "push" technology instead of a "pull" technology. And in the distant future, e-commerce will become known simply as commerce (without the "e").

E-CASH
Will We Ever Do Away with Folding Cash and Coins?
Using cash or checks to pay for products in an electronic commerce world is a bit of an oxymoron, like jumbo shrimp, freezer burn, even odds, and ill health. Of course, you can use a credit card to buy products on the Web,

F I G U R E   9.8

E-cash facilitates transactions on the Web by using files that represent money.

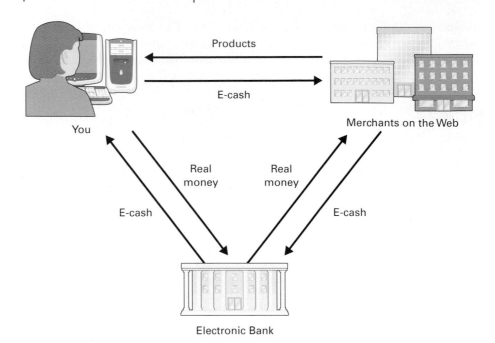

Products

E-cash

You   Merchants on the Web

Real money   Real money

E-cash   E-cash

Electronic Bank

but you still receive a paper credit card balance statement, and you must write a check to pay your balance.

The alternative is e-cash. **E-cash** (**electronic cash** or **digital cash**) is exactly what its name implies—an electronic representation of cash. This electronic representation of cash is nothing more than a file that says you have a certain amount of money in electronic form. You can then buy products on the Web by sending the e-cash file to a merchant. E-cash is certainly far beyond digital money and digital wallets, which we discussed in Chapter 4.

To use e-cash on the Web, the first thing you have to do is obtain e-cash from an electronic bank. You can buy e-cash in a variety of ways—send real cash through the mail, provide your debit or credit card number as if you were making a regular purchase, or actually open an account with the electronic bank and request that an amount of e-cash be deducted from your account and sent to you.

Once you have your e-cash, all you have to do is find a product to purchase on the Web and send the appropriate number of e-cash files to the merchant. For example, a $40 purchase would require that you send two $20 e-cash files. In turn, the merchant can use the e-cash to purchase products and services from other merchants or return it to the electronic bank for real money (see Figure 9.8).

What's Holding Up E-Cash?

E-cash and its use look simple enough. And someday it will be simple and commonplace. However, we first have many hurdles to overcome.

- **Anyone Can Be an Electronic Bank**—The FDIC and FSLIC have yet to establish strict guidelines by which an organization can become an electronic bank and offer e-cash. Be careful here—buy e-cash only from an established and well-known electronic bank.
- **There Are No E-Cash Standards**—Many electronic banks on the Web are offering their own versions of e-cash. So, e-cash from one electronic bank will look different from another electronic bank's

e-cash. This makes merchants hesitant—dealing with different forms of e-cash is almost like accepting different forms of international currency.

- **Merchants Must Have Accounts with Electronic Banks**—To accept e-cash, a merchant must have an account with an electronic bank. This is necessary if the merchant wants to convert the e-cash to real money.

- **E-Cash Makes Money Laundering Easy**—E-cash files include no information about you. So, the owner of e-cash can use it for any purpose and it can't be traced. This will make money laundering very simple on the Web.

- **E-Cash Is Easy to Lose, Impossible to Replace**—E-cash is a file on your hard disk. If your hard disk crashes and you lose your information (some of that information is actually e-cash), you've lost your money. Don't expect an electronic bank to replace it.

In spite of these hurdles, we firmly believe that e-cash will become the standard form of currency on the Web in the very near future. What do you think?

BUYING SERVICES INSTEAD OF SOFTWARE

Will I Always Have to Buy Software?

The answer here is definitely no. All of computing is becoming Web-based. That statement alone and the fact that it's true will soon change how we acquire and use software.

Many people today don't get their money's worth when they purchase software (especially software suites). You may, for example, use presentation software only a couple of times a year to create a slide presentation. So, why not rent the software you need instead of buying it?

That will become a reality in the very near future. Microsoft, for example, as well as many other large software publishers, is already planning to release "pay-for-use" software over the Web. So, you won't buy all

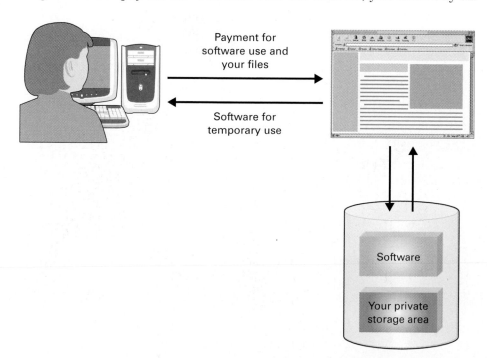

Payment for software use and your files

Software for temporary use

Software

Your private storage area

FIGURE 9.9

Software may someday become a commodity that you rent on the Web.

the software you need. Instead, you'll simply connect to a site and rent software that you use infrequently. When you rent software like this, you may pay only $.95 per hour-long session. And that may certainly be cheaper than buying the software.

When renting software becomes widespread, so will the proliferation of Web-oriented devices such as smart phones, pagers, and PDAs. These types of devices don't have enough disk storage space or RAM to hold certain types of software. But if you're using a site that supplies the software, Web devices won't need the extra storage capacity. Many sites that plan on letting you rent software will also provide you with a secure area where you can store your documents. So, you may not even need a disk drive to store any files you create.

PUSH (NOT PULL) TECHNOLOGIES
When Will Businesses Know Exactly What I Want?

Right now, the Internet and the World Wide Web are "pull" technologies. That is, you visit a specific site and request information, services, and products. So, you're literally "pulling" what you want. In the future, the emphasis will be on "push" technologies. In a ***push technology*** environment, businesses and organizations come to you with information, services, and product offerings based on your profile. If this sounds like advertisements you receive in the mail or door-to-door salespeople, it's not the same at all.

For example, right now you can subscribe to a cell phone service that pushes information to you. When you drive by your favorite video store, that service sends you a recorded message on your cell phone with a list of newly released videos, a list customized to your preferences, based on what type of movies you most often rent at that video store.

Push technologies have far-reaching implications. They will further enable the concept of one-to-one marketing, which we discussed in Chapter 8. Can you imagine watching a ballgame on TV and having a message

F I G U R E   9.10

Today, you "pull" information from Web sites. In the future, Web sites will know enough about you to "push" customized information and offerings to you.

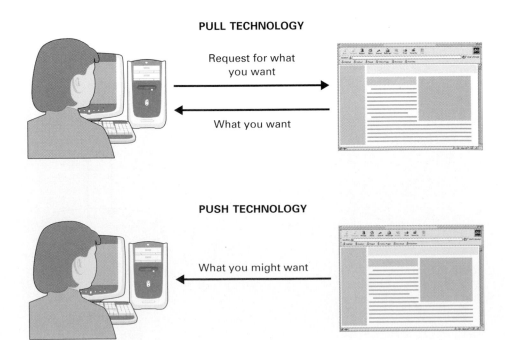

PULL TECHNOLOGY

Request for what you want

What you want

PUSH TECHNOLOGY

What you might want

flash on your screen that says, "We'll deliver your favorite sausage and mushroom pizza to your doorstep within 30 minutes. On your remote control, press the ORDER NOW button." That message is an example of a push technology. A local pizza delivery service would have determined that you like sausage and mushroom pizza and that you order it most often while watching a ballgame.

Push technologies rely on an organization's ability to really know its customers, their likes and dislikes, and how often they order certain types of products or services. This is what business to consumer electronic commerce is all about.

NO MORE E-COMMERCE; JUST COMMERCE
Is Electronic Commerce Just a Fad?

Right now, electronic commerce accounts for a very small percentage of purchases made worldwide by consumers. But that percentage is doubling and even tripling every year.

Certainly in your lifetime, e-commerce will become just commerce. That is, we believe someday e-commerce purchases will be greater than brick-and-mortar store purchases. If that does indeed come to pass, what will happen to commercial real estate prices? What will happen to malls? Is there room in this world for both e-commerce and traditional commerce? What do you think will happen?

---

making the grade   SECTION B://

1. _____ is an electronic representation of cash.

2. If you lose your e-cash, an electronic bank will not _____ it.

3. In the future, you'll be able to _____ software on the Web that you use infrequently.

4. In a _____ technology environment, businesses and organizations come to you with information, services, and product offerings based on your profile.

5. Someday, e-commerce will become just _____.

C://YOUR INTELLIGENT HOME

Technology is no longer just for the workplace or school. It's for your home. And we're not simply talking about having a notebook or desktop computer in your home. We're talking about a home based completely on (and run by) technology.

INFORMATION SUPPLIER CONVERGENCE
Will I Get All the Information I Need from One Source?

Information supplier convergence isn't really an emerging technology. Rather, it is a merging of technologies—a trend that suggests that someday you'll receive all the information you need from a single organization. Right now, you get your mail from the postal service, your cable TV from one organization, your telephone service from another provider, and your newspaper from yet another source. We certainly expect that to change.

F I G U R E   9.11

You may someday receive all your information needs from a single supplier.

The IT and telecommunications industry is changing dramatically today, mainly through mergers and acquisitions. Telephone service providers such as AT&T are buying cable TV companies (and vice versa). As this shakes out in the coming years, a single organization may very well provide you with all the information you need and want. Your cable TV provider, your Internet service provider, and your utility company may be rolled into one. As your ISP, it will offer you access to electronic newspapers and magazines and deliver much of your mail in the form of e-mail.

This convergence of information suppliers is an important trend that the whole world is watching. Can you imagine receiving a single monthly bill (that you'll pay electronically) that includes all the information services you use today?

TALK TO YOUR HOME

If My Home Is Computer-Based, Will I Talk to It?

Right now, your home has a number of seemingly simple and insignificant input and output devices. For example, you have light switches, stereo controls, thermostat controls, sprinkler system controls, and the familiar array of others. When your home does become completely technology-based, you'll be able to interact with all those controls in one simple way—by speaking.

When you walk into a room, you'll say "lights" and the room will come alight. Some new homes now have sensors that turn the lights on and off automatically as you enter or leave a room. Lying in bed at night, you won't need to get up to turn the heat down. Instead, you'll simply say, "Turn the heat down two degrees."

You'll control your TV and stereo with your voice. From the kitchen, you'll be able to speak the appropriate commands to turn on the TV in another room or turn up the volume on the stereo. This is not far-fetched—it's just around the corner.

STAYING IN TOUCH WITH YOUR HOME

Will I Be Able to Communicate with My Home Even When I'm Not There?

Because your home will be technology-based and you'll probably have a single information service, you'll be able to communicate with your home from anywhere in the world. By using a simple device such as your cell phone, you'll be able to start the water sprinklers, randomly turn on and off lights to keep burglars away, and perform numerous other tasks in your home while you're away from it.

Many new homes today come with video cameras that you can access through the Web. Child care centers already offer this convenience to parents who want to watch their children throughout the day. So, you'll soon

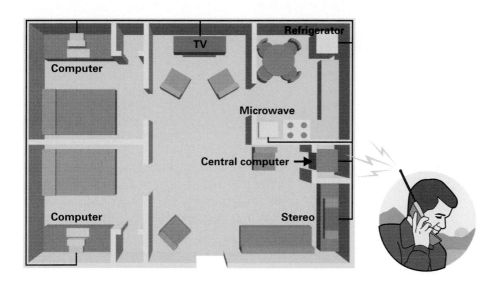

Homes of the future will certainly have all their electronic devices controlled and connected via technology.

be able to connect to a Web site, enter your password (or biometrics), and watch a video of your home. Again, this will be possible because your home will be computer-controlled and because you have a single information service.

APPLIANCES THAT KNOW AND DO

Will My Refrigerator Do My Shopping?

Finally, in your home of the future, you'll interact with a variety of intelligent home appliances. An *intelligent home appliance* contains embedded computer technology that controls numerous functions and is capable of making some decisions. Consider the following examples:

- Smart vacuum cleaners that automatically adjust settings based on the naps or densities of your carpet, varying densities and weights of dirt, and collection bag fullness.
- Hand-held digital video cameras that make sure your movie never jumps around. These cameras compare frames to each other to determine if the movement of objects is caused by hand movement jitters, and, if so, they eliminate the problem.
- Gas ranges that detect when water is about to boil, regulate simmering, and adjust settings for a variety of cookware and foods.
- Clothes washers that automatically balance loads and determine dirt content to add detergent, the appropriate cycle for the type of clothes, and the amount of water based on clothes weight.

Some appliance manufacturers are even developing "smelling" refrigerators. These refrigerators can detect when food is spoiling and can even tell you which type of food it may be (milk or produce).

Also, keep in mind that these intelligent home appliances will be wired to your home and capable of responding to voice commands. All you have to tell your microwave is "pop popcorn." It will adjust its settings and even shut itself off when all the kernels are popped—no more burned popcorn in the microwave. And you'll even be able to start the clothes washer or preheat your oven by making a simple phone call on your cell phone.

making the grade

1. _____ refers to the trend that suggests that someday you'll receive all the information you need from a single organization.

2. Homes of the future will include _____ recognition so you can literally talk to your home.

3. In the future, you'll be able to watch a _____ of your home by connecting to a Web site.

4. A(n) _____ contains embedded computer technology that controls numerous functions and is capable of making some decisions.

D://PUSHING THE ENVELOPE

In a chapter like this, you should really start to think "beyond your ears" (that's our version of thinking outside the box). How technology will change and change our lives is simply going to be unbelievable and unpredictable. So why not step out and make a few bold predictions? They may just come true. Here are a few of ours.

TECHNOLOGY IN THE WALLS

Will Technology Someday Be Everywhere at Our Fingertips?

With the coming miniaturization of technology, you'll be able to find computers in every product imaginable. We believe that someday you'll have technology wired throughout your walls, with very small input/output devices literally embedded into the wallpaper, sheet rock, and plaster.

You also may not have a television. Instead, you'll use your finger to draw an outline of where you want your TV to appear on your wall. Then, using voice recognition, you'll turn on your TV and it will show on the wall where you drew the outline. If you walk into a different room, you'll just draw a new screen on the wall.

FIGURE   9.13

What if you could use your finger to draw an outline on the wall of where you want your TV screen to appear?

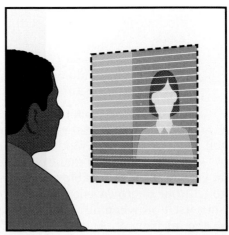

i·series insights

Ethics, Security & Privacy

Do You Really Want a Chip in Your Body?

Implant chips are the central issue of much debate, mainly in the area of privacy. On an implant chip, you can store a wealth of information about yourself, including your medical history and other forms of personal information. Then, if you ever need that information, it can easily be scanned.

Most people are in favor of that use of the technology. But many want it to stop there, while others see more applications. For example, that same implant chip could be used (in conjunction with satellites) to track the movement of people. So, we could easily find lost skiers and hikers, tell who burglarized a home, and find a lost or kidnapped child. Those sound like good uses of technology.

However, if we can track anyone anywhere, what's to stop certain people or organizations from tracking others for the wrong reasons? Couldn't the government easily follow you wherever you go? Couldn't your school easily track you to see where you are when you're supposed to be in class? Couldn't the ATF (Bureau of Alcohol, Tobacco, and Firearms) use those implant chips to determine who should be able to drink alcohol or own a gun?

What do you think? Is this technology that we should repress or ignore because it can potentially be

used in a bad way? Or should we move forward with its use while enacting legislation to control its use?

How's that for stepping out and making a bold prediction? For some interesting (and well-founded) reading along these lines, we recommend Michio Kaku's book *Visions: How Science Will Revolutionize the 21st Century.*

IMPLANT CHIPS

Is the "Terminator" a Realistic Possibility?

Futuristic movies and shows such as *The Six Million Dollar Man* and *Terminator* paint a pretty interesting picture of the future. In that future, technology will become increasingly a part of the human body (perhaps the entire human body as in the *Terminator*). Who knows if that will in fact ever become a reality? We do know, however, that current exploration is under way to implant chips in human bodies.

These chips will have several purposes. First, these chips will contain vitally important information about you. So, if you get ill while on vacation, a doctor can simply scan your chip and view your complete medical history, including any allergic reactions you may have to certain types of drugs. That's the smaller scale of implant chips.

On a grander scale, many people propose that these chips be used to track the movement of people by satellite. And this has raised much concern in the area of privacy. Most people don't want the government or any organization to have the ability to monitor their movements. But there are arguments for it. For example, we could easily locate missing children. If someone were to break into your house, the police could tell who it was.

FIGURE 9.14

Implant chips in your body may
contain all your vital information.

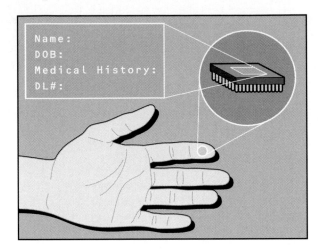

FIGURE 9.14

Implant chips in your body may
contain all your vital information.

Technology coming together with the human body will physically aid
people in many ways. Today, there are implant chips that block pain for
people who suffer severe spinal injuries. Doctors are exploring the use of
implant chips to help paralyzed people walk. And there are even implant
chips that can help people see. Technology such as implant chips in the
right hands used for the right purposes can increase our quality of life.
Technology in the wrong hands used for the wrong purposes can be disastrous.

HOLOGRAPHIC DEVICES

What if I Don't Want to Read a Newspaper on My Screen?

Holographic devices create, capture, and/or display images in true three-
dimensional form. One such holographic device is a CAVE. A **CAVE (cave
automatic virtual environment)** is a special 3-D virtual reality room that
can display images of other people and objects located in other CAVEs all
over the world.

In working form, you would enter a CAVE room. At the same time,
someone else would enter another CAVE room in another location. Numerous digital video cameras would capture the likenesses of both of you
and re-create and send those images with holographic devices. Then, you
and the other person could see and carry on a normal conversation with
each other. You would feel as if that other person were in the same room
with you.

FIGURE 9.15

CAVEs will give you the
complete illusion that you're with
someone miles away.

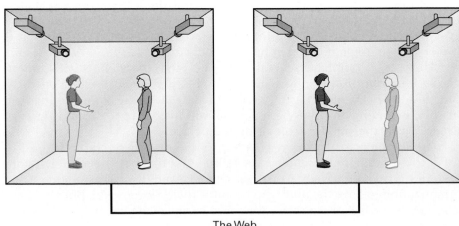

The Web

Unlike basic virtual reality, you won't need to wear any special gear. Can you imagine the possibilities with CAVEs? You could visit relatives without ever getting on a plane. You could experience vacation destinations and resorts before making a decision about which one to go to. CAVEs clearly have great potential. Someday, you may have a CAVE in your house and simply connect to the Web to visit a friend.

Holographic devices have other applications beyond CAVEs. Someday, your screen or monitor will actually be a holographic device. So, when you read your virtual newspaper, your holographic device will create a real-life version of the newspaper suspended in the air. If you really like the feel of a paper book, holographic devices can help you make the jump from physical to virtual products.

AUTOMATIC PILOT IN YOUR CAR

Can We Expect to See More Computers in Cars?

Out in California, researchers are exploring the use of computer-controlled cars on highways. But the computer controlling the car isn't the real invention. Rather, researchers have placed small sensors on the road (about every six feet) that communicate with and then tell the computer in the car what to do.

With this combination of technology, researchers have succeeded in moving a line of cars down the road at over 100 miles per hour. Even more significant, these cars are only three feet apart, and the computer system controls when they pass, when they accelerate, and when they slow down.

In the future, you may get in your car and tell it where you want to go. Your car computer will then take over, determine the best route to get there, and begin driving for you. It will know where stop signs are, know how to avoid a slow car, and may even take you on a short detour to get gas.

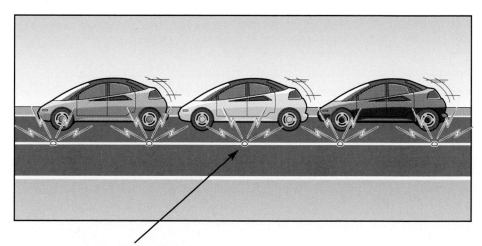

F I G U R E   9.16

Computer-controlled cars will drive themselves.

Computers in the road will control cars by communicating with the computers in the cars.

COMPUTERS IN YOUR SHOES

How Portable Will Technology Really Become?

Technology will someday become so portable that you may wear a computer in the heel of your shoe. This computer will have a permanent storage device as well as a wireless modem. So, all you have to do is speak a message to someone. Your shoe (or rather the computer in your shoe) will capture the contents of your message and then use its wireless modem to send that person an e-mail message.

That's not really a far-fetched idea. Of course, we may not actually put computers in the heels of our shoes. But technology will become so small that you may wear your computer on your wrist (watch out, Dick Tracy) or keep it in your pocket much like you would a pen.

F I G U R E   9.17

As technology becomes increasingly small, expect to wear your computer.

Levi Strauss is making jackets with portable music players.

Charmed Technology wants you to wear your CPU on your belt.

With your CPU on your belt, you'll use special eyeglasses to see information.

SECTION D : //   *making* **the grade**

1. Someday technology will become so small that you'll have _____ devices literally embedded into the wallpaper, sheet rock, and plaster of your home.
2. Many people today are exploring the implanting of chips into the _____.
3. _____ devices create, capture, and/or display images in true three-dimensional form.
4. A _____ is a special 3-D virtual reality room that can display images of other people and objects located in other parts of the world.

i·witness

An Up-Close Look at Web Sites

Framing a Web Site

To frame or not to frame Web sites is a question that Web developers can't seem to agree on. But they do agree that if you choose to use frames, you need to use them well.

To frame a Web site means you provide areas surrounding the main part of the site that are always present. An example of framing in the accompanying Web site shows how you could place links in Section A and a logo in Section B. The main content of your site would be in Section C. As you click though the links, both Section A and Section B remain on the Web browser. Only Section C changes according to the link you choose.

Why frame a Web site? You may want to improve its navigability by providing ready-to-use links. Or maybe you want to use the top section of your e-commerce site for a business logo or banner ads. In either case, you'll need to use frames effectively. Take a look at some quick tips for building an effectively framed Web site:

- Limit the number of frames.
- Load Web pages in the correct framed area.
- Avoid loading Web sites other than your own without proper planning.

We offer three framed Web sites for you to review. Two of the Web sites don't follow the above guidelines, but one does.

www.mhhe.com/i-series/I-Witness/9-A.html
www.mhhe.com/i-series/I-Witness/9-B.html
www.mhhe.com/i-series/I-Witness/9-C.html

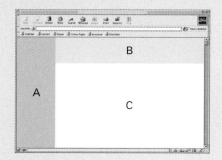

Try all three of the examples. Which one works best? Why? What's wrong with the other two? What advice do you have to fix them?

You can download these examples, but follow the directions on the Web site carefully to get all of the HTML files.

E://SUMMARY AND KEY TERMS

In this chapter, we hope we have opened your eyes to the possibilities of emerging technologies in the future. Technology will definitely change, and those changes will greatly affect how you live your life. We know that many of our predictions will come true, and you should embrace them. Others may seem a bit far-fetched, but so was the whole idea of a "home computer" not long ago.

Emerging technologies in the area of "touching your senses" include:

- **Automatic speech recognition (ASR)**—which captures your speech and can distinguish your words and word groupings to form sentences.

- **Three-dimensional (3-D) technology**—which presents information to you in such a way that you have the illusion that the object you're viewing is actually in the room with you.

- **Biometrics**—the use of physical characteristics, such as your fingerprint, the blood vessels in the retina of your eye, or perhaps the sound of your voice, to provide identification.

- **Virtual reality**—a three-dimensional computer simulation in which you actively and physically participate.

Emerging technologies for electronic commerce include:

- *E-cash*—an electronic representation of cash you'll use to make purchases on the Web.
- *Renting software*—for software you use infrequently.
- *Push technologies*—when businesses and organizations come to you with information, services, and product offerings based on your profile.
- *Just plain commerce*—when e-commerce becomes so commonplace that we drop the "e."

Emerging technologies for your intelligent home include:

- *Information supplier convergence*—getting all the information you need from a single source.
- *Homes that respond to your voice*—you'll be speaking to your home and it will respond.
- *Staying in touch with your home while you're gone*—taking care of your home through the Web.
- *Intelligent home appliances*—that contain embedded computer technology that controls numerous functions and is capable of making some decisions.

Some extreme emerging technologies may include:

- *Technology in the walls*—literally so small that devices are embedded in wallpaper, sheet rock, and plaster.
- *Implant chips*—in the human body that contain vitally important information.
- *Holographic devices*—that create, capture, and/or display images in true three-dimensional form.
- *Computer-controlled cars*—that will take over much of the driving for you.
- *Portable technologies*—so small that you may wear them in your shoe.

On the Web site for this text at www.mhhe.com/i-series, you can find more information about the topics in this chapter including automatic speech recognition and 3-D images.

KEY TERMS

automatic speech recognition (ASR) (p. 9.3)

biometrics (p. 9.6)

CAVE (cave automatic virtual environment) (p. 9.18)

e-cash (electronic cash or digital cash) (p. 9.10)

feature analysis (p. 9.3)

glove (p. 9.7)

headset (p. 9.7)

holographic device (p. 9.18)

intelligent home appliance (p. 9.15)

language processing (p. 9.4)

pattern classification (p. 9.3)

push technology (p. 9.12)

three-dimensional (3-D) (p. 9.6)

virtual reality (p. 9.7)

walker (p. 9.7)

CROSSWORD PUZZLE

Across

4. Display true 3-D images
5. Virtual reality room
6. Physical characteristics for ID
7. Opposite of pull
8. Step #3 in ASR
9. Step #1 in ASR
11. VR device for your feet
12. Step #2 in ASR

Down

1. VR device for your hand
2. Simulation in which you physically participate
3. Electronic money
4. VR device for your eyes
10. Verbal communication to a computer

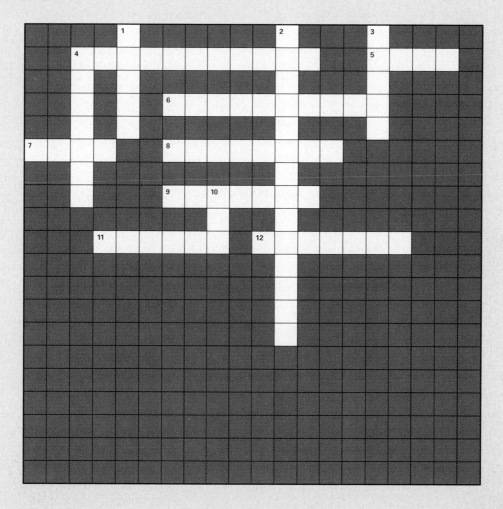

QUESTIONS AND EXERCISES

Multiple Choice

1. The second step of automatic speech recognition is
   a. feature analysis.
   b. pattern classification.
   c. language processing.
   d. acoustic modeling.
   e. none of the above.

2. In an ASR system, the vocabulary is stored in a(n)
   a. acoustic model database.
   b. language model database.
   c. implanted chip.
   d. virtual reality glove.
   e. walker.

3. Biometrics involve
   a. fingerprints.
   b. blood vessels in the retina.
   c. the sound of your voice.
   d. all of the above.
   e. none of the above.

4. Special hardware devices for virtual reality include
   a. gloves.
   b. headsets.
   c. walkers.
   d. all of the above.
   e. only a. and b.

5. E-cash is
   a. a fad that will not come to pass.
   b. an electronic representation of cash.
   c. different from digital cash.
   d. now widely used on the Web to make purchases.
   e. used only with cell phones that can access the Web.

6. In a(n) _____ technology environment, businesses and organizations come to you with information, services, and product offerings based on your profile.
   a. pull
   b. nano
   c. push
   d. emerging
   e. CAVE

7. In the future, you may receive all your information needs from
   a. the government.
   b. your school.
   c. one supplier.
   d. two suppliers.
   e. a local grocery store.

8. A(n) _____ contains embedded computer technology that controls numerous functions and is capable of making some decisions.
   a. CAVE
   b. ASR system
   c. 3-D system
   d. intelligent home appliance
   e. glove

9. Chips within your body that contain vitally important information about you are called
   a. implant chips.
   b. nano chips.
   c. ASR chips.
   d. gloves.
   e. headsets.

10. A device that creates, captures, and/or displays images in true three-dimensional form is a(n)
    a. ASR system.
    b. glove.
    c. holographic device.
    d. input device.
    e. storage device.

True/False

11. ____ A discrete ASR system can process continuous streams of words (that is, normal speech).

12. ____ Real 2-D technology presents information to you in such a way that you have the illusion that the object you're viewing is actually in the room with you.

13. ____ During and after virtual reality, you can experience eyestrain, simulator sickness, and flashbacks.

14. ____ Computers someday may become so small that we'll wear them in our shoes.

15. ____ Automatic speech understanding will occur before automatic speech recognition.

QUESTIONS AND EXERCISES

1. Below is a list of 17 emerging technologies and emerging uses of technologies we discussed in this chapter. In what order do you think they will become a reality? In the right-hand column provide a number between 1 and 17. The number 1 will represent the technology or use of technology you believe will become a reality first, and the number 17 will represent the one you believe will become a reality last. Essentially, you're building a timeline for the emerging technologies and emerging uses of technology.

EMERGING TECHNOLOGY	TIMELINE NUMBER
Automatic speech recognition	_____
3-D	_____
Biometrics	_____
Virtual reality	_____
E-cash	_____
Renting software	_____
Push technologies	_____
Just commerce (without the "e")	_____
Information supplier convergence	_____
Talking to your home	_____
Staying in touch with your home	_____
Intelligent home appliances	_____
Technology in the walls	_____
Implant chips	_____
Holographic devices	_____
Computer-controlled cars	_____
Computers in your shoe	_____

2. For each of the following answers, create the question:

ANSWER	QUESTION
A. It can capture my words and form sentences.	_____
B. Fingerprints or the blood vessels in my retina.	_____
C. It will be cheaper than buying software.	_____
D. Finally, I can read in my car.	_____
E. Using it, I won't get ink on my hands from the newspaper.	_____
F. It'll be just like the Jetsons.	_____
G. The scariest of all the emerging technologies.	_____
H. I may never have to go on vacation again.	_____

e-commerce

1. Stock Trading

Stock trading on the Web is already widespread, with one of every three stock transactions occurring through the Web as opposed to through a traditional stockbroker. Setting up an account with a Web-based trading house is easy, and you can do it for as little as $500. Below, we've listed four Web-based stock brokerage firms.

- Charles Schwab—www.schwab.com
- E*Trade—www.etrade.com
- Ameritrade—www.ameritrade.com
- Merrill Lynch—www.ml.com

Question Set #1

Connect to at least two of the sites and answer the following questions for each:

a. What is the minimum investment to open an account?

b. What services does the site offer in addition to buying and selling stocks?

c. What type of support does the site provide? 24-hour toll-free? E-mail? Other?

d. How can you retrieve stock quotes? By company name? By stock ticker symbol?

e. How do you apply electronically? Do you still have to sign a paper form?

f. How do you transfer money into your new account?

Question Set #2

Now, consider all of the sites and answer the following questions:

a. Which are only "click-and-mortar" brokerage houses and which have "brick-and-mortar" establishments?

b. Which is easiest in terms of getting stock quotes?

c. What is the delay for stock quote figures or are they real-time?

d. How would you rank the sites from the one you'd be most interested in using to the one you'd be least interested in using?

2. Making Long-Distance Phone Calls

Someday you may never pay for another long-distance phone call. By paying only your ISP monthly fee, you'll be able to use the Web to make "free" long-distance phones calls. Sound too good to be true? Well, it's already happening and many people are doing it. Below, we've provided four Web sites that support using the Web for making long-distance phone calls.

- EuroCall—www.eurocall.com
- DialPad—www.dialpad.com
- InetPhone—www.inetphone.com
- Ezfone—www.ezfone.com

Question Set #1

Connect to any one of the sites and answer the following questions:

a. Are calls really free or do you have to pay some sort of fee? If you have to pay a fee, what is it?

b. What sort of special computer equipment do you need to make a Web-based phone call?

c. Can you make local calls as well as long-distance calls?

d. Can you use a cell phone to make phone calls on the Web?

e. Does the person you're calling also have to be connected to the Web when you call them?

Question Set #2

Now, consider the current long-distance phone call industry and be prepared to answer the following questions:

a. How can Web sites offering free long-distance phone calls make any money?

b. Will traditional long-distance phone call companies eventually begin offering their services on the Web for free?

c. How does making long-distance phone calls on the Web support the concept of information supplier convergence?

e-commerce

3. Buying Stamps on the Web

We may never completely replace the United States Postal Service in favor of communicating electronically through the Web. However, there are many products and services that the postal service offers that will become Web-based (perhaps completely). For example, you can connect to the postal service (www.usps.gov) and calculate rates for sending packages and look up zip codes. And now you can buy stamps on the Web and use those electronic stamps for sending letters through the postal service. Below are four sites that sell these stamps.

- Stamps.com—www.stamps.com
- E-Stamp—www.e-stamp.com
- VirtualStoreUs—
  www.virtualstoreus.com/stamps.htm
- BeautifulShopping—
  www.beautifulshopping.com/stamps.shtml

Connect to any one of these sites and answer the following questions:

a. In what denominations can you buy electronic stamps?

b. Do you have to have special hardware or software to use electronic stamps?

c. How does the whole process work? How do you buy and download stamps? How do you get them on an envelope?

d. What sort of security does each site use to ensure that you don't reuse electronic stamps?

e. Can you send electronic stamps to friends so they can use them?

4. Sending and Receiving Electronic Greeting Cards

Another type of traditional mailing that we do may someday be completely replaced by Web mail—sending and receiving greeting cards. Today, you can send electronic versions of birth-day cards, get-well cards, congratulations cards, and any other type of card you can think of. And it's all free. Most even include sound and some sort of animation. Below are four sites that offer free greeting card services on the Web.

- BlueMountain—www.bluemountain.com
- Greetings-Cards—www.greeting-cards.com
- Cyber Greeting Cards—
  www.cyber-greeting-cards.com
- Amazon—www.amazon.com

For this project, team up with a classmate and send each other a greeting card. To do so, follow these steps:

a. Record each other's e-mail address.

b. Connect to any one of the sites listed above.

c. Choose and send a greeting card to each other.

d. Check your e-mail to view the card you receive.

What did you think of the experience? Are electronic greeting cards more fun to receive (and send) than paper greeting cards? What's going to happen to the paper-based greeting card industry?

on the web

1. E-Publishing on the Web

E-publishing is an emerging technology that we didn't discuss specifically in this chapter. E-publishing is simply the development, authoring, distribution, and use of traditional print products in electronic form. For example, you can now buy some textbooks in electronic form and download them to your computer. Do some research on the Web concerning e-publishing. What organizations seem to be leading the way? What Web sites offer e-books? Can you find fiction, nonfiction, textbooks, and magazines? What measures are e-publishers implementing to ensure that you pay for your e-book and then don't make a copy of it for someone else? What's a rocket book? What's a soft book?

2. Finding Virtual Reality Applications

On the Web, you can find a variety of virtual reality applications. Some you can download for free, while you have to buy others. Connect to your favorite search engine and type in "virtual reality." What did you find? What are the best sites for finding virtual reality applications? What sites sell virtual reality gear such as a glove or headset? What about user groups—how many did you find for virtual reality?

3. E-Cash Providers

E-cash will forever change how you buy products and services on the Web. Connect to your favorite search engine and type in "e-cash." What providers did you find? Were those providers targeting consumers or businesses that want to use e-cash? Follow through the process of buying e-cash. How does it work? Now, connect to PayPal at www.paypal.com. How is PayPal an intermediate step between using folding cash to pay for merchandise and using e-cash to pay for merchandise? What other sites offer services similar to PayPal?

4. Desktop Videoconferencing

Home or desktop videoconferencing systems with the Web are an emerging technology that will someday allow you to have conversations over the Web with another person while seeing that person on your screen. What is the state of this emerging technology? How much does it cost to buy a Web cam? What sort of special software do you need to have? Do most ISPs support home videoconferencing? Now, connect to CUseeMe at www.cuseeme.com. What services does it provide to help you with videoconferencing? What are its fees?

5. Electronic Coupons

When you receive your local Sunday newspaper, it probably comes with a host of coupons you can clip and take to the store. When we finally arrive at completely electronic newspapers, those coupons will also have to be electronic. Right now, you can find electronic coupons on the Web. Connect to Coupons.com at www.coupons.com. What sort of coupons did you find? How are they organized? How do you download the coupons and print them? Now, connect to your favorite search engine and types in "coupons." What other sites did you find that offer electronic coupons?

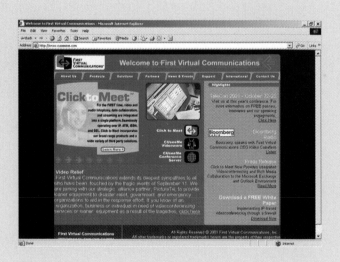

ethics, security & privacy

1. DNA Testing

In the movie *Gattica*, biometrics was carried to its extreme logical conclusion. In that movie, all people were identified through a quick check of their DNA. A girl on a date even had her boyfriend's DNA checked for any flaws or deficiencies. People were given jobs according to their DNA testing. Those people with DNAs that showed physical or mental deficiencies of any kind were given simple tasks such as collecting trash. Those with good DNAs were given the opportunity to work in an office, make a lot of money, and live a nice life.

Consider, answer, and debate the following questions:

a. Should we use DNA testing as the ultimate form of biometrics? It will certainly make it almost impossible for anyone to imitate you.

b. Should we use DNA testing to determine what types of jobs people should have?

c. Should we use DNA testing to determine what schools people are allowed to go to?

d. Should the poultry industry be allowed to use DNA testing on chickens and other forms of fowl to determine which birds will yield you the greatest nutritional value?

e. In general, isn't DNA testing another form of discrimination, no matter how it's used?

2. Watching Live Videos on the Web

Watching videos on the Web will someday be commonplace. We provided one such example in this chapter—of your being able to watch your home while you're away. That sounds good enough, but can it be carried too far? Consider, answer, and debate the following questions:

a. Should you be able to watch a video of a house cleaner while he or she is in your home?

b. Should you be able to watch a video of a baby sitter taking care of your kids in your home?

c. Should you be able to watch a video of a baby sitter taking care of your kids while he or she (the baby sitter) is in his or her own home?

d. Should your boss be able to watch a video of you at work?

e. Should the police be able to watch a video of you while you're at a bar and then follow you home if they believe you've had too much to drink?

f. Should the police be able to watch a video of you as you drive through an intersection to see if you're following all the rules?

g. Should your teacher be able to review a video of your class as you take an exam to determine if anyone is cheating?

h. Before doing any of the above, should the people being watched on a video be required to sign a consent form?

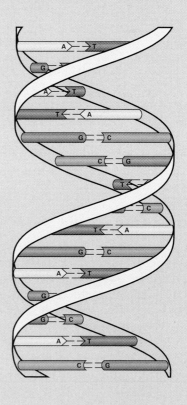

w w w . m h h e . c o m / i - s e r i e s

group activities

1. Your Future Home and Emerging Technologies

The home of the future is certainly going to be different from any home you've probably lived in. Right now, the home construction industry is leading the way in innovating emerging technologies for your home of the future. Do some looking around and prepare a list of specific emerging technologies and uses of technology that will appear in the home of the future. As a starting place, you can search the Web and perhaps even visit new model homes in your area. As you prepare your list, write a short description concerning how the home of the future will look and work.

2. The Information Supplier Convergence

In your part of the country, you're probably already witnessing the "information supplier convergence." That is, there are most likely companies providing you with information that are also buying or merging with other information suppliers. Create a list of all the companies that provide you with information in your home—your ISP, your telephone service, your cable TV service, and any others. Do any of them happen to be the same? If they're all different, do some researching to see if any of those companies plan to merge with, acquire, or be acquired by other companies who also provide information.

3. Intelligent Home Appliances

Take a short trip to a local appliance store. What sort of intelligent home appliances are for sale? For each appliance you find, write down its characteristics, how the embedded computer technology can make decisions, and whether or not the appliance is voice-controlled. For each that you find, also find a corresponding appliance that is not "intelligent." What's the price difference? Does the increased functionality of the intelligent home appliance make you want to spend more money?

4. Creating Three-Dimensional Graphs

Creating two-dimensional and pseudo three-dimensional graphs in spreadsheet software such as Excel or Lotus 1-2-3 is easy. Using your spreadsheet software, type in the following information:

Territory	Sales in $ millions
East	$10
West	12
North	31
South	17
International	4

Create the following graphs: (1) a two-dimensional bar graph of sales, (2) a two-dimensional bar graph of sales with the bars running horizontally, (3) a three-dimensional bar graph, (4) a two-dimensional pie chart, and (5) an exploded three-dimensional pie chart. You should be able to create just the first graph and then simply change the graph or chart type to view the other four. Do the three-dimensional graphs do a better job of conveying information or are they simply more appealing to the eye?

5. Wireless Mice and Keyboards

Wireless keyboards and mice are emerging technologies. Of course, you use a keyboard and mouse every day—the emerging part is the wireless aspect. Visit a local computer store (or perhaps a few Web sites) and do some fact finding about wireless mice and keyboards. How do they work? How much do they cost? How far away can you be from your computer and still use a wireless mouse or keyboard? Do they work well all the time or can some sort of interference stop their transmission to your computer?

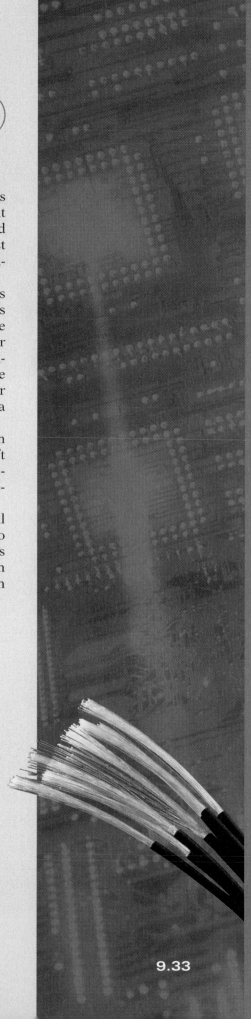

Looking Back/Looking Ahead

The Life and Times of a Dot-Com Entrepreneur

Joann has been hard at work determining her current technology needs and how she'll set up shop on the Web. Along the way, she's learned about application and operating system software, built her Web site, determined her exact hardware needs, learned how to store information, and—most important—learned to view technology within the context of ethics, security, and privacy.

But Joann knows that technology is changing every day. That means she needs to stay current and she needs to think about how her visitors will use her site in the future. So, Joann is already making plans. First, she wants her Web site to respond to voice commands because many of her visitors will be using _____. Her visitors will demand high-quality images, art, and photos, as well. So, she's learning how to create _____ objects. She also wants her visitors to experience her product and service offerings before buying them. So, she's building a _____ application so her visitors can do just that.

Many of her future visitors won't be using credit cards or paying with a check. Instead, they'll be using _____. And Joann doesn't want a passive Web site waiting around for visitors. So, she plans to incorporate _____ technologies so she can go to her visitors before they come to her.

As Joann looks forward to learning more, she realizes that she still needs to learn more about developing software systems. She also needs to take an organizational perspective of herself and her business if she plans to grow in size. Finally, she knows intelligent technologies exist that can help her make effective business decisions. She'll find her answers in Chapters 10, 11, 12, and 13.

CHAPTER

10

ten

Systems Development

Why Is Packaged Software Sometimes Not Enough?

Software doesn't just magically appear. Someone has to determine a need for it. Then someone has to specify in excruciating detail how the software must work, what information it should capture and display, and the steps within each process. Next, someone must write the actual software code. Then, it has to be tested, tested, and retested. And that only covers the software aspect—there's just as much to do for hardware.

Many organizations today have spent billions of dollars developing computer systems, from seemingly simple payroll systems to elaborate customer-integrated systems that run on the Web. These are definitely nontrivial efforts.

In this chapter, we'll focus on how organizations go about developing new computer systems. Although you may not want to develop computer systems for a living, this is still an important topic for you. Why? Mainly because you'll be using those systems. If they meet your needs, you'll be more productive. If they don't meet your needs, you'll experience many hours of frustration.

As we look at how organizations develop computer systems, we'll do so from a very broad perspective, covering the major steps and some tasks within each step. In the chapter to follow, we'll closely examine the programming function and different programming languages.

A://WHY ORGANIZATIONS DEVELOP SYSTEMS

Before we explore *how* organizations build computer systems, let's first answer the following question, "*Why* do organizations need computer systems?" That's a really great question; after all, if you don't know why you're developing something, you typically question the need for it. Organizations today develop new computer systems for three primary reasons:

1. To remain efficient.
2. To level the competitive playing field.
3. To achieve an advantage through innovation.

DEVELOPING SYSTEMS TO REMAIN EFFICIENT
Do Organizations Develop Systems Just for Efficiency?

Many organizations today do indeed develop some systems just to be more efficient in their internal processes. For example, an organization may create a new payroll system that streamlines the submission and processing of time sheets. The previous payroll system may have been working well but required employees to submit written paper time sheets. While entering the time sheet information, people made mistakes that later had to be fixed. By reducing the number of errors, the new system made the whole process more efficient.

Systems developed for the sake of efficiency may not actually yield an advantage in the marketplace. But they do add to the bottom line of an organization in terms of dollars.

DEVELOPING SYSTEMS TO LEVEL THE COMPETITIVE PLAYING FIELD

Do Organizations Develop Systems Just to Stay Up with the Competition?

In many instances, organizations develop new systems just to stay competitive. This is typically a "reactionary" measure by which an organization sees that a competitor has developed a new system and, in turn, develops its own just to stay competitive. For example, shipping organizations, such as UPS and the U.S. Postal Service, noticed several years ago that FedEx had developed a new system that allowed customers to request a parcel pick-up and to track a parcel throughout the shipment process by simply accessing the Web and entering a parcel tracking number (see Figure 10.1).

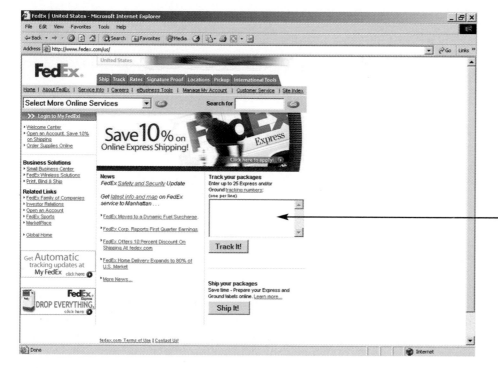

FIGURE   10.1

FedEx's customer-oriented parcel tracking software helped it achieve a competitive advantage in the marketplace.

Track your package here.

Just to stay competitive and not lose customers to FedEx, UPS and the others were forced to develop similar systems. This may not seem like the ideal situation under which to develop a new system (and it isn't), but sometimes organizations find themselves reacting to what the competition is doing.

DEVELOPING SYSTEMS TO ACHIEVE AN ADVANTAGE THROUGH INNOVATION

Can Organizations Achieve an Advantage by Developing a New System?

The best reason for an organization to develop a new system is for the purpose of gaining an advantage in the marketplace through innovation. Our previous example of FedEx is a good one. FedEx developed its new customer-oriented parcel tracking software (which is an example of a customer-integrated system) to achieve an advantage over its competitors. Until UPS and the others were able to develop similar systems, FedEx attracted many new customers (away from its competition).

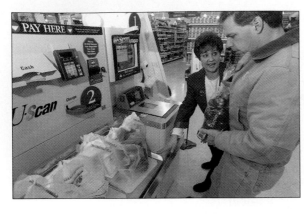

Almost by their nature these types of new systems also increase the efficiency of an organization. Because of its customer-oriented "do it yourself" software, FedEx was able to reduce the number of people handling incoming phone calls for parcel pick-up and tracking.

Another excellent example of achieving an advantage through the development of a new computer system is self-scanning systems at a grocery store. Again, this new system allows you (as the customer) to process your own grocery purchase, including scanning items and paying. Many people needing only a few grocery items specifically visit stores with self-scanning facilities. They do this because they believe they can get through the checkout process more quickly.

SECTION A://   *making the grade*

1. Many organizations today develop some systems just to be more _efficient_ in their internal processes.
2. When organizations develop new systems just to stay competitive, it is typically a _reactionary_ measure.
3. The best reason for an organization to develop a new system is for the purpose of gaining an _advantage_ in the marketplace through innovation.

B://WHY YOUR PARTICIPATION IS IMPORTANT

Now that you know "why" organizations develop new systems, let's answer another question: "*Why* is your participation important as your organization develops a new system?" That's another really great question; if you understand why your participation is important, you'll be more inclined to add as much value as you can to the systems development process. Your participation during the systems development process is important because you are (or will be) a

- Business process expert.
- Quality control analyst.
- Manager of other people.

YOU ARE A BUSINESS PROCESS EXPERT
What Valuable Input Can I Provide about Business Processes?

First and foremost, your participation is important because you are a business process expert. For example, let's suppose your job includes managing accounts receivables (what your customers owe your organization). Who knows better than you how that particular business process should work in the most efficient and effective way?

In most systems development efforts, a team of technology specialists is charged with actually designing the new system, buying the right hardware, and writing the necessary software. But those technology specialists are—by their very name—specialists in technology and not in business

Systems Development Process

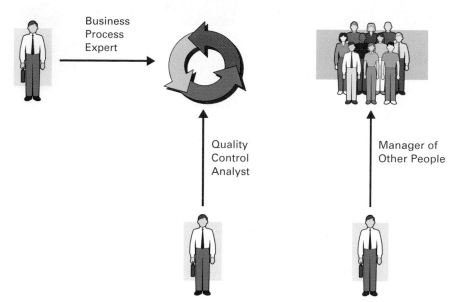

During the development of systems, you have three primary roles.

processes such as accounts receivable. So, your job is to inform those people exactly how the process you know about should work. You are the business process expert, and your input into the systems development process is vital and invaluable.

YOU ARE A QUALITY CONTROL ANALYST

How Can I Ensure That the System Is Developed Correctly?

Throughout the systems development process, it is also your responsibility to review and suggest changes to the system as it's being developed. For example, that team of technology specialists will periodically ask you to review sample screens for inputting information and the content and format of sample reports. You must ensure that those screens capture the appropriate information and that those reports include the information you want to see.

It's rather like having a home custom built. You initially provide the builder with the characteristics of the home you want (a version of being a business process expert). You must then review architectural drawings and the like to ensure that the home meets your original specifications.

You may also be asked to review process specifications for software. In this instance, you'll be verifying that business rules are being captured—such as notifying customers of an outstanding balance after 45 days, in our example of someone with expertise in the management of accounts receivables.

YOU ARE A MANAGER OF OTHER PEOPLE

What Responsibilities Do I Have for the People I Manage?

Finally, you have responsibilities to those people you manage. In today's technology-based business world, all the employees you manage will be using computer systems in some fashion. It's up to you to ensure that those systems meet people's needs, allowing them to be efficient and innovative in the ways in which they carry out their tasks.

Managing people today extends beyond traditional "human resource management" such as hiring and training. You must also ensure that your employees have the technology they need to do their work.

1. When you provide input concerning how a computer system should work, you are acting as a ___business process expert___

2. When you ensure that a system is being developed correctly, you are acting as a ___quality control analyst.___

3. As a manager of other people, you must ensure that your employees have the ___technology___ they need to do their work.

C://THE TRADITIONAL SYSTEMS DEVELOPMENT LIFE CYCLE

The most common way in which organizations develop systems today is through the traditional systems development life cycle. The ***traditional systems development life cycle (SDLC)*** is a structured step-by-step approach to developing systems that creates a separation of duties among technology specialists and users. In the SDLC, users (such as yourself) are the business process experts and quality control analysts, whereas the technology specialists are responsible for the actual design, construction, and support of the system.

Again, it's like having a home custom built. You are the expert in what you want and it's up to you to ensure that the house is built to meet your needs and specifications. The builder, including all the various crews, is then responsible for the actual design and construction of your home along the lines you have laid out.

Using the SDLC, your organization follows six phases (see Figure 10.3):

1. Investigation
2. Analysis
3. Design
4. Construction
5. Implementation
6. Support

FIGURE 10.3

The traditional systems development life cycle (SDLC) includes six phases.

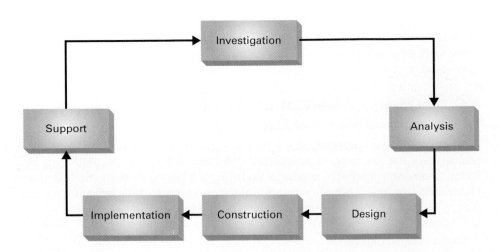

To illustrate some key concepts and techniques in the SDLC, let's follow the Richmond Blood Center as it went about developing a new system for tracking donors, inventory, and requests from local hospitals. The Richmond Blood Center is a nonprofit organization that maintains an inventory of blood by accepting donations and fills requests for blood from local hospitals. Please review Figure 10.4.

FIGURE   10.4

The Richmond Blood Center needs a new system for tracking donors, inventory, and requests from local hospitals.

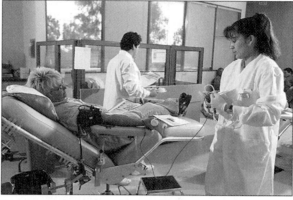

Donors who are acceptable are then taken to a waiting room, and, from there, on to a donating room. Once the donor has given blood, Richmond logs the pint of blood into its inventory and updates information for the donor.

When a potential donor arrives, Richmond goes through a series of checks. For a new donor, Richmond gathers a variety of information, including name, address, age, and medical history. If the new donor is not acceptable, Richmond provides a written reason why and the donor is excused. For a repeat donor, Richmond verifies that enough time has elapsed since that donor last gave blood. If enough time has not elapsed, Richmond provides a written statement to that effect and the donor is excused.

Periodically, Richmond receives requests for blood from local hospitals. If Richmond has sufficient blood in inventory, it fills the requests and updates its blood inventory information. If there is insufficient inventory, Richmond backlogs the requests. On a daily basis, Richmond evaluates the backlogged requests to see which—if any—it can fill.

On a daily basis, Richmond checks its inventory status by blood type. If inventory levels for any blood type fall below 10 pints, Richmond generates appeal letters to previous donors with the given blood type.

SYSTEMS INVESTIGATION

How Does the Systems Development Process Begin in an Organization?

In the first phase of the SDLC—*systems investigation*—you seek to lay the foundation for the systems development process by performing four tasks (see the four tasks in Figure 10.5). All four tasks are equally important, but at the outset *defining the problem* or opportunity is most crucial.

A ***problem/opportunity statement*** is a concise document that describes the exact nature of the problem or opportunity and provides broad statements concerning how the proposed system will benefit the organization. What is key here is that you define the problem or opportunity and <u>not</u> symptoms. Many systems development efforts fail today because people don't truly understand the nature of the problem or opportunity. So, they end up developing a system that treats only symptoms.

FIGURE   10.5

Systems investigation is the phase that starts the systems development life cycle.

- Define the Problem/Opportunity
- Assess Initial Feasibility
- Build the Project Team
- Create a Systems Development Project Plan

Second, you must create an *initial feasibility assessment* from several points of view, taking into account the time, technical, and fiscal aspects.

- A ***time feasibility assessment*** determines if your organization can develop the proposed system while meeting certain deadlines.

- A ***technical feasibility assessment*** determines if your organization has access to or can acquire the necessary hardware and software for the proposed system.

- A ***fiscal feasibility assessment*** determines if your organization has sufficient resources to develop the proposed system and if the total cost of those resources falls within an allocated budget.

If the proposed system is infeasible for any of the above reasons, you may choose to abandon its development or seek other development means such as end user development and outsourcing (which we'll discuss in later sections).

Once you've determined that a proposed system is feasible, it's time to *build a project team.* Most project teams include the following people:

- *A champion*—a **system champion** is a management person within your organization who (1) believes in the worth of the system and (2) has the "organizational muscle" to pull together the necessary resources. This may often be the chief information officer. A **chief information officer (CIO)** is the person within your organization who oversees the use of information as a resource.

- *Several users*—users are simply those people who will eventually be responsible for interacting with the system on a daily basis.

- *One or more systems analysts*—a **systems analyst** is a technology specialist who understands both technology and business processes. This person is responsible for gathering requirements from users and ensuring that other specialists understand those requirements.

- *One or more programmers*—a **programmer** is a technology specialist whose expertise lies in taking user requirements and writing software to match those requirements. Your team may include both **application programmers** (programmers who write application software) and **system programmers** (programmers who write operating system and utility software).

- *One or more hardware specialists*—a hardware specialist has expertise in different types and platforms of hardware, perhaps networking units or server computers.

- *Project manager*—the **project manager** is the person who oversees the project from beginning through implementation and support.

All these people are vitally important to the systems development process, with perhaps the most important being the systems analyst. A systems analyst must be able to speak two languages—business and technical. That person is responsible for creating the communications bridge between users (business process experts) and technology experts.

As the fourth and final task, you must create a *systems development project plan.* A **systems development project plan** is a document that includes a list of the project team, the problem/opportunity statement, the project budget, the feasibility assessments, and project timetable (see Figure 10.6). In each subsequent phase of the SDLC, you'll revisit this project plan and perhaps update it in light of new considerations.

At the Richmond Blood Center gaining a competitive advantage in the marketplace was not a concern. It had a manual and paper-based process for tracking donors, handling blood requests from hospitals, managing inventory, and generating appeal letters that worked just fine. The real goal of the new system was simply to streamline processes and work more efficiently.

FIGURE 10.6

The systems development project plan is the document you create in systems investigation.

1. **Problem/Opportunity Statement**
2. **Feasibility Statement**
   - Time
   - Technical
   - Fiscal
3. **Project Team**
   - Champion
   - Users
   - Systems Analysts
   - Programmers (Application and System)
   - Hardware Specialists
   - Project Manager
4. **Project Budget**
5. **Project Timetable**
   - Milestones

SYSTEMS ANALYSIS

How Does an Organization Study the Current System?

The ***systems analysis phase*** of the systems development life cycle (SDLC) involves modeling how the current system works from a logical (not physical) point of view, identifying its weaknesses and the opportunities to improve, creating a logical model of the new system, and reviewing the project plan (see Figure 10.7).

FIGURE 10.7

During systems analysis, you logically model the current and proposed systems.

- Model How the Current System Works
- Identify Weaknesses and Opportunities
- Create a Model of the New System
- Review the Project Plan

There are two keys here. First, you can't simply ignore the current system. It undoubtedly has some value. And when you model it, you can gain insight into its weaknesses and opportunities for improvement.

Second, the real goal of systems analysis is to develop an understanding of the current and proposed system from a logical, not physical, point of view. That is, at this point you shouldn't concern yourself with technical issues such as hardware and software. You should focus first on business processes and business information without regard to the hardware and software that does or will support them. In doing so, you allow your business needs to drive your technology decisions, not the other way around.

During this phase, you can employ a variety of modeling techniques—one of the more popular ones is data flow diagramming. ***Data flow diagramming (DFD)*** is a modeling technique for illustrating how information moves through various processes and how people outside the system provide and receive information. In Figure 10.8 you can see a data flow diagram (DFD) for the Richmond Blood Center. Notice that it really has no starting or ending point and that it makes no reference to technology. So, DFDs are great tools for modeling a system from a logical perspective without regard to any of its physical or technical characteristics.

F I G U R E   10.8

The Richmond Blood Center data flow diagram (DFD) shows major processes and the flows of information among them.

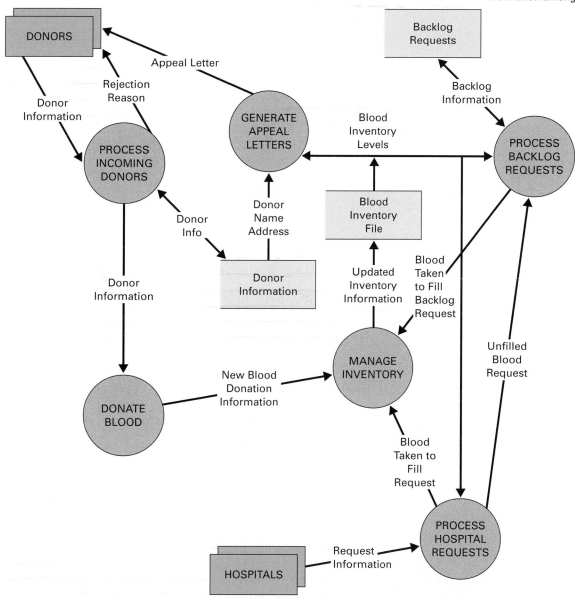

In a DFD, processes are represented as circles and information repositories are represented as open-ended rectangles. Players that are external to the system are represented as rectangles.

It was during this process that the receptionist for the Richmond Blood Center noted that repeat donors often became a bit miffed after driving to the blood center to give blood only to find that not enough time had elapsed since their last donation. So, the receptionist suggested that creating a Web site might be a good idea. Then, donors could type in a special password and determine if it was time to give blood again.

SYSTEMS DESIGN

How Does an Organization Create a "Blueprint" for the New System?

The **_systems design phase_** of the systems development life cycle (SDLC) involves generating several alternative technical solutions for the new logical model, selecting the best technical alternative, developing detailed software specifications, and—once again—reviewing the project plan (see Figure 10.9).

FIGURE   10.9

During systems design, you build the technical blueprint for the new system.

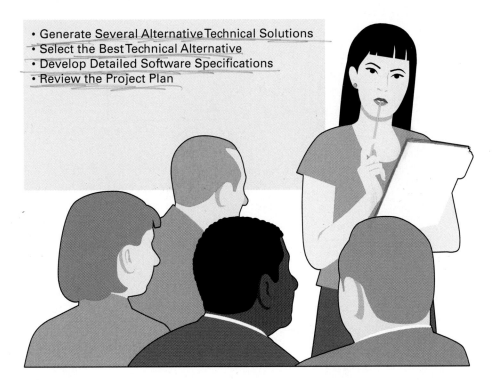

- Generate Several Alternative Technical Solutions
- Select the Best Technical Alternative
- Develop Detailed Software Specifications
- Review the Project Plan

At this point, your role as a business process expert diminishes and your role as a quality control analyst increases. That is, most of the work during this phase is performed by the technology specialists. Your role becomes one of reviewing the technical alternatives, the chosen technical alternative, and the software specifications to ensure that they meet your logical business needs.

As the technology specialists generate the software specifications, they will often create sample input screens, sample report formats, and program flowcharts. It is your responsibility to review all of these. A **_program flowchart_** is a graphical depiction of the detailed steps that software will perform. In Figure 10.10 you can see a partial program flowchart for the Richmond Blood Center for the software that accepts a hospital request for blood, determines if it can be filled, and backlogs the request if it cannot be filled, or fills the order and updates the inventory to reflect that inventory has been reduced.

This flowchart shows the process the Richmond Blood Center follows to process blood requests from hospitals.

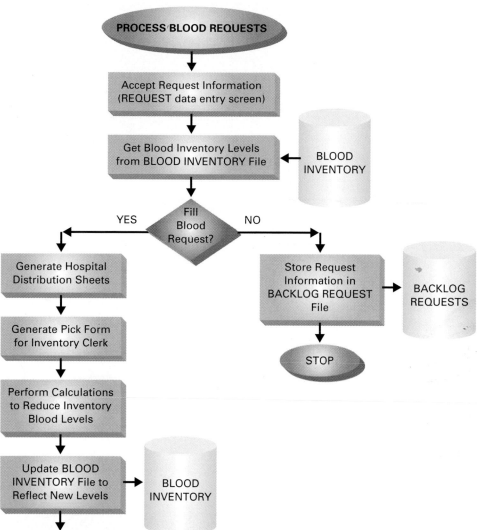

There are numerous other ways besides program flowcharting to create software specifications. We'll be covering some of these in the next chapter on programming and programming languages.

In generating and evaluating technical designs, your project team will probably look at such options as creating an intranet, a completely private system that runs on a network or perhaps a system that runs on a Web site for everyone on the Web to see and use. Whatever the case, there are more alternatives than you can imagine. It's up to your technology specialists to identify a group of the best, and then it's up to the entire project team (including users) to choose absolutely the best one given the constraints of your project plan.

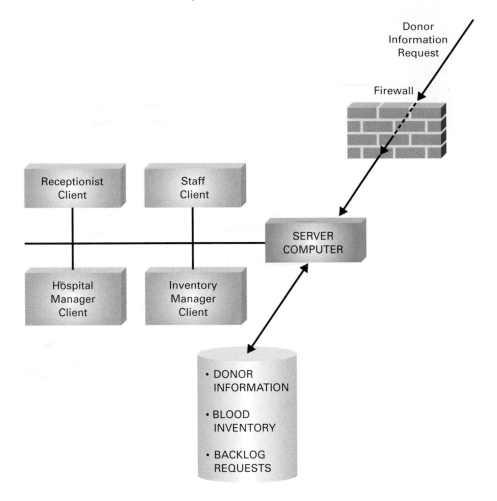

The Richmond Blood Center
technical design shows an
intranet protected by a firewall.

At the Richmond Blood Center it became obvious that the system had
to be an intranet-based application that would allow donors to enter a
special password to determine if they could give blood again. Figure 10.11
shows the technical design for Richmond's new system with that feature
included.

SYSTEMS CONSTRUCTION

How Do Technology Specialists Build the New System?

The goal of the *systems construction phase* of the systems development
life cycle (SDLC) is to actually create the new system. This will involve a
number of tasks including acquiring and installing any new hardware,
writing software, testing the software, and reviewing the project plan (see
Figure 10.12). This is the phase in the SDLC that requires the most time.
According to most experts, 80 to 90 percent of all efforts are devoted to
this phase. Why? Because writing and testing software is a labor-intensive
task.

During systems construction, you actually build the new system.

Writing software requires that programmers use the software specifications and a programming language or tool to actually create the working software. That is no small task. Consider this—the typical large-organization payroll software includes somewhere between 500,000 and 1 million lines of software code. And all that code must work perfectly.

That's also why testing is so important during this phase. As a user, you'll be called on to test the software. At this point, you'll need to make sure that the software doesn't allow you to enter bad information (such as a series of numbers for a name or the letter "Q" for a blood type). You'll also want to test the software for range validity—for example, the system for the Richmond Blood Center should not allow the entry of new donors who are under the age of 18. Basically, you have to look at every field and determine what it cannot accept and then try it.

As you do this, hardware specialists will be acquiring, installing, and testing any new hardware. Eventually, you'll have to test the software again (in the next phase) on the new hardware under operational conditions.

SYSTEMS IMPLEMENTATION

What Steps Must an Organization Take to Start Using the New System?

The ***systems implementation phase*** of the systems development life cycle (SDLC) involves training users, converting existing information to the new system, converting users, acceptance testing, and reviewing the project plan (see Figure 10.13). At this point, your project team brings the new system to life in your organization. The project team installs the new software on the new hardware, trains all users how to use the software, and goes through a process of acceptance testing.

Acceptance testing is a formal, documented process in which users use the new system, verify that it works correctly under operational conditions, and note any errors that need to be fixed.

A key in this phase is moving from the old way of doing things to the new system. We call this *conversion*. There are four popular conversion techniques:

1. ***Parallel conversion***—in which you run both the old and new systems until you're sure the new system works correctly.

2. ***Plunge conversion***—you unplug the old system and use the new system exclusively.

3. ***Pilot conversion***—you target a select group of users to convert to the new system before converting everyone.

4. ***Piecemeal conversion***—you target only a portion of the new system for conversion, ensure that it works correctly, and then convert the remaining system.

Each method has its advantages and disadvantages. For example, parallel conversion is the safest but also the most expensive procedure. Plunge conversion (sometimes called "cold turkey" conversion) is the cheapest but also the most dangerous if the new system fails. Many or-

FIGURE 10.13

During systems implementation, you test the new system and bring it to life in your organization.

- Train Users
- Convert Information
- Convert Users
- Perform Acceptance Testing
- Review the Project Plan

ganizations combine several. For example, an international organization may convert its home office in Tokyo using a parallel conversion method before converting the rest of its offices (pilot approach).

The Richmond Blood Center, because its old system was paper-based, decided to use a parallel conversion method. So, employees at each process gathered and recorded information using both the old paper system and the new computerized system until it was verified that the new system worked correctly.

SYSTEMS SUPPORT

What Happens When the New System Needs Modification?

No system is ever complete. Why? Because the way your organization works and the processes it performs are constantly evolving and changing. So, your computer systems must change as well. It may be that your systems are fairly robust and adaptable to change. But it is entirely possible that a given system may need a complete overhaul at some time.

During systems support, your tasks are four-fold (see Figure 10.14). First, your organization must provide a formal mechanism for the periodic review of the system. Your organization will be interested in answering such questions as "Does this system still support the overall business goals?" and "Do modifications need to be made to this system in light of changes to business processes?" These are very important questions, and your organization should provide answers to them on a frequent basis.

Second, as users use the system they may notice changes that need to be made. Some of these are quite simple, such as adding a new report. Others may be more complex, such as adding new business rules to meet federal reporting requirements for tax purposes. Whatever the case, your organization must provide a formal mechanism through which users can request changes. You can certainly achieve this by creating a change

- Provide a Mechanism for System Review
- Provide a Mechanism for Requesting Changes
- Evaluate Proposed System Changes
- Initiate System Changes

FIGURE 10.14

Systems support includes a variety of ongoing tasks.

FIGURE   10.15

Support costs for a system vary over time.

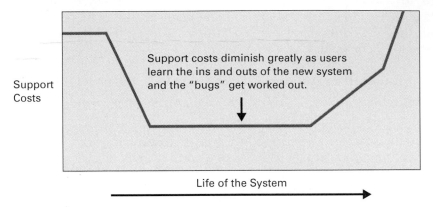

For a period of time after implementation, support costs may be relatively high for further user training and eliminating "bugs."

Nearing the end of the useful life of a system, support costs will begin to skyrocket. It's definitely time to consider a complete overhaul.

Support costs diminish greatly as users learn the ins and outs of the new system and the "bugs" get worked out.

Support Costs

Life of the System

request form or by holding meetings in which users provide feedback concerning the system and its operation.

Third, as changes are proposed your organization must evaluate them and determine which (if any) to undertake. As we've stated, even seemingly minor modifications require time and money. Your organization must constantly balance proposed changes against limited resources.

Finally, your organization must initiate system change. This is usually achieved in one of two ways. First, if the change is minor, such as adding a report, the new requirements would go immediately to the construction phase for the writing and testing of the necessary software. On the other hand, major changes require you to start the SDLC all over again with the investigation phase. This often occurs when the technology on which the original system was built becomes obsolete and hard to maintain (see Figure 10.15). If this is the case, starting over may very well be the best way to implement change.

What you have just read is a brief introduction to the SDLC. What's important is for you to understand what goes on during each phase and—most important—what your roles are. In the early phases of the SDLC, you'll act primarily as a business process expert. In the later phases, you'll act primarily as a quality control analyst. Both roles are vitally important.

SECTION C:// making the grade

1. A _____ feasibility assessment determines if your organization can develop the proposed system while meeting certain deadlines.
2. A _System analyst_ is a technology specialist who understands both technology and business processes.
3. _DFD_ _____ is a modeling technique for illustrating how information moves through various processes and how people outside the system provide and receive information.
4. Using the _Plunge_ _____ conversion method you literally unplug the old system and use the new system exclusively.

D://END USER DEVELOPMENT AND PROTOTYPING

The systems development life cycle (SDLC) is indeed the most popular way in which organizations develop computer systems. Two other popular alternatives are outsourcing (which we'll discuss in the next section) and end user development. **_End user development_** is the development and support of computer systems by users (such as yourself) with little or no help from technology specialists.

End user development is growing in popularity. Today, it's estimated that most organizations have so many new proposed systems that it would take them an average of five years to complete them all. So, many organizations are empowering employees to develop many smaller systems themselves. This is the concept of end user development.

You must be prepared for this. Although you won't be developing large-scale systems that support hundreds of users, you'll probably be developing smaller systems such as a customer information tracking system for the marketing department or perhaps a maintenance scheduling system for equipment on the production floor. These are definitely important systems.

PROTOTYPING

Will I Follow the SDLC while Performing End User Development?

When you perform the process of end user development, you'll almost always build prototypes. **_Prototyping_** is the process of building a model that demonstrates the features of a proposed product, service, or system. A **_prototype_**, then, is a model of a proposed product (which can be a computer system).

FIGURE   10.16

In prototyping, you start with basic requirements and continually add new features and processes.

End User Development

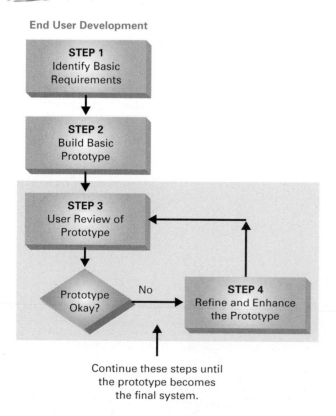

Continue these steps until the prototype becomes the final system.

SDLC

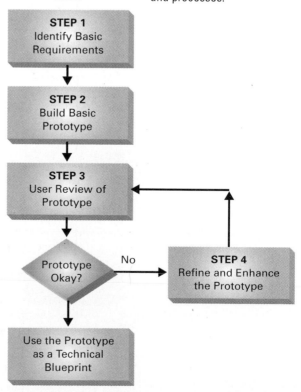

People and organizations perform prototyping all the time. Automobile manufacturers build prototypes of cars to demonstrate safety features. Building contractors construct models of bridges to test their strength in adverse weather conditions. Your instructor may give you sample test questions for an upcoming exam. Those sample questions are a model or prototype of what you can expect.

In systems development, prototyping is an iterative process in which you (see Figure 10.16):

1. Identify the basic requirements of the system.
2. Build a prototype from basic requirements.
3. Have other users review the prototype and suggest changes.
4. Refine and enhance the prototype until it's complete.

The iterative process occurs between steps #3 and #4. So, as your fellow users review your prototype and suggest changes, you refine and enhance your prototype and then have the users once again review the updated prototype. This iterative process continues until the prototype is complete and can become the final system (see the right side of Figure 10.16 on the previous page).

Prototyping is also widely used in the SDLC. However, as the left side of Figure 10.16 shows, the final prototype in the SDLC acts only as the technical blueprint from which the eventual system is developed. So, during the SDLC, prototyping is used for the analysis and design phases. For end user development, you'll most often use prototyping for analysis, design, and construction.

THE END USER DEVELOPMENT PROCESS
What Steps Will I Follow while Performing End User Development?

In Figure 10.17, you can see the phases of end user development including the prototyping process. It's actually quite similar to the SDLC, except that analysis, design, and construction are replaced by the four steps of prototyping.

FIGURE 10.17

End user development looks similar to the traditional systems development life cycle (SDLC).

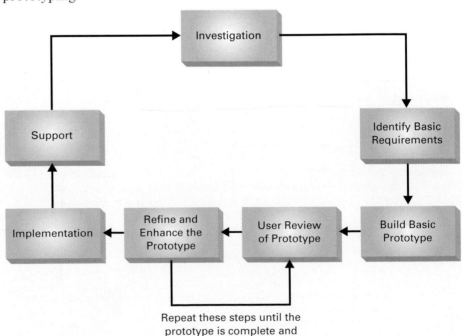

Repeat these steps until the prototype is complete and becomes the final system.

During end user development—as its name implies—the burden of all development tasks falls on your shoulders. These tasks include identifying potential hardware and choosing the best, writing any necessary software, training other users, converting existing information to the new system, testing the new system, and completely documenting how the new system works, just to name a few.

These are not insignificant tasks, and you shouldn't take them lightly. End user development is an empowering process. But it comes with increased responsibility.

END USER DEVELOPMENT ADVANTAGES AND DISADVANTEGES

Is There a Good Side and a Bad Side to End User Development?

As always, there are two sides to a coin. The same is true for end user development. It has both advantages and disadvantages.

The Advantages of End User Development

If undertaken carefully and correctly, you can develop the systems you need through end user development. Below are other advantages of end user development.

- **Encourages active user participation**—when users develop their own systems, they definitely increase their participation in the systems development process.

- **Improves requirements determination**—during end user development, users essentially tell themselves what they want. This greatly improves the effectiveness of capturing requirements.

- **Strengthens user sense of ownership**—no matter what you do, if you do it yourself, you take pride in your work.

- **Increases speed of systems development**—many small systems do not lend themselves well to the SDLC. These smaller systems may suffer from "analysis paralysis" because they don't require a structured step-by-step approach.

The Disadvantages of End User Development

If you're not careful, you can waste a lot of time developing a system that doesn't work. Below are other disadvantages of end user development.

- **Inadequate expertise leads to undeveloped systems**—many end user development systems are never completed because users lack the real expertise to utilize the most appropriate IT tools. If you spend time developing a system that you never complete, you have indeed wasted time.

- **Lack of organizational focus creates "privatized" systems**—when you develop a system for yourself, you must ensure that it interacts with other organizational systems. If you don't, you may create a "privatized" system that includes redundant information or performs redundant processes.

- **Insufficient analysis and design leads to subpar systems**—some users jump to conclusions about the hardware and software they should use without carefully analyzing all the alternatives. If this happens, your system may work but not as efficiently as it could.

i·buy

Surge Suppressors and Uninterruptible Power Supplies

If you're developing your own systems, you want to make sure they work correctly—and you also want to make sure they don't "freeze up" or "lock up" on you because of a power surge or even a sudden loss of power. To avoid these problems, you might want to consider getting a surge suppressor and/or an uninterruptible power supply.

A surge suppressor looks like a strip of electrical outlets. You plug devices into the surge suppressor and plug the surge suppressor into a wall outlet. If a sudden surge of electricity occurs, the surge suppressor blocks it.

An uninterruptible power supply (UPS) works differently. If you lose power, your UPS feeds electricity to whatever devices you've plugged into it. Today's UPSs can supply power from 10 minutes to two hours.

So, do you need either or both? You should at least purchase a surge suppressor for your computer. They cost only about $25. UPSs, however, can cost several hundred dollars. Businesses can justify that expense but you may not be able to.

If you decide against a UPS, you should at least save your information frequently (every five min-

utes or so). You can set your software so that it will automatically back up your information every few minutes.

Technology is an important part of your life. Investing so that it stays up and doesn't go down is a wise move.

- **Lack of documentation and support leads to short-lived systems**—when users develop their own systems, they often forgo documentation of how the system works and fail to realize that they can expect little or no support from technology specialists. All systems must change over time. Those changes are your responsibility to foresee in end user development.

SECTION D:// making the grade

1. _____ is the development and support of computer systems by users with little or no help from technology specialists.
2. A _prototype_ is a model of a proposed system.
3. In prototyping, you must first identify the _basic requirements_
4. In prototyping, the iterative process occurs between steps _____ and _____.

E://OUTSOURCING

A final alternative to developing a computer system is outsourcing. ***Outsourcing*** is the delegation of work to a group outside your organization for (1) a specified length of time, (2) a specified cost, and (3) a specified level of service.

Outsourcing is big business, and not just limited to the technology area. According to a Yankee Group survey of 500 companies, 90 percent stated that they had outsourced at least one major business function and 45 percent stated that they had outsourced some major portion of their technology environment. In just the IT area, a survey estimated that outsourcing exceeded $120 billion in the year 2000.

As you can see in Figure 10.18, there are various ways an organization can outsource some of its IT operations:

1. Purchasing ***horizontal market software,*** or general business software that has application in many industries. Horizontal market software includes accounts receivable, payroll, inventory management, logistics, and customer relationship management.

2. Purchasing ***vertical market software,*** or software that is unique to a particular industry. In the medical field, for example, an organization can purchase radiology software, nursing scheduling software, and patient admission software. These types of applications are definitely unique to the medical field (you wouldn't buy nursing scheduling software to help you schedule production equipment on a manufacturing floor).

3. Hiring an outsourcing vendor to develop software from scratch—when no prewritten software is available, an organization may choose to hire an organization to create the system from scratch.

FIGURE   10.18

Outsourcing systems development can take on many forms.

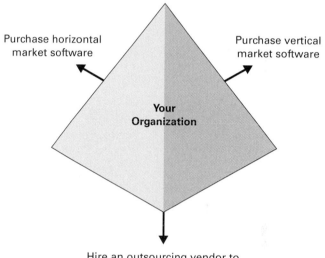

Purchase horizontal market software

Purchase vertical market software

Your Organization

Hire an outsourcing vendor to develop software from scratch

THE OUTSOURCING PROCESS

How Is the Process of Outsourcing Different from and Similar to the SDLC?

In most instances, outsourcing is similar to the systems development life cycle (SDLC), except that your organization turns over much of the design, construction, implementation, and support steps to another organization. However, your organization is still responsible for investigation, analysis, and a few new steps centered on a *request for proposal* (see Figure 10.19 on the next page).

Systems Investigation

No matter who will develop the proposed system, you must always perform systems investigation. Recall from our discussion of the SDLC that systems investigation includes performing an initial feasibility assessment. It is while assessing the initial feasibility of a proposal that you might target a system for outsourcing.

FIGURE   10.19

Like end user development, outsourcing looks similar to the traditional systems development life cycle (SDLC).

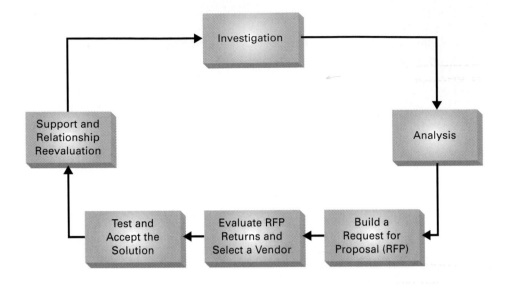

FIGURE   10.20

A request for proposal (RFP) is the most important document in outsourcing.

1. **Organizational Overview**

2. **Problem Statement**

3. **Description of Current System**
   - Business Processes
   - Hardware
   - Software (Application and System)
   - Information
   - System Interfaces

4. **Request for New System Characteristics**
   - Hardware
   - Software
   - Business Processes
   - Information
   - System Interfaces

5. **Request for Implementation Plan**
   - Training
   - Conversion

6. **Request for Support Plan**
   - Hardware
   - Software
   - Training

7. **Request for Development Time Frame**

8. **Request for Statement of Outsourcing Costs**

9. **How RFP Returns Will Be Scored**

10. **Deadline for RFP Returns**

11. **Primary Contact Person**

For example, you could determine that your IT specialists haven't enough time or resources to build a system. You could also determine that your organization doesn't possess the expertise to develop a given system. You may also find that it's simply cheaper to buy prewritten horizontal or vertical market software than it is to develop it from scratch. These are all good reasons why your organization would target the development of a proposed system for outsourcing.

Systems Analysis

As with systems investigation, you must still perform the systems analysis phase for any proposed system. That is, you must still be able to document how a current system works in order to develop specifications for how the new system should work.

The documentation you create during systems analysis will become the foundation for the most important outsourcing document—a request for proposal.

Build a Request for Proposal (RFP)

To tell an outsourcing vendor what you want, you must create a request for proposal. A **_request for proposal (RFP)_** is a formal document that outlines your logical requirements for the proposed system and invites outsourcing vendors to bid on its development. An RFP is not a small document—some will exceed several hundred pages and require months for your organization to create. Here, take all the time you need. The more complete and thorough your RFP, the more likely an outsourcing vendor will be able to define and develop a system that meets all your needs. Figure 10.20 shows the general outline of content for an RFP. Notice that it includes such information as an organizational overview, description of the current system, and requests for new systems characteristics.

It also includes other important information such as the deadline for RFP returns, how RFP returns will be evaluated, and a primary contact person.

Evaluate Request for Proposal Returns and Select a Vendor

Once you receive RFP returns from several potential outsourcing vendors, you must evaluate those and decide on which outsourcing vendor to use. Again, this is not a simple process. One outsourcing vendor may be the cheapest but may not offer a system with everything you want. Another outsourcing vendor may offer exactly the system you want but cannot develop it within your desired time frame. So, you must prioritize your requirements and choose an outsourcing vendor that meets most of your needs.

Once you've chosen an outsourcing vendor, a lengthy and legal process follows during which you must create a legally binding document that both organizations sign stating exactly what work is to be carried out, how and when payments will be made, the project time frame, and how your organization can get out of the contract if the outsourcing vendor is not living up to its end.

With that legal document in place, the outsourcing vendor will set out to create the system you want. Now, representatives from your organization will get together with representatives from the outsourcing vendor and review software, screens, and reports.

Test and Accept the Solution

Once the outsourcing vendor has completed the system, it will turn it over to you for testing and acceptance. It is during this time that you'll completely test the software, train users, convert old information to the new system, and convert users to the new system (through one or some combination of the parallel, plunge, pilot, and piecemeal conversion methods).

Your most important task here is to completely test the software. If something doesn't work right, do not accept the system. Instead, have the outsourcing vendor fix the problem(s) immediately. Eventually, you must "sign off" on the system, which states that you're completely happy with the new system and that you release the outsourcing vendor from any other work.

Systems Support and Relationship Reevaluation

As you move forward in using the new system, you'll want to provide for the many support tasks we discussed with the SDLC, including performing a periodic review of the system, providing a formal mechanism through which users can request changes, and evaluating the worth of proposed changes.

Most important, you'll want to constantly reevaluate your relationship with the outsourcing vendor. Many such organizations include support and maintenance activities as part of the overall cost of the system. Is the outsourcing vendor providing support when it stated it would? Is the outsourcing vendor willing to help you evaluate the worth of proposed changes as it stated it would? These are important questions you must consistently answer as you go along. In a way, the outsourcing vendor is now one of your business partners, and you must determine if it's a partnership worth keeping.

i·series insights

Ethics, Security & Privacy

Outsourcing Gone Bad

Outsourcing can be a very effective systems development technique. It enables your organization to focus on its unique core competencies and hire another organization to perform processes, take over business activities, and also develop systems that are important but not in a strategic sense. For example, your school may outsource its food operations and perhaps security. Why? Because your school is not in the business of providing food—it's in the business of providing you with an education. So, your school can focus on that primary task and let someone else make your lunch.

But there are significant downsides to outsourcing for systems development related to the compe-

Outsourcing

tence of the outside source. For example, in 1996, Duke Power Co. hired an outsourcing vendor to develop a customer relationship management system. The outsourcing vendor did deliver the system but it didn't work correctly. The vendor then wanted another two years to make modifications. Duke Power had no choice but to abandon the

project, and it lost $12 million in the process.

This problem of course occurs in all business environments. A couple of years ago GE was all set to introduce a new washing machine, but it couldn't because GE had outsourced some of the parts development and the vendor was late in delivering the parts. So, GE had to delay its product introduction and lost money on marketing and advertising.

It may not always be true that if you want something done right you should do it yourself. But just because you hire someone else to do your work doesn't necessarily mean that it will get done right or on time.

FIGURE 10.21

Outsourcing has both advantages and disadvantages.

ADVANTAGES: Outsourcing Allows Your Organization to . . .
- Focus on unique core competencies.
- Exploit the intellect of another organization.
- Better predict future costs.
- Acquire leading-edge technology.
- Reduce costs.
- Improve performance accountability.

DISADVANTAGES: Your Organization May Suffer Because Outsourcing . . .
- Reduces technical know-how for future innovation.
- Reduces degree of control.
- Increases vulnerability of strategic information.
- Increases dependency on other organizations.

SECTION E:// making the grade

1. _Outsourcing_ is the delegation of work to a group outside your organization.
2. _Horizontal_ market software is general business software that has application in many industries.
3. _Vertical_ market software is software that is unique to a particular industry.
4. The most important document in the outsourcing process is a _RFP_.

i·witness

An Up-Close Look at Web Sites

Rollovers

You've seen ways to use HTML to organize information on the Web. And you know part of the Web's appeal is its graphics and colors. But what about interactivity? Interactivity occurs when something on a Web page changes in response to what you do. A common interactivity element is a *rollover*. A rollover occurs when something changes as you move your mouse pointer over it. You've experienced a rollover when hyperlinks change color or an image lights up.

You'll need more than just basic HMTL to create a rollover on your Web page, but not much more. Using JavaScript (which we discuss in the next chapter) you can easily add some interactivity to your Web page. Let's say you'd like a message to appear when people place their mouse on a hyperlink.

• www.mhhe.com/i-series
Come on over to our Web site!

You can use the following Java-Script as a start:

```
<A HREF ="http://www.mhhe.com/
i-series"
ONMOUSEOVER="window.
status='Come over to our Web
site!'; return true"
ONMOUSEOUT="window.
status="; return true">www.mhhe.
com/i-series</A>
```

Using the ONMOUSEOVER and ONMOUSEOUT JavaScript commands, you're able to control what happens when people place their mouse pointer over a hyperlink.

We've designed two Web pages to help you learn more about using rollovers in JavaScript:

www.mhhe.com/i-series/I-Witness/10-A.html

www.mhhe.com/i-series/I-Witness/10-B.html

The first page has rollovers while the second does not. You'll want to locate all the rollovers that are on the first page and then decide which you'd like to try to create on the second page.

We've also provided links to Web pages and tutorials to help you learn more about JavaScript at www.mhhe.com/i-series.

F://SUMMARY AND KEY TERMS

Organizations need computer systems today for three reasons: (1) to remain efficient, (2) to level the competitive playing field, and (3) to achieve an advantage through innovation. Your participation in the systems development process is important because you are (or will be): (1) a business process expert, (2) a quality control analyst, and (3) a manager of other people.

The most common way in which organizations develop systems is through the ***traditional systems development life cycle (SDLC)***—a structured step-by-step approach to developing systems that creates a separation of duties among technology specialists and users. The SDLC includes six phases:

1. ***Systems investigation***—laying the foundation for the systems development process. In it you create a problem/opportunity statement; perform time, technical, and fiscal feasibility assessments; gather a project team; and create a systems development project plan.

2. ***Systems analysis***—modeling how the current system works, identifying weaknesses and opportunities, creating a model of the new system, and reviewing the project plan.

3. *Systems design*—generating several alternative technical solutions, selecting the best alternative, developing detailed software specifications, and reviewing the project plan.

4. *Systems construction*—creating the new system, including acquiring and installing any new hardware, writing software, testing software, and reviewing the project plan.

5. *Systems implementation*—training users, converting existing information to the new system, converting users, acceptance testing, and reviewing the project plan.

6. *Systems support*—maintaining and supporting the system over time.

Because most organizations don't have the IT resources to develop all proposed systems, they are turning to end user development. *End user development* is the development and support of computer systems by users (such as yourself) with little or no help from technology specialists. As you perform this process, you'll most often be *prototyping,* building a model that demonstrates the features of a proposed system. As you continually refine the prototype, you eventually create a complete and working system.

Still other organizations are turning to outsourcing. *Outsourcing* is the delegation of work to a group outside your organization for (1) a specified length of time, (2) a specified cost, and (3) a specified level of service. The most important document in outsourcing is a request for proposal. *A request for proposal (RFP)* is a formal document that outlines your logical requirements for the proposed system and invites outsourcing vendors to bid on its development.

On the Web site for this text at www.mhhe.com/i-series, we've provided a great deal of support for this chapter including how you can learn more about JavaScript.

KEY TERMS

acceptance testing (p. 10.16)

application programmer (p. 10.9)

chief information officer (CIO) (p. 10.9)

data flow diagramming (p. 10.10)

end user development (p. 10.19)

fiscal feasibility assessment (p. 10.8)

horizontal market software (p. 10.23)

outsourcing (p. 10.23)

parallel conversion (p. 10.16)

piecemeal conversion (p. 10.16)

pilot conversion (p. 10.16)

plunge conversion (p. 10.16)

problem/opportunity statement (p. 10.8)

program flowchart (p. 10.12)

programmer (p. 10.9)

project manager (p. 10.9)

prototype (p. 10.19)

prototyping (p. 10.19)

request for proposal (RFP) (p. 10.24)

system champion (p. 10.9)

system programmer (p. 10.9)

systems analysis phase (p. 10.10)

systems analyst (p. 10.9)

systems construction phase (p. 10.14)

systems design phase (p. 10.12)

systems development project plan (p. 10.9)

systems implementation phase (p. 10.16)

systems investigation (p. 10.8)

technical feasibility assessment (p. 10.8)

time feasibility assessment (p. 10.8)

traditional systems development life cycle (SDLC) (p. 10.6)

vertical market software (p. 10.23)

CROSSWORD PUZZLE

Across

1. SDLC phase in which you develop the problem/opportunity statement
5. Building a model
7. Conversion method installing one part of a system at a time
8. Model for how information moves within the system
11. SDLC phase in which you build the system
12. How users test a system
14. Software for wide variety of industries
16. SDLC phase in which you focus on logical needs
18. Does your organization have the necessary hardware/ software?
19. Can your organization meet deadlines?
21. Conversion method for unplugging the old and plugging in the new
23. Software for a specific industry
24. Does your organization have the money?
25. SDLC phase in which you build a technical blueprint

Down

1. SDLC in which you bring the new system to life
2. Programmer who writes OS software
3. Delegating work
4. Opposite of system programmer
6. Model
9. Design tool
10. Conversion method in which you run both systems
13. Overseer of the use of information
15. Management person with "organizational muscle"
16. Understands both technology and business
17. Structured step-by-step development approach
20. Conversion method using only a group of users
22. Most important document in outsourcing

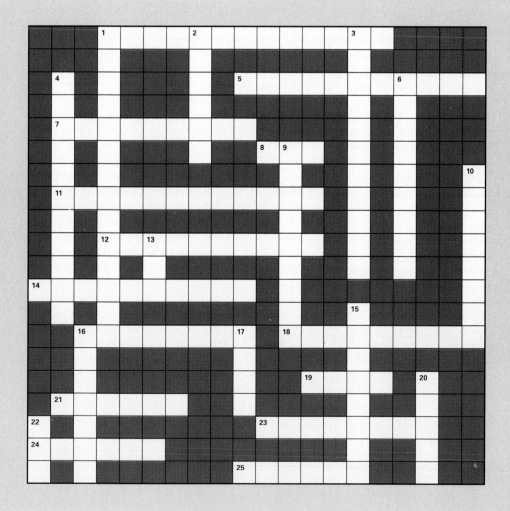

QUESTIONS AND EXERCISES

Multiple Choice

1. Organizations develop new computer systems
   a. to remain efficient.
   b. to level the competitive playing field.
   c. to achieve an advantage through innovation.
   d. for all of the above reasons.
   e. for none of the above reasons.

2. Laying the foundation for the systems development process is the purpose of which phase of the SDLC?
   a. systems investigation
   b. systems analysis
   c. systems design
   d. systems construction
   e. systems implementation

3. In which phase of the SDLC do you model the current and proposed system only from a logical point of view?
   a. systems investigation
   b. systems analysis
   c. systems design
   d. systems construction
   e. systems implementation

4. A(n) _____ is a graphical depiction of the detailed steps that software will perform.
   a. data flow diagram
   b. structure chart
   c. English narrative
   d. program flowchart
   e. problem/opportunity statement

5. In which phase of the SDLC do you write the software?
   a. systems investigation
   b. systems analysis
   c. systems design
   d. systems construction
   e. systems implementation

6. Targeting a select group of users for conversion to the new system before converting everyone is which type of conversion method?
   a. parallel
   b. plunge
   c. pilot
   d. piecemeal
   e. proactive

7. When performing end user development, you'll most often be
   a. confused.
   b. prototyping.
   c. outsourcing.
   d. insourcing.
   e. relying on technology specialists.

8. Outsourcing is the delegation of work to a group outside your organization for
   a. a specified length of time.
   b. a specified cost.
   c. a specified level of service.
   d. all of the above.
   e. none of the above.

9. General business software that has application in many industries is
   a. vertical market software.
   b. industrial software.
   c. industry-compliant software.
   d. horizontal market software.
   e. none of the above.

10. Determining if your organization can develop the proposed system while meeting certain deadlines is
    a. organizational feasibility assessment.
    b. deadline feasibility assessment.
    c. time feasibility assessment.
    d. technical feasibility assessment.
    e. fiscal feasibility assessment.

True/False

11. _____ During the early phases of the SDLC, you'll act primarily as a business process expert.

12. _____ Fiscal feasibility assessment determines if the proposed system will fit within your organization's culture.

13. _____ A chief information officer is the person within your organization who oversees the use of information as a resource.

14. _____ Data flow diagramming is a modeling technique for illustrating how data entry screens interact with databases.

15. _____ During systems construction, you model the system from a logical point of view only.

QUESTIONS AND EXERCISES

1. For each of the following steps in the left column identify in which phase of the SDLC they occur (given in the right column).

STEP		SDLC PHASE
A. _____ Build the project team		1. Systems Investigation
B. _____ Create a model of the new system		2. Systems Analysis
C. _____ Write software		3. Systems Design
D. _____ Initiate system changes		4. Systems Construction
E. _____ Identify weaknesses and opportunities		5. Systems Implementation
F. _____ Create a systems development project plan		6. Systems Support
G. _____ Select the best technical alternative		
H. _____ Provide a mechanism for requesting changes		
I. _____ Model how the current system works		
J. _____ Assess initial feasibility		
K. _____ Develop detailed software specifications		
L. _____ Train users		
M. _____ Perform acceptance testing		
N. _____ Acquire and install new hardware		
O. _____ Convert users		
P. _____ Generate several alternative technical solutions		
Q. _____ Define the problem/opportunity		
R. _____ Provide a mechanism for system review		
S. _____ Convert information		
T. _____ Evaluate proposed system changes		

2. Believe it or not, every day you outsource many aspects of your life. In the table below, list several aspects of your life that you outsource and then include a description of the outsourcing organization, what you pay, the specified length of time, and the specified level of service.

ASPECT OUTSOURCED	ORGANIZATION, COST, TIME, AND SERVICE
_____	_____
_____	_____
_____	_____
_____	_____
_____	_____

e-commerce

1. Buying Organic Foods

Everyone seems to be eating healthier these days—and you can eat healthy on the Web. Well, not exactly, but you can order organic foods from numerous Web sites. These sites are essentially specialty online grocery stores that sell just organic products (supposedly). Below are four such sites.

- www.goodeats.com
- www.allherb.com
- www.bioshop.org
- website.lineone.net/~organic.direct/index.htm

Connect to each of these sites or any others of your choosing and answer the following questions:

a. Can you order organic nonfood items such as T-shirts?

b. What is the delivery time?

c. Is there a delivery charge? If so, how much?

d. Does the site display a TRUSTe logo or some other form of privacy guarantee?

e. Is the site actually supported by a larger regular online grocer?

f. How are foods organized?

g. Does the site offer any information related to fitness and wellness?

h. Do any links on the site take you to other sites that are organic-related?

Now visit a "traditional" online grocer such as Peapod (www.peapod.com). How would you compare the sites? Do traditional online grocers such as Peapod have better-looking and easier-to-navigate sites than organic food sites? If there is a difference, why do you think it exists?

2. Donating to a Charity

The Web is full of business opportunities and exciting and fascinating places for you to visit. You can also use the Web for the betterment of people and society around the world. One such way is to donate to charities. Many charities and nonprofit organizations have created Web sites so that you can make donations over the Web. Below are four such sites.

- www.giveonline.org
- www.give.org
- www.helping.org
- www.charitiestoday.com

As you visit each site answer the following questions:

a. How can you search for your favorite charity?

b. Does the site provide full disclosure concerning its use of your money and your information?

c. Can you request that e-mails be sent to you periodically concerning new donation opportunities?

d. How do you make a donation—credit card over the Web, request a form, etc.?

e. How comfortable do you feel donating money at the site?

Of course, the Web also has some shady sites that may be posing as charities in an attempt to get your money. How can you be sure you're donating to a legitimate charity? Do you think charity donations will actually increase because charities advertise on the Web? Why or why not?

3. Getting Tutored on the Web

It only makes sense—you can find just about any information you want on the Web, especially for helping you with class work—so, why not be able to get online tutoring assistance? You can. Many Web sites provide online assistance, while others will help you find tutors in your area. Below are four tutor-oriented sites.

- www.tutor.com
- www.alt-tutor.com
- www.tutor2000.com
- www.tutoraid.org

e-commerce

As you visit each site, answer the following questions:

a. Does the site provide online tutoring?

b. Will the site help you find a tutor in your area?

c. What are the costs of tutoring or matching services?

d. How do you pay for services?

e. For what topics can you find tutoring assistance?

f. What sort of credentials does the site offer?

Let's think about this for a moment. Tutoring is a very individualized activity that usually requires a lot of one-on-one interaction. Do you think you can receive the same level of quality over the Web? Why or why not?

4. Writing Books on the Web

You know by now that you can buy and/or read books on the Web. If you're an aspiring author, you can also write books and have them published just on the Web too. The big advantage to this is that you don't have to be a Stephen King to publish a book on the Web. You simply provide the e-publisher with your manuscript and the e-publisher places it on the Web for people to pay

for and enjoy. The e-publisher loses very little money if your book sells only a few copies. Below are the sites for a few e-publishers.

- www.rocketebook.com
- www.mightywords.com
- www.ebooksonthe.net
- www.infinitypublishing.com

As you visit each site, answer the following questions:

a. Do you have to pay any sort of fee to publish a book?

b. What royalty rate will you receive for your book?

c. Do you retain the intellectual property rights to your book?

d. Will your book be registered with the Library of Congress?

e. Will the site do any advertising on behalf of your book?

f. Do you believe that the next wave of great writers will start by publishing their books on the Web? Will they really be as credible as today's current best-selling authors? Why or why not?

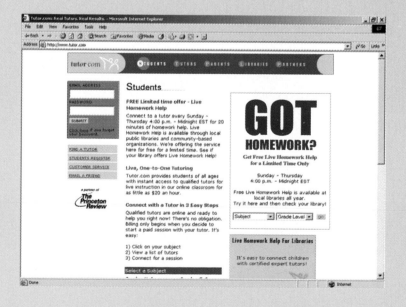

on the web

1. A Career as a Chief Information Officer

Chief information officers (CIOs) are among the highest paid of all technology professionals, with some salaries exceeding $1 million annually. Connect to a couple of your favorite job databases and perform a search for "chief information officer" or "CIO." Prepare a report for your class that includes such information as required skills, required number of years of employment, preferred degree(s), and salary range.

2. Finding Vertical Market Software

Search the Web for vertical market software providers. You'll undoubtedly find many, so you can refine your search just to a particular industry such as health care or manufacturing. Who seem to be the best organizations for providing vertical market software? Does the organization list other organizations that have purchased its software? What sort of support does the organization provide to other organizations that purchase its software? Does the organization post any sort of pricing on its Web site?

3. Finding Free Flowcharting and Data Flow Diagramming Tools

There is indeed a lot of free software on the Web, including everything from checkbook software to card games. You can also find a variety of freeware for drawing diagrams such as flowcharts and data flow diagrams (DFDs). Search the Web for one or two examples of this type of software and download one to your computer. Now, try to re-create the drawings in Figures 10.8 and 10.10 on pages 10.11 and 10.13. How successful were you? Did you find the drawing tool easy or difficult to use?

4. Joint Application Development

Joint application development (JAD) is a technique that many organizations use to determine requirements and generate technical alternatives quickly. Do some research on the Web and find out more about joint application development. Develop a short report that details the participants in a JAD session, the typical length of a JAD session, and at least one organization that has successfully used JAD.

5. Building Synergistic Teams

Most systems development efforts are successful because they were carried out by people who worked effectively as a team. You've probably experienced this in school. Some of your projects may have been great because you could work easily with your other team members. And you may have been on a team that never seemed to get anywhere for a variety of reasons. So, to effectively develop systems or work on any kind of team, you need to choose team members carefully. Do some research on the Web for team-building information. As you find sites that discuss the characteristics of a good team, create a list of helpful suggestions for creating the best team.

ethics, security & privacy

1. What to Do When Software Produces the Wrong Results

People create software. And people make mistakes. So, it's entirely possible that some software will not work correctly. What should you do when that happens? How responsible is an organization for its software that doesn't work right? What you do about it or what the organization does may be a question not of law but of ethics. It may be difficult to determine the correct course of action. Consider the scenarios below. For each, determine what action you would take (if any) and determine what action the organization should take (if any).

a. Your state's lottery software accidentally generates thousands of winning numbers. You have one of those numbers.

b. Your state's lottery software accidentally generates thousands of winning numbers. You have a ticket but not a winning number.

c. Your organization's payroll software overpays you by $10.

d. Your organization's payroll software overpays you by $100.

e. Your organization's payroll software overpays you by $1000.

f. A grocery store scanning system doesn't charge you enough for a certain product. You notice the error when you get home.

g. A grocery store scanning system charges you too much for a certain product. You notice the error when you get home.

h. Your utility bill is $600 when it should be only $60.

i. Your school notifies you in writing that you will graduate at the end of the term because you've taken all your classes. You plan a big party, and then receive a second letter stating that the first was an error.

j. As you review your bank statement, you notice a check written for $100 that your bank processed for only $10. It was a check you wrote.

k. As you review your bank statement, you notice a check written for $100 that your bank processed for only $10. It was a check you deposited.

2. What to Do When Users Won't Convert

Here's a true story. A few years ago a small auto parts store hired a contract programmer to create an inventory tracking system. When the system was complete (and it did work perfectly), the contract programmer unveiled it and set out to train the user. The user was the mother of the parts store owner and she refused to use a computer.

What should the owner do? His mother doesn't have much money and is probably not employable in very many places. However, he just spent $20,000 on a new computer system to stay up with the competition. If he doesn't use the new system he will have wasted $20,000 and he will probably be out of business within a year.

What should the contract programmer do? Should he give the money back since the system may not be used?

group activities

1. Everyday Prototyping

Throughout your life, you've performed the process of prototyping many times. For example, you may have created a resume, had several people evaluate it, and then refined it for another round of reviews. Think of at least three more instances in which you've performed prototyping. For each answer the following questions:

a. What basic requirements did you start with?

b. Who reviewed the prototype?

c. Approximately how many times did you refine and enhance the prototype?

d. What was the role of technology as you performed prototyping? If you didn't use any technology, could you have benefited from its use? Why or why not?

2. Interviewing a Systems Analyst

In your community or perhaps at your school, interview a systems analyst. In preparing for your interview, think of a number of questions regarding his/her background, degree, major responsibilities, and so on. As you do the interview, determine which skills you would need to acquire to become a systems analyst. Does this type of job appeal to you? Why or why not?

3. Creating a Data Flow Diagram for a Vending Machine

In Figure 10.8 on page 10.11, we provided a data flow diagram (DFD) for the Richmond Blood Center. Now it's your turn to attempt to draw a DFD. For your exercise, consider a vending machine that sells candy bars. The external players will include the person who fills the machine and empties the money and consumers such as your group. What are the processes you identified (there should be approximately five to seven)? What information repositories did you identify? Compare your DFD with that of another group. How similar and different are the two DFDs?

4. Creating a Program Flowchart

Consider the process you go through to register at your school for classes. Using Figure 10.10 on page 10.13 as a guide, create two different flowcharts. The first should detail the steps you go through to register for classes. The second should detail how the software works that supports your registering for classes. Now, compare the two. How are they different? How are they the same? Do you think organizations can benefit by first flowcharting what process a customer follows and then building software around that process? As a final task, create a flowchart of the ideal registration process from your point of view. How different is it from your current registration process?

5. Advantages and Disadvantages of the Traditional Systems Development Life Cycle

In this chapter, we listed various advantages and disadvantages for end user development and outsourcing. We did not, however, provide those same lists for the traditional systems development life cycle (SDLC). Your task is first to create a list of advantages of the SDLC, and second, for each advantage think of a corresponding disadvantage. Now, see if you come up with any further disadvantages. For each, create a corresponding advantage.

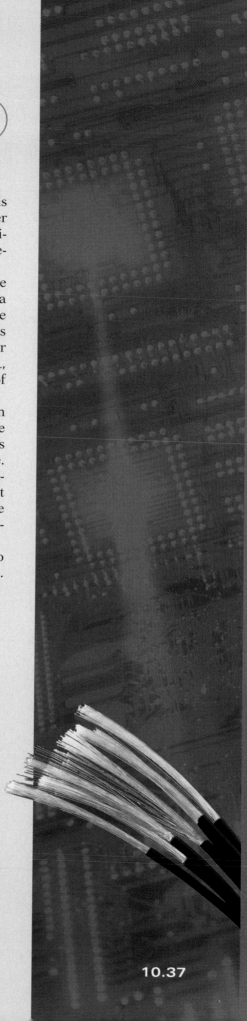

Looking Back/Looking Ahead

The Life and Times of a Dot-Com Entrepreneur

Joann's business is moving along quite nicely now. Her customer base is growing every day and she hopes to make a profit in about a year. As her business grows, Joann realizes that she'll need software to help her business run internally. So, she's set about the process of learning how to develop unique software for her unique needs.

Because most of her systems will be small and designed for just one person, Joann has decided not to use the traditional _____, a methodology really designed for users and technology specialists on the same team. However, Joann knows that there are many important facets of this methodology that she would like to follow while developing her software. Most important, she wants to develop a good _____, which will include milestones, feasibility assessments, and a statement of her problem/opportunity.

As for her specific systems development approach, she has chosen _____ because she will develop the systems for herself. As she creates her software, she'll be _____ or building models. This will allow her to continually refine the software until it becomes complete.

If she ever finds that she doesn't possess the time or expertise to develop a system, she'll look toward _____. It is quite likely that she can purchase _____ market software that has a wide range of applications to all industries or _____ market software that may be unique to her particular business.

If she does develop systems for herself, she realizes that she'll need to learn more about programming and programming languages and tools. She'll find out more about those in the next chapter.

For as long as computers have been around, the challenge for programmers has been to make software that effectively instructs computers what to do. You'll learn much about developing software in this chapter, but let's start with a few interesting facts:

software *development has definitely improved. Forty years ago creating computer programs required hundreds of programmers to code them on long strands of ticker-tape.*

to *avoid investing in an expensive supercomputer, corporations are now recruiting thousands of PC owners to do contract work for them over the Internet.*

fewer *women are becoming programmers and designers. In 2000, 28 percent of computer science graduates were women, a 9 percent drop from 1984.*

end users *typically use only 30 percent of the code that developers produce for application software. Perhaps developers don't understand what users need.*

the *first computer "bug" really was—a moth, caught in a computer relay switch.*

producing *a Sega Genesis game in the 90s cost $200,000. By 2000, the Playstation and Nintendo 64 games cost $2 million to develop. Today it costs ?? to produce a video game.*

To find out how much it costs to make your favorite video games, visit www.mhhe.com/i-series.

CHAPTER

11

eleven

Computer Programming

How Can You Create Your Own Software?

Without software, your computer is nothing more than a doorstop. Hardware is important, but without software, it won't do much. In Chapter 2, you learned how to use Web browser and connectivity software. In Chapter 3, you learned about application and system software. In Chapter 8, you worked with database management software. You've seen that the right software plus the right hardware makes your computer powerful.

In the previous chapter, we presented a broad overview of the systems development process. One of the most time-consuming aspects of the process is writing the software—software development or programming—which occurs in the construction phase.

In this chapter, we'll tackle the vitally important business of writing software. We'll explore basic programming techniques and how programmers create software. We'll look at programming languages available to you, and we'll look at languages programmers use to create Web applications.

A://PROGRAMMER'S VIEW OF INVESTIGATION, ANALYSIS, AND DESIGN

Let's assume that you're an applications programmer who must create a new payroll system. You join the project team in the investigation phase. In this section, we'll look at systems investigation, analysis, and design from your point of view.

SYSTEMS INVESTIGATION

How Can a Programmer Help Lay the Foundation for a New Systems Development Effort?

Recall from Chapter 10 that there are four key tasks performed in systems investigation, including defining the problem/opportunity, assessing initial feasibility, building the project team, and creating a systems development project plan. As a programmer, your primary focus should be on defining the problem/opportunity. To write the software correctly, you'll need to understand the exact nature of the problem or opportunity.

Does the new payroll system need to calculate weekly wages? Should it print payroll checks? How does it handle overtime? As a programmer, you'll need to ask these kinds of questions. Your goal is to build an effective and complete problem/opportunity statement. Have a close look at Figure 11.1, which shows how to do this for the proposed payroll system.

Figure 11.1 shows that with a few simple questions you can identify key pieces of information. Without this process, you wouldn't have known about overtime, the hours per week restriction, or that the software didn't need to print payroll checks.

It takes four months to two years for a typical software engineer to become comfortable with object-oriented programming.

did you know?

FIGURE 11.1

As a programmer you'll frequently create problem/opportunity statements.

Client's Request

Please create software to calculate employees' payroll.

Questions to Ask

Your Question	Client's Response
How often are employees paid?	Weekly.
Are they paid by the hour or salaried?	Both, but this program will only be for the hourly employees.
How much can an employee make per hour?	No more than $75 an hour and no less than $10.
Do the employees earn overtime?	Yes. Any hours over 40 are paid as time and a half.
How much overtime can an employee make?	An employee can work no more than 80 hours total in one week.
Will this program need to print out the paychecks?	No. Just send the information to Payroll. They will run the checks the same time they do the salaried paychecks.
What about employee benefits?	No. Payroll already has software for this as well.

Problem/Opportunity Statement

Create a program that gets an employee's identification, pay rate, and number of hours worked in one week.

Assume that employees are hourly workers.

If an employee works over 40 hours in a week, calculate for overtime pay. No employee can work over 80 hours in one week. No employee can earn less than $10 an hour or more than $75 an hour.

Send the weekly payroll totals to the Payroll department so they can calculate benefits and print the paychecks. Make sure that this software's output is portable to the Payroll software.

SYSTEMS ANALYSIS

How Does a Programmer Model the Logical, Not Physical, System?

During systems analysis, your focus is on the information and information-processing requirements of the new system. You want to develop these specifications *logically*, without worrying about the physical details such as amount of storage space, type of network software, or speed of the CPU.

So, in analysis you need to define: (1) what information will go into the software, (2) how the software will process information, and (3) what information the software will generate.

In the previous chapter, you saw how to do this with a data flow diagram. However, programmers usually use other modeling techniques called pseudocode and program flowcharts.

Pseudocode

We have noted that as a programmer you wouldn't concern yourself with the physical details of a system during systems analysis. You also wouldn't worry yet about how your software will interact with the operating system.

Instead, you focus on what the program should do. For this you can write pseudocode. *Pseudocode* uses English statements to create an outline of the necessary steps for a piece of software to operate. Programmers call these steps an algorithm. An *algorithm* is a set of specific steps that solves a problem or carries out a task. An algorithm is like a cooking recipe. It lists in order the steps to create a scrumptious dessert. In our case, the sweet reward is a working piece of software.

When you read about SQL statements in Chapter 8, you learned to use a form of structured English to ask the DBMS to perform tasks. You used specific words such as **SELECT, FROM,** and **SORT.** Pseudocode is like structured English, but it's not as strict. As a programmer, you can choose whatever notation works best for you as long as it's not ambiguous.

Look at the pseudocode for the payroll software in Figure 11.2. Notice that even though there's no set of rules for writing pseudocode, the pseudocode in Figure 11.2 does follow some rules:

- Use simple English.
- Put one command on a line.
- Place any important words in bold.
- Start from the top and work toward the bottom.
- Separate processes with spaces to form modules.

FIGURE 11.2

Pseudocode is one method programmers use to express an algorithm.

```
START PROGRAM

GET INPUT FROM EMPLOYEE (NAME, HOURS WORKED, PAY RATE)

CHECK IF INPUT MEETS EMPLOYER'S CONDITIONS

    If Hours Worked > 80 hours Then
        Inform the user to see manager or re-enter hours

    If Pay Rate < $10 OR Pay Rate > $75 Then
        Inform the user to see manager or re-enter pay rate

CALCULATE EMPLOYEE'S PAY

    If Hours Worked <= 40 Then
        Weekly Pay = Hours Worked * Pay Rate
    Else
        Overtime = Hours Worked – 40
        Overtime Pay = Overtime * Pay Rate * 1.5
        Weekly Pay = (Pay Rate * 40) + Overtime Pay

DISPLAY RESULTS ON SCREEN

ASK EMPLOYEE IF INFORMATION IS CORRECT
    If information is correct Then
        Submit Information to Payroll
    Else
        Have Employee Repeat Process

STOP PROGRAM
```

Program Flowcharts

Programmers also use program flowcharts to plot the software's algorithm. As we discussed in Chapter 10, a ***program flowchart*** is a graphical depiction of the detailed steps that software will perform. Unlike pseudocode, which has less structure, in flowcharts programmers must use symbols. Figure 11.3 shows the payroll software flowchart. Compare the flowchart in Figure 11.3 with the pseudocode in Figure 11.2. You'll see identical logic in each.

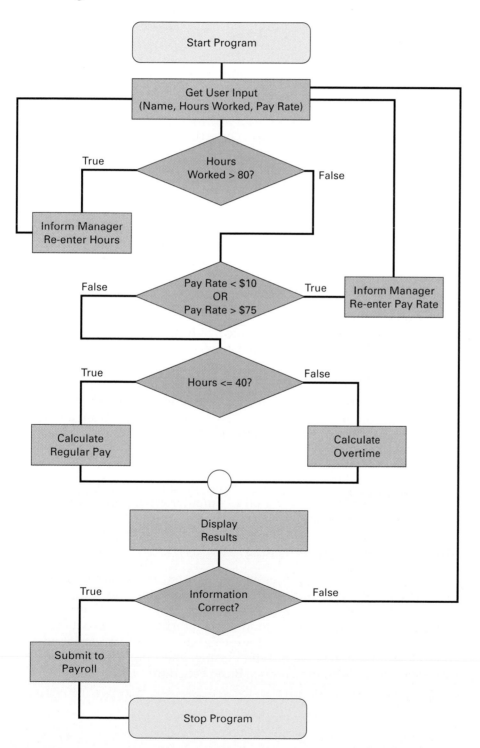

F I G U R E   11.3

Program flowcharts graphically express algorithms.

Testing the Algorithm

After you've completed your algorithm, check its logic. In the payroll software, calculating overtime for anyone working more than 20 hours instead of more than 40 hours would be a logic error. A *logic error* is a mistake in the way an algorithm solves a problem.

Logic errors can be hard to find once you begin writing your program, so it's best to catch them in the algorithm. Programmers check their algorithms by inputting test data and checking the logic by hand or with a calculator. Come up with some test data (employee name, hours worked, and pay rate) and run it through our pseudocode (Figure 11.2 on page 11.4) or program flowchart (Figure 11.3 on page 11.5). Did everything work?

SYSTEMS DESIGN

How Does a Programmer Create a Technical Design for the New Software?

As you move into design, it's time to convert your logical description of the proposed software into technical software specifications. Now you must concern yourself with the physical characteristics of the system—the filenames, variable names, and the like.

Basic Software Needs

You know that in the analysis phase you must know what information will go into the software, how it will process that information, and what will result. In other words, you're looking at input, processing, and output. All software must work with these three concepts to be successful.

- *Input* is information that comes from an external source and enters the software. Input can come from your typing on your keyboard, from records in a database, or from clicking on an image with your mouse.

- *Processing* manages information according to a piece of software's logic. In other words, processing is what the software does to the input it receives. This can be anything from adding a few numbers together to mapping the earth's climate. In the payroll software, processing involves calculating an employee's pay.

- *Output* is the information software produces after it has processed input. Output can appear on a computer screen, in a printout, or in records in a database.

Input-Process-Output Tables

As you work with input, processing, and output in the design phase, you can include them in input-process-output tables. An *input-process-output (IPO) table* shows what information a piece of software takes in, how it processes information, and what information it produces. We've created such a table in Figure 11.4 for the variable **Hours_Worked.**

To learn more about input, processing, and output, visit the Interactive Companion Labs and choose "Basic Programming."

Input	Processing	Output

Hours_Worked	If Hours_Worked <= 40
	　　Weekly_Pay = Hours_Worked * Pay_Rate
	Else
	　　Overtime = Hours_Worked – 40
	　　Overtime_Pay = Overtime * Pay_Rate * 1.5
	　　Weekly_Pay = (Pay_Rate * 40) + Overtime_Pay
	End If
		Hours_Worked
		Weekly_Pay
		Overtime
		Overtime_Pay

FIGURE 11.4

An IPO table assists programmers as they design the software.

making the grade

SECTION A://

1. _____ uses English statements to create an outline of an algorithm.
2. An _____ is a set of specific steps to solve a problem.
3. A _____ is a mistake in the way an algorithm solves a problem.
4. Managing information according to software's logic is _____.

B://WRITING COMPUTER SOFTWARE

After you test your algorithm and start to determine basic software needs, it's time to write the software. This is the construction phase, the fourth phase, of the systems development life cycle. In this section, we'll show you some of the basic programming techniques or structures you'll need to create software.

CODING

How Do I Explain My Algorithm to the Computer?

Once you've written your algorithm using pseudocode or a flowchart, it's time to explain your algorithm in terms a computer can understand. To accomplish this, you'll write software using a programming language. A **programming language** contains specific rules and words that express the logical steps of an algorithm. We'll discuss the many languages later.

Most programmers call writing the software program "coding." **_Coding_** is when you translate your algorithm into a programming language. Figure 11.5 (on the next page) shows the application and part of the code for our payroll program, which we wrote in Visual Basic (VB). The complete software program is available at the text Web site at www.mhhe.com/i-series.

F I G U R E   11.5

F I G U R E   11.5

Notice how the reserved words and comments are colored.

```
Private Sub cmdProcess_Click()

' Get input from the Employee.

    strEmployee_Name = txtName.Text
    sngHours_Worked = Val(txtHours.Text)
    curPay_Rate = Val(txtPay_Rate.Text)

' Make sure employer's conditions are met before proceeding employee data.

    If sngHours_Worked > 80 Then

        MsgBox "You cannot work over 80 hours a week. " + vbNewLine + _
        "Please see your manager or adjust your hours.", vbExclamation, "Too many Hours"
        txtHours.Text = ""
        lblPay_Out = ""
        Exit Sub
    End If

    If (curPay_Rate < 10) Or (curPay_Rate > 75) Then

        MsgBox "You have entered an invalid Pay Rate. " + vbNewLine + _
        "Please see your manager or adjust your Pay Rate.", vbExclamation, "Invalid Pay Rate"
        txtPay_Rate.Text = ""
        lblPay_Out = ""
        Exit Sub
    End If

' Calculate Employee's Pay

    If sngHours_Worked <= 40 Then

        curWeekly_Pay = sngHours_Worked * curPay_Rate

    Else

        sngOvertime = sngHours_Worked - 40
        curOvertime_Pay = sngOvertime * curPay_Rate * 1.5
        curWeekly_Pay = (curPay_Rate * 40) + curOvertime_Pay

    End If

' Output the Weekly Pay to the form and write it to a Payroll file.
```

Comments

Check for and compute overtime pay if necessary.

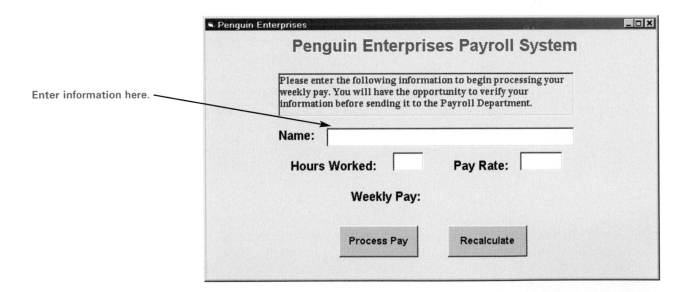

Penguin Enterprises Payroll System

Please enter the following information to begin processing your weekly pay. You will have the opportunity to verify your information before sending it to the Payroll Department.

Name:

Hours Worked: **Pay Rate:**

Weekly Pay:

Process Pay   Recalculate

Enter information here.

Notice that some words appear blue. These are reserved words. ***Reserved words*** are words that a programming language has set aside for its own use. In Figure 11.5, you'll notice **If** is colored blue. **If** is a reserved word VB uses to create a logical test. For example, determining if an employee should receive overtime pay is achieved using **If**. Notice also that many lines start with a single apostrophe and are a different color (green). Programmers call these explanations comments. ***Comments*** are explanations that tell other programmers what's happening in software code. The computer ignores the comment lines when it runs the code.

CONTROL STRUCTURES

How Do I Tell the Computer How to Read My Algorithm?

Unless told otherwise, most computers will read code like you're reading this textbook. Programmers refer to this as sequential execution. *Sequential execution* is when a computer performs each line of software code in the order it appears. However, this wasn't always the case. It wasn't until programming languages adopted control structures that you could assume a certain sequence of execution. *Control structures* specify the order in which a computer will execute each line of software code. Let's look at the three basic control structures you can use.

Sequence Control Structure

The sequence control structure is the most basic. The *sequence control structure* makes sure that a computer executes software code from top to bottom, left to right. It enforces sequential execution. Figure 11.6 is an example of how the sequential control structure works.

But what happens if the logic in your algorithm requires the program to execute the code in a different order or skip sections if a certain condition exists? For this you'll need other control structures: selection or repetition. We'll discuss these two below. You can see all three control structures in action at the Web site at www.mhhe.com/i-series.

Selection Control Structure

Every day you make decisions. Should you sleep in or should you go to class? Should you eat that last piece of pizza? You make your decision based on some condition: Are you sleepy? Do you have a test? Are you hungry? This is similar to how software uses a selection control structure. A *selection control structure* uses an existing condition to decide how a computer will execute software code.

In our payroll software, we asked how much each person worked. If it's more than 40 hours, we calculate overtime; if it's less or equal to 40, we don't. Based on that condition the software decides what code to execute. Figure 11.7 shows how the code handles this condition.

FIGURE   11.6

The sequential control structure is the most basic programming control structure.

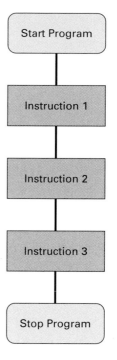

```
If  Hours_Worked <= 40 Then
    Weekly_Pay = Hours_Worked * Pay_Rate
Else
    Overtime = Hours_Worked - 40
    Overtime_Pay = Overtime * Pay_Rate * 1.5
    Weekly_Pay = (Pay_Rate * 40) + Overtime_Pay
End If
```

In this code, you only pay an employee overtime if Hours_Worked is NOT less than or equal to 40. In other words, they worked more than 40 hours.

FIGURE   11.7

The selection control structure makes a decision based on a condition.

FIGURE   11.8

The if-then-else control
structure tests a true/false
condition.

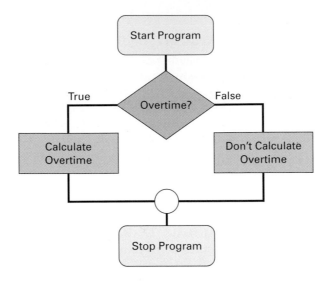

Look at the **If**, **Then**, **Else**, and **End If** reserved words in Figure 11.7
(on the previous page). These indicate the if-then-else control structure.
The ***if-then-else control structure*** tests a condition in software code that
results in a true or a false. Figure 11.8 is a flowchart of the if-then-else control structure.,

The ***case control structure*** tests a condition that can result in more
than a true or false answer. For example, you might need to determine
shipping costs based on an item's weight. Figure 11.9 shows the case control structure in action.

FIGURE   11.9

The case control structure tests
a condition that has more than a
true or false answer.

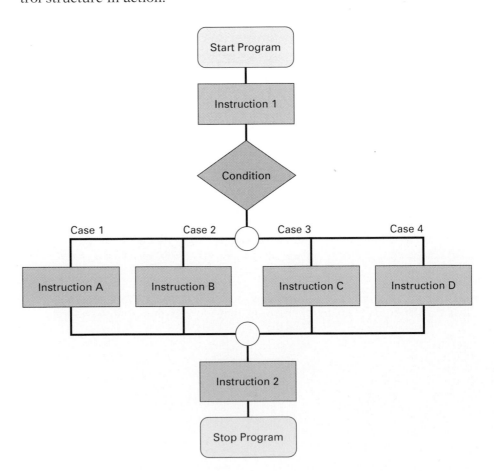

Repetition Control Structure

Have you ever read the instructions on a shampoo bottle? You'd most likely see (1) Lather, (2) Rinse, (3) Repeat if necessary. You're to use the shampoo until you meet a condition (let's assume it's clean hair).

Similarly, in coding, the ***repetition control structure*** instructs a piece of software to repeat a series of instructions until it fulfills a condition or while a condition exists. Programmers also call the repetition control structure an ***iteration control*** or a simply a ***loop.*** There are three variations of repetition control structures: (1) the do-while control structure, (2) the do-until control structure, and (3) the for-next control structure. Figure 11.10 shows a flowchart of a repetition control structure and code for each iteration control variation.

The ***do-while control structure*** repeats a portion of software code as long as a certain condition exists. If the condition is true, the software program executes the lines of code. It then tests the condition again. If it's still true, the software program executes the code again. In our do-while loop code in Figure 11.10, as long as **X** is less than or equal to **10,** the loop will repeat. If it's false **(X>10),** the software program moves to the next set of commands. In this case, the loop ends.

In contrast, the ***do-until control structure*** repeats a portion of a software code as long as a certain condition doesn't exist. In Figure 11.10, as long as **X** is not greater than **10,** the software will execute the code. As

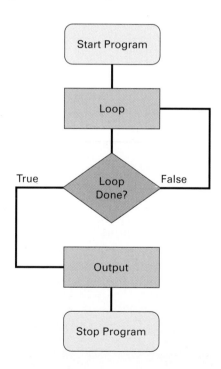

FIGURE   11.10

Programmers use loops when they need to repeat a process a certain number of times or as long as a condition exists.

All three loops will print the numbers 1–10

Do-While Control Structure	Do-Until Control Structure	For-Next Control Structure
| ```
X = 0
DO WHILE X <= 10
   PRINT X
   X=X+1
LOOP
``` | ```
X = 0
DO UNTIL X > 10
   PRINT X
   X=X+1
LOOP
``` | ```
FOR X = 1 TO 10
   PRINT X
NEXT
``` |
```

i·series insights

Ethics, Security & Privacy

Programming Backdoors

You know how difficult it can be to write just a few lines of code that result in a working, bug-free software program. Imagine that you're working on a project team whose job is to create software containing millions of lines of code. How can you make sure that if something bad happens when you run the program, you'll be able to stop it and fix it?

You might consider creating a backdoor. A **backdoor** is an undocumented method a programmer uses to gain access to a program or a computer. The backdoor in your house is another way to enter besides the front door. A programming backdoor is a way to enter that no one except the programmer knows about.

The concept is simple. Programmers create a command that

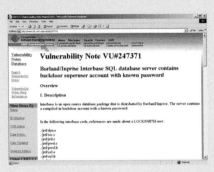

allows them to enter a program or a computer and fix any errors or check up on the program. However, people other than the programmers can find the backdoor and use it for purposes other than maintenance or troubleshooting. Hackers routinely find backdoors in software and exploit their discovery. Maybe they just explore the pro-

gram, but maybe they decide to take information.

Backdoors also can cause other problems. Many viruses use backdoors to access e-mail or credit card information or steal information from corporate databases. What programmers designed to help can become hurtful instead.

But backdoors can indeed be helpful. When programs cease to work and there's a possibility of a system crash, programmers can use a backdoor to enter the program and save important information. Perhaps a hacker seizes control of a company's Web server. A backdoor could help the company take its server back.

You must decide whether you think programming backdoors are beneficial or too risky.

---

soon as **X** is greater than **10 (X=11),** the condition no longer exists and the loop ends.

The *for-next control structure* repeats a portion of software code a precise number of times. The for-next control structure uses a counter to check the condition. A **counter** is a numerical value that tracks the number of iterations in a software code.

To learn more about control structures and other programming techniques, visit the Interactive Companion Labs and choose "Programming II."

SECTION B://   *making the grade*

1. _____ is when you translate your algorithm into a programming language.

2. Programming languages have _____ for certain purposes.

3. The _____ structure tests a condition that can result in more than a true or false answer.

4. Repetition control structures are also called _____.

C://TESTING, IMPLEMENTING, AND MAINTAINING SOFTWARE

In the remaining systems development life cycle, you'll need people to help you test your software (phase #4—construction), implement it in your organization (phase #5—implementation), and provide you feedback so you can maintain the software over time (phase #6—support).

TESTING SOFTWARE

How Do I Make Sure a Piece of Software Works?

You tested your algorithm before you began coding, but now you'll want to test—or debug—your written code. **Debugging** is the process of finding errors in software code. **Bugs** are a common name for software errors. When you debug your code, you look for syntax, run-time, and logic errors.

Syntax Errors

Syntax errors are mistakes in a software code's grammar. Just as misspelling a word is a mistake when writing, misspelling a command word or forgetting to close a module will cause a syntax error. If you're supposed to use a semi-colon (;) and you use a colon (:) instead, you've made a syntax error.

Run-Time Errors

Run-time errors are mistakes that occur when you run the software code. Software not displaying a window correctly is a run-time error. Another common error is not matching variables in a calculation. Figure 11.11 shows what happens when you try to add a number and a letter.

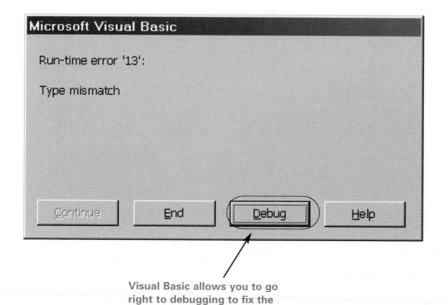

FIGURE 11.11

This run-time error occurs when you add a number and a letter.

Visual Basic allows you to go right to debugging to fix the run-time error.

Logic Errors

You checked for logic errors when you designed your algorithm. Remember that a logic error is a mistake made in the way an algorithm solves a problem. You should test for logic errors as part of the debugging process. Figure 11.12 has some common programming errors. Notice the marked logic error in the program. What happens when this software checks how many hours the employee worked?

FIGURE 11.12

A major task for programmers is debugging the code. In many development environments syntax errors appear in red.

Looks like the programmer made a logic error. Can you find another?

Notice the syntax errors in red.

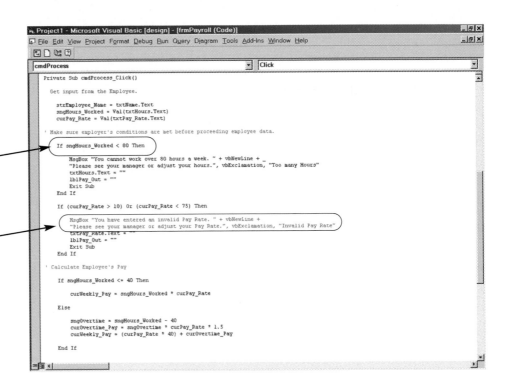

```
Project1 - Microsoft Visual Basic [design] - [frmPayroll (Code)]
File  Edit  View  Project  Format  Debug  Run  Query  Diagram  Tools  Add-Ins  Window  Help

cmdProcess                                          Click

   Private Sub cmdProcess_Click()

   ' Get input from the Employee.

      strEmployee_Name = txtName.Text
      sngHours_Worked = Val(txtHours.Text)
      curPay_Rate = Val(txtPay_Rate.Text)

   ' Make sure employer's conditions are met before proceeding employee data.

      If sngHours_Worked < 80 Then

         MsgBox "You cannot work over 80 hours a week. " + vbNewLine + _
         "Please see your manager or adjust your hours.", vbExclamation, "Too many Hours"
         txtHours.Text = ""
         lblPay_Out = ""
         Exit Sub
      End If

      If (curPay_Rate > 10) Or (curPay_Rate < 75) Then

         MsgBox "You have entered an invalid Pay Rate. " + vbNewLine +
         "Please see your manager or adjust your Pay Rate.", vbExclamation, "Invalid Pay Rate"
         txtPay_Rate.Text = ""
         lblPay_Out = ""
         Exit Sub
      End If

   ' Calculate Employee's Pay

      If sngHours_Worked <= 40 Then

         curWeekly_Pay = sngHours_Worked * curPay_Rate

      Else

         sngOvertime = sngHours_Worked - 40
         curOvertime_Pay = sngOvertime * curPay_Rate * 1.5
         curWeekly_Pay = (curPay_Rate * 40) + curOvertime_Pay

      End If
```

User Testing

After programmers have fixed the errors, users will test the software to make sure it meets their needs. As we discussed in Chapter 10, users must test it and "sign off" that the software works correctly. This is called acceptance testing.

SOFTWARE DEVELOPMENT ENVIRONMENT
How Do I Find Errors and Manage My Code?

You could write code in a simple text editor such as Notepad. However, most programmers use a software development environment. A **software development environment** is an application that provides programming tools to debug and manage software programs.

Debugging Help

In Figure 11.12, some code is in red. You know that this identifies syntax errors in the code. If you were to execute this code, you'd also get run-time errors. And although they're not easy to see, logic errors exist. Unlike a syntax or a run-time error, the software development environment won't alert you to a logic error. We've placed the code for Figure 11.12 at www.mhhe.com/i-series so you can find all the errors.

Managing Development

Many software development environments also help you manage your software development. Some have powerful programming features, such as graphical interfaces and tools to help link the software to other software. For example, you could make sure that your payroll software works with the Payroll department's software. Figure 11.13 shows some of the tools available to you in Microsoft's Visual Basic development environment.

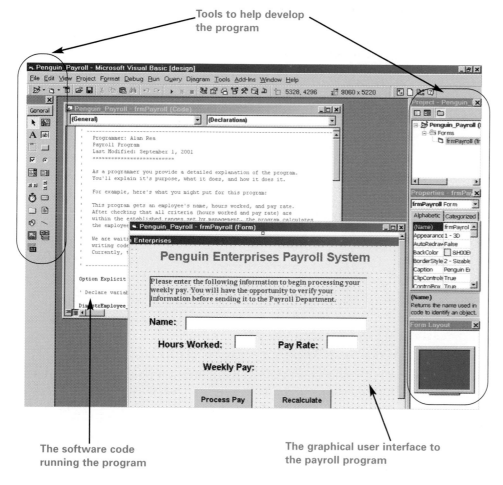

Tools to help develop the program

The software code running the program

The graphical user interface to the payroll program

FIGURE 11.13

Programmers use the Microsoft VB development environment to write code and design graphical interfaces for software.

Because of its power, programmers use the software development environment for prototyping. As discussed in Chapter 10, users can "try out" a prototype to see if the software meets their needs. If it doesn't, the programmer makes changes and sends out another prototype. Programmers refer to this as rapid application development. **_Rapid application development (RAD)_** uses prototypes to test software components until they meet specifications. To learn more about software development environments (and to try one yourself), visit the Interactive Companion Labs and choose "Programming Overview."

CASE Tools

In certain organizations, programmers use sophisticated CASE tools (see Figure 11.14). ***CASE, or computer aided software engineering, tools*** are software applications that help prepare reports, draw program flowcharts, and generate software code for prototypes.

F I G U R E   11.14

Microsoft Visio is one of the CASE tools available to programmers.

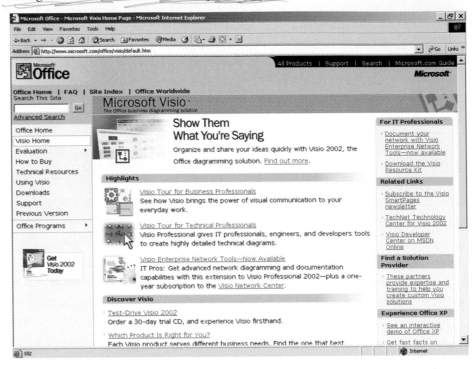

IMPLEMENTING SOFTWARE

How Can I Make Sure There's a Smooth Transition?

One task the programmer has in the implementation phase is writing documentation. ***Documentation*** is a collection of instructions and explanations relevant to a piece of software. Programmers must produce or help produce various forms of documentation during software implementation. These are comments, program manuals, and user manuals.

Comments

As we discussed earlier, comments are explanations within code that tell other programmers what's happening. Comments can be a single line or a large portion of text explaining what's happening in a section of code.

Program Manual

Programmers also must create documentation for other programmers. The ***program manual*** is a technical manual for programmers. It can be print or electronic. The program manual contains the problem/opportunity statement, algorithms, flowcharts, and copies of older versions of the code.

User Manual

Usually the programmer doesn't write the user manual. Instead companies employ technical writers. ***Technical writers*** explain concepts and procedures to non-technical software users. The technical writer will work with programmers and others to produce the user manual. The ***user manual*** tells users how to use a software program. When you buy software, it comes with a user manual. More frequently, it comes on a CD or is on a Web site. You can see program and user manuals in Figure 11.15.

MAINTAINING SOFTWARE
How Do I Keep Software Fresh?

In Chapter 10 you learned about systems support and maintenance. As a programmer, you help support and maintain a system by making sure the software functions correctly and meets business needs. To do this, you'll need to code and implement software patches and updates.

FIGURE 11.15

Program manuals and user manuals are very different in their focus. Most manuals are on CDs and Web sites.

Software Patches

In the support phase, employees use the software. They might find a problem with how the software interacts with a system or another piece of software. Maybe the payroll software doesn't connect to and send information to the Payroll system in the correct format. If it's a minor fix, programmers will patch the software. A *software patch* is a small fix to a problem using a piece of software code.

Software Upgrades

When patches are no longer enough, programmers must upgrade software. A *software upgrade* is a substantial revision of existing software to improve its usefulness. Often software companies release upgrades because they've made major improvements since the last version. For example, Microsoft Office XP is an upgrade to Microsoft Office 2000.

---

making the grade

1. _____ errors are mistakes in a software code's grammar.
2. A _____ is an application that provides programming tools to debug and manage software programs.
3. A _____ is a technical manual for programmers.
4. A _____ is a small fix to a software problem.

D://PROGRAMMING LANGUAGES

Earlier we used Visual Basic to write the payroll software, but we had many other choices. You choose a certain programming language depending on system requirements and how the software must function. In this section, we'll explore programming language generations, look at programming language characteristics, and describe the notion of object-oriented programming. These concepts will help you choose the right programming language for the job.

PROGRAMMING LANGUAGE GENERATIONS
How Have Languages Evolved?

If you're reading this textbook, you're familiar with the rules of the English language. Sentences, spelling, and grammar come together to create meaning. Think of programming languages as something like English, French, or Spanish. Just as human languages have rules and grammar, so do programming languages.

In international business, people use English more often because it's more widely understood. Programmers have hundreds of programming languages to choose from, but they use some more often because of their flexibility and portability. ***Portability*** means a programming language has the ability to work on a variety of computer hardware and operating systems. Because of the diversity of computer systems available today, programmers must think about portability when deciding which programming language will work best in a given situation. To help make this decision, you'll need to know something about how programming languages have evolved. Let's look at the four generations of languages: machine, assembly, and third and fourth generation languages.

Machine Language

Just as you can't understand a language you've never learned, a computer can't understand any language but its own. A ***machine-dependent language*** is a programming language that works only on a specific computer system and its components. Languages that work only on a certain computer system are low-level languages. A ***low-level language*** requires programmers to code at a basic level that a computer can understand.

The most basic programming language is machine language. ***Machine language*** is a machine-dependent, low-level language that uses binary code to interact with a specific computer system. If you thought about writing the payroll software in machine language, you'd write it in binary because binary code is the only language computers can understand. You learned about binary code in Chapter 6. Programmers don't use binary to code software, but they must translate all software into machine code so computers can use it.

Assembly Language

Since no one can easily code in binary, programmers developed another low-level programming language: assembly language. ***Assembly language*** is a machine-dependent, low-level language that uses words instead of binary numbers to program a specific computer system. Programmers can use words such as **start** or abbreviations such as **mov** (move) to tell the computer what to do. Assembly language is considered "once removed" from machine language so it's placed in the next generation. Figure 11.16 is assembly language that tells the computer to print "Hello World" on your screen.

For the computer to read assembly language you must run the code through an assembler. An ***assembler*** is a utility program that converts assembly language into machine language that the computer can then use to run software.

Third Generation Languages

Can you imagine the task of writing assembly language for every type of computer today? Neither can programmers. Instead they use programming languages that many different computers can use. These

FIGURE   11.16

This assembly language program prints "Hello World" on the screen. It works only on a certain computer system.

```
.text
.align 4
.global start
start:
mov 0, %o0
set string, %o1
mov 14, %o2
mov 4, %g1
ta 0
mov 0, %o0
mov 1, %g1
ta 0
.align 4
string:
.ascii "Hello, World!\n"
```

are machine-independent languages. A ***machine-independent language*** is a programming language that works on different computer systems regardless of their components.

With machine-independent languages, you can use words closer to human language, such as **ADD, DIVIDE,** and **PRINT,** and mathematical symbols such as **(+)** and **(–)** for addition and subtraction. A ***high-level language*** allows programmers to use words and symbols closer to human language to code software.

Machine independence and high level in these languages distinguish them from machine and assembly languages. The move to these languages (in the 1950s) marks another generation: third generation languages. A ***third generation language (3GL)*** is a machine-independent, high-level procedural language that uses human words and symbols to program diverse computer systems.

All 3GLs are also procedural languages. A ***procedural language*** requires that a programmer write code to tell software *what* to accomplish and *how* to accomplish it. In other words, if you wanted to create software to get a sum of numbers, you'd have to tell the software what you wanted (a sum of numbers) and then how to accomplish it (add the numbers together).

The collection of 3GLs is immense. Most programmers cannot be proficient in all of them. You've already used Visual Basic for the payroll program, but it's not your only choice. Depending on the computer system and business needs, you can choose from languages such as COBOL, C++, Fortran, or Java, to name a few.

For example, if you wanted to design business application software for a mainframe computer, you'd probably use COBOL. ***COBOL*** stands for **C**ommon **B**usiness **O**riented **L**anguage and works best for business applications on mainframe computers. It's the most common programming language in the world. Compare the COBOL code in Figure 11.17 to the Visual Basic code in Figure 11.5 (on page 11.8) and the assembly code in Figure 11.16 (on page 11.18). Which would you rather use?

FIGURE 11.17

COBOL programs are primarily used for business applications.

```
IDENTIFICATION DIVISION
PROGRAM-ID. SUM-OF-PRICES.
AUTHOR.
SOURCE.
ENVIRONMENT DIVISION.
INPUT-OUTPUT SECTION.
FILE-CONTROL.
    SELECT INP-DATA ASSIGN TO INPUT.
    SELECT RESULT-FILE ASSIGN TO OUTPUT.
DATA DIVISION.
FILE SECTION.
FD INP-DATA LABEL RECORD IS OMITTED.
01 ITEM-PRICE
    02 ITEM PICTURE X(30).
    02 PRICE PICTURE 9999V99.
    02 FILLER PICTURE X(44).
FD RESULT-FILE LABEL RECORD IS OMITTED.
01 RESULT-LINE PICTURE X(132).
WORKING-STORAGE SECTION.
77 TOT PICTURE 999999V99, VALUE 0, USAGE IS
COMPUTATIONAL.
77 COUNT PICTURE 9999, VALUE 0, USAGE IS
COMPUTATIONAL.
01 SUM-LINE.
    02 FILLER VALUE ' SUM ='PICTURE X(12).
    02 SUM-OUT PICTURE $$,$$$,$$9.99.
    02 FILLER VALUE ' NO. OF ITEMS ='PICTURE X(21).
    02 COUNT-OUT PICTURE ZZZ9.99.
01 ITEM-LINE.
    02 ITEM-OUT PICTURE X(30).
    02 PRICE-OUT PICTURE ZZZ9.99.
PROCEDURE DIVISION.
START.
    OPEN INPUT INP-DATA AND OUTPUT RESULT-FILE.
READ-DATA.
    READ INP-DATA AT END GO TO PRINT-LINE.
    ADD PRICE TO TOT.
    ADD 1 TO COUNT.
    MOVE PRICE TO PRICE-OUT.
    MOVE ITEM TO ITEM-OUT.
    WRITE RESULT-LINE FROM ITEM-LINE.
    GO TO READ-DATA.
PRINT-LINE.
    MOVE TOT TO SUM-OUT.
    MOVE COUNT TO COUNT-OUT.
    WRITE RESULT-LINE FROM SUM-LINE.
    CLOSE INP-DATA AND RESULT-FILE.
    STOP RUN.
```

Fourth Generation Languages

With a 3GL you can use words resembling human language. However, you still specifically instruct the software *what* to do and *how* to do it because 3GLs are procedural languages. Wouldn't it be easier if you could just write software that tells the computer system *what* you want and let the software figure out *how* to get it?

Fourth generation languages are nonprocedural languages. A *nonprocedural language* requires that a programmer write code to tell the software only what it should accomplish. So a *fourth generation language (4GL)* is a machine-independent, high-level nonprocedural language that uses human words and symbols to program diverse computer systems.

You've already used a 4GL in Chapter 8 when you wrote SQL to create statements such as

```
SELECT Name, Address, Phone FROM "cars.dat" WHERE
Purchased < 1995
```

Here you didn't need to instruct the database *how* you wanted it to find the **Name, Address,** and **Phone** number for people who bought cars before 1995. You just had to tell the database *what* you wanted and SQL did the rest.

FIGURE 11.18

As a programmer you can choose from various programming languages. Here are some of them.

BASIC	Stands for Beginner's All-purpose Symbolic Instruction Code. BASIC was developed in 1964 and is still in use today. Many variations of it exist and it's on most desktop and notebook computers. It's a procedural, interpreted language.
Visual Basic	Developed by Microsoft, VB uses a graphical interface to develop event-driven Windows programs. Visual Basic for Applications (VBA) is a subset of VB that allows programmers to develop macros in the Microsoft Office environment.
COBOL	Stands for Common Business Oriented Language. COBOL is a widely used procedural language in business applications. It's primarily used on mainframe computers.
C	C is a compiled procedural program used to develop operating systems and application software. It is a powerful and efficient program, but it's difficult to use.
C++	An object-oriented version of C. It's used for many of the same applications as C as well as database and Internet programs. You don't need to know C to learn C++.
FORTRAN	Stands for Formula Translator. FORTRAN is the oldest (developed in 1954) high-level language still in use. Scientists and engineers use it to handle complex mathematical and scientific calculations.
Pascal	Developed in the late 1960s to help students learn structured programming concepts. It's named after the 17th-century French mathematician Blaise Pascal. Turbo Pascal is an object-oriented version.
Java	A high-level, object-oriented programming language based on C++. Java is optimized for Web and Internet appliance applications.
SQL	Stands for Structured Query Language. SQL was developed to provide a common means to work with databases. SQL is a declarative fourth generation language that assists programmers in deriving the necessary information from databases.

Experts are using human language to instruct a computer and make programming easier. ***Natural languages*** are human languages that can program a computer. For example, instead of the SQL statement above, a natural language command might be

```
TELL me the NAME, ADDRESS, and PHONE number for
EVERYONE who bought a car BEFORE 1995.
```

Figure 11.18 (on the previous page) lists some of the programming languages you can choose from. We've listed other languages and more information about the ones in Figure 11.18 at the Web site for this text at www.mhhe.com/i-series.

PROGRAMMING LANGUAGE CHARACTERISTICS
What Distinguishes Languages from Each Other?

You can see how programmers can distinguish languages depending on the generation the languages come from. But how can you determine which language you'd need to write a software application program for a Windows operating system? You'd probably pick a 3GL, since machine language or assembly language wouldn't be as portable for the many computers that use Windows. A 4GL might be a good choice if you're working with databases. But how would you know to use a 3GL for a certain application? To make this decision you'll need to know a bit more about programming language characteristics.

Compiled

You know that computers can understand only machine language (binary). So when you code in a high-level language such as C++ you must get it into a form the computer can understand. With assembly language you can use an assembler. With a high-level language you use a compiler. A ***compiler*** simultaneously translates high-level programming languages into machine language. In other words, your 3GL or 4GL is completely translated into machine language all at once.

When you write your code in a programming language, you're writing the source code. Your ***source code*** contains all the commands and comments a programmer used to code the software. The ***object code*** is the machine language the computer uses to run your program. To get from the source code to the object code, you must compile your source code into the object code. Most software development environments come with a compiler.

Interpreted

With other programming languages, such as JavaScript, the computer uses an interpreter to convert the source code into object code. An ***interpreter*** translates one line of source code into object code at a time. In other words, the computer translates a line of source code into object code, then executes it, and then goes to the next line of code and repeats the process. Running interpreted software on a computer does take longer than running compiled software. However, with the speed of today's systems the loss isn't noticeable.

Scripted

Because today's computer systems can run interpreted languages efficiently, you will see many programs written with scripting languages. A *scripting language* is an interpreted programming language that works within another application to perform tasks. These tasks are often referred to as macros. A ***macro*** is a scripting language program that executes a task or set of tasks within a software application.

In Chapter 10, you learned that end user development is one way some businesses choose to develop software applications. Since many businesses use the Microsoft Office suite of applications, Visual Basic for Applications is often the choice for end user development. ***Visual Basic for Applications (VBA)*** is an interpreted scripting language that works within Microsoft Office applications. For example, you can use VBA in Microsoft Excel to create a payroll spreadsheet macro (Figure 11.19) much like the payroll software.

F I G U R E   11.19

With some minor VBA modifications of the payroll program you now can use the program in Microsoft Excel.

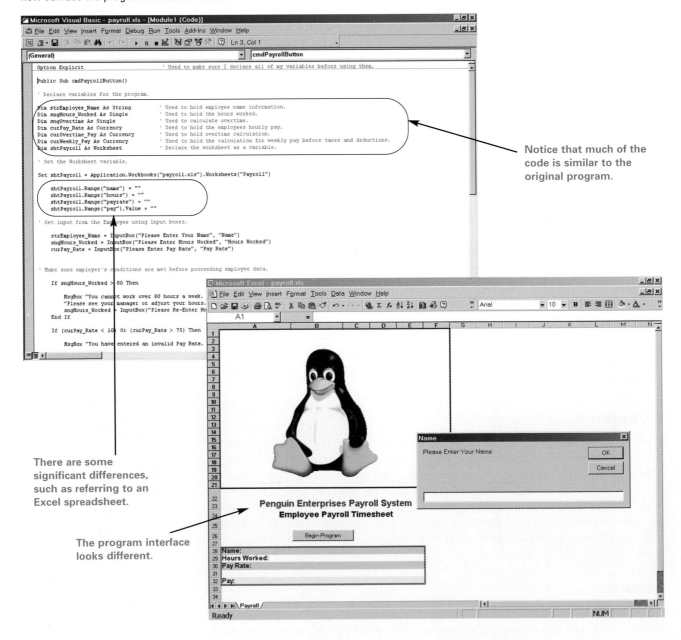

To learn more about compiling and interpreting, as well as the characteristics of programming languages, visit the Interactive Companion Labs and choose "Programming Overview."

OBJECT-ORIENTED PROGRAMMING

How Can I Reuse Parts of Programs?

Even though programmers found earlier 3GLs such as COBOL much easier to use to code software than assembly or machine language, they found they needed to rewrite the same type of code even when they wrote similar software. For example, if they wrote software to sort employee information alphabetically, they would still need to code different software to sort client information alphabetically. It became even more complicated when either of these programs stored its information in a database or file.

Objects

In response to this need, programmers created objects. You learned in Chapter 8 that an object is one item that contains distinct information. In programming, this distinct information contains procedures used in a software program. ***Procedures*** are instructions that manipulate an object's information. ***Object-oriented programming (OOP)*** is any programming language that uses objects to code software.

Let's think back to our sorting dilemma. Now you can write a **namesort** object (you can call it whatever you'd like) and reuse it whenever you need to sort items in software. Your **namesort** object contains the information and the procedures to manipulate the information. You can use a copy of the **namesort** object in your software to sort employee information and another copy of the **namesort** object in your client software program. Figure 11.20 illustrates how objects can help you in programming.

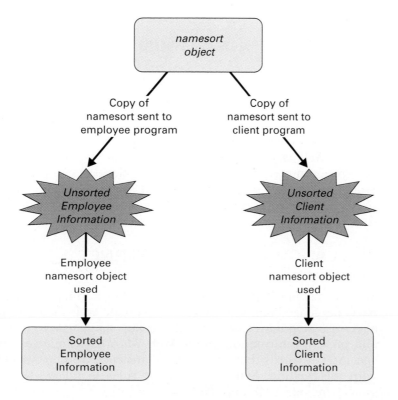

F I G U R E   11.20

OOP objects can be reused in different software programs.

Object Instance

When you make a copy of an object you create an object instance. An ***object instance*** is an exact copy of an object in OOP. Even if you have two different databases of information to access, each **namesort** object will know what to do because they have the same procedures.

Event-Driven

The most common OOP languages are event-driven. An ***event-driven language*** responds to actions users perform on the program. It's an event when you click on a button, use a pull-down menu, or scroll down a window. In an event-driven language, each of these events triggers the program to action.

There's more to OOP than what we've discussed here, but it's a concept that you'll encounter either as a programmer or working with programmers so it's good to be familiar with the term. If you'd like to learn more about programming languages and how to use them, visit the text Web site at www.mhhe.com/i-series.

SECTION D://　　*making the grade*

1. A _____ language works only on a specific computer system.
2. A(n) _____ is a utility program that converts assembly language into machine language.
3. A _____ translates a high-level programming language into machine language.
4. A(n) _____ is an item that contains information and procedures.

E://WEB PROGRAMMING

You learned in Chapter 4 the many ways you've come to depend on the Web for researching, shopping (e-commerce), and communicating with others. You also learned how to use HTML to create your own Web resume and were introduced to some of the multimedia software that you can use to make your Web site interactive.

But Web users are demanding even more from Web sites. Fortunately Web programmers (also called Web developers) can use a variety of new programming languages. In this final section we'll take a quick look at some of the newest programming languages you can use to improve a Web site.

THE LANGUAGE OF THE INTERNET

How Do I Program Web Pages?

You learned in Chapter 4 that Hypertext Markup Language (HTML) is the basic language Web developers use to create Web sites. But programmers also are using newer versions of markup languages to organize, format, and present information on the Web. ***Markup languages*** contain sets of specific key words that use syntax to instruct Web browsers how to work with information. ***Syntax*** is a set of rules to follow. New markup languages include XML and XHTML.

Language Translators

You now see the many decisions you must make when translating an algorithm into error-free software. Whether it's choosing the correct programming language or debugging and testing the code, there's no room for error. Can you imagine the challenge of coding software that can translate one human language to another? Such software is available and can be of use to you. Consider the following mistakes people made (without the help of software):

- When KFC wanted to translate its slogan "finger-lickin' good" into Chinese, it came out as "eat your fingers off."
- Scandinavian vacuum manufacturer Electrolux launched an ad campaign in the United States with the slogan "nothing sucks like an Electrolux."
- When General Motors tried to sell the Chevy Nova in South America, people didn't buy it. "No va" means "it won't go" in Spanish. GM changed the name to Caribe for its Spanish markets.

These examples show that translating one language into another is tricky—even for people with huge resources. Idioms are particularly difficult. Even simple Web-related terms can be difficult to translate into a different language.

Language translator software can help. Such software will translate Web pages, e-mail, reports, manuals, and books into another language. You can also get multilingual word processors, encyclopedias, dictionaries, and writing tools. And some Web sites will translate text for a fee.

For translation of short blocks of text, try InterTran's Web site (www.tranexp.com), which can translate your text into 26 languages. If your text requires foreign characters, make sure you install them on your computer before you start. Both Netscape and Internet Explorer can show Web sites in languages other than English. You just have to add the language to your Web browser.

Be wary about using language translation software if you don't know the target language well. Undoubtedly, some language translation software tools will also translate the phrase "finger-lickin' good" into "eat your fingers off." If you're in doubt, proceed with caution using language translation software, being sure to check with someone who's fluent in the language before you use the translated text. Our personal and business worlds are global and cross-cultural. You don't want to risk offending someone because you used language translation software and didn't verify the result.

eXtensible Markup Language (XML)

You learned about eXtensible Markup Language in Chapters 4 and 8. Using key words, or tags, XML allows you to identify each piece of information found on your Web page or Web site. This makes it easier to organize and search for information.

eXtensible HTML

What if you could combine the formatting power of HTML with the organizing power of XML? You can with XHTML. *eXtensible HTML (XHTML)* combines the formatting power of HTML with the strict syntax of XML and allows users to access a Web site from almost any Internet device. If you use a computer, a mobile phone, a PDA, or any type of Internet appliance, you'll be able to view and use XHTML Web sites. This is especially important with the focus on mobile commerce (m-commerce). You know from Chapter 4 that businesses want you to be able to purchase goods and services whether you're accessing their Web sites with your notebook, mobile phone, or PDA. Figure 11.21 shows how your PDA will become a valuable tool for Web access and communication.

FIGURE   11.21

With XHTML, PDAs will be able to access even more Web sites.

PDAs are able to surf XHTML-enabled Web sites.

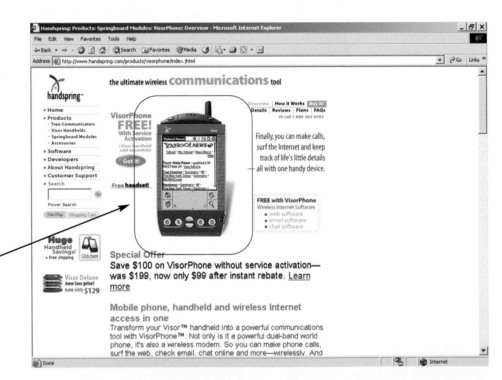

CLIENT-SIDE WEB PROGRAMMING LANGUAGES
How Do I Use a Web Browser's Power?

Web developers know that Web browser applications can do more than just display information. But they also know they can't increase interactivity at the expense of a Web server's resources. Client-side Web programming languages avoid this problem. *Client-side Web programming languages* employ users' Web browsers to add interactivity and new functions to Web pages. We discussed JavaScript and Java applets in Chapter

4, but Web developers also depend on Dynamic HTML (DHTML) and VBScript:

- **Dynamic HTML (DHTML)** combines cascading style sheets (CSS), JavaScript, specific tag extensions, and other markup languages to bring high interactivity to Web sites. Figure 11.22 is not only a DHTML reference site but also a Web site that offers high interactivity through DHTML.

- **VBScript** is an interpreted scripting language based on Visual Basic. VBScript is similar to JavaScript but only Microsoft's Internet Explorer Web browser can use it.

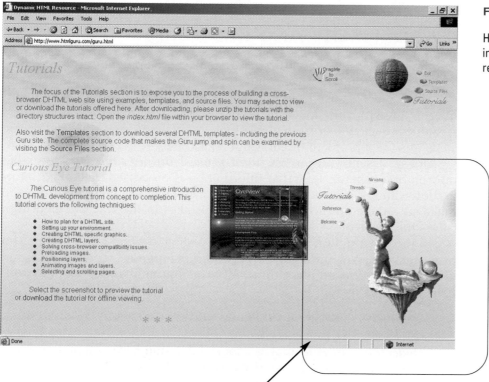

FIGURE   11.22

HTMLGURU.com offers high interactivity and DHTML resources.

The DHMTL resource site is also written in DHTML. Notice the high level of interactivity.

SERVER-SIDE WEB PROGRAMMING LANGUAGES

How Do I Supplement the Web with Web Servers?

As powerful as Web browsers are, not all programming is on the client side. You do need Web servers to run certain applications. **Server-side Web programming** uses Web server resources to retrieve information, process information, and output customized Web pages. Web developers use a variety of programming languages and scripts. You don't need to concern yourself with these server-side programming and scripting languages unless you plan to program advanced applications and tasks into your Web pages. Most users can accomplish their goals with a combination of markup and client-side scripting languages.

Although we didn't cover all Web programming languages and scripts, you can find out how to use many of the languages and keep up with the newest programming techniques in *Life-Long Learning Module A*, "Enhanced Web Development," introduced at the end of the text and continued on the text Web site at www.mhhe.com/i-series.

making the grade

1. _____ combines HTML with XML.

2. _____ Web programming languages use Web browser resources to add interactivity and new functions to Web pages.

3. _____ is an interpreted scripting language based on Visual Basic.

4. _____ programming uses Web server resources.

F://SUMMARY AND KEY TERMS

Within the various phases of the systems development life cycle, programmers have many responsibilities and many tools to work with. In analysis, you often use *pseudocode* (English statements to create an outline of an algorithm for a piece of software) or *program flowcharts* (graphical depictions of the algorithm). An *algorithm* is a set of specific steps to solve a problem or carry out a task.

During design, you can use *input-process-output tables* to show what information is input, how that information is processed, and what information is then displayed or printed. You also must test your algorithms to make sure there are no *logic errors*—mistakes in the way the algorithm solves the problem.

In the construction phase you begin coding. *Coding* occurs when you translate your algorithm into a *programming language* (specific rules and words that express an algorithm). All programming languages have *control structures* including:

- *Sequence control*—a command word to instruct the program to go to another line of code.

- *Selection control*—makes a logical decision based on an existing condition (these include *if-then-else* and *case*).

- *Repetition control*—instructs the software program to repeat a series of instructions until you fulfill a condition or while a condition exists (these include *do-while*, *do-until*, and *for-next*).

When testing software, you find software errors or *bugs.* Software errors include *syntax errors* (mistakes in the programming language's grammar), *run-time errors* (mistakes that occur when you run the software code), and *logic errors.*

Many programmers today write software in a *software development environment*—an environment that provides programming tools to *debug* and manage software programs. A common software development environment is a CASE tool. *Computer aided software engineering (CASE) tools* help prepare reports, draw flowcharts, and generate software code from prototypes. Maintaining software often involves creating *software patches* (a small fix to a problem) and *software upgrades* (a substantial revision of existing software).

Depending on your system and software needs, you can choose from *machine, assembly, third generation (3GL),* and *fourth generation (4GL)* programming languages. If it's a 3GL you'll need to *compile* or *interpret* the *source code* to create *object code.* Many programmers use

i·witness

An Up-Close Look at Web Sites

How Do You Get Your Web Site Noticed?

You've spent hours creating your Web site. It's exactly how you want it. You place it on the Web, set up your Web counter, and wait. A week later, only you and your friends have visited the Web site. What can you do to get it noticed?

Search engines allow people to find Web sites, but you need to help search engines find your site. You can do this by using HTML meta tags. **Meta tags** provide information to search engines about your Web site. Meta tags don't appear on the Web site, but they tell search engines what's in your Web site.

You need to place meta tags between the <title></title> tags in your Web page. Yours could look like this:

```
<meta name="keywords"
contents="programming,
computers, technology">
```

You can list as many key words as you'd like about the content in your Web site. You can vary them for each Web page as well. Search engines use these key words to categorize your site.

But meta tags can do more. You also can change the **name** attribute to include **description, copyright,** and **author:**

```
<meta
name="description"
contents="This Web
page contains
information about
programming.">
<meta name="copyright"
contents="Copyright
2002 McGraw-Hill">
<meta name="author"
contents="Alan Rea">
```

Meta tags can also make sure there's always a new copy of your Web page loaded in a Web browser. They can even send people to another Web site. We've included ex-

amples of how to do this on our Web site (*Life-Long Learning Module A* "Enhanced Web Development" at www.mhhe.com/i-series).

We've also included two Web pages to help you learn more about meta tags:

www.mhhe.com/i-series/I-Witness/11-A.html

www.mhhe.com/i-series/I-Witness/11-B.html

The first page contains no meta tags and the second one does. Create some meta tags for the page without any.

---

object-oriented programming (OOP) because they can use objects to make their code reusable.

Web developers use **markup languages** to present information on the Web. You also can use **client-side programming languages** such as **VBScript** and **Dynamic HTML (DHTML)** to add interactivity and new functions to Web pages. You also can use **server-side Web programming** languages to retrieve information, process information, and output customized Web pages.

At www.mhhe.com/i-series, we provide additional resources for this chapter on topics including:

- Programming languages
- Sample software code

KEY TERMS

algorithm (p. 11.4)

assembler (p. 11.18)

assembly language (p. 11.18)

backdoor (p. 11.12)

bug (p. 11.13)

CASE (computer aided software engineering) tool (p. 11.16)

case control structure (p. 11.10)

client-side Web programming language (p. 11.26)

COBOL (p. 11.19)

coding (p. 11.7)

comment (p. 11.8)

compiler (p. 11.21)

control structure (p. 11.9)

counter (p. 11.12)

debugging (p. 11.13)

documentation (p. 11.16)

do-until control structure
(p. 11.11)

do-while control structure
(p. 11.11)

Dynamic HTML (DHTML)
(p. 11.27)

event-driven language (p. 11.24)

eXtensible HTML (p. 11.26)

for-next control structure
(p. 11.12)

fourth generation language
(4GL) (p. 11.20)

high-level language (p. 11.19)

if-then-else control structure
(p. 11.10)

input (p. 11.6)

input-process-output (IPO)
table (p. 11.6)

interpreter (p. 11.21)

iteration control (loop)
(p. 11.11)

logic error (p. 11.6)

low-level language (p. 11.18)

machine language (p. 11.18)

machine-dependent language
(p. 11.18)

machine-independent language
(p. 11.19)

macro (p. 11.22)

markup language (p. 11.24)

meta tag (p. 11.29)

natural language (p. 11.21)

nonprocedural language
(p. 11.20)

object code (p. 11.21)

object instance (p. 11.24)

object-oriented programming
(OOP) (p. 11.23)

output (p. 11.6)

portability (p. 11.18)

procedural language (p. 11.19)

procedure (p. 11.23)

processing (p. 11.6)

program flowchart (p. 11.5)

program manual (p. 11.16)

programming language
(p. 11.7)

pseudocode (p. 11.4)

rapid application development
(RAD) (p. 11.15)

repetition control structure
(p. 11.11)

reserved word (p. 11.8)

run-time error (p. 11.13)

scripting language (p. 11.22)

selection control structure
(p. 11.9)

sequence control structure
(p. 11.9)

sequential execution (p. 11.9)

server-side Web programming
(p. 11.27)

software development
environment (p. 11.14)

software patch (p. 11.17)

software upgrade (p. 11.17)

source code (p. 11.21)

syntax (p. 11.24)

syntax error (p. 11.13)

technical writer (p. 11.16)

third generation language
(3GL) (p. 11.19)

user manual (p. 11.16)

VBScript (p. 11.27)

Visual Basic for Applications
(VBA) (p. 11.22)

CROSSWORD PUZZLE

Across

2. A programming language's ability to work on a variety of computer hardware and operating systems
5. A word that a programming language has set aside for its own use
7. A common name for a software error
8. This uses English statements to create an outline of the necessary steps for a piece of software to operate
10. Information software produces after it has processed input
11. Finding errors in software code
14. A set of specific steps that solves a problem or carries out a task
16. A numerical value that tracks the number of iterations in a software code
17. An interpreted scripting language based on Visual Basic
18. Translating your algorithm into a programming language
19. Information that comes from an external source that enters the software
21. An explanation that tells other programmers what's happening in software code
23. Computer aided software engineering
24. eXtensible HTML
25. Another word for repetition control structure

Down

1. A collection of instructions and explanations relevant to a piece of software
3. Translates one line of source code into object code at a time
4. A utility program that converts assembly language into machine language
6. Visual Basic for Applications
9. Dynamic HTML
12. This control structure uses an existing condition to decide how a computer will execute software code
13. A set of rules to follow
15. A writer who explains concepts and procedures to non-technical software users
20. Common Business Oriented Language
22. A scripting language program that executes a task or set of tasks within a software application

QUESTIONS AND EXERCISES

Multiple Choice

1. A(n) _____ is a set of specific steps to solve a problem or carry out a task.
   a. algorithm
   b. procedural language
   c. loop
   d. program flowchart
   e. iteration

2. Errors that occur when you execute software code are _____ errors.
   a. syntax
   b. run-time
   c. logic
   d. procedural
   e. control

3. A _____ error is a mistake in the way that an algorithm solves a problem.
   a. syntax
   b. run-time
   c. logic
   d. miscellaneous
   e. grammar

4. _____ is when you translate your algorithm into a programming language.
   a. Assembly
   b. Scripting
   c. Coding
   d. Compiling
   e. Interpreting

5. The if-then-else control structure is an example of what kind of structure?
   a. sequence control
   b. selection control
   c. repetition control
   d. flowcharting control
   e. logic control

6. Repetition control structures include
   a. do-until.
   b. do-while.
   c. for-next.
   d. all of the above.
   e. none of the above.

7. A(n) _____ is a numerical value that tracks the number of iterations.
   a. counter
   b. loop
   c. repetition
   d. VBScript
   e. object

8. COBOL is an example of what kind of language?
   a. first generation
   b. second generation
   c. third generation
   d. fourth generation
   e. natural language

9. _____ languages are human languages that can program a computer.
   a. Machine-independent
   b. Machine-dependent
   c. Natural
   d. Procedural
   e. OOP

10. _____ is an interpreted scripting language based on Visual Basic.
    a. JavaScript
    b. XHTML
    c. COBOL
    d. DHTML
    e. VBScript

True/False

11. ____ Programmers debug a program to locate errors in the code.

12. ____ Low-level programming languages are machine-dependent.

13. ____ Programming environments contain debugging tools.

14. ____ Control structures specify a code's sequence of execution.

15. ____ Procedural languages aren't portable.

QUESTIONS AND EXERCISES

1. Explain a programmer's role in each phase of the systems development life cycle.

PHASE	YOUR EXPLANATION
Investigation	_____
Analysis	_____
Design	_____
Construction	_____
Implementation	_____
Support	_____

2. Identify a computer problem you had recently. Create a problem statement describing the problem. Then use pseudocode to describe the steps you took to solve the problem. If you never solved the problem, use pseudocode to discuss what steps you tried. Bring the problem statement and pseudocode to class.

3. Develop a pseudocode and a flowchart using one of the problem/opportunity statements at www.mhhe.com/i-series (click on "Chapter 11"). Which technique did you prefer? Why?

4. Go to the list of programming languages at www.mhhe.com/i-series. Using the languages for reference, fill in this table:

GENERATION/CHARACTERISTIC	PROGRAMMING LANGUAGE
Procedural	_____
Compiled	_____
Interpreted	_____
Scripting	_____
Object-oriented	_____
Machine	_____
Assembly	_____
3GL	_____
4GL	_____

5. Testing the software code is an important part of the systems development life cycle. At www.mhhe.com/i-series you'll find two programs in Visual Basic for Applications. This interpreted scripting language is a part of Microsoft Office XP. For our purposes open Microsoft Excel and then open the code you've downloaded from the site. Note the following:

A. What are the syntax errors? How did you know?

B. What are the run-time errors? How did you know?

C. Are there any logic errors? Should there be any logic errors at this point in the SDLC?

After you've answered these questions, see if you can fix the errors and make the program work.

LEVEL THREE

e-commerce

1. Consumer Rights on the Web

Shopping on the Web doesn't have to be a "click in the dark." Be an informed consumer to make sure you get what you want. Lucky for you, there are Web sites to help:

- Consumer Reports— www.consumerreports.org
- Consumer World—www.consumerworld.org
- The Better Business Bureau—www.bbb.org

Think about how you'd use these sites to research an item you'd like to buy. Consider these questions:

a. Is there enough information on the Web to help you make an informed purchase?

b. Can you make a decision on a product solely on the Web or do you want to try it first? Why do you feel you need to try the product?

c. Once you decide on an item, was it easy to find a highly rated e-commerce Web site to buy it from? Would you feel comfortable buying this item from the Web site?

d. Did you later buy the item? If so, where did you buy it?

If you aren't satisfied with an item you've purchased, there are Web sites to help you, if the merchant will not:

- National Fraud Information Center— www.fraud.org
- FirstGov for Consumers—www.consumer.gov

2. Taking College Courses on the Web

You've probably had an instructor who places materials on the Web for you to use. You may have taken exams over the Web or joined in Web discussion groups. But did you know that many schools offer entire classes over the Web? Some schools even offer online degrees. You could go to college without ever leaving home. We've listed some of these Web sites:

- The Open University—www.open.edu
- The University of Phoenix—www.phoenix.edu
- Capella University—www.capella.edu

As you look at these schools, consider these questions:

a. What types of courses or degrees do they offer?

b. Can you get the degree you're pursuing at an online school?

c. Would you rather get your degree at an online school than the one you're at now? Why or why not?

d. Can you think of people who might benefit from taking courses online? Who might they be? What are the benefits?

e. What would be the differences between taking a course online and taking one in a classroom?

f. What would be the differences between getting an entire degree online and getting one where you are now?

3. Putting Your Book on the Web

You want to write the Great American Novel. Or maybe you'd like to publish your poems or your mom's recipes. Most publishing houses won't talk to you, but you always have the Web.

To publish a book on the Web, you can convert it to HTML and put it up as Web pages. However, for a fee, there are companies that will publish your book, market it, and make printed copies for people who want it. Take a look at these:

- Iuniverse—www.iuniverse.com
- XLibris—www.xlibris.com
- Trafford Publishing Service—
  www.trafford.com

Consider the following questions:

a. What are the advantages of using a service like this?

b. Are there disadvantages?

c. Do you think writers should consider these options or use a more traditional route? Why or why not?

d. Would you buy a book from one of these Web sites? Would you order an electronic or print copy? Why?

4. Using Interlibrary Loan

You've spent hours doing research for your paper. After searching databases, you have a list of books and articles that will help. You trudge off to the library and begin your search.

But you can find only some of the books and magazines that you need. Instead of giving up, try interlibrary loan. Interlibrary loan is a service that lets member universities share books and articles with each other. Here are a few:

- Library of Congress—www.loc.gov/rr/loan
- OhioLink (All Ohio Universities)—
  olc1.ohiolink.edu
- Penn State University—
  www.libraries.psu.edu/iasweb/ill/illmain.htm
- Western Michigan University—
  www.wmich.edu/library/interlib-loan.html

After looking at these Web sites, go to your university's library Web site and look for information on interlibrary loans. Answer the following questions:

a. What are your library's policies on requesting books? Do they differ from the Web sites listed above? How?

b. What are your library's policies on requesting articles? Do they differ from the Web sites listed above? How?

c. How long will it take you to get a book? An article?

Some libraries will allow you to request a book or an article over the Web. Although you still need to go to the library for many things, the Web makes finding information in your library much easier.

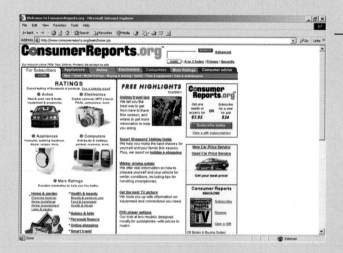

on the web

1. Finding a Programming Job Online

Programmers are in high demand. Search on job Web sites for programmers and Web developers. Start with these Web sites:

- ComputerJobs.com—www.computerjobs.com
- Dice.com—www.dice.com
- Monster.com—www.monster.com

Consider the following questions:

a. What types of jobs did you find?

b. Are they what you expected?

c. What type of skills, education, and experience are employers looking for?

Report to the class the five most interesting opportunities you found.

2. Finding the Top 5 Programming Languages

Hundreds of programming languages exist, but programmers use only a few for certain tasks. Conduct a Web search for the top five programming languages in business. Not everyone's list will be the same, so make sure you justify why you chose the five that you did. Present your findings to the class. Were there any programming languages that showed up on everyone's list?

3. Finding a Software Development Environment

Programmers rely on a development environment to help them write efficient software code. Development environments consist of debugging utilities, text editing programs, compilers, and interpreters. Conduct a Web search for development environments. What did you find? How much did they cost? Which languages are programmers able to use in the development environments? Report your findings to the class.

4. Top Choices for Web Programming

Web developers depend on the Web for information they need to program effectively. Choose three of the Web programming languages we discussed and find three Web sites for each one. Prepare a short presentation that discusses why each Web site may help programmers. Make sure you explain why the Web sites are so important. Prepare a short presentation that discusses why you chose these Web sites. If you have access to the Web in the classroom, show the Web sites.

5. Finding Code on the Web

Many programmers will share code (or portions of it) on the Web. Find five Web sites that share or discuss programming. Consider:

a. Were you able to download the complete code for a program? If so, why do you think programmers made it available? If not, why do you think they haven't shared it?

b. Did programmers share code from certain programming languages more often than others? Which ones? Why?

6. What Is Open Source?

Do a search for information on "open source" software. What is it? Why do people use it? Which languages do people use to write open source software? Would you use open source software? Prepare a short report on your findings. If it's possible, show some of the open source Web sites you found to the class.

ethics, security & privacy

1. Are You Giving Out More Information than You Want To?

You've probably filled out registration forms or contest entries on the Web. Most likely you've used a Web form to enter the information and then submitted it. Web developers collect and process your information with these forms. Using form validation, they can make sure you've entered a name, e-mail address, or zip code. But did you know they can also get information such as your Web browser version, computer system, and even the time and your location on the Internet when you submitted the form?

In other chapters we've discussed cookies and security and privacy issues associated with them. But with forms and certain Web programs, Web developers take information without even asking. What are your thoughts on this? Is it wrong to do all the time? When should it be done?

After you answer these questions look at www.mhhe.com/i-series (click on "Chapter 11") to see what Web developers can get when you submit a form or even just visit their site. Now what are your thoughts on the same questions? Have they changed?

2. To Install or Not to Install: That's the Question

We read of ethical, security, and privacy violations almost every day. Hackers, software pirates, and identity fraud all make headlines. Although this is unfortunate, we don't always think about the decisions programmers, systems analysts, and software engineers quietly make on a daily basis.

Suppose you landed a job as a programmer at a good company. On your first day, your manager hands you an application package and asks you to customize the application with macros and then install the customized application on all the computers in the business. When you ask about the software licensing agreement, your manager tells you not to worry about it. You're not quite sure what your manager means by this. What do you do? You want the job, but you're not sure if this request is ethical (or legal). How can you get some guidance?

Fortunately, there are ethical standards for IT professionals to follow. These come from the Association for Computing Machinery (ACM), the Institute of Electrical and Electronics Engineers (IEEE), and the British Computer Society (BCS):

- ACM Code of Ethics and Professional Conduct—
  www.acm.org/constitution/code.html
- IEEE Code of Ethics—
  www.ieee.org/about/whatis/code.html
- BCS Codes of Practice—
  www1.bcs.org/docs/01100/1194/Cop.htm

Choose one of the societies listed above and then apply their guidelines to your situation. What's your answer now? What might you say to your manager? Can you think of other ethical IT dilemmas you may encounter as an IT professional or even as a computer user?

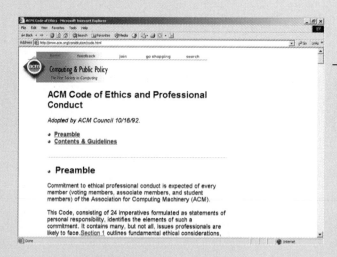

group activities

1. An Interview with a Programmer

Find a programmer or software engineer either on your campus or at a local business. Prepare a set of questions about job responsibilities and software development. You might want to ask how his or her SDLC is the same or different from the one in this text. Or maybe see what types of programming languages he or she prefers.

Interview the programmer or software engineer and present your findings to the class. Make sure to compare your findings to your classmates' interviews. Does the programmer's or software engineer's role vary? Did he or she mention specific programming languages? What about how he or she conducted software development? Was it the same as in this text?

2. Solve a Programming Problem

Programmers solve problems by creating software. Identify a problem or opportunity that you can solve by creating a new software program or by upgrading an older software program. Your group isn't expected to actually code, test, implement, or maintain the program. However, you should analyze the situation, create a problem/opportunity statement, and design the pseudocode and flowchart.

3. Choose a Language

Choose one procedural and one nonprocedural language. For example, you could choose COBOL and Java. Conduct research on both the Web and in programming journals. Identify uses for each language. Compare and contrast each of the languages in a report and presentation to the class. Note the strengths and weaknesses of each programming language.

4. Predict the Future of XML and XHTML

In this chapter you saw that many newer Web programming languages such as XML and XHTML aren't entirely supported in Web browsers. Start with the W3C (www.w3c.org) to learn more about XML and XHTML. Continue to explore how Web developers use these two interpreted scripting languages. Also study how developers intend to use them in the future. Prepare your findings in a report and presentation to the class. If Web access is available, show some Web sites that discuss or use these languages.

5. Proprietary versus Open Source Software

In this chapter we've discussed programming languages and how programmers can use a language to create software. Currently, there's much discussion among programmers about proprietary versus open source software.

Compare and contrast the philosophy behind proprietary software such as Windows with open source software such as Linux. Which would you use for your operating system? What about application software or utilities? Find one operating system, one word processing program, one spreadsheet, and one DBMS for each type. Which would the group use? (You can choose proprietary for some and open source for others.) Why?

Looking Back/Looking Ahead

The Life and Times of a Dot-Com Entrepreneur

Joann's business has been extremely successful. But now her software is no longer meeting her system's needs. She knows that she needs new software or at least an _____ to her existing software, but she's not sure how to begin.

Joann contacts her programmer friend Lavar. After asking Joann some questions, he tells her that she needs new software. They both know it's time to begin systems _____ to model the _____ system before any programming takes place.

After Lavar makes sure that the software meets Joann's needs, he develops his _____ in outline form. He also uses a _____, or a graphical representation of the program logic.

After testing the algorithm, Lavar begins writing, or _____, the software. He uses Visual Basic, a _____-level programming language that he needs to compile from the _____ code to _____ code before the computer can run the software.

Lavar uses Visual Basic because he can use objects he has created before. The ability to reuse objects is a basic tenet of _____ programming. He also likes Visual Basic because Joann can use a GUI interface to interact with menus and buttons. The ability to interact with Visual Basic in this way makes it an _____-driven language.

After Lavar has written the code, he uses his _____ environment to _____, or test, the code. Once it has no errors, Lavar moves to the _____ or installs the software. Throughout the coding, Lavar has written _____ in the code, and kept _____ to make sure he can explain the program to a _____ writer who will write the _____ manual.

Joann is satisfied with her new software, but knows she'll need to _____ her software soon because she wants to deploy more of the components over the Web. She'd like to use _____ to create Web pages her customers can access with their PDAs. She also wants to add more interactivity using _____, a scripting language based on Visual Basic.

As Joann's business grows she'll need to increase her computing needs and hire staff. Luckily she'll learn how to manage information in a larger organization in Chapter 12.

CHAPTER

12

twelve

Organizational Information Systems

Why Are Computers the Heavy Artillery in Business?

Computers are today the heavy artillery in business. In the information age, knowledge is power. Remember the old saying, "What you don't know can't hurt you." Well, in business today the new saying is, "What you don't know can and will put you out of business."

Computers and technology are the tools businesses use to gather, store, manage, and manipulate vitally important information. This information includes (1) transactions with customers and other businesses, (2) knowledge about the competition and other external forces, and (3) knowledge about how the business works internally. Successful businesses today keep a wealth of information about all three. They provide employees the technology and technology know-how to access and use that information.

As you prepare to move into the business world, you need to understand how and why businesses gather, store, manage, and manipulate information with technology. In previous chapters, we've discussed some of these issues, especially in regards to databases in Chapter 8. Now, we want to take a very specific look at the structure of a business and what computer systems businesses use in the information age.

In this chapter, we'll first survey the broad picture, the nature and structure of an organization, decentralized computing and shared information, and characteristics of information (see Figure 12.1). Next, we'll look at how businesses track transaction information, what computer systems managers use, and then various computer systems that support organizational logistics. Finally, we'll see how businesses are using technology to spread out around the globe.

FIGURE   12.1

Your focus in this chapter starts with a look internally at organizations and then expands to businesses spreading out nationally and around the globe.

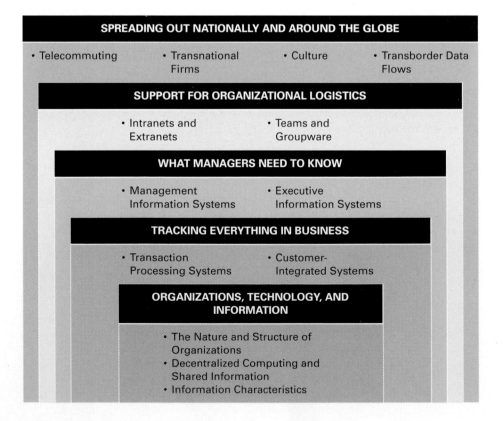

SPREADING OUT NATIONALLY AND AROUND THE GLOBE

- Telecommuting
- Transnational Firms
- Culture
- Transborder Data Flows

SUPPORT FOR ORGANIZATIONAL LOGISTICS

- Intranets and Extranets
- Teams and Groupware

WHAT MANAGERS NEED TO KNOW

- Management Information Systems
- Executive Information Systems

TRACKING EVERYTHING IN BUSINESS

- Transaction Processing Systems
- Customer-Integrated Systems

ORGANIZATIONS, TECHNOLOGY, AND INFORMATION

- The Nature and Structure of Organizations
- Decentralized Computing and Shared Information
- Information Characteristics

A://ORGANIZATIONS, TECHNOLOGY, AND INFORMATION

The use of technology to manage information in an organization doesn't just happen. It must be carefully thought out and planned. Organizations can't simply decide they need technology because everyone else seems to have it, just as you shouldn't buy a home computer because everyone else seems to have one. Organizations must first understand their nature and structure, the information requirements of their employees, and then how technology can support what they do.

THE NATURE AND STRUCTURE OF ORGANIZATIONS

How Are Organizations "Organized" Today?

A traditional organization is usually viewed as a four-level pyramid (see Figure 12.2). At the top is **strategic management,** which provides an organization with overall direction and guidance. Strategic management is responsible for developing the long-range plans of the organization. Typical strategic-level managers include the CEO (Chief Executive Officer), CIO (Chief Information Officer), CFO (Chief Financial Officer), and COO (Chief Operating Officer). It may also include people who have the title of "vice president."

The second level of an organization is often called **tactical management,** which develops the goals and strategies outlined by strategic management. So, tactical management may set goals for sales over the next several years. The third level is **operational management,** which manages and directs the day-to-day operations and implementation of the goals and strategies. So, operational management might determine the sales goals for each region (East, West, North, and South) that would meet the overall sales goals set by tactical management.

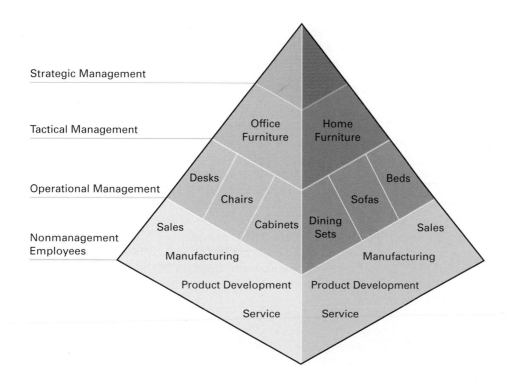

FIGURE 12.2

Typical organizational structures are in the form of a pyramid with several levels.

Strategic Management

Tactical Management

Operational Management

Nonmanagement Employees

Office Furniture

Home Furniture

Desks

Beds

Chairs

Sofas

Sales

Cabinets

Dining Sets

Sales

Manufacturing

Manufacturing

Product Development

Product Development

Service

Service

At the fourth level of an organization are nonmanagement employees, those people who perform all the productive daily activities such as order processing, manufacturing line work, customer service, and so on. You should notice in Figure 12.2 that organizations also exhibit depth. In our example, the organization is structured according to product lines.

DECENTRALIZED COMPUTING AND SHARED INFORMATION

How Do Organizations Get Technology and Information into the Hands of Their Employees?

In today's business world, technology is in the hands of all employees, so information must be in their hands as well. All employees—regardless of their level—can help an organization be successful, but they can do it only if they can use technology to access the right information. Organizations achieve this goal through the practices of decentralized computing and shared information.

Decentralized Computing

Decentralized computing is the placement of technology into the hands of those people in an organization who need it in order to do their jobs effectively and efficiently. This is really all about empowering employees through the use of technology. If you need access to information, then your organization should provide you with the technology to access it. Organizations need to train employees to use the technology in the most efficient and optimal way, too.

Shared Information

Shared information is the concept that employees should have access to whatever information they need when they need it (see Figure 12.3). For example, sales people need to access inventory information to determine if products are on hand, and they need to access manufacturing information to determine when products will be available.

In a shared information and decentralized computing environment, you'll typically find a large central database that contains all the information anyone may need to access. You'll also find smaller departmental databases that contain information that only employees in a particular department need to access. For example, Bass Brewery—one of England's largest beer manufacturers—uses decentralized computing, shared information, and a state-of-the-art computer system to produce more than 50 types of beer in more than 150 different packages. With the touch of a computer screen, production managers control both the brew house and packaging hall, selecting the volume run, type of beer, and type of packaging. The appropriate recipes alter the contents fed into the vats. Information concerning bottling sizes and labels is sent to the packaging hall. Cleaning fluid is automatically released to the vats in the brew house. The entire process depends on decentralized computing, shared information, and the touch of a finger.

FIGURE   12.3

Decentralized computing and shared information give all employees the ability to access whatever information they need whenever they need it.

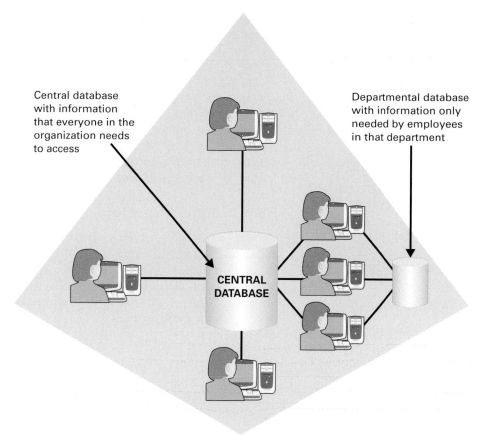

Central database with information that everyone in the organization needs to access

Departmental database with information only needed by employees in that department

CENTRAL DATABASE

INFORMATION CHARACTERISTICS

Do People in Organizations Have Different Information Needs?

People within an organization have different information needs according to their responsibilities. Thus, information within an organization takes on different attributes and flows in different directions.

Differing Information Needs

Depending on your responsibilities within your organization, you need information of varying specificity, or "granularity." ***Information granularity*** refers to the degree of detail information contains. For example, non-management employees and operational managers need information with a fine level of granularity, perhaps sales on a daily basis. Tactical managers make use of information with a coarser granularity, perhaps sales by product line on a monthly or quarterly basis. Strategic managers work with information that exhibits a very coarse level of granularity, perhaps total sales by year.

F I G U R E   12.4

Information granularity varies according to the organizational level.

Coarsest granularity—
greatly summarized

Finest granularity—
greatly detailed

So, if you think of an organization from top to bottom, people at the highest or strategic levels need more general information with the coarsest granularity, while nonmanagement or line people who work with daily processes need the finest level of granularity (see Figure 12.4). Strategic managers don't need to know the details of every sale; they need to know total sales by some time period in order to set overall goals and directions. Operational managers and nonmanagement employees need to know the details of every sale because they are charged with the day-to-day business activities.

Information Attributes

People in different jobs in an organization need information that covers different areas or that describes different aspects of the business. We say that information can be internal, external, objective, or subjective.

Internal information describes specific operational aspects of an organization. *External information,* on the other hand, describes the environment surrounding an organization. *Objective information* quantifiably describes something that is known, while *subjective information* attempts to describe something that is currently unknown.

Let's consider these information attributes within the context of the levels of an organization. Strategic managers need internal and objective information that describes how the organization is performing its activities, albeit objective information with a coarse level of granularity. Strategic managers also need external and subjective information, however. For example, the CFO needs to know how interest rates will probably move in the coming months, which would be external and subjective information.

As you move down through the levels of an organization, people typically need more internal and objective information and less subjective and external information. For example, operational managers and nonmanagement employees may need to know exact sales figures on a daily basis (internal and objective), not projected sales (which would be subjective information), which would serve a strategic planning function.

F I G U R E   12.5

Information within an organization flows up, down, and horizontally.

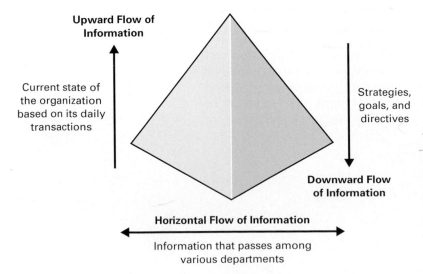

Upward Flow of
Information

Current state of
the organization
based on its daily
transactions

Strategies,
goals, and
directives

Downward Flow
of Information

Horizontal Flow of Information

Information that passes among
various departments

The Flows of Information

Information in organizations flows continuously in various directions—up, down, and horizontally (see Figure 12.5). The *upward flow of information* describes the current state of the organization based on its daily transactions (such as sales). So, people at the lower level of the organization capture that information and store it in the central database. Then, people in the upper levels can access and use that information.

i·series insights

Ethics, Security & Privacy

Who's Looking at Your Medical Records?

According to one poll, 85 percent of surveyed doctors said that protecting the confidentiality of patient medical records was very essential and high on their priority list. That sounds good, doesn't it? Think again. If there are 35 students in your class, then 85 percent means that 5 of you have doctors who don't care about protecting the confidentiality of your medical records.

Long before the use of computers in the medical field became widespread, record confidentiality was suspect. For example, your doctor's handwritten notes about you could be subpoenaed by a court without your permission or knowledge. This happened to a woman in California whose medical records were subpoenaed after a car accident. Her records revealed that she had given up a child for adoption 30 years earlier, information that should not have been relevant.

Telemedicine—which can electronically transfer your records to any doctor in the country at any time—is a great concept. For example, if you live in Montana and become ill while on vacation in Florida, your medical records can easily be transferred. But beware—perhaps your most sensitive information is now traveling throughout a vast network of computers and computer users.

If you're concerned about the confidentiality of your medical records, take action. These suggestions provide a starting point.

1. Never disclose anything to your doctor that is not health-related. It may be recorded in your file, which can be transferred to another organization such as an insurance carrier.

2. Ask your doctor if any of your records can be accessed by individuals or organizations outside his or her office. If they can, ask for what purpose.

3. Always ask to review your medical records for accuracy and content.

4. Ask your doctor to notify you in writing if your records are ever subpoenaed.

The **downward flow of information** consists of the strategies, goals, and directives that originate at one level and are passed to lower levels. So, an overall sales goal might originate at the strategic management level. That goal would flow down to tactical management, which would develop more specific sales goals and pass them to operational management. That level would then develop daily or weekly sales goals and pass them to nonmanagement employees (the lowest level).

The **horizontal flow of information** refers to information that passes among various departments. If you consider our organizational structure in Figure 12.2 on page 12.3, there would be a constant horizontal flow of information between the product development departments in the office furniture and home furniture product lines. Why? Because there is probably some overlap of business intelligence here. Perhaps the office furniture department has determined a way to make a better office chair that can be used by the home furniture product development team to make a better sofa.

SECTION A://   *making* the grade

1. _Tactical_ management develops the goals and strategies outlined by strategic management.
2. _Decentralized_ is the placement of technology in the hands of those people in an organization who need it in order to do their jobs effectively and efficiently.
3. Information _granularity_ refers to the level of detail the information contains.
4. _External_ information describes the environment surrounding an organization.
5. The _downward_ flow of information consists of the strategies, goals, and directives that originate at one level and are passed to lower levels.

B://TRACKING EVERYTHING IN BUSINESS

At the very heart of a business are systems that process daily transactions, such as sales to customers, inventory updating, and billing. These systems are most often a business's primary interface to its customers. If these systems don't work correctly or are slow to work, your customers won't be your customers anymore. They'll simply go someplace else to buy their products and services. Computer systems for tracking daily transactions include transaction processing systems and customer-integrated systems.

TRANSACTION PROCESSING SYSTEMS
What Computer Systems Process Daily Transactions?
A ***transaction processing system (TPS)*** is exactly what its name implies—a system that processes transactions that occur within an organization. Types of TPS transactions include processing sales orders, paying accounts payable, creating billing for accounts receivable, tracking hours and generating checks for payroll, and ordering more inventory and raw materials.

At a minimum, a TPS includes hardware and software components for

1. Gathering input information.
2. Processing information.
3. Presenting information.
4. Storing information.

In Figure 12.6, you can see a TPS order-entry system that performs those four functions for Avon products. Notice that Avon's TPS uses a document-imaging system to gather the input information from orders. In previous years, order entry clerks had to type in handwritten information from orders. This was an extremely slow process and created many errors. With the document-imaging TPS system, Avon reports that accuracy has improved by 76 percent, productivity has improved by 75 percent, order-processing times have increased by 67 percent, and order-entry costs have decreased by 65 percent.

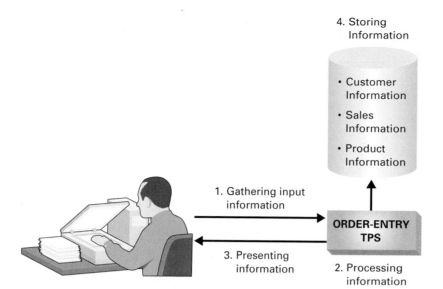

FIGURE   12.6

Avon's transaction processing system (TPS) includes digital imaging for gathering input information.

In any organization, once information enters a central database through a TPS, that information can then be used throughout the organization. For example, managers at all levels can generate whatever reports they need to make better decisions.

Transaction processing systems are found in all functions of an organization. And again, these systems must work correctly and efficiently. Not only will your customers leave you if they don't, you could very well go out of business. In the manufacturing industry, losses because of TPS downtime during 1992 were estimated at almost $2.5 billion. In another study, Dr. Stephen Lunce found that most businesses estimated they would lose 50 percent of their revenues if their IT systems failed for only 15 days.

CUSTOMER-INTEGRATED SYSTEMS

Are There Computer Systems That Allow Customers to Process Their Own Transactions?

One of the newest computer systems in the business world today is a customer-integrated system. A ***customer-integrated system (CIS)*** is an extension of a transaction processing system that places technology in the hands of an organization's customers and allows them to process their own transactions. ATMs are perhaps the most common example of a CIS. ATMs provide you with the ability to do your own banking anywhere at any time. What's really interesting is that ATMs actually do nothing "new," but they give you greater flexibility in accessing and using your money.

For a bank, an ATM represents greater customer satisfaction and cost savings. If you're using an ATM instead of a teller inside a bank, then the bank may not need as many tellers. You essentially become your own teller when you use an ATM. It's a win-win situation for everyone.

CISs further decentralize computing power in an organization by placing that power in the hands of customers (see Figure 12.7 on page 12.10). For that reason, CISs are also responsible for *communicating* information. Consider ATMs again. You can use an ATM literally anywhere in the world. So, ATMs must include the ability to communicate information from one location to another.

F I G U R E   12.7

Customer-integrated systems (CISs) allow customers to process their own transactions.

- Customer information
- Sales information
- Product information

CUSTOMER-INTEGRATED SYSTEM

You can find other great examples of customer-integrated systems all over the Web. Throughout this text, you've been experiencing CISs by completing the e-commerce projects at the end of each chapter.

Transaction processing and customer-integrated systems capture vitally important information that helps an organization ensure quality and undertake various reengineering efforts. To learn more about quality and reengineering efforts such as total quality management and business process reengineering, visit the Web site for this text at www.mhhe.com/i-series.

SECTION B : //   *making the grade*

1. A _____*C.IS*_____ is an extension of a TPS that places technology in the hands of an organization's customers.

2. A _____*TPS*_____ is exactly what its name implies—a system that processes transactions that occur within an organization.

3. CISs further *decentralized* computing power in an organization by placing that power in the hands of customers.

4. The Web is a common place to find all kinds of _____*CIS*_____.

C://WHAT MANAGERS NEED TO KNOW

Before, during, and after daily activities occur within an organization, managers have many responsibilities. Among them is to identify and solve problems, and identify and take advantage of opportunities. But problems and opportunities won't arrive at your desk in an envelope marked "URGENT." Instead, you need to constantly monitor your surroundings. A problem solved before it becomes a problem is the best problem to have. An opportunity that everyone knows about is no longer an opportunity. There are computer systems that can help you with your responsibilities as a manager—these are management information systems and executive information systems.

MANAGEMENT INFORMATION SYSTEMS

What Systems Help Managers Manage?

A *management information system (MIS)* is a system that provides periodic and predetermined reports that summarize information. In an organization, this information comes from a database that gathers and stores daily information from transaction processing and customer-integrated systems (see Figure 12.8).

So, MISs are systems that process and create new information (by manipulating existing information) and present information to whoever needs it. MISs are often called *management alerting systems* because they are designed to alert people (usually managers) to the existence or potential existence of problems and opportunities. However, MIS reports can rarely tell you as a manager why a problem has occurred or how to take advantage of an opportunity. That's your job, and that's why an organization is willing to pay you a nice large salary.

Types of Management Information System Reports

Management information systems provide reports in many different forms—periodic, summarized, exception, and comparative. A *periodic report* is a report that is produced at a predetermined time interval—daily, weekly, monthly, yearly, and so on. A *summarized report* is simply a report that aggregates information in some way. For example, sales by sales people, returns by product line, and the number of students enrolled in a class are all examples of summarized reports.

An *exception report* is a report that shows only a subset of available information based on some selection criteria. For example, a report showing all sales people who did not meet their quotas is an exception report. Finally, a *comparative report* is a report that shows two or more sets of similar information in an attempt to illustrate a relationship.

FIGURE   12.8

Management information systems (MISs) summarize information contained within a central database.

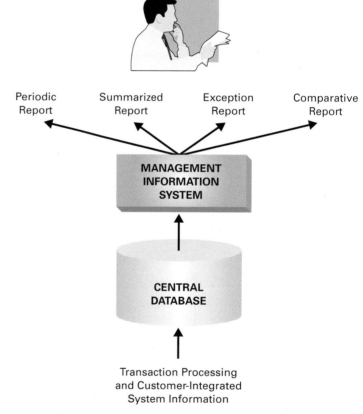

Periodic Report   Summarized Report   Exception Report   Comparative Report

MANAGEMENT INFORMATION SYSTEM

CENTRAL DATABASE

Transaction Processing and Customer-Integrated System Information

FIGURE 12.9

An accounting aging schedule is an example of a periodic, summarized, exception, and comparative report.

	MAXIMUM OFFICE PRODUCTS For Period Ending January 31, 2002					
CUSTOMER	**0–10 Days***	**11–30 Days**	**31–60 Days**	**61–90 Days**	**91–120 Days**	**120+ Days**
Shutt's Co.		$2,400				
Bellows Meats		700	$300			
Darian Publicity						$2,000
Federal Drivers	$1,400					
Jake's Toys	7,000					
Malloy Realty		1,600				
P.J.'s Floral				$600	$200	
Trevor Landscape						
Whitt Federal						
Yellow Truck	9,500					1,500
Zeno Fishery		6,000				
Totals:	$17,900	$10,700	$300	$600	$200	$3,500

Total Sales: $33,200

% of Total Sales:	53.9%	32.2%	0.9%	1.8%	0.6%	10.5%

*Terms are given 2/10, net 30. $358 total discounted for payments within 10 days.

FIGURE 12.10

Executive information systems (EISs) help managers solve problems and take advantage of opportunities.

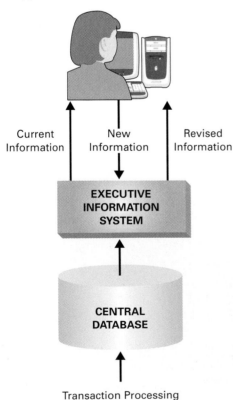

Current Information — New Information — Revised Information

EXECUTIVE INFORMATION SYSTEM

CENTRAL DATABASE

Transaction Processing and Customer-Integrated System Information

In Figure 12.9, you can see an example of an MIS report that is summarized, periodic, exception, and comparative. In accounting, this type of report is called an "aging schedule." It summarizes sales by customer. It's periodic because it's generated at the end of the month (notice the title). It's an exception report because it groups payments according to when they were made (the selection criterion is time). And it's also a comparative report because it shows percentages of total sales by time period. From this report, do you see any potential or real problems or opportunities?

EXECUTIVE INFORMATION SYSTEMS

What Sort of Computer Systems Help Strategic Managers?

An ***executive information system (EIS)*** is a highly interactive MIS that helps managers solve problems and take advantage of opportunities (see Figure 12.10). Like a management information system, an EIS creates new information (by manipulating existing information) and presents information to the user. Unlike an MIS, however, EISs give you the ability to enter new information and perform scenario analysis such as "what if?" analysis. So, you could view a sales report for last quarter and easily increase sales by 10 percent to understand the net effect on sales for the year.

An EIS allows you to "drill down" through information, as well, to better determine causes of problems and determine how to take advantage of an opportunity. In Figure 12.11 you can see an illustration of drilling down. In the first report, you can see sales by year. By clicking on any year, you can see sales for that year by territory (the second report). Finally, you can click on any territory and see sales by product line within that territory (the third report). So, drilling down is essentially looking first at the forest and choosing which trees to explore.

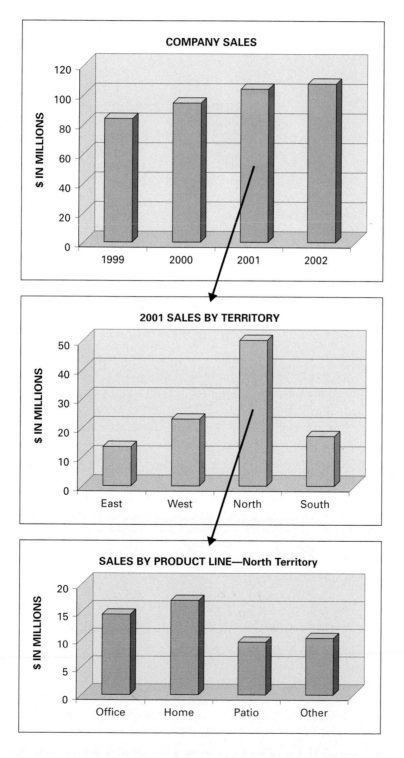

FIGURE 12.11

With an executive information system (EIS), you can "drill down" through information.

i·buy

Lease versus Buy

In many instances, businesses choose to lease the hardware and software that make up such systems as transaction processing, customer-integrated, management information, and executive information systems. When a business leases hardware or software, it makes relatively small monthly payments but does not own the technology. You have the same option. That is, you can buy a personal computer (and thus own it) or you can lease a computer.

When you lease a computer, there are both advantages and disadvantages. The advantages include (1) good support while you lease the computer; (2) lack of technology obsolescence; and (3) lower cost.

It's true. While you lease a computer, you do get good around-the-clock support if you have any problems. And in a couple of years, you simply trade in your old computer and begin making lease pay-

ments on a new computer (avoiding technology obsolescence). Finally, leased computers are typically cheaper than a purchased computer. Today, you can lease a computer for about $25 per month and that includes free unlimited Web access.

On the downside, leasing means that you don't own your computer. So, you can't resell it at a later date. As well, you must often receive approval from the leasing company if you want to upgrade your computer or add additional software.

If you're interested in leasing a home computer, start at the Web site for this text at www.mhhe. com/i-series.

Calgary Co-op—a small retail chain based in Canada—uses an EIS to effectively compete against the larger chains such as REI, Cub Foods, and Sam's Club. Calgary's EIS constantly displays and updates a large "quick-look monitor board." The board highlights the best and worst product performers on a minute-by-minute basis. Calgary's product managers can use their desktop computers to drill down through information to determine why some products are performing poorly and forecast needed inventory levels for products that are moving quickly. With its EIS, Calgary can now analyze sales information in a matter of minutes, a process that once required over two weeks of effort.

SECTION C://   *making the grade*

1. A ___MIS___ is a system that provides periodic and predetermined reports that summarize information.
2. A ___Summarize___ is simply a report that aggregates information in some way.
3. An ___Exception___ is a report that shows only a subset of available information based on some selection criteria.
4. A ___Comparative___ is a report that shows two or more sets of similar information in an attempt to illustrate a relationship.
5. An EIS allows you to "_____" through information to better determine causes of problems and determine how to take advantage of an opportunity.

D://SUPPORT FOR ORGANIZATIONAL LOGISTICS

Businesses today need to move quickly to succeed and survive. Few businesses have the luxury of waiting years for buildings to be constructed. They need teams of people scattered all over the city, country, and perhaps world to meet and work together. These same businesses also need to distribute information to employees in a secure fashion no matter where they are. And businesses today need to let their customers and suppliers "inside" the organization to run application software.

This is all about organizational logistics. There are computer systems and technology to help businesses today operate without regard to where their employees, customers, and suppliers may be.

INTRANETS AND EXTRANETS

Can Organizations "Carve Out" Their Own Internet?

From a business point of view, what's the number-one best thing about the Internet? You can undoubtedly answer that question in many ways. From a business point of view, the best thing about the Internet is that it's *platform independent*. That simply means anyone can use any type of operating system and any computer or computer-related device made by any manufacturer to access the Internet. It doesn't matter if you use a Mac, an IBM, a Compaq, or a Nokia cell phone—you can access the Internet.

For businesses, that's important because they have a variety of different types of hardware and software within them. For example, the production and design department may use Macs because they provide really great CAD/CAM (computer-aided design/computer-aided manufacturing) software, while the accounting department uses IBMs (or IBM compatibles) because of the wide range of available application software.

So, many organizations have begun to "internalize" the Internet, essentially creating their own private Internet. To do this, you create an intranet. An **intranet** is an internal organizational Internet that is guarded against outside access by a special security mechanism (see Figure 12.12). A firewall is the technical term for the special security mechanism that protects against outside access. As we discussed in Chapter 6, a firewall can be either software or hardware.

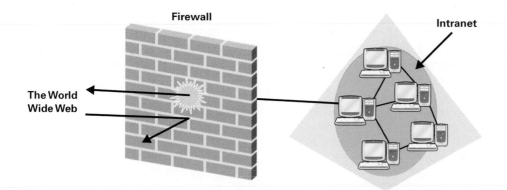

Firewall

Intranet

The World Wide Web

FIGURE 12.12

Intranets use a firewall for protection.

With an intranet, you can post sensitive and strategic information for everyone in your organization to see and use, without worrying about that information falling into the hands of your competitors. And intranets look and work exactly like the Internet and Web. You can create elaborate Web pages with links and downloadable files.

U.S. West's intranet—called the *Global Village*—connects over 20,000 employees in 14 different states. The employees can meet in private online chat rooms, exchange documents, and discuss ongoing projects. U.S. West employees can also use the Global Village to request vacation leave, check on their sick day accumulation, and even change their withholding tax. And U.S. West's firewall keeps all the information safe and secure.

Letting Your Suppliers and Customers inside Your Intranet

Carrying the concept of an intranet even further, many organizations are also creating extranets. An ***extranet*** is an extension of an intranet that allows other organizations and people access to information and application software on an internal intranet (see Figure 12.13). For example, you can allow your customers to use your internal order-entry TPS by giving them extranet access to your intranet.

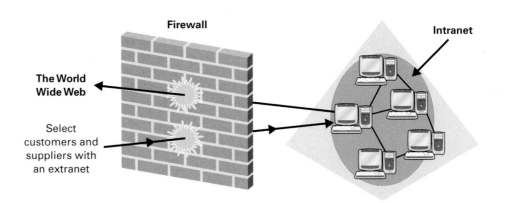

FIGURE 12.13

If you have an extranet, the firewall allows select customers and suppliers to enter your intranet.

This is a common application for organizations that have other organizations as customers (business to business). In this case, you don't want to let just anyone see and use your internal order-entry transaction processing system. So, you provide your organizational customers with extranet access, ensuring that no other organizations or people can use your order-entry TPS.

As the business world moves more toward electronic commerce, intranets and extranets will become commonplace. Over a two-year period, the percentage of businesses reporting they had intranet capabilities grew from 16 percent to 70 percent.

The average strategic manager spends between 50 and 80 percent of his or her time in meetings.

did you know?

SUPPORTING TEAMS WITH GROUPWARE

What Computer Systems Help Groups of People Work Together?

A **workgroup support system (WSS)** is a system that is designed to improve the performance of teams by supporting the sharing and flow of information. With a WSS, team members can be in the same office or spread out around the globe. This is why we say WSSs support organizational logistics. The foundation of any workgroup support system is **groupware**—the popular term for the software component that supports team efforts. Popular groupware suites include Lotus Notes/Domino, Microsoft Exchange, Novell Groupwise, and NetSys WebWare. For a review of these suites and a few more, visit the Web site for this text at www.mhhe.com/i-series.

Groupware suites contain software components for supporting the following three functions (see Figure 12.14):

1. Team dynamics
2. Document management
3. Applications development

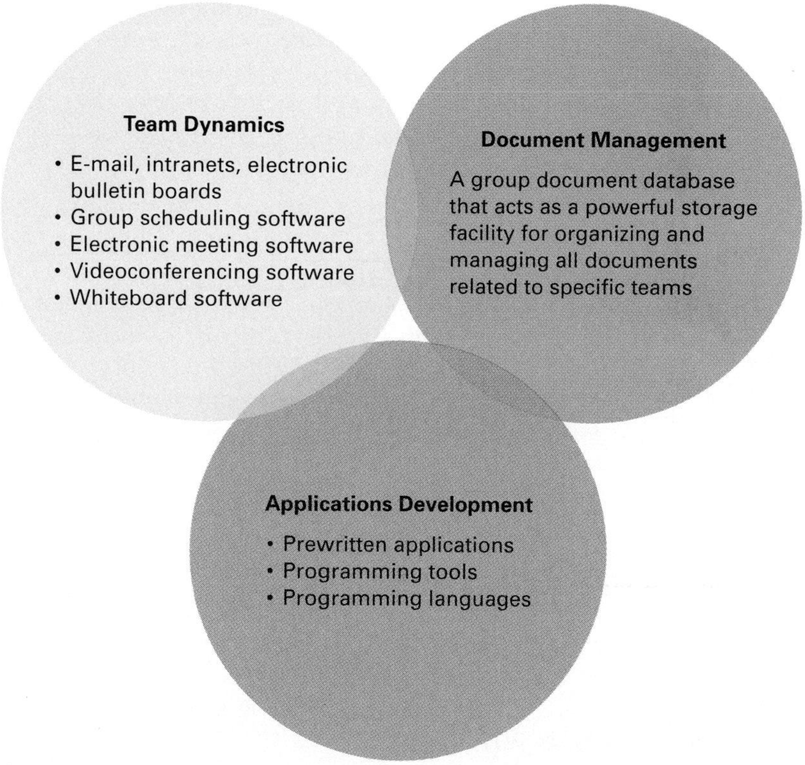

FIGURE   12.14

Groupware supports team dynamics, document management, and applications development.

Team Dynamics

- E-mail, intranets, electronic bulletin boards
- Group scheduling software
- Electronic meeting software
- Videoconferencing software
- Whiteboard software

Document Management

A group document database that acts as a powerful storage facility for organizing and managing all documents related to specific teams

Applications Development

- Prewritten applications
- Programming tools
- Programming languages

Team Dynamics

Team dynamics is the most basic and fundamental support provided by groupware. Team dynamics includes (1) any communications that occur between team members and (2) the facilitation and execution of meetings. For communications, groupware supports such technologies as intranets (which we discussed), e-mail (which you already know about), and electronic bulletin boards.

F I G U R E   12.15

Videoconferencing software allows people to meet face-to-face while in different locations.

An ***electronic bulletin board*** is a shared message space where you can post inquiries and schedules for events, and participate in discussion threads and chat rooms. Basically, electronic bulletin boards are bulletin boards with electronic capabilities.

For facilitating and executing meetings, groupware suites include:

- ***Group scheduling software***—provides facilities for maintaining the day-to-day electronic calendars of team members. You can easily use group scheduling software and request a meeting of several team members on a given day. The group scheduling software will look at everyone's calendar, inform you of the best meeting time, send an e-mail to everyone notifying them of the meeting time, and even block that time off on everyone's calendar.

- ***Electronic meeting software***—lets a team have a "virtual" meeting. For example, electronic meeting software helps you develop an agenda and send it to everyone. In turn, other team members read the agenda and provide an electronic response to those items they wish to discuss. This type of meeting can go on for several days and doesn't require that everyone attend an actual meeting in the same place or at the same time.

- ***Videoconferencing software***—allows a team to have a face-to-face meeting when members are geographically dispersed (see Figure 12.15). Videoconferencing software uses video cameras and large-screen monitors to allow everyone to see all the participants. Like electronic meeting software, videoconferencing software doesn't require that everyone attend an actual meeting in the same place.

- ***Whiteboard software***—lets team members meet, view a presentation, and record electronic notes on a large board called a whiteboard. So, you can make a PowerPoint presentation to your team, write on the whiteboard where your presentation appears, and have your writing captured as notes and sent to all team members.

Document Management

Perhaps the most critical component of any groupware suite is document management, achieved through a group document database. A ***group document database*** is a powerful storage facility for organizing and managing all documents related to specific teams. An organizationwide group document database may include documents from many different teams, some of which may be shared among many of the teams (see Figure 12.16 on the next page).

did you know? The *average real estate cost for having a single employee in a central office is about $3,000 per month.*

Because of the sharing of information, group document databases support many levels of security to control access to documents. In our example in Figure 12.16, the production team would have access to its documents as well as the shared documents, but not to documents specific to the distribution team.

Your team can store, access, track, and organize a wealth of information in a group document database. You can include word processing documents, spreadsheets, PowerPoint slides, and even audio and video files. Some groupware suites allow you to search all these file types for a specific word. In doing so, it will return to you the location of the word, even to the point that it will tell you where in a video a certain word appears.

Applications Development

Finally, groupware suites provide you with software development tools so your team can build applications quickly. These tools come in the form of prewritten applications (such as customer relationship management) and actual programming tools and languages. You can use these programming tools and languages to build applications from scratch or modify the existing prewritten applications. We discussed the process of creating software and applications in Chapters 10 and 11.

FIGURE   12.16

In a group document database, different teams can share information and protect private information.

Production Team Document Database

- Bill of materials
- Equipment maintenance
- Material requirements planning

Distribution Team Document Database

- Truck maintenance
- Routing schedules
- Driver allocation

Shared Information

- Work in progress
- Inventory status
- Customer orders

---

making the grade   SECTION D://

1. An <u>intranet</u> is an internal organizational Internet that is guarded against outside access by a special security mechanism.

2. An <u>Extranet</u> is an extension of an intranet that allows other organizations and people access to information and application software on an intranet.

3. <u>Group Web</u> is the popular term for the software component that supports team efforts.

4. <u>Group Scheduli</u>software provides facilities for maintaining the day-to-day electronic calendars of team members.

5. A <u>Group document</u> database is a powerful storage facility for organizing and managing all documents related to specific teams.

E://SPREADING OUT NATIONALLY AND AROUND THE GLOBE

Very few businesses today are "local." No matter what you do, you may have national and international customers, suppliers, employees, and (most important) competition. On a national scale, there are over 270,000,000 people in the United States. But there are over 5,600,000,000 (that's 5+ billion) people worldwide. Why not go after that vast international market? Why not start by capturing more of those 270,000,000 U.S. consumers? And while you're going after that bigger market, consider letting your employees work wherever they need to through telecommuting.

TELECOMMUTING

Do All Employees Have to Work in a Central Office?

Telecommuting is another business innovation supported by technology. **Telecommuting** is the use of various technologies (especially telecommunications technologies) to allow employees to work in a place other than a central location. So, **telecommuters** are people who work outside the central office some of the time while connected to the central office through technology.

Telecommuting is big business. Over 15 million people in the United States telecommute at least 50 percent of their workweek. And that number is expected to grow by 20 percent per year for the next several years.

For some jobs, telecommuting makes obvious sense. For example, sales people need to be "on the road" and in front of their customers more than they need to be sitting in an office. So, many in today's sales workforce are telecommuters. But there are other jobs that are not so obvious for which telecommuting is a great fit.

For example, JCPenney lets catalog sales people work from home. These people simply wait in their homes for the phone to ring. As a customer, when you call the 800 number to order JCPenney merchandise from its catalog, your phone call is routed to someone's home. That person uses a computer (which is connected to the central database at JCPenney) to take your order. In Figure 12.17 you can see that almost every business segment plans on implementing telecommuting in the near future.

FIGURE 12.17

It seems that all industries plan to implement telecommuting.

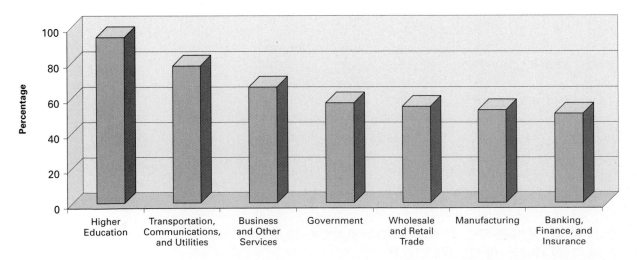

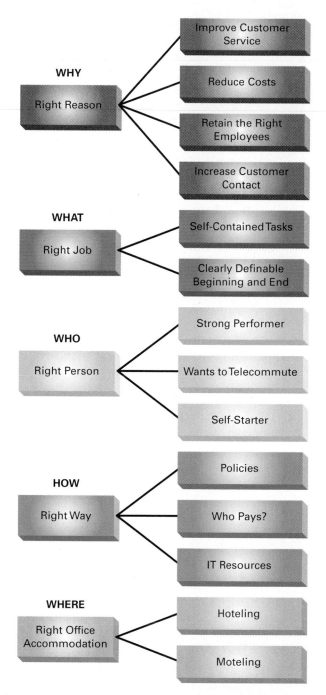

F I G U R E   12.18

Before implementing any telecommuting program, always ask yourself why, what, who, how, and where.

You must implement telecommuting carefully. Not everyone will make a good telecommuter. And some types of jobs don't lend themselves to telecommuting. When considering telecommuting in your organization, ask yourself five questions (see Figure 12.18):

- Why would you want to implement a telecommuting program? Good reasons include improving customer service, reducing costs, retaining employees, and increasing customer contact. A bad reason is because everyone else is doing it.

- What jobs or projects are suited to telecommuting? Good telecommuting jobs and projects include those with self-contained tasks and a clearly definable beginning and end.

- <u>Who</u> is best suited to telecommuting? Characteristics of good telecommuters include strong performers, a desire to telecommute, and self-starters.
- <u>How</u> can you best implement telecommuting? You must consider new policies that you'll need to have in place, who pays for mobile technology and perhaps office furniture in a telecommuter's home, and what new IT resources you'll need to handle the necessary telecommunications.
- <u>Where</u> will you locate telecommuters when they do come into the office? You have a variety of options here including hoteling (equipped offices that telecommuters reserve in advance) and moteling (equipped offices that are allocated on a first-come, first-serve basis).

Answering these five questions will definitely help you develop a successful telecommuting program.

TRANSNATIONAL FIRMS

What Businesses Operate throughout the World?

A ***transnational firm*** produces and sells products and services in countries all over the world (see Figure 12.19), so much so that it's difficult to know which country is the firm's home country. That's certainly true for Honda, an auto manufacturer headquartered in Japan that is now producing more cars outside than inside Japan. In fact, Honda exports more cars from the United States than does General Motors, Ford, or Chrysler. Did you know that?

Operating internationally, a business benefits in many ways. It gains access to a larger market of customers. It can utilize a larger workforce that may be cheaper than in its home country. It can also tap into the intellectual expertise of a workforce in a given country. That's true of many "U.S." software publishers who write and produce much of their software in such countries as India and Pakistan.

To effectively produce and sell products and services all over the world, a transnational firm faces many challenges. These include cultural differences (see Figure 12.20) and issues surrounding transborder data flows.

FIGURE   12.19

Transnational firms operate all over the world.

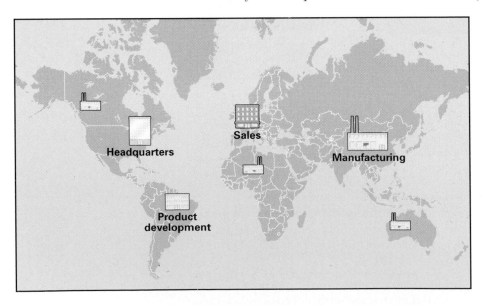

Culture is the collective personality of a nation or society that encompasses language, traditions, currency, religion, history, music, and acceptable behavior. Consider these cultural differences:

Gestures:
A raised or a waggling hand:
• In the United States, it says "goodbye."
• In India and South America it's a beckoning gesture.
• In much of Europe it's a signal for "no."

Handshake:
• United States: Should be firm and strong.
• East Africa: Light palm touch with the fingers hardly bending.
• Morocco: Kiss the back of the hand being shaken.

Insulting gestures:
• United States: Middle finger thrust upward.
• Britain: First two fingers thrust upward with the palm of the hand facing the body.
• Italy: First and little finger form "horns" to signify the object of the insult being gored by a bull.
• Turkey: Whole arm, with clenched fist, thrust out aggressively.

For more cultural oddities, visit the Web site for this text at www.mhhe.com/i-series.

FIGURE   12.20

Culture makes societies interesting and unique.

Transborder Data Flows

Transnational firms must consider their information and technology assets as they operate around the globe. The popular term for this is transborder data flows. But transborder data flows don't just deal with "data" (or information). They also deal with the technology that supports the movement of information.

As organizations begin to move information around the world, they must consider political and legal barriers. For example, in Canada banks cannot transmit financial information out of the country for processing. Instead, it must first be processed in Canada. So, banks with ATMs in Canada must also have processing centers in Canada to process the transactions as they occur. Other countries choose to transmit ATM transaction information to processing centers in the United States. That information is then processed in the United States and transmitted back to the original country.

As organizations move information around the globe, they must also consider the quality and type of technology. Some countries have high-quality technology for moving information, while others do not. And some countries have slow-moving phone lines only for moving information, while others support satellite transmission. Whatever the case, transborder data flows are a challenge for any transnational firm.

making **the grade**   SECTION E://

1. _telocomuth_ is the use of various technologies to allow employees to work in a place other than a central location.
2. A _transnationall firm_ produces and sells products and services in countries all over the world.
3. _____ is the collective personality of a nation or society.
4. _____ is the popular term for considering the movement of information around the globe and the technologies that do it.

i·witness

An Up-Close Look at Web Sites

Web Hosting

Once you've developed your Web site, you'll want to share it with others by placing it on the Web. To do this, you may need a Web hosting service or Web host. As we discussed in Chapter 4, a Web host is a service that provides disk space to you for your Web site on a Web server.

To choose a Web host, ask yourself a few questions about your needs and your budget.

Do I Need a Web Host?

If you want to post your Web site just for friends or family, see if your school or your ISP already provides Web space. Having 5 or 10MB is plenty of room for a Web site with a few pages and photos.

If you're starting your own e-business, you'll need to purchase space from a Web host and get a domain name.

How Much Should I Pay?

If you don't have much money, consider using a free Web host. Places such as www.geocities.com offer free personal Web space and www.bizland.com offers free space for businesses.

Free Web hosts make money by displaying banner ads on your Web site. For a monthly fee ($20 and up), you can use a Web host that doesn't display banner ads.

How Much Web Space Do I Need?

This depends on what you want to do with your Web site. You'll need a lot of space if you plan on storing images, video, audio, and other multimedia elements. An e-business may need to store Web catalogs and a Web database. For most people, though, 10MB is plenty of room.

The links below show different types of Web hosting plans. These may include secure transactions, Microsoft FrontPage support, and databases.

- www.tripod.com
- www.123hostme.com
- www.interland.net

In one year, 440 IRS employees were investigated for browsing through the tax records of neighbors, acquaintances, or celebrities.

did you know?

F://SUMMARY AND KEY TERMS

Computers are in fact the heavy artillery in business, supporting everything from tracking internal quality information to transborder data flows.

An organization typically consists of four levels:

- *Strategic management*—which provides an organization with overall direction and guidance.
- *Tactical management*—which develops the goals and strategies outlined by strategic management.
- *Operational management*—which manages and directs the day-to-day operations and implementation of the goals and strategies.
- *Nonmanagement employees*—who actually perform daily activities.

Today, organizations employ a combination of ***decentralized computing*** and ***shared information*** so that employees can access whatever information they need. That information may be ***internal***, ***external***, ***objective***, ***subjective***, or some combination of the four. And as information moves throughout the organization, it does so in an upward, downward, and/or horizontal fashion.

Computer systems help organizations track all types of information:

- **Transaction processing system**—a system that processes transactions that occur within an organization.
- **Customer-integrated system**—an extension of a transaction processing system that places technology in the hands of an organization's customers.
- **Management information system**—a system that provides periodic and predetermined reports that summarize information.
- **Executive information system**—a highly flexible management information system that helps managers solve problems and take advantage of opportunities.

Computer systems and technologies can also support organizational logistics:

- **Intranet**—an internal organizational Internet that is guarded against outside access by a special security mechanism.
- **Extranet**—an extension of an intranet that allows other organizations and people access to information and application software on an internal intranet.
- **Workgroup support system**—a system that is designed to improve the performance of teams by supporting the sharing and flow of information (includes the software component of **groupware**).

Finally, computer systems and technologies support organizations as they spread out nationally and around the globe. In either case, technology supports **telecommuting**—the use of various technologies (especially telecommunications technologies) to allow employees **(telecommuters)** to work in a place other than a central location. A **transnational firm** produces and sells products and services in countries all over the world. To do this, transnational firms face the challenges of cultural differences and transborder data flows.

On the Web site for this text at www.mhhe.com/i-series, we've provided a great deal of support. There, you can learn more about:

- Total quality management and business process reengineering
- Leasing a computer
- Groupware suites
- Cultural oddities
- Web hosting services

KEY TERMS

comparative report (p. 12.11)

culture (p. 12.23)

customer-integrated system (CIS) (p. 12.9)

decentralized computing (p. 12.4)

downward flow of information (p. 12.7)

electronic bulletin board (p. 12.18)

electronic meeting software (p. 12.18)

exception report (p. 12.11)

executive information system (EIS) (p. 12.12)

external information (p. 12.6)

extranet (p. 12.16)

group document database (p. 12.18)

group scheduling software (p. 12.18)

groupware (p. 12.17)

horizontal flow of information (p. 12.7)

information granularity (p. 12.5)

internal information (p. 12.6)

intranet (p. 12.15)

management information system (MIS) (p. 12.11)

objective information (p. 12.6)

operational management (p. 12.3)

periodic report (p. 12.11)

shared information (p. 12.4)

strategic management (p. 12.3)

subjective information (p. 12.6)

summarized report (p. 12.11)

tactical management (p. 12.3)

telecommuter (p. 12.20)

telecommuting (p. 12.20)

transaction processing system (TPS) (p. 12.8)

transnational firm (p. 12.22)

upward flow of information (p. 12.6)

videoconferencing software (p. 12.18)

whiteboard software (p. 12.18)

workgroup support system (WSS) (p. 12.17)

CROSSWORD PUZZLE

Across

1. Software for writing and recording notes on a presentation
3. Extension of a TPS
7. Collective personality of a group of people
8. Person who doesn't work in the office
9. Report that illustrates a relationship
11. Unknown information
13. Side-to-side flow of information
14. Report produced at a regular time interval
16. Flow of information from the top to bottom
18. Report that uses selection criteria
19. System for supporting groups
21. Technology spread throughout the organization
23. System that processes transactions
24. Lets your customers into your intranet
25. Information that describes the workings of your organization
26. Internal Internet

Down

2. Lowest level of management
4. Report that aggregates information
5. Top-level management
6. Level of information detail
8. Firm that operates all over the world
10. System that produces reports
12. Highly flexible MIS
15. Information surrounding your organization
17. Quantifiably known information
20. Information that everyone can use
22. Information flow that starts at the bottom

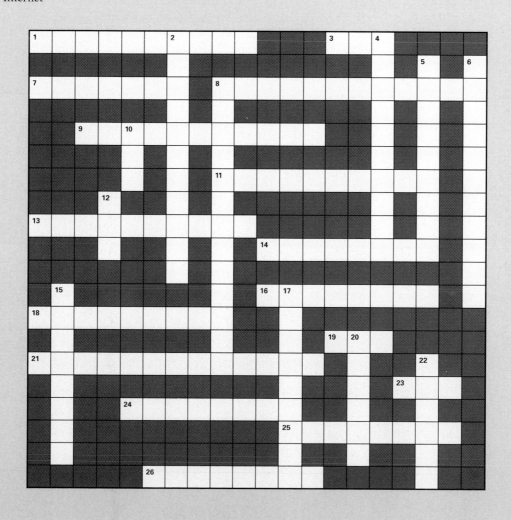

QUESTIONS AND EXERCISES

Multiple Choice

1. The concept that states that employees should have access to whatever information they need is

   a. shared information.
   b. decentralized computing.
   c. drilling down.
   d. transborder data flow.
   e. upward flow of information.

2. Detailed information exhibits

   a. objective information only.
   b. a coarse level of granularity.
   c. a fine level of granularity.
   d. subjective information only.
   e. internal information only.

3. The _____ flow of information describes the state of the organization based on its transactions.

   a. downward
   b. horizontal
   c. upward
   d. internal
   e. sideways

4. A customer-integrated system (CIS) is an extension of a(n)

   a. TPS.
   b. MIS.
   c. WSS.
   d. EIS.
   e. BIS.

5. A _____ report shows two or more sets of information in an attempt to illustrate a relationship.

   a. comparative
   b. exception
   c. internal
   d. periodic
   e. summarized

6. You can allow people and organizations access to information and application software on an intranet through a(n)

   a. firewall.
   b. TPS.
   c. MIS.
   d. extranet.
   e. EIS.

7. Groupware suites include support for

   a. team dynamics.
   b. document management.
   c. applications development.
   d. all of the above.
   e. none of the above.

8. For communications, groupware supports such technologies as

   a. intranets.
   b. e-mail.
   c. electronic bulletin boards.
   d. all of the above.
   e. none of the above.

9. Software that helps a team have a face-to-face meeting when members are geographically dispersed is

   a. videoconferencing.
   b. virtual.
   c. electronic meeting.
   d. group scheduling.
   e. whiteboard.

10. Software that lets a team have a meeting, view a presentation, and record electronic notes is called

    a. videoconferencing.
    b. virtual.
    c. electronic meeting.
    d. group scheduling.
    e. whiteboard.

True/False

11. ____ Business today is global business.

12. ____ CISs can be found only on extranets.

13. ____ The chief operating officer (COO) is a part of tactical management.

14. ____ EISs can summarize information but cannot help solve problems or take advantage of opportunities.

15. ____ A periodic report is produced at a predetermined time.

QUESTIONS AND EXERCISES

1. In the table, we've listed the major types of computer systems we discussed in this chapter in the rows. The columns identify five major information-processing tasks—gathering, presenting, processing to create new information, storing, and communicating. Identify which of the information-processing tasks each system is primarily responsible for by placing a "P" (for primary) in the appropriate blank or blanks. If you think a given system includes one or more secondary responsibilities, place an "S" in the appropriate blank or blanks.

System	Gathering	Presenting	Processing to Create New	Storing	Communicating
Transaction processing	_____	_____	_____	_____	_____
Customer-integrated	_____	_____	_____	_____	_____
Management information	_____	_____	_____	_____	_____
Executive information	_____	_____	_____	_____	_____
Workgroup support	_____	_____	_____	_____	_____

2. Types of information include internal, external, objective, and subjective. And often you need them all to make an effective decision. Consider a local convenience store that sells gasoline. What information does it need to set the price per gallon? Complete the table below by listing the specific pieces of information in the appropriate area.

INTERNAL

_____

_____

_____

EXTERNAL

_____

_____

_____

OBJECTIVE

_____

_____

_____

SUBJECTIVE

_____

_____

_____

3. For each of the following answers, create the question:

ANSWER	QUESTION
A. CIO, for example.	_____
B. Detailed sales transactions.	_____
C. Closing price of a stock.	_____
D. Accounts payable.	_____
E. Buying concert tickets on the Web.	_____
F. The same as an MIS but more flexible with drilling down capabilities.	_____

e-commerce

1. Buying a Car

Buying a car has typically been an "experiential" shopping excursion. That is, most people really need to drive different cars, get a feel for how they handle, and just smell the interior. Of course, you have to put up with a salesperson, but nonetheless when it comes to a car, most people want to "try before they buy." Well, once you do decide on the perfect car, you should still shop the Web for the best deal and financing. Below, we've listed four Web sites where you can do just that.

- CarsDirect—www.carsdirect.com
- AutoWeb—www.autoweb.lycos.com
- autobytel—www.autobytel.com
- Edmunds.com—www.edmunds.com

Think of a car you'd like to own (realistically), visit each site, and answer the following questions.

a. How do you search for a car?

b. Does the site inform you of the closest dealer who has the car you want?

c. Can you simply buy your car on the Web and have it delivered to your driveway?

d. What about financing options? Does the site offer you those?

e. Does the site provide unbiased rankings of automobiles?

f. Can you find used cars?

Would you ever really consider buying a car on the Web without first test-driving one at a local dealership? And what about your local dealership? How does its prices compare to the prices on the Web? Cheaper? More expensive?

2. Finding Pet Supplies

Many of us love pets and have one. According to one poll, almost 70 percent of American households have pets. Actually there are more pets in the United States than there are households. So, it only makes sense that you would find pet stores on the Web. Some even sell pets and ship them to you—don't worry, it's safe. Below, we've listed four pet store Web sites.

- PetProducts.com—www.petsupplies.com
- PETsMART.com—www.petsmart.com
- Noah's Pets—www.noahpets.com
- PetMarket—www.petmarket.com

Think about the type of pet products you buy and visit a couple of these Web sites to see what they offer. If you don't have a pet, think about the products you would need if you did. Answer the following questions for each Web site you visit.

a. Can you find the pet products you need?

b. How do you search for products—by pet, by manufacturer, or by other means?

c. How do you pay for products you want?

d. What is the shipping time for products?

e. Do you have to pay for shipping?

f. Can you register yourself as a pet owner and receive e-mails about product promotions?

g. Can you find medical advice for an ill pet?

e-commerce

3. Buying Sports Gear

Sports is big business on the Web. You can check scores, visit your favorite team, and even place legal bets on games around the world. You can also find sites dedicated to selling you sports gear—equipment you need for playing sports, sports memorabilia, and sports apparel such as sweatshirts and T-shirts. Below, we've listed four such sites.

- Gear.com—www.gear.com
- MVP.com—www.mvp.com
- Foot Locker—www.footlocker.com
- Sports fan—www.sportsfan.com

Visit two of these sites and answer the following questions.

a. Can you find sports equipment? If so, for what sports?

b. Can you find sports memorabilia?

c. Can you find sports apparel?

d. Is the sports apparel "official" merchandise of a certain league?

e. Can you search for products by team name? By player name? By sport?

f. Do any of these sites give you the ability to read about players or perhaps talk with them in a chat room? How about live video?

g. Can you watch games at any of these sites or perhaps highlights of games?

4. Finding Your Dream Home

You can't actually live on or in the Web, although some people seem to try. But on the Web you can find real estate for sale and rent. For example, you can search apartment complexes in your neighborhood, buy a timeshare condo in Florida (or just about anywhere else in the world), and find homes for sale. Let's concentrate on residential homes for sale. Connect to two of the sites listed below.

- iOwn.com—www.homescoutiown.com
- Home Connections—www.ihomes.com
- homebuilder.com—www.homebuilder.com
- homestore.com—www.homestore.com

Pick anywhere in the United States you'd like to live. Now, search your chosen sites for available homes. As you do, perform the following tasks.

a. Search for a home in a particular price range.

b. Search for a home according to a time period in which it was built.

c. Search for a home with special features such as a swimming pool or a view of the mountains.

d. Check for available financing options and interest rates.

Did you find any homes? Were you able to view photos of various homes from the interior, exterior, or both? What did you think of your home shopping experience? If you moved to a new city and needed a home, would you start shopping on the Web first? Why or why not?

on the web

1. Customer-Integrated Systems on the Web

Examples of customer-integrated systems (CISs) are all over the Web. These systems simply give you the ability to perform your own transaction processing. Prepare for your class a demonstration of a Web site with CIS capabilities. As you provide your demonstration, point out the aspects of the Web site that include gathering, presenting, processing to create new information, storing, and communicating information. Finally, many people say that CISs must be "idiot proof," because anyone should be able to use them without any training. How would you evaluate the Web site you've chosen? Is it really idiot proof? What defines a Web site as being idiot proof?

2. Learning about Quality Awards

Organizations wanting to improve their quality and demonstrate it to their customers often follow the guidelines of various quality awards. Two such awards are the Baldrige Award and the Deming Award. Choose one and do a little research on the Web. Your report should include (1) the nature of the award, (2) the criteria for winning the award, (3) the organization which sponsors the award, and (4) past winners of the award. Does winning a quality award really mean that an organization produces quality? Does it mean that an organization will be successful? What Web sites did you find that were the most comprehensive in covering quality awards?

3. Shared Information at Your School

In some form or fashion, your school provides shared information on its Web site. Visit your school's Web site and find examples of shared information that you have access to. What type of information is it? Why would your school allow students to have access to that information? Now, what information does your school not provide on its Web site that you would like to see? Should your school be sharing this type of information on its Web site? Are there any legal or ethical ramifications if your school were to make this type of information available?

4. Illustrating Executive Information System "Drilling Down"

On the Web site for this text at www.mhhe.com/i-series (click on "Chapter 12"), you'll find a spreadsheet named CH12eis.xls. It includes information concerning a call center. The following specific information is provided:

Column A—the date a call came in

Column B—the employee who answered the call

Column C—the customer who made the call

Column D—the length of the call

Column E—the nature of the call

Your task is to develop a series of three or four graphs that illustrate the concept of drilling down in an EIS. So, your first graph should provide highly summarized information, and your last graph should provide the most detail. You can refer back to Figure 12.11 on page 12.13 for an example of drilling down with an EIS.

ethics, security & privacy

1. The Ethics of Business Process Reengineering

Many times, a business process reengineering (BPR) effort not only streamlines processes but also puts people out of a job. Indeed, many businesses have undergone BPR efforts and been able to cut hundreds of employees. The question becomes an ethical one. Should employees lose their jobs because a business finds a better way to use fewer employees and more technology? Should businesses be responsible for "retooling" employees and finding them other jobs? For each of the following real-life BPR efforts that have reduced the number of employees, be prepared to justify what you think the organization should do with displaced employees.

a. Wireless meter reading—no longer do meter readers have to walk through a neighborhood. Instead, just a few drive through and capture the readings with wireless technologies.

b. Computer-aided manufacturing—essentially robotics in manufacturing that make many assembly line workers unnecessary.

c. Self-scanning at a grocery store—meaning that fewer checkout clerks are needed.

d. School registration on the Web—which means your school doesn't need as many clerks to register you for classes.

e. Electronic tax filing—meaning the government will need fewer IRS workers.

f. ATMs—so banks don't have to have as many tellers.

g. Automated directory assistance—so phone companies don't have to have as many operators.

2. Breaking through a Firewall

Many businesses today boast of secure and private intranets. On these intranets, employees can share vitally important and sensitive organizational and personal information. But what if a hacker figures out how to break into an intranet? Consider the following question: Is the organization responsible to its employees in some way for the loss of the privacy of their personal information caused by a hacker? Answer the preceding question for each of the following scenarios:

a. The firewall implemented by the organization is known to be easy to break through.

b. An employee inside the organization shut down the firewall letting anyone in.

c. The firewall had heretofore never been breached in any of its implementations.

d. It took a team of 100 hackers over six months to break through the firewall.

e. Some sort of "computer glitch" caused the firewall to shut down. The nature of the glitch was never discovered and simply went away over time.

f. The organization had required every employee to sign a release stating that the organization was not responsible if the firewall failed.

g. A new computer virus caused the firewall to fail.

h. The intranet was actually an extranet and one of the organization's customers gave away the password.

group activities

1. Your School's Organizational Structure

Organizations come in all shapes, sizes, forms, and structures. What does your school's organizational structure look like? Draw its structure in the form of a hierarchy from the very top down to the departmental level. How many levels are there? What is considered strategic management, tactical management, and operational management? What are some upward, downward, and horizontal flows of information that occur within your school? Does your school use any subjective or external information to make decisions? What is that information and what decisions do they support?

2. Evaluating a Utility Bill

Find a utility bill, perhaps for your electricity, cable TV, or phone. As you examine it, answer the following questions:

a. What parts of it constitute a report from a transaction processing system?

b. What parts of it constitute a report from a management information system?

c. Is the MIS portion periodic, comparative, exception, summarized, or some combination of the four?

d. Why would an organization provide you as a customer with a form of an MIS report? How does that information help you?

3. Building Management Information System Reports

On the Web site for this text at www.mhhe.com/i-series (click on "Chapter 12"), you'll find a spreadsheet file called ch12mis.xls. It contains a list of real estate transactions for an area of the country. The following specific information is provided:

> Column A—county name in which the home resides
>
> Column B—name of builder of the home
>
> Column C—year in which the home was built
>
> Column D—asking price for the home
>
> Column E—selling price for the home
>
> Column F—days it took to sell the home

Your task is to download that file (the instructions are on the Web site), use your spreadsheet software, and generate MIS reports. You must generate at least five reports—one summarized, one exception, one comparative, one periodic, and one that's some combination of at least two of the others. Did any of your reports reveal problems or opportunities?

4. Types of Information for Setting Interest Rates

Consider a bank that offers interest rates on CDs. Banks do have some flexibility in setting those interest rates. What sort of information do you think a bank uses to set interest rates? Complete the table below. In the first column, identify specific information that would go into the decision-making process. In the remaining columns, place a check mark identifying what type of information it is.

Information Used	Internal	External	Objective	Subjective
_____	_____	_____	_____	_____
_____	_____	_____	_____	_____
_____	_____	_____	_____	_____
_____	_____	_____	_____	_____
_____	_____	_____	_____	_____

Looking Back/Looking Ahead

The Life and Times of a Dot-Com Entrepreneur

Joann is really getting excited about her new Web-based business. She's developed or acquired all the hardware and software she needs, and she's built her Web site. Customers are beginning to find her Web site, and she's starting to make money.

Now, Joann is focusing on her needs as an organization. She's the only person in her business right now, so she's a(n) _____ manager, a(n) _____ manager, a(n) _____ manager, and the employee who does all the work. As she sets goals and directions, she needs information with a _____ granularity, while she needs information with a _____ granularity to process her daily transactions.

For processing her daily transactions, Joann uses a _____ internally. And she's given her customers the ability to process their own transactions by providing a _____ on the Web.

As a manager, she needs to make decisions. So, she generates several different types of reports with a _____. These reports can be _____, _____, _____, _____, or perhaps some combination of the four. Her _____ is also flexible so she can _____ through information to determine the causes of problems and how to take advantage of an opportunity. This makes her _____ an _____.

Because she's the only employee, Joann doesn't have much need for a _____ that supports team efforts. However, she can use _____ software to have meetings with her suppliers.

Finally, Joann knows she needs to expand internationally, making her business a _____. As she does, she'll have to modify the way she performs some business aspects to take into account the _____ of the people she's doing business with.

As Joann looks forward, she has one remaining task. She needs to learn about various computer systems that can aid her in making good business decisions. She'll learn about those in Chapter 13.

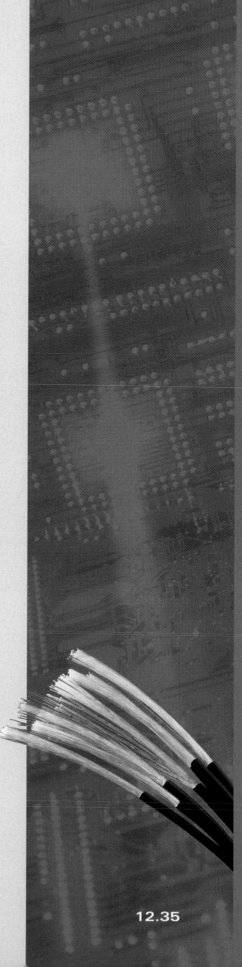

CHAPTER

13

thirteen

Computer Brainpower

How Can You Use Your Computer to Help You Think?

You make countless ordinary decisions every day. You also make decisions from time to time that are not everyday decisions—where you should send your college application, what job to take, whom to marry. Your decisions affect your future and every action has consequences. For the serious situations, if you don't make the right decision, you have to fix it, find a way out or a way to live with the consequences.

In the business world, it's no different. Managers make decisions every day, some more consequential than others. For the complicated decisions, computers can help. Computer-aided decision software falls into four major categories.

1. Decision support software that helps you analyze information to aid your decision-making. For example,

    • Specific decision support systems such as those for financial planning.

    • Geographic information systems that show information in map form.

2. Artificial intelligence software that can make decisions or perform tasks for you on its own. Examples of this software are

    • Expert systems

    • Neural networks

    • Genetic algorithms

    • Fuzzy logic

3. Intelligent agent software that handles repetitive tasks such as searching and retrieving, and monitoring.

4. Data mining software that uses analysis and artificial intelligence tools to predict trends and discover new relationships in the information stored in a data warehouse.

The CEO of Intel predicts that there will be 1 billion computers connected to the Internet by the year 2004.

did you know?

A://DECISION SUPPORT SOFTWARE

In this section we'll first examine a relatively simple decision situation to see how decision support software can help you. Then we'll discuss decision support systems (DSS) in general. We'll finish with geographic information systems which show information in map form. But first a few words about types of decisions.

Decisions can be structured or unstructured or somewhere in between (see Figure 13.1). A *structured decision* is one that you can make by applying a formula. With a structured decision you punch in the right numbers, do the arithmetic correctly, and get the right answer—guaranteed. An *unstructured decision* is one for which there is no guaranteed way to get a precise right answer. In fact, there may be many "right" answers. You can only guess since none of us knows for sure what the future holds (psychics notwithstanding). In reality, most decisions have structured and unstructured parts. The following situation is an example.

WHAT JOB DO I TAKE?

Advancement Opportunity   Salary

Nonstructured   Somewhere in between   Structured

FIGURE   13.1

Decisions range from the totally unstructured to the totally structured. Most decisions fall somewhere in between.

DECISION MAKING WITH PERSONAL PRODUCTIVITY SOFTWARE

How Could I Use a Decision Support System?

Suppose you're trying to decide on financing for a car that costs $10,000. Your choices are

- Three years at 8.25 percent interest.
- Four years at 9.25 percent interest.
- $1,000 down and three years at 8 percent interest.

Which option should you take? This is an example of a decision that has structured and unstructured parts. The structured part is calculating the monthly payments and what the total amount you pay for the car will be when you're finished making the payments.

The unstructured part of this car-buying decision is determining what's best for your financial situation. That's not as easy as applying a formula. This decision requires knowledge about your current financial situation, assumptions about the future, and some good guesses.

An ordinary spreadsheet, such as Microsoft's Excel, is an example of software that you can use to construct your own decision support system and analyze your options. You can look at the numbers, try different possibilities, and compare the results. But first, you need to build an amortization table (see Figure 13.2 at the top of the next page) which shows, in tabular form, the progress of your loan during the loan period.

F I G U R E   13.2

You can use a spreadsheet to analyze your car-buying options.

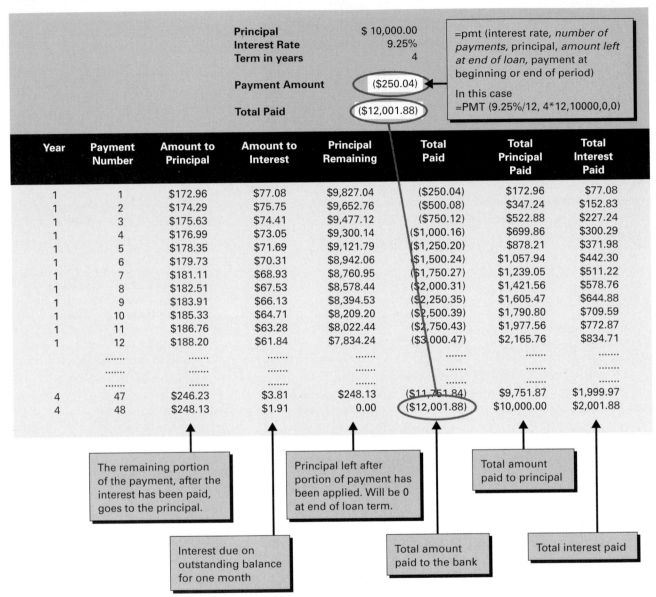

Year	Payment Number	Amount to Principal	Amount to Interest	Principal Remaining	Total Paid	Total Principal Paid	Total Interest Paid
				Principal	$ 10,000.00		
				Interest Rate	9.25%		
				Term in years	4		
				Payment Amount	($250.04)		
				Total Paid	($12,001.88)		
1	1	$172.96	$77.08	$9,827.04	($250.04)	$172.96	$77.08
1	2	$174.29	$75.75	$9,652.76	($500.08)	$347.24	$152.83
1	3	$175.63	$74.41	$9,477.12	($750.12)	$522.88	$227.24
1	4	$176.99	$73.05	$9,300.14	($1,000.16)	$699.86	$300.29
1	5	$178.35	$71.69	$9,121.79	($1,250.20)	$878.21	$371.98
1	6	$179.73	$70.31	$8,942.06	($1,500.24)	$1,057.94	$442.30
1	7	$181.11	$68.93	$8,760.95	($1,750.27)	$1,239.05	$511.22
1	8	$182.51	$67.53	$8,578.44	($2,000.31)	$1,421.56	$578.76
1	9	$183.91	$66.13	$8,394.53	($2,250.35)	$1,605.47	$644.88
1	10	$185.33	$64.71	$8,209.20	($2,500.39)	$1,790.80	$709.59
1	11	$186.76	$63.28	$8,022.44	($2,750.43)	$1,977.56	$772.87
1	12	$188.20	$61.84	$7,834.24	($3,000.47)	$2,165.76	$834.71
...	...	...	...	...	...	...	...
4	47	$246.23	$3.81	$248.13	($11,751.84)	$9,751.87	$1,999.97
4	48	$248.13	$1.91	0.00	($12,001.88)	$10,000.00	$2,001.88

=pmt (interest rate, *number of payments*, principal, *amount left at end of loan*, payment at beginning or end of period)

In this case
=PMT (9.25%/12, 4*12,10000,0,0)

The remaining portion of the payment, after the interest has been paid, goes to the principal.

Principal left after portion of payment has been applied. Will be 0 at end of loan term.

Total amount paid to principal

Interest due on outstanding balance for one month

Total amount paid to the bank

Total interest paid

The amortization table will be the basis of your DSS. To construct it, you need to know what information is important and understand the relationships inherent in that information. For example, you need to relate principal, interest rate, loan term, and payments. Fortunately, Excel has a function (the PMT function) to calculate your payment. You need to know that car loan interest rates are usually quoted as yearly rates, but for the Excel PMT function you need to divide the annual rate by 12 to achieve a monthly rate, since car payments are usually monthly.

When you've entered the data and formulas, you're ready to analyze the information—that's the decision support part of the exercise. You would enter different values for the variables to see how the payments and total amount you'll pay for the car vary. The amortization table enhanced with the ability to change values and view the results constitutes a decision support system.

	Options	Payment	Total Cost of Car
Option 1	$10,000 @ 8.25% for 3 years	$314.52	$11,322.66
Option 2	$10,000 @ 9.25% for 4 years	$250.04	$12,001.88
Option 3	$9,000 @ 8% for 3 years with $1,000 down	$282.03	$10,152.98 + $1,000 (to the bank) (down)

FIGURE   13.3

With option 3 you'll pay the lowest total amount for the car, but the lowest monthly payments come from option 2.

When you've tried several different values, you'll have a concrete basis for making your decision. This type of analysis is called a "what-if analysis" and helps you to decide between different options.

The lowest payments come from the second option of $10,000 at 9.25 percent for four years (see Figure 13.3). And the lowest overall total cost of the car is in the third option ($1,000 down and $9,000 at 8 percent for three years). The shorter the loan term, the less it costs in the long run, other things being equal.

Of course, getting those numbers is only half the battle. You still have to decide what's right for you. You may not have $1,000 right now that you can use as a down payment. You may be living on a restricted budget that makes the lowest possible payments your immediate concern. You'll also need to estimate your financial future. The idea of a DSS is to let you look at alternatives, taking all relevant circumstances into consideration, so that you can make a more informed, and therefore better, decision.

DECISION SUPPORT SYSTEMS

What's a Decision Support System?

In its narrowest sense, a **decision support system (DSS)** is software that uses models, information, and an interactive user interface to help you make decisions. A DSS lets you look at information in different ways to help you come to a conclusion about what the best course of action might be for a certain situation. Usually a DSS is software that requires a lot of input from you (see Figure 13.4).

You Contribute . . .	. . . and Gain the Advantages of a DSS
• Experience	• Increased productivity
• Intuition	• Increased understanding
• Judgment	• Increased speed
• Knowledge	• Increased flexibility
	• Reduced problem complexity
	• Reduced cost

FIGURE   13.4

Decision support software helps you make the most of your own decision-making talents.

F I G U R E   13.5

A decision support system helps you analyze options and make a decision.

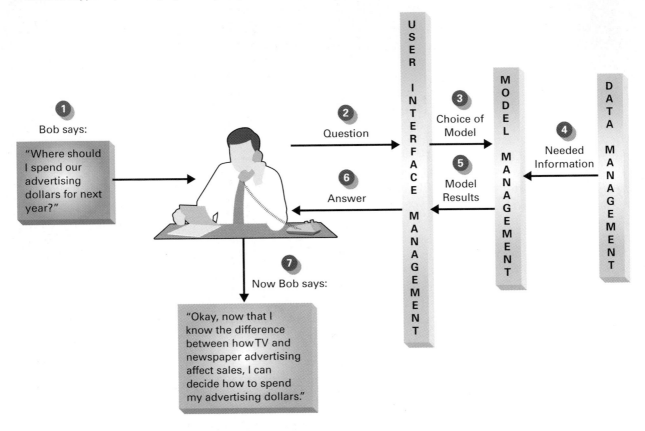

Decision Support System Components

Our Excel DSS from the last section has the three features that you expect to find in a DSS. It has a model, data, and a user interface (see Figure 13.5).

1. **Model Management:** The model management component of a DSS handles the models. A *model* is a representation of reality. Model airplanes and cars are small physical versions of the real thing. Mathematical or financial models are representations of the relationship between variables. In our example, the formulas of the amortization table form the model. The model is simply the mathematical representation of how the different values, such as the principal and monthly payments, are linked to each other.

2. **Data Management:** Data or information, in this case, consists of the details of the particular case you're interested in and other pertinent information. The information that we used in the example was the numeric values of the variables, that is, the set of numbers that fit each of the three cases—principal, interest rate, and term of the loan.

3. **User Interface Management:** A *user interface* is the manner in which you communicate with the software package. It's what you use to manipulate the information. The Excel screen with its rows and columns, menus and buttons, is the user interface in our example. You can use the user interface to change numbers and see the results

of the changes in the DSS we created. A DSS typically has an interactive user interface so that you can change values easily as we did in the car-buying example.

Business Decision Support Systems

There are many other types of decision support systems besides the one we built for the car-buying "what-if" analysis. A DSS is often very sophisticated software for analyzing information. For example, an insurance company constantly assesses its risk when selling different policies. That's why your age, the type of car, and perhaps your marital status will all be factors the company will use to decide how much you'll have to pay for car insurance. For example, someone probably used a DSS to determine that young single men who drive performance vehicles are the most likely to have accidents and how much it costs to insure those drivers. Examples of other business tasks that lend themselves to the use of a DSS are:

- Deciding where to spend advertising dollars.
- Analyzing sales trend information.
- Analyzing drug interactions.
- Developing airline schedules.
- Developing asset portfolios.

You can easily think of others. A DSS usually gets the information it analyzes from the transaction processing systems (which we discussed in the previous chapter) of the organization. But while a transaction processing system (TPS) provides great detail and a management information system (MIS) summarizes what happened, a DSS tries to use the past to peek into the future and decide how best to proceed.

The types of models that a DSS uses include simulation, optimization, goal-seeking, and statistical techniques, as well as "what-if" models (see Figure 13.6). For example, suppose you just bought a newsstand and are trying to decide which newspapers and magazines to stock and how many of each. If you have too few copies of a popular magazine and run out of it, customers will go elsewhere and you'll lose those sales and possibly future sales too. If you have too many copies of the magazine, however, you'll either have to absorb the loss or, at the very least, pay for shipping the extra copies back to the publisher.

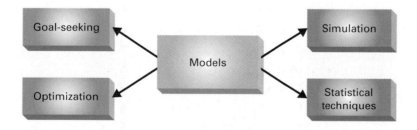

FIGURE 13.6

Types of decision support system models are many and varied.

You could use a simulation to help you decide. That would involve estimating demand, which may be constant or changing, and calculating the profit or loss at varying levels of inventory. You could "run the stand" electronically for a number of months and see how it turns out.

i·series insights

Ethics, Security & Privacy

Mapping Your Nose

You might be surprised to learn that one of the surgical procedures most prone to malpractice lawsuits is the nasal surgery that is done to alleviate allergy symptoms or to improve breathing. One of the big problems with nasal surgery is simply the location of the nose. It's so close to the eyes and brain that mishaps can turn into tragedies. Occasionally the optic nerve is accidentally cut during nasal surgery, resulting in blindness or near blindness for the patient.

Many nasal surgeries are conducted with an endoscope, a thin, flexible wire with a tiny camera on the tip, which allows the surgeon to "see" inside small tight places such as nasal passages. With the image from the camera displayed on a

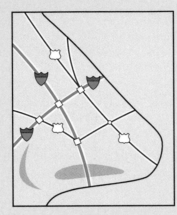

large monitor, the surgeon can use scalpels, needles, and forceps to perform the necessary procedure.

To allow surgeons to train for this tricky procedure, Lockheed Martin has developed a nasal cavity simulation "road map." Many,

many razor-thin cross-sectional pictures of actual nasal passages are stored in a database and can be viewed as a three-dimensional picture. To allow surgeons to practice their skills, Lockheed installed this picture of nasal terrain into a mannequin that is used for virtual nasal operations at training hospitals.

The nasal-terrain simulator is an adaptation of a system that Lockheed developed for the Swedish Air Force. That system mapped the terrain of northern Europe. The main alteration that Lockheed made was to shift the emphasis from speed, which the fighter pilots need most, to precision, which the surgeons need most. Whether it's Europe or your nose— help with navigation is the key.

Alternatively, you could use an optimization model, which if properly constructed, would give you the optimum number of newspapers and magazines to stock and sell for the greatest profit. Optimization models are used to calculate the most profitable, or least costly, mix of products.

Of course, the accuracy and helpfulness of the results of any model depend on the correctness of the relationships or formulas, how accurate the estimates are, and the validity of any underlying assumptions. For more information on decision support systems, visit our Web site at www.mhhe.com/i-series.

GEOGRAPHIC INFORMATION SYSTEMS (GIS)

What's a Geographic Information System?

Suppose you drive a delivery van. Which of the following would you rather have?

1. A table that shows a list of the pickup and delivery addresses with text information about where each is located.

2. A map that shows the location of all your customers and what you're supposed to pick up or deliver.

Probably you'd rather have the map, as most people would. This kind of flexible map information is called a geographic information system.

F I G U R E   13.7

A geographic information system
represents information in layers.

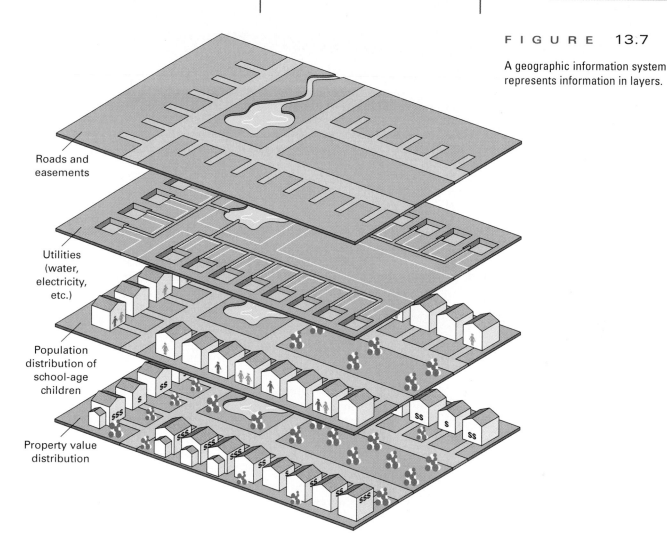

Roads and
easements

Utilities
(water,
electricity,
etc.)

Population
distribution of
school-age
children

Property value
distribution

A *geographic information system (GIS)* is software that allows you
to see information in map form. The value of a GIS is in its visual representation of information. A GIS takes traditional map information and
combines it with other information from databases or spreadsheets and
represents the information in layers. You can choose the layers you want
to see in the picture and thus get a complete image of all the information
you need in graphic form (see Figure 13.7). A GIS can take thousands of
rows of spreadsheet information and display it in map form, perhaps even
with 3-D graphics and animation. You can usually see more information
more quickly this way than you can with huge tables.

You can also combine a GIS with a global positioning system. A *global
positioning system (GPS)* is a device that tells you your current latitude,
longitude, speed, and direction of movement. Companies that deal in
transportation use GISs combined with database and GPS technology. For
example, airlines and shipping companies can plot routes with up-to-the-
minute information on the location of all their transport vehicles. Hospitals can keep track of where personnel are located by using a GIS and sensors in the ceiling that pick up the transmissions of badges worn by
hospital staff. It's almost like *Star Trek* except that the computers don't
hold everyday conversations with you.

making **the grade**

1. Software that has models, information, and a user interface to help you make decisions is called a(n) _____.
2. A(n) _____ is a representation of reality.
3. Information is stored in layers in a(n) _____.
4. A(n) _____ is a device that tells you where you are.

B://ARTIFICIAL INTELLIGENCE

As you saw in the last section, a decision support system augments your own brainpower. It allows you to analyze information as an aid to decision making, but you have to make the final decision.

A different type of computer-aided decision software is artificial intelligence. ***Artificial intelligence (AI)*** is the science of making machines imitate human thinking and behavior. Robots are an example of an artificial intelligence system. A ***robot*** is an artificial intelligence device with simulated human senses capable of taking action on its own. For example, bomb squads use a bomb-retrieving robot. When they get a report that there's a bomb in a building, they can send in the robot equipped with cameras to "take a look." Some of these robots are also able to disarm or even bring out the bomb by acting on commands sent by remote control. This keeps human beings out of harm's way.

ARTIFICIAL INTELLIGENCE SYSTEMS IN BUSINESS
How Does Business Use Artificial Intelligence?

In business decision-making, artificial intelligence is usually in software form. Financial analysts use a variety of artificial intelligence software to manage assets, invest in the stock market, and perform other financial operations. Hospitals use artificial intelligence in many capacities—scheduling staff, assigning beds, and diagnosing and treating illnesses. Many government agencies, including the IRS and the armed forces, use AI. Credit card companies use artificial intelligence to detect credit card fraud, and insurance companies use artificial intelligence techniques and software to ferret out fraudulent claims. Artificial intelligence lends itself to tasks as diverse as airline ticket pricing, food preparation, oil exploration, and child protection.

There is not yet any AI system that can truly replace human thinking, reasoning, and creativity. However, each AI system mimics some specific aspect of human thinking. The major categories of artificial intelligence software that people use in the decision-making process are

- *Expert systems,* which reason through problems and offer advice in the form of a conclusion or recommendation.
- *Neural networks,* which can be "trained" to recognize patterns.
- *Genetic algorithms,* which "learn" and produce increasingly better solutions to problems in a manner similar to the evolutionary process.
- *Fuzzy logic,* which is a way of reasoning with imprecise or partial information.

EXPERT SYSTEMS

What's "Expert" about an Expert System?

An **expert system,** also called a **knowledge-based system,** is an artificial intelligence system that applies reasoning capabilities to reach a conclusion. Expert systems are built for specific application areas, called *domains,* such as diagnosing a disease or determining how to fix a faulty engine. A common type of expert system is a rule-based expert system, which consists of a set of IF . . . THEN questions, called "rules." You answer those questions or rules according to your situation, and the expert system then reaches a conclusion.

Here's an example. Suppose you had an expert system in your car that would tell you what to do when approaching a traffic light. In this case, negotiating traffic lights would be the domain of the expert system. As you approach a green traffic light, you'll most likely proceed on through. If the light is red, you'll stop. If the light is yellow, however, you'll probably try to gauge whether you'll be able to make it through the intersection in time. Your traffic-light expert system would have a set of rules or questions—the kind of questions that you unconsciously ask yourself every time you sit behind the wheel of a vehicle, like "Can I stop without causing havoc or should I continue through the intersection on this yellow light?"

Look at Figure 13.8 for the sequence of questions.

FIGURE   13.8

An expert system asks the user questions and reaches a conclusion based on the answers.

Rule	Question	Yes	No	Explanation
1	Is the light green?	Go through the intersection.	Go to Rule 2.	Should be safe if light is green. If not, need more information.
2	Is the light red?	Go to Rule 4.	Go to Rule 3.	Should stop, may not be able to.
3	Is the light likely to change to red before you get through the intersection?	Go to Rule 4.	Go through the intersection.	Will only reach this point if light is yellow, then you'll have two choices.
4	Can you stop before entering the intersection?	Stop.	Go to Rule 5.	Should stop, but there may be a problem if you can't.
5	Is traffic approaching from either side?	Prepare to crash.	Go through the intersection.	Unless the intersection is clear of traffic, you're likely to crash.

Expert Systems are used in
- *Accounting,* for auditing, tax planning, and so on.
- *Medicine,* to prescribe antibiotics, taking into account the patient's medical history, source of the infection, the price of available drugs, and so on.
- *Process control,* for example, in lithographic printing.
- *Human resource management,* perhaps to determine if the organization is in compliance with federal employment laws.
- *Forestry management,* to plan tree cutting and planting.

Applications of **Neural Networks** include use
- In airports to find bombs in luggage by detecting their distinctive chemical patterns.
- By medical technicians to check for irregularities in human tissue in an effort to find early warning signs of cancer and other diseases.
- In the business world to assemble stock portfolios, detect fraud, evaluate credit applications, appraise real estate, and even read handwriting.

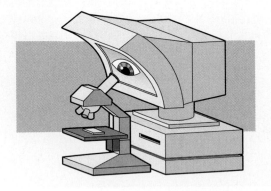

You use expert systems mainly to solve one of two kinds of problems: diagnostic and prescriptive. A diagnostic problem asks the question "what's wrong?" For example, if a car's transmission doesn't work, the car mechanic will ask you several questions and based on your answers to those questions he/she will ask some more questions. Eventually the mechanic may be able to tell what the problem is. Prescriptive problems ask the question "what to do?" like our traffic-light expert system did.

NEURAL NETWORKS

Doesn't "Neural" Have Something to Do with My Brain?

A neural network is so called because it simulates the human ability to classify. You learned to differentiate cars from trucks by seeing lots of examples of each type. You learned to look for certain discriminating characteristics, the truck bed or the distinctive cab, and used that information to tell the difference. In other words, you used pattern recognition to tell one type of vehicle from another.

A *neural network* is an artificial intelligence system that is capable of learning how to differentiate patterns. You would use a neural network when you have a vast amount of information to analyze and your objective is identification or classification. You train a neural network by feeding it hundreds, or thousands, of examples telling it what category each one belongs to. Then, on its own, the neural network "learns" what characteristics are important in differentiating type A from type B—just as you once did with cars and trucks.

Have you ever received a call from your credit card company asking you if a particular purchase was okay because the purchase was out of the ordinary? If so, the credit card company may well have been responding to its neural network's alert. Credit card companies use neural networks to compare past patterns of credit card usage with incoming purchase transactions. To train the neural network, the company provides it with details of numerous credit card histories and tells it which transactions are fraudulent. Eventually the neural network will learn to identify suspicious transactions on its own.

Another application area of neural networks is in spotting computer viruses. Symantec Corp. has introduced a version of its Norton AntiVirus software, which includes a neural network to help determine if a virus has found its way into your computer. The software, which was patented by IBM, can identify known and *unknown* viruses within minutes, allowing the company to provide a fix for the virus faster than the advertised 24 to 48 hours.

Automatic Speech Understanding

It is an old and often asked question—"Will we ever carry on normal conversations with our computers?" Many people will answer emphatically no. Their reasoning is simple. Carrying on a conversation requires intelligence, and computers do not have nor will they ever have true intelligence. Right now, they possess artificial intelligence, but the key word is "artificial," not intelligence.

For example, if someone says to you, "I have four computers," you would understand that the word "four" is in fact a number, not the word "for" as a preposition, or the word "fore." How do you know that? You know because of years of learning the differences and the meanings of the words.

So, the question really becomes, "Can we create computers that are capable of learning?" You've been exploring types of systems that mimic learning processes in this chapter. Genetic algorithms learn (after a fashion) by simply exhausting all possibilities to determine an optimal solution (we discuss these next). Expert systems use a set of rules (another type of learning) to reach a conclusion, and neural networks perform the learning process by creating associations with patterns.

If we combine all these, perhaps it is possible that we could create a "hybrid" intelligence system capable of true learning. If that's the case, then you will be able some day to carry on a normal conversation with your computer.

In that instance, your computer would literally learn along with you, from birth through the rest of your life. As an infant begins to make simple associations with words and later comes to understand rules of grammar, so would that infant's computer. And don't forget, computers will some day be so small that we'll carry them around with us (perhaps in the heels of our shoes).

So, what do we think? We believe that automatic speech understanding is a realistic possibility. When will it happen? Probably in your lifetime, maybe even 10 or so years from now. Current exploration and research are making great strides in the area of artificial intelligence. The goal of that research is to remove the term "artificial," making computers truly intelligent.

If that happens, you'll be carrying on conversations with your computer around 2010 or 2015.

GENETIC ALGORITHMS
What Does Genetics Have to Do with Computers?

When avid rose growers develop new roses, they usually try to grow a flower with one or more specific characteristics—no thorns, stronger stem, yellow flower, and so on. They combine individual roses that already have the desired characteristics to get a new rose. This is evolution, helped by humans. Believe it or not, businesses use a type of software that is based on the same evolutionary principle, called genetic algorithms. A *genetic algorithm* is an artificial intelligence system that mimics the evolutionary, survival-of-the-fittest process to generate increasingly better solutions to a problem.

Many problems exist that have an almost infinite number of possible solutions and it's very hard to find the one that's best. What managers usually do is find a solution that is as good as it can be, given the time constraints of producing it. But with a genetic algorithm, you let the computer use its extraordinary speed to examine many more solutions. The software evaluates these new solutions and, based on the best of those, generates even more solutions, repeating the process until it finds the best one it can.

Let's take an example using business finance. Suppose you were trying to decide what to put into your stock portfolio. You have countless stocks to choose from and a limited amount of money to invest. You might decide that you'd like to start with 20 stocks and you want a portfolio growth rate of at least 7.5 percent.

Probably you'd start by examining historic information on the stocks. You would take some number of stocks and combine them, 20 at a time, to see what happens with each grouping. If you wanted to choose from a pool of 30 stocks, you would have to examine 30,045,015 different combi-

nations. For a 40-stock pool, the number of combinations rises to 137,846,500,000. It would be an impossibly time-consuming, not to mention numbingly tedious, task to look at this many combinations and evaluate your overall return for each one. However, this is just the sort of repetitive number crunching task at which computers excel.

So instead of a pencil, paper, and calculator, you might use a genetic algorithm. You could input the appropriate information on the stocks, such as the number of years the company has been in business, the performance of the stock over the last five years, price to earnings ratios, and other information.

You would also have to tell the genetic algorithm your exact "success" criteria such as stock price growth rate. You could also use a revenue growth rate in the company over the last year of at least 10 percent, a presence in the marketplace going back at least three years, a connection to the computer industry, etc. The genetic algorithm would simply combine and recombine stocks eliminating any combinations that don't fit your criteria and continuing to the next iteration with the acceptable combinations—in our example those that give an aggregate growth rate of at least 7.5 percent while aiming for as high a stock price growth rate as possible.

A note of caution here: It's important to understand that this method of stock selection is based on past information and assumes that things will not change. That may or may not be a good assumption.

FUZZY LOGIC

Is That like Fuzzy Thinking?

Fuzzy logic is a way of dealing with uncertainty and imprecision. If you've ever mistyped a Web address, you've had personal experience of the level of precision that computers require. People, on the other hand, talk in subjective, imprecise ways all the time. You've surely used terms such as "bright lights," "cold winters," "big rooms," "tasty food," and "small cars," and other people pretty much understand what you're talking about. However, computer software can't cope with these vague types of terms without fuzzy logic.

Fuzzy logic is a mathematical method of handling imprecise or subjective information. Using fuzzy logic, it's possible for computers to deal with circumstances that are not simple "either/or" situations. Take room temperature for example. Most people would consider a room in which the thermostat is set at 75 degrees Fahrenheit to be warm. If you lower the temperature one degree, the room is still warm. If you keep lowering the temperature until the air in the room is only 40 degrees, most people would say it's cold. At what number of degrees did the temperature go from warm to cold? Was it at 50 degrees, or 60 degrees, or some other number? In truth, there is no hairline warm/cold point. In the real world, the room becomes "less" or "more" warm and gradually becomes "less" or "more" cold. It's this sort of situation that fuzzy logic can handle. If you had a fuzzy logic thermostat, you wouldn't set it to a certain degree setting. You'd set it to "warm" or "cool" and the fuzzy logic would take care of the rest.

A good example of fuzzy logic in action is Matsushita's Aisaigo Day washing machine. The name of the washing machine actually means "beloved wife's machine." This washing machine uses sensors to determine what sort of dirt is on the clothes (oily or muddy), how much water will be needed, and how hot the water should be. The machine uses IF . . . THEN rules as our expert system did, but these rules are much more flexible and deal in shades of gray instead of black or white.

Fuzzy logic is best for situations in which the variables are shifting constantly and a decision must be made quickly. For example, fuzzy logic is built into antilock brakes, giving them control to apply breaking pressure appropriate to the level of skid of the tires. Normally, a computer could handle only input of skid or no-skid, but fuzzy logic adds the ability to differentiate between a road surface that is a little bit slippery, pretty slippery, and very slippery.

For more information on artificial intelligence, visit our Web site at www.mhhe.com/i-series.

Genetic Algorithms are used to
- Minimize the amount of cable that needs to be laid over a wide geographic area.
- Schedule commercials at radio stations.
- Minimize the movement of whiskey casks around a distiller's warehouse.
- Schedule the rotation of trains in France.

SECTION B://   *making the grade*

1. A(n) _____ is an artificial intelligence system that is capable of learning to differentiate patterns.
2. A(n) _____ is an artificial intelligence system that mimics the evolutionary process.
3. A mathematical method of handling imprecise or subjective information is called _____.
4. An artificial intelligence system that applies reasoning capabilities to reach a conclusion is a(n) _____.

C://INTELLIGENT AGENTS OR BOTS

You're probably already familiar with Clippy, an early version of an intelligent agent. Clippy is that shifty-eyed paper clip that pops itself up in many versions of Word. If the document you're typing looks like the beginning of a letter, the animated paper clip will offer helpful suggestions on how to write letters. Another example of a primitive intelligent agent is the software on Amazon.com's Web site that automatically suggests books for you to purchase on the basis of your previous purchases.

An *intelligent agent* or *bot* is software that will automatically perform repetitive tasks on your computer for you. The tasks usually involve finding and collecting information, rather as if you had a very intelligent, well-trained, tracking "software dog" in your computer.

To be truly "intelligent" systems, intelligent agents must learn. For example, if you had an intelligent agent that made travel arrangements for you, it might learn that you like to fly at night. Intelligent agent technology is still in its early stages and there is great disagreement on what actually constitutes an "intelligent agent." Some software that is popularly called "intelligent" doesn't learn, which, according to many, is the foundation of intelligence—natural or artificial.

Intelligent agents usually work in the background, so your computer is still available to you for use. For example, your intelligent agent might search the Internet every morning for information about your state senators, your favorite sports team, the comic strip you like the most, and so on, presenting you with a customized newspaper to read with your morning coffee.

There are four major types of intelligent agents:

- Find-and-retrieve agents.
- User agents.
- Monitor and surveillance agents.
- Data-mining agents.

In this section we'll discuss the first three above. Data-mining agents appear in the next section on data warehouses and data mining. For more information on intelligent agents, visit our Web site at www.mhhe.com/i-series.

FIND-AND-RETRIEVE AGENTS

Is a Shopping Bot a Find-and-Retrieve Agent?

Find-and-retrieve agents travel around a network (very likely the Internet) finding information and bringing it back to you. If you're looking for a particular vintage car, you might send a bot out to find one for you. This would be a **buyer agent** or **shopping bot.** These are intelligent agents that look on the Web for the product of your choice and bring the information back to you. These agents are essentially specialized search engines and work very efficiently for commodity products such as CDs, books, electronic components, and other one-size-fits-all products.

Shopping bots make money by selling advertising space, special promotions in cooperation with merchants, or click-through fees. Click-through fees are fees that the merchant pays the site that provided the link to the merchant site. Some shopping bots give preference to certain sites for a financial consideration.

MySimon.com is the most successful shopping bot to date with more than a million visitors a month according to Nielsen/NetRatings. MySimon searches for millions of products on thousands of Web sites. Government sites also have search-and-retrieve agents you can use to get the information you need. FERRET (Federal Electronic Research and Review Extraction Tool)

was developed jointly by the Census Bureau and the Bureau of Labor Statistics. With FERRET you can find information on employment, health care, education, race and ethnicity, health insurance, housing, income and poverty, aging, marriages, and family.

USER AGENTS

What Can User Agents Do for Me?

User agents are intelligent agents that help an individual perform computer-related tasks. Again, intelligent agents usually work in the background, so you can still use your computer while they operate. In this category belong those intelligent agents that check your e-mail, sort it according to priority (your priority), and alert you when good stuff comes through—like college acceptance notifications.

If you're a gamer, you might want to have a bot that will patrol game areas for you or act as your opponent. For your daily news requirements, you might want to bypass the TV and newspaper altogether with a news bot. There are several versions of these. A CNN Custom News bot will gather news from CNN on the topics you want to read about—and only those. Others search all types of sources for news on your chosen subjects.

You can find many other types of user agents including

- Agents that fill out forms on the Web automatically for you. They even store your information for future reference.
- Agents that scan Web pages looking for and highlighting the text that constitutes the "important" part of the information there.
- Chat agents that will discuss topics with you from your deepest fears to sports.

MONITORING AND SURVEILLANCE AGENTS

What Do These Agents Monitor?

Monitoring and surveillance agents are intelligent agents that perform diagnostic and housekeeping in the background, alerting you when they find something of interest. Agents that monitor large networks for potential problems belong in this category. For example, Computer Associates International (CA) has a monitoring agent that watches its huge network 24 hours a day. Every five seconds, the agent measures 1,200 data points and can predict a system crash 45 minutes before it happens. NASA's Jet Propulsion Laboratory has an agent that monitors inventory, planning, and scheduling equipment ordering to keep costs down.

Other types of monitoring and surveillance agents include agents that monitor

- Your competition and bring back price changes and special-offer information.
- Web sites, discussion groups, mailing lists, etc., for stock manipulation, insider training, and rumors that might affect stock prices.
- Web sites for updated information on the topic of your choice.
- Particular products and bring back price or term changes.
- Auction sites for products or prices that you want.

SECTION C://   *making the grade*

1. Specialized search engines that look at products and prices on many Web sites and bring back information on what they found are called _____.
2. Gaming bots are an example of _____ agents.
3. Software that will automatically perform repetitive tasks on your computer for you is called a(n) _____.
4. To be truly "intelligent," software must be able to _____.

D://DATA WAREHOUSES AND DATA MINING

Data mining is such an important part of decision making in business that we discuss it separately in its own section. In data mining, various decision support systems and AI systems combine to help you work with massive amounts of information.

DATA WAREHOUSES

Is a Data Warehouse a Physical Building?

You've already learned in Chapter 8 about databases and query facilities and how important they are to businesses. Since organizations store untold amounts of information in various databases, the next logical step would be to bring at least some of those databases together so that you could ask questions of (or query) a larger pool of information. Such an information pool is called a data warehouse.

A *data warehouse* is a collection of information from internal and/or external sources organized specifically for decision-making purposes. For example, a bank might be trying to segment its customer base in an effort to aim specific products and services at those customers most likely to buy them. The bank would have historic and current information on its customers in its own databases. It might buy information about outstanding debt and credit ratings from a credit bureau and information about competitors' products and services from a public database. Then the bank would bring all of this information together into a data warehouse so that personnel could analyze the information to decide whom to target, how to price products and services, and how to market them.

Another company might want to bring together only internal database information. That company might want to combine sales, marketing, and customer information to find out which marketing strategies are working well (see Figure 13.9).

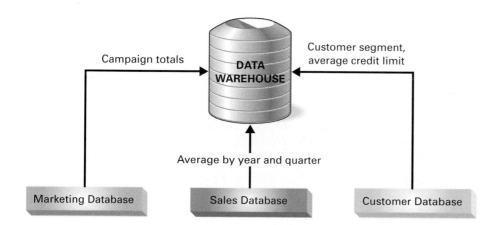

FIGURE 13.9

The information in a data warehouse can come from other databases within the organization.

A data warehouse is multidimensional in that there are layers of columns and rows instead of just one set of rows and columns as in a spreadsheet. This allows you to look at relationships in the information that are not easy to see in a two-dimensional structure (see Figure 13.10).

FIGURE   13.10

A data warehouse is multidimensional with layers of rows and columns.

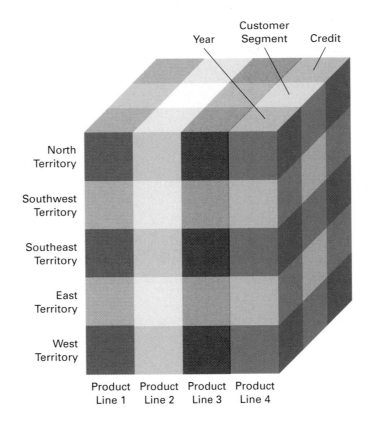

DATA MARTS

How Is a Data Mart Different from a Data Warehouse?

A ***data mart*** is a miniature data warehouse with a special focus. If you think of a data warehouse as a Wal-Mart superstore, selling everything from peaches to table lamps to hub caps, then a data mart is like a convenience store catering to a subgroup of shoppers. Similarly, a data mart would usually be a subset of a data warehouse. It would have information from a select set of databases to aid decision making in a specific focus area, such as one sales region of a national store chain.

DATA MINING

What Is Data Mining?

Data mining is the process of extracting information from a data warehouse for decision-making purposes. It's the process of searching and exploring information electronically to discover new information and relationships. Try this analogy: Think of going to a huge store with a diverse range of goods to get a housewarming gift for a friend. Say you've decided to get a kitchen trash can and fill it with "stuff." You're planning to decide on the exact stuff when you see what's available. While in the trash can aisle, you see some kitchen utensils and gather some of those. Then, you walk through the clothes section and see aprons and add one to your shopping basket. Later, as you wander through the electronics section, you get a hands-free phone so that your friend can talk on the phone and cook at the same time. Maybe that leads you to think of placemats to set under the cooked meal, and dish cloths for cleanup, and so on and so forth. When you're finished, you've got a unique gift made up of lots of different types of goods.

Data mining works in a similar fashion. You "slice and dice" through the information, electronically looking at it in different ways, getting ideas about how to manipulate it further and discovering new relationships (see Figure 13.11). You may end up with information that you didn't specifically search for.

Data-mining tools are designed specifically to work with a large amount of information where a gigantic number of permutations and combinations are possible. The two main objectives of data mining are prediction and discovery.

Data mining can predict probable outcomes. This means that by analyzing past trends with statistical methods, you can calculate the likelihood of future trends. Data mining can tell you something interesting that you didn't know before. For example, supermarket executives might discover that sales of sports magazines go up when displayed near diapers. The reason might be that fathers of young children on their way home pick up some diapers and then see the magazines and pick up one for themselves. Since neural networks are designed to find patterns in information, an important application of neural networks is in data mining.

Searching for and collecting information is what intelligent agents or bots do best. In fact, a special class of intelligent agents called data-mining bots is dedicated to data-mining applications. **Data-mining bots** search through data warehouses to discover new information. An intelligent agent may detect a major shift in a trend or a key indicator. Intelligent agents work well with neural networks. The agents find and bring back the information and the neural network detects patterns.

A data-mining bot can detect the presence of new information and alert you. For example, Volkswagen uses an intelligent agent system that acts as an early-warning system about market conditions. If conditions become such that the assumptions underlying the company's strategy are no longer true, the intelligent agent alerts managers.

For more information on data mining, visit our Web site at www.mhhe.com/i-series.

F I G U R E 13.11

Data-mining tools are many and varied.

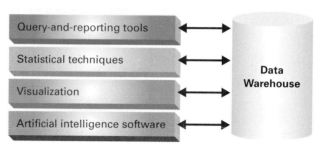

making the grade

1. The process of extracting new information from a data warehouse is called _____.

2. A _____ is a miniature data warehouse with a specific focus.

3. The two main objectives of data mining are _____ and prediction.

4. A collection of information organized for decision-making purposes is a(n) _____.

E://SUMMARY AND KEY TERMS

Information technology can offer help in decision making in various forms. The three categories of computer-aided decision making software are decision support software that helps you analyze options; artificial intelligence software that makes the decision for you; and data-mining software that helps you analyze information in a data warehouse.

A *decision support system (DSS)* is software that uses models, information, and an interactive user interface to help you make decisions. Some business information is easier to comprehend and analyze in map form. A *geographic information system (GIS)* is software that allows you to see information in map form. It's sometimes used in conjunction with a *global positioning system (GPS).*

You don't always need to know enough to do your own analysis. *Artificial intelligence (AI)* is the science of making machines imitate human thinking and behavior. There are four major categories.

- An *expert system,* also known as a *knowledge-based system,* is an artificial intelligence system that applies reasoning capabilities to reach a conclusion.

- A *neural network* is an artificial intelligence system that is capable of learning to differentiate patterns.

- A *genetic algorithm* is an artificial intelligence system that mimics the evolutionary, "survival-of-the-fittest" process to generate increasingly better solutions to a problem.

- *Fuzzy logic* is a mathematical method of handling imprecise or subjective information.

For tasks and decision making that are continuously ongoing, an *intelligent agent* can help. There are four types.

- A *buyer agent* or *shopping bot* (also called *find-and-retrieve agents*) is an intelligent agent that looks on the Web for the product of your choice and brings the information back to you.

- *User agents* are intelligent agents that help an individual in performing computer-related tasks.

- *Monitoring and surveillance agents* are intelligent agents that perform diagnostic and housekeeping in the background, alerting you when they find something of interest.

i·witness

An Up-Close Look at Web Sites

Getting Your Site on a Search Engine

Throughout this text, we've been exploring with you how to build an effective Web site. The HTML code you use and design rules you follow are the most important aspects of building a Web site that your visitors will want to return to again and again. Now, let's look at helping your visitors find your Web site by placing it on a search engine.

All search engines, such as WebCrawler, allow you to easily add your site to their database. When you do, you can provide a description as well as key words and terms by which you want your site to be found. Unfortunately, these services may not be free. WebCrawler, for example, charges

a one-time fee that can range from $99 to $199. Other search engine sites have similar charges (and a few are free).

For a good, easy beginning, we suggest you use a service that will register your site with numerous search engines all at once. Once such service is Free Mania (www.freemania.net), which does in fact register your site on over 40 different search engines for free. Another site you might try is Submit It! (www.submit-it.com). For additional sites that provide these services and what they charge, visit the Web site for this text at www.mhhe.com/i-series.

Once visitors begin reaching your site, you should determine which search engine they used to find you. Then you can target that search engine specifically with more information and key words.

- **Data-mining bots** search through data warehouses to discover new information. **Data mining** is the process of extracting information from a data warehouse for decision-making purposes.

A **data warehouse** is a collection of information from internal and/or external sources organized specifically for decision-making purposes. A **data mart** is a miniature data warehouse with a special focus.

As added support, we've provided more information on the Web site that supports this text at www.mhhe.com/i-series on the following topics:

- Decision support systems
- Artificial intelligence systems
- Intelligent agents
- Data mining

KEY TERMS

artificial intelligence (AI) (p. 13.10)

buyer agent (shopping bot) (p. 13.17)

data mart (p. 13.20)

data mining (p. 13.20)

data-mining bot (p. 13.21)

data warehouse (p. 13.19)

decision support system (DSS) (p. 13.5)

expert system (knowledge-based system) (p. 13.11)

find-and-retrieve agent
(p. 13.17)

fuzzy logic (p. 13.15)

genetic algorithm (p. 13.14)

geographic information system
(GIS) (p. 13.9)

global positioning system (GPS)
(p. 13.9)

intelligent agent (bot) (p. 13.16)

monitoring and surveillance agent
(p. 13.18)

neural network (p. 13.12)

robot (p. 13.10)

structured decision (p. 13.3)

unstructured decision (p. 13.3)

user agent (p. 13.17)

user interface (p. 13.6)

CROSSWORD PUZZLE

Across

2. _____ and surveillance agent
6. These agents can play games with you
7. This type of decision is reached by applying a formula
10. This type of system is good for diagnostic and prescriptive problems
11. This kind of logic handles concepts like "warm" and "hot"
12. Shows information in map form
14. A data _____ is a collection of lots of information
16. This type of mining finds information

Down

1. A software tool to help you analyze information
2. A miniature data warehouse
3. This type of agent performs repetitive tasks on your computer
4. An algorithm based on evolution
5. A network that "learns"
8. Can tell you what longitude and latitude you're in
9. This type of agent is also called a shopping bot
13. This machine has simulated human senses
15. Stands for artificial intelligence

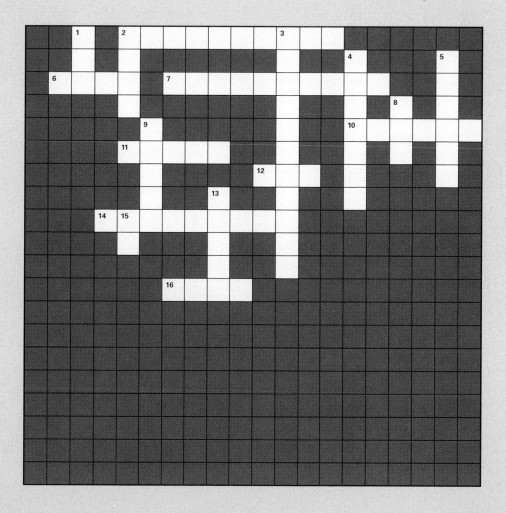

QUESTIONS AND EXERCISES

Multiple Choice

1. A collection of information from internal and external sources organized specifically for decision-making purposes is called a(n)
   a. DSS.
   b. data warehouse.
   c. geographic information system.
   d. artificial intelligence.
   e. model.

2. The extraction of new information from a data warehouse is
   a. neural networking.
   b. data mining.
   c. visualization.
   d. data marting.
   e. none of the above.

3. The tasks that data mining is best at are
   a. prediction and discovery.
   b. diagnostic and predictive.
   c. diagnostic and discovery.
   d. prediction and pattern recognition.
   e. none of the above.

4. Intelligent agents can be
   a. shopping bots.
   b. monitoring and surveillance agents.
   c. data-mining bots.
   d. all of the above.
   e. none of the above.

5. A DSS has
   a. models.
   b. information.
   c. a user interface.
   d. all of the above.
   e. none of the above.

6. Software that lets you see information in map form is a(n)
   a. DSS.
   b. genetic algorithm.
   c. neural network.
   d. geographic information system.
   e. mapping agent.

7. The science of making machines imitate human thinking and behavior is called
   a. artificial intelligence.
   b. genetic algorithm.
   c. neural network.
   d. expert systems.
   e. all of the above.

8. An AI system that learns to recognize patterns is a(n)
   a. genetic algorithm.
   b. neural network.
   c. expert system.
   d. geographic information system.
   e. bot.

9. A knowledge-based system is also known as a(n)
   a. genetic algorithm.
   b. neural network.
   c. expert system.
   d. geographic information system.
   e. DSS.

10. Software that helps you analyze information so that you can make better decisions is a(n)
    a. GIS.
    b. DSS.
    c. neural network.
    d. genetic algorithm.
    e. expert system.

True/False

11. _____ The strength of a genetic algorithm lies in its ability to recognize patterns.

12. _____ A genetic algorithm is based on the evolutionary process.

13. _____ A neural network can learn to recognize patterns on its own.

14. _____ Fuzzy logic is a mathematical method for handling imprecise or subjective information.

15. _____ A shopping bot is a type of find-and-retrieve intelligent agent.

QUESTIONS AND EXERCISES

1. Look at each situation and pick the appropriate decision support or AI tool and specify why it's suitable (several tools may be applicable).

   A. To compare the cost of four vacation plans.
   B. To turn your lights on when it's "pretty dark."
   C. To verify signatures on checks.
   D. To diagnose problems with the washing machine.
   E. To tell you what to do to fix the washing machine.

   F. To decide on the best locations for bus stops in a city.
   G. To decide on the wiring layout for a large campus network that uses the least amount of cable.
   H. To help you fix your car when something goes wrong.

2. For each of the following answers, create the question:

ANSWER	QUESTION
A. Software that will automatically perform repetitive tasks on your computer for you.	
B. Software that helps you analyze alternatives.	
C. Software that shows information in map form.	
D. Software that recognizes patterns.	
E. Software that operates with rules.	
F. Software that checks large networks for problems.	
G. Software that finds new information in data warehouses.	
H. A collection of information from many databases.	
I. A miniature data warehouse.	
J. 51	
K. Software that generates several generations of solutions.	
L. Classification and identification.	
M. Prediction and discovery.	
N. User agents.	
O. Neural networks and genetic algorithms.	

e-commerce

1. Magazine Subscriptions

Many people predicted that we would soon be a "paperless" society because of computers. That hasn't happened yet. Magazines, for example, rather than going away, are proliferating. They are also becoming more specialized. You can find magazine subscriptions for sale by student and civic organizations, at central clearinghouses, and online.

Look at these Web sites and for each answer the questions that follow.

- NBAF Magazine Subscriptions—nbaf.com
- Magazine Subscriptions Store— www.super-stuff.com/magazines/index.html
- Newsweek—www.msnbc.com
- InformationWeek— www.informationweek.com

a. Does the site say how many magazines it sells?

b. Does the site mention a discount off the newsstand price?

c. Does the site specialize in a particular interest group or population segment?

d. Can you read part of the magazine online?

e. Do you need a password to read articles online?

2. Shopping Bots

Have you ever found something you wanted in a store only to wonder if you could get it at a better price elsewhere? To find out, you'd have to go to other stores and compare prices. Or perhaps you could look through catalogs and find the information there. If you've had that feeling while visiting a Web site, your task is much easier. Perhaps what you found was on an e-tailer site (e-commerce site) or an auction site such as eBay. All you have to do for extensive comparison-shopping is to send a shopping bot in search of a better deal.

Following are some shopping bot sites. Choose three items to search for: one music-related item, one clothing item, and one household item. Search for them with each site. Then answer the questions that follow for each site.

- Bottom Dollar—www.bottomdollar.com
- MySimon—www.mysimon.com
- Yahoo Shopping—shopping.yahoo.com
- Pricing Central—www.pricingcentral.com

a. How many hits did you get at each site for each item?

b. Are tax, postage, and handling charges included in the quoted price?

c. Can you sort in order of price?

d. Does the shopping site specialize in a particular kind of item?

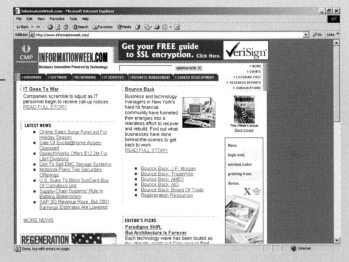

3. Everything for Taxes

One of the two constants in this world is taxes. We all have to pay them in various forms. If you work, you pay federal and perhaps state tax. If you buy anything, you may have to pay sales tax. If you're lucky and inherit big-time money, you may have to pay estate taxes. If you use toll roads you may have to pay highway tax. If you're drawing a paycheck, you know that the printed amount isn't the same as the number of hours you worked times your pay rate. In between that calculation and your actual check amount are tax deductions. Not only that, but you have to file a tax return every year.

Tax codes can be very complicated, so much so that a whole army of accountants and lawyers devote their professional lives to sorting it all out. But, you may be able to find out much of what you want to know about taxes on the Internet.

Here are some sites for you to look at. Then answer the questions that follow for each.

- The Internal Revenue Service (IRS)— www.irs.ustreas.gov
- TaxInteractive— www.irs.ustreas.gov/taxi/index.html
- Quicken.com—www.quicken.com
- Tax Resources—www.taxresources.com
- Ernst & Young—www.ey.com

a. Is this a commercial or an informational site?

b. If it's commercial, what is the Web site trying to sell?

c. Can you download tax forms from this site?

d. Does it explain things such as Roth IRAs and mutual funds?

e. Is the site primarily for individuals or businesses?

4. Online Photos

Most people love to have photos. Photos serve to remind us of people, places, and events that we want to remember. In this information age we have more choices than ever in photos we can have and how we display them. With digital photos you can even change the image easily.

You can get your film photos developed by processing businesses that are online. They will let you retrieve your photos from the Internet or put them onto a CD-ROM for you.

Here are some photo-related sites. Have a look at each and answer the questions that follow.

- Photo Works—www.photoworks.com
- Photo Alley—www.photoalley.com
- Shop@kodak—www.kodak.com
- Timeless Photo & Imaging— timelessphoto.com

a. Does the site develop rolls of film?

b. Can you view your photos online?

c. Does the site offer a "smart" frame? (*Hint:* Try the Kodak site.)

d. Will the site make calendars for you?

e. Will the site make greeting cards out of your photos for you?

1. Data Mining Software

Find three business data mining tools. Compare them in terms of characteristics and price. Here are a few Web sites you could try:

- IBM's Intelligent Miner— www.4.ibm.com/software/data/iminer
- KD Nuggets—www.kdnuggets.com
- Smart Drill—www.smartdrill.com

2. Intelligent Agents

Here are some shopping bot sites. Find the ones that have the characteristics listed in the table below.

- www.bestbookbuys.com
- www.shopper.com
- www.onsale.com
- www.bizrate.com
- www.whenushop.com
- www.nextag.com

QUESTION	WEB SITE(S)
a. Which sites specialize in computers and electronics?	_____
b. Which sites review e-tailers based on customer feedback?	_____
c. Which sites tell you about discount coupons?	_____
d. Which sites pay the return postage if you're unhappy with your purchase?	_____
e. Which sites let you negotiate a better price if you don't like the quoted one?	_____

3. Types of Decision Support

Go to a Web site such as InformationWeek's at www.informationweek.com or www.techtv.com and look up articles on decision support systems. Classify the articles you find as follows into the categories on the left-hand side of the table and put the number that you find into the right-hand side column.

TYPE OF ARTICLE	NUMBER
a. Number that mention data mining.	_____
b. Number that deal with financial applications.	_____
c. Number that are for manufacturing applications.	_____
d. Number that mention global information systems.	_____

4. Expert Systems

In the text we discussed rule-based expert systems. These are expert systems that go through lists of questions and use the answers to reach a solution. However, not all expert systems are rule-based. Case-based reasoning is the basis of another type of expert system. This type of expert system looks at prior similar situations to find one that matches the problem situation and from that comparison it reaches a conclusion. This works similarly to the way lawyers find precedent cases similar enough to the current case to make the precedent applicable to the current case. Find some Web sites that discuss expert systems. Find three expert systems. What are the domains of the expert systems? Does the description say whether these expert systems are rule-based (like the ones discussed in the chapter) or use some other method of handling knowledge (such as case-based reasoning)?

ethics, security & privacy

1. Carnivore

Carnivore is a sniffer program developed by the FBI to covertly search for e-mails and other computer messages from those suspected of criminal acts. It can scan millions of e-mails per second. The *Carnivore* computer connects to the suspect's ISP and is controlled and configured remotely by FBI agents. The system can monitor a suspect's e-mail headers and/or content as well as access to FTP and other Web sites.

Carnivore has generated howls of protest from privacy advocates about the danger inherent in invading the privacy of law-abiding citizens. The FBI maintains that to deal with crime in the information age, it has to use the tools of the information age. Privacy advocates want the FBI to publish the *Carnivore* code, but the FBI says that if it were to publish the code of *Carnivore*, then those who wanted to could defeat it, which in turn would defeat its purpose.

Following are some of the FBI's arguments for keeping *Carnivore*.

- *Carnivore* is necessary to fight crime, and its use is very restricted.
- *Carnivore* cannot be installed without the help of the target ISP and remains connected only for the duration of the court order.
- *Carnivore* doesn't look for key words or even search the subject lines of e-mails.
- *Carnivore* is used very sparingly—in the year 2000, it was applied only 16 times. It's used only for serious crimes and only after law enforcement can demonstrate to a judge that it's absolutely necessary.
- *Carnivore* does not look at everyone's e-mail in hopes of finding criminal activity—that would be highly illegal.
- *Carnivore* is necessary to fight foreign terrorists and espionage, dangers that the FBI considers to be the greatest potential cyberthreats to our national security.

Privacy advocates and other groups, while they recognize the FBI's need for surveillance of suspected criminals, don't believe that *Carnivore* has sufficient safeguards in place. Some of their arguments are as follows:

- No one outside the FBI knows exactly how *Carnivore* works. This means that no one but the FBI can tell if it's actually doing what the court order says it can do.
- Any searches for specific e-mails mean that the addresses of all e-mail going in and out of an ISP must be scanned. This amounts to government surveillance of e-mail not covered by the court order.
- The chances of examining only a suspect's messages are remote since it's very difficult to capture and reassemble one person's messages when they flow in an information stream shared by many ISP customers.
- A third party could alter, forge, or misroute messages.
- The risk of criminals being able to intercept the system for their own ends is high since the system is operated remotely.

What do you think? Should the FBI be allowed to proceed with *Carnivore?* Which arguments do you find compelling? Are there some good ones on each side? Which ones?

group activities

1. Ordering Videos

A video storeowner wants to have enough of the hottest videos in stock so that people who come in to rent a particular video won't be disappointed and the store won't lose profits. Videos just sit on shelves after their popularity has faded, however, so the owner wants to keep the number of copies of any one movie as low as possible. If the owner wants to design a decision support system to try to predict how many copies to purchase, what information will be needed? For starters, it would be good to know (1) the population of the target market and (2) sales for horror films in similar markets. What else?

2. Mortgage Time Line

Use the car-buying decision support system spreadsheet in the chapter to calculate the difference in the price of a house if you take out a 15-year loan versus a 30-year loan. Try the exercise for a $50,000 home, a $100,000 home, and a $450,000 home. Try interest rates at 6.5 percent, 8 percent, and 10 percent.

3. Extend the Traffic-Light Expert System

Add more rules (questions) to the traffic-light expert system in the chapter. (What else can happen at a traffic light besides the events discussed in that expert system?) Would you like to have an expert system to do your driving for you? Would you feel safe? If so, why? If not, why not?

4. A GIS Map

Make a GIS-type map (you can draw it by hand or use a computer) by taking a map of your campus and adding information to it. Plot the activities that take place in each of the buildings. Also plot some events in the lives of each team member that took place at various parts of campus. Lastly, plot the percentage of one team member's week spent in each of those places.

5. Which AI System to Use

Suggest three real-life situations in which it would be helpful to have a neural network, a genetic algorithm, an expert system, and a geographic information system. You should have 12 examples total.

6. Conduct a Meeting via Computer

Put together a two-page paper on intelligent agents using computers as your only form of communication. With your partner or partners, hold a series of online meetings. You can use e-mail, set up a chat room, or use any computer-related electronic form of contact to write the paper—just don't discuss the project face-to-face. What were the advantages of your electronic meetings? What were the disadvantages?

7. Neural Networks and Genetic Algorithms

Look on the Web for neural networks and genetic algorithms. Find one of each. What is the application area (financial, manufacturing, environmental, etc.)? Is the product free? If not, how much does it cost?

Looking Back/Looking Ahead

The Life and Times of a Dot-Com Entrepreneur

Joann has learned a lot by now, and so have you. You've learned about the World Wide Web, electronic commerce, Web authoring and multimedia, what to look for when buying a computer, how a computer works, how to protect yourself, how to use databases, programming and software development, how businesses use information technology, and what technological developments are just around the corner.

It's our hope that you will use most, if not all, of what you have learned to be successful in your chosen career. We've covered the basics on how to get started and now it's up to you to develop your Web site and perhaps even your own business.

The best part of information technology is that it's changing and improving all the time. But that's also the most challenging part because it takes a concerted effort to keep up with new developments. Information technology is a freight train loaded with good things coming in your direction. Will you jump aboard? Don't let it pass you by.

We'd like to help you keep as current as possible concerning information technology. So, we've developed six Life-Long Learning modules. You'll find an introduction to each of these next. But the really valuable and up-to-date information is on our Web site at www.mhhe.com/i-series. Please visit our site regularly, even long after you've completed your education.

Today's world—both academic and business—is certainly characterized as one of "life-long learning." Simply put, you can't stop learning. Even when you graduate from school and start that perfect job, you need to keep learning to compete effectively.

You must be a life-long learner in your personal life. You need to stay up-to-date on world events, politics, and other such matters. Our world is changing fast and in so many ways that affect you.

Of course, as you already know from reading this textbook, technology is changing on a daily basis. That means the business world and your personal life are also changing because of new advances in technology. It's up to you to keep pace, in ways that are appropriate for your life and career.

In the following pages, you'll read brief introductions to our *Life-Long Learning Modules,* a comprehensive set of materials you'll find on the Web site that supports this text at www.mhhe.com/i-series. In these *Modules* on the Web, we provide more state-of-the-art information concerning the vast field of information technology.

These *Life-Long Learning Modules* will definitely help keep you current.

The information provided in the *Modules* will enhance the material you've been reading. The practical reality of a textbook is that we are constrained in the number of pages we can write. After all, you don't want to buy a text (and carry it around) several thousand pages long. If you've benefited from the discussions in the text, keep on learning at our Web site.

Long after you've finished this class, you'll need to refresh your knowledge and keep on learning. We encourage you to revisit the Web-based *Life-Long Learning Modules.* They're free, full of valuable information, and always up to date.

Please visit us at www.mhhe.com/i-series.

life-long learning modules

www.mhhe.com/ i-series

module

a://

ENHANCED WEB DEVELOPMENT

You know how much the Web is now a part of our lives. You can use the Web to find information, buy goods and services, download software, and play games with friends.

Every day people put more Web sites online. You're probably one of them. We designed some Web pages together in Chapter 4. And you learned about Web design in the I-Witness boxes throughout the book.

With all the Web sites out there, how can you make yours stand out from the rest? You can redesign your Web site to make it easier for users to navigate. Or you can add some multimedia to make your Web site more interactive. Maybe you want to create electronic shopping carts to allow customers to buy things at your own e-commerce business. In this *Life-Long Learning Module*, we'll show you how you can accomplish all this and more.

We'll keep you informed of new Web technologies to make your Web site sizzle. Think of your Web site as your electronic business card. The better the information you can put on it and the easier it is to read, the more people you'll attract and retain. Come join us at www.mhhe.com/i-series as we explore making Web sites sizzle.

DEVELOPMENT TOOLS

Your choice of a Web development tool is an important one if you want to make your site sizzle. You have many options to choose from. In this section we'll explore many of them including HTML and WYSIWYG editors (Notepad, BBEdit, Dreamweaver, and FrontPage), image and photo editors (Photoshop, Fireworks, and Illustrator are a few), and Web site management tools such as link checkers and site mapping software. We'll also show you how to get by on $0.00 a day with freeware and open source solutions.

WEB SCRIPTING AND PROGRAMMING

Web scripting and programming are all about defining the structure and layout of your Web site and creating interactivity. A well-designed Web site is easy to use, encouraging your readers to visit again and again. Interactivity is also key in retaining readers. Come with us and explore HTML, XHTML, XML, DHTML, JavaScript, VBScript, CGI, Java, and many other scripting and programming tools.

DESIGN GUIDES

Anyone can build a Web site, but doing it *effectively* is another story. It's rather like creating an advertising flyer. You can easily create such a flyer and include all the necessary information. What's key is doing it in such a way that people will want to buy your products or services. In Web site design, important considerations include image sizes and placements, use of color, and streamlining Web sites. We'll discuss these issues and much more at www.mhhe.com/i-series.

MULTIMEDIA

The technology world is now multimedia. Almost all presentations of information include some combination of text, art, video, sound, and animation. Your Web site can definitely benefit from the use of multimedia elements. These may include animated GIFs, audio, streaming media, and perhaps even virtual reality. In this section we'll explore these as well as some multimedia development tools such as Flash and Shockwave.

BEHIND THE SCENES

As you increase your use of multimedia and other interactive elements, you need to begin to understand what goes on behind the scenes. That is, if you understand the technical infrastructure, you can more readily take advantage of multimedia and interactivity in creating your Web site. Important "behind the scenes" topics include Web servers (and server farms), Web databases, Web security, and Web site architectures.

Why Do Things Go Wrong?

module

b://

CARE AND FEEDING OF YOUR COMPUTER

Your computer is your thinking and working machine, and it needs maintenance and care. It's like your car, which as you know needs maintenance and care. For your car, some of it you do yourself, such as filling the gas tank and maybe even changing the spark plugs and oil. Some of the upgrading and maintenance tasks that your computer needs you can also take care of yourself; for others you may want some professional help. It mostly depends on how technically oriented you are, how much you know about computers, and how much experience you have.

Just as you probably pump your own gas, you'll need to manage your computer storage space yourself, dividing the space into folders and keeping files orderly (as we discussed in Chapters 3 and 8). You'll also have to swap out cartridges for your printer when the need arises.

Beyond these routine tasks, many people prefer to handle computer maintenance the way most of us take care of car maintenance—with professional help. Perhaps you can change the oil and maybe a tire, but after that you might like a mechanic to take over. Similarly, when you want more memory or a CD-ROM drive installed, you might want to bring your computer to a service center or get help from someone who knows more than you do.

At www.mhhe.com/i-series, we'll discuss the care and feeding of your computer and help you decide what you want to do yourself and for what you may want professional help.

UPGRADING YOUR HARDWARE AND SOFTWARE

Upgrading your computer can run the gamut from replacing your CPU and motherboard and adding more memory to adding a DVD drive or replacing a mouse with a trackball. If it's a new CPU or more memory you want, you'll have to be sure you have the right kind. You may want a better video card so that gaming or video is faster and better quality. From time to time, you'll also need to upgrade your software, both application and system. Let us help you decide what you can do yourself and for which tasks you might want professional help.

TROUBLESHOOTING

Since a computer is such a sophisticated and complicated machine, there are umpteen things that can go wrong with it. Each component has its own special list. For example, if your printer doesn't work, it could be that it's not plugged securely into the wall outlet or into the back of the system unit. It could be that you forgot to install the printer driver, or the fan is broken, or any one of a dozen other things. Let's discuss some troubleshooting issues such as common warning beeps, BIOS problems, modem problems, and many more.

OPERATING SYSTEM CONSIDERATIONS

Your operating system handles many "behind the scenes" tasks as you use your application software. Just like any other part of your computer, you need to care for and feed your operating system. For example, you'll need to install new drivers if you add new hardware. You may also want to change your screen saver. Your operating system can also help you un-delete files, essentially allowing you to retrieve them after performing a delete. Although your operating system isn't a personal productivity tool in the strictest sense, it can in fact help you be more productive as you use your application software. We'll show you many features of your operating system at www.mhhe.com/i-series.

GENERAL MAINTENANCE

You can perform many general maintenance tasks yourself. We encourage you to do so. If you take your keyboard to a computer repair shop to have it cleaned, you'll probably be charged more than the cost of a new keyboard. On the other hand, you can do it yourself in a matter of minutes with a few simple instructions. In this section we'll explore many general maintenance activities you can perform yourself including cleaning your mouse and monitor, defragmenting your hard disk, and changing printer cartridges. All of these are simple tasks, and we want to help you perform them correctly.

PROTECTION

Finally, you definitely need to protect your computer—not only from viruses but from the harmful effects of weather and even magnets. In this section, we'll discuss the best ways to protect your computer using UPSs (uninterruptible power supplies), firewalls, and anti-virus software.

What's Your Dream Job?

CAREERS IN INFORMATION TECHNOLOGY

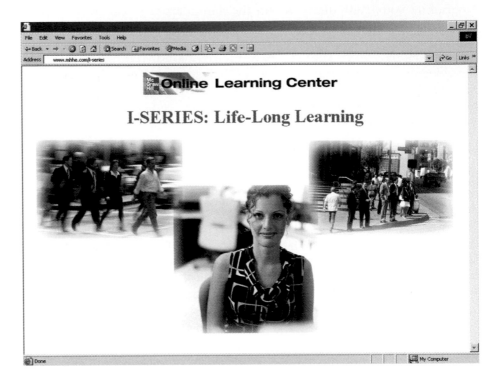

The field of information technology can be a great place to work, and the opportunities you have are enormous. By 2005, there will be an estimated 1 million unfilled jobs that require Internet expertise. In Silicon Valley, hi-tech firms are hiring sharp young students fresh out of high school. Some firms are even paying parents if their children agree to work for them. Don't worry—it's not child labor all over again. It's simply hiring the best for the job at hand. After all, in electronic commerce one slogan is "hire the children."

To prepare for a career in information technology you must in fact "prepare." You need to carefully select your classes and devote your time and energies to making the best grades. You also need to be aware of what jobs are available, what skills you need, and how you can best position yourself to land that job you dream of.

In this *Life-Long Learning Module*, we inform you of career opportunities in the field of information technology.

IT specialists today are among the highest paid of all occupations. See how and why at www.mhhe.com/i-series.

module

C://

JOB TITLES, DESCRIPTIONS, AND SALARIES

The technology field holds a variety of different jobs for you. The field is so new that some job titles seem to overlap or perhaps don't make any sense. But the jobs are there waiting for you. Each has its own set of responsibilities and comes with a rewarding paycheck. Your focus is on understanding what jobs are available and which seem to be of interest to you.

THE SKILLS YOU NEED

To prepare for an IT job, you need two sets of skills—technology skills and people skills. The technology skills are easy to come by—you can learn them in class. The people skills may be more difficult to acquire. Don't think that technology specialists don't need people skills. If you can't communicate with your customers, no one will visit your Web site to buy your products. You need a solid people-skill set, and that includes finance, accounting, marketing, human resource management, and production and logistics, just to name a few. We'll explore both technology skills and people skills at www.mhhe.com/i-series.

SEARCHING FOR JOBS

The Web is a great place to look for employment. Thousands of Web sites offer searchable databases of job opportunities and internships. Knowing which sites to visit and how to build an electronic resume are important. In this section, we'll guide you to some of the better job database sites and offer you points for building an effective electronic resume.

LEARNING BEYOND YOUR EDUCATION

Once you graduate, you can't stop learning. The advancements in technology aren't going to suddenly halt just because you have a diploma in hand. If technology continues to change, then you must be prepared to continue to learn and change with it. That's one of the key reasons why we developed these *Life-Long Learning Modules*. Here, we explore some of the fascinating ways you can stay up with technology.

THOUGHTS FROM THE AUTHORS

Let it not be said that we (as authors) don't care about you as a student and a person. We do receive royalties for writing this book, but our true love is education. Between the three of us, we have almost 40 years of dedicated teaching experience. Please let us offer you some of our thoughts as you prepare for your future. And if you have some of your own thoughts that you feel other students would benefit from, please send us an e-mail at i-series@mcgraw-hill.com. We'd love to hear from you and post your thoughts along with ours.

How Did We Get Here?

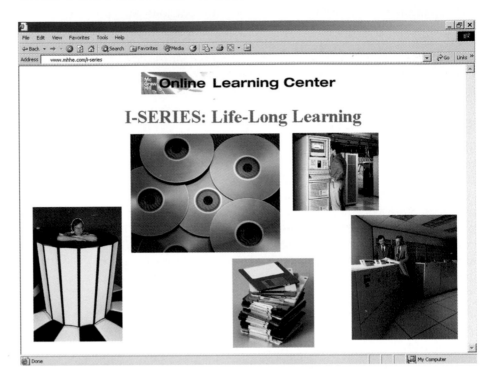

In textbooks, you often read a historical perspective on a particular subject. And it really does help you to better understand what you're studying today if you know something of the past. In technology, history is yesterday. The computer you bought yesterday is probably already slow compared to today's machines. The printer you bought yesterday probably doesn't have the quality of today's printers.

The Web changes on a daily basis too. Hundreds of new Web sites pop up every day, and hundreds of yesterday's Web sites are no longer accessible. Even the technologies we use to access the Web are changing at ferocious speeds.

Technology and computers, as we know them today, have been around for only about 60 years. And in those 60 years, we've moved from computers that weighed several tons to personal digital assistants (PDAs) that weigh less than a pound. Even more important, the speed of technology has changed dramatically.

In this *Life-Long Learning Module*, we'll take a tour of the past through the previous generations of technology up through today's generation. And we'll even look at what tomorrow may bring. You can see tomorrow at www.mhhe.com/i-series.

module

d://

FIRST GENERATION

The first generation of computer technology actually only began in the 1940s. And in the 1950s, when businesses began to buy computers, computers were used mostly for accounting purposes only. These original computers weighed thousands of pounds. In fact, one of the first computers required so much electricity that it dimmed the lights of the city every time it was turned on. This generation of technology was based on vacuum tubes (and they were not used in vacuum cleaners).

SECOND GENERATION

We didn't stay long in the first generation of computers. In spite of the fact that many people believed computers would never catch on, researchers continued their efforts to build better, cheaper, and faster computers. Some of these even operated at or near 250,000 instructions per second. How fast is your computer today—2 billion or more instructions per second? This generation of technology was based on transistors—a term and technology first associated with radios.

THIRD GENERATION

The third generation of computers ushered in an entirely new era of technology—the integrated circuit. Then, computers became much faster, but they also overcame a fundamental problem of all previous computer generations—heat. First and second generation computers had to be cooled with internal air-conditioning systems. The integrated circuit helped alleviate much of that need. Computer technologies in this era no longer needed to be housed in an entire room.

FOURTH GENERATION

Today, we are in the fourth generation of technology, characterized by very-large-scale integration (VLSI). Parallel processing systems and systems that "piggy-back" multiple CPUs enable us to work at unbelievable speeds. Only in this generation can we now work with information in the form of sound and high-quality images. Previously, we worked with computers through a character-based interface; now we use a graphical user interface (GUI). Come see how our current generation compares to previous generations at www.mhhe.com/i-series.

THE GENERATION TO COME

Where to from here? Probably organic or membrane-based technologies. That is, the future of technology and its next level of innovation may very well be "grown," just as you would grow flowers or vegetables in a garden. If that idea piques your interest, you'll find this section worth reading. When we do move into the next generation of technologies, complete computing will become microscopic in size. Join us at www.mhhe.com/i-series as we predict the generation of technology for tomorrow.

What's Going On around You Today?

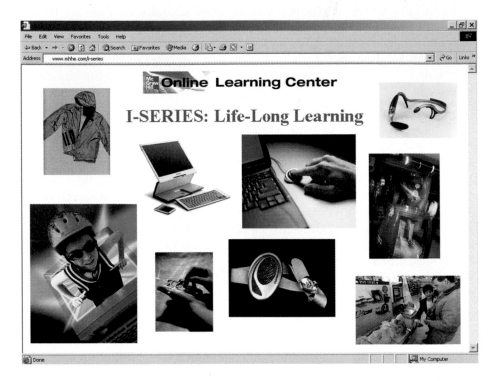

From the point of view of information technology, this is a great time to be alive, and an even better time to be young. So many aspects of our lives are improved by IT and the list is growing every day.

Technology is giving us hope that people without eyes will be able to see. Trials are under way which involve connecting a computer directly into the visual cortex of the brain. A new computerized wheelchair goes up stairs—yes, right up stairs!

Less dramatically, we'll soon be able to get hundreds of radio stations via satellite no matter where we go. No more out-of-range problems in the car. Wireless Web appliances will let you wander around your house and have Internet access from anywhere—even the shower. A "SmartBox" will sit outside your door ready to receive packages for you from a delivery service like FedEx. It will even contact you by e-mail or pager when the package arrives. You'll be able to get a small portable lie detector that uses voice recognition software to sense whether someone is lying to you. If it's warm outside and you want moist towels, we've got computerized dispensers that fit the bill. These products have already been developed.

In this *Life-Long Learning Module,* we'll explore many new technologies in your life today. Join us at www.mhhe.com/i-series.

module

e://

PORTABLE COMPUTING

Bigger is not always better with technology. As CPUs become more powerful yet smaller, developers are finding ways to help you access the information you need. Want to check e-mail or surf the Web as you lounge by the pool? You don't need a computer anymore. Perhaps you'll use your cell phone or PDA. And soon those may seem quite cumbersome compared to a portable computer you'll wear on your wrist. In this section we'll explore what's out there and what's coming.

INTERNET AND HOUSEHOLD APPLIANCES

Want to check your e-mail in the kitchen, but you'd rather not set a desktop computer by the sink? You could use a device designed only to check e-mail and surf the Web. Such Internet appliances are quickly replacing a second, or sometimes a first, computer in households. Appliances themselves are becoming smarter too. Who ever thought there'd be a day when your refrigerator could remind you by e-mail to buy milk? In this section we'll explore many Internet and intelligent home appliances such as smart lock boxes, electronic photo frames and paintings, Web stations, and much more.

ENTERTAINMENT TECHNOLOGY

You already know you can use your computer for more than just work. You can play video games and leisurely surf the Web for relaxation. You can also find other computer-based entertainment technologies such as robotics toys, Playstations, Xboxes, and multiuser Internet games. We'll discuss many of these as well as special types of equipment you may need including gamepads, sounds cards, and audio systems. Come see how you can enjoy entertainment technologies at www.mhhe.com/i-series.

VIRTUAL REALITY AND PERCEPTUAL USER INTERFACES

Technology is also changing daily with respect to how we physically interface with it. In a few short years, you may no longer use a mouse or keyboard. Instead, you'll use speech recognition and eye-tracking devices. Using these eye-tracking devices, you'll simply focus on a button and your software will initiate that function. Of course, virtual reality will become common (and inexpensive). Come explore these new advancements and many others with us.

LIFE-ENHANCING TECHNOLOGIES

Finally, we are beginning to see a rich and well-developed set of technologies that are life-enhancing. These new technologies are exploding in the medical field, including camera pills that you swallow to telemedicine applications such as remote triage virtual reality. Other new technologies are being developed in the automotive and aviation industries. Here's your chance to learn more about the latest and greatest life-enhancing technologies. You can find them at www.mhhe.com/i-series.

Do You Have a Crystal Ball?

module

f://

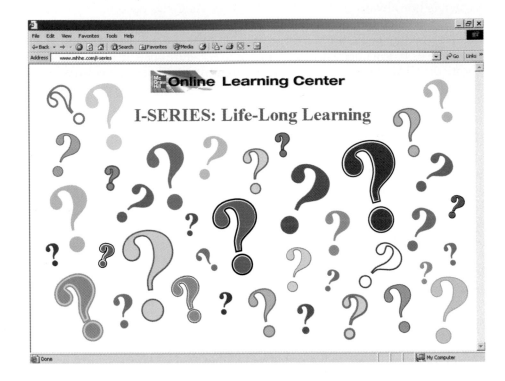

Well, if you do have a crystal ball, we'd certainly like to borrow it sometime. The simple fact of the matter is that no one can predict the future with any real consistency, especially with respect to technology.

However, we can make some statements regarding the future of technology in general. For example, we know that future technologies will begin to incorporate more of your senses (speech for example), just as we discussed in Chapter 9. We also know that complete and high-speed wireless communications are just around the corner. But how those will come about and exactly when is a mystery.

This *Life-Long Learning Module* will take you on a whirlwind tour of what we think the future holds for technology. More important, we want to alert you to how the future of technology will impact your personal life, the life of business, and your career.

We call these *Life-Long Learning Modules* because we want you to visit them long after you've completed your computer class. The content in this particular module will change frequently, and perhaps dramatically. Bookmark it (www.mhhe.com/i-series) and drop back in for a visit from time to time.

BIG TODAY—HOW SMALL TOMORROW?

Technology today is still relatively "big." Although you may think that a PDA that weighs less than a pound is small, tomorrow's PDAs will be about the size of a credit card and weigh about the same amount. Sound too good to be true? Not so. Technology tomorrow may become so small that you won't even be aware of its existence. What's even more important is that those "hard to see" computers will process billions and billions of instructions in a single second.

HERE TODAY—NOWHERE TOMORROW?

We still live in a world of physical boundaries—homes, states, and even countries. Of course, technologies such as the Web have helped eliminate many of those boundaries. But we have a long way to go. Imagine living in a world where location doesn't matter, a world in which you can run the world's largest organization from your garage or in a wheat field in Kansas. Imagine, too, a world in which language limitations are no longer an issue—it's coming sooner than you think. Come with us and explore a "locationless" tomorrow.

INTERNET TIME TODAY—WHEN TOMORROW?

As with physical boundaries, we also operate in a world constrained by time. But soon time will also become irrelevant. It's not that we'll operate 24 hours a day—it's that we'll operate without regard for even the day of the week, the month of the year, or perhaps even the year. In the virtual world, there are no physical limitations or boundaries—time is one such limitation that will not be present (past or future) in a virtual world. Let's explore a "timeless" tomorrow.

SEE TECHNOLOGY TODAY—TRANSPARENT TECHNOLOGY TOMORROW?

Transparent technology refers to the fact that technology may become such an integral and everyday part of our lives that we won't even acknowledge its existence. Think about electricity. Every organization needs it to survive, but how many organizations include electricity in their strategic plans? None, because electricity is transparent after a fashion. At www.mhhe.com/i-series, let's explore how technology can become transparent in the business world.

TECHNOLOGY FOCUS TODAY—WHAT TOMORROW?

Today, technology is such a hot buzzword that everyone seems to be focusing more on it than the most important issue—how to use technology for the betterment of people, society, and the business world. Let's take a glimpse into the future and see what it looks like when technology becomes transparent from a societal point of view.

making the grade answers

CHAPTER ONE

SECTION A://

1. Web site
2. Web site address
3. link
4. chat room

SECTION B://

1. Application software
2. vocal cords
3. telecommunications
4. Supercomputers
5. hardware, software

SECTION C://

1. under
2. ab
3. virus
4. Ethics

SECTION D://

1. graphical user interface (GUI)
2. button
3. twice
4. Text

SECTION E://

1. personal
2. need
3. service
4. warranty

CHAPTER TWO

SECTION A://

1. Internet
2. Web page

3. Favorites
4. search engine
5. directory search engine

SECTION B://

1. modem
2. Web computer
3. WebTV
4. microbrowser
5. Blackberry

SECTION C://

1. Internet service provider
2. Commercial
3. Web space
4. free
5. work

SECTION D://

1. Web server
2. network access point (NAP)
3. uniform resource locator (URL)
4. communications protocol
5. Hypertext transfer protocol (http)

SECTION E://

1. E-mail
2. e-mail address
3. Web portal
4. Bandwidth

CHAPTER THREE

SECTION A://

1. Desktop publishing
2. Graphics
3. cells
4. Electronic banking

SECTION B://

1. Multitasking
2. Windows XP Home
3. Utility software
4. Anti-virus software, viruses

SECTION C://

1. file
2. extension
3. directory
4. folder (subdirectory)

SECTION D://

1. control
2. microphone
3. digital camera
4. Multimedia authoring software

SECTION E://

1. software license
2. Shareware
3. Freeware
4. shrink-wrap

CHAPTER FOUR

SECTION A://

1. technology
2. click-and-order
3. eBay

4. shopping cart

5. Opting out

SECTION B://

1. Web multimedia

2. plug-in

3. player (or viewer)

4. Streaming media

5. VRML (or Virtual Reality Modeling Language)

SECTION C://

1. HTML (Hypertext Markup Language)

2. XML (eXtensible Markup Language)

3. Image

4. FTP program

5. applets

SECTION D://

1. theme

2. different/both

3. key words

4. Web developer

CHAPTER FIVE

SECTION A://

1. CPU or processor

2. RAM or memory

3. trillion

4. magnetic

5. one

SECTION B://

1. optical

2. resolution

3. Inkjet

4. USB

5. wireless

SECTION C://

1. battery

2. portability

3. touchpad

4. PC

5. hot swap

SECTION D://

1. input

2. sound

3. megapixels

4. memory or RAM

5. docking

CHAPTER SIX

SECTION A://

1. bit

2. byte

3. ASCII

4. expansion

SECTION B://

1. network interface card (NIC)

2. router

3. network operating system (NOS)

4. Ethernet

SECTION C://

1. network administrator

2. Bluetooth or WiFi

3. local area network (LAN)

4. network operating system (NOS)

SECTION D://

1. telephone

2. cable

3. wireless ISP

4. Windows CE

CHAPTER SEVEN

SECTION A://

1. ethics

2. Fair Use Doctrine

3. right

4. Pirated software

SECTION B://

1. Identity

2. hacker

3. virus

4. denial-of-service

SECTION C://

1. Privacy

2. sniffer

3. Spam

4. Spoofing

SECTION D://

1. firewall

2. Anti-tracking

3. Federal Trade Commission (FTC)

4. social security number

CHAPTER EIGHT

SECTION A://

1. database
2. field
3. property
4. record
5. entity

SECTION B://

1. network database
2. Relational databases
3. relationship
4. primary key

SECTION C://

1. database management system (DBMS)
2. data dictionary
3. reports
4. data security
5. query language

SECTION D://

1. Database administrators (DBAs)
2. Web-enabled databases
3. Middleware
4. Web personalization
5. One-to-one marketing

SECTION E://

1. file management system
2. Access speed
3. FAT
4. fragments
5. decompress (or unzip)

CHAPTER NINE

SECTION A://

1. automatic speech recognition (ASR)
2. 3-D
3. Biometrics
4. Virtual reality
5. walker

SECTION B://

1. E-cash (Electronic cash, Digital cash)
2. replace
3. rent
4. push
5. commerce

SECTION C://

1. Information supplier convergence
2. speech
3. video
4. intelligent home appliance

SECTION D://

1. input/output
2. human body
3. Holographic
4. CAVE

CHAPTER TEN

SECTION A://

1. efficient
2. reactionary
3. advantage

SECTION B://

1. business process expert
2. quality control analyst
3. technology

SECTION C://

1. time
2. systems analyst
3. Data flow diagramming
4. plunge

SECTION D://

1. End user development
2. prototype
3. basic requirements
4. 3, 4

SECTION E://

1. Outsourcing
2. Horizontal
3. Vertical
4. request for proposal (RFP)

CHAPTER ELEVEN

SECTION A://

1. Pseudocode
2. algorithm
3. logic error
4. processing

SECTION B://

1. Coding
2. reserved words
3. case control
4. iteration control or loops

SECTION C://

1. Syntax
2. software development environment
3. program manual
4. software patch

SECTION D://

1. machine-dependent
2. assembler
3. compiler
4. object

SECTION E://

1. XHTML (eXtensible HTML)
2. Client-side
3. VBScript
4. Server-side

CHAPTER TWELVE

SECTION A://

1. Tactical
2. Decentralized computing
3. granularity
4. External
5. downward

SECTION B://

1. customer-integrated system (CIS)
2. transaction processing system (TPS)
3. decentralize
4. customer-integrated systems (CISs)

SECTION C://

1. management information system (MIS)
2. summarized report
3. exception report
4. comparative report
5. drill down

SECTION D://

1. intranet
2. extranet
3. Groupware
4. Group scheduling
5. group document database

SECTION E://

1. Telecommuting
2. transnational firm
3. Culture
4. Transborder data flows

CHAPTER THIRTEEN

SECTION A://

1. decision support system (DSS)
2. model
3. geographic information system
4. global positioning system (GPS)

SECTION B://

1. neural network
2. genetic algorithm
3. fuzzy logic
4. expert system

SECTION C://

1. buyer agents or shopping bots
2. user
3. intelligent agent or bot
4. learn

SECTION D://

1. data mining
2. data mart
3. discovery
4. data warehouse

glossary

Acceptance testing Formal, documented process in which users use the new system, verify that it works correctly under operational conditions, and note any errors that need to be fixed.

Access speed The time between when you ask for a file and when the computer delivers it to you.

Active matrix screen Screen that has a separate transistor for every pixel, or dot, on the screen and updates faster providing a higher-quality, crisper image.

Affiliate program (associate program) Allows you to sell goods and services via another e-commerce site.

AGP (accelerated graphics port) bus Dedicated to carrying complex graphics between the CPU and the AGP video card in the AGP slot on the motherboard.

AGP slot An expansion slot that terminates the AGP bus.

Algorithm Set of specific steps that solves a problem or carries out a task.

Alphabetic validation Makes sure only letters appear in a field.

Anti-virus software Utility software that scans for and often eliminates viruses in your RAM and on your storage devices.

Application software Software that allows you to perform specific tasks such as writing a term paper, surfing the Web, keeping a home budget, and creating slides for a presentation.

Applications programmer Programmer who writes application software.

Archive A copy of older data that becomes historical records.

Arithmetic logic unit (ALU) Component of the CPU that performs arithmetic operations.

Artificial intelligence (AI) The science of making machines imitate human thinking and behavior.

ASCII (American Standard Code for Information Interchange) Coding system that most personal computers and minicomputers use. Pronounced ASK-ee.

Assembler Utility program that converts assembly language into machine language that the computer can then use to run software.

Assembly language A machine-dependent, low-level language that uses words instead of binary numbers to program a specific computer system.

Attribute A quality that an object possesses.

Automatic speech recognition (ASR) Captures your speech and can distinguish your words and word groupings to form sentences.

Backdoor An undocumented method a programmer uses to gain access to a program or a computer.

Bandwidth The amount of information that can travel from one place to another in a given amount of time.

Banner ad Graphical advertisement that will take you to an e-commerce site if you click on it.

Basic formatting tag An HTML tag that tells a Web browser how to display text in formats such as bold, italics, and underline.

Bay Place in the system unit reserved for a storage unit.

Biometrics The use of physical characteristics, such as your fingerprint, the blood vessels in the retina of your eye, or perhaps the sound of your voice, to provide identification.

Bit (or binary digit) A one or a zero.

Black-hat hackers Hackers with malicious intent—they're cyber-vandals.

Bluetooth Technology that provides entirely wireless connections for all kinds of communication devices.

Brick-and-mortar business Exists only in the physical world and performs no e-commerce functions.

Bug Common name for a software error.

Business to business electronic commerce (B2B e-commerce) Occurs when a business sells products and services through e-commerce to customers who are primarily other businesses.

Business to consumer electronic commerce (B2C e-commerce) Occurs when a business sells products and services through e-commerce to customers who are primarily individuals.

Button Graphic representation of something that you click on once with the left mouse button.

Buyer agent or **shopping bot** Intelligent agent that looks on the Web for the product of your choice and brings the information back to you.

Byte A group of 8 bits that represents one natural language character.

Cable modem Device that uses your TV cable to produce an Internet connection.

Cache Memory where instructions and information wait for processing after they arrive in the CPU from RAM.

Cascading style sheet (CSS) Method of creating one file that contains your entire theme (color, fonts, etc.) for your Web site.

Case control structure Tests a condition that can result in more than a true or false answer. For example, you might need to determine shipping costs based on an item's weight.

CASE (computer aided software engineering) tool Software application that helps prepare reports, draw program flowcharts, and generate software code for prototypes.

Cat 5 or **Category 5 cable** (also called **Ethernet cable**) Twisted pair cable (like phone cable), except that there are more pairs of wires, and the pairs are twisted around each other.

CAVE (cave automatic virtual environment) A special 3-D virtual reality room that can display images of other people and objects located in other CAVEs all over the world.

CD-R (compact disc—recordable) Optical disc to which you can write one time only.

CD-ROM (compact disc read-only memory) Optical or laser disc whose information cannot be changed once it has been created.

CD-RW (compact disc—rewritable) Compact disc storage medium that allows you to save, change, and delete files.

Central processing unit (**CPU** or **microprocessor** or **processor**) Chip that carries out instructions it receives from your software.

Chat room Virtual meeting place on the Web in which you can communicate live with other people who happen to be on the Web at the same time.

Chief information officer (CIO) The person within your organization who oversees the use of information as a resource.

Children A subdirectory or subfolder.

Class Collection of similar objects.

Click-and-mortar business Has both a presence in the physical world (such as a store) and a Web site that supports some type of e-commerce.

Click-and-order business Exists solely on the Web with no physical presence that you can visit to buy products and services.

Click-through Information that is captured when you click on a banner ad to go from one Web site to another.

Client computer The computer you use to move around the Internet and access the information and services on a server computer.

Client/server network Network in which one or more computers are servers and provide services to the other computers, which are called clients.

Client-side Web programming language Employs users' Web browsers to add interactivity and new functions to Web pages.

Clock cycle Equivalent to a CPU cycle or machine cycle.

Cluster Organized collection of sectors.

COBOL Stands for Common Business Oriented Language and works best for business applications on mainframe computers.

Coding When you translate your algorithm into a programming language.

Comment An explanation that tells other programmers what's happening in software code.

Communications protocol (protocol) A set of rules that every computer follows to transfer information.

Communications software Software that helps you communicate with other people through the use of your computer.

Comparative report A report that shows two or more sets of similar information in an attempt to illustrate a relationship.

Compiler Simultaneously translates high-level programming languages into machine language.

Compound primary key Occurs when two or more fields identify a distinct record.

Compressed file A file made smaller by file compression.

Compression ratio Determines how small you want a compressed file to be.

Compression software Utility software that allows you to compress a file or files.

Computer (or **computer system**) Set of tools that helps you perform information-related tasks.

Computer network (or **network**) A collection of computers that support the sharing of information and hardware devices.

Computer system Set of tools that helps you perform information-related tasks.

Computer virus (virus) Software that was designed intentionally to cause annoyance or damage.

Connectivity software Enables you to use your computer to "dial up" or connect to another computer.

Consumer to consumer electronic commerce (C2C e-commerce) Occurs when a person (such as you) sells products and services to another person through e-commerce.

Control structure Specifies the order in which a computer will execute each line of software code.

Cookie Small text file containing specific information about you that's stored on your computer's hard drive.

Copyright Type of legal protection accorded to intellectual property.

Counter Numerical value that tracks the number of iterations in a software code.

CPU clock A sliver of quartz that beats at regular intervals in response to an electrical charge.

Crackers Hackers who hack for profit.

Crash-proof software Utility software that helps you save information if your system crashes and you're forced to turn it off and then back on again.

CRT Monitor that looks like a TV set. It's the most common type of monitor.

Culture The collective personality of a nation or society that encompasses language, traditions, currency, religion, history, music, and acceptable behavior.

Customer service Makes sure that a customer knows about the product and has no questions about buying it or what happens afterward.

Customer-integrated system (CIS) An extension of a transaction processing system that places technology in the hands of an organization's customers and allows them to process their own transactions.

Data Distinct times that don't have much meaning to you in a given context.

Data broker A company that searches many databases and returns information to you.

Data dictionary Defines the basic organization of a database.

Data file Contains organized data destined for use in a database.

Data flow diagramming (DFD) Modeling technique for illustrating how information moves through various processes and how people outside the system provide and receive information.

Data integrity Makes sure the right type of data is in each field.

Data mart Miniature data warehouse with a special focus.

Data mining The process of extracting information from a data warehouse for decision-making purposes.

Data security Restricts database access for viewing, organizing and updating data files.

Data structure Organizes data in a uniform manner.

Data warehouse Collection of information from internal and/or external sources organized specifically for decision-making purposes.

Database Stores and organizes data.

Database administrator (DBA) Designs, implements, and maintains solutions to business challenges using databases.

Database management system (DBMS) Application software that allows you to arrange, modify, and extract data from a database to create information.

Data-mining bot Searches through data warehouses to discover new information.

Debugging The process of finding errors in software code.

Decentralized computing The placement of technology into the hands of those people in an organization who need it in order to do their jobs effectively and efficiently.

Decision support system (DSS) Software that uses models, information, and an interactive user interface to help you make decisions.

Decompress "Unshrinking" a compressed file back to its original size.

Defragmentation program Reallocates file clusters and decreases fragmentation.

Denial-of-service (DoS) attack Causes thousands of access attempts to a Web site over a very short period of time, overloading the target site and shutting it down.

Desktop computer The most popular choice for personal computing needs, with prices ranging from about $500 to several thousand dollars.

Desktop publishing software Extends word processing by including design and formatting techniques to enhance the layout and appearance of a document.

Device letter Unique identifier for each different storage device on your computer.

Digital camera Input device that helps you capture live photos or pictures and transfer them directly to your computer.

Digital money Allows you to purchase items using a bank account balance instead of a credit card.

Digital video camera Input device that helps you capture live video and transfer them directly to your computer.

Directory List of the files on a particular storage device.

Directory search engine Organizes listings of Web sites into hierarchical lists.

Disk compression utility Operates between the compressed files and the operating system.

Disk optimization software Utility software that organizes your information on your hard disk in the most efficient way.

Docking station Small platform into which you can plug your whole notebook computer.

Documentation Collection of instructions and explanations relevant to a piece of software.

Domain name Identifies a specific computer on the Internet and the main page for an entire site.

Dot pitch Distance between the centers of a pair of like-colored pixels.

Do-until control structure Repeats a portion of a software code as long as a certain condition doesn't exist.

Do-while control structure Repeats a portion of software code as long as a certain condition exists.

Downward flow of information Consists of the strategies, goals, and directives that originate at one level and are passed to lower levels.

DSL (Digital Subscriber Line) High-speed Internet connection using the phone line, which allows you to use your phone for voice communication at the same time.

DVD-R (DVD—recordable) Optical disc to which you can write one time only and which has a higher capacity than a CD.

DVD-ROM Optical storage medium whose information can't be changed, but which has a larger capacity than a CD-ROM.

DVD-RW (also called **DVD-RAM,** or **DVD+RW** by different manufacturers) Optical storage medium that allows you to save, change, and delete files but has a larger capacity than a CD-RW.

Dynamic HTML (DHTML) Combines cascading style sheets (CSS), JavaScript, specific tag extensions, and other markup languages to bring high interactivity to Web sites.

EBCDIC The set of patterns that IBM mainframes use to represent characters.

E-cash (electronic cash or **digital cash)** Electronic representation or equivalent of cash.

E-commerce enabled Web site host Allows you to build a virtual storefront, create a catalog, process secure payments, provide customer service, and manage your e-commerce Web site.

Electronic bulletin board A shared message space where you can post inquiries and schedules for events and participate in discussion threads and chat rooms.

Electronic commerce (e-commerce) Commerce that technology facilitates and enhances.

Electronic data interchange (EDI) A set of guidelines for electronically handling the ordering, billing, and paying for goods and services.

Electronic meeting software Lets a team have a "virtual" meeting.

E-mail (short for **electronic mail)** Software you use to electronically communicate with other people.

E-mail address Unique address for a person using an e-mail system.

Encryption Technology used to hide the information and make it secure.

End user development The development and support of computer systems by users (such as yourself) with little or no help from technology specialists.

Entity A distinct item in a database.

Ergonomics Deals with how you arrange and use your technology to reduce discomfort and avoid health problems.

Ethernet card The most common type of network interface card.

Ethics Set of principles and standards we use in deciding what to do in situations that affect other people.

Event-driven language Responds to actions users perform on the program. It's an event when you click on a button, use a pull-down menu, or scroll down a window.

Exception report Report that shows only a subset of available information based on some selection criteria.

Executive information system (EIS) Highly interactive MIS that helps managers solve problems and take advantage of opportunities.

Expansion board (or **card)** A circuit board that you insert into an expansion slot on the motherboard and to which you connect a peripheral device.

Expansion bus Forms the highway system on the motherboard that moves information coming from and going to devices outside the motherboard such as your microphone or printer.

Expansion slot Long skinny socket on the motherboard into which you insert an expansion board.

Expert system (also called a **knowledge-based system)** Artificial intelligence system that applies reasoning capabilities to reach a conclusion.

eXtensible HTML (XHTML) Combines the formatting power of HTML with the strict syntax of XML and allows users to access a Web site from almost any Internet device.

External information Describes the environment surrounding an organization.

Extranet Extension of an intranet that allows other organizations and people access to information and application software on an internal intranet.

Fair Use Doctrine Defines the situations in which copyrighted material may be used.

Feature analysis Captures your words as you speak, converting the digital signals of your speech into phonemes.

Field The smallest piece of meaningful data.

Field name Describes what's in the field.

File A collection of information you need to effectively use your computer.

File allocation table (FAT) File that stores information about the physical location of every file on the computer's hard disk.

File backup system Copies files and stores them in a safe place.

File compression Shrinks a file or files into a smaller file.

File management system Coordinates how the computer organizes and keeps track of files.

File manager utility software Utility software that helps you manage, organize, find, copy, move, rename, and delete files on your computer.

File transfer protocol (FTP) The communications protocol that allows you to transfer files of information from one computer to another.

Filename Unique name that you give to a file of information.

Filename extension (most often just called an **extension**) Further identifies the contents of your file usually by specifying the file type.

Find-and-retrieve agents These travel around a network (very likely the Internet) finding information and bringing it back to you.

Firewall Hardware and/or software that protects computers from intruders.

Firewire Connectors that are similar to USB connectors, except they're faster.

Fiscal feasibility assessment Determines if your organization has sufficient resources to develop the proposed system and if the total cost of those resources falls within an allocated budget.

Flash Software that helps you create animated and interactive Web pages.

Flat-panel display Thin, lightweight monitor that takes up much less space than a CRT.

Floppy disks (also called simply **floppies** or **diskettes**) Removable magnetic storage media.

Folder Special portion of your root directory into which you can place files that have similar information (which your operating system will display as a manila folder icon).

Font tag An HTML tag that allows you to change the size of your text, specify a font type, and/or specify a color.

Form Graphical interface that makes it easy to add or delete data.

For-next control structure Repeats a portion of software code a precise number of times. It uses a counter to check the condition.

Fourth generation language (4GL) Machine-independent, high-level nonprocedural language that uses human words and symbols to program diverse computer systems.

Fragmentation Occurs when your computer places parts of files over many hard disk areas.

Freeware Software that is also public domain software, meaning you can use it as you wish free of charge.

FTP program Moves files from your computer to your Web server so people can view them on the Web.

FTP server Maintains a collection of files that you can download.

Fuzzy logic Mathematical method of handling imprecise or subjective information.

Gas plasma display Shines light through gas to make an image.

Genetic algorithm Artificial intelligence system that mimics the evolutionary, survival-of-the-fittest process to generate increasingly better solutions to a problem.

Geographic information system (GIS) Software that allows you to see information in map form.

Gigabyte (GB or **Gig)** About 1 billion bytes.

Gigahertz (GHz) The number of *billions* of CPU cycles per second.

Global positioning system (GPS) Device that tells you your current latitude, longitude, speed, and direction of movement.

Glove Input device that captures the shape and movements of your hand and fingers.

Graphical user interface (GUI) Graphic or icon-driven interface on which you use your mouse to start software (such as a Web browser), use that software, and initiate various other functions.

Graphics software Helps you create and edit photos and art.

Group document database Powerful storage facility for organizing and managing all documents related to specific teams.

Group scheduling software Provides facilities for maintaining the day-to-day electronic calendars of team members.

Groupware The popular term for the software component that supports team efforts.

Hackers Very knowledgeable computer users who use their knowledge to invade other people's computers.

Hacktivists (or **cyber terrorists**) Politically motivated hackers.

Handspring A type of PDA that uses the Palm OS.

Hard disk Magnetic storage medium, usually fixed inside the system unit, consisting of one or more thin platters or disks that store information.

Hardware The physical devices that make up your computer system.

Heading tag An HTML tag that makes certain information, such as titles, stand out on your Web page.

Headset Combined input and output device that (1) captures the movement of your head from side to side and up and down and (2) includes a special screen that covers your entire field of vision.

Hierarchical database Uses an inverted directory tree structure to organize data under different directories.

High-level language Allows programmers to use words and symbols closer to human language to code software.

Holographic device Creates, captures, and/or displays images in true three-dimensional form.

Horizontal flow of information Refers to information that passes among various departments.

Horizontal market software General business software that has application in many industries.

Hot-swap Means that you can change, or swap out, cards without shutting your computer down.

HTML (Hypertext Markup Language) The basic language used to create Web pages.

HTML document File that contains HTML tags and the information you want to appear on your Web page.

HTML tag Specifies the formatting and presentation of information on a Web page.

Hypertext database Lists each Web address as an object linked to its respective Web page.

Hypertext transfer protocol (http) The communications protocol that supports the movement of information over the Web, essentially from a Web server to you.

Icon Graphic representation of something that you click on twice or double-click.

Identity theft The impersonation by a thief of someone with good credit.

If-then-else control structure Tests a condition in software code that results in a true or false.

Image format Contains instructions to create and store information about an image.

Image tag An HTML tag you use to insert photos and other images onto your Web page.

Information Organized data whose meaning is clear and useful to you in a given context.

Information granularity Refers to the degree of detail information contains.

Inkjet printers Make images by forcing ink droplets through nozzles.

Input Information that comes from an external source and enters the software.

Input device Captures information and translates it into a form that can be processed and used by other parts of your computer.

Input-process-output (IPO) table Shows what information a piece of software takes in, how it processes information, and what information it produces.

Intelligent agent or **bot** Software that will automatically perform repetitive tasks on your computer for you.

Intelligent home appliance Contains embedded computer technology that controls numerous functions and is capable of making some decisions.

Interface hardware The hardware that connects external devices to the motherboard.

Internal information Describes specific operational aspects of an organization.

Internet A vast network of networked computers (hardware and software) that connects millions of people all over the world.

Internet backbone The major set of connections for computers on the Internet.

Internet mall Provides the Web space and utilities (in this case, software) and you supply the information and products.

Internet service provider (ISP) A company that provides individuals, organizations, and businesses access to the Internet.

Interpreter Translates one line of source code into object code at a time.

Intranet An internal organizational Internet that is guarded against outside access by a special security mechanism.

IRC (Internet relay chat) server Supports your use of discussion groups and chat rooms.

IrDA (infrared data association) Port for wireless devices, and works in essentially the same way as the remote control to your TV does.

ISA (industry standard architecture) bus The oldest and slowest type of expansion bus.

ISA slot An expansion slot that is usually black and terminates the ISA bus.

Iteration control (loop) Another word for repetition control structure. It instructs a piece of software to repeat a series of instructions until it fulfills a condition or while a condition exists.

Java applet A small piece of software that enables applications to run on a Web page.

JavaScript A scripting language that allows you to add interactivity and other features to a Web page.

Kilobyte (KB or K) About 1,000 bytes (a kilobyte is exactly 1,024 bytes, but we round down to 1,000 for the sake of simplicity).

Language processing Attempts to make sense of what you're saying by comparing the possible word phonemes to rules in a language model database.

Laser printer Forms images using an electrostatic process, the same way a photocopier works.

LCD (liquid crystal display) Screen that shines light through a layer of crystalline liquid to make an image.

Link (the technical term is hyperlink) Clickable text or an image that allows you to move from one Web site to another or move to different places within the same Web site.

Link tag An HTML tag that you use to create links on your Web page to other sites, pages, downloadable files such as audio and video, and e-mail.

Linux An open-source operating system that provides a rich operating environment for high-end workstations and network servers.

List tag An HTML tag that allows you to present information in the form of a list, either numbered or unnumbered.

Local area network (LAN) Network of computers that are contained within a limited geographic area, a building or a campus.

Logic error A mistake in the way an algorithm solves a problem.

Low-level language Requires programmers to code at a basic level that a computer can understand.

Mac OS The operating system for today's Apple computers.

Machine cycle (or CPU cycle of clock cycle) Consists of retrieving, decoding, and executing the instruction, and returning the result to RAM.

Machine language Machine-dependent, low-level language that uses binary code to interact with a specific computer system.

Machine-dependent language Programming language that works only on a specific computer system and its components.

Machine-independent language Programming language that works on different computer systems regardless of their components.

Macro Scripting language program that executes a task or set of tasks within a software application.

Macro virus Virus that spreads by binding itself to software such as Word or Excel.

Mail server Provides e-mail services and accounts.

Mainframe computer (sometimes just called a **mainframe)** Computer designed to meet the computing needs of hundreds of people in a large business environment.

Malware Malicious software that is designed by people to attack some part of a computer system.

Management information system (MIS) System that provides periodic and predetermined reports that summarize information.

Many-to-many relationship Many records of a record type can be related to many records in another record type.

Markup language Contains sets of specific key words that use syntax to instruct Web browsers to work with information.

M-commerce (mobile e-commerce) Allows you to use wireless devices such as cell phones or PDAs to buy and sell products and services.

Megabyte (MB or **M** or **Meg)** Roughly 1 million bytes.

Megahertz (MHz) The number of *millions* of CPU cycles per second.

Megapixels Maximum number of dots, in millions, that make up the image in a digital camera.

Meta tag Provides information to search engines about your Web site.

Microbrowser Web browser software for Web phones that can display text information in a small amount of space.

Microphone Input device that captures live sounds such as your voice or perhaps a dog barking.

Microsoft Windows 2000 Millennium (Windows 2000 Me) An operating system for a home computer user with utilities for setting up a home network and performing video, photo, and music editing and cataloging.

Microsoft Windows 2000 Professional (Windows 2000 Pro) An operating system for people who have a personal computer connected to a network of other computers at work or at school.

Microsoft Windows XP Home (Windows XP Home) Microsoft's newest home computer user operating system.

Microsoft Windows XP Professional (Windows XP Pro) Microsoft's newest recommendation for people who have a personal computer connected to a network of other computers at work or at school.

Middleware Software application that works between two different software applications and allows them to talk to each other.

Minicomputer (sometimes called a **mid-range computer)** Designed to meet the computing needs for several people simultaneously in a small- to medium-size business environment.

Modem Device that connects your computer through a phone line to a network of other computers.

Monitoring and surveillance agent Intelligent agent that performs diagnostic and housekeeping in the background, alerting you when it finds something of interest.

Motherboard (also called the **main board,** or **system board)** The large circuit board inside your system unit that holds the CPU, memory, and other essential electronic components.

Mouse An input device that has a ball on the bottom that causes the cursor on the screen to move as the ball rolls.

Multifunction printer A printer that will scan, copy, fax, as well as print.

Multimedia Presentation of information which can include sound, text, graphics, video, and animation and over which you have some sort of control.

Multimedia authoring software Software that you use to build your multimedia application.

Multitasking Operating system function that allows you to work with more than one piece of software at a time.

Natural language Human language that can program a computer.

Navigation Refers to how easily surfers can find what they need on a Web page or Web site.

NCIC (National Crime Information Center) A huge database with information on the criminal records of more than 20 million people.

Netiquette Good manners or courtesy in cyberspace.

Network A collection of computers that support the sharing of information and hardware devices.

Network access point (NAP) Point on the Internet where several connections converge.

Network administrator The person in charge of the network.

Network database Uses a tree structure similar to the hierarchical database but its children can have more than one parent.

Network hub Device that connects multiple computers into a network.

Network interface card (NIC) Expansion card or PC Card (for a notebook) that connects your computer to a network and allows information to flow between your computer and the rest of the network.

Network operating system (NOS) The operating system that runs a network, steering information between computers and managing security and users.

Network service provider (NSP) Owns and maintains routing computers at NAPs and even the lines that connect the NAPs to each other (such as MCI or AT&T).

Neural network An artificial intelligence system that is capable of learning how to differentiate patterns.

Nonprocedural language Requires that a programmer write code to tell the software only what it should accomplish.

Notebook computer (sometimes called **a laptop computer)** Small, portable, fully-functional computer designed for you to carry around and run on battery power.

Numeric validation Makes sure only numbers appear in a field.

Object One item that contains distinct information.

Object code The machine language the computer uses to run your program.

Object instance An exact copy of an object in object-oriented programming.

Objective information Quantifiably describes something that is known.

Object-oriented database Uses objects to represent entities rather than fields in tables.

Object-oriented programming (OOP) Any programming language that uses objects to code software.

One-to-many relationship One record of a record type can be related to many records of another record type.

One-to-one marketing Allows businesses to provide you with goods and services they tailor to your buying habits.

One-to-one relationship One record of a record type can be related to only one other record in a record type.

Online banking The use of your computer system to interact with your bank electronically, including writing checks, transferring funds, and obtaining a list of your account transactions.

Operating system software System software that controls your application software and manages how your hardware devices work together.

Operational management The level of management which manages and directs the day-to-day operations and implementation of the goals and strategies.

Optical mouse An input device that senses movement with red light and moves the cursor accordingly.

Opting in When you give permission for alternative uses of your personal information.

Opting out When you say no to alternative uses of your personal information.

Output The information software produces after it has processed input. Output can appear on a computer screen, in a printout, or in records in a database.

Output device Takes information within your computer and presents it to you in a form that you can understand.

Outsourcing The delegation of work to a group outside your organization for (1) a specified length of time, (2) a specified cost, and (3) a specified level of service.

Palm A type of PDA that uses the Palm OS.

Palm Operating System (Palm OS) The type of operating system that Palm/Handspring-type PDAs run on.

Parallel connector Plugs into a parallel port, has 25 pins, which fit into the holes that are in the port.

Parallel conversion Conversion method in which you run both the old and new systems until you're sure the new system works correctly.

Parent Directory similar to a folder in file systems.

Pathname The device letter, folder, subfolder (if present), filename, and extension that describes a particular file and its location.

Pattern classification Attempts to recognize your spoken phonemes by locating a matching phoneme (or phoneme sequence) among words stored in an acoustic model database.

PC Card (which is an updated version of the traditional **PCMCIA card**) Expansion card you use to add devices to your notebook computer.

PCI (peripheral component interconnect) bus The most common in modern computers.

PCI slot An expansion slot that terminates the PCI bus.

Peer-to-peer network Network in which a small number of computers share hardware (perhaps a printer) and information.

Periodic report Report that is produced at a predetermined time interval—daily, weekly, monthly, yearly, and so on.

Personal digital assistant (PDA) Small hand-held computer that helps you surf the Web and perform simple tasks such as note taking, calendaring and appointment scheduling, and maintaining an address book.

Personal finance software Offers you capabilities for maintaining your checkbook, preparing a budget, tracking investments, monitoring your credit card balances, and even paying bills electronically.

Personal information management (PIM) software Helps you create and maintain (1) to-do lists, (2) appointments and calendars, and (3) points of contact.

Personal portal Integrates all of your information into one Web site.

Personal productivity software Helps you with personal tasks that you can probably perform even if you don't own a computer.

Personalization The process of customizing a Web page or series of Web pages according to a customer's preferences.

Piecemeal conversion Conversion method in which you target only a portion of the new system for conversion, ensure that it works correctly, and then convert the remaining system.

Pilot conversion Conversion method in which you target a select group of users to convert to the new system before converting everyone.

Pirated software Copyrighted software that is copied and distributed without permission of the owner.

Pixels (picture elements) The dots that make up the image on your screen.

Player (viewer) Software that works outside your Web browser to play multimedia.

Plug and Play You can add devices to your computer and the operating system will find and install the drivers automatically without your having to go through a manual installation.

Plug-in Software that works within your Web browser to play multimedia.

Plunge conversion Conversion method in which you literally unplug the old system and use the new system exclusively.

PocketPC A type of PDA that uses Windows CE or PocketPC OS.

Pop-up ad Small Web page containing an advertisement that appears on your computer screen outside of the current Web site loaded in your Web browser.

Portability When a programming language has the ability to work on a variety of computer hardware and operating systems.

Presentation software Helps you create and edit information that will appear in electronic slides.

Primary key The field in a table that is specific to only one record in the table.

Privacy The right to be left alone when you want to be, to have control over your own personal information, and not to be observed without your consent.

Problem/opportunity statement Concise document that describes the exact nature of the problem or opportunity and provides broad statements concerning how the proposed system will benefit the organization.

Procedural language Requires that a programmer write code to tell software what to accomplish and how to accomplish it.

Procedure Instructions that manipulate an object's information.

Processing Manages information according to a piece of software's logic. In other words, processing is what the software does to the input it receives.

Program flowchart Graphical depiction of the detailed steps that software will perform.

Program manual Technical manual for programmers. It contains a problem/opportunity statement, algorithms, flowcharts, and copies of older versions of the code.

Programmer Technology specialist whose expertise lies in taking user requirements and writing software to match those requirements.

Programming language Contains specific rules and words that express the logical steps of an algorithm.

Project manager The person who oversees the project from beginning through implementation and support.

Property The type of data in a field (for example, numeric, date, and currency).

Prototype Model of a proposed product (which can be a computer system).

Prototyping The process of building a model that demonstrates the features of a proposed product, service, or system.

Pseudocode Uses English statements to create an outline of the necessary steps for a piece of software to operate.

Public domain software Software that you can copy, distribute, and even modify without obtaining permission.

Push technology Businesses and organizations come to you with information, services, and product offerings based on your profile.

Query Asks a question to a database in a language it understands—query language.

Query language Uses English statements to extract data from a database and create information.

Query-by-example (QBE) Allows you to graphically represent what information you'd like to see from the database.

RAM (random access memory) Temporary memory that holds software instructions and information for the CPU.

Rapid application development (RAD) Uses prototypes to test software components until they meet specifications.

Record Complete data entry.

Relational database Stores data in tables that have rows and columns.

Relationship An association between database entities.

Repetition control structure Instructs a piece of software to repeat a series of instructions until it fulfills a condition or while a condition exists.

Report A graphical display of your data.

Report generator Creates a written or Web report of information you request.

Request for proposal (RFP) Formal document that outlines your logical requirements for the proposed system and invites outsourcing vendors to bid on its development.

Reserved word A word that a programming language has set aside for its own use.

Resolution of a printer Number of dots per inch (dpi) it produces.

Resolution of a screen Number of pixels it has.

RJ-45 connector (also called an **Ethernet connector)** Looks like a telephone connector except that it's larger.

Robot An artificial intelligence device with simulated human senses capable of taking action on its own.

Router Device that acts as a smart hub connecting computers into a network, and goes a step further by separating your network from any other network it's connected to.

Run-time error A mistake that occurs when you run the software code.

Satellite modem Modem that allows you to get Internet access using a satellite dish.

Scanner Input device that helps you copy or capture images, photos, and artwork that exist on paper.

Script bunny (or script kiddie) Someone who would like to be a hacker but doesn't have much technical expertise.

Scripting language An interpreted programming language that works within another application to perform tasks.

Search engine Facility on the Web that allows you to find Web sites by key word or words.

Sector Single area that can hold a certain number of bytes of data.

Secure transaction Uses specific protocols to transfer sensitive information.

Selection control structure Uses an existing condition to decide how a computer will execute software code.

Sequence control structure Makes sure that a computer executes software code from top to bottom, left to right.

Sequential execution When a computer performs each line of software code in the order it appears.

Serial connector Plugs into a serial port, usually has 9 holes but may have 25, which fit the corresponding number of pins in the port.

Server computer (also called a **host computer)** Computer on the Internet that provides information and services to other computers and Internet users such as you.

Server-side Web programming Uses Web server resources to retrieve information, process information, and output customized Web pages.

Shared information Concept that employees should have access to whatever information they need when they need it.

Shareware Software that you can "test drive" or "try before you buy."

Shockwave Software that helps you create Web pages with significant interactivity through Web multimedia.

Shopping cart Software that stores information about your e-commerce purchases.

Shrink-wrap license Document that is shrink-wrapped to the outside of the software box.

Site map Sketch or diagram of how all of your Web pages work together.

Sniffer Software that sits on the Internet analyzing traffic.

Software The set of instructions that your computer hardware executes to process information for you.

Software development environment An application that provides programming tools to debug and manage software programs.

Software license Defines the way in which you can use the software.

Software patch A small fix to a problem using a piece of software code.

Software suites "Bundles" of related software packages that are sold together.

Software upgrade A substantial revision of existing software to improve its usefulness.

Software version (version) Tells you which iteration of the software you're using.

Source code Contains all the commands and comments a programmer used to code the software.

Spam Electronic junk mail or unsolicited mail, usually from commercial businesses attempting to sell you products and services.

Spoofing Forging the return address on an e-mail so that the e-mail message appears to come from someone other than the sender.

Spreadsheet software Helps you work primarily with numbers, including performing calculations and creating graphs.

Storage device Stores information so you can recall and use that information at a later time.

Strategic management The level of management which provides an organization with overall direction and guidance.

Streaming media Continually sends small parts of a large file to your Web browser as you watch or listen to what you've already downloaded.

Structured decision Decision you make by applying a formula. With a structured decision you punch in the right numbers, do the arithmetic correctly, and get the right answer—guaranteed.

Structured Query Language (SQL) The default query language for most databases.

Subjective information Attempts to describe something that is currently unknown.

Summarized report Report that aggregates information in some way.

Supercomputer The fastest, most powerful, and most expensive type of computer.

Syntax A set of rules to follow.

Syntax error A mistake in a software code's grammar.

System bus Consists of electrical pathways which move information between basic components of the motherboard, including between RAM and the CPU.

System champion Management person within your organization who (1) believes in the worth of the system and (2) has the "organizational muscle" to pull together the necessary resources.

System programmer Programmer who writes operating system and utility software.

System software The software that details how your computer carries out technology-specific tasks.

System unit The case or box in which the motherboard and storage units are housed.

Systems analysis phase Systems development life cycle (SDLC) phase that involves modeling how the current system works from a logical (not physical) point of view, identifying its weaknesses and the opportunities to improve, creating a logical model of the new system, and reviewing the project plan.

Systems analyst Technology specialist who understands both technology and business processes.

Systems construction phase Systems development life cycle (SDLC) phase in which you actually create the new system.

Systems design phase Systems development life cycle (SDLC) phase that involves generating several alternative technical solutions for the new logical model, selecting the best technical alternative, developing detailed software specifications, and—once again—reviewing the project plan.

Systems development project plan Document that includes a list of the project team, the problem/opportunity statement, the project budget, the feasibility assessments, and project timetable.

Systems implementation phase Systems development life cycle (SDLC) phase that involves training users, converting existing information to the new system, converting users, acceptance testing, and reviewing the project plan.

Systems investigation The first phase of the traditional systems development life cycle (SDLC) in which you seek to lay the foundation for the systems development process.

Table Organized collection of records.

Tactical management The level of management which develops the goals and strategies outlined by strategic management.

TCP/IP (Transport Control Protocol/Internet Protocol) The basic communications protocol that makes the Internet work.

Technical feasibility assessment Determines if your organization has access to or can acquire the necessary hardware and software for the proposed system.

Technical writer Explains concepts and procedures to non-technical software users.

Telecommunications device Helps you communicate information to people in other locations.

Telecommuter Person who works outside the central office some of the time while connected to the central office through technology.

Telecommuting The use of various technologies (especially telecommunications technologies) to allow employees to work in a place other than a central location.

Telephone modem (modem) Device that connects your computer through a phone line to a network of other computers.

Terabyte (TB) Approximately 1 trillion bytes.

TFT (thin film transistor) Flat-panel display with an active matrix screen.

Theme Coordinated presentation of colors, text, and other elements that appear on your Web site.

Third generation language (3GL) Machine-independent, high-level procedural language that uses human words and symbols to program diverse computer systems.

Three-dimensional (3-D) Technology that presents information to you in such a way that you have the illusion that the object you're viewing is actually in the room with you.

Time feasibility assessment Determines if your organization can develop the proposed system while meeting certain deadlines.

Top-level domain Three-character extension of a Web site address.

Touchpad A little dark gray rectangle on which you move your finger around and the cursor moves accordingly.

Trackball A mouse with the ball on the top, and you move it with your fingers or thumb.

Traditional systems development life cycle (SDLC) A structured step-by-step approach to developing systems that creates a separation of duties among technology specialists and users.

Transaction processing system (TPS) System that processes transactions that occur within an organization.

Transnational firm Produces and sells products and services in countries all over the world.

True search engine Uses software agent technologies to search the Web for key words and place them into indexes.

Unicode Coding system that uses 16 bits instead of 8, allowing for approximately 65,000 (2^{16}) different patterns.

Uninstaller software Utility software that you can use to remove software from your hard disk you no longer want.

Unstructured decision Decision for which there is no guaranteed way to get a precise right answer.

Unzipping Another word for decompressing a file.

Upward flow of information Describes the current state of the organization based on its daily transactions (such as sales).

URL (uniform resource locator) Address for a specific Web page or document within a Web site.

Usability Refers to how easy or difficult it is to use a Web page or site.

USB (universal serial bus) Connectors and ports that are becoming the most popular means of connecting devices to computers.

User agent Intelligent agent that helps an individual perform computer-related tasks.

User interface The manner in which you communicate with the software package.

User manual Tells users how to use a software program.

Utility software Software that provides additional functionality to your operating system.

VBScript An interpreted scripting language based on Visual Basic.

Vertical market software Software that is unique to a particular industry.

Videoconferencing software Allows a team to have a face-to-face meeting when members are geographically dispersed.

Viral marketing Technique that e-commerce businesses use to gather personal information about you, use that information in their own promotional campaigns, and sell that information to other e-commerce businesses.

Virtual memory Space on your hard disk space that holds software instructions for a program currently in use.

Virtual reality Three-dimensional computer simulation in which you actively and physically participate.

Virus hoax E-mail distributed with the intention of frightening people about a nonexistent virus.

Visual Basic for Applications (VBA) An interpreted scripting language that works within Microsoft Office applications.

VRML (Virtual Reality Modeling Language) Creates a virtual world in which users have the illusion that they are physically participating in the presentation of the Web multimedia.

Walker Captures the movement of your feet and body as you walk or turn in different directions.

Web audio All of the sounds and music on the Web.

Web authoring software Helps you design and develop Web sites and pages that you publish on the Web.

Web browser software (or a Web browser) Software that allows you to surf the Web.

Web catalog Uses a database to provide images, information, and pricing on available items.

Web computer Scaled-down version of today's typical computer system that provides Web access and costs about half the price.

Web developer Professional who creates Web sites.

Web multimedia The use of audio, video, animation, and other elements to allow interactivity on a Web site or page.

Web page Specific portion of a Web site that deals with a certain topic.

Web phone Special type of cell phone that allows you to access the Web.

Web portal Site that provides a wide range of services, including search engines, free e-mail, chat rooms, discussion boards, and links to hundreds of different sites.

Web server Provides information and services to Web surfers.

Web site Specific location on the Web where you visit, gather information, and perhaps order products.

Web site address (or **site address)** Unique name that identifies a specific Web site on the Web.

Web site management software Allows you to create, update, and manage all of your Web pages quickly and efficiently.

Web space Storage area where you keep your Web site.

Web video All of the movies on the Web.

Web-enabled database Accesses, modifies, and presents information through a Web browser.

Whiteboard software Lets team members meet, view a presentation, and record electronic notes on a large board called a whiteboard.

White-hat hackers Follow a "hackers' code" and, while they break into computers they have no right to access, they often report the security leaks to the victims.

Wide area network (WAN) Network of networks that extends over a large geographic area.

WiFi A way of transmitting information in radio wave form that is reasonably fast and is often used for notebooks (formerly known as IEEE 802.11b).

Windows CE (also called **Pocket PC OS)** The type of operating system that PocketPCs run on.

Wireless adapter for your desktop computer or a **wireless PC Card** for your notebook that lets you wirelessly access a network.

Wireless Internet service provider (wireless ISP) Does the same job as a standard Internet service provider except that you don't need a wired connection for access.

Wireless mouse An input device that sends signals to the computer by means of waves.

Wireless network access point Device that allows computers to access a wired network using radio waves.

Word processing software Helps you create papers, letters, memos, and other basic documents.

Workgroup support system (WSS) System that is designed to improve the performance of teams by supporting the sharing and flow of information.

World Wide Web (Web) The Internet in a linked multimedia form.

Worm Computer virus that spreads itself, not only from file to file, but from computer to computer via e-mail and other Internet traffic.

WYSIWYG HTML editor "What You See Is What You Get" HTML editor, displays how your Web pages will look.

XML (eXtensible Markup Language) Allows you to use key words to identify similar items and organize information on the Web.

Zipping Another word for compressing a file.

photo credits

index

geographic information system (GIS), 13.8–13.9

gestures, cultural differences demonstrated by, 12.23

GHz, 5.4

GIFs, 4.22

gifts, Web sites for buying, 6.30

Gifts of History Web site, 6.30

gigabyte (GB or Gig), 5.6, 5.10

Gigahertz (GHz), 5.4

GIS (geographic information system), 13.8–13.9

giveonline.org, 10.32

give.org, 10.32

Glassbook Web site, 6.31

global positioning system (GPS), 5.35, 13.9

Global Village, 12.16

gloves for virtual reality, 9.7

goal setting, 13.7

good manners. *See* manners

goodeats.com, 10.32

Google, 8.18

gov top-level domain, 2.19

government agencies on the Web, 2.35

government entities, paying online, 1.4

government records on individuals, 7.19–7.21

Go.Web wireless ISP, 6.23

GPS (global positioning system), 5.35, 13.9

Grab.com, 4.12

grammar for software code, 11.13

"granularity," 12.5–12.6

graphical links, 1.20, 1.21

graphical user interface. *See* GUI

Graphics Interchange Format (GIFs), 4.22

graphics software, 3.5, 3.6

graphs, creating with spreadsheet software, 3.8

greeting cards, sending and receiving electronic, 9.27

Greetings-Cards Web site, 9.27

Grocer Online Web site, 1.28, 5.33

groceries, buying on the Web, 1.28–1.29

Groceries Express Web site, 1.28

grocery stores, self-scanning systems, 10.4

group document databases, 12.18–12.19

group scheduling software, 12.18

groupware, 12.17

GUI, 1.19–1.20, 2.2

GUI elements in Yahoo!, 1.20–1.21

h

hackers, 1.17, 7.7, 7.14–7.15

"hackers' code," 7.14

hacking, 7.2

hacktivists, 7.14

hand-held devices, distinctions between, 6.22

Handspring PDAs, 6.22

hard disks, 1.12, 5.8, 5.9–5.11

  buying as much space as possible, 5.10

  capacities of, 5.10

  drive letters for, 3.17

  files deleted from, 5.14

  finding files on, 8.23

  removable, 5.11

  rotation speed (RPM) of, 5.10

hardware, 1.7, 1.9

  categories of, 1.9–1.13

  consumer's guide to buying, 5.2

  leasing, 12.14

  for viewing multimedia, 3.21

  for Web surfing, 2.11–2.13

hardware specialists, 10.9

HDSL, 6.19–6.20

HDTV, 5.17

headhunter.net, 2.4

heading tags in HTML, 4.19, 4.20, 4.21

headset, 9.7

health care agencies, privacy standards for, 7.32

Health Insurance Portability and Accountability Act, 7.21, 7.32

heat sink, 6.6

"heavy" files, storing, 5.12

helping.org, 10.32

hierarchical database, 8.5

hierarchical form, Web pages in, 2.3

hierarchical lists, organizing listings of Web sites into, 2.7, 2.8

hierarchical tree structure, 3.18

high-bit-rate DSL (HDSL), 6.19–6.20

high-capacity floppy disks, 5.11

high-level language, 11.19

Hilton Group Web site, 7.30

HIPAA, 7.32

Holiday Inn Web site, 7.30

holographic devices, 9.18–9.19

home, communicating with, 9.14–9.15

Home Connections Web site, 12.31

"Home" link, including on each Web page, 4.26, 4.28

home networks, 6.12–6.14, 6.15–6.16

Home Page, 4.27

homebuilder.com, 12.31

HomeGrocer Web site, 1.28

homes

  buying on the Web, 12.31

  intelligent, 9.13–9.15

HomeStore.com, 8.31, 12.31

Honda, 12.23

Honolulu Advertiser.com, 4.34

horizontal flow of information, 12.6, 12.7

horizontal market software, 10.23

host computers. *See* servers

hot-swapping devices, 5.22

HotBot search engine, 1.30, 2.9

hotels, Web sites for, 7.30

hotjobs.com, 2.4

HotWire Web site, 2.7

How to Write a Good Resume Web site, 5.32

HTML (Hypertext Markup Language), 4.18

  blink tag, 7.24

  building tables, 8.25

  creating Web pages with, 4.19–4.22

  documents, 4.19

  editing software, 3.5–3.6, 4.22–4.23

  font styles and sizes, 5.26

  for images, 2.26

  meta tags, 11.28

  tags, 4.20–4.21

HTMLGURU.com, 11.27

HTTP (hypertext transfer protocol), 2.22

https://, indicating a secure site, 7.8, 7.9

hub, 6.13

human bodies, implanting chips in, 9.17–9.18